NONTIMBER FOREST PRODUCTS IN THE UNITED STATES

DEVELOPMENT OF WESTERN RESOURCES

The Development of Western Resources is an interdisciplinary series focusing on the use and misuse of resources in the American West. Written for a broad readership of humanists, social scientists, and resource specialists, the books in this series emphasize both historical and contemporary perspectives as they explore the interplay between resource exploitation and economic, social, and political experiences.

John G. Clark, University of Kansas, Founding Editor
Hal K. Rothman, University of Nevada, Las Vegas, Series Editor

NONTIMBER FOREST PRODUCTS IN THE UNITED STATES

Edited by Eric T. Jones,
Rebecca J. McLain, and
James Weigand

University Press of Kansas

Published by the University Press of Kansas (Lawrence, Kansas 66049), which was organized by the Kansas Board of Regents and is operated and funded by Emporia State University, Fort Hays State University, Kansas State University, Pittsburg State University, the University of Kansas, and Wichita State University.

Library of Congress Cataloging-in-Publication Data

Nontimber forest products in the United States / edited by Eric T. Jones, Rebecca J. McLain, and James Weigand.
p. cm. — (Development of western resources)
Includes bibliographical references and index.
ISBN 0-7006-1165-7 (cloth : alk. paper) — ISBN 0-7006-1166-5 (pbk. : alk. paper)
1. Forest products industry—United States. I. Jones, Eric T., 1965–
II. McLain, Rebecca J. (Rebecca Jean). III. Weigand, James F.
IV. Series.

HD9755.N66 2002
338.1'7498'0973—dc21
2001007416

British Library Cataloguing in Publication Data is available.

Printed in the United States of America

10 9 8 7 6 5 4 3 2 1

The paper used in this publication meets the minimum requirements of the American National Standard for Permanence of Paper for Printed Library Materials

Our sincerest gratitude is extended to
Roger Fight of the USDA Forest Sciences Lab
for project consultation and in-kind support.

CONTENTS

TABLES AND FIGURES

TABLES

FIGURES

PREFACE

Since the late 1980s, the Non-Wood Forest Products Program of the United Nations Food and Agricultural Organization (FAO) has been sponsoring international workshops on nontimber forest products (NTFPs) around the world. The first series of workshops took place in Asia, Africa, and Latin America. Emphasis on these regions gives the impression that managing NTFPs is a Third World forestry policy issue with little relevance for forest managers and policy makers in industrialized countries. Yet during the 1980s and 1990s, stories about local and regional conflicts over NTFPs—Pacific yew, wild mushrooms, beargrass, and ginseng, for example—made front-page news in many U.S. newspapers. Loss of natural productivity for other important traditional nontimber forest products, such as maple syrup, butternuts, and pine nuts, from plant pests, disease, and environmental decline began to alarm both forest scientists and forest product dealers. Thus in 1997, when the FAO Non-Wood Forest Products Program office announced an international NTFP workshop for North America, a small group of scientists active in NTFP research in the United States, including a number of the contributors to this volume, decided to assemble a series of papers addressing some of the major biological, ecological, economic, cultural, historical, and political issues surrounding NTFP management in the United States.

When the FAO postponed the North American workshop in the fall of 1997, Roger Fight, the NTFP representative from the United States on the FAO's North American Forestry Committee, used that opportunity to initiate a three-country document comparing NTFP management concerns and issues across Mexico, Canada, and the United States. During 1998, representatives from Canada, Mexico, and the United States crafted an outline for what we began to call the North American NTFP Assessment, a document describing state-of-the-art scientific and management knowledge about NTFPs for each of the three countries. By late 1998, Jim Weigand, coeditor of the assessment, acquired funding from the U.S. Forest Service, the North American Commission on Environmental Cooperation, and the Turner Fund to produce the U.S. portion of the assessment. However, in 1999, FAO canceled plans to sponsor the NTFP workshop in North America, and the Canadian and Mexican partners withdrew from the assessment project due to lack of funding. The U.S. team decided to go forward with the U.S. portion of the NTFP Assessment as planned; this book is the product of that effort.

Over the next two years, the NTFP Assessment changed in structure and focus. Originally conceived of as a comprehensive state-of-the-art description of scientific and management knowledge of NTFPs in the United States, the assessment eventually evolved into an analysis of key U.S. policy issues, research directions, and management concerns. The shift from a text describing current NTFP management conditions to a much more analytical text proceeded in fits and starts as the contributors and editors struggled to develop a common vision of the document's purposes and a strategy for how the team could best achieve them.

Scientific research on nontimber forest products in the United States is fragmented and underfunded, and the number of scholars with expertise in NTFP issues in the United States is small. To provide a cohesive and vital picture of the current and potential role of NTFPs, we have brought together in one volume research from multiple scientific disciplines and analytical perspectives. We chose to organize the book under the one idea that all of the contributors hold in common: NTFPs are important to U.S. society and to sustainable forest management. The primary purpose of the book is to illustrate the many different ways in which NTFPs are important, to whom they are important, and the steps that different individuals and interest groups are taking or have taken to ensure that they have access to these products now and in the future.

One dilemma was how to achieve a balance between description and analysis. Much of the scientific community and the general public remains unaware that the activities that surround NTFPs are increasingly important topics for scientific research and management. Most people have some acquaintance with nontimber forest products in their lives, but few have given serious thought to NTFPs as a general category of natural resource management. We felt obligated to include sufficient descriptive details in each section to provide the reader with the context needed to understand the logic of the analysis presented in that section. Anticipating a fairly diverse audience for this work, we also sought to maintain a structure in which each major section could function as a stand-alone set of readings yet still flow smoothly and without repetition into the entire collection.

A second dilemma was how to bring cohesion to a book composed of sections written by more than twenty contributors drawn from fields as diverse as economics, mycology, history, ecology, law, entomology, forestry, geography, and anthropology. The interdisciplinary backgrounds of the coeditors, as well as the use of an informal interdisciplinary peer review process for each contribution, allowed us to construct a reasonably cohesive and integrated volume despite authors' differences in analytical styles.

The methods of research used by contributors to this book varied enormously. The Maidu case and the environmental justice case, for example, draw primarily upon data obtained through in-depth interviews and long-term participant observation. The history chapter, the Yakama case study, and the sections on Indian reserved rights and customary law are based mainly on analyses of historical and legal documents; the federal NTFP policy section is a composite of data obtained through phone interviews, website analyses, and a review of relevant public laws and regulations. The commerce chapter includes trade and agricultural statistical data, supplemented by data obtained through surveys of various segments of the NTFP industry. The inventory and monitoring chapter draws upon a review of relevant literature as well as upon data obtained through field experimentations. In short, the research methods used to develop each contribution reflect the eclectic nature of the topic itself.

Eric Jones, the primary coordinator of this collaboration, constructed a physically separate but nonetheless integral part of the volume in the form of an NTFP website. The website, *www.ifcae.org/ntfp*, initially served to let others know that a team of people had begun working on a book about U.S. NTFPs and to provide a forum in which contributors could fine-tune their work in response to comments by others. Due to some of the team members' concerns about copyright issues, however, we opted not to use the website for the peer review process. Instead, it became a repository for data useful to all of the authors as well as to others. Hosted by the Institute for Culture and Ecology in Portland, Oregon, the site currently includes two databases, one containing annotated citations for books and articles on NTFPs and the other a prototype database of these products harvested in the United States.

We would like to thank Paul Vantomme and FAO Non-Wood Forest Products colleagues in Rome, Italy, for their efforts to make linkages between North America and NTFP activities in other parts of the world and for announcing this project in their international newsletter. Special thanks are extended to Nancy Turner and Will McWilliams for their comments on an early draft of "Historical Overview of Nontimber Forest Product Uses in the Northeastern United States." "Business As Usual: The Exclusion of Mushroom Pickers in Wild Mushroom Management in Oregon's National Forests" was funded through an honorarium from the Natural Resources Law Center, University of Colorado at Boulder. The chapter is based upon data gathered as part of a project funded by the EPA STAR Graduate Fellowship Program (1997–2000) and the USDA–Forest Service's Social and Economic Values Program in the Pacific Northwest Research Station, Portland, Oregon (1995–1997).

The following reviewers supplied important input on the case studies:

Kim McDonald, Beverly Brown, Su Alexander, Marla Emery, and Kathy Patterson. The following legal scholars provided guidance for the chapter "Nontimber Forest Products Customary Claims": Michael Blumm, Northwestern School of Law, Lewis and Clark College; Chris Wold, Northwestern School of Law, Lewis and Clark College; Ileana Porras, University of Utah College of Law; Karen Engle, University of Utah College of Law; Arthur McEvoy, University of Wisconsin Land Tenure Center; John Bruce, University of Wisconsin Land Tenure Center; Louise Fortmann, University of California–Berkeley.

Thank you to Jack Anderson, photographer and beekeeper in Anchorage, Alaska; Torey Johnson of Ruhl Bee Supply, beekeeper and former president of the Oregon State Beekeepers Association; and Joanne Olstrom of Joanne's Honey. The helpful comments of Rosemary A. Marshall, Susan R. Kephart, and James F. Weigand improved the honey case study. Thanks to Justin Umholtz for information about recent changes in western Washington NTFPs. Thank you to the Great Lakes Indian Fish and Wildlife Commission—particularly Jim Zorn, Neil Kmiecik, Sue Erickson, and Peter David—for their invaluable insights and recommended revisions on the Ojibwe case study. Thank you to Martha Osgood, Doug Stienbarger, Ron and Shirley Jones, Char Eickholt, Robin Smith, William and Reathie McLain, and many others who helped support this project.

Major financial and in-kind contributions came from ArrowWood Associates; Institute for Culture and Ecology; North American Fund for Environmental Cooperation; Pacific Forest Trust; Pinchot Institute for Conservation; Turner Foundation; and USDA Forest Service State and Private Forestry.

INTRODUCTION

Rebecca J. McLain and Eric T. Jones

Once found primarily in specialty shops, nontimber forest products (NTFPs), such as medicinal herbs and edible wild mushrooms, now figure among the offerings on the shelves of mainstream drug and grocery stores. Simultaneously, subsistence and recreational demands for products derived from plant, fungi, and lichen species gathered in forest, woodland, or savanna ecosystems have also expanded. Examples of NTFPs include ferns, mosses, wild mushrooms, cones, boughs, maple syrup, bark, and hundreds of medicinal plants, such as ginseng and goldenseal. Although greater attention to NTFPs on the part of forest managers can contribute toward increased ecosystem biodiversity, the rapidly rising demands for these products pose the risk that market expansion will outpace the knowledge needed for sensible management. To that end this book attempts to examine some of the major social, economic, and biological benefits of nontimber forest products while simultaneously addressing the potential negative consequences of NTFP harvesting on forest ecosystems, NTFP species populations, and the sociopolitical systems in which they are embedded.

In the United States, where timber management has long dominated public and private forestry, forest stakeholders are now seeking to restructure forest management in ways that more explicitly fulfill a broader variety of an increasingly diverse American society's needs. Forest-based employment is also changing. Timber harvesting has become more mechanized and requires less labor than ever before, while current timber harvests, especially from federal public lands, are greatly reduced from those of fifteen years ago. Americans are asking public land managers to reduce timber harvests as one way to ensure that natural processes of forest ecosystems remain intact. Forest managers must now manage forests in ways that simultaneously allow for the production of commodities (fisheries, clean water, timber) and services (recreation opportunities, solitude) while conserving amenities (aesthetic landscapes, cultural heritage sites). As this shift has occurred, requests for commercial access to NTFPs on both public and private lands have risen exponentially in the past two decades. Private landowners are also exploring options for using incomes from NTFPs to supplement or supplant revenues from timber harvests.

The Working Group on Criteria and Indicators for the Conservation and Sustainable Management of Temperate and Boreal Forests for the Montreal Process (to which the United States is a signatory) has cited the lack of adequate information about NTFPs as a critical gap in knowledge upon which to judge sustainability of forest management. The limited research that has been done on nontimber forest products has focused almost exclusively on the existing and potential roles that NTFPs play in economic development and ecosystem sustainability in Third World countries. Quantifiable data about changes and presumed growth in NTFP sectors in industrialized economies are sketchy at best. Little organized information exists about the benefits, trade-offs, risks, and constraints stemming from subsistence and commercial harvests of U.S. NTFPs. Lack of well-organized and easily accessible information extends to the number of jobs and amount of income generated from economic uses of nontimber forest products. Are the benefits on the order of hundreds of millions or billions of dollars? Managing forests in ways that expand the availability of NTFP species for raw materials may substitute in part for jobs lost in wood-products industries. However, we have a poor understanding of the roles that NTFPs can play in diversifying forest economies. Without adequate information about conservation and management of NTFP resources, we cannot evaluate the sustainability of forest practices and management in the United States.

The primary purpose of this book is to illustrate the many different ways in which nontimber forest products are important in the United States, to whom they are important, and the steps that various social actors are taking or have taken to ensure that they have access to NTFPs now and in the future. Our expectation is that the book will be a seminal work for orienting future NTFP research within and across the social and natural sciences. By providing managers and researchers with deeper understandings of the complexities of social, ecological, and economic aspects of NTFPs, we hope that the book will contribute toward the development of more sophisticated forest policy and management frameworks. We see the contributions to this volume as useful to a broad audience, ranging from NTFP harvesters and buyers to environmentalist organizations, rural development groups, Native American tribal members, scientists, and public and private forest land managers.

DEFINING NTFPS

The natural resource management category "nontimber forest product" encompasses a broad range of species and their constituent parts. For the purposes of this volume, we use the term "nontimber forest products," as defined by the United Nations Food and Agricultural Organization, to encompass five broad product categories: foods, such as wild edible mushrooms, fruits, nuts, and berries; medicinal plants and fungi; floral greenery and horticultural stocks; fiber and dye plants, lichens, and fungi; and oils, resins, and other chemical extracts from plants, lichens, and fungi. This definition is broad in the sense that we include all organisms and their parts found in forest environments—ranging from forests relatively unmodified by human activity to farm-forestry systems substantially modified or created by humans to urban forests and forest plantations existing solely because of human intervention. Our definition is narrow in that, with the exception of a case study on honey production, we limit our discussion to botanical species. We include the discussion on honey since it is a product that insects and plants produce jointly.

OVERALL FRAMEWORK

Given that this volume constitutes the first extensive national overview of nontimber forest product policy and management specific to the United States, we chose to focus on aspects directly linked to sustainable NTFP management, including existing use, trade, and management patterns; ecological and cultural/spiritual concerns that increased demands for NTFPs have engendered; and tensions among the different claimants to these products, particularly on federally managed lands. The first two sections thus describe the ways in which NTFPs are important in the United States, including their sociocultural, economic, and ecological values. The last three sections focus on NTFP-related tenure conflicts, including tensions over who has a voice in policy and management decisions that affect NTFPs and their harvesters, buyers, and processors.

In Part One, Emery's overview of historical uses of nontimber forest products in the northeastern United States sets the stage for the rest of the volume by illustrating the myriad ways in which NTFPs and activities related to their harvest, use, and enjoyment have been important in the past. Jones and Lynch's discussion of contemporary sociocultural aspects of NTFPs, along with case studies by Weigand, Jahnige, and Spero and Fleming about their uses and harvesters in a variety of settings in the United States, illustrates how these products continue to be important in the everyday lives of many Americans. The key themes emerging from Part One include the notions that NTFP gathering and use traditions are long-standing and common to most, if not all, American subcultures, old and new, and that such traditions cross not only cultural but also class, gender, age, and urban-rural residence lines.

Part Two demonstrates that nontimber forest products constitute important components of both formal and informal American trade and commerce systems. In their chapter, Alexander, Weigand, and Blatner describe structural characteristics of various NTFP markets, many of which function simultaneously in formal and informal economic sectors. They then provide an overview of the scope and key aspects of domestic economic exchange patterns for these products and illustrate the extent to which many NTFPs harvested in the United States are integrated into international trade circuits.

The remaining chapters in Part Two outline some of the major ecological concerns associated with the expansion of NTFP markets as well as the continuance of old cultural traditions and the development of new ones centered around NTFP harvesting or processing activities. Vance begins with an overview of ecological sustainability issues associated with rising consumer demand for nontimber forest products. Crook and Clapp follow with a critique of market-based conservation, an approach that has gained popularity among some environmental organizations, such as Conservation International and the World Wildlife Fund, as a solution to tropical deforestation and that has been suggested as a means for addressing concerns about NTFP overharvesting in the United States. Extractive reserves also have gained popularity as a mechanism for addressing ecological sustainability questions in tropical forests, particularly in the Amazon. Love's contribution thus examines the relevance of extractive reserve systems to the U.S. context. Forest product certification constitutes a third widely used policy mechanism for addressing ecological concerns about harvesting NTFPs for which there are global markets. Mallet outlines the three major approaches used to certify forest and agricultural products and ends with a discussion of the strengths and weaknesses of such systems for NTFPs.

Sustainability discussions would not be complete without touching on the circumstances under which domestication or semidomestication of wild plants, lichen, or fungi might serve as a solution to concerns about endangered or threatened species. Teel and Buck address the issue of domestication and semidomestication of NTFPs in their overview of the different kinds of agroforestry systems. These range from types, such as hedgerows or windbreaks, where nontimber forest products are a component of fully domesticated farm-forest systems, to others, such as riparian buffer zones, where NTFP species form a wild or semiwild component of such systems. Honey is a product that has long been associated with farm-forest systems in many parts of the world. The Alexanders' case study of honey bees, which are non-native to the United States but which have become pollinators of native and non-native plants alike, illustrates the dynamic and adaptive nature of ecosystems, as well as the blurring between commercial and noncommercial aspects of NTFP harvesting activities. A common theme in Part Two is the notion that inventory and monitoring efforts are essential to sustainable NTFP management. Kerns, Liegal, Pilz, and Alexander explain how to design appropriate inventory and monitoring systems as well as provide a number of concrete examples drawn from the authors' experiences in the Pacific Northwest.

Part Three explores NTFP tenure issues on federally managed lands. Due to the critical role that Native American claims to nontimber forest products play in shaping the contours of federal NTFP policies, this section begins with a chapter by Goodman outlining the concept and application of Indian reserved rights, particularly as they pertain to wild plants, lichens, and fungi within the formal legal system of the United States. A series of case studies complements this overview, providing a sense of the complexities associated with Native American claims to NTFPs on federally managed forests. The cases include a contribution from Danielsen and Gilbert on the off-reservation harvest of wild plants among the Ojibwe in the Great Lakes region, Fisher's discussion of the 1932 Handshake Agreement between the Yakama in central Washington and the U.S. Forest Service over rights to huckleberry gathering grounds in the southern Washington Cascades, Schroeder's summary of subsistence rights of Alaskan natives, and London's analysis of the Maidu's attempts to assert their traditional claims to gathering grounds on national forests in northern California.

Part Four focuses on NTFP tenure issues at the federal level. Antypas, McLain, Gilden, and Dyson begin the section with an overview of federal resource management policies that directly or indirectly affect nontimber forest product use and management. The authors argue that the various federal agencies with land management responsibilities play an important role in shaping the conditions of access to NTFPs, particularly in the West where a large percentage of forested land is administered by federal agencies. They note that the adoption of ecosystem management as the guiding principle for federal land management during the early 1990s has increased the visibility of NTFPs in federal forest planning and decision-making processes. At the same time, the issuance of an executive order requiring federal agencies to take into account issues of environmental justice when making resource management decisions has brought the question of how to expand public participation opportunities into the policy limelight. McLain's case on wild mushroom picker participation in forest management in central Oregon illustrates the flaws of current public participation processes where migrant and/or politically and economically weak stakeholders are involved. Ringgold's piece on stewardship contracting examines the issue of expanding participation in federal forest management to include the ability of smaller-scale businesses to compete for contracts aimed at holistic management of specific areas of ground rather than the traditional forest product sales contracts.

In Part Five, Goodman's chapter on customary claims and legal pluralism provides an alternative view to the prevailing tendency on the part of U.S. policy makers and managers to think of policy and management decisions and implementation efforts as actions that take place, or that should take place, solely within formal legal frameworks. Goodman suggests the need for policy makers, land managers, and researchers to acknowledge the existence of often long-standing customary claims to NTFPs, including claims of non-native Americans, on federal lands. His review of the international literature on customary claims and legal pluralism also strongly suggests that recognition and embracement of some elements of informal legal systems may allow for the development of viable approaches to sustainable NTFP management.

KEY TOPIC AREAS NOT INCLUDED IN THIS VOLUME

Although this book covers a wide range of material related to NTFPs in the United States, it barely scratches the surface of the issues and concerns surrounding NTFPs. When we began discussing materials to include in this volume, the list included all of the topics noted above as well as numerous other aspects of nontimber forest products, ranging from state and private NTFP management and policy to transportation and import-export policies. In the course of putting this book together, we gathered data in three of these areas—state, private, and international NTFP policy—but lacked the resources to develop the analyses as well as the space to include them in this volume. The following summaries of the key themes we identified in each of these areas, however, illustrate the need for scientists and policy analysts to begin focusing greater attention on these sectors of society.

State Resource Management Policies

In the United States, state-level NTFP policies are critical components of the overall management regimes that govern who has access to which products, as well as the incentives that various landowners have for managing their lands for NTFP production or protection. Many states have laws regulating the transport of nontimber forest products across ownership boundaries; others have laws that require NTFP buyers to keep track of the quantities they purchase, as well as who they buy them from and how much they pay for products. State policies regarding NTFP harvesting vary widely depending on their natural resources and their involvement in environmental conservation. Many states have no policies directly related to NTFPs but do have endangered species, weed control, or quarantine laws that are relevant to these products. Some states have highly detailed regulations concerning harvesting certain NTFPs, such as ginseng, wildflowers, or cacti, and most, if not all, require landowner permission before harvesting on private lands. Most states regulate nontimber forest products through their forestry or natural resources departments. However, a few, such as Delaware, consider NTFPs agricultural products and thus address them through their agricultural regulations. Many states have forest products legislation, but for the most part such laws tend to be directed primarily at the harvest of wood products and, in some cases, the certification of timber workers. In short, the state NTFP policy arena is extremely complex but critical to adequate understanding of the political context in which NTFP harvesting takes place in the United States.

Private and NGO Sector Resource Management Policies

Most published NTFP policy research examines either federal or state-level policies, yet private citizens and corporations own and manage more than 71 percent of the nation's commercial forests. In addition, a number of conservation-oriented nongovernmental organizations either own property outright or have acquired important conservation easements on lands scattered across the United States. Private and nongovernmental-sector NTFP policies have the capacity to greatly constrain or facilitate harvester access to these products on much of the nation's forested holdings. In the Pacific Northwest, for example, large private landholdings functioned as de facto commons during much of the twentieth century, with timber companies allowing relatively unrestricted access to many NTFPs on their lands. In the past two decades, however, access to nontimber forest products on private lands in the Pacific Northwest has become increasingly limited: some timberland owners have developed permit systems for people wishing to acquire NTFPs from their lands, while others have shut down their lands to all NTFP harvesting, often due to concerns over liability if harvesters get hurt while on their property or to concerns about vandalism to company property and equipment. Given the large percentage of forested land in private hands, research that examines NTFP policies and management on private lands constitutes a priority for future work.

International Policies: Resource Management and Trade Policies

As nations assume greater responsibilities to each other in terms of how they regulate commerce, production, and consumption, all activities that have direct or indirect effects beyond the borders of a single nation are being swept into the domain of international regulation. The internationalization of environmental protection and trade has significant implications for the conservation and marketing of NTFPs in the longer term. International regimes for trade and for endangered species have demonstrated significant authority to impact the domestic policies of nations party to relevant treaties and members of relevant international organizations. Specifically, the World Trade Organization (WTO) and the Convention on International Trade in Endangered Species (CITES) can exercise direct and binding restrictions on domestic policy. What is not yet clear is how well environmental and trade regimes can be integrated into one another. Conflicts between the two have already occurred, and more are certain in the future.

The world trading regime is currently not designed to be very sensitive to environmental protection policies that implicate trade. The WTO is concerned exclusively with promoting and managing trade liberalization, making sure, among other things, that nations do not use trade restrictions against other nations for activities that are legal, even if environmentally harmful. For instance, products derived from exploitative mining of renewable resources cannot be excluded from international markets because of the way they were produced unless such production methods are prohibited under some other international treaty. The inability to protect domestic natural resource producers who incur greater expenses due to conservation restrictions can have deleterious consequences for both resources and producers.

The ability of environmental treaties such as CITES to prevent export-driven overexploitation is relatively weak, though once species come under the protection of the treaty their trade can be regulated under its tiered protection system. Two important NTFPs harvested in the United States, American ginseng *(Panax quinquefolius)* and goldenseal *(Hydrastis canadensis),* receive limited protection under CITES, which extends only to whole and sliced roots and parts of roots, not manufactured parts or derivatives such as powders, pills, extracts, tonics, teas and confectionery. CITES protects only individual species and not habitats, and it cannot affect management regimes for species that are not yet listed. More comprehensive agreements such as the Convention on Biological Diversity and the Rio Forest Principles, a nonbinding agreement signed at the UN Conference on Environment and Development in 1992, may become important components in the international conservation mix in the future. Developing better understandings of how international trade and environmental policies influence and are influenced by local and national nontimber forest product politics is a third critical area of investigation for additional work on U.S. NTFPs.

Other Important NTFP-Related Topics

In addition to the above three areas, topics that we strongly feel would be useful to examine further in a volume similar in scope and detail to this one include human health and safety issues associated with expanding NTFP use, phytosanitary concerns of changing transportation and marketing patterns for nontimber forest products, approaches for integrating NTFPs into resource management curricula and cooperative extension research and education programs, and the effects of current taxation and labor policies on NTFP conservation and economic development incentives for nontimber forest products.

Part One

PAST AND PRESENT

Historical Overview of Nontimber Forest Product Uses in the Northeastern United States

Marla R. Emery

Nontimber forest product (NTFP) uses in the United States are neither new nor merely quaint relics of some distant cultural and economic past. As the other chapters in this book make clear, there is a plethora of NTFPs in use at the beginning of the twenty-first century. They contribute to the livelihoods of individuals from diverse ethnic backgrounds in a variety of ways, and the social and ecological contexts within which these uses occur have profound implications for their future. However, today's uses and issues also have a past. Human reliance on nonagricultural plants has a deep and evolving history throughout North America. The story of these uses is fundamentally about relationships—between people and plants and the social structures and interactions within which those uses are embedded. It also is about movement, through both time and space. Examining those relationships and movements in the past provides insights into present-day NTFP issues and suggests questions that must be addressed as we think about their future.

In the United States, NTFPs have been derived from biomes as disparate as the temperate rain forests of the Pacific Northwest, the deserts of the Southwest, the prairie grasslands, and the New England coast. Regional NTFP uses reflect these biotic differences as well as multiple cultural traditions and their interactions. Native Americans had (and continue to have) strong local traditions that drew on a deep knowledge of the plants in their environment and incorporated practices from other peoples with whom they came into contact. Immigrant groups, whether their arrival was voluntary or forced, brought their own NTFP knowledge and practices with them, adapting them to a new environment and borrowing others from the people they encountered.

The long history of human migration has seen an accompanying movement of plant material, especially of species that people used and valued. Well before European contact, NTFPs moved along trade routes throughout North America (Turner and Loewen 1998). Within given regions, the ranges of valued species were extended by people transporting seeds or stock of individual plants with propitious characteristics to locations outside the area of a species' previous occurrence (Black 1978; Erichsen-Brown 1979; Gilmore 1931). Species arrived from other continents whenever there was a major movement of people (Crosby 1986; Grimé 1979). Many of these naturalized rapidly and were adopted into the material cultures of others. Often, gatherers actively managed NTFP species to produce desired characteristics and increase their availability (Anderson 1996; Peacock and Turner 2000).

In this chapter I provide an overview of the historical relationships between people and plants and the associated social interactions that today we would classify as NTFP uses. I examine the many material ways in which nonagricultural plants have been vital to peoples of the United States as food, medicine, and utilitarian and ceremonial materials. I also consider the range of economic modalities through which people have derived livelihood resources, from subsistence to global commodity. From the outset, I intended to explore the NTFP uses of the greatest possible range of cultural groups. This historical, multicultural approach led to consideration of both the discrete development of NTFP practices in particular locations (social as well as geographic) and the flows of material and knowledge between them.

The review focuses on the northeastern United States, including the Upper Midwest. This emphasis reflects personal research interests and location rather than the relative importance of NTFPs in a region or the availability of references on them. I have made use of ethnobotanical texts and archaeological records as well as primary narratives such as explorers' logs, traders' journals, settlers' diaries, and the promotional tracts of officials trying to encourage settlement in "new" areas. Ethnographies published in outlets like U.S. Bureau of Ethnology annual reports and the pages of *American Anthropologist* recorded plant uses of many Native American groups in the nineteenth and early twentieth centuries. Records of nondomesticated plant uses by immigrant populations from Africa, Asia, and Europe, as well as all cultural groups prior to the 1800s, were generally embedded in broader narratives. My purpose here is to be suggestive rather than exhaustive. I hope to broadly outline the area, identify topics for further investigation by others, and highlight historical processes that have direct bearing on key issues in contemporary NTFP management and policy discussions.

NORTHEAST

Since the retreat of the Wisconsin Ice Sheet, human inhabitants of northeastern North America (present-day New York and New England states) have been drawing on the region's plant life to support their existence. By approximately 3000 B.P., floral composition and locational zones were roughly similar to those of the present time (Funk 1978; Trigger 1978). Generally, deciduous tree species predominate in richer and more southerly locations, while coniferous species are more prevalent on poorer soils and at higher elevations and latitudes (Bailey 1995).

Archaeological work in New York and New England evidences the use of NTFPs as edibles and cultural materials from early prehistory to the time of European contact (Bolian and Gengras 1994; Haviland and Power 1994; Nicholas 1999; Ritchie 1969; Snow 1978). Early Woodland Era (circa 3000–2000 B.P.) burial sites have yielded shrouds and other artifacts made of bark and fiber textiles, suggesting the cultural importance of these materials. Basswood *(Tilia americana),* slippery elm *(Ulmus rubra),* Indian hemp *(Apocynum cannabinum),* and milkweed (*Asclepias* sp.) were used for cordage and textiles, the former two producing a coarse cordage while the latter two were used to make fine cordage.

It has long been held that meat and fish constituted the largest part of Early Woodland diets. However, nut remains are almost omnipresent in middens and hearth pits of the period, and Nicholas (1999) states that "the gathering of wild foods and other resources was unquestionably the economic foundation of most hunting-and-gathering systems" (p. 34). Excavations at later Woodland sites in central New York and Vermont reveal seeds or shells of an increasing variety of plant foods, including acorns (*Quercus* spp.), hickory nuts (*Carya* spp.), butternuts *(Juglans cinerea),* walnuts *(Juglans nigra),* hazelnuts (*Corylus* sp.), hawthorn (*Crataegus* sp.), cherries and plums (*Prunus* spp.), grapes (*Vitis* spp.), strawberries (*Fragaria* sp.), blueberries (*Vaccinium* spp. and *Gaylussacia* spp.), raspberries and blackberries (*Rubus* spp.), elderberries *(Sambucus canadensis),* hog peanuts *(Amphicarpa bracteata),* pigweeds (*Chenopodium album, C.* sp.), dropseeds (*Sporobolus* spp.), dock (*Rumex* sp.), roses (*Rosa* spp.), sassafras *(Sassafras albidum),* and staghorn sumac *(Rhus typhina).*

Pits lined with bark and grass indicate that NTFPs also were vital storage materials used to preserve seasonal foods and other items. Among the foods dried for later consumption were raspberries, blackberries, elderberries, grapes, chokecherries, chestnuts *(Castanea dentata),* and butternuts. NTFPs also provided material for fishing equipment. Nets and lines were made of twisted Indian hemp fiber, and hooks made of hawthorn spines have been found in at least one location. Baskets and bags made from twisted Indian hemp and basswood fibers continued to be important functional and aesthetic items well into historical times. Shelters, whether longhouses or smaller structures, generally were constructed of bark or rush mats secured to a pole frame with flooring of mats or skins, often insulated by an underlayer of evergreen boughs in cold and damp seasons.

Extensive, well-documented contact by Europeans with northeastern North America dates to about 1600 B.P. Firsthand chroniclers of this period describe Native American NTFP uses through the filters of their own cultures and interests, principally immediate survival and the long-term prospects for commercial development and colonization. Several sources (Champlain 1603; DeForest 1851; Ruttenber 1872; Society of Jesus 1898; Williams [1643] 1936) describe the use of the same construction materials that archaeological evidence suggests were used in prehistoric times. For example, writing in 1616, a missionary describes the relocation of camps in Acadia (present-day Nova Scotia, New Brunswick, and Maine):

> Arrived at a certain place, the first thing they do is to build a fire and arrange their camp. . . . The women go to the woods and bring back some poles which are stuck into the ground in a circle around the fire, and at the top are interlaced, . . . Upon the poles they throw some skins, matting or bark. . . . All the space around the fire is strewn with leaves of the fir tree, so they will not feel the dampness of the ground; over these leaves are often thrown some mats. . . . In Summer . . . they nearly always cover them with bark, or mats made of tender reeds, finer and more delicate than ours made of straw, and so skillfully woven, that when they are hung up the water runs along their surface without penetrating them. (Society of Jesus 1898, 3:77)

The use of wild edibles by Native Americans and European settlers also was documented during this period. Writing of his voyage down the St. Lawrence River in 1603, Champlain notes the abundance of wild foods in rich soils at its confluence with the St. Croix, including grapes (*Vitis* spp.), serviceberry *(Amelanchier canadensis),* hazelnuts (*Corylus* sp.), cherries (*Prunus* sp.), and currants *(Ribes oxyacanthoides* and *triste).* His description of the culinary virtues of "certain small roots, the size of a small nut, tasting like truffles, which are very good roasted or boiled" (Champlain 1603, 131) suggests that, like other explorers, he and his crew made use of NTFPs to sustain themselves. Jesuit epistolaries also mention potato- or truffle-like roots on at least three occasions between 1612 and 1616. Describing European settlers' and missionaries' efforts to dig enough to feed themselves at times when their own agricultural efforts and transatlantic food shipments frequently left them hungry, more than one of these accounts displays resentment toward indigenous inhabitants who had arrived at productive patches before them (Society of Jesus 1898).

Drawing on accounts by early English settlers in New England, DeForest (1851) indicates that Connecticut tribes sometimes mixed ground nuts *(Apios americana)* and Jerusalem artichokes *(Helianthus tuberosus)* in their succotash (a mixture of the agricultural crops corn and beans) and thickened it with flour made from walnuts, chestnuts, or acorns. In 1643, Roger Williams included numerous edibles in his guide to the Narraganset language and culture.[1] He notes that fruits and nuts—including chestnuts, acorns, and currants (*Ribes* spp.)—were dried for later consumption. He further notes that the Narraganset made oil from walnuts, while English settlers brewed a beer from chips of the tree's wood. His comments about strawberries raise interesting issues about the relationship between field agriculture, wild edibles, and indigenous management of native vegetation (all spellings as in the original): "This Berry [strawberry] is the wonder of all the Fruits growing naturally in those parts: . . . In some parts where the *Natives* have planted, I have many times seen as many as would fill a good ship within few miles compasse: the *Indians* bruise them in a Morter, and mixe them with meale [presumably corn] and make Strawberry bread" (Williams [1643] 1936, 96; emphasis in the original).

Although early English, Dutch, and Swedish immigrants to northeastern North America set out to duplicate European agricultural practices, they also relied on NTFPs. Undomesticated plant material was not only a recourse in times of crisis but also a regular complement to agricultural products. Berries, nuts, and maple sugar *(Acer saccharum)* were valuable sources of food for humans, while forests provided forage for cattle and pigs (Thompson 1853; Williams 1989). Settlers' reliance on NTFPs for both food and medicine is evident in the account of an early European resident of Long Island (all spellings as in the original; see Table 1 for Latin names):

> The Fruits natural to the Island are Mulberries, Posimons, Grapes great and small, Huckleberries, Cramberries, Plums of several sorts, Rosberries and Strawberries, of which last is such abundance in June, that the Fields and Woods are died red: Which the Countrey-people perceiving, instantly arm themselves with bottles of Wine, Cream, and Sugar . . . and so rushing violently into the fields, never leave till they have disrob'd them of their red colours, and turned them into the old habit. . . . The Herbs which the Countrey naturally afford, are Purslain, white Orage, Egrimony, Violets, Penniroyal, Alicampane,[2] besides Saxaparilla very common, with many more. . . . did we know the vertue of all those Plants and Herbs growing there (which time may more discover) many are of opinion, and the Natives do affirm, that there is no disease common to the Countrey, but may be cured without Materials from other Nations. (Denton 1670, 3–4)

The activities of Jesuit missionaries in the early 1700s were responsible for the first documented entry of a North American NTFP into the international commodity market. Petrus Jartoux, a missionary in northern

Table 1. Historical and probable Latin names

Historical name	Probable Latin name
Mulberries	*Morus* spp.
Posimons	*Diospyros virginiana*
Grapes	*Vitis* spp.
Huckleberries	*Gaylussacia* and/or *Vaccinium* spp.
Cramberries	*Vaccinium* spp.
Plums	*Prunus* spp.
Rosberries	*Rubus* spp.
Strawberries	*Fragaria* spp.
Purslain	*Portulaca oleracea*
White Orage	*Atriplex patula*[?]
Egrimony	*Agrimonia parviflora*[?]
Violets	*Viola* spp.
Penniroyal	*Hedeoma pulegioides*
Alicampane	*Inula helenium*
Saxaparilla	*Aralia nudicalis*
Linden-tree	*Tilia americana*

China, described the use and harvest of Asian ginseng *(Panax ginseng)*, surmising that it should likewise be found in northeastern North America. Joseph Francois Lafitau, a Jesuit working in New France, found that a similar root *(Panax quinquefolius)* grew in the forests of northeastern North America. Lafitau arranged for the first export to China in 1720, a trade that persists today (Foster 1995). Some decades later, George Washington is reported to have participated in the ginseng trade (Wigginton 1975).

Writing in 1853, a Vermont clergyman and schoolmaster says: "Upon the settlement of this state the ginseng was found to grow here in great plenty and perfection, and it soon began to be sought with eagerness for exportation. For many years it was purchased at nearly all the retail stores in the state, and was sent to the seaports to be shipped to China" (Thompson 1853, 221). However, he notes that heavy harvesting and forest clearing had rendered it scarce by his time. Although ginseng was much esteemed as a medicine in China, it does not appear to have been used widely in the United States. Moerman includes ginseng on the list of medicinals used by several Native American groups (1998). However, it is notably absent from Erichsen-Brown's authoritative *Medicinal and Other Uses of North American Plants* (1979), and Charles F. Millspaugh (1892), a physician and botanist writing at the end of the nineteenth century, notes that ginseng was removed from the 1882 revision of the *Pharmacopeia of the United States.*

In the 1800s, many settlers in the Northeast continued to rely on NTFPs. Thompson (1853) describes the uses of nineteen tree species found in Vermont's forests for medicinals, foodstuffs, fodder, tanning material, paper substitutes, and roofing material. Following a brief presentation of more than twenty wild fruits and berries eaten by residents, he laments, "We had intended in this place to notice a few of the many herbs and roots which are, or have been, of repute for their medicinal virtues, but we have not room" (p. 221).

As this statement suggests, native and naturalized plants may have been especially widely used for their healing properties by settler populations in the nineteenth century. Among the competing medical schools of the time, the Eclectics championed what was known as a vegetal materia medica (Foster 1995). By 1892, Millspaugh's classic text, *American Medicinal Plants,* listed 180 plants indigenous to or widely naturalized in the United States. Those who did not prepare their own herbal medicines might purchase them from organizations such as Lloyd Brothers Pharmacists or the Shakers at New Lebanon, New Hampshire (Erichsen-Brown 1979; Foster 1995). The latter produced plant-based medicines using both gathered and cultivated sources of northeastern species for domestic and export sales. Other healers and lay people relied on their own preparations, with results ranging from the proverbial "snake oil" to carefully prepared and time-tested remedies.

James Still (1877) provides an example of the latter. The son of former slaves, he served as a medical practitioner in the New Jersey pinelands. At an early stage in his professional life he distilled sassafras root, peppermint *(Mentha piperita),* and other herbs for sale to the Philadelphia pharmaceutical market. After studying a medical botany text and a medical formulary, he began to prepare remedies for his family using native and naturalized species as well as cultivars. Eventually he was pressed into service for a larger community. Throughout his several decades of practice, he said, "It has always been my delight to prepare my own medicines. . . . By this means I had the pleasant satisfaction of knowing what I was giving to my patients, and I always knew it to be a good and pure article" (p. 130).

Further evidence of immigrant populations' uses of NTFPs during this time is gleaned from the 1863 proceedings of the Farmers' Club (American Institute 1864). More than three hundred pages of letters between farmers and the club's officers demonstrate the punctuated flow of NTFP knowledge and plant materials as well as the relationship between "wild" species, agriculture, and people. Kansas wildflower seeds were mailed to New York gardeners, and considerable interest was expressed in the "discovery" of a "new" fibrous plant—Indian hemp—which, as previously noted, had been used by Native Americans as a cordage and textile fiber from prehistoric times. A New Hampshire farmer described maple sugar production at length, recommending it for both personal consumption and sale.

By this time, the region's Native American population had been severely displaced both geographically and culturally. However, ethnographers working into the first decades of the twentieth century documented their use of NTFPs in the recent past and at the turn of the century. Morgan (1901) provides detailed descriptions and diagrams of Iroquois material culture employing NTFPs. These include the continued manufacture of cordage from slippery elm and basswood, which was used for items ranging from tump straps to bird traps. He notes that tobacco, an important cultivated ceremonial plant, was cut with sumac "to diminish its stimulating properties" (p. 34), while maple sugar and ground nuts continued to be important food items. During research conducted in the 1920s and 1930s, Tantaquidgeon (1972) documented the survival of medicinal-plant knowledge and use among members of northeastern Native American groups. Describing Delaware and Mohegan practices, she notes the highly personal and proprietary nature of much medicinal knowledge. Additional detailed descriptions of NTFP uses by northeastern tribes in this period can be found in annual reports of the Bureau of American Ethnology and the *American Anthropologist* (old series).

The use of NTFPs by northeastern Native Americans and immigrant Americans alike throughout the twentieth century and into the twenty-first demonstrates both change and continuity. The *Handbook of North American Indians* documents the contemporary importance of NTFPs to northeastern tribes in the 1970s (Trigger 1978). The continued Iroquois observance of maple and strawberry ceremonies and the inclusion of medicinal herbs in ritual prayer demonstrates the ongoing importance of gathering as a spiritual and practical act (Tooker 1978). Production of ash baskets has great cultural and economic importance for skilled individuals on and off reservations throughout the region (Benedict and David 2000; Fenton 1978; Hofman 1999; Woods 1994). However, like all cultural practices, basketry traditions in the region have evolved with their social and ecological contexts. Today, fancy baskets may follow traditional designs but are as likely to be colored with commercially purchased dyes as with vegetable and mineral preparations (Hofman 1999).

Among peoples from a variety of origins outside the North American continent, medicinal and edible uses of NTFPs may be especially important. A 1983 study of the health care beliefs and practices of Puerto Ricans, Haitians, and low-income African Americans in the greater New York City area documented herbal medicinal practices by each of these cultural groups. Haitian immigrants may consult with *Docteur-feuilles,* literally "leaf doctors," and *Sages-femmes,* or lay midwives, who use medicinal plants, herbs, and roots in their treatment of patients. Latino immigrants may seek remedies at botánicas located throughout Spanish-speaking neighborhoods. African American home remedies and traditional healers often use herb teas (John Snow Public Health Group 1983). Although sources for these medicinals are unclear, some may be harvested in the region's urban and/or rural forests.

The contemporary use of wild edibles is not confined to rural environments or any one ethnic group. The plethora of field guides and how-to books on wild edibles, epitomized by Euell Gibbons's much reprinted *Stalking the Wild Asparagus* (1962), demonstrates the continued vitality of wild edibles as a broadly cherished notion, if probably somewhat less widely utilized food source. However, observations throughout the Northeast indicate that even in postindustrial cities, individuals from a variety of ethnic groups do continue to seek out and consume edible and medicinal NTFPs (Brill and Dean 1994; Emery 1999; Jahnige 1999; Tritton 2000).

UPPER MIDWEST

The mixed hardwood forests of the Great Lakes region also have supported humans since the emergence of woodlands following the last glacial retreat. Archaeological evidence provides clues to some NTFPs in use by humans in this region before written documentation is available. As in the Northeast, excavations from the late Archaic period (3000–1000 B.P.) in the Upper Midwest indicate extensive use of wild plant foods including hickory nuts, acorns, butternuts, and walnuts. Excavations of Middle Woodland sites (circa 100 B.P.) suggest that the seeds of marsh elder *(Iva frutescens),* giant ragweed *(Ambrosia trifida),* and pigweed were important food sources in this period, as were nuts, tubers, and berries (Cleland 1992; Keene 1981). Artifacts from sites dating to the early to mid-1600s include vegetable fiber cordage as well as gathered foodstuffs (Mason 1986).

Jesuit missionaries, chronicling their activities and observations for European readers, provide what is probably the earliest written documentation of NTFP use in the North Woods. Arriving in the upper Great Lakes region in the first half of the 1600s, their letters are peppered with descriptions of Native American uses of plant materials, which also helped to sustain the missionaries. Birch bark *(Betula papyrifera)* was used as a building material for housing and canoes as well as for baskets for food storage and cooking. Berries (eaten fresh and dried), wild rice *(Zizania palustris),* and maple sugar receive frequent mention as dietary staples. The Jesuits also noted medicinal plant uses as well as a root sometimes employed to poison enemies or commit suicide (Society of Jesus 1898).

By the 1800s, the westward expansion of the United States brought European American merchants, travelers, and government functionaries to the region in increasing numbers. Many of their journals and other records are preserved in the Library of Congress (1999) collection *Pioneering the Upper Midwest: Books from Michigan, Minnesota, and Wisconsin, ca. 1820–1910.* This collection documents the use of NTFPs for food, medicine, building materials, ceremonial and other cultural uses, and their important role in subsistence and commerce for both Native Americans and European Americans during that period.

Cranberries (*Vaccinium* spp.), maple sap, and wild rice are perhaps the most prominently mentioned NTFPs in these texts. Cranberries figure in writings as diverse as tracts designed to attract settlers to the North Woods (Henry 1896; McClung 1870) and travel logs (Michigan State Historical Society 1908; Seymour 1850). Citing an article in the September 29, 1849, issue of the *Minnesota Chronicle,* Seymour (1850) indicates that in that season Native American women were arriving daily in St. Paul to exchange cranberries for (unspecified) goods. As of that date, 2,135 barrels of the berries had been shipped from the area. Some twenty years later, McClung stated that "from the cranberry marsh on his farm, many a farmer makes more money than on his crop" (1870, 150).

Maple sap was processed into at least three forms: sugar, syrup, and vinegar. Sugar has the advantage of superior resistance to spoilage and ease of storage as compared to syrup. According to Seymour, maple sugar was a principal component of the northern Minnesota Chippewa (Ojibwa) diet. He reported that "some Indian families manufacture 1000 pounds annually" (1850, 195). Autobiographical accounts of life in mid- to late-1800s Michigan make it clear that maple sugar also was important to European American settlers (Hufford 1950; Michigan State Historical Society 1908; Nowlin 1876). Raised by Scottish parents on a homestead near Petoskey, Michigan, in the last decades of the nineteenth century, Hufford indicated that her family avoided the expense of purchasing sweetener by making maple sugar. They ate cakes of their sugar as candy, sometimes pressing it into iron muffin molds to produce attractive forms. In his 1876 narrative of growing up on a farm near Dearborn, Michigan, Nowlin recounted how his family derived much needed income by making and selling as many as three hundred to four hundred pounds of maple sugar in some years. The risk of spoilage notwithstanding, maple syrup was also a favored food item. Hufford reported that her family of thirteen enjoyed syrup on pancakes and hosted syrup-on-snow parties for their entire community. Both Native Americans and settlers also converted maple sap's sweetness into vinegar. Moerman (1998) indicates that the Ojibwa and Potowatomis permitted maple sap to sour into vinegar. Hufford and Nowlin each mention making maple vinegar. According to Hufford, "After the buds commenced to come out on the trees, the sap did not make such good syrup. Instead of making the sap from the last run into syrup, it was stored in barrels and made a very nice grade of vinegar" (1950, 106).

Additional NTFPs were important in the processing and trade of maple items. Sap-collecting implements were made from forest plant material including hollowed birch blocks and basswood branches shaped into spouts (Hufford 1950). Seymour's description of Ojibwa sap troughs illustrates the role of other NTFPs in the collection of maple sap: "A rectangular piece of birch bark, about eighteen by twenty inches, is plaited with two folds at each end, which are secured in their places by a string made of the bark of the linden-tree; thus forming a tight and elastic square vessel, capable of holding a gallon or more" (1850, 195). Schoolcraft (1821) and Kinzie (1873) each report that mococks[3]—birch bark baskets often embellished with porcupine-quill designs—were filled with maple sugar and traded at Michilimackinac (Mackinaw, MI). Kinzie notes that Native American women brought them as commodities to exchange for other goods.

Wild rice, also known by the French term "folle avoine," was a staple of Native American diets in the Great Lakes region. Its importance is evidenced by the frequency with which it is mentioned in European Americans' descriptions throughout the 1800s (Keating 1824; Kinzie 1873; McClung 1870; Schoolcraft 1821; Seymour 1850; State Historical Society of Wisconsin 1804). Indeed, wild rice was so prominent a feature of regional Native American cuisine that both the Menominee in upper Wisconsin and the Ojibwa of the St. Croix River area frequently were referred to as the Folle Avoine (State Historical Society of Wisconsin 1804).

Throughout the 1800s, wild rice was a vital subsistence resource and commodity for trade. In a region where growing seasons are too short for most domesticated grains, this wild grass seed provided the staple carbohydrate of Native Americans and also was consumed by European American settlers (Seymour 1850). Chroniclers included in the *Pioneering the Upper Midwest* collection describe several variations on the basic three-part rice processing sequence of toasting, threshing, and winnowing. Processed wild rice was (and is) durable and easily portable. Other NTFPs no doubt played a role in its storage for subsistence use, as McClung reported that processed rice was stored in baskets (1870) and Kinzie observed that it was kept in cordage bags (1873). Several entries in the journal of French-speaking trader Michel Curot suggest that in the early years of the century, fawn skins, removed virtually whole and sewn shut, provided the container and unit of measure for trade in wild rice. For example, his entry of Tuesday, October 20, 1803, notes, "I traded for the Rum Four fawn-skins of wild rice" (State Historical Society of Wisconsin 1804, 410).

Ethnobotanical studies written in the early twentieth century for the Bureau of American Ethnology (Densmore 1974) and the Public Museum of the City of Milwaukee (Smith 1923, 1928) attest to the continued importance of NTFPs for Native Americans of the region. On the basis of studies conducted between 1907 and 1922, Densmore documented the ongoing use of 208 botanical species or groups of species by Chippewa (Ojibwa) peoples for such uses as amusement, antidote, ceremonial, charm, dye, food, medicine, pleasure, smoked, toys, and utility. Her exhaustive work, first published in 1928 in the *Forty-fourth Annual Report of the Bureau of American Ethnology* and later reprinted by Dover Publications

(1974), provides detailed descriptions of the preparation and use of many NTFPs, copiously illustrated by photographs of plant materials, equipment, and people, often engaged in processing NTFPs.

Densmore states that "the two most important vegetable foods were maple sugar and wild rice" (p. 308) and describes the preparation of these foods, including timing, social organization, processes, structures, and equipment. As her photographs of birch bark lodges for boiling maple sap and basswood fiber used for hooking and tying wild rice indicate, structures and equipment for processing edibles were made from other NTFPs. Densmore also details Chippewa use of plants as medicine. She notes two broad types of medical practice involving plant material: the specialized and proprietary cures of the trained medical society, the Midewiwin, and generally known household remedies for common ailments. On the basis of descriptions provided by Midewiwin affiliates and others, she describes the preparation and storage of medicinal barks, roots, flowers, leaves, and stalks. Brief sections also document the use of plants for dyes, charms, and "useful and decorative arts." Noting that "the uses of birch bark are many and various" (p. 387), she also describes birch bark harvesting and processing in detail.

Botanist Huron Smith identifies plants and plant uses described to him between 1921 and 1923 by Menominee on their reservation in northwest Wisconsin and Meskwaki (a.k.a. Fox) on tribal lands in Tama, Iowa (1923, 1928). Following multiple three- to four-week field trips to each location, Smith lists 277 and 267 plant species for the Menominee[4] and Meskwaki, respectively, documenting their uses through the categories of dyes, fibers, foods, medicinals, and miscellaneous practices (including charms and ceremonials). Focused particularly on medicinal plant species and their uses, Smith notes the individuality of cures employed by skilled healers in both tribes and their predominant use of remedies that combined several plant ingredients.[5] Both he and Densmore (1974) indicate that skilled medical practitioners would suspend the use of a treatment after approximately eight days if a patient's condition did not appear to improve. According to Smith, skilled medical practitioners "understand that there is a proper season for gathering the various medicines, when the medicinal principles are the most active," and interrupt or defer other activities to harvest at this time. He reports somewhat bemusedly that Meskwaki medicine men and women observe "certain rules about gathering these medicines, which they still follow religiously" (1928, 191), including harvesting no more than a specified amount even when the supply was abundant and a long journey was required to reach the site.

Like conservation biologists today (Cox 2000; Nabhan et al. 1991), Smith lamented the loss of traditional knowledge and practice due to the passing of tribal elders and the impingement, both physical and social, of European American culture:

> The young people are not interested in retaining the lore of their grandparents. . . . The older people, who have this lore, are fast dying out. (1928, 180)

> With encroaching civilization, these [wild] foods are becoming harder to find. . . . Then, too, last year, the game warden who patrols the reservation warned them that they could not gather their wild rice as before, for he said it was against the law, and that he would arrest them and throw them in jail, if they did. Imagine a whole tribe of 1800 Indians, named after the wild rice and forbidden to gather it on their own reservation. (1923, 59)

Although much knowledge was surely lost, many practices may simply have gone unlooked for and, consequently, largely unnoticed in the industrial and postindustrial 1900s. Evidence that Native Americans and European Americans in the region continued to rely on NTFPs is found in photographs and formal studies. In 1937, Farm Security Administration photographer Russell Lee captured Red Lake Ojibwa (Chippewa) picking blueberries in the cutover region around Little Fork, Minnesota, and the archives of the Hiawatha National Forest include photographs of European Americans picking berries in Michigan's Upper Peninsula two years later. Nor was NTFP use erased by the second half of the century. I documented the continued use of over 130 NTFPs from more than 100 botanical species by people of diverse cultures in the mid-1990s (Emery 1999). The gatherers I interviewed in upper Michigan ranged in age from sixteen to seventy-six and harvested NTFPs to preserve family and personal customs as well as to obtain vital livelihood resources (Emery 1998).

INSIGHTS FROM THE PAST, QUESTIONS FOR THE PRESENT

The history of NTFP use in the northeastern United States provides several insights into the relationships between people and plants and associated social processes that are germane to contemporary debates throughout the nation. The patterns of the past help clarify the complexity of many current issues and model the range of potential futures for NTFP use and management.

Relationships between People and Plants

NTFP uses have been an important factor in the development and maintenance of many past and present plant assemblages. For example, immigrants to North America transported valued plant species such as traditional culinary and medicinal herbs between continents. With time such species can become so integral to the landscapes within which they are found that it may be difficult to ascertain their origin and not altogether sufficient in assessing their biological importance. Thus, a noted nineteenth-century botanist and physician wrote in the introduction to his edition of a Virginia flora:

> My *Flora* professes to be principally an outline of the *indigenous* plants of Virginia. . . . Concerning not a few of the other plants which I have described in the following pages, I have found it much more difficult to determine, in what light I ought to consider them; whether as truly indigenous, or as foreigners which have early made their way into the country, and have now completely established themselves in the new soil, mixing and even breeding, with the natives. (Barton 1812; emphasis in the original)

Movement of plant material also has occurred at intracontinental scales, as valued plant material was transported along regional trade routes. Within small territories, people moved individuals of favored species for ease of access and ensured availability. Indeed, human cultures and forests may reasonably be considered to have coevolved in glaciated regions. Not infrequently, the movement of NTFP species was designed to integrate them functionally and geographically with other livelihood activities. Such was the case when Algonquin farmers in the Northeast promoted the growth of strawberries near their cornfields, preserving them for the production of strawberry bread outside of their growing season.

In addition to the deliberate transport of NTFP species, people have historically tended the individual plants they relied on and used other techniques to manage the landscape for species they valued. For example, Native Americans in California pruned favored shrub species and managed their landscapes to produce basket-making materials (Anderson 1999).

Observations of the role of humans in moving and tending plant material suggest a set of interrelated questions that probe the terms "native," "natural," and "wild" and their implications for contemporary NTFP management.

- How long must a plant species have been present in an area to be considered "native"? Are there scalar issues in that designation (i.e., how far must a plant species have been moved before it leaves its "native" territory)? Does the transport vector make a difference (i.e., nonhuman animal or weather/hydrologic versus human action)?
- What makes a plant assemblage "natural"? What distinguishes an introduced species that is considered invasive and a target for eradication from one that is designated ecologically benign or valuable and, thus, to

be maintained? What kinds and levels of human intervention can be accommodated within the term "natural"?

- What are the salient characteristics of a "wild" plant? Is a plant wild if its form is to some extent the result of human manipulations? Are there meaningful gradations in human management from entirely unmanaged to semicultivated to fully domesticated?[6] How are these expressed ecologically? How do they interact?
- What role might human activity have played in the establishment and maintenance of ecological communities that we value today? Does the discovery of human agency change our sense of its value? By what criteria do we judge such value?
- As we negotiate and renegotiate the answers to these questions, what guidance, if any, do they offer for making decisions about vegetative management and NTFP policy?

Relationships between People Involving NTFPs

It is particularly striking that people of diverse ancestral origins have used nontimber forest products. The NTFP practices of cultural groups developed in the places they inhabited, using the plant material in their environments with the knowledge acquired through experience. But just as plant material has been deliberately (and accidentally) moved through space, so too have knowledge and practice. Thus, NTFP uses have been both culturally distinctive and reflective of intercultural exchange.

Development and transfer of traditional knowledge are important factors in the dynamics of NTFP use. In some cases, the exchange of knowledge has been multidirectional. Drawing on early historical records and experiments with precontact cooking technologies, Munson (1989) suggests that early Native Americans consumed processed maple sap only as syrup. European settlers, who learned to harvest and process maple from the region's first inhabitants, introduced the iron kettle for boiling. This change in processing technology may have led to the first production of maple sugar by both cultural groups. However, knowledge "flow" has not always been continuous and unbroken. Rather, it has been conveyed again and again between individuals and groups, sometimes being reinvented or transformed in the process. For example, as noted earlier, Native Americans had used Indian hemp to make cordage for millennia before European American settlers in the early 1800s wrote enthusiastic letters to Farmers' Club officers about a wonderful "new" fiber.[7] Further, while some NTFP knowledge has historically been widely available, other knowledge has been regarded as highly specialized and proprietary. Thus, the identity of edible berries and simple herbal remedies were broadly known, while complex medicinal preparations and their proper harvesting and administration were not.

Diversity is a feature of past NTFP economic uses. From early history to the present, NTFPs have contributed to livelihoods through a variety of exchanges between people that include family-centered subsistence, gift giving, barter, petty commodity production, and sale as global commodities. One or more of these economic uses often were integrated with other livelihood strategies, as attested to by the diaries of midwestern settlers who describe farming, consuming their own maple sugar to avoid the expense of purchasing sweetener, and selling some for much needed cash. NTFPs also have been central to the maintenance of social and spiritual life. The smoking of tobaccos, in which the domestic species and nondomesticated species such as sumac and mullein *(Verbascum thapsus)*[8] often were mixed, was an essential element in many Native American spiritual ceremonies and social negotiations.

Numerous historical examples suggest that NTFPs may be particularly important livelihood resources in times of crisis and for individuals with limited access to other economic strategies. For example, Turner documented the use of famine foods by indigenous peoples in the Pacific Northwest (Turner and Davis 1993). Malcolm X reported that when he was a child his family ate dandelion greens picked in the yards of their Lansing, Michigan, neighborhood when they faced extreme hunger (Haley and X 1964). Biographers of Bonnie and Clyde noted that during the Depression "jobless American families were forced to survive in any way possible. Sending children into the woods to pick dandelions, wild mushrooms and onions for 'Hoover Soup' was common" (Steele, Scoma, and Scoma 1999, 11).

Notwithstanding the importance of the multiple economic uses of NTFPs, the global commodity status of some products has long commanded special attention. Ginseng provides the most notorious historical example of the promise and pitfalls of global commodity status. North American ginseng has had a sustained international market, if fluctuating prices, for more than three centuries. Figures as noteworthy as George Washington and as unsung as Appalachian woodsfolk have profited from the sale of this prized root. However, their respective positions in the commodification process were quite distinct as, no doubt, were their earnings. Sustained demand, heavy harvesting, and conversion of forestland eventually led to the development of agricultural production systems that currently satisfy much of the market demand.

Unfortunately, there is nothing new about conflicts over access to NTFPs. And as the notes of hungry Jesuits suggest, neither are the racial overtones to these conflicts. Traditional gathering systems often included strategies for allocating access to an NTFP and harvesting for sustained availability (Densmore 1974; Peacock and Turner 2000). The long histories of many gathering systems suggest that where gatherers understood these strategies and complied with them, they were both socially and ecologically effective. However, the example of the game warden who threatened to arrest Great Lakes Ojibwa if they harvested wild rice in the early decades of the twentieth century is illustrative of one of the many ways that the social structures and processes of NTFP use have been disrupted in the past. These include the criminalization of gathering and the imposition of an alternative land use/land cover on gathering grounds.

Again, historical observations raise questions that are central to the development of contemporary NTFP policy:

- Who has valuable information about nontimber forest products? What kinds of NTFP knowledge are there and how are they produced? How is such knowledge disseminated? To whom? By whom? To whom does that knowledge belong? What is the relationship between knowledge, harvesting practices, and ecological results?
- How is access to NTFPs established and controlled? What are the historical patterns of access? What shaped them? What are the respective needs and interests of groups that harvest or seek to harvest NTFPs? What kinds of criteria are accepted as legitimate claims? What is the relationship, if any, between different types of access regimes and social and ecological results?
- How do the economics of NTFP use affect associated social and ecological patterns? Are different economic uses associated with different social groups? Do different economic uses tend to produce correspondingly different ecological patterns? What are the spatial and social dynamics of different economic uses? Are they mutually exclusive or can they cohabit the same space?
- What role do NTFPs play in gatherers' material and cultural lives? How do vegetative management and regulatory policies affect the viability of those roles? What responsibility, if any, do public land managers and policy makers have to understand and incorporate gatherers' concerns into their decisions? How can, or should, the episodic nature of much NTFP use—particularly that associated with economic crisis—be factored into management and policy?

OPPORTUNITIES FOR FUTURE RESEARCH

This overview of historical NTFP use suggests the fallacy of simplistic assumptions about the relationship between people and plants. The history of ginseng harvesting in the Northeast makes it clear that NTFP use can deplete a plant population. However, the use and active management of other species has demonstrably increased their populations and enhanced biodiversity at the community and landscape scales (Peacock and Turner 2000). Thus, the historical evidence indicates that the ecological results of NTFP use are contingent upon the interaction of biophysical and social structures and processes. The reproductive characteristics of a species and its role(s) in the ecological community and landscape, the plant part being harvested and the manner and timing of harvest, all have a bearing on the results of NTFP use for the plants in question and the people who rely on them.

The historical record also sheds light on the types of people who use nontimber forest products and the variety of their functional and livelihood uses. Indigenous peoples were the first to rely on North America's NTFPs, and they continue to have special importance for many Native Americans today. However, virtually every immigrant group to arrive on the continent has made use of its nondomesticated plants. NTFPs have been consumed directly, given as gifts, and exchanged for cash and other goods. They have been notably important livelihood resources for individuals at times when the market economy has failed to provide adequate means of existence. At the start of the twenty-first century, they continue to be important to rural and urban residents from a variety of ethnic backgrounds.

This chapter has only scratched the surface of the lessons of the past. The opportunities for more research on historical NTFP uses are great, and in-depth regional studies that explore the full range of such uses by multiple cultural groups have yet to be written. Perhaps more sorely needed, however, are critical historical studies that probe the questions above. The potential value of such studies is great. Policies that fail to acknowledge the biophysical and social complexity of NTFP use run the risk of creating results that are ecologically perverse or socially unjust or both. History cannot provide easy answers to our current dilemmas, but it can help to put them in context and point the way toward workable solutions for tomorrow.

NOTES

1. The Narraganset lands were located in present-day Rhode Island.
2. The inclusion of Elecampane *(Inula helenium),* a species indigenous to Europe, and its medicinal use by several eastern tribes (Moerman 1998; Tantaquidgeon 1972) illustrates the multidirectional flow of plant material and use knowledge between people and places.
3. Spelled "makuk" by Densmore (1974).
4. However, Smith did not document a use for all species listed in the Menominee ethnobotany. Citing the common experience of ethnographic scholars, who learn new information with each subsequent visit, he indicates that "the writer has decided that plants not known to be used by the Menomini [*sic*] should be included in the various lists, so that future investigators may discover and record names and uses of such plants" (1923, 13–14).

5. Smith's descriptive lists of individual medicinal species also mention European American pharmacological uses where he was aware of them.

6. Ford (1985) suggests that human behavior toward plants may be viewed along a continuum of degrees of human manipulation from simple foraging to cultivation to domestication.

7. Although use of Indian hemp for fiber clearly was not new, the proposal that it be converted to a fully domesticated field crop likely did constitute a new relationship between people and the species, with attendant changes in the social structures and processes that would surround its use.

8. Mullein was introduced to North America from Europe.

REFERENCES

American Institute. 1864. *Annual Report of the American Institute of the City of New York*. Albany, NY: Comstock and Cassidy.

Anderson, M. K. 1996. "Tending the Wilderness." *Restoration and Management Notes* 14(2): 154–166.

———. 1999. "The Fire, Pruning, and Coppice Management of Temperate Ecosystems for Basketry Material by California Indian Tribes." *Human Ecology* 27(1): 79–113.

Bailey, R. G. 1995. *Description of the Ecoregions of the United States*. Washington, DC: USDA Forest Service.

Barton, B. S. 1812. *Flora Virginica*. Philadelphia: D. Heartt.

Benedict, L., and R. David. 2000. *Handbook for Black Ash Preservation, Reforestation/Regeneration*. Mohawk Council of Akwesasne, Department of the Environment. New York: Hogansburg.

Black, Michael J. 1978. *Plant Dispersal by Native North Americans in the Canadian Subarctic*. Ann Arbor: Museum of Anthropology, University of Michigan.

Bolian, C. E., and J. B. Gengras. 1994. *Early and Middle Woodland Occupation in the Upper Connecticut Valley*. Concord, NH: New Hampshire Department of Transportation.

Brill, S., and E. Dean. 1994. *Identifying and Harvesting Edible and Medicinal Plants in Wild (And Not So Wild) Places*. New York: Hearst Books.

Champlain, S. de. 1603. *Of Savages or Voyage of the Sieur de Champlain Made in the Year 1603*. Toronto: Champlain Society.

Cleland, C. E. 1992. *Rites of Conquest: The History of Michigan's Native Americans*. Ann Arbor: University of Michigan Press.

Cox, P. A. 2000. "Will Tribal Knowledge Survive the Millennium?" *Science* 287: 44–45.

Crosby, A. W. 1986. *Ecological Imperialism: The Biological Expansion of Europe, 900–1900*. Cambridge, UK: Cambridge University Press.

DeForest, J. W. 1851. *History of the Indians of Connecticut: From the Earliest Known Period to 1850*. Hamden, CT: Shoe String Press.

Densmore, F. 1974. *How Indians Use Wild Plants for Food* and *Crafts* (formerly titled *Uses of Plants by the Chippewa Indians*). New York: Dover Publications.

Denton, D. 1670. *A Brief Description of New York, Formerly Called New Netherlands, with Places Thereunto Adjoining*. New York: M. Gowan.

Emery, Marla R. 1998. *Invisible Livelihoods: Nontimber Forest Products in Michigan's Upper Peninsula.* Ann Arbor, MI: UMI Dissertation Services.

———. 1999. Interview with George Leduc regarding his nontimber forest product gathering in the greater Burlington, Vermont, area.

Erichsen-Brown, C. 1979. *Medicinal and Other Uses of North American Plants: A Historical Survey with Special Reference to the Eastern Indian Tribes.* New York: Dover Publications.

Fenton, W. N. 1978. "Northern Iroquoian Culture Patterns." In *Handbook of North American Indians: Northeast,* ed. B. G. Trigger, pp. 296–321. Washington, DC: Smithsonian Institution.

Ford, R. I. 1985. "The Processes of Plant Food Production in Prehistoric North America." In *Prehistoric Food Production in North America,* ed. R. I. Ford, p. 411. Ann Arbor: Museum of Anthropology, University of Michigan.

Foster, S. 1995. *Forest Pharmacy: Medicinal Plants in American Forests.* Durham, NC: Forest History Society.

Funk, R. E. 1978. "Post-Pleistocene Adaptations." In *Handbook of North American Indians: Northeast,* ed. B. G. Trigger, pp. 16–27. Washington, DC: Smithsonian Institution.

Gibbons, E. 1962. *Stalking the Wild Asparagus.* Putney, VT: Alan C. Hood.

Gilmore, M. R. 1931. *Dispersal by Indians a Factor in the Extension of Discontinuous Distribution of Certain Species of Native Plants.* Ann Arbor, MI: Michigan Academy of Science, Arts and Letters.

Gleason, H. A., and A. Cronquist. 1991. *Manual of Vascular Plants of Northeastern United States and Adjacent Canada.* Bronx, NY: New York Botanical Garden.

Grimé, W. E. 1979. *Ethno-Botany of the Black Americans.* Algonac, MI: Reference Publications.

Haley, A., and Malcolm X. 1964. *The Autobiography of Malcolm X.* New York: Ballantine Books.

Haviland, W. A., and M. W. Power. 1994. *The Original Vermonters: Native Inhabitants, Past and Present.* Hanover, NH: University Press of New England.

Henry, W. A. 1896. *Northern Wisconsin: A Hand-Book for the Homeseeker.* Washington, DC: Library of Congress.

Hofman, T. 1999. Maine Indian Basketmakers Alliance. Personal communication.

Hufford, G. H. 1950. *Then Came May.* Washington, DC: Library of Congress.

Jahnige, Paul. 1999. *Nontimber Forest Product Uses and Values in Baltimore, Maryland.* Baltimore, MD: Community Resources.

John Snow Public Health Group. 1983. "Common Health Care Beliefs and Practices of Puerto Ricans, Haitians, and Low-Income Blacks Living in the New York/New Jersey Area." Report prepared for the National Health Service Corps, Department of Health and Human Services, Region II, contract no. 120-83-0011.

Keating, W. H. 1824. "Narrative of an expedition to the source of St. Peter's River, Lake Winnepeck, Lake of the Woods, &c. &c. performed in the year 1823 by order of the Hon. J. D. Calhoun, Secretary of War, under the command of Stephen H. Long, Major U.S.T.E. Volume 2. compiled from the notes of Major Long, Messrs. Say, Keating, and Calhoun." From "Pioneering the Upper Midwest: Books from Michigan, Minnesota, and Wisconsin, ca. 1820–1910," at *http://memory.loc.gov/ammem/umhtml/umhome.html.* Washington, DC: Library of Congress.

Keene, A. S. 1981. *Prehistoric Foraging in a Temperate Forest: A Linear Programming Model.* New York: Academic Press.

Kinzie, J. A. M. 1873. *Wau-Bun: The Early Days in the Northwest.* Washington, DC: Library of Congress.

Library of Congress. 1999. *Pioneering the Upper Midwest: Books from Michigan, Minnesota, and Wisconsin, ca. 1820–1910.* Washington, DC: Library of Congress.

Mason, R. J. 1986. *Rock Island: Historical Indian Archaeology in the Northern Lake Michigan Basin.* Kent, OH: Kent State University Press.

McClung, J. W. 1870. "Minnesota As It Is in 1870. Its General Resources and Atractions with Special Descriptions of All Its Counties and Towns." From "Pioneering the Upper Midwest: Books from Michigan, Minnesota, and Wisconsin, ca. 1820–1910," at *http://memory.loc.gov/ammem/umhtml/umhome.html.* Washington, DC: Library of Congress.

Michigan State Historical Society. 1908. *Pioneer Collections.* Vol. 10. Washington, DC: Library of Congress.

Millspaugh, C. F. 1892. *American Medicinal Plants.* New York: Dover Publications.

Moerman, Daniel E. 1998. *Native American Ethnobotany.* Portland, OR: Timber Press.

Morgan, L. H. 1901. *League of the Ho-De-No-Sau-Nee or Iroquois.* New York: Dodd, Mead.

Munson, P. J. 1989. "Still More on the Antiquity of Maple Sugar and Syrup in Aboriginal Eastern North America." *Journal of Ethnobiology* 9:159–170.

Nabhan, G. P., D. House, H. S. A., W. Hodgson, L. H. S., and G. Malda. 1991. "Conservation and Use of Rare Plants by Traditional Cultures of the U.S./Mexico Borderlands." In *Biodiversity: Culture, Conservation, and Ecodevelopment,* ed. M. L. Oldfield and J. B. Alcorn, pp. 127–146. Boulder, CO: Westview Press.

Nicholas, G. P. 1999. "A Light but Lasting Footprint: Human Influences on the Northeastern Landscape." In *The Archaeological Northeast,* ed. M. A. Levine, K. E. Sassaman, and M. S. Nassaney, pp. 25–38. Westport, CT: Bergin and Garvey.

Nowlin, W. 1876. *The Bark Covered House, or Back in the Woods Again; Being a Graphic and Thrilling Description of Real Pioneer Life in the Wilderness of Michigan.* Washington, DC: Library of Congress.

Peacock, S. L., and N. J. Turner. 2000. "'Just Like A Garden': Traditional Resource Management and Biodiversity Conservation on the Interior Plateau of British Columbia." In *Biodiversity and Native America,* ed. P. E. Minnis and W. J. Elisens, pp. 133–179. Norman: University of Oklahoma Press.

Reid, R. L. 1989. *Picturing Minnesota 1936–1943: Photographs from the Farm Security Administration.* St. Paul: Minnesota Historical Society Press.

Ritchie, W. A. 1969. *The Archaeology of New York State.* New York: Natural History Press.

Ruttenber, E. M. 1872. *History of the Indian Tribes of Hudson's River; Their Ori-*

gin, Manners and Customs; Tribal and Sub-Tribal Organizations; Wars, Treaties, Etc., Etc. Port Washington, NY: Kennikat Press.

Schoolcraft, H. R. 1821. *Narrative Journal of Travels through the Northwestern Regions of the United States: Extending from Detroit through the Great Chain of American Lakes to the Sources of the Mississippi River, Performed as a Member of the Expedition under Governor Cass in the Year 1820.* Washington, DC: Library of Congress.

Seymour, E. S. 1850. *Sketches of Minnesota, the New England of the West. With Incidents of Travel in That Territory during the Summer of 1849.* Washington, DC: Library of Congress.

Smith, H. H. 1923. *Ethnobotany of the Menomini Indians.* Milwaukee: Public Museum of the City of Milwaukee.

———. 1928. *Ethnobotany of the Meskwaki Indians.* Milwaukee: Public Museum of the City of Milwaukee.

Snow, D. R. 1978. "Late Prehistory of the East Coast." In *Handbook of North American Indians: Northeast,* ed. B. G. Trigger, pp. 58–69. Washington, DC: Smithsonian Institution.

Society of Jesus. 1898. *Travels and Explorations of the Jesuit Missionaries in New France, 1610–1791: The Original French, Latin, and Italian Texts, with English Translations and Notes; Illustrated by Portraits, Maps, and Facsimiles.* Cleveland: Burrows Brothers.

State Historical Society of Wisconsin. 1804. *Collections of the State Historical Society of Wisconsin.* Vol. 20, *A Wisconsin Fur-Trader's Journal, 1803–1804.* Washington, DC: Library of Congress.

Steele, P. W., B. Scoma, and M. Scoma. 1999. *The Family Story of Bonnie and Clyde.* Gretna, LA: Pelican Publishing.

Still, J. 1877. *Early Recollections and Life of Dr. James Still.* New Brunswick, NJ: Rutgers University Press.

Tantaquidgeon, G. 1972. *Folk Medicine of the Delaware and Related Algonkian Indians.* Harrisburg, PA: Pennsylvania Historical and Museum Commission.

Thompson, Z. 1853. *Natural History of Vermont.* Rutland, VT: Charles E. Tuttle.

Tooker, E. 1978. "Iroquois since 1820." In *Handbook of North American Indians: Northeast,* ed. B. G. Trigger, pp. 449–465. Washington, DC: Smithsonian Institution.

Trigger, B. G. 1978. *Handbook of North American Indians: Northeast.* Washington, DC: Smithsonian Institution.

Tritton, L. 2000. Nontimber forest product harvesting in Philadelphia. Personal communication.

Turner, Nancy J., and A. Davis. 1993. "'When Everything Was Scarce': The Role of Plants as Famine Foods in Northwestern North America." *Journal of Ethnobiology* 13:171–201.

Turner, Nancy J., and D. C. Loewen. 1998. "The Original 'Free Trade': Exchange of Botanical Products and Associated Plant Knowledge in Northwestern North America." *Anthropologica* 40:49–70.

Wigginton, E. 1975. *Foxfire 3.* New York: Anchor Books.

Williams, M. 1989. *Americans* and *Their Forests: A Historical Geography.* Cambridge, UK: Cambridge University Press.

Williams, R. [1643] 1936. *A Key into the Language of America*. Providence: Rhode Island and Providence Plantations Tercentenary Committee.
Woods, L. 1994. "A History in Fragments: Following the Forgotten Trail of Native Adirondack Cultures." *Adirondack Life* (November/December):30–38, 61, 68–73.

The Relevance of Sociocultural Variables to Nontimber Forest Product Research, Policy, and Management

Eric T. Jones and Kathryn Lynch

The intent of this chapter is to highlight the critical need to understand and incorporate sociocultural issues associated with NTFP harvesting in forestry research, management, and policy making. We begin by examining the relevance of several political ecology approaches to the study of nontimber forest products. Building on this theoretical foundation, we discuss the challenges of conceptualizing and categorizing NTFP harvesters and then illustrate the relevance to policy making of some specific demographic variables. We highlight the need for data that are disaggregated by age, ethnicity, and gender while illustrating the complexity of such variables for NTFP research. We also examine the importance of understanding livelihood strategies and harvester culture and conclude with a discussion regarding the interrelationship of traditional ecological knowledge (TEK), tenure theory on self-regulation, and stewardship behaviors.

Nontimber forest product harvesters do not operate in a vacuum but are embedded within larger human social networks. Likewise, cultural phenomena such as rituals and traditions that involve NTFPs are produced from the interplay of social networks. In fact, contemporary NTFP harvesting in the United States often is rooted in traditions that have persisted against great odds, including shrinking resource bases, loss of rural knowledge, and the hegemony of timber production, cattle grazing, and recreational activities on U.S. forestlands. Yet, with few exceptions, natural resource policy makers and managers either have not had sufficient sociocultural data or have ignored sociocultural issues in regard to NTFPs, which has often resulted in the creation of less than favorable environments for harvesting. Ignorance about cultural use patterns has meant that there has been a lack of successful long-term nontimber forest product management and policy or even formal scientific study of NTFP ecological systems. Without understanding these patterns it is difficult to identify who harvests, their motivations, their traditions, or how they will be impacted by policy and management. Given that local, indigenous, and traditional ecological knowledge about NTFP resources is a major feature of sociocultural processes, policies developed without incorporating such information miss an opportunity to provide incentives for ecological conservation and use. Furthermore, to develop NTFP policies and manage these resources without paying attention to the types of knowledge that are available effectively disenfranchises important forest users from critical forest management decision-making processes (see McLain on environmental justice, part four of this volume).

EXAMINING NTFPS THROUGH A POLITICAL ECOLOGY LENS

Political ecology stresses the interconnections of cultural and ecological systems and posits that it is necessary to understand the dialectical interactions between these two systems to fully comprehend the dynamics of resource use, management, and conservation. Therefore, looking at the question of NTFP use through a political ecology lens draws attention to both the sociostructural and environmental contexts. The sociostructural context includes such diverse variables as household consumption patterns, local and international market prices, labor availability, migration patterns, local, national, and international policy and law, and the presence and strength of civil society in an area. Local, national, and international political and economic stability are also critical factors. The environmental context includes everything from the list of resources found in an area to flood cycles, seasonal fruiting patterns, game abundance, and migration patterns. Taken together, the political ecology framework provides a more holistic understanding of the factors influencing resource use and ultimately conservation. In the following section we provide an overview of several main approaches to political ecology that have developed and suggest ways in which they can inform sociocultural research and analysis of NTFPs.

One political ecology approach situates local human ecological dynamics within the macropolitical economies in which they are embedded (Greenberg and Park 1994). It attempts to capture how local human variation, adaptations, and microlevel power dynamics closely linked to ecological systems are affected by varying levels (e.g., local and regional) and types of power associated with global political economic processes, such as the expansion of capitalism (Greenberg and Park 1994; Watts and Peet 1993; Wolf 1982). For example, ongoing research by Jones[1] with commercial NTFP harvesters in the Pacific Northwest suggests that multiple modes of production[2] occur at the local community level, despite pressures to conform to global economic trends. Individuals working alone through extended kinship networks, cooperatives, and other social institutions extract forest species for subsistence and exchange in noncash trade. Native

Americans and Caucasians with long-standing traditional use patterns often value maintaining these gathering traditions, with many Caucasians openly looking, as a means to preserve their independent lifestyles, to use a mixture of NTFP cash and noncash trade as an alternative to full participation in the formal economy. Yet, these forms of production are often overlooked or dismissed by economic development and forest management policies that favor formal business structures.

Political ecology provides a useful framework for looking at the social stratification of the NTFP arena by wealth (i.e., capital) and prestige. For example, a key concern is the differential access and control over resources among NTFP stakeholders of different classes. Historically, timber interests dominated public land management (Hays 1989; Hirt 1994). In recent decades, this control has gradually eroded as other interests such as recreation and conservation groups have gained power and influence, especially with regard to public land policy (Hays 1989; Keiter 1990). Forest recreation has increased substantially through the years with greater public interest, more opportunities (e.g., ski parks), and effective lobbying efforts by special interest groups. At the same time, conservation political movements have helped elevate the status and influence of forest science in the formulation of forest management and policies (Antypas 1998).

Some NTFP recreational harvesters have benefited from the increased power of conservation science and recreation. McLain, Christensen, and Shannon (1998) point out that amateur mycologists in mushroom clubs are often active participants in scientific studies and identify themselves as conservationists. A related study found that recreational harvesters have much stronger ties to government agencies than commercial harvesters (Love, Jones, and Liegel 1998). In the early 1990s, mycology clubs in western Washington used this power to help pass new regulatory measures governing commercial harvests of wild mushrooms. Commercial mushroom harvesters for the most part were unable to organize themselves into a powerful enough voice to influence the formation of the regulations. In the wake of the law, some highly productive local mushroom economies such as the Olympic Peninsula have basically collapsed.

Another example of social stratification and differential power between harvesters is the ability of scientists to secure research areas. Vast amounts of lands in the United States are set aside for formal scientific studies. In New Mexico alone over a million hectares of land (3.3 percent of the state) are designated for research (Harrington 1996). In many cases these areas attempt to preclude or strictly limit nonresearch activities. The degree to which such barriers can be effectively enforced or whether nonscientific NTFP harvesters stay out of research areas is an area ripe for study.

Building on the political economy orientation, another approach examines human ecological relationships through a hierarchy of scales (Blaikie and Brookfield 1987; Bryant 1992). Political ecologists working in this tradition focus on constructing chains of explanations for environmental degradation that link together different social, economic, political, ecological, and geographic levels. These chains of explanations range from describing local land management (e.g., small forest owners) to outlining the interrelations among local managers and other groups that have power to influence or control local land management to the interactions that make up larger state and global political economies (Stonich 1993). Applied to non-timber forest products, "chains of explanations could be created to analyze the power dynamics of institutional arrangements that mediate" between harvesters and the NTFP resources at different scales (Stonich 1993).

For example, with many NTFPs, the buying stations where the product is bought from harvesters are often a central link between local harvesters and the multitude of regional entities that affect local activities.[3] Buying stations may be field stations for regional buyers or may themselves be direct connections to national and international distributors and retail markets. Buying station operators and distributors often exchange information about local harvest conditions, product quality, and regional, national, and international product prices. In addition, buying stations serve not only as points where products are exchanged for cash but also as points where equipment (e.g., baskets) is supplied, where harvesters and buyers can socialize, and where new harvesters can learn trade secrets. Since it is difficult for scientists, managers, and economic developers to find and talk with harvesters, researchers typically seek out buying station operators, who tend to know a lot about NTFP harvesters because of their daily interactions with them. However, it is important to recognize that buyers often have reciprocal relationships with harvesters and may protect them by limiting the types of information they divulge to researchers, or if necessary, by providing misleading information.

A number of political ecology theorists focus on discourse analysis, and the ways in which discourse is a form of power, to examine the interconnection of production systems, views of nature, and resource use (Escobar 1996; Havelkov and Escobar 1998; Heller 1996). Escobar (1996) suggests that the ways in which nature is socially constructed through modern forms of knowledge or epistemological lenses (e.g., western scientific methods) are forms of power perpetuated by social institutions that can invalidate other epistemologies (e.g., harvester's view of nature). He further argues that developer narratives of planning and management are presented as "rational" and "objective," leading to normalization and control of the social world. One effect of the use of this discourse is that the local context of "remote" or rural communities is redefined as a "resource" to be planned and managed by outsiders.

Another useful approach in political ecology relevant to sociocultural analyses of NTFP use and management is influenced by Foucault's theory of disciplinary power (1995), which refers to the disciplinary character of power and the forms of knowledge produced through institutional practices. McLain (2000) argues that this approach offers a way to examine everyday and informal politics and power. It is characterized by looking at practices and mechanisms of power (e.g., harvesting permits or regulations governing resource access) and how they work to shape the fields of power (e.g., management and traditions) in which resource systems are embedded.

In a recent study of wild mushroom politics in central Oregon, McLain (2000) identities five key elements of disciplinary power that, when applied in combination, serve to facilitate greater control over wild mushrooms by the nation-state management regime. These elements include categorization and ranking of wild mushroom pickers, segregation of pickers in time and space from other forest users, development of systems for tracking pickers and their actions within the forest, creation of a personnel and resource-efficient monitoring and enforcement system, and professionalization of knowledge and occupations associated with wild mushroom harvesting and management.

Inherent in the disciplinary power perspective is the recognition of many important levels and kinds of power, not just those of formal law. For example, harvesters might ignore new policies requiring them to obtain permits, particularly if those policies concern harvesting from a favorite forest patch that they have been using for years. By ignoring the requirement, the harvester is exercising a form of power that Scott calls "everyday resistance" (1990). From a sociocultural perspective, the challenge to resource managers is to explore why the regulation is resulting in the behavior before invoking actions that may hasten "the problem."

Foucault argues that it is useful to construct policy genealogies that examine how connected past events have led us to think a particular management practice or set of regulations is self-evident or natural when in fact they are merely the result of a specific set of social and ecological circumstances coming together at a particular point in time (McLain 2000, 100). "In essence, genealogy transforms knowledge claims, and the status that is attached to them, into objects of critical reflection and thus opens up new possibilities for political change" (Ransom 1997). For the manager, the construction of such genealogies can expose wrongful assumptions about the appropriateness of certain types of regulations for manipulating the behavior of local resource users. For the harvester, genealogies might reveal the chain of historical or traditional practices that results in a belief about access and land use rights.

The political ecology approach used by biocultural anthropologists offers a strategy for studying the sociocultural linkages to human and environmental health as well as risk factors. Leatherman and Thomas (1996) identify three key elements of this approach: expanding analyses to include social contexts beyond proximal indicators of socioeconomic status (wealth, health); exploring the ways in which environmental and historical contexts shape local environmental processes and social relations over time and the impacts they have on human biology; and including human agency as a variable in understanding individual and social responses and adaptation to environmental stressors. For example, a biocultural anthropologist might undertake a risk assessment of a rural community to look at how reciprocal exchanges of nontimber forest products could increase food supplies or provide raw materials to create exchangeable goods. Another relevant application to the NTFP arena would be to examine the health impacts of harvesting in forest areas sprayed with herbicides. Leatherman and Thomas go on to suggest that "deconstructing and following the consequences of coping actions of human agents is an informative approach for understanding human biology and behavior." Applied to the NTFP arena, researchers might follow the physical reactions (e.g., sickness) and social responses of harvesters regularly working in cold and wet weather with inferior gear, unreliable transportation, and a poor diet.

In addition, the biocultural political ecology approach could be applied in the NTFP arena by looking at dialectical relationships between harvester health and forest health. To what degree does the harvesting of NTFPs require and promote forest biodiversity in a biological stewardship sense as well as influencing management decisions? How in turn does that translate to increasing biological stability in individuals and overall community health? Such a study would benefit from a theoretical framework and set of integrated methods that could measure human health, profile harvester behaviors (e.g., micromanagement of the forest for multiple species through selective harvesting), and map the flow of knowledge between harvesters, scientists, and managers.

Although biocultural anthropology is focused primarily on human biology, it is a relevant scientific approach that treats human ecological systems as dynamic, embedded in varying scales of social, economic, and political complexity, and at the same time does not overlook the individual. It is also one of the more sophisticated examples of a truly integrated, interdisciplinary scientific research approach.

These various works illustrate the diverse applications of political ecology. Regardless of the particular issue or geographic location, the common theme is that political, economic, and ideological structures influence human-environment interactions. As forest management and policies seek to influence human-environment interactions, understanding how political, economic, and cultural variables impact human behavior becomes necessary for designing successful programs. Indeed, we argue that is it imperative that researchers, managers, and policy makers understand both the cultural and the environmental contexts in which they work. By looking at the use of natural resources, embedded in complex social systems of political, economic, and cultural opportunities and constraints, incentives, and disincentives, it is possible to illuminate variables that might act as restraints or that might influence the efficacy of policy and management. Overall, it is clear that forestland management does not take place in a vacuum, but within particular cultural and environmental contexts, and that the interrelation of these variables at different scales of analysis needs to be acknowledged and incorporated within natural resource policies.

WHAT IS A HARVESTER?

A central problem in sociocultural analyses of nontimber forest product networks has been the inability of researchers to provide "thick" descriptions of NTFP harvesters. Lack of funding for social science natural resource research is a significant barrier, which can lead researchers to employ cost-effective but often inappropriate methodologies. For example, the use of written surveys with commercial wild mushroom harvesters in a sustainability study on the Olympic Peninsula had close to a zero response rate (Love, Jones, and Liegel 1998). In contrast, the use of ethnographic methods during the same study yielded extensive data about harvester livelihoods, harvest methods, household income, ethnic variability, and so forth. This disparity illustrates that although ethnographic methods are more time-intensive than survey methods, they are probably the most effective way to get quality data on NTFP harvesters.

Beyond financial and logistical constraints, there are also significant conceptual considerations when attempting to define NTFP harvesters. In thinking of the political ecology of discourse analysis, several considerations arise. The first is that how we categorize resource users has political and ultimately cultural and ecological consequences. Thus, the categories we use are not neutral or value-free categories, but rather have significant importance in defining the management issues. Second, attempts to categorize harvesters are problematic since they are extremely diverse. Exploratory research and reviews of the literature reveal that the motivations for contemporary NTFP harvesters are highly variable (Emery 1998; Hansis 1998; Richards and Creasy 1996). Because of this heterogeneity, it is problematic both to have simplistic or vague categories (e.g., commercial versus noncommercial) that tell us little about the harvesters, as well as to deconstruct harvesters into smaller and smaller units for analysis. In addition, harvester types are not mutually exclusive of each other, as an extraction activity may have (and usually does have) many purposes. For example, quite often plants collected for purposes of healing also satisfy a spiritual need.

Cognizant of these challenges and limitations, we present a categorization of harvesters that we have found to be useful for recognizing general intent and probable behavior. The following list deconstructs "harvester" into a more descriptively useful set of six major types, primarily based on extraction purpose or motivation. These categories should be used only as a beginning framework for organizing more detailed descriptions of variability such as mobility patterns, ethnicity, gender, age, class, and cultural identity.

- Subsistence Harvester—Subsistence harvesting refers to the collection of plant foods for household consumption for reasons of sustenance (i.e., food and nourishment). In its pure form, subsistence does not involve market exchange for cash or trade. In reality, subsistence gathering is often linked with patterns of reciprocity through trade, gift giving, and sharing within social networks.
- Commercial Harvester—Commercial harvesting refers to NTFP collection to exchange or trade for any form of payment. Cash exchange is the most obvious and possibly dominant form of commercial activity, but cannot be said with any certainty, given only scant research into harvester household economics. Preliminary research with mushroom harvester networks suggests frequent trading of products for goods and services.
- Recreational Harvester—This type of gathering is motivated by the pursuit of pleasure or exercise. Typically, the quantities of resource that are removed are small (e.g., a couple gallons of mushrooms). If more is removed, it might also be considered a subsistence or commercial activity.
- Spiritual Harvester—Individuals who fall into this category view harvesting activities as a spiritual endeavor or treat NTFPs as sacred objects. Harvesters across all ages, ethnicities, and genders have described gathering as a spiritual experience, even if it is also subsistence, recreational, or commercial in nature. For example, women from the Hoh tribe in northwest Washington still journey to specific areas of the forests as they have for generations to harvest sacred bear grass and peel cedar for their baskets.
- Healer—Healers are individuals who gather nontimber forest products for the purpose of healing, using plant products to cure sickness or disorder in other people, animals, or some entity.
- Scientific Harvester—Scientific harvester refers to individuals who collect NTFPs or reserve resource areas for scientific observation. This category includes formal scientists and amateur or informal scientists. Although traditional ecological knowledge (TEK) arguably is a form of science, it is treated separately in this chapter. Our intent here is to get the reader to conceive of formal and amateur scientists as a harvester category.

DEMOGRAPHICS

Estimations of the overall harvester population and breakdown by type are somewhat speculative given the lack of reliable demographic data. However, since markets for NTFPs have expanded substantially in recent years (Von Hagen and Fight 1999), it is likely that harvester populations would have seen parallel growth. Automation is unlikely to have replaced harvester labor since nontimber forest products generally require manual extraction methods. As cultivatable alternatives become available for wild counterparts, it is possible there will be an increase in mechanized harvesting, or at least more intensive management of units in an agroindustrial sense (see Teel and Buck, this volume). With known quantities of NTFPs in the millions of dollars shipped domestically and internationally (Alexander, Weigand, and Blatner, this volume; Schlosser and Blatner 1995; Von Hagen and Fight 1999), it is likely that the part- and full-time workforce population numbers in the tens of thousands.

Mushroom clubs are found in every state, with some like the Puget Sound Mycological Society having several hundred members. As previously mentioned, many club members also engage in amateur science, thus adding to the numbers of harvesters who could be considered to be engaging in NTFP science. It is readily apparent that nontimber forest product recreational activities such as berry gathering figure prominently in thousands of people's lives throughout the country. If occasional berry picking were considered, the number of NTFPs harvested for recreational purposes would surely number in the millions. Factoring in the large Native American population of Alaska (Schroeder, this volume), undoubtedly there must be thousands of subsistence harvesters. Demographic numbers for spiritual harvesters and healers are even more speculative.

With the exception of Native American ethnographies, little literature discusses age as a variable in NTFP harvester research. However, through participant observation in the field and in conversations with research colleagues throughout the United States, it is clear that NTFP harvesting is spread across a broad age range and is a culturally significant variable. A few examples drawn from ongoing research begin to illustrate this claim. A number of kids have described harvesting as a source of fun and a way to make a little spending money. Even within the confines of child labor laws, many kids are able to contribute to their family's overall household economy through subsistence gathering. Many retired natural resource workers enjoy NTFP harvesting as a way to retain a working relationship with the forest. In some families and cultural groups, the age range represents generational knowledge flows when children follow family elders to the forest to learn where patches are and how to harvest.

ETHNICITY

Ethnicity is characterized by individuals or populations who identify with a common ancestry, language, and custom (American Anthropological Association 2001). Since resource use patterns, motivations, group organization, and the sexual division of labor vary across ethnic groups, understanding these differences should help policy makers and resource managers make more informed decisions. However, although ethnic analysis may suggest that certain groups might behave in certain ways, it is an area of research requiring extreme caution. For one, ethnicity is exceedingly difficult to ascribe to individuals since it is based on how people perceive their ethnic origin. Sometimes ethnicity is relatively synonymous with nationality, but nations are typically made up of many ethnic groups (e.g., India has hundreds). Thus, it is important to clarify the use of labels such as Japanese or Peruvian and to use clear criteria for what constitutes an ethnic division.

From a political ecology perspective, it is valuable to examine how some individuals or groups might be privileged or discriminated against based on cultural backgrounds or phenotype or both. For example, U.S. citizens who are harvesters and of Mexican and Central American ethnic origin are often presumed to be undocumented illegal aliens. This supposition illustrates how management, law enforcement, scientists, and others have labeled harvesters as belonging to particular ethnic groups based on subjective observations such as phenotype (e.g., skin color). However, phenotypic markers are rarely confined to a single ethnic group and so are risky to use as ethnic descriptors. Language and customs are more viable markers of ethnicity but should also be exercised with caution. As Paulson (1992) illustrates, ethnic identity is not fixed but rather quite malleable. She points out that gender and ethnicity are negotiable dimensions of identity that shift through space and time. Likewise, Stronza (2000, 169) demonstrates that people can shape and manipulate ethnicity to accommodate certain situations or achieve particular goals.

One perfect illustration of the relevance of this type of analysis to NTFP harvesting in the United States occurred several years ago. Within a national park, a sign regarding harvesting had been posted in multiple languages. On the one hand, this was an important step forward, in that a government agency was recognizing that there was ethnic variability in the NTFP harvester population and that many could not read English well. On the other hand, however, the languages on the sign (Korean, Vietnamese, Spanish, and English) did not reflect the dominant harvester languages in the area (Lao, Khmer, Spanish, and English), which illustrates once again the critical need for accurate sociocultural data in forestry research, management, and policy making.

GENDER

Recent research has also demonstrated the critical role that gender plays in differentiating resource use. Gender is commonly understood to be socially constructed and to include all of the socially given attributes, roles, activities, and responsibilities connected to being a male or a female in a given society. These socially constructed differences and relations between men and women are understood to be dynamic and to vary by situation and context (Oxfam 1994; Parker et al. 1995). As Margaret Andersen writes, "Gender is a dynamic concept: its meaning in any culture varies across time and a variety of other social concepts of differentiation, such as race, ethnicity, age, class and others. And like race, ethnicity, class and other social concepts, gender assigns people to social categories that establish our life chances and direct our social relations with others" (1993, 75).

Joan Scott puts forth two propositions that help to frame the issues surrounding gender: first, "gender is a constitutive element of social relationships based upon perceived differences between the sexes," and second, "gender is a primary way of signifying relationships of power" (1988, 42). The emphasis on understanding power relations is a critical focal point. Gender analysis thus asks some basic questions: Who does what? When do they do it? Who has what? Who decides what? These questions illuminate the sexual division of labor and gender roles as well as differential opportunities and power between men and women. Yet, as the Managing Ecosystems and Resources with a Gender Emphasis (MERGE) Program[4] notes, gender analysis "requires going beyond statements about 'women' and 'men' to understand how historical, demographic, institutional, cultural, socioeconomic and ecological factors affect relations between women and men of different groups, which partly determine forms of natural resource management" (Schmink 1999, 2).

Since the 1970s, conservation and development practitioners have paid increasing attention to the variable of gender. New theoretical frameworks as well as tools for data collection and analysis have been developed in order to capture the complexity of gender relations (March, Smyth, and Mukhopadhyay 1999; Paulson 1996; Thomas-Slayter, Esser, and Shields 1993). These tools are now proving to be useful in providing data on the complexity of gender relations in the management of natural resources.

A significant amount of research has demonstrated the theoretical basis and practical necessity for inclusion of gender as a variable in research on conservation and development (Buvinic 1986; Kabeer 1994; Moser 1993; Overholt et al. 1991; Slocum et al. 1995; Leach 1994). These studies show how gender is central to the issue of who participates and who benefits from conservation and development projects and have illustrated that resource use is often differentiated by gender. For example, research conducted by the Ecology, Community Organization, and Gender (ECOGEN) project[5] illustrates how effective resource management, including consideration for productivity as well as long-term sustainability and equitability, is strengthened through explicit attention to gender (Thomas-Slayter, Esser, and Shields 1993, 2).

Buenavista and Flora found that "activities, control of resources, and responses to increased environmental degradation all had gender-related aspects" (1994, 43). They note that traditional field methods would have missed the critical role women play in resource management, and that without an understanding of how women manage natural resources and adapt to changes in the availability of those resources, designing and implementing strategies to improve resource management would fail. Likewise, Muirragui and Anderson (1995) found that "without specific attention to gender and women in development issues, socio-economic research does not necessarily provide information on differences between men's and women's roles, responsibilities and rights, and women may continue to remain 'invisible' and by-passed by technical assistance and other project activities." These examples reflect a growing body of literature that seeks to document how gender systems interact with environmental and agricultural systems (Netherlands Development Assistance 1997; Rocheleau 1988; Sachs 1996).

Although this work has primarily been conducted in developing countries, the frameworks and tools are applicable and relevant to NTFP management issues in the United States. Unfortunately, U.S. policy makers are missing the opportunity to learn from the wealth of experiences offered by the international conservation and development arenas. This absence of gender analysis and ethnographic research has meant that our understanding of NTFP systems remains rudimentary. At this point, managers and policy makers are unable to answer the most fundamental questions regarding NTFP harvesters and their resource use patterns. In the context of U.S. nontimber forest products, not only must we understand the specific habitats being utilized by harvesters, but we also must identify who in the household is using these forest resources as well as who benefits and who bears the costs. Understanding these dynamics allows us to comment on the impact of this resource use at the different levels of biodiversity. We then must move beyond the catalogue of "who does what?" and "who has access and control?" to an analysis of the underlying power structures that determine such relationships, and from this understanding it is possible to confront the power structures that reproduce inequality.

To date, only exploratory research has been conducted in this arena. Yet, this research suggests that commercial NTFP harvesting affords economic opportunities for some women, even in cultural contexts where they traditionally have not been involved in natural resource–related work. This is especially true in rural settings where men have dominated such work (Gilden 1996). For example, although in the Pacific Northwest the majority of NTFP harvesters are men, in certain sectors, such as commercial mushroom harvesting, women appear to have greater opportunities and may outnumber men. For example, many of the commercial mushroom field buyers are women, as are the employees of many brush sheds where floral green processing takes place (e.g., manufacturing wreaths).

As Thomas-Slayter, Esser, and Shields note, "Gender analysis increases our understanding of gender-based division of labor, indigenous knowledge, resource access and control, and participation in community institutions with respect to natural resource management" (1993, 1). These are all critical elements necessary for efficient and equitable forest management. Without gender-differentiated data regarding roles and responsibilities within the NTFP community, managers cannot develop appropriate policies and programs. Thus, the absence of gender analysis about NTFPs in the United States represents a critical failure of natural resource managers in this country.

To conclude this section on demographics—in which we looked only briefly at the specific variables of age, ethnicity, and gender—we would like to reiterate that harvesters are not a homogeneous category. Rather a person's identity is defined by a multitude of factors including age, ethnicity, sex, class, and so on, all of which play a role in defining an individual's relationships, roles, responsibilities, and location within power structures. Likewise, all of these variables help define a person's relationships to natural resources. These variables do not operate in isolation, but in tandem. For example, women are seldom observed among Latino mushroom harvesters in the Pacific Northwest, whereas Southeast Asian–American women are highly visible pickers alongside their families or extended family networks.

We now move from demonstrating the relevance and some of the challenges of incorporating sociocultural variables such as age, ethnicity, and gender analysis into NTFP research and policy making processes to examining livelihood strategies and issues of quality of life.

LIVELIHOOD STRATEGIES AND QUALITY OF LIFE

In her research on NTFP harvesters in the Upper Peninsula of Michigan, Emery (1988) defined livelihood strategies as the actions of people to secure a living inside and outside of marketplaces. A broad interpretation of this concept encompasses a range of interlocking behaviors such as household economic strategies (e.g., commercial harvesting, reciprocal gift giving, part-time jobs), networking and knowledge sharing, and human-ecological relationships and attitudes. The following quote from Jones's personal experiences points to some of the complex motivations that can underlie livelihood strategies.

> It was another long day of lousy mushroom picking. It was one thing the weather hadn't cooperated, you can't control that. It's quite another all those gates turning up on the forest access roads. A bunch of us were standing around the evening campfire when we heard that folks in Tok, Alaska were walking out their backdoors and picking hundreds of dollars worth of morels. Revelry broke out and everyone got excited wishing they could go. Two days later two of us were fully packed and caravanning the 2,500 mile journey north to Alaska. Fifty-two hours later with stops only for fuel, we drove straight into the heart of a 100,000 square acre burn producing morels as far as the eye could see. The feeling that comes over you when you hit the motherlode is like no other. It isn't just that you might make some money, but that you get to be out in the woods, doing something you love that is constructive, not destructive to the earth. And we got to spend two months in beautiful Alaska. (Mushroom harvester 1992)[6]

This story shows how livelihood strategies may be embedded in values and a concern for quality of life. Though the trip to Alaska may have offered financial opportunities, the traveling, fun, and working in the woods were also important factors. These things are often overlooked or bypassed by scientists and managers because they are not easily quantified like economic statistics. Similarly, mainstream social values may not reflect values found among many NTFP harvesters. For example, some policy makers and managers have suggested that commercial nontimber forest products do not provide ample income possibilities. However, a harvester's view of what is important for a high quality of life often indicates that income potential in the NTFP industry is only one consideration out of many. These views bring into question mainstream values such as the notion of poverty. For many harvesters, poverty is often less about financial status than it is having the means (e.g., access to the resource) to fulfill their livelihood less burdened by social and political constraints.

NTFP commercial extractors often describe how they value their status as independent contractors, the power of being their own boss, and deciding when, how, and where to work. Even though most harvesters would welcome the opportunity to make greater revenue, many have stated in interviews that they would make less money to continue harvesting because of the joy they get from the type of work. They recognize that few work opportunities exist where you can spend entire days off of trails, largely apart from civilization, as an active participant in a forest ecosystem. The following quote illustrates this preference and typifies a common interview response when asked if money was a primary motivation for picking:

> No, I just enjoy picking. As a matter of fact, when I was first approached about being a buyer I told the company owner that despite the fact I'd

> make a lot more money as a buyer, if it ever interfered with my picking and I cannot get out in the woods as often as I want, I'll quit. I do it because I just enjoy it out there. I walk and exercise. I like to have a work-oriented purpose associated with going to the woods. I could work harder, and pick all the small ones as well, and then I'd make a lot more money . . . but I prefer to make just enough so I can keep going out.

Preliminary data from research currently under way by Jones suggest that many rural residents near forests are using NTFP harvesting as a way to supplement income and avoid taking part-time jobs or moving to urban areas with more work opportunities. Emery (1998) and others have found that many NTFP harvesters (and sometimes buyers) employ subsistence and commercial gathering strategies as economic buffers through such things as supplemental food, cash trade, or using raw materials to make reciprocal exchange items (Love and Jones 1995; McLain 2000; Wigginton 1973). Research is desperately needed to clarify the degree to which NTFP harvesting is a safety net by which rural cultural fabric is held together in hard times.

Another important area of future research is to look at how natural resource policy and management that makes NTFP harvesting more difficult (e.g., road closures) might contribute to the destablization of rural economies and encourage the problems that often accompany such downturns (e.g., increasing domestic violence, theft). Research by Gilden (1997) found that timber harvest declines in Oregon's Santiam Canyon in the 1990s led to increased community and social stress such as unemployment, underemployment, increased levels of domestic violence, and broken families. A combined lack of activities, jobs, and parental guidance has contributed to severe problems among many of the canyon's youth, including alcohol and drug abuse, early motherhood, and gang-related activities. However, in this example the canyon communities were arguably at risk by being dependent on large logging companies controlling the area economy. Policies decreasing the supply of logs from the local national forest possibly accelerated trends toward automation and employee layoffs that were under way in the region. Yet, clearly there can be negative social consequences to environmental policies, and in the case of NTFP harvesting impacts, it remains unclear just how significant they can be to the stability of the broader sociocultural fabric.

Many harvesters share similar values and attitudes about the forest. In hundreds of interviews of mushroom pickers across all harvester types, nearly everyone talked about their love of being out in nature. Although "environmentalist" carries the social stigma of antiforest worker for many harvesters, even many commercial harvesters cautiously refer to themselves as environmentalists. Their descriptions of the forests and recognition of the importance of conservation are often indistinguishable from the values expressed by the voices of environmental movements (e.g., William Cronon, Gray Snyder, and Aldo Leopold). For example:

> Some of my favorite, most productive patches have been destroyed by logging. I've been able to harvest in the same patches for 15 years, and made good money at it, and then, wham, it's clearcut and rendered useless to me and any other harvesters picking other things in the area. If anybody bothered to add up all the special forest products (aka NTFP) gathered in that area they logged I'll bet over 50 years it would be a lot more sustainable. And furthermore all the critters would still have food and nesting materials. Yep, the overall ecosystem would be better off and a lot nicer to look at. (Mushroom harvester 1995)

Quality of life motivations are often spiritual in nature. Spirituality is used broadly here to depict any sort of worship, metaphysical connection, deification, or sacred meaning attached to objects, activities, or places associated with nontimber forest products. Moerman (1998) lists hundreds of NTFPs used by Native American tribes as ceremonial and witchcraft medicine, charms, magic, and sacred items. Many Japanese Americans retain matsutake mushroom gift-giving traditions dating back over a thousand years in Japan. According to Hosford et al., "Matsutake have been used and revered by the Japanese people for more than a millennium and have become more than just a seasonal delicacy. They also symbolize fertility, and by extension, good fortune and happiness" (1997). Spiritual motivations even underlie scientific pursuits, as posited by a mycology colleague who said that "the process of searching for hidden gems in the forest can connect one to the marvels and sacredness of the natural world."

Quality of life can be reflected in the rituals of some NTFP harvesters. In its formal sense, ritual is the observance of a set form or system of rites, religious or otherwise (*Webster's* 1983). Interpreted more broadly, ritual involves forms of action or purpose different from everyday life (Mitchell 1996). Theorists have widely debated the purpose of ritual—from serving to attach individuals to society (Emile Durkheim), to being a process for transcending social structure (Victor Turner), to being performance or political theater (Richard Schechner) (Mitchell 1996). As Rappaport (1968) argued, rituals in some cultural groups can be of such central importance as to facilitate the regulation of their universe. For Native Americans, NTFPs are often used as sacred objects in rituals and are embedded in spiritual belief. For example, the Ojibwa place sweet birch bark on coffins when burying the deceased (Moerman 1998). In discussions with Nez Perce women gatherers, they describe performing a ritual whereby strict codes of conduct are handed down between elders and new inductees to their circle. Outside of Native American descriptions, discussion of NTFP harvester rituals is minimal, yet broadly interpreted rituals occur frequently across all harvester types. For example, several mushroom harvesters (unknown to each other) have indicated in interviews that out of respect for the forest they never take the first mushroom of the season. In New England, many families have described how the art of maple syrup tapping is often passed down from parents to children.[7]

Quality of life is also reflected in contemporary NTFP cultural institutions such as the festivals and celebrations that evolve around seasonal harvests of regionally specific species. Examples include ramp (wild leek) festivals in Appalachia, filbert fairs in the Northwest, and wild blueberry festivals and pancake feeds at maple syrup houses in New England. Wild mushroom festivals can be found in Michigan, Colorado, Virginia, Oregon, and many other states, not to mention the fact that mycology clubs across the country frequently host public gatherings displaying regional mushrooms. In addition to fostering community well-being through the expression of a common cultural identity, these events may be a critical link for perpetuating NTFP harvest traditions. Viewed through a political ecology lens, it is then peculiar that the widespread occurrence of nontimber forest product events does not seem to bring greater visibility or recognition of their cultural importance with federal land management agencies.

A unique facet of NTFP gathering is that both urban and rural people engage in the activity, and these urban-rural linkages promote connections between people and between people and nature. In addition to harvesting within urban boundaries (see Jahnige, this volume), many city dwellers visit forests to harvest mushrooms, berries, and other plant resources. A broad interpretation of this point would include the millions of tourists to U.S. parks, wilderness areas, and public forests who stop on the trail to pick huckleberries and other wild berries or to collect a few ferns, cones, or moss to bring home for crafts. Many commercial harvesters are based in urban areas and commute to distant forests in their vehicles (Hansis 1995; Love, Jones, and Liegel 1998), while rural harvesters often travel to urban centers to sell the day's harvest. Mushroom clubs are often located in cities and organize forays to regional forests throughout the year for seasonal fungi (McLain, Christensen, and Shannon 1998).

KNOWLEDGE AND STEWARDSHIP

Anthropologists have long documented the significance of local institutions and local knowledge to resource stewardship (King 1997). People living and interacting as part of an ecosystem often have highly developed knowledge about elements within it (Anderson 1996; Johnson 1992; Reed 1997).

These systems of traditional ecological knowledge (TEK), as they are increasingly referred to, are really informal sciences where users learn through processes of trial and error, categorize, and share knowledge through social networks. Perhaps the only real difference is the controlled replicability of the experiments that characterize modern science. Thus, the indigenous traditions and science are epistemologically closer to each other than most scientists will acknowledge (Balick and Cox 1996). Berlin (1992), speaking specifically to folk classification, suggests that the common denominator for informal and formal science rests with the inescapable and largely unconscious appreciation of the inherent structure of biological reality that humans possess.

Increasingly, conservation groups have tended to valorize the notion of indigenous groups as models of environmental stewardship (Sillitoe 1998). Although indigenous does not necessarily equate with ecological knowledge of good stewardship practice, certainly indigenous groups have been able to live in the same natural area for generations. Furthermore, they have done so as an integral part of its evolution (Rappaport 1993). What is significant about these indigenous knowledge systems are the attitudes, motivations, intimate connections, and cultural influences that underlie the daily interactions between the human and nonhuman elements. Understanding an ecosystem and its successful management is more than just understanding the biological processes; it is about understanding and respecting the interconnection of all its elements, including its people and their beliefs and behaviors (Gaul and Thomas 1991). Anderson (1996) argues that recognizing and developing relationships with TEK systems, rooted in local culture, are necessary precursors to sustainable management of ecosystems.

TEK is generally thought of in terms of cultural groups interacting with an ecological area for generations (Turner 1997). As indicated earlier, many NTFP harvesters have traditions that have persisted over long periods of time (see Emery, this volume). Ethnoecologists (e.g., Brent Berlin, Virginia Nazara, Nancy Turner) have put out excellent research demonstrating the traditional ecological knowledge that characterizes many of these cultural groups. However, less clear is how quickly knowledge develops in the relatively recent social networks that characterize many of the commercial harvesters in the nontimber forest product arena. Ethnographic research on the Olympic Peninsula with commercial wild mushroom harvesters found individuals making astute observations and regularly performing semisystematic experiments to better understand the productivity of the resource (Love and Jones 1995). These experientially based behaviors combined with access to formal scientific information give many commercial harvesters a broad-range of knowledge that facilitates successful extraction strategies. Ongoing research reveals that mobile mushroom harvesters following fruiting cycles over many states often study topography maps, review mycological literature pertaining to given areas, and sometimes consult with professional mycologists. In contrast, few scientists mention contacting harvesters for input on their studies.

A major consideration affecting NTFP social networks and the production of ecological knowledge is the issue of access to the land and resources. From a political ecology perspective, natural resource policy and the prevailing science that underlies it are structured in ways that undermine sociocultural processes that could be establishing sustainable relationships with the land. To illustrate this argument, it is necessary to briefly review some recent claims by scholars working on land tenure and common property issues.

Broadening Malinowski's definition beyond cultivation, land tenure is the relation of human beings, individuals, and groups to the soil they inhabit (Hann 1996). The vast public lands of the United States on which a lot of NTFP tenure patterns unfold are common property systems. Scholars divide common property systems into open access where few well-defined property rights exist; private property where an individual or corporation has exclusive rights to regulate and exclude others; communal property where rights and access are determined by a community of users; and state property where government controls access and use rights[8] (Berkes 1996). In the United States, large portions of forested lands are controlled by federal and state governments (the state) and large private timber companies. Nontimber forest product extraction has principally occurred under a de facto open access system on these lands, meaning the lands were heavily regulated but NTFP harvesting was largely overlooked. From the harvester's perspective it meant the forest was a public commons, and, as such, harvester cultural beliefs, behaviors, and household economic systems have evolved usufruct traditions on the land.

The forest "commons" are increasingly in transition to what might be called state and private regulated tenure regimes (McLain 2000). A number of factors have combined to lead state and private forest managers to begin regulating access. These include the need to replace shrinking revenues from decreased logging; conflicts between different user types (e.g., recreational); liability concerns with theft, vandalism, and injury; concern over harvesters assuming property rights; and, perhaps most prevalent, fear of a "tragedy of the commons" due to the dramatic increase in commercial extraction.

Garret Hardin claimed in his influential work "The Tragedy of the Commons" (1968) that users dependent on public commons are locked into a system that compels them to increase their resource consumption without limit, inevitably leading to ruin for all unless regulated by outside forces (e.g., the state or privatization). The reasoning that markets will fail without well-defined property rights came to dominate natural resource economics and ultimately management for the last thirty years (Fortmann 1998). Anthropologists have argued that followers in the Hardin vein too often try to explain resource use with simple deterministic bioeconomic models that ignore complex socioecological systems (Berkes et al. 1989). Hardin himself discussed commons as if there was only one type, open access, implying a system in which users can do anything they like (McCay and Jentoft 1998). In fact, open access is somewhat of a myth, and researchers are finding that in almost all commons systems cultural responses are usually at play that attempt to control overexploitation (Ostrom 1999).

Recent research with important implications for NTFPs suggests that under certain conditions, local cultural institutions develop that allow resource users to successfully manage the resource themselves (McCay and Jentoft 1998). Resource users have a propensity for stewardship, and generally, it is in their best interests to manage a resource sustainably over time, as profit is often not the sole (sometimes not at all) motivating factor. However, the macroscale variables (political, economic, and social) that a political ecology approach highlights often undermine or complicate resource users' ability to manage a resource sustainably or for stewardship behaviors to manifest themselves. Incorporating gender analysis and other participatory techniques within a political ecology framework could illuminate the needs and constraints of harvesters and thus could help facilitate their successful comanagement of the resource. In this way, a more efficient, more economical, more equitable system is developed that complements harvesters' propensity to protect the resources they depend upon. An example relevant to this discussion is drawn from studies of lobster fisheries in Maine.

Despite no licensing requirements, lobster stocks in Maine have remained stable since 1947 because of the traditional fishing rights created by local communities (Berkes et al. 1989). Though individuals fish alone generally, they work with other fishers to set ground rules, minimize risks such as reducing price fluctuations by not flooding the market, share knowledge about shifting fishing conditions, and work together to exclude outsiders not participating in their system of controls (Acheson 1988). Rather than regulator, the state's role has been primarily to assist the local cultural system with information and monitoring. The result is that comparisons with other fisheries finds that productivity is better with significantly more and larger lobsters caught with less overall effort (Berkes et al. 1989).

Anthropologists using ethnographic methods have been able to reveal how the underlying social complexities of self-regulation and the outcomes of commons problems are significantly rooted in a community of users (McCay and Jentoft 1998). Where other scholars have tended to essentialize human communities as a static or bounded phenomenon, anthropologists acknowledge that they are often fluid, overlapping systems of social networks. Thus, it is not inconceivable that nontimber forest product networks are employing mechanisms of self-regulation and producing traditional ecological knowledge. If this is in fact the case, as research is beginning to suggest, then key sources of knowledge about ecosystem processes and sustainable use of NTFP resources are being left out of formal science, policy making, and management.

CONCLUSION

The intent of this chapter was to highlight the critical need to understand and incorporate sociocultural variables associated with NTFP harvesting in forestry research, management, and policy making. We began by examining the relevance of several political ecology frameworks to understanding nontimber forest product issues. We then argued that policy makers and resource managers have a critical need for demographic data, including data dissaggregated by age, ethnicity, and gender, while at the same time pointing toward the complexities facing demographic research with nontimber forest product harvesters. The almost complete lack of basic demographic information on harvesters in the United States and ignorance about cultural use patterns has meant that policy makers and resource managers have not been able to accurately gauge the social and economic impacts of their policies. Finally, we argue that the lack of sociocultural information is not only detrimental to NTFP harvesters but also to policy makers and resource managers, who are missing an opportunity to work with stakeholders who have valuable knowledge of the resource ecology. To conclude, we strongly believe that understanding the cultural complexities and nuances of NTFP resource use will facilitate the development of management policies that can be both efficient and equitable.

NOTES

1. Eric Jones has been involved in research with Pacific Northwest wild mushroom harvesting for fifteen years and with nontimber forest products in general for the last seven years.

2. Mode of production is defined as the relationship between the relations of production (e.g., managers versus laborers) and the forces of production (e.g., tools, land, materials) (Abercrombie, Hill, and Turner 1984, 57–58).

3. This example is based on Eric Jones's fifteen years of experience in the industry as a harvester, buyer, and research anthropologist.

4. MERGE began in 1994 as an innovative collaborative project between the University of Florida, the Facultad de Ciencias Sociales in Quito, Ecuador, Conser-

vation International in Peru, the Nature Conservancy, and a network of collaborating organizations in Ecuador, Brazil, Peru, and the United States. This program focused on strengthening the understanding of gender issues in natural resource management in tropical areas through both training and research initiatives.

5. A joint research project of Clark University and Virginia Polytechnic Institute and State University.

6. This quote comes from Eric Jones's journals before he was involved in formal social science reseach on NTFPs. From 1983 to the present, he has harvested a variety of NTFPs commercially and noncommercially throughout the western United States. The contentions the authors make are supported by data from hundreds of ethnographic interviews with mushroom harvesters over the last seven years.

7. Eric Jones visited with many NTFP gatherers in New England over a seven-year period in the 1990s.

8. In practice, resources are often held in overlapping combinations of these systems (Berkes et al. 1989).

REFERENCES

Abercrombie, Nicholas, Stephen Hill, and Bryan Turner. 1984. *Dictionary of Sociology.* 2d ed. London: Penguin Books.

Acheson, James M. 1988. *The Lobster Gangs of Maine.* Hanover, NH: University Press of New England.

American Anthropological Association. 2001. Response to OMB Directive 15, "Race and Ethnic Standards for Federal Statistics." *http://www.aaanet.org/gvt/ombdraft.htm.*

Andersen, Margaret L. 1993. *Thinking about Women: Sociological Perspectives on Sex and Gender.* New York: Macmillan.

Anderson, E. N. 1996. *Ecologies of the Heart.* Oxford: Oxford University Press.

Antypas, Alexios R. 1998. "Translating Ecosystem Science into Ecosystem Management and Policy: A Case Study of Network Formation." Ph.D. diss., University of Washington.

Balick, Michael J., and P. A. Cox. 1996. *Plants, People, and Culture.* New York: Scientific American Library.

Berkes, Fikret. 1996. "Social Systems, Ecological Systems, and Property Rights." In *Rights to Nature,* ed. Susan S. Hanna, C. Folke, and K.-G. Mäler, pp. 87–107. Washington, DC: Island Press.

Berkes, Fikret, David Feeny, Bonnie J. McCay, and James M. Acheson. 1989. "The Benefits of the Commons." *Nature* 340:91–93.

Berlin, B. 1992. *Ethnobotanical Classification.* Princeton, NJ: Princeton University Press.

Blaikie, Piers, and Harold Brookfield. 1987. *Land Degradation and Society.* London: Methuen.

Bryant, Raymond L. 1992. "Political Ecology: An Emerging Research Agenda in Third World Studies." *Political Geography* 11(1): 12–36.

Buenavista, Gladys, and Cornelia Butler Flora. 1994. "Participatory Methodologies for Analyzing Household Activities, Resources, and Benefits." In *Tools for the Field: Methodologies Handbook for Gender Analysis in Agriculture*, ed. Hilary Sims Feldstein and Janice Jiggins, pp. 36–44. West Hartford, CT: Kumarian Press.

Buvinic, M. 1986. "Projects for Women in the Third World: Explaining Their Misbehavior." *World Development* 14(5): 653–664.

Emery, Marla R. 1998. *Invisible Livelihoods: Nontimber Forest Products in Michigan's Upper Peninsula*. Ann Arbor, MI: UMI Dissertation Services.

Escobar, Arturo. 1996. "Constructing Nature: Elements for a Post-Structuralist Political Ecology." *Pergamon* 28(4): 325–343.

Fortmann, L. 1998. "Bonanza! The Unasked Questions: Domestic Land Tenure Through International Lenses." In *Who Owns America: Social Conflict Over Property Rights,* ed. H. M. Jacobs, pp. 3–18. Madison: University of Wisconsin Press.

Foucault, Michael. [1979] 1995. *Discipline and Punish: The Birth of a Prison.* Trans. Alan Sheridan. Reprint, New York: Vintage Books.

Gaul, Karen, and R. Brooke Thomas. 1991. "Indigenous Perspectives: Ecology, Economy, and Ethics." *Journal of Human Ecology* (Special Issue): 73–83.

Gilden, Jennifer. 1996. "Environment, Symbolism, and Changing Gender Roles in Oregon's Santiam Canyon." Master's thesis, Oregon State University.

——. 1997. "An Oregon Case Study: Families, Gender Roles, and Timber Communities in Transformation." In *Public Lands Management in the West: Citizens, Interest Groups, and Values,* ed. Brent S. Steel, pp. 173–184. Westport, CT: Praeger.

Greenberg, James B., and Thomas K. Park. 1994. "Political Ecology." *Journal of Political Ecology* 1:1–12.

Hann, C. M. 1996. "Land Tenure." In *Encyclopedia of Social and Cultural Anthropology,* ed. Alan Barnard and Jonathan Spencer, pp. 321–323. New York: Routledge.

Hansis, Richard. 1995. "The Harvesting of Special Forest Products by Latinos and Southeast Asians in the Pacific Northwest: Preliminary Observations." *Society and Natural Resources* 9:611–615.

——. 1998. "A Political Ecology of Picking: Nontimber Forest Products in the Pacific Northwest." *Human Ecology* 26:67–86.

Hardin, Garrett. 1968. "The Tragedy of the Commons." *Science* 162:1243–1248.

Harrington, L. M. B. 1996. "Regarding Research as a Land Use." *Applied Geography* 16:265–277.

Havelkov, Soren, and Arturo Escobar. 1998. "Nature, Political Ecology, and Social Practice: Toward an Academic and Political Agenda." In *Building a New Biocultural Synthesis,* ed. Alan H. Goodman and Thomas L. Leatherman, pp. 425–450. Ann Arbor: University of Michigan Press.

Hays, Samuel P. 1989. "Three Decades of Environmental Politics: The Historical Context." In *Government and Environmental Politics: Essays on Historical Developments since World War Two,* ed. Michael J. Lacey, pp. 19–79. Washington, DC: Woodrow Wilson International Center for Scholars.

Heller, Chaia. 1996. "Political Ecology, Anthropology, and Social Ecology: Toward a Post-Scarcity Discussion of Globalization and Development." Paper presented at the American Anthropology Association annual meeting, San Francisco.

Hirt, Paul W. 1994. *A Conspiracy of Optimism: Management of the National Forests since World War Two*. Lincoln: University of Nebraska Press.

Hosford, David, David Pilz, Randy Molina, and Michael Amaranthus. 1997. *Ecology and Management of the Commercially Harvested American Matsutake Mushroom*. U.S. Department of Agriculture–Forest Service General Technical Report No. 412. Portland, OR: Pacific Northwest Research Station.

Johnson, M. 1992. "Research on Traditional Environmental Knowledge: Its Development and Role." In *Capturing Traditional Environmental Knowledge,* ed. M. Johnson, pp. 1–22. Ottawa: International Development Research Centre.

Kabeer, N. 1994. *Reversed Realities: Gender Hierarchies in Development Thought*. London: Verso.

Keiter, Robert B. 1990. "NEPA and the Emerging Concept of Ecosystem Management on the Public Lands." *Land and Water Law Review* 25(1): 43–60.

King, Thomas D. 1997. "Folk Management among Belizean Lobster Fisherman: Success and Resilience or Decline and Depletion." *Human Organization* 56(4): 418–427.

Leach, Melissa. 1994. *Rainforest Relations: Gender and Resource Use among the Mende of Gola, Sierra Leone*. Washington, DC: Smithsonian Institution Press.

Leatherman, Thomas, and R. Brooke Thomas. Forthcoming. "Political Ecology and Constructions of Environment in Biological Anthropology." In *Human Dimensions of Environmental Change,* ed. Carole Crumley. Walnut Creek, CA: Altamira Press.

Love, Thomas, and Eric T. Jones. 1995. "Grounds for Argument: Local Understandings, Science, and Global Processes in Special Forest Products Harvesting." In *Special Forest Products: Biodiversity Meets the Marketplace,* ed. Nan Vance and J. Thomas, pp. 70–87. Pub. no. GTR-WO-63. Washington, DC: USDA Forest Service.

Love, Thomas, Eric T. Jones, and Leon Liegel. 1998. "Valuing the Temperate Rainforest: Wild Mushrooming on the Olympic Peninsula Biosphere Reserve." *Ambio Special Report* 9:16–25.

March, Candida, Ines Smyth, and Maitrayee Mukhopadhyay. 1999. *A Guide to Gender-Analysis Frameworks*. Oxford: Oxfam GB.

McCay, Bonnie J., and Svein Jentoft. 1998. "Market or Community Failure? Critical Perspectives on Common Property Research." In *Human Organization* 57(1): 21–29.

McLain, Rebecca J. 2000. "Controlling the Forest Understory: Wild Mushroom Politics in Central Oregon." Ph.D diss., University of Washington.

McLain, Rebecca J., Harriet H. Christensen, and Margaret A. Shannon. 1998. "When Amateurs Are the Experts: Amateur Mycologists and Wild Mushroom Politics in the Pacific Northwest, USA." *Society and Natural Resources* 11:615–626.

McLain, Rebecca J., and Eric T. Jones. 1997. *Challenging "Community" Definitions in Sustainable Natural Resource Management: The Case of Wild Mushroom Harvesting in the USA*. Gatekeeper Series, no. 68, pp. 1–19. London: International Institute for Environment and Development, Sustainable Agriculture Programme.

———. 1998. "Participatory Non-Wood Forest Product Management: Experiences from the Pacific Northwest." In *Sustainable Development of Non-Wood Goods from Boreal and Cold Temperate Forests,* ed. G. Lund, B. Pajari, and M. Korhonen, pp. 189–196. Joensuu, Finland: European Forest Institute.

McLain, Rebecca J., Eric T. Jones, and Leon Liegel. 1998. "The MAB Mushroom Study as a Teaching Case Example of Interdisciplinary and Sustainable Forestry Research." *Ambio* 9:34–35.

Mitchell, Jon P. 1996. "Ritual." In *Encyclopedia of Social and Cultural Anthropology,* ed. Alan Barnard and Jonathan Spencer, pp. 490–493. New York: Routledge.

Moerman, Daniel. 1998. *Native American Ethnobotany*. Portland, OR: Timber Press.

Moser, C. O. N. 1993. *Gender Planning and Development: Theory, Practice and Training*. London: Routledge.

Muirragui, Eileen I., and E. Suely Anderson. 1995. "Gender and Socio-Economic Considerations in Environmental Programs and Projects: Lessons Learned in the Brazilian Amazon." GENESYS Special Study no. 14. Washington, DC: U.S. Agency for International Development.

Netherlands Development Assistance, Development Cooperation Information Department and Ministry of Foreign Affairs. 1997. In collaboration with Margreet Moolhuyzen and July Leesberg, consultants. "Gender and Environment: A Delicate Balance between Profit and Loss." *Working Paper no. 1*. The Hague: Ministry of Foreign Affairs.

Ostrom, Elinor. 1999. "Self-Governance and Forest Resources." *Occasional Paper no. 20*. Jakarta, Indonesia: Center for International Forestry Research.

Overholt, C. A., K. Cloud, M. B. Anderson, and J. E. Austin. 1991. "Gender Analysis Framework." In *Gender Analysis in Development Planning: A Case Book,* ed. A. Rao, M. B. Anderson, and C. A. Overholt, pp. 9–20. West Hartford, CT: Kumarian Press.

Parker, A. Rani, Itziar Lozano, and Lyn A. Messner. 1995. *Gender Relations Analysis: A Guide for Trainers*. Westport, CT: Save the Children.

Paulson, Susan. 1992. "Gender and Ethnicity in Motion: Identity and Integration in Andean Households." Ph.D. diss., University of Chicago.

———. 1996. "Reflexiones sobre Metodologías para Género y Forestería Comunal. Desarrollo Agroforestal y Comunidad Campesina." *Revista del Proyecto Desarrollo Agroforestal en Comunidades Rurales del NOA Año* 5(22): 10–15.

Ransom, John S. 1997. *Foucault's Discipline: The Politics of Subjectivity*. Durham, NC: Duke University Press.

Rappaport, Roy A. 1968. *Pigs for the Ancestors*. New Haven, CT: Yale University Press.

———. 1993. "Ecosystems, Populations, and People." In *The Ecosystem Approach in Anthropology: From Concept to Practice,* ed. Emilio Moran, pp. 435–458. Ann Arbor: University of Michigan Press.

Reed, R. 1997. *Forest Dwellers, Forest Protectors*. Boston: Allyn and Bacon.

Richards, Rebecca T. 1997. "What the Natives Know: Wild Mushrooms and Forest Health." *Journal of Forestry* 95(9): 4–26.

Richards, Rebecca T., and Max Creasy. 1996. "Ethnic Diversity, Resource Values, and Ecosystem Management: Matsutake Mushroom Harvesting in the Klamath Bioregion." *Society and Natural Resources* 9:359–374.

Rocheleau, Dianne E. 1988. "Gender, Resource Management and the Rural Landscape: Implications for Agroforestry and Farming Systems Research." In *Gender Issues in Farming Systems Research and Extension,* ed. Susan Poats, Marianne Schmink, and Anita Spring, pp. 149–169. Boulder, CO: Westview Press.

Sachs, Carolyn. 1996. *Gendered Fields: Rural Women, Agriculture, and Environment.* Boulder, CO: Westview Press.

Schlosser, William E., and Keith A. Blatner. 1995. "The Wild Edible Mushroom Industry of Washington, Oregon, and Idaho." *Journal of Forestry* 93(3): 31–36.

Schmink, Marianne. 1999. "Conceptual Framework for Gender and Community-Based Conservation." *Case Study No. 1: Managing Ecosystems and Resources with a Gender Emphasis,* MERGE Program, University of Florida.

Scott, James C. 1990. *Domination and the Arts of Resistance: Hidden Transcripts.* New Haven, CT: Yale University Press.

Scott, Joan Wallach. 1988. *Gender and the Politics of History.* New York: Columbia University Press.

Sillitoe, Paul. 1998. "The Development of Indigenous Knowledge: A New Applied Anthropology." *Current Anthropology* 39(4): 223–252.

Slocum, Rachel, Lori Wichhart, Diane Rocheleau, and Barbara Thomas-Slayter, eds. 1995. *Power, Process, and Participation: Tools for Change.* London: Intermediate Technology Publications.

Stonich, Susan C. 1993. *I Am Destroying the Land! The Political Ecology of Poverty and Environmental Destruction in Honduras.* Boulder, CO: Westview Press.

Stronza, Amanda Lee. 2000. "'Because It Is Ours': Community-Based Ecotoursim in the Peruvian Amazon." Ph.D. diss., University of Florida.

Thomas-Slayter, Barbara, A. L. Esser, and M. D. Shields. 1993. "Tools of Gender Analysis: A Guide to Field Methods for Bringing Gender into Sustainable Resource Management." ECOGEN Research Project, International Development Program, Clark University.

Turner, Nancy J. 1997. "Traditional Ecological Knowledge." In *The Rainforests of Home: Profile of a North American Bioregion,* ed. Peter K. Schoonmaker, Bettina von Hagen, and Edward C. Wolf, pp. 275–298. Washington, DC: Island Press.

Von Hagen, Bettina, and Roger Fight. 1999. *Opportunities for Conservation-Based Development of Nontimber Forest Products in the Pacific Northwest.* Pub. no. PNW-GTR-473. Portland, OR: USDA Forest Service.

Watts, Michael, and Richard Peet. 1993. "Liberation Ecology: Development, Sustainability, and Environment in an Age of Market Triumphalism." In *Liberation Ecologies,* ed. M. Watts and R. Peet, pp. 1–45. London: Routledge.

Webster's New Universal Unabridged Dictionary. 2d ed. 1983. New York: Simon and Schuster.

Wigginton, Eliot, ed. 1973. *Foxfire 2.* New York: Anchor Press.

Williams, Suzanne, with Janet Seed and Adelina Mwau. 1994. *The Oxfam Gender Training Manual.* Oxford: Oxfam.

Wolf, Eric R. 1982. *Europe and the People without History.* Berkeley: University of California Press.

CASE STUDY

Workers in the Woods: Confronting Rapid Change

Richard Hansis

One of the trends in recent years in the United States is the large increase in the participation of non–European American ethnic groups in forest work. For most of the twentieth century, most commercial as well as subsistence pickers were primarily European Americans, plus a number of African Americans living in the southern part of the country, from rural areas and small towns. Many recreational pickers, predominantly European American as well, dwelled in large cities. Native Americans also continued to gather NTFPs for spiritual and subsistence purposes and small amounts for sale. Over the past decade, these demographics have shifted rapidly in parts of the United States with the entry of large numbers of immigrants from Southeast Asia and Latin America, especially Mexico and Guatemala, into forest occupations in the Pacific West region. The first wave of immigrant harvesters consisted mainly of peoples who came as refugees from Cambodia and Laos. These immigrants began by picking wild forest mushrooms as well as beargrass for the floral greens industry.

To a lesser extent, a few Southeast Asian groups were also picking salal, ferns, tree boughs, mosses, and huckleberries. Many of these immigrants live in large and medium-sized cities as well as some smaller towns on the West Coast of the United States but often come from smaller cities and villages in their country of birth. Some harvest only during certain seasons, specializing in the harvest of select species of wild mushrooms. Others engage in NTFP harvesting on a year-round or nearly year-round basis, harvesting a variety of NTFPs over the course of the year. For those immigrants with few skills applicable to the U.S. economy and who do not read, write, or speak English well, NTFP harvesting provides an opportunity to earn money in a self-directed activity rather than working as a menial laborer in the city. For others, NTFP picking allows them to supplement their other sources of income. For both groups, going to the forest to pick may also serve to maintain extended family bonds because NTFP work can often be done as a family or extended family activity. For those families who enjoy forest settings or who wish to escape urban life for a short time, NTFP harvesting also makes it possible for them to afford to spend time in remote rural settings.

Latinos first entered the forest workforce in the United States as reforestation workers and as workers on Christmas tree farms. Over time Latino immigrants expanded into other forest work, including the harvesting of floral greens. In the past five years, they have also begun to take on a more prominent role in harvesting wild mushrooms. Some Latinos engage in NTFP harvesting as an alternative to farmwork, a common occupation for new immigrants from Mexico and Central America. More recently, settled Latino farmworkers have turned to NTFP harvesting for additional or alternative sources of income when agricultural work is not available owing to poor harvests or increased competition for the farm jobs. In the Cascade range of Washington and Oregon, for example, many Latino farmworkers started by picking huckleberries but now are beginning to harvest many other NTFPs.

The larger numbers of potential pickers have brought with them both increased cooperation among ethnic groups and conflict between groups. In the late 1980s, bear grass became a large-volume commodity, due in large part to the presence of a new labor supply consisting primarily of Cambodian immigrants. Over the years, some Cambodian immigrants working in beargrass harvesting have begun to assume the role of labor brokers–crew foremen rather than harvesters. In this new role, the Cambodian immigrants recruit young Latino immigrants to do the heavy, sometimes cold and wet work of harvesting bear grass. Latinos who participated in preliminary investigations of an NTFP study in the eastern Cascades indicated that their wages are very low, whether in bear grass, floral greens, or bough harvesting.

In other parts of the United States, as in the Pacific West, unlawful harvesting of NTFP is a major issue. When prices for products such as wild ginseng reach into the hundreds of dollars per pound, the incentive for people with small and sometimes irregular sources of income to harvest without permits, out of season, on lands prohibited for harvesting (Late Successional Reserves on federal forestlands in the Pacific Northwest; private lands all over the country), or with methods that are rapid but destructive increases exponentially.

Harvesting salal for floral greens is a major industry in a large portion of western Washington. Much of the land in the area is privately owned by timber companies as well as by some smaller landowners. Other harvested lands belong to the public, mainly the USDA Forest Service and the state department of natural resources. The large buying companies have had the most success obtaining access to the timberlands at least in part because dealing with fewer permit holders is easier for the timber company managers. One common arrangement is that the floral green companies informally "contract" with individual harvesters or a crew leader to harvest the salal from the land the company has leased from the timber company. The harvesters or crews must bring their bunches to sell to that same company in addition to paying three to five cents per bunch or 10 percent of their total to pay for their secondary permit. Harvesters are considered self-employed informal "contractors." When harvesting on public land, they pay a permit fee and then can sell to whatever buying shed they wish. Although there are many more complexities to these labor relationships, these are the basic outlines. Over the past ten years as this industry has grown into a multimillion-dollar business, the harvester labor force has been primarily Latino, both local community members and members of the mobile labor force. Harvesters work in crews or alone depending on documentation, language, and contacts. Often the crew leader will be the only one who deals with the transactions needed to access land and get paid. The crews are made up of friends or relatives for the most part.

The Department of Labor has been looking into the employment relationship between salal/NTFP harvesters and the buying sheds/companies in western Washington. They are in the initial stages of gathering information on the industry and providing education and outreach on labor law to contractors, buying sheds, and other parties. It is possible that floral greens will fall under agriculture laws, and thus the Labor Department may view labor relationships from that legal standpoint. If so, the informal nature of the industry will be changing. Under agricultural law, if a shed/company permits control of an area and harvesters pick under that permit as self-employed contractors, they become an employee of the company as soon as they sell the brush back. Harvesters will likely make less money in this relationship but will also gain benefits such as workers' compensation. In addition, if harvesters are not employees of a company, they must get a business and contractor's license in order to obtain a permit to access the land. People working as contractors for the sheds who have the true copy of the permit must also have a license to be eligible to pick on private land. Nothing is known yet about public land.

The landowners are now in a position where they need to be very careful about liability. They may find that they suddenly are responsible for three hundred employees they never hired. Hence, companies are shifting their policy to clarify that those permitted will not be employees and are trying to comply with the Labor Department. They had to cancel some of their permits with people who did not have a contractor's license.

Harvesters are in another position entirely. Those without documents (which is unofficially estimated to be rather high, perhaps 80 percent) will have a hard time staying in the industry, which has been an easily entered job. Getting a contractor's license will be tricky, and working as an employee with the companies will open people up to the INS Social Security checks, which require employers to ask new employees for verification that they are in the United States legally. There are going to be major changes for undocumented and documented workers.

According to one source in the industry, at least a few harvesters with documents are glad to see the change because they feel that wages and working conditions have been undercut by the large undocumented workforce. One person who contracts for tree planting and thinning in the area actually had a hard time keeping a work crew together because they would leave at certain times each year to make more money picking salal and getting paid under the table.

A recent change in some sheds is to weigh out brush to charge for the permit at the same 10 percent or five cents per bunch, but the harvester can then sell to anyone. Another new system is the harvester takes brush anywhere and then takes the receipt to the shed that permitted the land access and pays five cents per bunch. This change may well push many to pick without permits already viewed by some in the area as a large problem. If there is already overharvesting, then it will be difficult for the companies to guarantee an hourly wage to their employees.

These changes will have benefits for some. Documented workers will suddenly be in a different power relation with employers and in contractor/employee relations that have been problematic in tree planting and related work. Undocumented workers, estimated at 80 percent of the workforce, will be in an even more difficult situation since they cannot get a contractor's license or be legally employed by the brush sheds or other contractors.

Complicating all of the flux in labor relations is Section 339 of the 2000 Appropriations Act, the Pilot Program of Charges and Fees for Harvest of Forest Botanical Products, which will be implemented throughout federal public lands. The program calls for charging fees that will cover the fair market value of the product to commercial harvesters. Enforcement of these new regulations, already strained by the increasing use of public lands for recreation, NTFP harvesting, and marijuana growing, will become more and more difficult. Harvesters, already at the margins of the economy, will be tempted to further noncompliance with regulations. The little progress that has been made in bringing public land management agencies to the table with a diverse harvesting population may be shattered.

Over the past six years or so, harvesters and forest workers other than timber cutters have begun to organize themselves in order to counteract the fragmented nature of their work. A fledgling organization, the Alliance of Forest Workers and Harvesters, has begun to reach out to the multiethnic workforce of the Pacific West. Its mission is to serve as a voice of social, environmental, and economic justice for forest harvesters. To do so it has begun to enhance communication and education among the different communities of harvesters in order to reduce the potential for conflict in the woods. In addition, it has established contacts with similar workers in other parts of the United States. The alliance has also helped create spaces where these usually unheard voices can speak with land managers and policy makers.

CASE STUDY

Overview of Cultural Traditions, Economic Trends, and Key Species in Nontimber Forest Products of the Pacific Northwest

James Weigand

The Pacific Northwest encompasses coastal temperate rain forests, oak savannas, and montane Mediterranean forests to the west of the Cascade Range crest and sagebrush desert, grassland steppes, and pine-dominated forests to the east. Diverse topography and climate bring to the region striking contrasts and natural biological richness in the variety of forest and woodland ecosystems. A heritage of federal public lands provides both residents and out-of-state visitors with opportunities to gather nontimber forest products for cultural, personal, and commercial uses.

Enduring interest among Indians in the Pacific Northwest for traditional resources and cultural products sustains contemporary uses of many plant, lichen, and fungi species. Scholarly literature on nontimber forest products and their uses by the Indian nations in Oregon and Washington is sparse in contrast to parallel research undertaken in adjacent British Columbia and California. Formal documentation of Indian uses began with Coville (1897), who recorded some of the ethnobotanical uses of the Klamath people, and with Barrett (1910), who reported on cultural plant uses of both the Klamath and Modoc tribes. Emanuel (1994) has compiled additional information about cultural uses of the Klamath people and their neighbors. Gunther (1973) and Turner, Bouchard, and Kennedy (1980) have described respectively the ethnobotany of Indians of western Washington and of the Okanagon and Colville Indians whose lands cross the border of British Columbia and Washington.

Many other in-depth studies of Indian ethnobotany in the Pacific Northwest are academic theses. Dickson (1946) researched diaries and other writings of early Euro-American explorers and settlers and recorded uses recounted by elders to compile principal Indian uses of plants in western Oregon. Zenk's (1976) work on Tualitin subsistence culture and Boyd's (1986) article on the Kalapuya people are virtually the only other works to document postcontact cultural uses of plants in western Oregon. Archaeological studies (Gill 1983; Cole 1990; Prouty 1995) of Indian settlement sites have also yielded information about past ethnobotanical uses by Northwest Indians. Theses by Mahar (1953) and Couture (1978) are contemporary accounts of Indian cultural uses from eastern Oregon. Couture, Ricks, and Housley (1986) describe gathering root crops in eastern Oregon for cultural and commercial uses among Paiute people.

The ecosystems of ancestral lands in large part determined the most significant cultural plant species for Pacific Northwest Indians. Active commercial activity among tribes on the Columbia River and across the interior basin of the Columbia Basin provided for opportunities to exchange food crops gathered by tribes east and west of the Cascade Divide. One important precontact trade food was camas (principally *Camassia quamash* and *C. leichtlinii*), which was so important as a staple food source that the Bannock-Shoshoni rebelled against losing access to their traditional camas fields (Smith 1978). Programs to restore camas prairies in western Oregon and Washington are currently under way by introducing frequent, low-intensity fires in Oregon white oak *(Quercus garryana)* savannas. Table 2 lists monographs on camas and other major cultural and economic plant and fungi species in the Pacific Northwest.

FLORAL PRODUCTS

In the early 1920s, floral products industries started up, principally in the Chehalis, Washington, area and in Kitsap and Mason counties at the southern end of the Olympic Peninsula (Allen 1950). Major species were, and remain to this day, salal *(Gautheria shallon)*, evergreen huckleberry *(Vaccinium ovatum)*, western red cedar *(Thuja plicata)*, tall Oregon-grape *(Mahonia aquifolium)*, and western sword fern *(Polystichum munitum)*—all low-elevation species of the coastal rain forest. In recent decades, higher-elevation species such as noble fir *(Abies nobilis)* and bear grass *(Xerophyllum tenax)* and plants more common in eastern Oregon and Washington, such as Oregon boxleaf *(Paxistima myrsinifolia)*, have become popular as well, and all of these species have international markets. Heckman (1951) offers a rare glimpse into the lifestyles of errant "brush pickers" who picked floral greenery when other work in forestry or timber mills was slow or who gathered brush as a way of sustaining a household economy based in the forest. Cones of all pine species also have commercial value, particularly sugar pine *(Pinus lambertiana)* and western white pine *(P. monticola)*.

Noble fir, once considered a timber species of minor importance, has become one of the two preferred commercial species in the European Community Christmas tree industry based in Denmark (Christiansen 1982). For citations on Danish research on plantation culture for noble fir,

Table 2. Monographs of economically and culturally important plant species of the Pacific Northwest

Latin name	NRCS name	References
PLANTS		
Camassia spp.	camas	Statham (1982), Thoms (1989)
Frangula purshiana	cascara sagrada (Pursh's buckthorn)	Arnst (1945)
Heracleum lamatum	common cowparsnip	Kuhnlein and Turner (1987)
Juniperus occidentalis	western juniper	Wilke (1988)
Lomatium spp.	biscuitroots	Hunn and French (1981)
Sagittaria latifolia	wapato	Darby (1996)
Taxus brevifolia	western yew	Wheeler et al. (1992) and many others
Thuja plicata	western red cedar	Stewart (1984)
Vaccinium membranaceum	thinleaf huckleberry	Minore (1972, 1984), Hunn and Norton (1984)
FUNGI		
Cantharellus formosus	Pacific golden chanterelle	Liegel et al. (1998), Redhead, Norvell, and Danell (1997)
Tricholoma magnivelare	American matsutake	Amaranthus, Weigand, and Abbott (1998), Hosford, Pilz, and Molina (1997)

grand fir, and Port Orford cedar Christmas trees and boughs, see von Hagen et al. (1996). Fischer (1992) provides a comparatively recent description of the international trade in floral greens from the Pacific Northwest in Germany. Cooperative extension staff and faculty at Washington State University have produced publications to inform people about economic opportunities and market developments in floral greens and conifer bough species from the Pacific Northwest and Idaho (Schlosser, Blatner, and Baumgartner 1992; Schlosser, Blatner, and Zamora 1992; Schlosser 1995; Schlosser and Blatner 1995).

WILD FOODS

Apart from camas, interest in traditional and modern uses of Pacific Northwest native plants and fungi is growing. Nutritionists and anthropologists teamed up to produce a series of articles in the 1980s about the nutritional value of major plants in the traditional diets of Indians in the Pacific Northwest (Keely et al. 1982; Norton et al. 1984). Minore (1972, 1984) and Hunn and Norton (1984) have focused on the most important berry for Indian people living at the intersection of the Columbia River and the Cascade Range.

Important research in recent years has focused on the ecology and commercial harvesting of edible fungi, especially morels (*Morchella* spp.), chanterelles (principally the Pacific golden chanterelle but also the white chanterelle *C. albidus*), and American matsutake. With only minor funding, a network of Forest Service scientists at the Pacific Northwest Research Station and their colleagues at the University of Washington, Central Washington State University, and Oregon State University have produced multidisciplinary publications on edible mushrooms, their management, and conservation (see especially Hosford, Pilz, and Molina 1997 and Liegal et al. 1998).

CURRENT MEDICINAL PLANT RESEARCH

Great interest in the uses of taxol from western yew *(Taxus brevifolia)* spurred intensive harvesting, some of it illegal, of yew bark from Pacific Northwest forests in the late 1980s and early 1990s. Publications reporting on research into the phytochemistry of Pacific yew have exceeded in number the publications on all other medicinal plants from the Pacific Northwest combined in recent years. Other recent research into the medical properties of Pacific Northwest native species has focused on species with traditional medicinal uses among the First Nations in British Columbia. Tribes in Oregon and Washington also used many of the same species. A series of papers by McCutcheon et al. (1992, 1994, 1995) surveys Pacific Northwest forest plants for antibacterial, antifungal, and antiviral activity. Joseph Karchesy and his colleagues and students at Oregon State University currently published research papers on the plant chemistry of key species emerging into prominence, such as red alder *(Alnus rubra)* (Chen, Karchesy, and González Laredo 1998), oceanspray *(Holodiscus discolor)* (González Laredo et al. 1997), and liverwort *(Chiloscyphus rivularis)* (Wu et al. 1997).

INNOVATION AND INFORMATION TRANSFER IN THE PACIFIC NORTHWEST

The Pacific Northwest has given rise to concerted efforts to manage nontimber forest products consciously for economic profit and as a tool for rural development. The U.S. Department of the Interior's Bureau of Land Management produced the BLM Task Force Final Report (1993) to guide the agency in managing nontimber products in Oregon and Washington in the context of existing environmental laws and regulations. As people, including many recent immigrants with diverse cultural backgrounds, increasingly participate in gathering these products, public land managers have concerns about sustainable harvesting and harvester safety. Outreach efforts to inform people about regulations, best harvesting methods, and civil rights have taken on new character. Gerald Smith, the special forest products program coordinator at the Chemult Ranger District in the

Winema National Forest, oversees complex operations to issue picking permits, instruct harvesters on regulations about picking American matsutake for commercial and personal use, and provide camping areas, water, and sanitary facilities for several hundred pickers during the peak matsutake season in September and October. Films in English, Cambodian, Vietnamese, and Hmong address policies and harvesting instructions to pickers with different cultural backgrounds and experiences in forests of their former homelands. Several social anthropologists (Hansis 1996, 1998; McLain and Jones 1998) have begun documenting the work of non-Indian hunters and gatherers. The Jefferson Institute in Grants Pass, Oregon, founded by Beverly Brown, has made great strides in bringing together people from different ethnic groups who are gathering nontimber forest products to cooperate on common issues to advance improvements in wages, workers' protection and safety, and civil rights.

REFERENCES

Allen, John W. 1950. *Marketing Woodlot Products in the State of Washington.* Bulletin 1. Olympia, WA: Washington Department of Conservation and Development, Institute of Forest Products.

Amaranthus, Michael P., James Weigand, and Rick Abbott. 1998. "Managing High-Elevation Forests to Produce American Matsutake *(Tricholoma magnivelare),* High-quality Timber, and Nontimber Forest Products." *Western Journal of Applied Forestry* 13(4): 120–128.

Arnst, Albert. 1945. "Cascara—A Crop from West Coast Tree Farms." *Journal of Forestry* 43(11): 805–811.

Barrett, Samuel A. 1910. "The Material Culture of the Klamath Lake and Modoc Indians of Northeastern California and Southern Oregon." *University of California Publications in American Archaeology and Ethnology* 5(4): 239–292.

BLM Task Force. 1993. *Managing Special Forest Products in Oregon and Washington: Final Report.* Portland, OR: Bureau of Land Management.

Boyd, Robert. 1986. "Strategies of Indian Burning in the Willamette Valley." *Canadian Journal of Anthropology* 5(1): 65–86.

Chen, J., J. J. Karchesy, and R. F. González Laredo. 1998. "Phenolic Diarylheptenones from *Alnus Rubra* Bark." *Planta Medica* 64(1): 74–75.

Christiansen, Paul. 1982. "Production and Marketing of Christmas Trees and Decorative Greenery in Denmark." *American Christmas Tree Journal* 26(4): 42–45.

Cole, Madeline L. 1990. "Megascopic Plant Remains from Three Housepits along the Applegate River, Southwest Oregon." Master's thesis, Oregon State University.

Couture, Marilyn Dunlap. 1978. "Recent and Contemporary Foraging Practices of the Harney Valley Paiute." Master's thesis, Portland State University.

Couture, Marilyn D., Mary F. Ricks, and Lucile Housley. 1986. "Foraging Behavior of a Contemporary Northern Great Basin Population." *Journal of California and Great Basin Anthropology* 8(2): 150–160.

Coville, Frederick Vernon. 1897. *Note on the Plants Used by the Klamath Indians of Oregon.* Contributions from the United States National Herbarium, vol. 5, part 2, pp. 87–108. Washington, DC: Government Printing Office.

Chu, A., J. Zajicek, L. B. Davin, N. G. Lewis, and R. B. Croteau. 1992. "Mixed Acetoxy-benzoxy Taxane Esters from *Taxus brevifolia.*" *Phytochemistry* 31(12): 4249–4252.

Darby, Melissa Cole. 1996. "Wapato for the People: An Ecological Approach to Understanding the Native American Use of *Sagittaria latifolia* on the Lower Columbia River." Master's thesis, Portland State University.

Dickson, Evelyn M. 1946. "Food Plants of Western Oregon Indians." Master's thesis, Stanford University.

Emanuel, Robert M. 1994. *A Field Guide to Ethnobotanical Plants of the Winema National Forest.* Pub. no. R6-WIN-TP 95-04. Portland, OR: USDA Forest Service, Pacific Northwest Region.

Fischer, Hartmut. 1992. *Schnittgrün aus Übersee: Transport per Flugzeug oder Schiffscontainer. Gärtnerbörse und Gartenwelt* 92(39): 1937–1940.

Gill, Steven J. 1983. "Ethnobotany of the Makah and Ozette people, Olympic Peninsula, Washington (USA)." Ph.D. diss., Washington State University.

González Laredo, R. F., J. Chaidez González, A. A. Ahmed, and J. J. Karchesy. 1997. "A Stilbene Xyloside from Holodiscus Discolor Bark." *Phytochemistry* 46(1): 175–176.

Gunther, Erna. 1973. *Ethnobotany of Western Washington: The Knowledge and Use of Indigenous Plants by Native Americans.* Rev. ed. Seattle: University of Washington Press.

Hansis, Richard. 1996. "The Harvesting of Special Forest Products by Latinos and Southeast Asians in the Pacific Northwest: Preliminary Observations." *Society and Natural Resources* 9(6): 611–615.

———. 1998. "A Political Ecology of Picking: Nontimber Forest Products in the Pacific Northwest." *Human Ecology* 26(1): 67–86.

Heckman, Hazel. 1951. "The Happy Brush Pickers of the High Cascades." *Saturday Evening Post,* October 6, 1951.

Hosford, David, David Pilz, and Randy Molina. 1997. *Ecology and Management of the Commercially Harvested American Matsutake Mushroom.* Pub. no. PNW-GTR-412. Portland, OR: USDA Forest Service, Pacific Northwest Research Station.

Hunn, Eugene, and David H. French. 1981. "Lomatium: A Key Resource for Columbia Plateau Native Subsistence." *Northwest Science* 55(2): 87–94.

Hunn, E., and H. H. Norton. 1984. "Impact of Mt. St. Helens Ashfall on Fruit Yield of Mountain Huckleberry, *Vaccinium membranaceum,* an Important Native American Food." *Economic Botany* 38(1): 121–127.

Keely, Patrick B., Charlen S. Martinsen, Eugene S. Hunn, and Helen H. Nortonelen. 1982. "Composition of Native American Fruits in the Pacific Northwest." *Journal of the American Dietetic Association* 81(5): 568–572.

Kuhnlein, Harriet V., and Nancy J. Turner. 1987. "Cow-parsnip (*Heracleum lanatum* Michx.): An Indigenous Vegetable of Native People of Northwestern North America." *Journal of Ethnobiology* 6(2): 309–324.

Liegal, Leon, David Pilz, and Thomas Love. 1998. "The Biological, Socioeconomic, and Managerial Aspects of Chanterelle Mushroom Harvesting: The Olympic Peninsula, Washington State, USA." *Ambio Special Report* 9:3–7.

Mahar, James. 1953. "Ethnobotany of the Oregon Paiutes of the Warm Springs Indian Reservation." B.A. thesis, Reed College, Portland, OR.

McCutcheon, A. R., S. M. Ellis, R. E. W. Hancock, and G. H. N. Towers. 1992. "Antibiotic Screening of Medicinal Plants of the British Columbian Native Peoples." *Journal of Ethnopharmacology* 37(3): 213–223.

———. 1994. "Antifungal Screening of Medicinal Plants of the British Columbian Native Peoples." *Journal of Ethnopharmacology* 44(3): 157–169.

McCutcheon, A. R., T. E. Roberts, E. Gibbons, S. M. Ellis, G. H. N. Towers, L. A. Babiuk, and R. E. W. Hancock. 1995. "Antiviral Screening of British Columbia Medicinal Plants." *Journal of Ethnopharmacology* 49(2): 101–110.

McLain, Rebecca J. and Eric T. Jones. 1997. *Challenging "Community" Definitions in Sustainable Natural Resource Management: The Case of Wild Mushroom Harvesting in the USA.* Gatekeeper Series, no. 68, pp. 1–19. London: International Institute for Environment and Development, Sustainable Agriculture Programme.

———. 1998. "Participatory Non-Wood Forest Products Management: Experiences from the Pacific Northwest. In *Sustainable Development of Non-Wood Goods from Boreal and Cold Temperate Forests,* ed. G. Lund, B. Pajari, and M. Korhonen, pp. 189–196. Joensuu, Finland: European Forest Institute.

Minore, Don. 1972. "Wild huckleberries of Oregon and Washington—A Dwindling Resource." Research paper no. 143. Portland, OR: USDA Forest Service, Pacific Northwest Forest and Range Experiment Station.

———. 1984. "*Vaccinium membranaceum* Berry Production Seven Years after Treatment to Reduce Overstory Tree Canopies." *Northwest Science* 58(3): 208–212.

Norton, H. H., E. S. Hunn, C. S. Martinsen, and P. B. Keely. 1984. "Vegetable Food Products of the Foraging Economies of the Pacific Northwest." *Ecology of Food and Nutrition* 14(3): 219–228.

Pilz, David, and Randy Molina. 1996. *Managing Forest Ecosystems to Conserve Fungus Diversity and Sustain Wild Mushroom Harvests.* Pub. no. PNW-GTR-371. Portland, OR: USDA Forest Service, Pacific Northwest Research Station.

Prouty, Guy Lee. 1995. "Roots and Tubers: Prehistoric Plant Use, Settlement and Subsistence Intensification, and Storage in the Fort Rock Basin, Northern Great Basin, Oregon." Ph.D. diss., Oregon State University.

Redhead, Scott, Lorelei L. Norvelle, and Eric Danell. 1997. "*Cantharellus formosus* and the Pacific Golden Chanterelle Harvest in Western North America." *Mycotaxon* 65:285–322.

Schlosser, William E. 1995. "Potential for Expansion of the Special Forest Products Industry in the Northern Rockies." *Western Journal of Applied Forestry* 10(4): 138–143.

Schlosser, William E., and Keith A. Blatner. 1995. "The Wild Edible Mushroom Industry of Washington, Oregon, and Idaho: A 1992 Survey." *Journal of Forestry* 93(3): 31–36.

Schlosser, William E., Keith A. Blatner, and D. M. Baumgartner. 1992. *Guide to Floral Greens: Special Forest Products.* WSU Cooperative Extension Bulletin

1659. Pullman, WA: Washington State University, Cooperative Extension Service.

Schlosser, William E., Keith A. Blatner, and B. Zamora. 1992. "Pacific Northwest Forest Lands' Potential for Floral Greenery." *Northwest Science* 66(1): 44–55.

Smith, Harriet Lummis. 1978. *Camas: The Plant That Caused Wars*. Lake Oswego, OR: Smith Publishing.

Statham, Dawn Stram. 1982. *Camas and the Northern Shoshoni: A Biogeographic and Socioeconomic Analysis*. Boise State University Archaeological Reports 10. Boise, ID: Boise State University.

Stewart, Hilary. 1984. *Cedar: Tree of Life to the Northwest Coast Indians*. Seattle: University of Washington Press.

Thoms, Alston Vern. 1989. "The Northern Roots of Hunter-Gatherer Intensification: Camas and the Pacific Northwest." Ph.D. diss., Washington State University.

Turner, Nancy J., Randy Bouchard, and Dorothy Kennedy. 1980. "Ethnobotany of the Okanagan-Colville Indians of British Columbia and Washington." *Occasional Papers of the British Columbia Provincial Museum 21*. Victoria, BC: British Columbia Provincial Museum.

Von Hagen, Bettina, James F. Weigand, Rebecca McLain, Roger Fight, and Harriet Christensen. 1996. *Conservation and Development of Nontimber Forest Products in the Pacific Northwest: An Annotated Bibliography.* Pub. no. PNW-GTR-375. Portland, OR: USDA Forest Service, Northwest Research Station.

Wheeler, N. C., K. Jech, S. Masters, S. W. Brobst, A. B. Alvarado, A. J. Hoover, and K. M. Snader. 1992. "Effects of Genetic, Epigenetic, and Environmental Factors on Taxol Content in *Taxus brevifolia* and Related Species." *Journal of Natural Products* 55(4): 432–490.

Wu, C., A. A. L. Gunatilaka, F. L. McCabe, R. K. Johnson, R. W. Spjut, and D. G. I. Kingston. 1997. "Bioactive and Other Sesquiterpenes from *Chiloscyphus rivularis*." *Journal of Natural Products* 60(12): 1281–1286.

Zenk, Henry Benjamin. 1976. "Contributions to Tualitin Ethnography: Subsistence and Ethnobiology." Master's thesis, Portland State University.

CASE STUDY

The American Southwest

James Weigand

Information about uses of native plants in colonial Mexico captured the interest of Spanish priests educated in medical botany. Possibilities for cures and remedies for maladies both familiar and newly encountered in the Americas made inquiries into Aztec and Mayan ethnobotany more than just a scholarly pursuit. Guerra (1973) has inventoried manuscripts from the Spanish colonial period to make them readily identifiable and accessible to researchers. These manuscripts provide an invaluable insight into the historic importance of plants to the Spanish colonizers of Mexico, including what is today the American Southwest and California. Of particular interest are three works: the Badianus manuscript by Martin de la Cruz (English translation 1940; Spanish translation 1964); the *Florentine Codex* of Aztec plant uses by Fray Bernardino de Sahagun (English translation of Book II, "The Earthly Things," by Dibble and Anderson 1963; Spanish translation by Estrada Lugo 1989); and the manuscript by Juan de Cárdenas (edited by Lozoya Legorreta 1980) on the "marvelous secrets" of Mexican herbal medicine.

The significance of these manuscripts remains today. For example, Heinrich et al. (1998) have used the *Florentine Codex* as a guide for their systematic search of phytochemicals from native species of Asteraceae in Mexico. Some medicinal Aztec plants are native to the American Southwest and have medicinal uses in the United States, for example, *Artemisia ludoviciana* (white sage brush, estafiate, iztauyatl) and *Achillea millefolium* (yarrow, mil hojas, tlaquequetzal). Early-nineteenth-century chronicles of plant uses (i.e., from the period before the Mexican-American War), are few in number, but Navarro (1992) and the Academia Médico-Quirúrgica de la Puebla de los Angeles (1832) list Southwest species in use or native to the United States within its post-1848 borders. One plant species from Mexico, wormseed or epazote *(Chenopodium ambrosioides),* deserves special mention. After introduction into eighteenth-century Anglo-America, wormseed attained commercial importance in Maryland as a crop plant for the emetic wormseed oil (Guenther 1950).

CONTEMPORARY CULTURES AND USES OF NATIVE PLANT SPECIES OF THE MEXICO–U.S. BORDERLANDS

In no other part of the United States is the confluence of multiple cultural traditions in plant uses so impressive as in the American Southwest. Medical anthropologists, in particular, have called attention to this confluence. Bauwens et al. (1977) have described the ethnically based medical traditions in the Southwest where most residents rely on available services from mainstream medical facilities, although belief in the beneficial effects of herbs, massage, and prayers also complements medical treatments for many Native American, Euro-American, Afro-American, and Mexican-American residents of Arizona and New Mexico. This eclectic approach to healing represents a risk-reducing strategy to guard against disease or to promote health. Velimirovic and colleagues (1978) have also investigated the societal responses to mainstream medicine and cultural attitudes and values in the borderlands between Mexico and the American Southwest. Kiev (1968) and Trotter and Chavira (1981) describe the social and medical effects of *curanderismo,* traditional healing practices in Mexico and in Mexican-American communities.

American anthropologists have recorded modern uses of plants in the Southwest, particularly among the Native American and Hispanic residents. The Bureau of Ethnology at the Smithsonian Institution published ethnobotanical research on a number of Indian tribes in Arizona and New Mexico in the early decades of the twentieth centuries: Zuni people (Stevenson 1915) and Tewa people (Robbins, Harrington, and Freire-Marreco 1916). Wyman and Harris (1941, 1951) introduced not only the species of plants used by Navajo communities to non-Navajo readers but also explained how the Navajo worldview underpins traditional Navajo medicine. Castetter and Bell (1942, 1951) studied agricultural systems of Indians of the Southwest during the 1930s through the 1950s. Curtin (1997) and Dunmire and Tierney (1997) have described the centuries-old ethnobotanical traditions of the Hispanic and Indian residents in the Four Corners Region. To better understand contemporary uses of the national forests in Arizona, the U.S. Forest Service commissioned Gallagher (1977) to compile contemporary plant uses by Apache people. Dunmire and Tierney (1995) and Rea (1997) continue the tradition of documenting contemporary uses of borderland plant species for food and medicine.

Cross-cultural and cross-border compilations of plant uses in the Mexican-American borderlands began with work by Burlage (1968), who incorporated information from Martínez (1989) about medicinal plants native to Texas. Ford (1975) and Kay (1996) have drawn on existing ethnobotanical literature and their own searches in marketplaces of plants sold as medicinals on both sides of the U.S.–Mexican border. Three other people have also been key to expanding people's awareness of cross-border connections in ethnobotany: Michael Moore, Gary Nabhan, and Robert Bye. Moore (1979, 1989, 1990, 1993) has been particularly active in promoting greater familiarity among the American public with the ethnobotanical resources of the Southwest and has advocated careful, sustainable harvesting of medicinal plants. Gary Nabhan (1979, 1983, 1985) has researched nutrition and health for Indian people in the Southwest and has advocated resuming diets of traditional foods from the Mexican–U.S. borderlands to prevent diabetes and to improve general health. A foundation established by Nabhan and others preserves traditional cultivars of major crop plants and distributes them to the public (see Table 3). Currently, that organization, Native Seeds/SEARCH, and the U.S. Forest Service are collaborating on establishing a preserve for wild populations of chili peppers *(Capsicum annuum).*

From his early work in the ethnobotany of the Tarahumara people in the Mexican state of Sonora, Robert Bye has been closely involved with the botany and the people of the Greater Southwest. In 1985, he edited the proceedings of the twenty-fifth annual meeting of the Society for Economic Botany, which are devoted to the ethnobotany and to the product development of plants native to the region. In both Mexico and the United States, Bye has contributed to training ethnobotanists focusing on the American Southwest and Mexico. Most recently, he and his coresearchers (1999) at the Universidad Nacional Autonoma de México (UNAM) published an overview of medicinal plant use in Mexico. This volume along with the work by Arqueta Villamar (1994) provide the most comprehensive and current information from Mexico about medicinal plants that co-occur in Mexico and the United States.

One important cultural food resource for people of the Southwest borderlands is pine nuts from native pinyon pines: *Pinus cembroides, P. edulis,* and *P. monophylla.* Several symposia in the Southwest have brought together researchers from multiple disciplines to summarize the latest science findings, new product uses, and integrated piñon management to benefit people and wildlife (Aldon and Loring 1977, Aldon and Shaw 1993, Everett 1986, and Shaw, Aldon, and LoSapio 1995).

Unlike in Arizona and New Mexico, native American ethnobotany has received little attention and documentation. Pannill (1983) has written an unpublished thesis about edible and dye plants from the Edwards Plateau region of Texas, and Williams-Dean (1978) completed a dissertation on the ethnobotany of prehistoric people in southwest Texas. Several recent works remedy that knowledge gap: Cheathem, Johnston, and Marshall (1995), Silverthorne (1996), and Tull (1999). Texas is fortunate, however, to have a journal, *Sabal,* devoted to native medicinal plants in the state. Covering not only the Southwest, Ebeling (1986) summarizes in an encyclopedic work the ethnobotanical uses of people in the Southwest and Great Basin.

Table 3. Traditional food plants from the Mexican–U.S. borderlands

Scientific name	NRCS name	Spanish names	Parts used as food
Capsicum annum var. *aviculare*	cayenne pepper	chili, chiltepines	fruits for culinary seasoning, decorative, medicinal
Chenopodium berlandieri	pitseed goosefoot	chual, huazontle, quelite	leaves, raw or cooked; seeds to season pinole and atole
Cucurbita pepo	field pumpkin	calabaza	acorn squash, summer squash, zucchini
Gossypium hirsutum	upland cotton		seeds, raw or parched, whole or ground
Helianthus annuus	common sunflower	girasol, mirasol	ray flowers for salads, seeds raw, roasted, or pressed for oil
Opuntia acanthocarpa	buckhorn cholla	cholla, nopal, tuna	flower buds, fruits, leaves (pads)
Opuntia echinocarpa	staghorn cholla		
Opuntia engelmannii	cactus apple		
Opuntia fulgida	jumping cholla		
Opuntia phaeacantha	tulip, pricklypear		
Opuntia spinosior	walkingstick, cactus		
Opuntia versicolor	staghorn cholla		
Panicum sonorum	sauwi		grain
Phaseolus acutifolius	tepary bean		seeds
Physalis philadelphica	Mexican groundcherry	tomatillo	sweet raw fruit, roasted for salsa
Pinus cembroides	Mexican pinyon	piñon	pine nuts
Pinus edulis	twoneedle pinyon	piñon	
Pinus monophylla	singleleaf pinyon	piñon	
Proboscidea parviflora	double claw		tender young fruits, dried seeds
Prosopis glandulosa	honey mesquite	mesquite	
Prosopis pubescens	screwbean mesquite	tornillo	fruits, honey from flowers, seeds
Prosopis velutina	velvet mesquite		
Salvia columbariae	chia	chia	seed mucilage for refreshing drinks; medicinal

Sources: Castetter and Bell (1942, 1951), Lanner (1981), Nabhan (1985), Native Seeds/SEARCH *(www.azstarnet.com/~nss),* Rea (1997).

LEARNING FROM MEXICO

Resources in Mexico are particularly important in the process of (re)discovering uses of plants, fungi, and lichens in the Mexico–U.S. borderlands. One resource remains the *Boletín de la Sociedad Mexicana de Micología,* published annually from 1968 to 1984, which includes unique information about uses of fungi, a topic largely neglected in ethnographic research in the United States. Since the 1970s, researchers in Mexico have been studying systematically indigenous medical systems and associated native medicinal plants (Lozoya Legorreta 1994). The Mexican federal government established the Institute for the Study of Medical Plants in 1975 to integrate botanical, chemical, and pharmacological studies on the Mexican flora. Diaz and Luis (1976a,b) rapidly produced databases on ethnobotanical information relating to Mexican medicinal plants from the medical literature of the sixteenth to the nineteenth centuries—during the time of Mexican sovereignty over the American Southwest—and on medicinal plants in current use.

At the same time, Lozoya Legorreta (1976) surveyed current knowledge about Mexican medicinal plants, while the Institute (1976) compiled a bibliography of theses on medicinal plants from students and faculty from the chemistry department at UNAM. About a thousand native plant species used in traditional medicine throughout Mexico for almost four hundred years were identified. By 1978, Viesca Treviño had completed a three-volume compendium of all ethnobotanic and medical anthropological studies conducted to date, and Ramírez had completed an annotated bibliography of work concerning traditional Mexican medicine since 1900. The Research Unit in Pharmacology of National Products under the Mexican Institute of Social Security now assumes centralized reporting on progress in multidisciplinary studies concerning nontimber plant products in Mexico.

In recent years, coverage of plant uses in Mexico has been rich in detail and breadth of scope. Many of these works are important contributions to plant knowledge in the United States, as many of the species also occur in the American Southwest. Table 4 lists major Mexican medicinal plants from arid ecosystems in the Mexican-American borderlands. Information about cross-border trade in these plants is poorly known. Many of the regional medicinal species reach their northernmost range listed just across the border in Arizona, New Mexico, and Texas. Harvesting wild populations in the United States may reduce the viability of native populations at their range limits and jeopardize commercial sustainability. Currently, grassroots efforts are under way in Mexico to generate sustainable crops of Mexican and American Southwest medicinal plant species (Betancourt Aguilar 1996) in Mexico. The Proyecto Mercados Verdes Herbolarios (PMVH) in Puebla State, for example, sponsored the First National Congress on Medicinal Plants in Mexico in 1996 to bring together traditional medicinal practitioners, medical doctors, researchers, and public health officials. PMVH is coordinating a Second National Congress for November 2002 in Guadalajara, Jalisco, in conjunction with the First Latin American Congress of Herbalism. These conventions strive for greater cooperation, exchange, and diffusion of information about scientific studies linked to herbalism and traditional medicine in Mexico and elsewhere in Latin America.

Table 4. Commercial medicinal plant species from arid regions of the Mexican–U.S. borderlands

Latin name	NRCS name	Spanish names	Family	Plant parts used	Conservation status
Bursera microphylla	elephant tree	copal, torote	Burseraceae	bark, gum	Plant Savers' WATCH List
Cardiospermum halicacabum	love in a puff	bombilla, farolito, rayo	Sapindaceae	roots	
Encelia farinosa	goldenhills	incienso	Asteraceae	plant gum	
Ephedra antisyphilitica	clapweed	popotillo	Ephedraceae	aboveground plant	
Eysenhardtia polystachya	kidneywood	palo cuate	Fabaceae	wood	
Fouquieria splendens	ocotillo	ocotillo	Fouqueriaceae	flowers, roots	
Gomphrena serrata	arrasa con todo	arrasa con todo	Amaranthaceae	roots	
Guazuma ulmifolia	bastardcedar	guacima	Sterculiaceae	bark, fruits, seeds	
Heliotropium angiospermum	scorpionstail		Boraginaceae	leaves	
Heteropteris laurifolia	dragonwith		Malphigiaceae	leaves	
Larrea tridentata	creosotebush	gober-nadora	Zygophyllaceae	whole plants	
Loeselia mexicana	Mexican false calico	hierba de la Virgen	Polemoniaceae	leaves	
Lophophora williamsii	peyote	peyote	Cactaceae	dried whole plants	
Milla biflora	Mexican star	carcoma, estrella	Liliaceae	flowers, fruits	
Opuntia imbricata	tree cholla	velas de coyote	Cactaceae	fruits	
Pithecellobium dulce	monkeypod		Fabaceae	bark	
Prosopis laevigata	smooth mesquite		Fabaceae	bark	
Prosopis pubescens	screwbean mesquite	tornillo	Fabaceae	roots	
Simmondsia chinensis	jojoba	jojoba	Simmondsiaceae	fruits	
Sophora secundiflora	mescal bean	frijolito	Fabaceae	seeds	
Turnera diffusa	damiana	damiana	Turneraceae	whole plant	

Source: Villaseñor Becerra (1993) for plants found in thorn forests (Texas) and xerophilous scrub (Arizona and New Mexico).

REFERENCES

Academia Médico-Quirúrgica de la Puebla de Los Angeles. 1832. *Ensayo para la Materia Medica Mexicana, Arreglado por una Comision Nombrada por la Academia Medico-Quirurgica de esta Capital, Quien ha Dispuesto se Imprima por Considerarlo Util.* Puebla, México: Oficina del Hospital de San Pedro, á cargo del C. Manuel Buen-Abad.

Aldon, Earl F,. and Thomas J. Loring. 1977. Ecology, Uses, and Management of Pinyon-Juniper Woodlands: Proceedings of the Workshop Held 24–25 March 1977 in Albuquerque, NM. General Technical Report RM-39. Fort Collins, CO: USDA Forest Service, Rocky Mountain Forest and Range Experiment Station.

Aldon, Earl F., and Douglas Shaw. 1993. *Managing Pinyon-Juniper Ecosystems for Sustainability and Social Needs: Proceedings of the Symposium Held 26–30 April 1993 in Santa Fe, NM.* General Technical Report RM-236. Fort Collins, CO: USDA Forest Service, Rocky Mountain Forest and Range Experiment Station.

Arqueta Villamar, Arturo. 1994. *Atlas de las Plantas de la Medicina Tradicional Mexicana.* 3 vols. México, DF: Instituto Nacional Indigenista.

Bauwens, Eleanor, Margarita Artschwager Kay, Mary Elizabeth Shutler, and Loudell F. Snow. 1977. *Ethnic Medicine in the Southwest.* Tucson: University of Arizona Press.

Betancourt Aguilar, Yolanda. 1996. Personal communication at the Internet website *www.personasenaccion.org/mensajes/796.html.*

Burlage, Henry M. 1968. *Index of Plants of Texas with Reputed Medicinal and Poisonous Properties.* Austin, TX: privately published.

Bye, Robert A., Jr., ed. 1985. "Symposium—Ethnobotany of the Greater Southwest." *Proceedings of the Society for Economic Botany, Twenty-fifth Annual Meeting, Texas A&M University, 1984.* Bronx, NY: New York Botanical Garden. Reprinted in *Economic Botany* 39(4): 375–581.

Bye, Robert A., Jr., Edelmira Linares, and Beatriz Florez. 1999. *Plantas Medicinales de México, Usos y Remedies Tradicionales.* México, DF: Universidad Nacional Autonoma de México, Instituto de Biología/Sistemas de Información Geográfica, S.A. de C.V.

Cárdenas, Juan de. 1980. *Primera Parte de los Problemas y Secretos Maravillosos de las Indias; Edición, Estudio Preliminary y Notas.* Ed. Xavier Lozoya Legorreta. México, DF: Academia Nacional de Medicina.

Castetter, E. F., and W. H. Bell. 1942. *Pima and Papago Indian Agriculture.* Albuquerque: University of New Mexico Press.

———. 1951. *Yuman Indian Agriculture: Primitive Subsistence on the Lower Colorado and Gila Rivers.* Albuquerque: University of New Mexico Press.

Cheathem, Scooter, Marshall C. Johnston, and Lynn Marshall. 1995. *The Useful Wild Plants of Texas, the Southeastern and Southwestern United States, the Southern Plains, and Northern Mexico.* Vol. 1. Austin, TX: Useful Wild Plants.

Cruz, Martin de la. 1940. *The Badianus Manuscript (Codex Barberini, Latin 241), Vatican Library: An Aztec Herbal of 1552.* Baltimore, MD: Johns Hopkins University Press.

———. 1964. *Libellus de Medicinalibus Indorum Herbis: Manuscrito Azteca de 1552*. México, DF: Instituto Mexicano del Seguro Social.

Curtin, Leonora Scott Muse. 1997. *Healing Herbs of the Upper Rio Grande: Traditional Medicine of the Southwest*. Rev. and ed. by Michael Moore. Santa Fe, NM: Western Edge Press.

Diaz Gomez, José Luis. 1976a. *Indice y Sinonimia de las Plantas Medicinales de Mexico. Monografias Cientificas I*. Mexico, DF: Instituto Mexicano para el Estudio de las Plantas Medicinales.

———. 1976b. *Usos de las Plantas Medicinales de México. Monografías Científicas II*. México, DF: Instituto Mexicano para el Estudio de las Plantas Medicinales.

Dunmire, William W., and Gail D. Tierney. 1995. *Wild Plants of the Pueblo Province: Exploring Ancient and Enduring Uses*. Santa Fe: Museum of New Mexico Press.

———. 1997. *Wild Plants and Native Peoples of the Four Corners*. Santa Fe: Museum of New Mexico Press.

Ebeling, Walter. 1986. *Handbook of Indian Foods and Fibers of Arid America*. Berkeley: University of California Press.

Everett, Richard L. 1986. *Proceedings of the Pinyon-Juniper Conference, 13–16 January 1986 in Reno, NV*. Ogden, UT: USDA Forest Service, Intermountain Research Station.

Ford, Karen Cowan. 1975. *Las Yerbas de la Gente: A Study of Hispano-American Medicinal Plants*. Anthropological paper no. 60. Ann Arbor: University of Michigan, Museum of Anthropology.

Gallagher, Marsha V. 1977. *Contemporary Ethnobotany among the Apache of the Clarkdale, Ariza Area: Coconino and Prescott National Forests*. Report no. 14. Albuquerque, NM: USDA Forest Service, Southwestern Region.

Guenther, Ernest. 1950. *The Essential Oils*. 6 vols. Princeton, NJ: D. Van Nostrand.

Guerra, Francisco. 1973. *Historia de la Materia Medica Hispano-Americana y Filipina en la Epoca Colonial; Inventario Crítico y Bibliográfico de Manuscritos*. Madrid: A. Aguado.

Heinrich, M., M. Robles, J. E. West, B. R. Ortiz de Montellano, and E. Rodriguez. 1998. "Ethnopharmacology of Mexican Asteraceae (Compositae)." *Annual Review of Pharmacology and Toxicology* 38:539–565.

Instituto Mexicano para el Estudio de las Plantas Medicinales. 1976. *Tesis Sobre Plantas Medicinales Realizadas en la Facultad Química de la UNAM, 1933–1975*. México, DF: Instituto Mexicano para el Estudio de las Plantas Medicinales.

Kay, Margarita Artschwager. 1996. *Healing with Plants in the American and Mexican West*. Tuscon: University of Arizona Press.

Kiev, Ari. 1968. *Curanderismo: Mexican-American Folk Psychiatry*. New York: Free Press.

Lanner, Ronald M. 1981. *The Piñon Pine: A Natural and Cultural History*. Reno: University of Nevada Press.

Lozoya Legorreta, Xavier. 1976. *Estado Actual del Conocimiento en Plantas Medicinales Mexicanas*. México, DF: Instituto Mexicano para el Estudio de las Plantas Medicinales.

———. 1994. "Two Decades of Mexican Ethnobotany and Research in Plant Drugs." *Ciba Foundation Symposium* 185:130–40, discussion at 140–152.

Lugo Estrada, Jane Ingrid. 1989. *El Códice florentino: Su Información Etnobotánica*. Montecillo, México: Colegio de Postgraduados, Institución de Enseñanza e Investigación en Ciencias.

Martínez, Maximino. 1989. *6a. ed. Las Plantas Medicinales de México*. México, DF: Ediciones Botas.

Moore, Michael. 1979. *Medicinal Plants of the Mountain West: A Guide to the Identification, Preparation, and Uses of Traditional Medicinal Plants Found in the Mountains, Foothills, and Upland Areas of the American West*. Santa Fe: Museum of New Mexico Press.

———. 1989. *Medicinal Plants of the Desert and Canyon West: A Guide to Identifying, Preparing, and Using Traditional Medicinal Plants Found in the Deserts and Canyon of the West and Southwest*. Santa Fe: Museum of New Mexico.

———. 1990. *Los Remedios de la Gente: Traditional Herbal Remedies of the Southwest*. Santa Fe, NM: Red Crane Books.

———. 1993. *Medicinal Plants of the Pacific West*. Santa Fe, NM: Red Crane Books.

Nabhan, Gary Paul. 1979. "Tepary Bean Domestication: Ecological and Nutritional Changes during Phaseolus Acutifolia Evolution." Master's thesis, University of Arizona.

———. 1983. "Papago Fields: Arid Lands Ethnobotany and Agricultural Ecology." Ph.D. diss., University of Arizona.

———. 1985. *Gathering the Desert*. Tucson: University of Arizona Press.

Navarro, Juan Fray. 1992. *Historia Natural, O Jardin Americano: Manuscrito de 1801*. México, DF: Universidad Nacional Autonoma de Mexico, Instituto Mexicano del Seguro Social, Instituto de Seguridad y Servicios Sociales de los Trabajadores del Estado.

Pannill, Mary Tudor. 1983. "A Guide to the Common Edible and Dye Plants of the Austin, Texas, Area." Master's thesis, University of Texas at Austin.

Ramírez, Axel. 1978. *Bibliografía Comentada de la Medicina Tradicional Mexicana (1900–1978). Monografías Científicas 3—Instituto Mexicano para el Estudio de las Plantas Medicinales 3*. México, DF: IMEPLAM.

Rea, Amadeo M. 1997. *At the Desert's Green Edge: An Ethnobotany of the Gila River Pima*. Tuscon: University of Arizona Press.

Robbins, W., J. P. Harrington, and B. Freire-Marreco, eds. 1916. *Ethnobotany of the Tewa Indians*. Bulletin 55. Washington, DC: Smithsonian Institution, Bureau of American Ethnology.

Sahagun, Fray Bernardino de. 1963. *Florentine Codex*. Trans. C. E. Dibble and A. J. O. Anderson. Book II, "The Earthly Things." Santa Fe, NM: School of American Research.

Shaw, Douglas W., Earl F. Aldon, amd Carol LoSapio. 1995. *Desired Future Conditions for Pinyon-Juniper Ecosystems*. General Technical Report RM-258. Fort Collins, CO: USDA Forest Service, Rocky Mountain Forest and Range Experiment Station.

Silverthorne, Elizabeth. 1996. *Legends and Lore of Texas Wildflowers*. College Station: Texas A&M University Press.

Stevenson, M. C. 1915. "Ethnobotany of the Zuni Indians." *Bureau of American Ethnology Annual Report* 30:31–102.

Trotter, Robert T., II, and Juan Antonio Chavira. 1981. *Curanderismo: Mexican American Folk Healing*. Athens: University of Georgia Press.

Tull, Delena. 1999. *Edible and Useful Plants of Texas and the Southwest*. Austin: University of Texas Press.

Velimirovic, Boris, ed. 1978. *Modern Medicine and Medical Anthropology in the United States–Mexico Border Population: Proceedings of a Workshop Held in El Paso, Texas (20–21 January 1977)*. Scientific Publication 359. Washington, DC: Pan American Health Organization.

Viesca Treviño, Carlos. 1976–1978. *Estudios Sobre Etnobotánica y Antropología Médica*. 3 vols. México, DF: Instituto Mexicano para el Estudio de las Plantas Medicinales.

Villaseñor Becerra, Alejandro. 1993. "Medicinal Flora of Mexico." *Journal of Herbs, Spices, and Medicinal Plants* 2(1): 55–91.

Williams-Dean, Glenna Joyce. 1978. "Ethnobotany and Cultural Ecology of Prehistoric Man in Southwest Texas." Ph.D. diss., Texas A&M University.

Wyman, Leland C., and Stuart K. Harris. 1941. *Navajo Indian Medical Ethnobotany*. Albuquerque: University of New Mexico Bulletin, Anthropological Series.

———. 1951. *The Ethnobotany of the Kayenta Navaho*. Albuquerque: University of New Mexico Press.

CASE STUDY

The Caribbean Basin: Florida, Puerto Rico, and the U.S. Virgin Islands

James Weigand

Although a comparatively small area in relation to the rest of the United States, portions of the Caribbean under U.S. sovereignty contribute greatly to the native plant species diversity in the United States. Florida, Puerto Rico, and the U.S. Virgin Islands provide links to other tropical and subtropical ecosystems of the Americas. At the same time, the multicultural confluence in the Caribbean Basin melds together Native American, European, and African customs and traditions of native plant use. Morton (1981) points to the three major sources of plants that constitute the medicinal plant heritage of Caribbean people: European medicinal herbs such as rosemary *(Rosmarinus officinalis)* and borage *(Borago officinalis)*, primarily from Spanish sources; wild and cultivated plants used by Caribbean native peoples; and an eclectic assortment of modern-day ornamental plants from around the world, for which Caribbean peoples have found medicinal uses as well. Consideration of food plants used in the region call to mind the wide variety of food plants from Africa and Asia that pervade the daily lives of people in the region, for example, sesame, okra, tamarind, and mangos.

The diaspora of Caribbean people to the continental United States—from Cuba, the Dominican Republic, Haiti, Puerto Rico, and the Lesser Antilles—has brought health care customs and uses of plants to cities of the East Coast and especially to Florida. The biotic continuity between Florida and the rest of the Caribbean Basin allows people from other Caribbean nations to find many of the same plant species from their home islands. In Miami, New York, Boston, and Philadelphia, medicinal plant shops called *botánicas* are part of inner-city commercial districts wherever Caribbean people live. Meeting the health care needs of Caribbean people, many of whom are poor, remains a challenge to social workers and health care providers in the United States (Delgado 1996). Traditional medicine from Caribbean-region plants may help elderly people in particular to find ease and comfort in the absence of access to mainstream medical care.

FLORIDA

Florida represents a geographic anomaly in the region as a peninsula, but especially in south Florida, the native flora resembles that of northern Caribbean islands. Most published works on the medicinal plants of the state (Christensen 1950; Demers 1997; Johnson 1967) have emphasized plant species in Florida that are also in the Southeast rather than those with Caribbean affinities. Historical and present-day uses of native flora by non-Anglo Floridians remains a mostly unexplored field of research. Ethnobotanical studies of Native Floridian people are scant, pioneered by Sturtevant's (1955) doctoral thesis on the Miccosukee Seminoles. Since then, archeological work in Florida has produced studies of native plant uses among Calusa people (Marquardt and Payne 1992) and uses during the Spanish colonial era (Hann 1986).

Economically, the most important medicinal plant from Florida is saw palmetto *(Serrenoa repens)*. Use of saw palmetto in recent years has become international. The Florida State Cooperative Extension Service provides training in silviculture of saw palmetto to respond to the demand for medicinal and medical uses. Florida also contributes significantly to the floral greens market worldwide. In Volusia, Putnam, and Lake counties, enterprising farmers established "ferneries"—farms and greenhouses devoted to culturing ferns and fernlike plants—at the turn of the twentieth century. Some two hundred growers produce fresh foliage for North American and European markets. While many species grown today are exotic, such as *Asparagus* spp. and many palms, the fernery industry has its base in native plants, in particular leatherleaf fern *(Rumohra adiantiformis)*, Boston sword fern *(Nephrolepis exaltata)*, coontie fern (actually a cycad *Zamia pumila*), Spanish moss *(Tillandsia usneoides)*, and saw palmetto. Florida ferneries have also expanded to include international marketing of domestic foliage greens from the Carolinas and the Pacific Northwest, the two other major supply centers for floral greens. Many of the native fern species produced grow under forest canopies in an agroforestry setting.

PUERTO RICO

Located at the axis between the Greater and Lesser Antilles, Puerto Rico contains a diverse tropical flora. Hernandez et al. (1984) found that 57 percent of their sample of Puerto Rican residents used medicinal plants regularly, especially for cardiovascular conditions. Núñez Melendez (1982) was the first to systematically compile the medicinal plant traditions of the island. Since then, Liogier (1990), Benedetti (1996, 1998), and

Dua (1996) have brought to bear a practical emphasis to link Puerto Rican horticulture and plant medicine with public health. The School of Pharmacy at the University of Puerto Rico currently maintains a database of several hundred native plants from the island (Guerrero et al. 1998) and conducts studies of native Puerto Rican plants (Antoun et al. 1993). Recent studies of medicinal plants in the marketplaces and medicinal plant shops are not available.

THE U.S. VIRGIN ISLANDS

Studies of the ethnobotany of residents of the Virgin Islands are few in number. The composite of African, Danish, and Anglo-American heritages make the islands a unique site for ethnobotanical study. Oakes and Morris (1958) introduce the role of "weedwomen" as healers in the Virgin Islands. Kuby (1979) provides an updated compendium of then current plant usage. The most recent medicinal plant work is by Thomas, O'Reilly, and Clarke (1997), published by the Cooperative Extension Service at the University of the Virgin Islands.

LEARNING FROM OTHER CARIBBEAN NATIONS

Many medicinal plants in the Caribbean Basin range widely across multiple islands. Understanding the context of diverse traditions and possibilities for new uses of native plants of U.S. territories in the Caribbean Basin requires accessing research works in English, Spanish, French, and Dutch from the remaining parts of the area. Virtually simultaneous publications by Morton (1981), Ayensu (1981), and Hirschhorn (1981, 1982) in the early 1980s contributed greatly to organizing indigenous knowledge and science research about native and non-native medicinal plants in the Caribbean Basin.

In 1982, a nongovernmental organization, Traditional Medicine for the Islands (TRAMIL), established a network of researchers and plant medicine practitioners first in the Dominican Republic, then Haiti, and subsequently in all Caribbean islands and mainland nations in Central and northern South America to promote research, organize existing data, and spread information about the benefits from and cautions about using Caribbean medicinal plants. Support for the organization has come from the French and Canadian governments. In the United States, faculty at the School of Pharmacy of the University of Puerto Rico and the Missouri Botanical Garden currently participate in the network.

By evaluating traditional uses of medicinal herbs, an information and support system parallel to Western medicine helps poor people in the region to find grassroots solutions to everyday health problems. Another benefit of the TRAMIL program has been to protect and validate the benefits of cultural heritages of Caribbean island peoples (Weniger 1991). Germonsen-Robineau (1996) has summarized the findings of nearly fifteen years of TRAMIL work.

LEARNING FROM AYURVEDIC MEDICINE

Another important information source, at first glance curious and inexplicable, is Ayurvedic medicine. Because many native medicinal plants in the Caribbean Basin are weedy, enabling them to spread more easily from one island to another in an environment characterized by frequent catastrophic disturbances from hurricanes, these so-called "pantropical weeds" arrived in India from the Americas during British, French, and Portuguese colonial rule. Although Indian in origin, Ayurvedic medicine remains receptive to new plant resources for its pharmacopeia. The subtropical and tropical ecosystems of India provided suitable sites for exotic introductions of West Indian and other tropical American plant species.

Species native to Florida, Puerto Rico, and the U.S. Virgin Islands and now part of Ayurvedic medicine include pond apple *(Annona glabra),* Mexican pricklypoppy *(Argemone mexicana),* herb-of-grace *(Bacopa monnieri),* red spiderling *(Boerhavia diffusa),* pillpod sandmat *(Chamaesyce [Euphorbia] hirta),* prostrate sandmat *(C. [E.] prostrata),* false daisy *(Eclipta prostrata = E. alba),* little hogweed *(Portulaca oleracea),* longleaf pondweed *(Potamogeton nodosus),* llima *(Sida cordifolia),* and desert horsepurslane *(Trianthema portlacastrum).* Medicinal plant stocks available commercially in the United States come from Indian rather than domestic sources. Also, in many instances, research undertaken on the Indian subcontinent is the only research on the medical efficacy of these native species.

REFERENCES

Antoun, M. D., N. T. Mendoza, Y. R. Rios, G. R. Proctor, D. B. Wickramaratue, J. M. Pezzuto, and A. D. Kinghoro. 1993. "Cytotoxicity of *Hymenocallis Expansa* Alkaloids." *Journal of Natural Products* 56(8): 1423–1425.

Ayensu, Edward S. 1981. *Medicinal Plants of the West Indies.* Algonac, MI: Reference Publications.

Benedetti, Maria Dolores Hajosy. 1996. *Sembrando y Sanando en Puerto Rico: Tradiciones y Visiones para un Futuro Verde.* Orocovis, PR: Verde Luz.

——. 1998. *Earth and Spirit: Medicinal Plants and Healing Lore from Puerto Rico.* Orocovis, PR: Verde Luz.

Christensen, Bernard Victor. 1950. *Collection and Cultivation of Medicinal Plants in Florida*. Orlando, FL: Cobb's Florida Press.

Delgado, M. 1996. "Puerto Rican Elders and Botanical Shops: A Community Resource or Liability?" *Social Work and Health Care* 23(1): 67–81.

Demers, Julie Anne Ferguson. 1997. "Medicinal Ethnobotany in North Florida." Master's thesis, University of Florida.

Dua, Mohammed. 1996. *Plantas Medicinales de Puerto Rico: Enfermedades, Remedios, Recetas, Consejos: Alimentos que Curan*. San Juan, PR: privately published

Germosen-Robineau, Lionel. 1996. *Farmacopea Vegetal Caribeña*. Santo Domingo, Républica Dominicana: Edna-Caribe.

Guerrero, R. O., R. Baez, M. Antoun, and A. Frame. 1998. *An Introductory Database on the Biological Activities of Plants from Puerto Rico. http://www.modern-natural.com/Chapter3f_May.htm.*

Hann, John H. 1986. "The Use and Processing of Plants by Indians of Spanish Florida." *Southeastern Archaeology* 5(2): 91–102.

Hazlett, Donald L. 1986. "Ethnobotanical Observations from Cabecar and Guaymi Settlements in Central America." *Economic Botany* 40(3): 339–352.

Hernandez L., R. A. Muñoz, G. Miró, M. Martinez, J. Silva-Parra, and P. I. Chavez. 1984. "Use of Medicinal Plants by Ambulatory Patients in Puerto Rico." *Am J Hosp Pharm* 41(10): 2060–2064.

Hirschhorn, H. H. 1981. "Botanical Remedies of South and Central America and the Caribbean: An Archival Analysis, I." *Journal of Ethnopharmacology* 4(2): 129–158.

———. 1982. "Botanical Remedies of South and Central America and the Caribbean: An Archival Analysis, II. Conclusion." *Journal of Ethnopharmacology* 5(2): 163–180.

Johnson, Carl Henry. 1967. *Important Medicinal Plants of Florida*. Tallahassee, FL: State of Florida, Department of Agriculture.

Kanth, V. R., and P. V. Diwan. 1999. "Analgesic, Anti-Inflammatory, and Hypoglycaemic Activities of *Sida cordifolia*." *Phytotherapy Research* 13(1): 75–77.

Kuby, Ronald L. 1979. *Folk Medicine on St. Croix: An Ethnobotanical Study*. Lawrence, KS: privately published.

Liogier, Alain H. 1990. *Plantas Medicinales de Puerto Rico y del Caribe*. San Juan, PR: Iberoamericana de Ediciones.

Marquardt, William H., and Claudine Payne, eds. 1992. *Culture and Environment in the Domain of the Calusa*. Monograph 1. Gainesville: University of Florida, Institute of Archaeology and Paleoenvironmental Studies.

Morton, Julia Frances. 1981. *Atlas of Medicinal Plants of Middle America: Bahamas to Yucatan*. Springfield, IL: C. C. Thomas.

Núñez Melendez, Esteban. 1982. *Plantas Medicinales de Puerto Rico: Folklore y Fundamentos Cientificos*. Rio Piedras, PR: Editorial de la Universidad de Puerto Rico.

Oakes, A. J., and M. P. Morris. 1958. "The West Indian Weedwoman of the U.S. Virgin Islands." *Bulletin of the History of Medicine* 32(2): 164–170.

Sturtevant, W. C. 1955. "The Mikasuki Seminole: Medical Beliefs and Practices." Ph.D. diss., Yale University.

Thomas, Toni, Rudy G. O'Reilly, and Clarice C. Clarke Jr. 1997. *Traditional Medicinal Plants of St. Croix, St. Thomas, and St. John: A Selection of 68 Plants.* St. Croix: University of the Virgin Islands Cooperative Extension Service.

Weniger, Bernard. 1991. "Interest and Limitation of a Global Ethnopharmacological Survey." *Journal of Ethnopharmacology* 32(1–3): 37–41.

CASE STUDY

California

James Weigand

California is a land of extreme physical and topographic contrasts that together provide biodiversity rich in endemic species, second only to Hawaii among all states. In addition, the state has arguably the most diverse traditions of plant uses among the ethnic and cultural heritages of its people. Traditional Indian uses of native plants, mushrooms, and lichens, for example, differ greatly among the biotic regions of California—from Paiute and Shoshone people on the east side of the Sierra Nevada at the interface with the Great Basin, to the tribes along the Klamath River in the plant-rich Klamath-Siskiyou Bioregion, to the Cahuilla and Kumeyaay people in borderland deserts and coast ranges of extreme southern California.

A careful tradition of documenting plant uses by California Indians dates back to records kept during the voyage of Sir Francis Drake along the California coast in 1570 (Allen 1971). Spanish evangelization and colonization of California, originally Alta California, in the eighteenth century brought European priests educated in plant medicine in contact with California Indians living close to El Camino Real and the Franciscan missions established along the trail at intervals of one-day's horse ride between San Diego and Sonoma. The missions functioned as technology and reeducation centers designed to transform the lives of mostly hunter-gatherer native peoples to sedentary, Christianized, agricultural slaves. A more benign service of the missions was as health care centers to heal Indians suffering from diseases brought by Spaniards (Westrich 1989). Although skeptical of the value of California Indian culture in general, Franciscan missionaries studied California Indian medicine carefully. Mission gardens contained both native medicinal and agricultural crops and those introduced from Spain.

Ethnobotanical knowledge of plants from the Mediterranean-climate region of California held promise as well for adaptation and application in Spain. Major native medicinal species of California known to Spanish settlers were commonly designated *yerbas* or medicinal plants (*hierbas* in contemporary Spanish). Medicinal plant names usually indicated their medicinal application—for example, *yerba del víbora* for American wild carrot *(Daucus pusillus)* used for snakebites—or described a quality—such as palliative for *yerba mansa (Amenopsis californica)*—in much the same manner as English-language names for medicinal plants in eastern North America. Other major California native medicinal plants that Spanish settlers used included yerba del pasmo or chamise *(Adenostoma fasciculatum),* yerba buena *(Clinopodium [Satureja] douglasii),* yerba del pescado or dove weed *(Croton setigerus),* copa de oro or California poppy *(Eschscholzia californica),* yerba santa (*Eriodictyon* spp., but mostly *E. californicum),* yerba del oso *(Frangula californica),* and cascara sagrada *(Frangula purshiana).*

A rich tradition of academic research by English-speaking anthropologists recording the diverse cultural uses among California Indians began at the turn of the twentieth century. Strike (1994) and Moerman (1998) summarize to date accounts of native plant use by California tribes. A commercial medicinal plant industry was also active in early twentieth-century California. Schneider (1912) provides an invaluable reference work, describing both the prospective and currently cultivated native and nonnative medicinal plants of that period. He notes that labor costs for gathering or growing medicinal products in California were already comparatively high in contrast to Europe and thus restricted the economic viability of many California species in the face of European competition. Some of these medicinal plant species have remained popular and available commercially a century later, notably California spikenard *(Aralia californica),* the gumweeds (*Grindelia* spp.), hollyleaved barberry *(Mahonia aquifolium),* and black sage *(Salvia mellifera).*

Early on, advocacy for exotic species with time-tested markets in eastern North America or Europe appealed to farmers wishing to diversify incomes but also wanting to reduce the risk of unsuccessful adaptations of native species. In addition to a market overview of more than 850 California native species and exotic introductions capable of commercial adaptation in the state, Schneider's work provides a definitive bibliography of literature about medicinal plant chemistry and culturing methods from the nineteenth and early twentieth centuries. Only after Grieve ([1931] 1971) highlighted California medicinal plants such as yerba santa did native medicinal flora receive much notice in the nonscholarly English-speaking world outside the state.

California Indian tribes have traditions of highly skilled weaving technology and aesthetic design for baskets. Regional surveys of traditional basket weaving (Kroeber 1905; Merrill 1923; Moser 1986, 1989, 1993; Bibby 1996) provide both historical and current overviews of this utilitarian art form. Weaving is currently undergoing a renaissance of interest and practice. The California Indian Basketweavers Association (CIBA) provides an umbrella organization for tribe members in California who share an interest in traditional basket weaving. As an advocacy group, CIBA has pushed for improving federal and tribal land management to conserve and increase populations of traditional fiber plants uncontaminated by herbicides and fire retardants and capable of producing high-quality fiber. Local community groups such as the Karuk Traditional Weavers continue weaving traditions and actively engage young people to learn the traditional methods of culturing, gathering, storing, preparing, and weaving baskets and hats with traditional fiber plant species.

Indigenous knowledge of Indian people in California is also proving critical for informing land managers about ways of managing the natural landscape for ecosystem conditions that produce key Indian cultural products. Shipek (1991) has recorded the personal ethnobotanical knowledge of a modern-day traditional Indian, Delfina Cuero. Anderson (1989, 1993, 1996) visits Sierra Nevada Indians to record traditional uses so that they may not disappear from the cultural landscape. Keator and Yamane (1995) provide glimpses into the lives of contemporary California Indians who maintain traditional indigenous knowledge. Heffner (1984) has described contemporary gathering of food, horticultural, medicinal, and traditional cultural species in northwest California. Blackburn and Anderson (1993) have collected important articles about timing and availability of key cultural species. Traditional management for cultural plant species through pruning, coppicing, and burning characterize the lives of an increasing number of Indians. Issues of *Notes from Native California* also contain articles about individual species of cultural importance. Balls (1962), Clarke (1977), Callegari and Durand (1977), Nyerges (1999), and Westrich (1989) have summarized the Indian, Hispanic, and Anglo-American plant uses from California in guidebooks for the general public.

Rural montane California has undergone a dramatic transformation since the late 1980s as the U.S. Forest Service first reduced timber sales in northwest California as part of the Northwest Forest Plan for the Conservation of the Northern Spotted Owl. After 1993, timber sales from federal lands in the Sierra Nevada also declined in response to the Interim Guidelines to Protect the California Spotted Owl. The loss of well-paying timber jobs in many communities brought attention to the need to create alternative sources of employment for rural residents. One potential source for alternative income is medicinal plants. In response, Everett (1997) has provided a management and culturing framework for sustainable harvests by categorizing medicinal plant species by their sensitivity to harvesting disturbance, growth pattern, and ecology.

As people have been exploring the possibilities for commercialization of nontimber forest products in California, developing or shifting markets for products have sometimes created conflicts among ethnic or cultural groups for access to plant and fungi resources. Richards and Creasy (1996) have described the different motivations of ethnic groups who harvest American matsutake *(Tricholoma magnivelare)* in the Klamath River Valley. Traditional subsistence use by Karuk, Yurok, and Hupa people competes with recently arriving commercial mushroom pickers coming from the California Central Valley and beyond. Issues of equity and priority in allocation remain at present unresolved on public lands. Growing Hispanic populations, especially in the Central Valley and southern California, have created new markets and encouraged new businesses that sell medicinal plants, herbs, and teas from native plants of California, principally from the Sierra Nevada, plus plants imported from Mexico and Central America (Richards 1996).

Research into new and expanded uses of medicinal plants from California is comparatively infrequent. Some medicinal plants, such as California poppy (Rolland et al. 1991), are attracting global attention. Much plant chemistry research on California native plants conducted since 1965 has originated in pharmacological schools at universities abroad.

REFERENCES

Allen, Robert W. 1971. *An Examination of the Botanical References in the Accounts Relating to Drake's Encampment at Nova Albion in 1579.* Point Reyes Station, CA: Drake Navigators Guild.

Anderson, Marion Kathleen. 1989. "Southern Sierra Miwok Plant Resource Use and Management of the Yosemite Region: A Study of the Biological and Cultural Bases for Plant Gathering, Field Horticulture, and Anthropogenic Impacts on Sierra Vegetation." Master's thesis, University of California at Berkeley.

———. 1993. "The Experimental Approach to Assessment of the Potential Ecological Effects of Horticultural Practices by Indigenous Peoples on California Wildlands." Ph.D. diss., University of California at Berkeley.

———. 1996. "The Ethnobotany of Deergrass, *Muhlenbergia rigens* (Poaceae): Its Uses and Fire Management by California Indian Tribes." *Economic Botany* 50(4): 409–422.

Balls, Edward K. 1962. *Early Uses of California Plants.* Berkeley: University of California Press.

Bibby, Brian. 1996. *The Fine Art of California Indian Basketry.* Sacramento, CA: Crocker Art Museum.

Blackburn, Thomas C., and Marion Kathleen Anderson, eds. 1993. *Before the Wilderness: Environmental Management by Native Californians.* Menlo Park, CA: Ballena Press.

Callegari, Jeff, and Keith Durand. 1977. *Wild Edible and Medicinal Plants of California.* El Cerrito, CA: Callegari and Durand.

Clarke, Charlotte Bringle. 1977. *Edible and Useful Plants of California.* Berkeley: University of California Press.

Everett, Yvonne. 1997. *A Guide to Selected Nontimber Forest Products of the Hayfork Adaptive Management Area, Shasta-Trinity and Six Rivers National Forests, California.* General Technical Report GTR-PSW-162. Albany, CA: USDA Forest Service, Pacific Southwest Research Station.

Grieve, Maud. [1931] 1971. *A Modern Herbal: The Medicinal, Culinary, Cosmetic and Economic Properties, Cultivation, and Folklore of Herbs, Grasses, Fungi, Shrubs, and Trees with All Their Modern Scientific Uses.* 2 vols. New York: Dover Publications.

Heffner, Kathey. 1984. *"Following the Smoke": Contemporary Plant Procurement by the Indians of Northwest California.* Eureka, CA: Six Rivers National Forest.

Keator, Glenn, and Linda Yamane. 1995. *Three Ways of Seeing California Plants.* Berkeley, CA: Heyday Books.

Kroeber, Alfred Louis. 1905. "Basket Designs of the Indians of Northwestern California." *University of California Publications in American Archaeology and Ethnology* 2(4): 105–164.

Merrill, Ruth Earl. 1923. *Plants Used in Basketry by the California Indians.* Berkeley: University of California Press.

Moerman, Daniel. 1998. *American Indian Ethnobotany.* Portland, OR: Timber Press.

Moser, Christopher L. 1986. *Native American Basketry of Central California.* Riverside, CA: Riverside Museum Press.

———. 1989. *Native American Basketry of Northern California.* Riverside, CA: Riverside Museum Press.

———. 1993. *Native American Basketry of Southern California.* Riverside, CA: Riverside Museum Press.

Nyerges, Christopher. 1999. *Guide to Wild Foods and Useful Plants.* Chicago: Chicago Review Press.

Richards, Rebecca T. 1996. "Special Forest Product Harvesting in the Sierra Nevada." In *Sierra Nevada Ecosystem Project, Final Report to Congress.* Vol. III: *Assessments, Commissioned Reports, and Background Information,* ed. Don C. Erman, pp. 787–884. Davis: University of California Centers for Water and Wildland Resources.

Richards, Rebecca T., and Max Creasy. 1996. "Ethnic Diversity, Resource Values, and Ecosystem Management: Matsutake Mushroom Harvesting in the Klamath Bioregion." *Society and Natural Resources* 9:359–374.

Rolland, A., J. Fleurentin, M. C. Lanhers, C. Younos, R. Misslin, F. Mortier, and J. M. Pelt. 1991. "Behavioral Effects of the American Traditional Plant *Eschscholzia californica:* Sedative and Anxiolytic Properties." *Planta Medica* 57(3): 212–216.

Schneider, Albert. 1912. *Pharmacal Plants and Their Culture.* California State Board of Forestry Bulletin 2. Sacramento, CA: Superintendent of State Printing.

Shipek, Florence C. 1991. *Delfino Cuero, Her Autobiography: An Account of Her Last Years and Her Ethnobotanic Contributions.* Menlo Park, CA: Ballena Press.

Strike, Sandra S. 1994. *Ethnobotany of the California Indians*. Vol. 2, *Aboriginal Uses of California's Indigenous Plants*. Champaign, IL: Koeltz Scientific Books.

Westrich, Lolo. 1989. *California Herbal Remedies: The History and Uses of Native Medicinal Plants*. Houston, TX: Gulf Publishing.

CASE STUDY

Culture and Nontimber Forest Products in the American Pacific Tropics

James Weigand

The vast Pacific Tropics is home to diverse peoples representing many indigenous and nonindigenous cultures. Cultural diversity in combination with both endemic and exotic plants creates a rich mix of human uses of nontimber forest products. Hawaii and the U.S. territories of American Samoa and Guam are the major island groups considered here.

HAWAII

The Pacific Ocean presents obstacles to the arrival of both plants and people in Hawaii, the archipelago most distant from any continental landmass in the world. Polynesian people reached the northeast extent of their migrations in the Hawaiian archipelago; only the distance to Easter Island was farther from their ancestral home in the western Pacific. From the earliest human settlement, beginning with Polynesians, people introduced new plants and animals to the Hawaiian ecosystems. Unlike Alaska, where documentation of introduced plants from in-migrating people has not been traced across time, anthropologists have charted the spread of the so-called "canoe plants," the plant species that Polynesians brought with them as they settled new islands such as Hawaii.

Some canoe plants are well known in the United States beyond the Pacific Islands: kukui or Indian walnut *(Aleurites moluccana),* used as a dye, fuel, and medicine; 'ape or giant taro *(Alocasia macrorrhizos)* for food and medicine; ulu or breadfruit *(Artocarpus altilis)* for food and fabric; taro, kalo, or coco yam *(Colocasia esculenta)* for dyes, food, and medicine; niu or coconut *(Cocos nucifera)* for fiber, food, medicine, and thatch; 'olena or common turmeric *(Curcuma longa)* for dyes, food, and medicine; 'uala or sweet potato *(Ipomoea batatas)* for food and medicine; mai'a or paradise banana *(Musa* x *paradisiacal)* for dyes, fiber, food, and medicine; and ko or sugar cane *(Saccharùm officinarum)* for food and medicine

(Whistler 1992). Other canoe plant species such as noni or Indian mulberry *(Morinda citrifolia)* and 'awa or kava *(Piper methysticum)* are becoming mainstream nutraceuticals, and 'awapuhi kuahiwi or bitter ginger *(Zingiber zerumbet)* appears in an increasing number of commercial shampoos. A major multinational drug company has been investigating kamani or Alexandrian laurel *(Calophyllum inophyllum)* for anti-HIV properties (Patil et al. 1993; Taylor et al. 1994; and Spino, Dodier, and Sotheeswaran 1998).

Without a definitive paleobotanical record, some botanists conjecture that culturally important plants such as ti-plant *(Cordyline fruticosa), Gardenia taihitensis, Heteropogon contortus, Pandanus tectorius,* and *Solanum viride* may have already reached Hawaii before the advent of the Polynesians. In contrast, no documentation shows that Polynesian people transported plants endemic to Hawaii back to earlier colonized islands such as Fiji, Tonga, and Samoa.

As the Native Hawaiian population became increasingly successful in adapting agricultural systems to their landscapes between 1100 and 1650 (Cuddihy and Stone 1990), the human population grew and altered native Hawaiian vegetation greatly. After the arrival of Captain Cook's fleet in 1778, the rate of introductions of non-native plants abruptly intensified again and initiated even greater transformations of the landscape, economy, and culture of the Hawaiian people. Agricultural, horticultural, and medicinal plants from temperate and tropical environments from around the world along with unintentional introductions of weed species plus goats drastically reduced the natural vegetative cover of many parts of Hawaii. Hawaiian residents have cultivated many plants introduced by non-Polynesians since the late eighteenth century for their nontimber uses; some species like ginger flowers in leis, although non-native, are icons of Hawaiian life.

Nineteenth-century scholars, such as John Papa I'i (1959), Samuel Kamakau (1964, 1976), and David Malo (1987), writing in Hawaiian-language newspapers, preserved accounts of traditional plant uses as one way of keeping Native Hawaiian culture vital. These accounts, now translated into English, provide the earliest detailed writings about Hawaiian cultural uses of plants. In addition, Malcolm Naea Chun has retranslated into English Hawaiian-language medicinal plant manuals by Kaaiakamanu and Akina (1994) and medical documents by anonymous authors (Chun 1986, 1994).

Whistler (1991b) notes that the food crops of Native Hawaiians consisted primarily of the canoe plants, that is, non-native species. Most of the non-native Polynesian food crops originated in South and Southeast Asia and were transported across the tropical Pacific Basin. The highly developed vocabulary for yams and sweet potato cultivars and their plant anatomy in Hawaii point to the sophisticated technology and dietary significance of these species (Handy 1940). Some native Hawaiian species, particularly ferns, have become part of Hawaiian diets: *Cibotium* spp., *Diplazium meyerianum, Marattia douglasii, Osteomeles anthillidifolia, Pneumatopteris sandwicensis* (Hawaiian air fern or ho'i'o kula), *Pritchardia* spp. (lo'ulu), *Rubus hawaiensis* and *R. macraei, Vaccinium reticulatum* (ohelo'ai), plus marine algae (Abbott 1996; Cuddihy and Stone 1990; Handy and Handy 1972; Neal 1976).

About one-third of medicinal plants used traditionally in Hawaii are species endemic to Hawaii (Whistler 1992). The traditional medicinal healer, or *kahuna lapa'au la'au,* uses medicine and ritual to expel demons that have invaded a person and caused him or her to overstep a *kapu* (taboo). Precontact plant medicines emphasized emetics, cathartics, and external dressings or salves. Early visitors to Hawaii noted the good health that people enjoyed, but the subsequent introduction of new diseases contracted after contact with white people taxed the native Hawaiian medical traditions. Whistler (1992) reports that much Hawaiian herbal medicine developed after contact with Europeans and North Americans. The body of plant medicine included new and old uses of native plants, plants from Polynesian introductions, and nineteenth- and twentieth-century introductions of tropical and semitropical plants from around the world. Most manuals about Hawaiian medicinal plants appeared after 1920, long after profound changes to indigenous Hawaiian culture occurred.

Many major medicinal plant species native to Hawaii have relatives on the North American mainland that are important medicinally or medically: *Argemone glauca* (pua kala or smooth pricklypoppy—roots, stem sap), *Artemisia australis* (ahinahina or Oahu wormwood—bark, leaves, roots), *Chamaesyce multiformis* (akoko or variable sandmat—buds, leaves, sap), *Chenopodium oahuense* (weoweo or alaweo—bark, buds), *Cuscuta sandwichiana* (kauna'oa—stems), *Rubus hawaiensis* (Hawaiian blackberry) and *R. macrei* (akala—whole plant), and *Vaccinium calycinum* (ohelo kau la'au—fruits). Other major species reflect Austral-Pacific flora not found elsewhere in the United States (Cambie and Brewis 1997; Handy 1940; McBride 1975; Neal 1976), such as beach naupaaka *(Scaevola sericea)* and ho'awa (*Pittosporum* spp.). Ferns in the genus Asplenium also figure prominently among medicinal plants, including *A. nidus,* the ekaha kuahiwi or bird's-nest fern.

Most dye plants for decorating tapa fabric or tattooing came from introduced plants, although native plants also produce quality dyes. Major native species used for dyes in traditional and modern clothing from Hawaii include *Dianella sandwichensis* ('uki 'uki—blue dye from fruit), *Gardenia remyi* (nau or Remy's gardenia—yellow dye from fruit), *Myrsine lessertiana* (kolea lau nui—red dye from bark), *Sadleria cyatheoides* (amaumau fern—red dye from stem sap), and *Solanum americanum* (popolo or

American black nightshade—green dye from unripe fruit) (Brigham 1911; Handy and Handy 1972; Krohn 1980).

Several native tree species of the Urticaceae (nettle family) provide high-quality cordage and fiber for multiple uses in Hawaiian technology: *Touchardia latifolia* (olona, considered the best native fiber species available), *Pipturus albidus* (Waimea pipturus or mamaki), and *Boehmeria grandis* (Hawaii false nettle). Funk (1979) has researched physical properties of fibers from these species and their continued use by Hawaiians.

Important fragrance plants are *Melicope anisata* (mokihana) with seed capsules or leafy branches smelling of anise, *Melicope sandwicensis* (Mt. Kaala melicope or alani leaves), *Alyxia oliviformis* (maile with fragrant branches), and *Santalum freycinetianum* and congeners (forest sandalwood or iliahi for fragrance from powdered heartwood) (Brigham 1911; Handy and Handy 1972). Many species with showy flowers capture the imagination of people for adornment in leis or for gardens. Unfortunately, many of these species are also federally designated as endangered or threatened with extinction. Many of the showiest native Hawaiian plants with traditional uses in horticulture and in adornment are endangered species of Malvaceae (mallow family), including *Abutilon menziesii* (ko'oloa 'ula), *Hibiscus arnottiianus* (pa makani or native white rosemallow), *H. brackenridgei* (ma'ohauhele or native yellow rosemallow), and *Kokia drynarioides* (Hawaii treecotton) (Handy and Handy 1972; Neal 1965).

Nineteenth-century exports of highly valued products altered population structures of native species. The two most affected species groups were the sandalwoods (*Santalum* spp.) for timber and fragrance and tree ferns (*Cibotium* spp.) for food, now listed as endangered by CITES. Efforts to develop sustainable agroforestry systems with these species have thus far failed to protect them in ecosystems and in the marketplace.

Several institutions in Hawaii actively conserve Hawaiian indigenous knowledge. Foremost is the Bernice P. Bishop Museum in Honolulu, which has supported research in Polynesian culture throughout the Tropical Pacific for nearly a century. The Center for Hawaiian Studies at the University of Hawaii at Manoa offers an academic major in Hawaiian studies. Course offerings include ethnobotany, plant autecology, and plant community ecology, plus specialized topic courses in cocoyam (taro) culture, Hawaiian medicinal plants and uses, traditional fiber artisanship, and traditional hula plants for adornments and implements. The Amy B. H. Greenwell Ethnobotanical Garden in Captain Cook, Hawaii, promotes Native Hawaiian cultural traditions of land use and plants and is actively conserving the plant resources of traditional Hawaiian cultural activities.

Nonprofit organizations and joint government-private partnerships are actively pursuing landscape restoration as a means to cultural restoration. Hawaii Ho'olau Hou (HHH), founded in 1993, is implementing a cultural landscape with the County of Kaua'i and the Hawaii Department of Land and Natural Resources, Division of State Parks, for part of Wailua River State Park. Another HHH project collaborates with the National Guard to restore the lowland dry shrubbery and wili wili *(Erythrina sandwichiana)* forest on the Kekaha Rifle Range.

AMERICAN SAMOA

American Samoa consists of the eastern islands of the Samoan archipelago, the largest of which are 'Aunu'u, Ofu, Olosega, Ta'ū, and Tutuila. Competing American and German colonial interests divided Samoa in the 1890s. After World War I, administration of German Samoa passed to New Zealand, and in 1961 it became the independent nation of Western Samoa.

A rich tradition of botanical studies from Samoa has developed since the late nineteenth century. Most early literature is in German, with Reinecke (1895, 1899), von Bülow (1896, 1899, 1900), and Krämer (1903) providing the earliest methodical ethnobotanical research. Ethnobotanical work in recent decades has concentrated in Western Samoa. As in Hawaii, Polynesian colonizers introduced many culturally important plants to the Samoan landscape. Many of these plants never reached Hawaii under the auspices of Polynesian colonizers: *Casuarina equisetifolia* (toa or beach seaoak), *Cucumis melo* ('atiu or cantaloupe), *Hibiscus rosasinensis* ('aute or shoebackplant), *Inocarpus fagifer* (ifi or Tahitian chesnut), and *Spondias dulcis* (vi or Jewish plum) (Whistler 1991b).

As in Hawaii, most Samoan medicinal plants are indigenous species, but the origins of many culturally important species are not clear. Ethnobotanists are unsure whether the following plant species are native to American Samoa: *Cocos nucifera* (niu or coconut), *Cordia subcordata, Cordyline fruticosa* (ti or tiplant), *Pandanus tectorius* (fasa or Tahitian screwpine), *Pipturus argenteus, Rorippa sarmentosa* (a'atasi or longrunner), *Terminalia catappa* (talie or tropical almond), and *Thespesia populnea* (milo or Portia tree) (Whistler 1991b). Dittmar (1998) describes modern applications of Samoan herbalism and the role of herbalism in Samoan cultural identity.

The American Pacific Project based at the University of Hawaii has been coordinating and sponsoring research for agricultural and agroforestry systems in the U.S. land grant colleges in the Pacific Tropics. The project has produced a handbook on medicinal plants and the Samoan healing arts (Harrington 1993). Cox (1990) emphasizes that Samoan traditional medical plant use is considerably more than a listing of specific plants and the maladies that they alleviate. He outlines Samoan medicine, including the sources of illness, classes of diseases, symptoms, and therapies, but as yet a written record of the orally transmitted traditional healing practices is not available.

GUAM

Very little information exists about the ethnobotany of Guam. Safford (1905) wrote the first study of ethnobotany in Guam soon after it was annexed by the United States following the Spanish-American War. Since his book, works in Japanese about cultural uses of plants in Guam have appeared (Kaisuke 1979), and Moody (1976) presented a master's thesis on contemporary Guamanian-Chomorro culture. The cycad *Cycas circinalis* is probably the best-known medicinal plant, and studies have been undertaken to define important compounds from it (Li, Brownson, and Mabry 1996; Oh, Brownson, and Mabry 1995).

LEARNING FROM THE ETHNOBOTANY OF THE TROPICAL PACIFIC REGION

Looking beyond the geographic scope of the three American territories in the Tropical Pacific Region provides additional information about potential or as yet undocumented uses of native plants from Hawaii, American Samoa, and Guam. Comparative works in anthropology and ethnobotany for the region (Strobel 1983; Whistler 1992, 1995; Yen 1993) or works for single Pacific island nations, such as the Cook Islands (Buck 1944), Fiji (Cambie and Ash 1994), and Tonga (Whistler 1991a), can supplement information about uses of species native to the United States and its territories.

For example, Cambie and Brewis (1997) at CSIRO, the Australian national forestry research institute, have summarized knowledge about plants across the Pacific Basin used to reduce human fertility. In the current political atmosphere of the United States, researchers at American national forest research institutes might avoid or suppress publication of information about controversial uses of native plants, such as human self-regulation of fecundity. Looking beyond national boundaries is another way for the interested public to gain otherwise hard-to-find information about cultural uses of plants.

REFERENCES

Abbott, Isabella Aiona. 1996. *Limu: An Ethnobotanical Study of Some Hawaiian Seaweeds*. 4th ed. Lawai, HI: National Tropical Botanical Garden.
Brigham, William Tufts. 1911. *Ka hana kapa: The Making of Bark-Cloth in*

Hawaii. Memoirs of the Bernice Pauahi Bishop Museum of Polynesian Ethnology and Natural History 3. Honolulu: Bishop Museum Press.

Buck, Peter H. 1944. *Arts and Crafts of the Cook Islands.* Bernice P. Bishop Museum Bulletin 179. Honolulu: Bishop Museum Press.

———. 1896. "Die Samoa-Inseln und Ihre Einheimischen Nutzpflanzen." *Gartenflora* (45): 412–415, 452–454, 518–520, 543–544, 574–575, 604–605, 628–633.

———. 1899. "Die Tapa-Bereitung." *Internationales Archiv für Ethnographie* (12): 66–75.

———. 1900. "Die Nahrungsquelle der Samoaner." *Internationales Archiv für Ethnographie* (13): 185–194.

Cambie, R. C., and J. Ash. 1994. *Fijian Medicinal Plants.* Collingwood, Victoria, Australia: CSIRO Press.

Cambie, R. C., and A. A. Brewis. 1997. *Anti-Fertility Plants of the Pacific.* Collingwood, Victoria, Australia: CSIRO Press.

Chun, Malcolm Naea. 1986. *The Hawaiian Medicine Book: He Buke Laau Lapaau.* Honolulu: Bess Press.

———, trans. 1994. *Must We Wait in Despair: The 1867 Report of the 'Ahahui La'au Lapa'au of Wailuku, Maui, on Native Hawaiian Health.* Honolulu: First People's Productions.

Cox, Paul Alan. 1990. "Samoan Ethnopharmacology." In *Economic and Medicinal Plant Research,* vol. 4, *Plants and Traditional Medicine,* ed. H. Wagner and N. R. Farnsworth, pp. 123–139. New York: Academic Press.

Cuddihy, Linda W., and Charles T. Stone. 1990. *Alteration of Native Hawaiian Vegetation: Effects of Humans, Their Activities, and Introductions.* Honolulu: University of Hawaii, Cooperative National Park Resources Studies Unit.

Dittmar, Alexandra. 1998. *Zur Traditionellen Heilkunde Samoas: Charakteristika und Strukturierung des Heilpflanzenuniversums.* Frankfurt: Verlag der deutschen Hochschulschriften.

Funk, Evangeline J. 1979. "Anatomical Variation of Fibers in Five Genera of Hawaiian Urticaceae and Its Significance to Ethnobotany." Master's thesis, University of Hawaii at Manoa.

Handy, Edward Smith Craighill. 1940. *The Hawaiian Planter: His Plants, Methods, and Areas of Cultivation.* Bernice P. Bishop Museum Bulletin 161. Honolulu: Bishop Museum Press.

Handy, Edward Smith Craighill, and Elizabeth Green Handy. 1972. *Native Planters in Old Hawaii: Their Life, Lore, and Environment.* Bernice P. Bishop Museum Bulletin 233. Honolulu: Bishop Museum Press.

Harrington, Michael T. 1993. *Samoan Medicinal Plants and Their Usage.* 2d ed. Agricultural Materials ADAP 93-1. Honolulu: University of Hawaii, Pacific Agricultural Development Office.

I'i, John Papa. 1959. *Fragments of Hawaiian History.* Trans. Mary Kawena Pukui. Honolulu: Bishop Museum Press.

Kaaiakamanu, David Kaluna M., and J. K. Akina. 1994. *Native Hawaiian Medicines: A New Revised and Enlarged Translation.* Trans. Malcolm Naea Chun. Honolulu: First People's Productions.

Kaisuke, Yoneda. 1979. *Guamu Rotato Shokubutsu Chosa Hokokusho* [in Japanese]. Tokyo: Nihon Shokubutsuen Kyokai. [in Japanese].

Kamakau, Samuel Manaiakalani. 1964. *Ka po'e kahiko: The People of Old.* Trans. Mary Kawena Pukui. Bernice P. Bishop Museum Special Publication 51. Honolulu: Bishop Museum Press.

———. 1976. *The Works of the People of Old* [Na hana a ka po'e kahiko]. Trans. Mary Kawena Pukui. Bernice P. Bishop Museum Special Publication 61. Honolulu: Bishop Museum Press.

Krämer, Augustin. 1903. *Die Samoa-Inseln. Entwurf einer Monographie mit Besonderer Berücksichtigung Deutsch-Samoas.* Vol. 2: *Ethnographie.* Stuttgart: E. Schweizerbarthsche Verlagsbuchhandlung.

Krohn, Val Frieling. 1980. *Hawaii Dye Plants and Dye Recipes.* Honolulu: University of Hawaii Press.

Li, C. J., D. M. Brownson, T. J. Mabry, C. Perera, and E. A. Bell. 1996. "Nonprotein Amino Acids from Seeds of *Cycas circinalis* and *Phaseolus vulgaris.*" *Phytochemistry* 42(2): 443–445.

Malo, David. 1987. *Hawaiian Antiquities [Ka mol'olelo Hawaii].* Trans. Malcolm Naea Chun. Honolulu: Kapiolani Community College Folk Press.

McBride, L. R. 1975. *Practical Folk Medicine of Hawaii.* Hilo, HI: Petroglyph Press.

Moody, John D., Jr. 1976. "Folk Botany of Guam: An Ethnobotanical Study of the Guamanian-Chamorro." Master's thesis, University of Guam.

Neal, Marie C. 1965. *In Gardens of Hawaii.* Honolulu: Bishop Museum Press.

———. 1976. "Plants Used Medicinally." In *Outline of Hawaiian Physical Therapeutics,* ed. E. S. Craighill Handy, Mary Kawena Pukui, and Katherine Livermore. Millwood, NY: Kraus Reprint.

Oh, C. H., D. M. Brownson, and T. J. Mabry. 1995. "Screening for Non-Protein Amino Acids in Seeds of the Guam Cycad, *Cycas circinalis,* by an Improved GC-MS Method." *Planta Medica* 61(1): 66–70.

Patil, A. D., and others. 1993. "The Inophyllums: Novel Inhibitors of HIV-1 Reverse Transcriptase Isolated from the Malaysian Tree, *Calophyllum inophyllum.*" *J Med Chem* 36(26): 4131–4138.

Reinecke, Franz. [1895] 1986. "Die Nutzpflanzen Samoas und Ihre Verwendung." *Jahresbericht der Schlesischen Gesellschaft für Vaterländische Cultur* 73: 22–46.

———. 1899. "Die Samoaner und die Kokospalme." *Globus* 75: 227–230.

Safford, W. 1905. *The Useful Plants of Guam with an Introductory Account of the Island Features and Natural History of the Island, of the Character and History of its People, and of Their Agriculture.* Contributions from the U.S. National Herbarium 9. Washington, DC: Government Printing Office.

Spino, C., M. Dodier, and S. Sotheeswaran. 1998. "Anti-HIV Coumarins from *Calophyllum* Seed Oil." *Bioorg Med Chem Lett* 8(24): 3475–3478.

Strobel, H. 1983. *Die Bedeutung von Fruchtbäumen in der Polynesischen Kultur.* Hohenschäftlarn, Germany: Renner Verlag.

Taylor, P. B., J. S. Culp, C. Debouck, R. K. Johnson, A. D. Patil, D. J. Woolf, I. Brooks, and R. P. Hertzberg. 1994. "Kinetic and Mutational Analysis of Human Immunodeficiency Virus Type 1 Reverse Transcriptase Inhibition by Inophyllums, a Novel Class of Non-Nucleoside Inhibitors." *J Biol Chem* 269(9): 6325–6331.

Whistler, W. Arthur. 1991a. *The Ethnobotany of Tonga: The Plants, Their Tongan Names, and Their Uses*. Honolulu: Bishop Museum Press.

———. 1991b. "Polynesian Plant Introductions." In *Islands, Plants, and Polynesians: Proceedings of a Symposium Sponsored by the Institute for Polynesian Studies, Brigham Young University, Hawaii Campus, Laia, HI,* ed. P. A. Cox and S. A. Banack. Portland, OR: Dioscorides Press.

———. 1992. *Polynesian Herbal Medicine*. Lawai, HI: National Tropical Botanical Garden.

———. 1995. *Wayside Plants of the Islands: A Guide to the Lowland Flora of the Pacific Islands: Including Hawai'i, Samoa, Tonga, Tahiti, Fiji, Guam, and Belau*. Honolulu: Isle Botanica.

Yen, D. E. 1993. "The Origins of Subsistence Agriculture in Oceania and the Potentials for Future Tropical Food Crops." *Economic Botany* 47(1): 3–14.

CASE STUDY

The Hidden Bounty of the Urban Forest

Paul Jahnige

Have you ever picked berries from the edge of a forest in a city park? Made a holiday wreath from wild grapevine growing in your backyard? Collected the nuts of a Chinese chestnut street tree? Or harvested pokeweed growing in an abandoned lot? Many people do collect such products—and others—in our cities. These urban nontimber forest products represent important economic, nutritional, biological, educational, and cultural resources for a diversity of urban residents (Community Resources 2000).

Within the past ten years, people have increasingly recognized nontimber forest products for the important cultural, subsistence, and market values that they add to rural forests and individual households worldwide. Nearly all ethnic groups around the globe rely on NTFPs for household income, food, medicine, construction supplies, and materials for decorative and ceremonial purposes. These resources are especially important during times of economic hardship or during lulls in agricultural production (Saxena 1986). Economically, the value of sustainably harvested NTFPs in tropical forests can often outweigh the value of other land uses such as logging, farming, or grazing (Peters, Gentry, and Mendelsohn 1989; Balick and Mendelsohn 1995; Grimes et al. 1994). Even in North American forests, NTFPs have been shown to provide significant opportunities for small entrepreneurs (Thomas and Schumann 1993; Shelly and Lubin 1995; Emery 1998). Indeed, NTFP markets have grown an estimated 20 percent in the last three years, and the U.S. herbal market has grown at an annual rate of 13 to 15 percent (Chamberlain, Bush, and Hammett 1998; Hammett, personal communication 1998).

Despite increasing use and recognition of NTFPs, they continue to be thought of as "rural" resources collected from rural areas and important to rural people (Guijt, Hinchcliffe, and Melnyk 1995). At the same time, research on the benefits of urban trees and forests typically includes beauty, increased property values, reduced noise pollution, improvements to water and air quality, and reduced energy costs but makes little or no mention of urban forest products (Moll and Young 1992; McPherson, Nowack, and Rowntree 1994).

This oversight does not reflect the actual popularity or value of urban forest products. In 1998, Community Resources (CR), an urban environmental nonprofit organization, began investigating urban NTFPs in Baltimore, Maryland, and other U.S. cities. The initial results of this study demonstrate that many urban residents collect and use a variety of NTFPs. These goods have significant value for individual collectors that policy makers, urban land managers, and even the general public have mostly overlooked.

DEFINING "URBAN FOREST" AND "URBAN NTFPS"

Some definitions of the urban forest account for all elements (biotic, abiotic, and social) of our urban ecosystems, while others refer only to large, closed-canopy forested areas. We define the urban forest as all trees and associated plants and animal species that live in our cities. This definition includes single street trees, yards, vacant lots, and landscaped areas as well as "forested" areas. We define an urban nontimber forest product as "any (nontimber) product collected, cultivated, or derived from the urban forest." For the purposes of our study in Baltimore, we narrowed this definition to exclude animals or animal products (except for honey and pollen), wood products, or products from actively cultivated gardens or orchards.

METHODS

CR initiated this project with seed funding from the National Urban and Community Forestry Advisory Council and the U.S. Forest Service. We focused our investigation on forest product collection in Baltimore but also collected information on forest products and relevant NTFP issues from other U.S. cities. We designed our methods to efficiently collect a relatively broad amount of information by drawing primarily on methods detailed in Emery (1998) and, to a lesser extent, on previous studies in tropical forests (Grimes et al. 1994; Godoy, Lubowski, and Markandya 1993; Guijt and Hinchcliffe 1998).

In Baltimore, we conducted semistructured, face-to-face interviews with more than eighty urban environmental professionals, community leaders, farmers' market vendors, and urban forest product collectors. In each interview, we briefly introduced ourselves, described our interests, and defined forest products. We then asked individuals to describe products they collect, products they know are collected by others, collection locations, uses, markets, prices, processing, collection times, tree or plant yields, and collection issues. We also conducted follow-ups with some individuals to get additional information. We identified interviewees through personal networks and contacts, field interviews with people found collecting, and also snowball contacts (from each person interviewed, we asked for names of additional people to contact).

We gathered information on product prices by scanning local farmers' markets and other vendors from August 1998 through September 1999. We gathered additional information about products, collection times, and plant yields through timed field collection; field observations of collection; estimates of product yields in the field; and a review of published literature. We also conducted phone interviews with urban environmental professionals, such as urban foresters, environmental educators, and park managers, in Philadelphia, New York, Boston, and Washington, D.C. (Community Resources, 2000). Examples of NTFPs collected in Baltimore include: edibles—peaches, figs, mulberries, wineberries, chestnuts, ginkgo nuts, maple syrup, honey, morels, and chanterelles; medicinals—sassafras bark, jewel weed, bee pollen, and maitake mushrooms; horticultural—ash seeds, walnuts, acorns, seeds of various cultivars, bamboo, ferns, dogwood seedlings, oak seedlings, and native azaleas; and craft—pine boughs, pinecones, boxwood, grapevine, forsythia sprigs, and willow bark.

RESULTS

Our interviews and observations documented at least 103 nontimber forest products currently collected by Baltimore residents. Discussions with key informants in other cities indicate that this number of products is not unique to Baltimore. A handful of phone interviews documented 57 products known to be collected in Philadelphia, and 26 edible products known to be collected in Boston.

SOURCES OF URBAN NTFPS

People collect urban NTFPs from diverse sites that span a range of ownership and management regimes—from public to private and from highly managed to unmanaged. Some products are collected from a variety of sites. For example, pokeweed is collected from yards, vacant lots, and roadsides. Other products are unique to a certain type of site. Peaches and figs appear mostly in private yards, and morels are found in closed-canopy forests. Generally, urban collection sites include:

- Street trees—publicly owned and tended, single trees planted in sidewalks and grass strips. These often include nut- and seed-producing trees, such as ginkgos, oaks, and walnuts.
- Yard trees and plants—privately owned and highly managed plant resources in front, side, or back yards. These often include fruiting plants, such as apples, pears, and berries. Yard and street trees often include exotic and ornamental plants.
- Vacant lots—publicly, privately, or community-owned lots, whether managed or wholly unmanaged. Species collected from lots include a variety of perennial and biennial plants, such as pokeweed and chicory.
- Open-grown park trees—publicly owned and managed, single trees grown in open park areas. These often include fruit- and nut-producing trees, as well as a variety of evergreen species providing decorative greens and cones.
- Open-grown trees on institutional properties—similar to open-grown park trees except that large private-sector businesses and institutions, including business parks, cemeteries, schools, and colleges, often own or care for the trees.
- Roadside and forest edge plants—both publicly and privately owned, and often unmanaged plant species growing along roadsides and forest edges. These plants often include berries, vines, and medicinal plants. Many urban roadside species are invasive.
- Closed-canopy forest plants—woodland trees, shrubs, herbs, and mushrooms that grow in both publicly and privately owned, usually unmanaged forest areas.

USE AND MARKETS FOR URBAN NTFPS

People collect urban NTFPs primarily for personal use. They pick berries as they walk through parks, collect chestnuts or edible mushrooms as ingredients for a special dinner, cut grapevines from roadsides to decorate their houses in the fall, or gather and can fruit for the winter.

Many people collect urban NTFPs to give as gifts and share their harvest bounty with neighbors or friends. Personally, I have given extra oyster mushrooms to neighbors and have received canned peaches in return. A friend collects chanterelles from her yard in Tampa and gives a wild mushroom party in season. Many people make natural crafts to give at holiday time. These include coasters from fallen twigs, pinecone baskets, and leaf-printed T-shirts. Sharing and gift giving is an important form of social reciprocity and an example of how urban NTFP collection can help build connections between people in urban communities.

Another prevalent use for urban NTFPs is to raise funds, both for organizations and for individuals. For example, the holiday greens sale is a common fund-raiser for churches, senior centers, garden clubs, and other organizations. In some cases, people gather greens from private neighborhood yards, but they also collect and gather NTFPs from parks, cemeteries, and hospital grounds. For fund-raising, many environmental nonprofit organizations sell seedlings at festivals. In some cases, organizations raise seedlings from seeds collected in local parks, and in other cases, people may dig up seedlings from yards or roadsides where seedlings are not wanted or are likely to be mowed or otherwise lost.

Finally, some collectors bring urban NTFPs to various markets for sale. Some make holiday wreaths and other natural decorations to supplement Christmas season incomes. Recreational beekeepers also sell their product locally to offset their costs. Some vendors include collected products as a part of their inventory at local farmers' markets. People report locally collected walnuts and chestnuts brought to market in Baltimore, and osage orange sold as a roach repellant in the St. Louis farmers' market. Others sell products such as pokeweed, wineberry, grapevine, and pinecones to various wholesale and retail vendors including greengrocers or specialty craft outlets. Frequently, individuals sell collected products, such as mushrooms and figs, directly to restaurants or other consumers.

URBAN NTFP COLLECTORS

Collectors of urban forest products are, in many ways, as invisible as collectors of forest products elsewhere. In fact, many urban harvesters do not identify themselves as collectors. Although our study focused more on forest products than their collectors, we learned much about the people who forage in the city.

Urban forest product collectors come from diverse socioeconomic and ethnic groups, and the products collected often reflect their socioeconomic and cultural heritage. For example, Korean collectors gather chestnuts and ginkgo nuts both because they are important ingredients for Asian cooking and because collecting is a traditional family activity. African Americans, with roots in the South, collect pokeweed as a traditional green. Many families of Greek descent grow figs, grapes, and other fruits in their mostly concrete backyards in Baltimore's Greektown.

Urban collectors come from inner-city communities and suburban developments, from poor neighborhoods and wealthy neighborhoods, and from probably every ethnic group that resides within a given city. In Baltimore, CR encountered Italian collectors who traveled from well outside Baltimore to gather chestnuts inside the city, inner-city residents who collect and can fruit from trees on vacant lots, New Englanders who made special trips to find ripe berries, and Native Americans who collect craft materials from city forests to make dream catchers.

Anecdotal evidence points to the particular importance of urban NTFPs for certain immigrant populations, especially eastern European, northeast Asian, and southeast Asian immigrants. People suspected to have more recent connections to rural life (for example, first-generation migrants to cities) are more likely to collect urban NTFPs than are long-term urban dwellers; however, this trend is not always the case. In interviews with Baltimore residents, we discovered many urbanites who were "rediscovering" collection as a new connection to the urban natural world as well as many recent migrants who were wary of urban collection.

A few people use the collection of urban forest products to boost their income. These include artisans, farmers' market vendors, and nature enthusiasts. In most cases, these folks are adding significant value to urban NTFPs through artistry, processing, education, and tourism.

One good example of urban NTFP entrepreneurship is Baltimore's "Mushroom Man." Every weekend, he loads up his old pickup truck with a grill, charcoal, tent canopy, and the bounty of his urban forest backyard. He tours the farmers' markets in Baltimore and Washington, D.C., selling woodland mushrooms to a wide diversity of buyers. In his backyard, on the edge of Baltimore's Woodbury Forest, he cultivates shiitake mushrooms on more than a thousand oak logs and oyster mushrooms on bags of inoculated straw. At market, he also sells chanterelles, morels, chicken of the woods, and hen of the woods, many of which he harvests from various sites around Baltimore and the mid-Atlantic region. He augments this cultivated and collected supply with mushrooms purchased from growers and collectors around the country. He calls this the "hobby that got out of control," but he also says it brings in much needed cash.

Another example of NTFP entrepreneurship is New York City's "Wildman" Steve Brill, who leads weekly urban forest foraging tours and sells books he has written on foraging. He also participates in education programs, tours, and talks. He uses urban NTFPs and his extensive knowledge of them as a way to earn income and find free food.

The number of people for whom collecting urban NTFPs is a significant portion of their livelihoods is relatively small, but CR's Baltimore investigations demonstrate how prevalent some sort of urban collection actually is. Far more people than we had expected occasionally collect edible, craft, and horticultural products from the urban forest.

THE VALUE OF URBAN NTFPS

Economic Value

In assessing the value of urban NTFPs, CR found that these products provide many kinds of benefits to harvesters. First and foremost, urban NTFPs have important economic values to harvesters. A product collected for personal use is a substitute for one otherwise purchased or is unique and cannot be purchased. Homemade or locally collected gifts have values that similar store-bought gifts do not capture. People selling urban NTFPs, either at fund-raisers or at local markets, earn cash from their products. Our ongoing investigation in Baltimore will quantify these economic values. CR's hypothesis is that the value to household economies is a substantial contribution in addition to the ecological/social values that urban trees provide. Table 5 shows some examples of this economic value.

Nutritional Value

Edible urban NTFPs provide important nutritional benefits to collectors (Guijt, Hinchcliffe, and Melnyk 1995). Urban NTFPs are collected and consumed fresh, and locally collected products may taste better than store-bought items. Urban NTFPs are often difficult or impossible to find in stores and thus represent greater product diversity and expanded consumer choices. Products such as fresh figs, berries, apricots, mushrooms, and nuts are excellent sources of vitamins, minerals, and proteins while being very low in fat. Finally, most urban NTFPs are grown without any chemical inputs and are thus organic. The CR study suggests that concerns about various forms of urban pollution are not a significant problem for most urban NTFPs.

Table 5. Examples of economic values of urban NTFPs

Product	Market price	Collection costs (time, processing, and equipment)	Net product value	Net est. avg. annual mature plant value
Chinese chestnuts collected for personal consumption/farmers' market	$3/lb.	$1.10/lb.	$1.90/lb.	$103/tree
Oyster mushrooms for personal consumption	$10/lb.	$0.91/lb.	$9.09/lb.	$111/fruiting log
Cones collected for gift decorations	$16/100 cones	$5.50/100 cones	$10.50/100 cones	$21/tree
Transplanted first-year seedlings	$5 each	$1.72 each	$3.28 each	N/A
Wineberry	$4.00/pint	$1.37/pint	$2.63/pint	$1.32/vine

Educational and Cultural Value

Searching for, collecting, and using forest products promotes a greater understanding of natural environments and the human connections to them. The educational value is particularly important in cities where many residents may not know nonurban environments. Urban NTFP harvesting can build and strengthen a sense of connection, as harvesting is often a multigenerational activity in which older family members teach younger ones about the natural world, family history, and their cultural heritage. One collector taps sugar maples and collects berries with his two-year-old daughter as a way to teach her about how trees work and where food comes from. Another person uses harvesting to teach his child about poisonous plants and berries. Others use collection to teach about traditional foods and nutrition.

Recreational Value

There is significant recreational value in collecting and in bringing home the harvest. Who does not enjoy chancing upon a patch of ripe berries? Or picking apples to take home for pie? Or bringing in fresh-cut blossoms to decorate the house? Collecting is fun. People will travel thirty or forty miles just to find a "u-pick-'em" place. In New York City, people pay to attend "Wildman" Steve Brill's foraging classes. Many people share harvesting and harvests with family and friends. Nearly all the collectors, we have observed, gathering chestnuts in Baltimore come in family groups of two or more. Because people perceive these products to be scarcer in the city and urban dwellers happen upon them less often, this recreational value is often greater for urban residents.

ISSUES FOR FUTURE EXPLORATION

Lack of Collector Empowerment

A wide variety of both ethnically and socioeconomically diverse people collect urban NTFPs. Unfortunately, public agencies, policy makers, urban land managers, or even a majority of people seldom recognize the importance of these products. Lack of awareness stems from several factors:

1. Forest product collection is decentralized. Collection sites are often hidden, changing constantly. Markets are decentralized, and sources of information about urban NTFPs are often scattered.
2. Many forest product collectors do not want others to know about their sites or activities for fear of jeopardizing their opportunities for collection.

3. Collectors of these products are often disenfranchised and minority individuals. They may not speak English well or are not a part of the mainstream "environmental" community or both. They too have little or no voice in policy making or urban forest management.
4. In urban areas of the United States, forest products usually do not figure prominently in people's minds whereas recreational values are uppermost.

Harvesters' lack of political organization and clout results in a dearth of broader public understanding and support for urban forest product collection. NTFP collectors are rarely considered as a stakeholder group in urban forest management, and NTFPs are not usually encouraged or managed for. Thus, collectors end up without a voice or an advocate in important decisions that affect the products they use and value.

Collector Conflicts in the Urban Environment

A number of different types of conflict can arise between groups of collectors, between collectors and private property owners, and between collectors and public property managers. Such conflicts are not particularly common, but the more prevalent collecting becomes, the more visible the conflicts may become.

Collector-collector conflicts arise when a scarce resource is in relatively high demand by different groups of collectors. For example, in Baltimore, Chinese chestnuts are relatively scarce compared to their demand, and conflicts occasionally arise at one particularly visible stand in Gwynns Falls/Leakin Park. Different groups of collectors sometimes compete for the nuts. Sometimes these conflicts escalate as one group resorts to more destructive harvesting techniques to bring the nuts down from the tree. In the urban context, informal ownership precedents for forest products on public property generally do not exist among harvester groups to address these kinds of conflicts.

A second potential conflict exists between collectors and private property owners. Our interviews suggest that most collectors ask for permission before collecting products from private yards. However, we have recorded cases of people stealing products from private property, especially if products are visible and easily gathered (i.e., fruit on backyard trees). In addition, damage to private property also occurs from collecting. For example, neighbors of "on-street" cherry trees in Baltimore sometimes complain about collectors standing on their cars to pick.

Finally, potential conflicts arise between collectors and public property managers. In many cities, local ordinances prohibit collecting from public lands, although urban land managers tend to ignore them. However, if urban collecting becomes more widespread or more attention is drawn to it (through publications such as this), urban land managers may crack down on collectors. Recently, in Baltimore, signs have been posted and police have been called to halt the collecting of chestnuts in Leakin Park.

Health Issues

Many people raise questions about health risks from using urban NTFPs. Some of the concerns include air pollution from automobile and industrial exhaust accumulating on or in edible products; lead and other heavy metals in soils from old paint, car exhaust, or illegal waste dumping; toxic chemicals from spraying insecticides or pesticides and from industrial contamination; and poisoning from eating misidentified products, especially mushrooms.

Some general guidelines for avoiding health risks include (Brill 1994): wash or peel all plants before eating them; don't collect within fifty feet of a major roadway; don't collect along railroad rights-of-way; don't collect water plants unless you have the water tested; always be sure about your plant or mushroom identification; know which parts of edible plants are edible and in what season; and collect only the plants you intend to use (Brill 1994). Uncertainty exists about serious health risks from air pollutants and heavy metal uptake by plants. Most collectors we interviewed felt that their health was not at risk, especially if simple precautions were followed.

Urban Advantages

CR investigations in Baltimore suggest, counterintuitively, that urban NTFPs may have advantages over rural NTFPs from the same region.

- Season extension—Urban "heat island" effects may make urban forest products available several weeks earlier in the spring and later in the fall than in adjacent rural areas. For example, cherries in Baltimore come into season about two weeks before other local cherries. This means that urban cherries are available when market prices are still relatively high at about five dollars a pound.
- Diversity—The urban forest contains diverse introduced species, many of which produce goods valued by a variety of ethnic groups and otherwise not available outside of the cities. For example, ginkgo trees, Chinese chestnuts, and figs are commonly found in the urban forest but are mostly absent in rural areas.
- Public management of single forest trees—Urban trees are managed as individuals, which makes them relatively easy to manage for product production.

- Access to products and markets—Urban NTFPs grow where many people live and shop. Very little travel time lowers costs for either collecting or selling these products.

Ecological Issues

As with other NTFP harvests, urban harvesting raises serious questions about sustainable harvesting and excessive harvesting. These concerns may be great given that the ratio of people to forest area is much higher in urban areas than in rural forested areas. Determining whether harvesting of a product is sustainable is never simple. In urban areas, many other factors affect sustainability: pollution, urban "heat island," invasive species, and so on. A complete understanding of the effects of human harvests on populations of urban NTFP species may be impossible.

On the other hand, forest product collection in urban areas may lead to a positive form of urban forest management. Many urban NTFPs come from planted trees or shrubs. Promoting the harvest value of these plants may actually lead to more planting and better stewardship of these resources. Other valuable urban NTFPs come from invasive species, such as mulberries, wineberries, and various vines. Intensively harvesting invasive species may actually reduce their reproduction and promote native forest diversity.

CONCLUSION

As we all work to better understand and promote the sustainable use of our forest resources, it is important to remember that the urban forest is an important component. In conclusion, we leave you with five key points from this chapter:

1. Nontimber forest product collection occurs in U.S. urban areas.
2. Diverse people collect many products from the urban forest.
3. Urban NTFPs have important economic, nutritional, educational, recreational, and cultural values.
4. Urban land and forest planners and managers should consider forest product collection and collectors as they work with communities, develop planting plans, and implement forest management strategies.
5. Further investigations can help people better understand urban NTFP issues, such as empowering harvesters, collector conflicts, health risks, and ecological and management issues in the urban context.

REFERENCES

Balick, Michael, and Robert O. Mendelsohn. 1995. "The Value of Undiscovered Pharmaceuticals in Tropical Forests." *Economic Botany* 49(2): 223–228.

Brill, "Wildman" S. 1994. *Identifying and Harvesting Edible and Medicinal Plants in Wild (and Not So Wild) Places.* New York: Hearst Books.

Chamberlain, Jim, R. Bush, and A. L. Hammett. 1998. "Nontimber Forest Products: The Other Forest Products." *Forest Products Journal* 48(10): 10–19.

Community Resources. 2000. "Working Paper: Exploring the Value of Urban Nontimber Forest Products," at *www.communityresources.org.*

Emery, Marla. 1998. "Invisible Livelihoods: Nontimber Forest Products in Michigan's Upper Peninsula." Ph.D. diss., Rutgers University.

Godoy, Ricardo, Ruben Lubowski, and Anil Markandya. 1993. "A Method for the Economic Valuation of Nontimber Tropical Forest Products." *Economic Botany* 47(3): 220–233.

Grimes, A., S. Loomis, P. Jahnige, M. Burnham, K. Onthank, R. Alarcon, W. Palacios Cuenca, C. Ceron Martinez, D. Neill, M. Balick, B. Bennett, and R. Mendelsohn. 1994. "Valuing the Rain Forest: The Economic Value of Nontimber Forest Products in Ecuador." *Ambio* 23(7): 405–410.

Guijt, Irene, and Fiona Hinchcliffe. 1998. *Participatory Valuation of Wild Resources: An Overview of the Hidden Harvest Methodology.* London: International Institute for Environment and Development.

Guijt, Irene, Fiona Hinchcliffe, and Mary Melnyk. 1995. *The Hidden Harvest: The Value of Wild Resources in Agricultural Systems.* London: International Institute for Environment and Development.

Hammett, A. L. 1998. Department of Wood Science and Forest Products, Virginia Tech, personal communication.

McPherson, E. G., D. J. Nowack, and R. A. Rowntree, eds. 1994. *Chicago's Urban Forest Ecosystem: Results of the Chicago Forest Climate Project.* General Technical Report NE-186. Radnor, PA: USDA Forest Service, Northeastern Forest Experiment Station.

Moll, G., and S. Young.1992. *Growing Greener Cities.* Los Angeles: Living Planet Press.

Peters, Charles M., Alwyn Gentry, and Robert Mendelsohn. 1989. "Valuation of an Amazonian Rainforest." *Nature* 339:655–656.

Saxena, S. 1986. "Desert Plants Used as Human Food during Scarcity and Famines." In *Desert Environment: Conservation and Management,* ed. K. A. Shankernarayan and V. Shanker, CAZRI pub. no. 26, Jodhpur, India.

Shelly, J. R., and D. M. Lubin. 1995. "California Hardwoods and Nontimber Forest Products, Final Report," University of California Forest Products Laboratory.

Thomas, Margaret G., and David R. Schumann. 1993. *Income Opportunities in Special Forest Products.* Agricultural Information Bulletin 666. Berkeley, CA: USDA Forest Service.

CASE STUDY

Rio Grande National Forest

Vince Spero and Carol Fleming

A team of social scientists is conducting research to determine the scope of nontimber forest product (also called special forest products) procurement in the Rio Grande National Forest (RGNF), located in south central Colorado. The following case study draws upon information gathered as part of that study from existing documents, the Internet, and interview data obtained from twenty local and regionally based people involved in different aspects of NTFP collection. The goals of the RGNF Nontimber Forest Products Project include determination of the present scope of NTFP procurement in the RGNF; development of an education plan for the public and Forest Service personnel, focusing on sustainable NTFP use of the forest and ethically sound collection methods; determination of the monetary value of nontimber forest products in order to help formulate commercial permit price structures; identification of sustainable rural economic development opportunities; and identification, and subsequent protection of, traditional uses of NTFPs by Native American and other traditional communities.

Managers of the RGNF felt that such a study was important due to a perceived upward trend, both nationally and locally, in demand for herbal and other products from the wild. Evidence of this upward trend at the local level is demonstrated by the attendance of two hundred people at the "Gathering on Traditional Uses of the Forest and Traditional Healing" conference held in Alamosa, Colorado, in September 1995. The rise in the number of participants attending the Creede, Colorado, Mushroom Foray from 20 people in 1996 to over 125 people in 1999 provides a further indication of the upward trend in local nontimber forest products. Staff at the Ranger District and Supervisor's Offices for the RGNF also report an increase in inquiries for a number of types of NTFPs.

A second reason for conducting the study is the general lack of treatment of NTFPs in the 1996 Rio Grande National Forest Revised Land and Resource Management Plan. The only mention of NTFPs in the plan is in the "Forestwide Desired Condition" section under the heading of "Special

Forest Products." This section simply states that the gathering of such products depends on the sustainable limits of the resource and that the RGNF recognizes the needs of the people of the San Luis Valley and surrounding areas for access to these products. The lack of basic management information, such as what specific NTFPs are collected, how they are collected, where they are collected, and what quantities are collected, prompted the development of this study as a means to begin gathering important baseline information. Inconsistent management of NTFPs on the RGNF, and within the Forest Service Rocky Mountain Region in general, also played a role in prompting the study. This lack of consistency has tended to frustrate the increasing number of people who inquire about obtaining permits for various NTFPs at the district and supervisor's office level.

Refinement of the NTFP policy in the Rio Grande National Forest is needed in order to clarify existing policies, which are vague, confusing, and incomplete; more clearly define the distinctions between traditional, personal/recreational, and commercial uses; assure the sustainability of ecosystems while providing NTFP harvesting opportunities for the public; and standardize product categories, terminology, and measurements used by NTFP program managers.

CATEGORIES OF HARVESTERS IN THE RGNF

Three classes of NTFP harvesters have been identified in the Rio Grande National Forest. These include traditional, personal, and commercial users, although it should be noted that overlap among classes occurs.

Traditional Users of NTFPs

Hispanic herbalists, craft people, and people of rural agricultural communities have utilized NTFPs traditionally for generations in the adjacent San Luis Valley of Colorado and New Mexico. In addition, Native American people of various local and regional tribes require certain materials found on RGNF administered lands. Such collected materials are considered essential to sustaining the traditional cultures of the groups. Some rural Hispanics presently choose to live in somewhat traditional ways by farming family plots, hunting and gathering to supplement their diet, gathering medicinal products, gathering wood for heating and cooking, grazing small herds of domestic animals, and obtaining materials for producing traditional cultural objects on nearby public lands. For example, one Hispanic Santero interviewed during the study uses a variety of botanical products to produce carved and painted depictions of saints.

Personal Users of NTFPs

Personal users are thought to be the fastest growing NTFP user group in the RGNF. Some gatherers are self-educated about product collection, some have attended herbal schools, and still others have learned about NTFP harvesting and processing through family or friends. Personal users generally harvest small quantities of nontimber forest products that are used by individuals, family units, or small groups of friends. Often they view collecting as a recreational experience. Most personal users interviewed stated that they adhered to some form of ethical standards when gathering.

Questionnaire results indicate that personal NTFP gatherers tend to collect medicinal plants as an alternative to buying pharmaceutical drugs and because of a preference for natural remedies. Food products, such as chokecherries, rose hips, berries, or potherb type plants, also figure among the NTFPs collected by personal use harvesters. A weaver interviewed collects plants in order to make natural dyes for dying fibers. A significant portion of the people interviewed collect a variety of edible mushrooms, including chanterelles, boletus, and other common types.

Commercial Users of NTFPs

Commercial users collect NTFPs for immediate sale, for further processing, or for resale as the raw material for other products. Known commercial users in the RGNF are considered small-scale operations, working part-time and on a limited scale in terms of quantities harvested, processed, or sold. What follows are examples of commercial NTFP businesses in the RGNF area.

The owners of one small local herb shop collect herbs and make them into a variety of tinctures, oils, salves, and ointments for internal and external uses. They also sell dried herbs for teas and ingestion as well as personalized mixtures of herbs. The shop owners have nursing backgrounds, and most of their herbal medicine experience comes from books, classes, herb walks, and other collectors of wild plants. They generally collect on private land but are an example of one type of potential commercial user on RGNF lands.

The owners of another small herbal business specialize in herbal teas and baths. The operator of the business learned about plants from her mother, who learned from her mother. She also instructs people about plant gathering and harvesting methods.

The owners of a somewhat larger herbal business, based in Taos, New Mexico, buy harvested plants from wildcrafters located in the RGNF area. They use these plants to produce tinctures and dried medicinal plants. They sell their products at retail prices in their own store in addition to selling products wholesale to other area stores.

A commercial mushroom buyer has operated in the RGNF for the past several years, selling his products wholesale to companies located on the East and West Coasts. Occasionally he employs five or six people during the picking season. His operation is small-scale, selling a few hundred pounds per year. He has obtained permits to pick in the RGNF in the past but is concerned about changes in permit requirements. He also notes that the permit fees do not adequately take into account the costs associated with harvesting and selling wild mushrooms.

Another commercial chanterelle mushroom harvester works out of the Creede, Colorado, area. He reportedly hires temporary help during the harvest season in August and has never obtained a Forest Service permit.

Commercial mushroom operations in the RGNF generally focus on bolete and chanterelle mushrooms, which pickers generally harvest in higher elevation spruce-fir stands. Common medicinal or edible plants collected commercially include yarrow, strawberry (whole plant), arnica, wild geranium, Oregon grape, violet, kinnikinnick, mariposa, cow parsnip, cinquefoil, juniper berries, Indian paintbrush, raspberry leaves, angelica, wild rose, juniper berries and stems, malva, tansy, and usnea. Some commercial users believe that osha, a plant commonly used among Hispanic, Native American, and Caucasian populations, is overharvested. Osha root is used in teas, tinctures, and poultices, and is eaten raw to treat arthritis, gum and lung infections, and insect bites.

OVERLAP OF HARVESTER TYPES

People who collect NTFPs for traditional uses sometimes enter the realm of commercial use by supplying medicines to the community, usually for a reasonable cost. Payments received are often low enough that harvesters recoup only a portion of the expenses they incur while obtaining the material. Some personal users also sell portions of their collected product to friends or relatives who do not harvest. Again, the payment received often does not cover all of the harvesting expenses. Serving the community as a healer may be the justification for some commercial harvesters to operate at a loss. In addition, some commercial users collect a part of the product for personal use.

CONCERNS OF NTFP HARVESTERS

Traditional users of nontimber forest products expressed five major concerns relating to harvesting: concern about the potential for overharvesting of certain plant species, especially osha, arnica, and bistort; concern about damage to ecosystems, including NTFP habitat, from the use of all-terrain vehicles and logging activity; among resident users, concern about people from other areas collecting medicinal plants in highland sites; concern that most people do not know how to collect using methods that assure plant sustainability and limit damage to the populations of plants gathered and to adjacent plant species; and concern about the need for preservation and protection of traditional gathering areas.

Personal users noted the following major concerns regarding NTFP harvesting: concern about the potential for an increase in the number of harvesters who do not adhere to ethical harvest methods; concern that relatively scarce plants, such as osha and wood lily, could disappear if overharvested; and concern that pollution from mining operations may contaminate plant populations.

Commercial users expressed concerns similar to those expressed by traditional and personal NTFP users: concern that uninformed collectors could cause damage without realizing it; concern about possible overharvesting by pharmaceutical companies that require large amounts of specific plant species; concern about the ecological damage caused by grazing livestock on Forest Service lands, including trampling of stream banks and overgrazing within riparian areas; concern about sustainable commercial gathering of osha because of its limited ecological niche; concern about logging impacts on the bolete mushroom supply; concern about conflicts between commercial and personal users; and concern that the changing permit requirements and permit fees are not reflective of the actual costs involved in harvesting and the timely shipping of the product.

FUTURE DIRECTIONS IN NTFP MANAGEMENT AND POLICY

Currently, NTFP users are not formally involved in forest product management and policy decisions because Rio Grande National Forest or Forest Service Regional Office managers have not identified public involvement as a priority. The RGNF nontimber forest product study is a beginning phase in expanding the involvement of various NTFP users in product management. The interview results will be used to inform RGNF managers of the interest and concerns of specific NTFP users.

The Rio Grande National Forest is planning to assess how the Ranger District and Supervisor's Offices implement their NTFP management programs. This assessment will assist RGNF staff in developing recommendations aimed at making NTFP policy consistent with regional and Washington office direction. If the RGNF amends its forest plan to include management guidelines aimed specifically at NTFPs, the general public will have the opportunity to be involved in developing such guidelines.

Part Two

COMMERCE AND CONSERVATION

Nontimber Forest Product Commerce

Susan J. Alexander, James Weigand, and Keith A. Blatner

Nontimber forest products include many plants, lichens, and fungi from forests, including understory species used in the floral market, boughs, fungi, stems, poles and posts, wild foods, medicinals, plant extracts, and transplants. Species with long traditions of use provide people with an identity that contrasts with other trends toward standardization, mass production, and uniformity. Such products evoke a connection to the land, in particular to rural and wilderness environments in the United States, at a time when the population of the United States is overwhelmingly urban. As the number of people desiring naturalness both in ecological and cultural senses grows, the value placed on these natural products increases. Markets for medicinal and many decorative plant species hark back to mainstream American traditions of herbal medicinal practices and tastes in floral decoration that were popular a hundred or more years ago. People may not find time to pick blueberries (*Vaccinium* spp.) or make a wreath, but wild blueberries and wreaths become important icons for a cultural connection to the land. Names of firms involved in native nontimber forest product industries often evoke the wildness of a frontier or the pastoral rural landscape of farms, creeks, or nearby mountains. In many parts of the United States, producing goods from native plants has become an active expression of cultural survival and conservation of indigenous knowledge.

Harvesters, biologists, and the general public have expressed concern about the commercial harvesting of NTFPs, particularly those for which little formal biological information exists. Information about what is being harvested, in what quantities, and the impact of harvesting on the species and its distribution is often not well researched or integrated across disciplines. Annual or regularly collected data on domestic production and prices for NTFPs are generally not available. Prices for many nontimber forest products in the United States are influenced by international supply and demand, by seasonal fluctuation in availability, and by rising domestic demand. Estimates have been made through the years, based on surveys or other means, of the scope of various segments of the nontimber forest product industry, particularly in the Pacific Northwest.

We will discuss NTFPs by several categories, including medicinals, food and forage species, floral and horticultural species, resins and oils, and arts and crafts. Market structure, domestic trade, and international trade are outlined for products originating in and primarily native to the United States. There are a multitude of products being harvested from U.S. forests for which relatively little is known, either from a biological, social, or economic viewpoint. With more information about the value and quantities of production of NTFPs, landowners and policy makers would be able to make better decisions about harvesting as well as policies that affect resource sustainability and income opportunities.

MARKET STRUCTURE

Economic theory defines market structure as the way firms operate in relation to buyers, sellers, and other firms. Market structure can be looked at in many ways. Two conceptual approaches, informal economies and commodity chains, are particularly helpful in examining how nontimber forest product markets function. Informal economies refer to unregulated or undocumented markets or labor activities in an environment where similar activities are regulated. In this chapter, as with this definition, we are referring to noncriminal activities. Commodity chains describe how a particular product moves through the market, from harvest and production through various stages of wholesale and retail to the final consumer.

It makes sense to weave the ideas of informal economies and commodity chains into the neoclassical concepts of competition. Markets can range from perfectly competitive to monopolies, in theory. An imperfect market is one in which any one of the following conditions, necessary for a perfect market, does not hold true: a homogeneous product; a large number of buyers and sellers; freedom of entry and exit for buyers and sellers; all buyers and sellers have perfect information and foresight with respect to the current and future array of prices; the sales or purchases of each market agent are insignificant in relation to the aggregate volume of transactions; there is no collusion amongst buyers and sellers; consumers maximize total utility and sellers maximize total profit; and the commodity is transferable. Markets tend to vary considerably with respect to these conditions (Pearce 1992). The degree to which a market, or a node along the commodity chain, is competitive can reveal a great deal of information about how the node functions. We will discuss informal economies and commodity chains and tie these concepts together as we use them to describe nontimber forest product markets.

Informal Economies

The informal economy is a commonsense notion with moving social boundaries, best understood as a process. Some activities in the informal sector are the result of desperate need, but a similar motivation can lead a worker to accept lower wages in the formal sector. The United States has been portrayed as the most likely country among developed nations for skilled workers to be underemployed, or to take part in the informal economy, because of deregulation (Leonard 1998). Studies in both advanced industrial and less developed countries have shown the economic dynamism of unregulated income-generating activities. Returns to labor are generally lower in the informal economy with the occasional highly successful entrepreneurs (Lozano 1985; Portes, Blitzer, and Curtis 1986). The informal economy is a specific set of relationships of production, not a euphemism for poverty; informal activities cut across the whole social structure. The informal economy is characterized by one central feature: it is unregulated by the state (i.e., government) in a legal and social environment in which similar activities are regulated (Castells and Portes 1989).

Businesses in the nontimber forest products industry are generally small, employing few people. There are, of course, exceptions, but most businesses are what are referred to as very small enterprises, employing fewer than ten people. As an example, in 1998, the U.S. Census Bureau's County Business Patterns data began to include the number of establishments by number of employees for the category "Forest Nurseries and Gathering Forest Products" as a new two-digit detail for sector 07 of the category "Agricultural Services, Forestry and Fishing." Of the firms that reported doing business as forest nurseries or gathering forest products in the United States in 1998, 82 percent had nine or fewer employees.

Very small enterprises are alive and well in the U.S. economy across all market sectors. Their relative number and the proportion of the economically active population employed by them have remained fairly stable over the last several decades (Castells and Portes 1989). This stability has been documented for small businesses in nontimber forest products in Michigan (Emery 1998). Very small enterprises are relevant to informality for two important reasons. First, because of their low visibility, ease of displacement, and other small business/low-capital investment characteristics, they provide the most appropriate setting for casual hiring, nonreported income, and other informal practices. Direct observational studies indicate that although many small concerns are forced to obtain licenses, their labor practices are often informal (Castells and Portes 1989). The second point is that it is easier to operate a very small enterprise as a totally underground business. Fully informal small enterprises escape government record keeping. It is important to note, however, that not all very small enterprises engage in informal practices.

Workers in the informal economy tend to have very specific characteristics that can be referred to as downgraded labor. Many receive fewer benefits or lower wages or experience worse working conditions than they would in the formal economy. Many work in the informal economy because they must. They might be undocumented immigrants or be a group that has been historically subject to stigmatization. Ethnic minorities, women, and youth are all potential candidates for working at home, part-time, and as temporary replacements (Castells and Portes 1989; Leonard 1998). Yet the boundaries of vulnerability are always historically specific. If workers in a highly structured industry become subject to structural unemployment, they will find whatever means they can to provide for their families. Emery (1998) found this to be true of miners in Michigan, harvesting nontimber forest products when the mines shut down.

Manufacture of grave blankets, a mat of evergreen boughs traditionally placed on graves in the winter, is one of many examples of the interwoven nature of formal and informal economies in NTFP primary production. Grave blankets are a very old tradition in Germany. Denmark exports noble fir *(Abies procera)* boughs to Germany for this use, among other traditional uses of bough materials. Emery (1998) reports that in Michigan, independent bough cutters and piece workers (mostly women) who assemble the blankets at home work in coordination with a buyer and distributor. The local distributor sells the blankets to brokers and cemeteries throughout the Midwest. In areas where other work is available, particularly wage-based jobs in the formal economy, buyers must depend even more on their relationships with harvesters to ensure a supply of boughs (Emery 1998). Grave blankets are manufactured in other parts of the United States, including the Pacific Northwest.

Networks of economic activities, networks of firms, and coordinated networks of workers are becoming recognized as a model of successful production and distribution. Firms that rely on such networks can be formal or informal, but there is a tendency for the informal economy to rely predominantly on social networks. Their connection to the formal economy is also through networks (Castells and Portes 1989). The reliance of many markets in the NTFP industry on relationships or networks of workers, buyers, producers, and distributors is well known. The nontimber forest products industry is a reflection of the greater society in which it functions, in that there is no clear-cut duality between the informal and formal sectors. There is, instead, a series of complex interactions.

The informal economy is a fundamental politico-economic process at the core of many societies, an integral component of total national economies rather than a marginal appendix to them (Castells and Portes 1989; Leonard 1998). Governments tolerate or even stimulate informal economic activities as a way to resolve potential social conflicts. The loss of formal control over these activities is compensated by the short-term potential for legitimation and renewed economic growth that they offer (Castells and Portes 1989).

Commodity Chains

Hopkins and Wallerstein (1986) define commodity chains as networks of labor and production processes resulting in a finished commodity. A global commodity chain, centered on one commodity or product, is a set of networks that link households, enterprises, and states within the world economy. An examination of these networks brings to light the social basis for economic activity.

Patterns of competition and innovation are crucial to understanding the organization and transformation of global commodity chains. Hopkins and Wallerstein (1994) point out that monopoly and competition are keys to understanding the distribution of wealth among the nodes along a commodity chain. Central nodes accrue more wealth than peripheral ones because competitive pressures are less pronounced in corelike nodes than in peripheral ones. The distribution of wealth within a commodity chain has often been portrayed as a reflection of the level of production, in that there is less wealth to producers of raw materials, and wealth (profits) increases through manufacturing, distribution, and so on. However, labor-intensive activities may be a more important growth area than manufacturing. Within a global commodity chain, profitability shifts from node to node according to competitive pressures, and industry is not always a determinant of development. Raynolds (1994) points out that commodity chains allow us to focus on the creation and distribution of global wealth as embodied in a multistage, multidimensional sequence of activities rather than as an outcome of industrialization alone.

By analyzing patterns of competition among specific enterprises, the global commodity approach can explore such issues as kinship and ethnic identity, crucial social resources that can be used by businesses in their efforts to sustain a competitive edge. The greatest virtue of a commodity-chain approach is its emphasis on process. Commodities move through the chains, which are not static. The capitalist world economy is revealed as a fast-moving network of relations, constantly reproducing a basic order that permits accumulation of capital in particular locations (Hopkins and Wallerstein 1994).

The global commodity chain approach highlights the need to look at the geographic spread of international trade, and at the linkages between raw material suppliers, factories, traders, and retailers, in order to understand sources of stability and change. Many, if not all, nontimber forest products exported from the United States go into buyer-driven commodity chains where large retailers, brand-name merchandisers, and trading companies set up decentralized production networks in a variety of exporting countries (Gereffi 1994).

Schlosser, Blatner, and Chapman (1991) and Schlosser and Blatner (1995) provide an overview of the distribution of floral and Christmas greens and wild edible mushrooms in the Pacific Northwest. The flow of materials begins at the forest, where independent harvesters cut the greens or pick the mushrooms. They sell the products to buyers, who process the materials. Processing may be as little as sorting or as much as creating a final product, such as a wreath. Following initial processing, plant materials move via one or more wholesalers/brokers to the retail market. Local producers also purchase from each other to obtain needed quantities of materials to fill specific orders. These commodity chains illustrate the networking that is such an integral part of NTFP businesses. In addition, products flow from the largely informal economy (independent harvesters) into the formal economy (the retail market) through these networks.

Harvest rights are usually secured in the form of leases or sales agreements or harvest permits, depending on the product. Leases and sales agreements are commonly used to secure the legal right to harvest floral and Christmas greens products. Large bough sales and long-term leases are typically purchased by producers in the region either on a lump-sum or weight-scale basis due to the amounts of capital required. Independent harvesters then harvest the boughs and other plant materials. They also purchase smaller bough sales and leases and harvest other nontimber forest products under harvest permits (Schlosser, Blatner, and Chapman 1991). Independent harvesters also harvest wild edible mushrooms under various permitting systems established by the landowner. The right to harvest wild edible mushrooms is not normally conveyed via leases because of the difficulty in predicting harvestable quantities in any given year (Schlosser and Blatner 1995).

Emery (1998) outlines commodity chains for cedar (eastern arborvitae, *Thuja occidentalis*) oil, fiddleheads *(Matteuccia struthiopteris)*, grave blankets made of boughs, princess pine *(Lycopodium obscurum)*, and blueberries in Michigan and Wisconsin. These products follow market networks similar to NTFPs harvested in the Pacific Northwest. Cedar boughs are harvested by independent harvesters and the oil is processed locally. The oil is then shipped to a New York distributor, where it is exported. Fiddleheads are harvested by independent harvesters, sold to a local processor, and then shipped as raw wild food products to restaurants in the United States. Princess pine, a club moss, is preserved for use in floral arrangements and wreaths and used as shrubbery in model railroads and dollhouses. Princess pine is gathered throughout the upper Midwest, processed in Wisconsin, and then sold through floral supply houses throughout the United States and Mexico.

Blueberries, huckleberries, cranberries (*Vaccinium* spp.), and other berries are processed locally into jams, jellies, and syrup in many parts of the United States, including the Pacific Northwest, the Northeast, and the Midwest. A large proportion of the product is sold locally or regionally by the producers through a variety of retail outlets or through mail order, instead of going through a broker or wholesaler. It is generally assumed that distribution channels for medicinal products follow a similar pattern with the exception of an additional processing phase prior to final sale, depending on the product.

DISCUSSION

The frameworks of commodity chains and informal economies give us useful tools to examine the structure and function of nontimber forest product markets. Hopkins and Wallerstein (1994) tell us that the separable processes constituting a commodity chain are nodes, and each is a separable production process. The boundaries are socially defined and can easily be redefined, or change, through technological or social organizational changes. They refer to "core" and "peripheral" nodes, where the most wealth (profits) accrues to core nodes. In core nodes there is less competition, among other characteristics.

Many of the characteristics of NTFP markets at the initial gathering, sale, and processing levels are those of peripheral nodes. There are many units of production (more competition), and labor is often done through nonwage agreements. Some of the aspects of leases, permits, and land ownership or access are also indicative of peripheral nodes. Floral, nursery, and craft businesses in the Upper Peninsula of Michigan and in the Pacific Northwest operate with small to medium short-term contracts, renegotiated regularly. Networks between raw product buyers and wholesale purchasers affect market stability (Emery 1998). Emery (1998) found that, in general, the structure of relationships moves from informal to formal as a nontimber forest product chain progresses from harvesting to distribution. In addition, returns increase as the chain progresses.

Two examples of markets in nontimber forest products can give us some insight as to how these concepts of informal markets and commodity chains can help assess market structure. As mentioned previously, the increase in demand for natural products has fueled a surge in the medicinal products markets, both in the United States and abroad. Independent harvesters often harvest raw products in the United States. Historically, informal labor supplied the producers with wild product until a species was felt to be in such decline that protection measures had to be implemented. With demand still high, many species were domesticated. As more people turn to a wider variety of wildcrafted medicinal products, more shifts in technology and redefinitions of social and organizational boundaries can be expected. The commodity chains for medicinal products include informal and formal aspects, with the informal aspects more common, but not limited to the earlier stages of the chain. The markets extend throughout the United States and into other countries, with peripheral and core nodes spread everywhere and shifting as the market expands.

Another example is the wild edible mushroom industry. Since demand in Europe and Japan increased in the 1980s, the markets have expanded rapidly, primarily as raw materials or lightly processed exports. Efforts to domesticate the primary species of interest have not been successful at a commercial scale. Some primary processing is done in the United States, but most of the wild edible mushroom market has been fresh or preserved bulk product shipped overseas. The U.S. part of the market is characterized by a network of informal and formal economic activities, mostly in very small enterprises. At the primary gathering and processing level, the wild edible mushroom market has many of the characteristics of peripheral nodes, which are quite vulnerable to shifts in labor availability, transportation costs, social structural change, and so on.

The U.S. wild mushroom industry has been hit hard in the past few years by two global economic and social structural changes. The depression in the Asian economies resulted in decreased demand for American matsutake *(Tricholoma magnivelare)* in Japan, causing prices to fall from their recent high points and dampen the wide fluctuations documented by Blatner and Alexander (1998). In addition, the high prices attracted supply from other countries, which can supply the preferred Japanese matsutake *(Tricholoma matsutake)* with lower transportation costs and, in many cases, lower wage expectations. The opening of trade with eastern bloc countries gave the European Union a supply of chanterelles (*Cantharellus* spp.), morels (*Morchella* spp.), and *Boletus* spp. that are closer, with lower transportation costs and lower wage expectations than the U.S. market. In response, U.S. producers are working to create product differentiation and expand domestic markets and are exploring further processing, packaging, and marketing options.

These two examples provide a fascinating snapshot of the fast-moving network of global commodity chains and their relationship to formal and informal economies, competition within the chains, and response to socioeconomic change and technological innovation. In the next sections of this chapter, we will discuss domestic and international trade.

DOMESTIC TRADE

Medicinals

Data on the size of the medicinal market are limited, but global markets are well developed (Lewington 1993). The medicinal market is composed of two sectors, the phytopharmaceutical and the botanical or herbal. The herbal medicine sector, which provides dietary and herbal supplements and alternative health care, is increasing rapidly in size, economic strength, and diversity (Foster 1995). The phytopharmaceutical sector has historically developed single-compound–based products with a high level of investment; conventional pharmaceuticals are subject to Food and Drug Administration (FDA) regulations. Herbal products are regulated under the Dietary Supplement Health and Education Act. Herbal products can claim to affect "structure or function" or aid in general well-being, but they cannot claim to cure a disease (von Hagen and Fight 1999).

No other use of the nontimber native flora of the United States has undergone such a rapid expansion in the last twenty years as the popular use of medicinal plants. Awareness and consumption of medicinal plants by Americans has been dynamic, reviving markets for plants that had wide use in the nineteenth century, such as goldenseal *(Hydrastis canadensis);* expanding markets nationally for plants with formerly regional markets, such as osha *(Ligusticum porteri);* or developing altogether new markets for species with little or no history of past use, such as Chamisso arnica *(Arnica chamissonis).* Thought to be a quaint profession seldom practiced anymore, gathering wild plants or plant parts, called wildcrafting, has become a viable livelihood strategy for rural residents in some parts of North America. Commercial gatherers grew in number, as did professional herbalists, trained at schools across the United States, and self-practitioners who gather for their personal and family use. Exact numbers and demographic profiles of people who are wildcrafters are unknown.

Several trends in popular culture have inspired the economic renaissance of medicinal plants in the United States. Landes (1986) remarks how the spice market changed from the 1950s to the 1980s. The American palette increasingly enjoyed spicier foods from more diverse cultural sources. An excellent indicator is the consumption of peppers (*Capsicum* spp.) in the United States, more than doubling from 2,340 metric tons in 1959 to more than 6,090 metric tons in 1984. Major domestic production hubs for hot peppers are centers of traditionally spicy foods, New Mexico and California. This trend was not limited to the United States, however. Freer access to products and increasing reliance on industrial production of spices rather than home cultivation saw the world production of tarragon *(Artemisia dracunculus),* a culinary and medicinal herb native to the United States, jump from 28 metric tons in 1974 to 853 metric tons in 1984 (Meares 1987).

Interest in the United States in medicinal plants began to rise rapidly in the early 1990s. As late as 1988, Landes and Blumenthal noted that potpourris were the strongest use for U.S. botanic products. By 1989, there were indications that consumer taste in the medicinal markets was changing in the United States. Products from native species such as berries from saw palmetto *(Serenoa repens)* and passion flower (mostly purple passionflower, *Passiflora incarnata*), most of which had been exported to Germany, began to have American producers. The rapidly increasing demand caused prices to rise sharply in 1989. By contrast the potpourri industry slumped.

For the first time, herbs previously confined to use in the American Southwest and northern Mexico found national exposure and popular reception, such as chaparral *(Larrea divaricata)*, damiana *(Turnera diffusa)*, and osha. The price of saw palmetto berries rose steeply again in early 1996 to fifty-five dollars per pound. In that same time period, goldenseal became scarce in places where it was widely harvested, leading to concern that natural populations of goldenseal were in jeopardy. Growing herbal medicinal consumption by Americans has spurred rapid progress toward developing domesticated crop production and simulated-wild agroforestry systems to accommodate demand while protecting wild populations. Domestication of medicinal species has led to technology transfer and greater internationalization of medicinal plant production. Commercial producers have been growing crops of some American species, such as common boneset *(Eupatorium perfoliatum)*, offshore for more than two decades.

Medicinal herbal products and plants have been and are big business in the United States, and demand for them has prompted protective measures. Many major herbal products important historically in the United States are mentioned in legislative laws in many states, including American ginseng *(Panax quinquefolius)*, goldenseal, cascara (*Rhamnus purshiana* DC), Saint-John's-wort *(Hypericum perforatum)*, and Sitka valerian (*Valeriana sitchensis* Bong.). Demand for these products continues to grow. According to Mater (1997), the herbal market in the United States was about $1 billion in 1992 and has been growing 13 to 15 percent per year. Klink (1997) estimated 1996 sales at $2.5 billion. Of the twenty-five top-selling botanicals in U.S. commerce, over 50 percent are plant species found in the United States. The domestic herbal market is experiencing consolidation and company mergers. There has been more emphasis on the pharmaceutical model of standardizing and quantifying active ingredients and an increased emphasis on quality as mainstream companies enter the marketplace (Brevoort 1996). There is some concern that the increasing demand will increase pressure on harvesters to supply large volumes to brokers (von Hagen and Fight 1999). Others see the opportunity for value-added processing by independent entrepreneurs (Mater 1994).

Brevoort (1998) provides the best overview of the dramatic change in the United States in public interest in and consumption of medicinal plant products. Between 1996 and 1998, national retail consumption of medicinal plant-based products rose from $1.8 billion to $4.0 billion. Much of the increase comes from valued-added processing, from fresh herbs all the way to standardized extracts and phytomedicines. From July 1997 to June 1998, American ginseng at $138 million, *Echinacea* species at $33 million, and saw palmetto at $27 million were the biggest sellers among the species native to the United States. Other prominent native species in the market are goldenseal, black cohosh *(Cimicifuga racemosa),* and cranberry (*Vaccinium* spp.). In 1998, annual retail sales of commercial herb species at $688 million were 55 percent higher than in 1997 (figures unadjusted for inflation). This huge increase, however, was followed in the first three quarters of 1999 with a virtually flat market (Blumenthal 1999). With the increasing participation of large multinational drug companies in the herbal plant products market, competition may compel smaller firms to redefine their product lines and species marketed.

Launching the mainstream herb market was not without problems. In the mid-1980s, the phenomenon of Chernobyl scared off many people both in Europe and North America from using medicinal plants grown traditionally in Eastern Europe. Although native to both the United States and Europe, mainstay medicinal species such as bilberry *(Vaccinium myrtillus),* kinnikinnick *(Arctostaphylos uva-ursi),* common elderberry (*Sambucus nigra*, now considered identical to *S. canadensis* and *S. mexicana*), nettles *(Urtica dioica),* and raspberry *(Rubus idaeus)* for sale as medicinals in the United States traditionally came from Bulgaria, Hungary, Poland, and the former Yugoslavia. A further destabilizing factor in the eastern European medicinal market was the restructuring of eastern European national economies after 1989. By 1999, however, production of medicinal plants from the region was in high gear again, and export markets were expanding for newly domesticated products such as common boneset, native to the United States but currently grown in Hungary and Poland. Domestic production, consumption, demand, and prices all affect and are affected by these shifts in the characteristics and nodes of the global commodity chains.

The number of medicinal species available to people in the United States is very large. Weigand and Alexander (forthcoming) cite more than five hundred plant species native to the United States that were commercially available during the second half of 1999. If non-native medicinal plant species from Chinese, European, Indian, and tropical American cultural traditions are added, the American public has well over a thousand medicinal plants to choose from. Consumer awareness of choices and impacts has critical implications for sustainability, product purity issues, equity and social issues, and many other concerns. Species used in the industry differ considerably in their cultural and geographic origins, current areas of production, availability, and product forms in which they arrive at the marketplace.

Multiple forms and combinations of herbal products are available in a variety of value-added products. Raw materials for these products are distinguished by the environment (wild-grown or farmed), by the manner in which they grew (organically or otherwise), and by how raw medicinal herb products were processed for consumers (dried whole, cut and sifted, or ground to a powder). Also available are bulk quantities from distributors and smaller quantities from herbolarias, botanicas, and health food stores. The types of value-added products available in the U.S. market include teas; herbal oils; infusions; salves, creams, and lotions; ointments; syrups; poultices; and tinctures. Access to the plant pharmacopoeia extends beyond just processed species. Companies now market live native species or seeds of species as medicinal herbs for people who want to grow their own. These horticultural and seed companies in effect pave the way for less common or as yet uncommercialized medicinal plant species into the U.S. market.

The number of fungi species in the American medicinal marketplace is much smaller than the number of plant species. Among lichens, only *Usnea barbata* or other related *Usnea* species appear commonly in U.S. herb stores. Chinese and Japanese medicine practitioners in the United States introduced medicinal applications of fungi species to the American public, and presently numerous firms are actively marketing fungi species for specific medical treatments. By contrast, in the world economy, the value of fungi in medical application far outweighs the value of mushrooms as foods. Worldwide, people spent more than $1.3 billion in 1997 on medical applications of fungi (Wills and Lipsey 1999). Many species used in the United States now are non-native species. Little information is available about Native American, Native Alaskan, or Native Hawaiian applications of native species of fungi for medicinal uses.

In addition to treating physiological dysfunctions, people are using native plants for altering emotional or psychological conditions. One of the critically endangered species within its small range in the United States is peyote *(Lophophora williamsii),* a native cactus with psychoactive properties that is used in religious ceremonies of the Native American church. Advocates of other healing applications of plants, such as aromatherapy, use plant-derived fragrances for achieving desired mental states. Practitioners blend essences from different species to achieve more subtle psychological benefits; blending also allows for product differentiation.

Flower essences (concentrated substances from distillation) frequently come from many of the same plant species used in medicinal products. Considerable concentration of production occurs in southwest Oregon and far northwestern California, where federal land management agencies have oversight over most land. Some species used in flower essences are rare, threatened, or endangered federally or in the states where people produce flower essences. Species used for flower essences include the California pitcherplant *(Darlingtonia californica)* and Humboldt's lily *(Lilium humboldtii),* both protected. Actual impacts from flower essence production on native populations of rare plant species are difficult to monitor and assess.

Some flower essence producers state that they create their essences in close proximity to a plant flower and therefore have little physical effect on the plant itself.

Food and Forage Species

Foods from native U.S. species provide a very small share of the food species consumed by Americans. Internationally important staple food species are also few in number: peppers, field pumpkins *(Cucurbita pepo),* and sunflower *(Helianthus annuus)* seeds. Introduction of new species into agricultural production in the United States is usually a very slow process. An important source of information on the status of advances in agriculture and commercialization of native plant species is the New Crops Center at Purdue University. The California Rare Fruit Society also tracks the history of uses and horticultural practices to facilitate private or commercial production of new or underutilized plant species. The most popular native fruits in the United States are species of berry genera also found in Europe: *Ribes, Rubus,* and *Vaccinium,* for example. Although information on the domestic wild berry trade is not generally available, several species are harvested for domestic use, including huckleberries and blackberries (*Rubus* spp). Most species have not found their way into mainstream American markets but are important in the Caribbean Basin or in markets in large eastern cities. The international trade section of this chapter gives an idea of the importance of wild berries to the U.S. export economy.

Edible wild-growing mushrooms also have wide popularity, especially in the North Central and Pacific Northwest states. Mushrooms that are popular include porcini (mostly king bolete, *Boletus edulis*), chanterelles, hedgehog mushroom *(Hydnum repandum),* Oregon white truffles *(Tuber gibbosum),* morels, American matsutake, and lobster mushrooms *(Hypomyces lactiflorum).* The biological aspects of commercial mushroom production have been explored by several studies (Norvell 1995; Pilz et al. 1999). So far, the conclusion is that yields fluctuate so widely that it is difficult to generalize, but estimates of productivity may be used to make local site-specific assessments of long-term productivity (Alexander et al. in review). Blatner and Alexander (1998) outline prices for some of the most significant commercially harvested fungi in the Pacific Northwest. It has been estimated that as many as thirty-six species are traded commercially but *Boletus,* chanterelles, morels, and American matsutake make up the bulk of the industry. The average price paid to harvesters in the Pacific Northwest from 1992 to 1996 was \$5.69 for *Boletus,* \$3.26 for chanterelles, \$5.04 for morels, and \$14.08 for American matsutake. The size of the wild mushroom market in Washington, Oregon, and Idaho was estimated at \$21.5 million in 1985 (McRobert 1985), \$38.6 million in

1989, and \$41.1 million in 1992 (Schlosser and Blatner 1995). Russel (1990) estimated that exports of American matsutake from British Columbia were worth \$9–10 million in 1989.

A few studies have attempted to estimate gross wages for wild edible mushroom harvesters. Acker (1986) states that an average wage for a mushroom picker in the mid-eighties was \$830 seasonally, with a few people earning a maximum of \$4,000. In an assessment of American matsutake in the Nass Valley in British Columbia, Meyer Resources (1995) found that pickers earned an estimated \$4,500 per season in the early 1990s. Love, Jones, and Liegel (1998) estimate wages for commercial mushroom harvesters in the Olympic Peninsula in Washington at about \$30 per day. Obst and Brown (2000) report an average wage of \$15 per hour (U.S.) for morel harvesters in the Northwest Territories of Canada. Other authors have found that while such wages may be standard for experienced pickers, the majority of mushroom harvesters earn far less and many, particularly those with little or no experience, lose money. Pickers are paid immediately in cash by mushroom buyers, who often handle tens of thousands of dollars each day in high-value, high-volume areas. Mushroom buying may represent the largest legal cash-based commerce in our society.

Mushroom buyers may work for a large broker, but most are small businesses that may be formal or informal. The vast majority of pickers are independent harvesters who use social networking to supply the formal economy with product. Commodity chains for wild edible mushrooms from the United States are strongly international; in many cases, the mushrooms are shipped to distribution points and then shipped overseas. Many successful small businesses supply both domestic and international markets with fresh or lightly processed mushrooms (e.g., dried or frozen), thus serving as peripheral nodes where the formal and informal economies interact.

Forage grass species are particularly important to federal and private land management in California and in the Pacific Northwest, Rocky Mountain, and Southwest regions where grazing in or near forest environments is a major land use activity and where native range restoration is a goal. The interactions and management of forage species, trees, and grazing animals are studied by agroforesters and silvopastural scientists. Common native grass species are available commercially and provide valuable forage for domesticated animals and wildlife species. Native grasses are used for range reclamation and restoration. Some species such as buffalo grass *(Buchloë dactyloides)* are used as turf and lawn grasses.

Native legumes are also commercially available, including milkvetches (*Astragalus* spp.), bundleflowers (*Desmanthus* spp.), and purple prairie clover *(Petalostemon purpureus)*. Mesquite (*Prosopis* spp.) is important forage for animals in Texas and the Southwest. California is the second most important region evolutionarily, after the Mediterranean Basin, for clover (*Trifolium* spp.) species diversity (Zohary and Heller 1984). None of the native clover species are used commercially as forage, although their role in landscape restoration is considerable. Some commercial grass forage species such as Indian ricegrass *(Achnantherum hymenoides)* are traditional staple crops of Native Americans. Programs for seeding lands with native forage accomplish two important elements of federal trust responsibilities to recognized Indian tribes: restoring ecosystems with traditional food species and providing high-quality forage for native game species such as buffalo and pronghorn antelope.

FLORAL AND HORTICULTURAL PRODUCTS

Plants native to the United States used for decorating and ornamenting homes and workplaces are as diverse as the decorative forms invented. Native species are used for Christmas trees, holiday greenery, and accent materials in holiday greenery. Species used in nonholiday decoration consist of both live and preserved foliage and flowers.

Christmas Trees

Native species used in Christmas trees come from three gymnosperm families: Cupressaceae, Pinaceae, and Taxodiaceae. True firs (*Abies* spp.), spruces (*Picea* spp.), pines (*Pinus* spp.), and Douglas firs *(Pseudotsuga menziesii)* are the major Christmas trees in all regions except in California, the Southeast, and Florida. In California, redwood *(Sequoia sempervirens)* and giant sequoia *(Sequoiadendron giganteum)* in the Taxodiaceae family are major Christmas tree species. In the Southeast and Florida, eastern red cedar *(Juniperus virginiana)* in the Cupressaceae family is one of the two most important Christmas trees regionally. Climatic conditions provide the major divisions for suites of species available in different regions of the United States. Important cultural distinctions and uses of Christmas trees also influence variations in uses between regions. For example, eastern red cedar is common as a Christmas tree only as far north as Virginia, although the species ranges on the Atlantic seaboard north to southern Maine. People in interior Alaska are accustomed to harvesting black and white spruces *(Picea glauca)* for personal use from public lands without charge or regulation. In the Southwest, juniper Christmas trees cut on rangelands helped to reduce woodland encroachment. In the West, Midwest, and Northeast, public land managers also permit individuals to cut trees for personal use with no or minimal charge.

Christmas trees are an example of an NTFP that has been increasingly cultivated in the United States, where most trees are pruned so that they are more dense than an unpruned forest-grown tree. There has been a dramatic shift in taste in the United States toward pruned, dense Christmas trees and away from open-grown trees. In Europe, cultivated Christmas trees are selected and grown for a more open appearance, like natural forest-grown trees. Particularly in northeastern Europe, there is still a tradition of placing lighted candles on the tree on Christmas Eve, and widely spaced branches are important. Some people in the United States go out in the forest and harvest their own Christmas tree. Many landowners have designated areas and issue permits, but some still experience problems with the theft of small trees from replanted areas.

The commercial range of many Christmas tree species frequently extends beyond the natural range of species. Major examples of American Christmas tree species planted regionally as exotics include eastern white pine *(Pinus strobus)* in the Prairie States, noble fir and Douglas fir in the Midwest and Northeast, and Arizona cypress *(Cupressus arizonica)* in the Southeast and Florida. These four species plus balsam fir *(Abies balsamea)*, Fraser fir *(Abies fraseri)*, Virginia pine *(Pinus virginiana)*, and eastern red cedar constitute the major commercial Christmas tree species nationally.

Increasingly, Christmas tree growers and vendors have created ensembles of experiences, particularly for families with children, at Christmas tree farms. People who do not own forestland of their own can travel to farms and arrange to select and cut trees of their choice. Entertainment and food services frequently accompany the experiences. Tie-in sales with Christmas greenery for wreath making and potpourri are also common.

Commercial Native Foliage Species

A considerable palette of native plant, lichen, and moss species supply commercial foliage, branches, stems, fruits, and pods for use in the winter holiday season and in the year-round floral industry. The diversity of forms in native plant materials has a strongly regional character, especially for the species that people wildcraft. Conifer species used for Christmas greens also have uses in floral arrangements, wreaths, and baskets. The major difference is that conifer materials central to holiday green uses have a subordinate role in floral market products. Any comprehensive list of floral products would quickly become incomplete because species availability and use can change quickly with variations in taste and with the creativity of individual firms introducing new items to the marketplace. Some of the species such as marubio and Florida hopbush have commercial use abroad, in these cases in the Philippines and Italy respectively, although they appear rarely if at all in U.S. markets.

Florida, the Southeast, and the Pacific Northwest are major centers for fresh foliage products, serving both domestic and foreign markets. These regions have many native nonconifer evergreen species for nearly year-round availability. American, Dutch, and German firms are present in Florida and California, and increasingly firms in Florida supply foliage products from both the Pacific Northwest and the Southeast to European markets. Pacific Northwest firms ship agriculturally grown or wildcrafted foliage species from the region. California, Florida, Minnesota, Oregon, Pennsylvania, and Texas are major centers for the dried foliage industry in the United States. This market provides mainly domestic consumers, as export markets emphasize fresh materials. Many plant materials used in dried plant design come from India.

The array of native species used as fresh foliage overlaps the species used as preserved foliage. For example, salal *(Gaultheria shallon),* bear grass *(Xerophyllum tenax),* and iron fern *(Rumohra adiantiformis),* all in the fresh foliage market, are widely available in the United States as preserved materials. Some firms supply both fresh and preserved plant materials to florists because contemporary decoration with plant materials frequently combines fresh and preserved species in a bouquet or wreath. One of the most important dried foliage products in the United States is white sagebrush *(Artemisia ludoviciana),* better known in the trade as silver king or silver queen and used as a filler to provide the body of a wreath or other display. Grass species are very common in dried floral markets. In the Southeast, native grape (*Vitis* spp.) vines are a widely used floral material.

Firms elaborate on the diversity of form in native plant species through different techniques to preserve plant materials. Various methods of preserving plants generate products with different shapes and colors. Materials that appear fresh may actually retain their natural or near-natural color using glycerin or another color fixative. Producers air dry or use desiccants such as sand, borax powder, and silica gels, depending upon species-specific requirements, to retain plant features or to create desired features. Subsequent steps may dye, bleach, gild, or silverize dried foliage, pods, and cones. Occasionally products are skeletonized, where chemicals selectively remove plant tissues to leave a netlike effect in preserved leaves. Recently, microwaving and freeze-drying plant materials have become popular.

Documentation of markets for floral NTFP products in the United States is scarce. According to Douglass (1975), the buying, selling, and shipping of native floral greenery was big business for several companies in the Pacific Northwest in the mid-1970s. It still is today, twenty-five years later. Emery (1998) found that bough gathering in the Upper Peninsula of Michigan was an important income source for many families. In addition, gathering boughs and greenery is an important source of income for many rural families, and thousands of others, such as loggers, fishermen, and housewives, pick floral greenery as a part-time occupation. Floral greenery leases help landowners in that they supply supplemental income and the pickers help patrol, report, and suppress fires as well as keep roads and trails open.

Douglass (1975) reports that floral greenery species suitable for the market and available in commercial quantities are limited in number, and he believes that new species are not likely to be found that would take up an appreciable market share. However, as subsequent studies have shown, existing species can be used in new ways, through preservation, dying, and new markets. As previously noted, the floral market changes quickly and is subject to style trends and variations in taste. The land base for floral greenery production changes due to temporary removal from timber harvesting and permanent removal due to conversion of lands to rural and agricultural use. The Pacific Northwest both markets to and experiences competition from other countries, and artificial species also affect demand.

Blatner and Schlosser (1997), in their most recent survey of the floral greens and Christmas greens market segments in the Pacific Northwest, found that the floral greens market appears to be decreasing (from 1989 to 1994), while the Christmas greens market is holding steady. They note that it is important to recognize the dynamic character of the nontimber forest product industry. Markets for all types of products continually expand and contract due to a wide variety of market forces, including nontimber forest product markets. The NTFP industry has been in existence in the Pacific Northwest since the early 1900s and in the east and south for much longer (see Emery, this volume). Cronemiller et al. (1950) and Shaw (1949) estimate that all NTFPs contributed about $5 million to Oregon's economy in 1950. Schlosser, Blatner, and Chapman (1991) estimate the size of the floral and Christmas greens markets in Washington, Oregon, and southwest British Columbia at $128.5 million in 1989, and Blatner and Schlosser (1997) estimate it at $106.8 million in 1994. The industry will likely remain an important component of regional economies for many years to come. Conversely, individual product markets will increase or decrease from year to year depending on changing market conditions and resource availability.

Although employment data are not available for most segments of the NTFP industry, there is a considerable amount of seasonal employment in the wild edibles and the medicinal markets as well as some in other segments, such as craft materials and transplants. The floral and holiday greens markets are also important in the United States, and although data are difficult to get about the industry nationwide, surveys for the Pacific Northwest give an idea of the potential size and importance in other regions such as the north central United States. Table 6 outlines available information on employment in Oregon and Washington in the floral and Christmas greens markets and includes data from the lumber and paper industries for comparison.

There is also little published information about wages paid to harvesters of Christmas greens and floral products. Heckman (1951) reports daily

Table 6. Forest products employment, Oregon and Washington

Year	Lumber and wood products	Paper and allied products	Floral and Christmas greens
1950	Not calculated	Not calculated	2,000[a]
1953	134,400[b]	2,100	N/A
1989	109,300[c]	26,500	10,300[d]
1990	103,600[e]	27,200	N/A
1994	91,100	26,300	5,800[f]

[a]Heckman 1951.
[b]U.S. Forest Service 1982.
[c]U.S. Forest Service 1990.
[d]Schlosser, Blatner, and Chapman 1991.
[e]Warren 1996.
[f]Estimated from Blatner and Schlosser (1997); includes Washington, Oregon, Idaho, and Montana.

wages of eighteen to forty dollars for people who harvested floral greens in the Pacific Northwest in 1950, with a weekly maximum of four hundred dollars. Tables 7 and 8 outline available prices paid to harvesters for a selected sample of floral plants collected in the forests of the Pacific Northwest. It has been estimated that about 80 percent of boughs are used during the Christmas holidays. The remaining 20 percent are used year-round by the floral market.

There are numerous conifer species used in both the holiday greens and the floral markets. Table 7 gives an idea of the range of prices across species and from year to year. The demand for Christmas greens is less subject to change than products used in the floral markets, as holiday uses are based on traditions that change slowly. However, early storms in the Cascade Mountains can limit harvested volumes in any given year. Further, changing resource management objectives on federal lands and the associated changes in the age-class distribution of the forest may result in the reduced availability of harvestable boughs from selected species.

Table 8 outlines prices paid to harvesters for selected floral greens. The species in this table have been important in the Pacific Northwest floral market since the market began there, but the volume of use and the way the products are utilized changes. For example, since Blatner and Alexander (1998) collected data, another size category ("shorts") for salal and huckleberry has become common. The use of sword fern *(Polystichum munitum)* has declined, and salal has become even more popular as a preserved product.

Resins and Oils

This section synthesizes current information on plant and lichen species native to the United States and its territories used as fragrances and flavors.

Table 7. Mean per-ton prices (current dollars) for Christmas greens harvested in Oregon, Washington, and Idaho

Common name	Latin name	1989	1994	1995	1996
Douglas fir	*Pseudotsuga menziesii*	200	315	234	338
Grand fir	*Abies grandis*	N/A	387	210	580
Incense cedar	*Libocedrus decurrens*	760	634	619	612
Noble fir	*Abies procera*	720	540	408	596
Western red cedar	*Thuja plicata*	460	406	295	433

Source: Blatner and Alexander 1998.

Table 8. Mean per-bunch prices (current dollars) for floral greens harvested in Oregon, Washington, and Idaho

Common name	Latin name	1950[a]	1972[b]	1989[c]	1994[c]	1995[c]	1996[c]
Bear grass	*Xerophyllum tenax*	N/A	N/A	0.90	0.56	0.44	0.43
Evergreen huckleberry sprays	*Vaccinium ovatum*	0.11–0.16	0.35	0.65	0.85	0.68	0.73
Evergreen huckleberry tips	*Vaccinium ovatum*	N/A	0.25	0.37	0.48	0.51	0.56
Red evergreen huckleberry	*Vaccinium ovatum*	N/A	0.35	0.65	0.92	0.66	0.79
Salal sprays	*Gaultheria shallon*	0.11–0.16	0.39	0.90	0.98	0.95	1.06
Salal tips	*Gaultheria shallon*	N/A	0.25	0.50	0.72	0.59	0.76
Scotch broom	*Cytisus scoparius*	N/A	0.28	0.40	0.41	0.42	0.51
Sword fern	*Polystichum munitum*	0.10–0.16	0.24	0.62	0.77	0.67	0.64
Moss (per lb.)	Various species	N/A	N/A	0.26	1.74	0.21	0.37

[a]Allen 1950.
[b]Douglass 1975.
[c]Blatner and Alexander 1998.

Many non-native species are also important in the domestic essential oils sector and are discussed briefly; medicinal and aromatherapy uses were discussed in the section about medicinals. The distinction between flavor and fragrance is not strict. Mints (*Mentha* spp.) frequently function as both olfactory and flavoring products. Carrier oils used in fragrance industries usually have uses in food preparation as well. The United States is a major producer of both plants and plant derivatives used in fragrance products. Most major commercial plant species in the plant fragrance industry are not native to the United States. The genera *Mentha* (true mints) and *Citrus* (citrus trees) dominate American commercial production. Complete listings of crop species, their commercial growing regions in the United States, crop volumes and values, and oil producers are difficult to ascertain (Simon 1990).

Products derived from native plant species fall into several broad categories. Different industrial methods of distillation concentrate natural compounds in plants for commercial uses as flavors and fragrances. Essential "oils" are not necessarily oil compounds. They consist of many volatile, that is, evaporating or atomizing, plant compounds that give a characteristic fragrance to plants. Many aromatic plant compounds repel animals and microbes. Industrial chemists use these plant compounds in air fresheners, bath products, diffusers, hair- and skin-care products, inhalants, massage oils, and perfumes. Food flavorists also use many of these same essential oils to flavor foods or to impart a combination of fragrance or flavor to pharmaceuticals.

Large commercial fragrance industries have been in business for many years, and their markets, often very specialized, extend around the world. A few species native to the United States have a long tradition of commercial industrial uses as fragrances and have international markets: eastern arborvitae and eastern redcedar, for example. Other species such as wintergreen *(Gaultheria procumbens)* and sassafras *(Sassafras albidum),* although native to North America, are increasingly grown commercially in other countries, in particular China and Vietnam. Many other species native to the United States and its territories are no longer produced commercially because costs of labor and production are prohibitive (Bauer, Garber, and Surburg 1997).

Rural residents can find employment in fragrance-related businesses in several ways. Certain common species such as balsam fir are still wildcrafted in the Northeast and the north central states. Large areas of black spruce *(Picea mariana)* forests in Alaska provide foliage boughs for distillation. Quality and sufficient quantity are best guaranteed when trees are tended for increased foliage production. Agricultural cultivation of native species can lessen the harvest pressure on wild populations. Another role for rural residents is to manage a collection site or "shed." This requires investments, such as storage for plant materials. Most large fragrance corporations are located close to major transportation centers, for example, the tri-state area around New York City. The likelihood of a rural entrepreneur establishing a lucrative business with large corporate firms at great distance from an urban center is small unless the entrepreneur can produce for established or niche markets. Setting up a distillation business requires even more resources, but there is potential for greater returns and for new job opportunities in rural communities. Expertise in organic chemistry, chemical engineering, fragrance marketing, and local flora are required for large-scale production. Some universities in France, such as in Clermont-Ferrand, offer degrees specifically in fragrance production. Commonly, producers of high-quality essential oils and related products in the United States have studied in Europe before undertaking a business venture.

Many plants native to North America have been cultivated elsewhere for oil production, such as grand fir. People have introduced exotic plant species with popular fragrances to the United States; many have escaped cultivation and are now growing wild. This stands in stark contrast to the many native species whose potential for flavoring and fragrance are barely, if at all, known. A partial list of species native to the United States used for essential oil production in North America includes balsam fir, sweet birch *(Betula lenta),* alligator juniper *(Juniperus deppeana),* eastern red cedar, Labrador-tea *(Ledum groenlandicum),* black spruce, eastern white pine, goldenrod *(Solidago canadensis),* northern white cedar *(Thuja occidentalis),* and eastern hemlock *(Tsuga canadensis).* The range of species currently used in the perfume industry is narrow, particularly when only North American species are considered. By contrast, resins and oils are important NTFPs in the United States. Opportunities exist for entrepreneurs interested in gathering, buying, and distilling plants and lichens from U.S. forests. Numerous native species are grown elsewhere and used for oil production, but there are still unexplored U.S. native plants with possibilities for oil production.

Diverse peoples in the United States have followed their cultural traditions for gathering wild plants historically for personal uses. Native Hawaiians, Native Alaskans, Hispanics in the American Southwest, and Indian nations across the United States are important bearers of traditional and subsistence use. Moerman (1998) provides a comprehensive summary of native plant species used as fragrances and incense that have subsistence and cultural importance. Conservation of many of these species is important for land managers and landowners, especially in areas that comprise ceded lands or customary use lands of Indian tribes as defined in treaties between the U.S. government and sovereign Indian tribes.

ARTS AND CRAFTS

The use of nontimber forest products in arts and crafts is an integral part of innumerable traditions in the United States. From Native American use of bark, willow, and branches in baskets, masks, traditional and ceremonial dress, to doll-making and baskets in the Appalachians, to furniture, birdhouses, bowls, and other well-known and admired Shaker products, the plants used are as varied as the products created. Many sources have documented the use of nontimber forest products in arts and crafts (e.g., Emery 1998; de Geus 1995). An Internet search yields innumerable sites for basket weaving, basket-making supplies, crafts, and cane chairs, to name a few products. Although many of the plant materials used in arts and crafts come from India, there are products in the United States that are unequalled anywhere else in the world, such as the pinecones from sugar pine *(Pinus lambertiana)* and western white pine *(Pinus monticola).* The arts and crafts markets have experienced great increases in demand. Since many of the products are created in rural communities and are traded or sold without records, information about these markets has not been summarized. In addition, the diversity of products makes these markets difficult to track as a group. It should be acknowledged, however, that these are significant products that contribute in important ways to household economies and have important meaning across U.S. cultures.

U.S. EXPORTS OF NTFPS

Markets abroad for native plant, lichen, and fungi species and products from the United States create export demand. Tracking products from individual species or from species groups nationally is usually difficult. No formal and uniform standards for collecting national production data and value are in place for most nontimber forest products, although there are notable exceptions such as maple syrup or pecan *(Carya illinoinensis)* production. For NTFPs exported from the United States, however, the situation is different. Since 1989, the United States has applied the Harmonized Tariff Schedule to track the values and quantities of all exports from and imports to the United States. The schedule sets international conventions to classify all internationally traded goods with a six-digit number. Each nation may then add four additional digits to track goods traded internationally that are of special concern or interest to that country.

Table 9 lists the Harmonized Tariff Codes (HTC) for the three kinds of export products covered in this section: NTFPs that come directly from native species growing wild in forests, forest openings, and woodlands; NTFPs from native species grown as agricultural row crops; and products from native species growing in nonforest environments, whether wild or domesticated. The table cannot be clearly organized to illustrate these three kinds of export products because of the aggregation of unlike materials, which is also a handicap in analyzing product data. For example, HTC 3301.29.5045 consists of cedar wood oil, a product from at least four species in the United States, with both clove oil and nutmeg oil, products derived from species not native to the United States. Some HTCs are so broad that it is impossible to describe trade in individual species. For example, fresh foliage and branches (HTC 0604.91.0000) covers many species with many different uses. Conclusions about such subgroups as floral greens or holiday greens must be drawn from other information sources. For product groups such as mosses and lichens (HTC 0604.10.0000), weights or volumes are meaningless because the range of water content differs substantially among products being exported. Only information on value for these products is available through the Harmonized Trade Schedule (HTS).

Table 9. Harmonized Tariff Codes (HTCs) in the Harmonized Tariff Schedule (HTS) for nontimber forest and other related products derived from native species and exported from the United States, 1989–1998

HTS number	Product description	Species included	Time series
0604.10.0000	Mosses and lichens	Various	1989–1998
0604.91.0000	Fresh foliage, branches	Various	1989–1998
0604.99.0000	Dried, dyed, bleached, impregnated, or otherwise prepared foliage and branches	Various	1989–1998
0709.51.0000	Mushrooms, fresh or chilled	Various	1989–1998
0709.52.0000	Truffles, fresh or chilled	Various	1989–1998
0810.40.0024	Wild blueberries, fresh	*Vaccinium* spp.	1993–1998
0810.40.0050	Cranberries, fresh	*Vaccinium macrocarpon, V. oxycoccos*	1989–1998
0811.40.0028	Cultivated blueberries, fresh	*Vaccinium* spp.	1993–1998
0811.90.2024	Wild blueberries, frozen	*Vaccinium* spp.	1993–1998
0811.90.2028	Cultivated blueberries, frozen	*Vaccinium* spp.	1993–1998
0813.40.2010	Wild blueberries, dried	*Vaccinium* spp.	1993–1998
0802.90.1000	Pecans, unshelled	*Carya illinoinensis*	1989–1998
0802.90.1500	Pecans, shelled	*Carya illinoinensis*	1989–1998
0905.00.0000	Vanilla beans	*Vanilla planifolia*	1989–1998
1211.20.0020	Cultivated ginseng, fresh or dried	*Panax quinquefolius, P. trifolius*	1989–1998
1211.20.0040	Wild ginseng, fresh or dried	*Panax quinquefolius, P. trifolius*	1989–1998
1515.60.0000	Jojoba oil	*Simmondsia chinensis*	1989–1998
1702.20.0000	Maple sugar and maple syrup	Mostly *Acer saccharum*	1989–1998
2008.19.3010	Pignolia (pine nuts)	Mostly *Pinus edulis*	1989–1998
2008.99.1910	Wild blueberries, canned	*Vaccinium* spp.	1992–1998
3201.30.0000	Oak or chestnut extracts for tanning	*Castanea* spp.; *Lithocarpus densiflorus, Quercus* spp.	1989–1998
3301.29.5045	Cedar wood oil, clove oil, nutmeg oil	*Juniperus virginiana, J. deppeana*	1989–1998
3805.10.0000	Gum, wood, or sulfate turpentine oils	Mostly *Pinus palustris*	1989–1998
3805.20.0000	Pine oil	*Pinus* spp.	1989–1998

Source: U.S. Department of Commerce, International Tariff Commission

This section will discuss exports from U.S. customs districts (CDs) for the following product categories: medicinal plants, foods, decorative foliage, and nonfood plant oils and extracts. Values of export products are expressed in 1995 dollars throughout this section to remove effects of inflation. Using HTS data to outline global commodity chains for NTFPs is a very useful starting point and, in most cases, is the best source of information available on these products. Many of the species have been domesticated and are commercially cultivated to varying degrees. Data are available separately for wild and cultivated products for only a few species, such as ginseng and blueberries.

Medicinal Plants

The U.S. HTS tracks only one medicinal plant, American ginseng, and distinguishes between wildcrafted and cultivated ginseng. The per-unit export price of wild ginseng is twice to four times greater than the price for cultivated ginseng. The largest share of wild ginseng leaves the United States from the Chicago CD. Since 1995, exports of wild ginseng have fallen in value from $30 million to less than $15 million. China (including Hong Kong) has been the major importing center. Production of wild ginseng for export has remained less than two hundred metric tons annually, reflecting a maximum capacity for limited national production. The volume of cultivated ginseng production is about ten times greater than wild ginseng in the export market. The Chicago CD exports the largest quantity of cultivated ginseng, reflecting the traditional agricultural production centers in the Upper Midwest. The price of cultivated ginseng has dropped 75 percent since its peak in 1992 at $80 million.

Foods

Most categories in the HTC system identifiable to species or to species groups refer to food. In the case of edible wild mushrooms, import data from Japan and from the European Community supplement data available from the U.S. Department of Commerce, International Trade Commission. Of all native fruit products explicitly named in the HTS system, blueberries have the largest number of classifications. The HTCs distinguish between wild and cultivated blueberry crops and whether crops are exported as fresh, frozen, canned, or dried products. The division into diverse types of blueberry products allows for a more detailed analysis of amounts and trends in export markets.

Since 1993, the quantity of fresh cultivated blueberries has averaged about eight thousand metric tons valued at about $3 million, with most going to Canada. The greatest growth in blueberry exports in recent years comes from exports of frozen, cultivated blueberries, mostly *Vaccinium corymbosum* cultivars. The export value of frozen, cultivated berries climbed from less than $1 million in 1993 to $24 million in 1998. In recent years, Japan has become a larger importer of cultivated blueberries as well. Together, Japan and Canada account for more than half of the volume of U.S. exports.

Most fresh wild blueberry exports come from northern New England and New York. The major wild export species is *V. angustifolium*. Exports of fresh wild blueberries have remained roughly constant since 1993 at less than one thousand metric tons, with the largest share going to Canada. The only exception was in 1994, when exports amounted to more than four thousand metric tons.

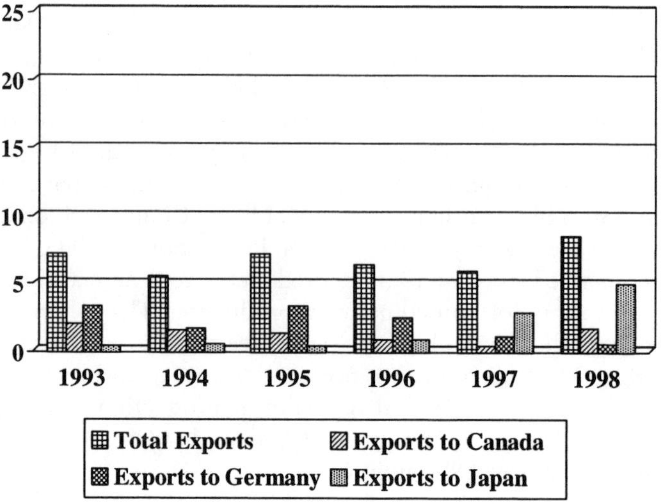

Figure 1. Value of frozen wild blueberry exports, 1993–1998, in millions of 1995 dollars.

The shift to exporting frozen products instead of fresh products has also occurred for wild blueberries. Most frozen wild blueberries are exported from Portland, Maine. In 1997 and 1998, Japan surged ahead of Canada and Germany as the leading trading partner for U.S. frozen wild blueberries. Dried wild blueberries do not have a major role in export markets. Except in 1995, dried exports amounted to less than $1 million. Canned wild blueberry exports rose steadily between 1993 and 1997, with about $4 million in sales in 1997. Japan is by far the largest importer of canned wild blueberries.

Figure 1 illustrates the extent of wild blueberry exports. Most U.S. exports of frozen wild blueberries are exported from the Portland, Maine, customs district, and most go to Germany, Canada, and Japan. The global commodity chain for wild blueberries illustrates their importance in the world market. Recent research shows that huckleberries and blueberries have high levels of antioxidants, so demand for wild *Vaccinium* leaves and berries may increase for medicinal and food uses.

Cranberries are an important export crop. Most cranberry exports consist of large cranberries *(Vaccinium macrocarpon)* from cultivated bogs, including bogs outside the natural range of the species. In recent years, exports of cranberries at higher than normal market prices from Alaska to Japan may constitute exports of small cranberries *(Vaccinium oxycoccos)*. Major crop production of large cranberries occurs in Massachusetts, New Jersey, Wisconsin, Oregon, and Washington. As with many agricultural crops of native species, pollination is essential for commercial production (see Alexander and Alexander, this volume). Canada and the United Kingdom are the largest trading partners for American cranberries. The export value in 1998 was nearly triple the real 1989 export value of $5 million. Export quantities for the same period ranged from five to eleven thousand metric tons annually, and Canada and the United Kingdom are the primary trading partners. One major factor in the growth in export sales of cranberries may stem from the increasing value placed on them for medicinal use, as cranberries are well known for their antioxidant properties.

Maple sugar and maple syrup (primarily from sugar maple, *Acer saccharum*) are produced in the United States; they are consumed domestically and exported. Under the HTC system, maple sugar and maple syrup together constitute a single product number. Quantities of sugar and syrup are not available; they would have no meaning, as quantities of liquids and solids would be combined. Since 1992, the value of maple product exports from the United States has consistently exceeded $3 million. Canada remains the largest trading partner, taking a third of all U.S. exports. Many other countries imported maple food products in small quantities from the United States.

Pecans are also consumed domestically and exported. The natural range of pecans covers the Southeast, Midwest, and Lower Prairie States. Most commercial pecans come from cultivars grown in orchards. Although pecan production remains important within the natural range of the species, considerable irrigated pecan production occurs in west Texas, New Mexico, Arizona, and increasingly in California. Australia is the only other major producer of pecans worldwide. Pecans are a delicacy in Europe as well as North America. Most pecan exports from the eastern United States leave the country shelled. Export quantities climbed from 1.5 thousand to 8 thousand metric tons between 1989 and 1998. Major trading partners are Canada, the Netherlands, and the United Kingdom. In 1998, the export value of shelled pecans equaled $48 million, in contrast to $6 million in 1989. In the Southwest, however, pecans in the shell are exported to Mexico for shelling (mostly in the state of Chihuahua) and then subsequently re-exported. The value and amount of unshelled pecan exports has fluctuated considerably from year to year. The export value of unshelled pecans is considerably smaller than the export value of shelled pecans. In 1998, unshelled pecans totaled $8 million for 4.26 metric tons.

Exports of edible wild mushrooms have surged in the past two decades. Most American exports of fresh or chilled edible mushrooms are cultivated *Agaricus* species, such as the field mushroom or champignon, and most of the volume goes to Canada. Wholesale values of cultivated mushroom species average between one and two dollars per kilogram. Markets for edible wild mushrooms from the United States, however, provide a disproportionately large share of the export value of all fresh or chilled edible mushrooms going to Japan and the European Community. This information is not discernible from the U.S. export trade data. Looking at import trade data from importing countries, however, provides one way of finding trends in wild edible mushroom exports from the United States.

In Japan, people revere matsutake or pine mushrooms as part of the entire experience of the autumn season. These wild-growing mushrooms are now rare in Japan, and most national demand there comes from imports, principally from China, North Korea, and South Korea. Smaller quantities come from Canada, the United States, and Morocco. Most commercially harvested American matsutake come from Oregon, Washington, and northwestern California. The only commercially collected species in the United States is American matsutake. In some years, American matsutake may be priced at thirty or more dollars per kilogram. Exports of American matsutake from the United States have increased greatly since 1988. However, in some years, such as 1991, 1994, and 1998, fall weather conditions may not favor fruiting of American matsutake, and over large regions, they become scarce. The Japan Tariff Organization, the Japanese equivalent of the U.S. International Trade Commission, has established a distinct HTC number for matsutake mushrooms. Tracking Japanese records of American matsutake imported to Japan from the United States allows people in both countries to know the value and volume of this U.S. export. Between 1989 and 1997, American matsutake exports to Japan from the United States climbed from $2.5 to $9.5 million. In 1997, more than 275 metric tons were exported to Japan.

Truffles (various species) are fungi that fruit primarily underground and have a pungent flavor. They have been harvested commercially in small quantities for some time. Most truffle exports come from wild-growing species from the Pacific Northwest and are exported to Canada. The value per kilogram of native truffles is very high, but production for export in most years continues to be very small.

Most edible wild mushrooms exported from the United States to the European Community come from the Pacific Northwest, and the majority are shipped from Seattle. Domestically cultivated *Agaricus* mushrooms find no market in the European Community because the product value is low and the shipping costs are high. Markets exist, however, for edible wild mushrooms. Values for chanterelles exported to the European Community may be eight to ten times greater per unit of weight than commercially grown *Agaricus* mushrooms and twice the value of chanterelles coming from major producer countries in Europe such as Poland and Lithuania (Weigand 2000). Figure 2 shows the monthly value of fresh (and presumably mostly wild) mushrooms from the Seattle CD to the original six countries of the European Community (EC-6): Belgium, France, Germany, Italy,

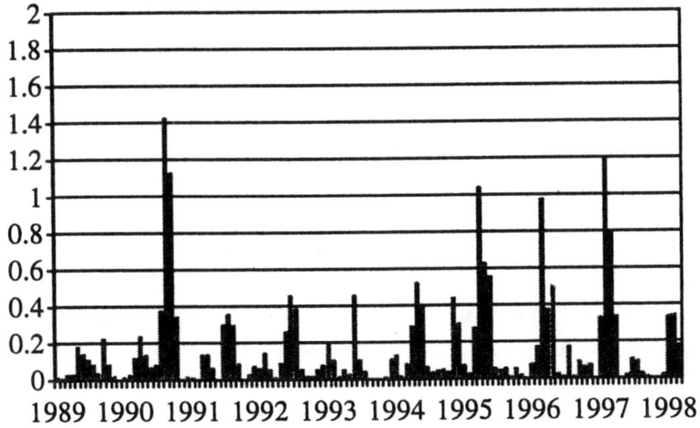

Figure 2. Value of monthly exports of fresh or chilled mushrooms from the Seattle Customs District to the EC-6 countries, in millions of 1995 dollars.

Luxembourg, and the Netherlands. Quantities produced for export differ considerably from year to year and also from month to month. Two peaks usually occur in each year—a smaller spring peak corresponding to morel harvests and a larger peak in the fall composed mostly of chanterelles. Interestingly, the mushroom export market to Italy is virtually closed. Exports of wild edible mushrooms to Italy are zero in most years in contrast to the other five EC countries.

Two other categories of food products of native plant species are part of the U.S. HTS: pinyon pine (mostly *Pinus edulis* and *P. monophylla*) nuts and vanilla *(Vanilla planifolia)* extract (native to Florida and Puerto Rico). Markets for U.S. pine nuts are largely domestic. In recent years small amounts have gone to Mexico. Although the flavor of pinyon pine nuts has international renown dating from the time of Spanish exploration, crops are unpredictable, labor costs are comparatively high in contrast to the major competitor nation, China, and traditional cultural uses by Southwest and California native peoples have the highest priority for use.

Vanilla, a vinelike orchid, reaches its natural northern and easternmost range limit in Florida and Puerto Rico. Commercial vanilla production occurs throughout the tropical Western Hemisphere, in Madagascar, and in Réunion in the Indian Ocean. The available land base in the United States and in Puerto Rico is small, and land prices and labor costs high; crop production, if it occurs at all, is very small. Any domestic production is difficult to detect in U.S. export trade data because vanilla beans and vanilla extract, products with quite different values and measures of quantity, are lumped together.

Floral and Horticultural Products

Many species constitute this broad category, and export amounts come from wildcrafted and cultivated plants, lichen, and fungi. U.S. export data for floral and horticultural products are reported in three categories: mosses and lichens; fresh foliage and branches; and preserved foliage, branches, and flowers.

Since 1992, the value of moss and lichen exports has been increasing steadily. Mosses and lichen are collected in nonagricultural environments. Most moss and lichen exports go to the Netherlands, the center of the horticultural and floral industries in the European Community. Much of the increase in exports is taking place in customs districts in the Pacific Northwest and New York. The major point of export for moss and lichen products from the Pacific Northwest en route to Europe is by way of New York, particularly during winter months when air temperature has less effect on product freshness. As much as $13 million worth of moss and lichens were exported from the Pacific Northwest in 1998, although data on the biomass removed to achieve this amount of values cannot be derived from the U.S. export data. The greatest amount of value in decorative plant exports comes from fresh foliage. The Netherlands, Canada, and Germany are the three major trading partners for American fresh foliage products. Within Europe, the Dutch flower markets are internationally famous and serve as a major resale/reexport point in the distribution channel for foliage products moving into other important European markets.

Exports of foliage and branch products to these countries have been fairly stable for the period 1989–1998. Foliage products come principally from Florida, the Southeast, and the Pacific Northwest. Many of the species grown commercially in Florida are exotic species grown horticulturally, but species exported from the Southeast and Pacific Northwest are wild-growing, mostly native species (Fischer 1992). Since 1993, the real value of exports has stabilized around $20 million annually.

Fresh-cut conifer boughs are generally not exported to Europe because of plant pest restrictions. Further, even if there were no pest restrictions, U.S. producers would have difficulty competing in Europe's well-established and highly competitive bough industry due to the high cost of shipping and the strong European preference for blue-green noble fir boughs grown primarily in Denmark.

Products that are categorized in the U.S. export data as dried, dyed, bleached, impregnated, preserved, or otherwise prepared flowers, foliage, and branches may be either native or exotic species and may originate from crop or wild populations. The volume of foreign trade in preserved floral products is lower than for fresh (or fresh-appearing) floral greens. Canada and Mexico have taken increasing shares of this export market since 1992.

Germany and the Netherlands are tied for third place in value of exports of preserved foliage. Exports to Europe fluctuate considerably from year to year, but the value of export production among the traditional producer regions has remained constant at about $15 million annually during the last decade.

Resins and Oils

The United States has several species and species groups that contribute to world markets for carrier oils, essential oils, and oleoresins, but very few of these species have individual HTCs. Jojoba *(Simmondsia chinensis)*, native to the deserts of California and Arizona as well as adjacent Mexico, is the most important native species. Two species, eastern redcedar and alligator juniper, constitute most of the production of cedar oil in the United States. Some production of cedar oil from western redcedar in the Pacific Northwest and from eastern arborvitae in the Upper Midwest may also be exported, but most production of oils of these two species comes from Canada. Unfortunately, clear conclusions about cedar oil export data are impossible because the same HTC code in the United States includes nutmeg oil and clove oil.

Pine oils can be produced from the foliage and bark of numerous pine species in the United States, but most comes from the Southeast, where pines are the major timber species. Pine oil is a by-product of the nontimber biomass from whole tree harvesting. Most exports leave by way of the Charleston, South Carolina, Savannah, Georgia, Miami, and Tampa, Florida, customs districts. The two major trading partner nations are Canada and the United Kingdom. Total export value has fluctuated between $6 and $9 million between 1989 and 1998.

Production of turpentines from gum and wood products, primarily from pine species and long-leaf pine *(Pinus palustris)* in particular, is concentrated in the Southeast. Target partner trading countries and ports of departure are different. On the one hand, the Savannah customs district is the major point of origin for export to France, the major European trading partner. Most turpentine destined for Mexico, the other major trading partner, passes through the Laredo, Texas, customs district. The total value of exports of turpentine differs considerably from year to year (between $3 and $8 million), and the total value is usually less than that of pine oil exports.

CONCLUSION

This overview of some of the many nontimber forest products and other native species from the United States captures only part of the economic activity in the domestic and international marketplace for these products. The export products specifically included in U.S. export data generally have long traditions of international trade. Products that have become important in export markets more recently include wild edible fungi, mosses, and lichens. Another distinction is that between wild and cultivated species. Commercial exportation of species such as pecans and cranberries relies almost entirely on agricultural crops. Blueberries and ginseng, in contrast, continue to maintain separate markets for both wild and cultivated crops, with the wild crop volume being considerably smaller and more valuable per unit of quantity than the cultivars or agriculturally grown product. The emerging significance in international trade of some crops from native species, such as American matsutake, appears to arise more from international demand than from any concerted marketing effort on the part of harvesters, landowners, or public land managers. In addition, there is little tradition in the United States of formal collective use rights to forest resources by local communities (see Love, this volume).

Scrutinizing biological diversity for new applications of natural products or for insights into new applications has not been national policy in the United States except in times of crisis such as the world wars of the twentieth century. Few countries have the diversity of ecosystems—crossing arctic, subarctic, temperate, subtropical, and tropical climate zones—that the United States has. In our moments of introspection apart from making or enjoying our wealth, a collective American discussion is perhaps in order concerning the conservation, enjoyment, and intelligent use of biological diversity. We might well ask if we are managing our biological diversity, and in particular our nontimber forest resources, in our own best interests. Do we see biological diversity as a source of wealth or as an obstacle to our wealth?

Countries such as Russia and India that have known famines and plagues pay attention to the role of forest resources as food and medical supplies for its people. By contrast, there is no national food policy in the United States in the event of crisis. A look to California reveals some noteworthy trends. The population of California is projected to double in thirty years. A culture with First World material expectations and Third World population growth taxes its natural environment. No major cultivated plant crop in California except jojoba is native to that state. However, the natural environment is replete with endemic species that are largely ignored. In California, soils salt, cropland, and savanna disappear, and the climate changes. Without concerted social policy, the elements for a crisis build themselves. Policies to avoid crises rather than policies to respond to crises are more likely to better conserve social values and personal security.

REFERENCES

Acker, Randy. 1986. *Harvesting Wild Edible Mushrooms in Washington: An Issue Paper*. Prepared for the Wild Edible Mushroom Task Group, November 3. Olympia, WA: Department of Natural Resources.

Alexander, S. J., D. Pilz, N. S. Weber, E. Brown, and V. A. Rockwell. In review. "Mushrooms, Trees and Money: Price Projections of Commercial Mushrooms and Timber in the Pacific Northwest."

Allen, John W. 1950. *Marketing Woodlot Products in the State of Washington*. Bulletin 1. Olympia, WA: Washington Department of Conservation and Development, Institute of Forest Products.

Bauer, K., D. Garbe, and H. Surburg. 1997. *Common Fragrance and Flavor Materials: Preparation, Properties, and Uses*. 3d ed., rev. New York: John Wiley and Sons.

Blatner, K. A., and S. Alexander. 1998. "Recent Price Trends for Nontimber Forest Products in the Pacific Northwest." *Forest Products Journal* 48(10): 28–34.

Blatner, K. A., and W. E. Schlosser. 1997. "The Floral and Christmas Greens Industry of the Pacific Northwest." Project report to the USDA Forest Service, Pacific Northwest Research Station.

Blumenthal, M. 1999. "Market Report: Herb Market Levels after Five Years of Boom." *HerbalGram* 47:64–65.

Brevoort, P. 1996. "The U.S. Botanical Market—An Overview." *HerbalGram* 36:49–57.

———. 1998. "The Booming U.S. Botanical Market: A New Overview." *HerbalGram* 44:33–44.

Castells, Manuel, and Alejandro Portes. 1989. "World Underneath: The Origins, Dynamics, and Effects of the Informal Economy." In *The Informal Economy: Studies in Advanced and Less Developed Countries*, ed. A. Portes, M. Castells, and L. A. Benton, pp. 11–37. Baltimore: Johns Hopkins University Press.

Chamberlin, E. H. 1933. *The Theory of Monopsolistic Competition*. Cambridge, MA: Harvard University Press.

Cronemiller, Lynn F., John B. Woods Jr., Charles H. Ladd, Alvin Parker, E. D. Hanneman, A. H. Sasser, C. W. Maus, and W. S. Phelps. 1950. *Secret Treasures in the Forest*. Bulletin 14. Salem, OR: Oregon State Board of Forestry.

De Geus, Nellie. 1995. *Botanical Forest Products in British Columbia: An Overview*. Victoria, BC: British Columbia Ministry of Forest, Integrated Resources Policy Branch.

Douglass, Bernard S. 1975. *Floral Greenery from Pacific Northwest Forests*. Portland, OR: U.S. Department of Agriculture, Forest Service, Pacific Northwest Region.

Emery, Marla. 1998. "Invisible Livelihoods: Nontimber Forest Products in Michigan's Upper Peninsula." Ph.D. diss., Rutgers University.

Fischer, Hartmut. 1992. "Schnittgrün aus Übersee: Transport per Flugzeug oder Schiffscontainer [Cut Greens from Overseas: Transport by Airplane or Ship Container]." In German. *Gärtnerbörse und Gartenwelt* 92(39): 1937–1940.

Foster, S. 1995. *Forest Pharmacy: Medicinal Plants in American Forests*. Durham, NC: Forest History Society.

Gereffi, Gary. 1994. "The Organization of Buyer-driven Global Commodity

Chains: How U.S. Retailers Shape Overseas Production Networks." In *Commodity Chains and Global Capitalism,* ed. G. Gereffi and M. Korzeniewicz, pp. 95–122. Westport, CT: Greenwood Press.

Grünwald, Jörg. 1994. "Europe: Phytomedicines, Market Growth, and Investment Opportunities." In *Proceedings: Drug Discovery and Commercial Opportunities in Medicinal Plants,* 19–20 September, Arlington, VA. Southborough, MA: International Business Communications.

Heckman, Hazel. 1951. "The Happy Brush Pickers of the High Cascades." *Saturday Evening Post,* October 6, 1951.

Hopkins, Terence K., and Immanuel Wallerstein. 1986. "Commodity Chains in the World Economy Prior to 1800." *Review* 10(1): 157–170.

———. 1994. "Commodity Chains: Construct and Research." In *Commodity Chains and Global Capitalism,* ed. G. Gereffi and M. Korzeniewicz, pp. 17–34. Westport, CT: Greenwood Press.

Klink, B. 1997. "Alternative Medicines: Is Natural Really Better?" *Drug Topics* 141(11): 99–103.

Landes, P. 1986. "An Overview of Spice Marketing in the Past Twenty Years." *HerbalGram* 10:7–10.

Landes, Peter, and Mark Blumenthal. 1988. "Market Report." *HerbalGram* 16:2.

Leonard, Madeline. 1998. *Invisible Work, Invisible Workers.* New York: St. Martins Press.

Lewington, A. 1993. *A Review of Importation of Medicinal Plants and Plant Extracts into Europe.* Gland, Swizerland: WWF/International Plant Program/ IUCN.

Love, T., E. Jones, and L. Liegel. 1998. "Valuing the Temperate Rainforest: Wild Mushrooming on the Olympic Peninsula Biosphere Reserve." *Ambio Special Report* 9:16–25.

Lozano, B. 1985. "High Technology, Cottage Industry." Ph.D. diss., University of California, Davis.

Mater, Catherine. 1994. "Factors Affecting Special Forest Products' Marketing and Business Management throughout North America." In *Proceedings: The Business and Science of Special Forest Products*, ed. C. Schepf, pp. 153–158. Portland, OR: Western Forestry and Conservation Association.

———. 1997. "Consumer Trends, Market Opportunities, and New Approaches to Sustainable Development of Special Forest Products." In *Special Forest Products: Biodiversity Meets the Marketplace*, ed. N. Vance and J. Thomas, pp. 8–25. General Technical Report GTR-WO-63. Washington, DC: U.S. Department of Agriculture, Forest Service.

McRobert, Gussie. 1985. "A Walk on the Wild Side." *Oregon Business* (October): 105–106.

Meares, Portia. 1987. "The Economic Significance of Herbs." *HerbalGram* 13:1, 6.

Meyer Resources. 1995. *A Preliminary Analysis of the Economic Importance of the 1994 Pine Mushroom Industry of the Nass Valley Area, British Columbia.* Victoria, BC: Meyer Resources.

Moerman, Daniel E. 1998. *Native American Ethnobotany.* Portland, OR: Timber Press.

Norvell, L. 1995. "Loving the Chanterelle to Death? The Ten-Year Oregon Chanterelle Project." *McIlvainea* 12(1): 6–25.

Obst, J., and W. Brown. 2000. *Feasibility of a Morel Mushroom Harvest in the Northwest Territories.* Yellowknife, Northwest Territories: Arctic Ecology and Development Consulting and Deton'cho Corporation.

Pearce, D. W., ed. 1992. *The MIT Dictionary of Modern Economics.* 4th ed. Cambridge, MA: MIT Press.

Pilz, D., J. Smith, M. P. Amaranthus, S. Alexander, R. Molina, and D. Luoma. 1999. "Mushrooms and Timber: Managing Commercial Harvesting in the Oregon Cascades." *Journal of Forestry* 97(3): 4–11.

Portes, A., S. Blitzer, and J. Curtis. 1986. "The Urban Informal Sector in Uruguay: Its Internal Structure, Characteristics, and Effects." *World Development* 14:727–741.

Raynolds, Laura T. 1994. "Institutionalizing Flexibility: A Comparative Analysis of Fordist and Post-Fordist Models of Third World Agro-Export Production." In *Commodity Chains and Global Capitalism,* ed. G. Gereffi and M. Korzeniewicz, pp. 143–161. Westport, CT: Greenwood Press.

Robinson, J. 1933. *The Economics of Imperfect Competition.* New York: Macmillan.

Russell, Kenelm. 1990. "Manufacturing, Marketing, and Regulatory Considerations: Forest Fungi." Remarks presented at the Special Forest Products Workshop, 8–10 February, Portland, OR.

Schlosser, William W., and Keith A. Blatner. 1995. "The Wild Edible Mushroom Industry of Washington, Oregon, and Idaho: A 1992 Survey of Processors." *Journal of Forestry* 93(3): 31–36.

Schlosser, William W., Keith A. Blatner, and R. Chapman. 1991. "Economic and Marketing Implications of Special Forest Products Harvest in the Coastal Pacific Northwest." *Western Journal of Applied Forestry* 6(3): 67–72.

Shaw, Elmer W. 1949. *Minor Forest Products of the Pacific Northwest.* Portland, OR: U.S. Department of Agriculture, Forest Service, Pacific Northwest Forest and Range Experiment Station.

Simon, J. E. 1990. "Essential Oils and Culinary Herbs." In *Advances in New Crops,* ed. J. Janick and J. E. Simon, pp. 472–483. Portland, OR: Timber Press.

USDA Forest Service. 1982. *An Analysis of the Timber Situation in the United States, 1989–2040.* General Technical Report RM-199. Fort Collins, CO: U.S. Department of Agriculture, Forest Service, Rocky Mountain Forest and Range Experiment Station.

USDA Forest Service. 1990. *An Analysis of the Timber Situation in the United States, 1952–2030.* Forest Resource Report 23. Washington, DC: U.S. Government Printing Office.

Von Hagen, B., and R. D. Fight. 1999. *Opportunities for Conservation-Based Development of Nontimber Forest Products in the Pacific Northwest.* General Technical Report PNW-GTR-473. Portland, OR: U.S. Department of Agriculture, Forest Service.

Warren, D. D. 1996. *Production, Prices, Employment and Trade in Northwest Forest Industries, First Quarter 1996.* Resource Bulletin PNW-RB-215. Portland, OR: U.S. Department of Agriculture, Forest Service, Pacific Northwest Research Station.

Weigand, James F. 2000. "Wild Edible Mushroom Harvests in North America: Market Econometric Analysis." In *Les Champignons Forestiers: Récolte, Com-*

mercialization et Conservation de la Resource, ed. J. A. Fortin and Y. Piché, pp. 35–43. Quebec: Université Laval.

Weigand, James F., and Susan J. Alexander. Forthcoming. *Categories and Commercial Species of Nontimber Forest Products in the United States.*

Wills, Russell M., and Richard G. Lipsey. 1999. "An Economic Strategy to Develop Nontimber Forest Products and Services in British Columbia." Report, Forest Renewal BC Project PA97538-ORE, Victoria, BC.

Zohary, M., and D. Heller. 1984. *The Genus Trifolium.* Jerusalem: Israel Academy of Sciences and Humanities.

Ecological Considerations in Sustainable Use of Wild Plants

Nan C. Vance

Wild collection of plants for a variety of uses is an enduring, if not sustainable, practice of rural and indigenous people worldwide. Wild harvest of plants and plant parts for botanical or nontimber forest products contributes to commercial trade in plant material amounting to thousands of tons of raw product valued at several billion dollars. At the same time, plant species in many parts of the globe are threatened by overexploitation, destructive harvesting techniques, and loss of habitat and genetic diversity (Lange 1998). In the United States, perceptions of opportunity in these markets and plentiful biotic resources are encouraging increasing numbers of people to collect wild plants and other organisms from public and private lands. Accountability for what is taken ostensibly resides with landowners, managers, harvesters, and processors. In reality, plants and plant parts are collected, processed, used, and marketed with relatively little inventory, monitoring, or effective oversight. On managed public or private forested lands in the United States, these conditions reflect past perceptions of how forests are to be managed and how forests are valued as a whole.

Throughout the United States, forest-based resources have sustained strong social structure and economic stability in rural communities, enabling them to retain their independence and identity. Maintenance of a sustainable ecological system should be compatible with the values and relations of these communities. But economic landscapes of diverse enterprises under local control can be overwhelmed by ventures capitalized outside the community, especially if the community has little control over the flow of raw material. The consequences of these inroads into the smaller, local commercial trade and communities are complex and not always predictable (Brown 1995). However, if a community's economy depends on producing large volumes of a single commodity and forest resources can no longer sustain those volumes, the effect on the community can be devastating (Jungwirth and Brown 1997; Robbins 1997).

Recently, rural communities whose economies were dependent upon timber resources for decades are being encouraged to diversify their portfolio of forest products. Promoting commodity production from diversified forest resources appears to be based on a growing perception that the species richness of northern temperate forests is an undertapped reservoir of potential products that could provide income, even if for the short term. This perception, if put into practice, could lead to mass and repeated removal of many more species growing in the wild even though the economic benefits have not been proven (Crook and Clapp 1998). It also brings into question the wisdom of expanding this system of wild harvest when previous extractive activities have resulted in deterioration of biological diversity, forest health, and watershed integrity (National Research Council 1998). It is a formidable challenge to avail society of the uses and benefits of forests, prairies, wetlands, and other ecosystems without degrading their many diverse attributes so essential to the quality of all terrestrial life.

SUSTAINABILITY FROM AN ECOLOGICAL PERSPECTIVE

The concepts "conservation" and "sustainable" as applied to developing or managing lands have coevolved through historically different but overlapping approaches to viewing the land and its resources. In nineteenth-century America, conservation as a concept was philosophically allied with preservation of natural systems, maintaining natural landscapes, and protecting biota; yet, conservation was also the conceptual keystone of leaders in forest management for achieving steady (sustainable) production of forest resources (Pisani 1997). Sustainability has been variously applied to managing resources, economic development, and forest and watershed management practices (Pfister 1993; Mangold 1995; National Research Council 1998). In need of a unifying concept, forestland management policies of federal agencies and forest-based industries have adopted the Brundtland Commission's definition of sustainability: "development to meet the needs of the present without compromising the ability of future generations to meet their own needs" (World Commission on Environment and Development 1987). For approximately seventy-eight million hectares of National Forest System land, sustainable forestry has become the linchpin of conservation and use (USDA Forest Service 2000).

For the Forest Service, sustainable management practices continue to need scientific validation. The scientific community is linked to sustainability in the Forest Service's most recent planning rules with the understanding that its contribution is necessary to the sustainable management of resources (USDA Forest Service 2000). This involves, of course, the management of all resources including that of hundreds of species collected on public lands for a wide array of uses. In its National Strategy for Special Forest Products, the Forest Service recognizes the key role of monitoring, inventories, and research. Legislation requiring "analyses to determine whether and how harvest of forest botanical products on National Forest System lands can be conducted on a sustainable basis" (FY 2000 Department of the Interior appropriations bill) will result in agency regulations calling for assessments to assure species viability. Implied is the broader role that ecological science will play in determining how sustainable management is to be achieved. But different philosophies of land use management often underlie how conservation-related concepts, such as the notion of sustainability, are applied to the harvest and use of forestry and watershed resources (Pfister 1993; Mangold 1995; National Research Council 1998; American Forest and Paper Association 2000).

From the ecologist's perspective, sustainable development may be too narrowly defined if the definition does not include protecting ecological complexity and biological diversity (Pfister 1993; Noss 1995; Struhsaker 1998; McLarney 1999). Consistent with this view, effective resource sustainability should also address the sustainability of natural communities, habitats, and environment. This approach suggests a broader view of ecosystems with their full range of values, but with ecological limits that should not be exceeded to provide social benefits. In natural systems, sustainability should be viewed as the degree of overlap between ecological possibilities and socially desired benefits (National Research Council 1998). However, the boundaries defining that overlap are fluid, and the ecological limits to land use are not easily or well understood. Whether managing land under multiple objectives or through partitioning land so different land use and conservation values can be met, there are always trade-offs (Hunter and Calhoun 1996). In addition, as society repeatedly seeks to renegotiate how lands and resources will be used, the ability of natural systems to support those uses will be changing as well.

Regardless of land management perspectives, ecological limits to use apply directly to each botanical resource as well as to the quality of the larger environment (Odum 1997). The consequences of ignoring such limits to resource sustainability have been demonstrated repeatedly throughout the history of settlement and land use in this country. Loss of soil fertility in land along the eastern seaboard improperly used for crops such as tobacco was in part an early driver of the westward migratory movement (Williams 1900). Loss of timbered lands and threats to water resources later became prominent issues while unnumbered plant species drifted to the brink of extinction virtually unnoticed. Nevertheless, toward the end of the nineteenth century, the scale at which forests and prairies were disappearing through land use conversion and degraded through unsustainable resource extraction propelled a conservation movement that led to the passage of the Forest Reserve Act of 1891. The intent of this legislation was to set aside publicly owned forestlands in the West as preserves to protect timberlands and watersheds (Steen 1997). Under this large-scale protection resided the fates of hundreds of plant species dependent upon the way these lands were managed for timber, range, or water resources.

Land management practices on forested lands in the twentieth century were commonly directed toward specific species or resources. In the Pacific Northwest, these practices appeared to have unpredictable if not profound effects on the distribution and abundance of nontarget species (Marcot 1997). Grazing practices and land management designed to improve grazing lands also tended to reduce total plant diversity (Moseley and Crawford 1995; Packard and Ross 1997). Until about the 1970s when an ecologically based system for weed management began to gain acceptance (Sheley, Kedzie-Webb, and Maxwell 1999), little value was attributed to maintaining floristic complexity on these lands.

That sustainable land management needed ecological tools to monitor and quantify land use was recognized as far back as early in the last century. It was out of concern for rangelands overgrazed by cattle in the Great Basin that the concept of "carrying capacity" then emerged (Young 1998). The concept suggests that land has a capacity to support a limited number of users but also a limited intensity of extractive use. Operationally defined by ecologists and wildlife biologists as the number of animals supported by an area (Young 1998), the focus was on the user. But the concept suggested that there were ecological limits on the land as well. Managing land for full productivity (in terms of the user) began to be viewed as not sustainable (Langston 1995).

Ecological studies conducted at the Forest Service's Great Basin Experiment Station in the early 1900s to determine the carrying capacity of a given area revealed that in fragile, arid intermountain lands, vegetation recovered slowly and frequent removal was detrimental to the native plant communities (Alexander 1997). Those research efforts scientifically validated that long-term sustainability is based on a biologically rational system supporting that which is being used and imposing limits on the user. Scientific investigations demonstrated how overuse of a resource resulted in wider consequences affecting plant communities, soil fertility, and watersheds but unfortunately, in many instances, not until serious ecological damage was done (Langston 1995).

SUSTAINABILITY FROM A USE PERSPECTIVE

Are there any intrinsic features of selective resource use that have elements of sustainability? Selection of plant resources for local availability, abundance, and quality of desirable species are energy-saving criteria for a variety of animals from insects to ungulates. As resources are depleted, animals migrate or select different species. If they cannot, their use is regulated by their failure to thrive or reproduce. Humans also have generally selected species that were abundant and accessible for use, not necessarily as a strategy to sustain the resource, but as a practical way of sustaining themselves. That indigenous people select from diverse and locally abundant plants suggests they might favor consistently available botanical resources that could sustain them at a most efficient level (Moran 1979; Phillips and Meilleur 1998; Salick et al. 1999). Plants that are widespread, abundant, and common usually have robust regeneration, reproduction, and growth.

In addition, spatially and seasonally selective user patterns, such as migrating to grassland areas for digging roots in the spring and to upland forests for harvesting berries in the fall, diffuse harvest over a variety of species and would tend to conserve plant resources (Turner and Efrat 1982; Hunn 1991). In many cases, setting spatially limited fires to open the understory would increase berry production or otherwise improve abundance of usable plants (Beckham and Shaffer 1991; Anderson 1996). Thus, selecting species that vary in food production over space and time and are common, abundant, and locally available as well as augmenting desired species' persistence through cultural treatments that maintain biocomplexity are practices that might contribute to sustainability of used species without detriment to whole plant communities.

Similar user practices may in some degree apply to traditional wildcrafting. In an assessment of over seventy floral and fungal species that supply many herbal and other commodities in the Pacific Northwest, most of the species harvested were found to be common and relatively abundant (Vance, Borsting, and Pilz 2001). Some of the most common and widely distributed understory plants of the Pacific Northwest coastal forests such as salal *(Gaultheria shalon)*, sword fern *(Polystichum munitum)*, and evergreen huckleberry *(Vaccinium ovatum)* have supported "brush pickers" in that region for decades (Shaw 1949; USDA 1963). Across the United States, herbalists and wildcrafters have been collecting, using, and selling products from local populations of plant species for generations (USDA 1963; Foster 1995; Emery 1998). Their livelihoods probably depended upon local trade and reliable markets, but they also depended upon the abundance, diversity, and availability of the local biota to provide a dependable resource without the expenditure of much economic energy (capital).

In addition, many of the products come from renewable portions of plants or their fruits. Forest managers concerned with other resources generally paid little attention to these wildcrafters; their activities to a large extent were self-regulated. This user behavior may contribute to sustainability but does not ensure it. Changes in climate or the environment, density of overstory canopy, intensity of disturbance, and normal demographic fluctuations can alter a plant species' abundance and distribution and thus its capacity to furnish resources. In addition, any model of sustainable use breaks down if the harvest/user population increases rapidly; scarcity is positively correlated with value, as with collectible orchids or wild ginseng; value to the user is short term and exacerbated by poverty; and users are not vested in the future of the land's resources (Freese 1996).

Commodification does not necessarily result in overharvesting, but if wild harvest levels increase for an appreciable period to compensate for low prices or to meet a growing or large demand, the levels may eventually exceed species' biological limits. A plant's life-form and parts used and the time it takes a plant to reach reproductive maturity also determine how soon a species' biological limits are reached (Cunningham 1991). Plant populations that are limited by reproduction, regeneration, and restricted habitat will be especially vulnerable. The consequences of unsustainable extraction can further strain native plant communities and habitats in sensitive and heavily disturbed areas and even place species at risk that heretofore have been regarded as common and abundant (Freese 1996).

If harvest and utilization practices exceed the biological limits of a species, they can lead to loss of genetic diversity, alterations and loss of plant communities, and degradation of habitat. An extreme example of this scenario as reported in April 1998 by the U.S. Embassy in Beijing is "facai grass," a small plant that grows on the arid, sandy grasslands of northeastern China. It is harvested for inclusion in meals desired by affluent Chinese. The gatherers rake the grasslands for the tiny shreds of facai, taking out grasses and other plants along with facai that stabilize the soil. The destruction of grasslands from a combination of facai gathering fueled by extreme poverty, logging, destructive farming and grazing practices, drought, and rising population was reported to have destroyed an estimated thirty-three million acres in Inner Mongolia alone.

SUSTAINABILITY FROM A MANAGEMENT PERSPECTIVE

Kinds and amounts of harvest and use that might sustain the user, plant resource, and habitat were suggested earlier. But how does one evaluate if sustainability is in effect? On managed but uncultivated forestlands, a largely unanswered question is how to measure sustainable harvest of botanically useful species. On timberlands, sustainability of a commercial species is quantified by the replacement of the species harvested in a purported sustained yield formula. Although monitoring harvest activities is important, monitoring a number of plant populations across a species' native range to determine the level at which extraction exceeds replacement may not be practicable or useful. As was true for calculating carrying capacity, harvest levels that begin to reach a plant population's replacement capacity may be too high for maintaining population viability in the long term. Accurate models of plant population response to harvest would have to account for climatic variations that affect population demographics, recruitment, mortality, and reproduction as well as other factors cited earlier that affect species distribution, abundance, and growth (Marcot and Murphy 1996).

Even if measurements could produce quantifiable data in monitoring the parameters considered best for indexing sustainability, theories and assumptions guide the choice of parameters to be measured. An important role of a biological scientist is to challenge prevailing theories and assumptions such as those that define forest health (Costanza 1992). Through this process, scientists may better define ecological relationships that would impose limitations on extractive practices (Noss 1995). This reevaluation is necessary. Consider that about one decade ago the prevailing view supported managing vegetation on public lands to enhance the survival and growth of a few key resources. A decade later managers on public lands who were charged primarily with sustained yield management of a limited number of species are being asked to manage forest ecosystems and to sustain a broad biocomplexity. This change in the way society views public lands suggests that consideration would have to be given to a wide array of organisms and a web of ecological interdependencies across diverse habitats. Whether it is the study of plant communities, pollination systems, or human collection and use of plants, there is insufficient research that has analyzed interactions among species and how they may be connected within a larger system (Willson 1996).

Complex and large-scale resource models are being developed, but models that incorporate ecological information are only as effective as the assumptions that underlie them. They will be of little value in projecting long-term species or ecosystem sustainability if they omit critical plant-animal interactions including those that involve human activities. Many plant-animal mutualisms in North American forests, such as plant-pollinator relationships so critical to the existence of flowering plants, are simply not known. There is evidence also that ecological theories of succession and widely used models of disturbance developed for forest landscapes do not apply well to herbs, small shrubs, and epiphytic plant communities. Understory and nonforest plant communities are highly variable within the temporal and spatial scales used to measure forests; in addition, their response to disturbances is likely to occur below detection at large spatial scales of forest organizational structure (Wimberly et al. 2000).

GLOBAL ISSUES

The connection of biology and ecology to cultural, social, and economic issues also should be reexamined as assumptions about the economics of use and ecological benefit are being challenged. The sociology of rural communities often underscores the need to understand more about the biota to which these communities are connected and ecosystems of which they are a part and a beneficiary (Crook and Clapp 1998). This integration of biology and sociology has appeared in ethnobotanical studies that investigate how indigenous people use and manage plants, modify natural landscapes, and retain their traditional knowledge (Turner and Bell 1973). Richards (1997) and Anderson and Rowney (1999) have investigated how harvest and use strategies of indigenous populations in the United States maintain a sustainable relationship with fungi and plants. By showing that the number of species useful to an indigenous tribe of people in Borneo strongly correlated with the number of species across all vegetation types, Salick et al. (1999) demonstrated how patterns of use interact with biological diversity. They further inquire if conservation of useful plant diversity is best served by focusing on patterns, processes, or people's uses of diversity.

In other parts of the globe, studies are evaluating ways to improve harvest practices, introduce agroforestry, and intensify management to sustain those resources that could support communities of people for whom a subsistence lifestyle is no longer possible (Srivastava, Lambert, and Vietmeyer 1995; Clay 1996). These strategies include using fewer species than traditionally employed in a subsistence lifestyle but more than in commodity-producing agriculture, and incorporating low-energy methods for enhancing resource productivity. Their success depends on locally common and abundant species, self-regulated user communities, and benefits of commodities that are directly realized by the users (Clay 1996). These commercial use strategies are largely experimental; whether they will remain viable within the carrying capacity of land partitioned out of increasingly fragmented landscapes remains an open question.

The contribution of ecology to the basic knowledge of traditional botanical harvest could be considerable but is not well supported by the beneficiaries of these harvested commodities. Conservation studies of medicinal plant resources are largely underfunded or a voluntary activity. The great majority of institutional funding is flowing into biotechnological solutions to the problems of human health and increasing food, fiber, and energy to meet continually growing consumption. It is no coincidence that the most studied plants represent the leading economic plant taxa in the world. Concurrent with increasing consumption is the changing status of biological systems of about 500 plant species at risk of going extinct in the United States, 404 are currently listed by the U.S. Fish and Wildlife Service as threatened (78) or endangered (326). Maintaining and increasing food production through developing agricultural and biological technologies will continue to be a global priority as global carrying capacity shrinks. But the loss of native plant diversity that accompanies the shrinking carrying capacity of nonagricultural systems may also have a bearing on the future health of human society (Phillips and Meilleur 1998).

The conservation and sustainable management of hundreds of commercially important native plant and fungal species depends upon implementing effective strategies not only for sustainable harvest, but also for species, habitat, and ecosystem protection. Although inventories, monitoring, and acquiring and applying ecological information will not guarantee that plant species, communities, and habitats will be sustained, they are at greater risk without these actions. If long-term sustainable harvest of wild plants and plant parts for a variety of human benefits is coupled with protecting forest flora and habitats and avoiding risk to the environment, it will save cost to society as well.

The challenge will be to accommodate the biological and ecological requirements of these species and their habitats as social and economic demands on resources continue to intensify. Biological and ecological understanding of plants, plant communities, or biological systems may be necessary but is certainly not sufficient for sustaining their capacity to provide for future generations. Knowledge in this case is not power. If the ecological feedbacks and the capacity of the system to sustain use are finessed or ignored, biological and ecological knowledge will only seek to explain why species disappear and land is degraded, but will be powerless to do anything about it.

REFERENCES

Alexander, T. G. 1997. "From Rule-of-Thumb to Scientific Range Management: The Case of the Intermountain Region of the Forest Service." In *American Forests: Nature, Culture, and Politics,* ed. C. Miller, pp. 179–194. Lawrence: University Press of Kansas.

American Forest and Paper Association. 2000. *Sustainable Forestry Initiative Program.* Washington, DC: American Forest and Paper Association.

Anderson, M. K. 1996. "The Ethnobotany of Deergrass, *Muhlenbergia rigens* (Poaceae): Its Uses and Fire Management by California Indian Tribes." *Economic Botany* 50:409–422.

Anderson, M. K., and D. L. Rowney. 1999. "The Edible Plant *Dichelostemma Capitatum:* Its Vegetative Reproduction Response to Different Indigenous Harvesting Regimes in California." *Restoration Ecology* 7:231–240.

Beckham, S. D., and S. Shaffer. 1991. "Patience and Persistence: The Cow Creek Band of Umpqua Tribe of Indians." In *The First Oregonians,* ed. C. M. Buan and R. Lewis, pp. 89–94. Portland, OR: Oregon Council for the Humanities.

Brown, B. A. 1995. *In Timber Country*. Philadelphia: Temple University Press.
Clay, Jason W. 1996. *Generating Income and Conserving Resources: 20 Lessons from the Field*. Washington, DC: World Wildlife Fund.
Costanza, R. 1992. "Toward an Operational Definition of Ecosystem Health." In *Ecosystem Health: New Goals for Environmental Management,* ed. R. Costanza, B. G. Norton, and B. D. Haskell, pp. 239–256. Washington, DC: Island Press.
Crook, Carolyn, and Roger Alex Clapp. 1998. "Is Market-Oriented Forest Conservation a Contradiction in Terms?" *Environmental Conservation* 25:131–145.
Cunningham, A. B. 1991. "Development of a Conservation Policy on Commercially Exploited Medicinal Plants: A Case Study from Southern Africa." In *The Conservation of Medicinal Plants,* ed. O. Akerele, V. Heywood, and H. Synge, pp. 337–351. London: Cambridge University Press.
Emery, Marla R. 1998. "Invisible Livelihoods: Nontimber Forest Products in Michigan's Upper Peninsula." Ph.D. diss., Rutgers University.
Foster, S. 1995. *Forest Pharmacy Medicinal Plants in American Forests*. Durham, NC: Forest History Society.
Freese, C. 1996. *The Commercial, Consumptive Use of Wild Species: Managing It for the Benefit of Biodiversity*. Washington, DC: World Wildlife Fund.
Hunn, E. 1991. "The Plateau." In *The First Oregonians,* ed. C. M. Buan and R. Lewis, pp. 9–14. Portland, OR: Oregon Council for the Humanities.
Hunter, M. L., and A. Calhoun. 1996. "A Triad Approach to Land-Use Allocation." In *Biodiversity in Managed Landscapes Theory and Practice,* ed. R. C. Szaro and D. W. Johnston, pp. 477–491. New York: Oxford University Press.
Jacobs, J. S., M. F. Carpinelli, and R. L. Sheley. 1999. "Revegetating Noxious Weed-Infested Rangeland." In *Biology and Management of Noxious Rangeland Weeds,* ed. R. L. Sheley and J. K. Petroff, pp. 133–141. Corvallis: Oregon State University Press.
Jungwirth, Lynn, and Beverly A. Brown. 1997. "Special Forest Products in a Forest Community Strategy and Co-Management Schemes Addressing Multicultural Conflicts." In *Special Forest Products—Biodiversity Meets the Marketplace,* ed. N. C. Vance and J. Thomas, pp. 88–107. Pub. no. GTR-WO-63. Washington, DC: U.S. Department of Agriculture, Forest Service.
Lange, D. 1998. *Europe's Medicinal and Aromatic Plants: Their Use, Trade, and Conservation*. Cambridge, UK: Traffic International Publishers.
Langston, N. 1995. *Forest Dreams, Forest Nightmares*. Seattle: University of Washington Press.
Mangold, R. D. 1995. "Sustainable Development: The Forest Service's Approach." *Journal of Forestry* 93:25–28.
Marcot, B. G. 1997. "Biodiversity of Old Forests of the West: A Lesson from Our Elders." In *Creating a Forestry for the 21st Century,* ed. K. A. Kohm and J. F. Franklin, pp. 87–105. Washington, DC: Island Press.
Marcot, B. G., and D. D. Murphy. 1996. "On Population Viability Analysis and Management." In *Biodiversity in Managed Landscapes: Theory and Practice,* ed. R. C. Szaro and D. W. Johnston, pp. 58–76. New York: Oxford University Press.
McLarney, W. O. 1999. "Sustainable Development: A Necessary Means for Effective Biological Conservation." *Conservation Biology* 13:4.

Moran, E. F. 1979. *Human Adaptability and Introduction to Ecological Anthropology*. Boulder, CO: Westview Press.

Moseley, R. K., and R. C. Crawford. 1995. "Fifteen-Year Population and Habitat Changes in a Narrow Idaho Endemic *Phlox idahonis* Wherry." *Bulletin of the Torrey Botanical Club* 122:109–114.

National Research Council. 1998. *Forested Landscapes in Perspective*. Board on Agriculture, National Research Council. Washington, DC: National Academy Press.

Noss, R. G. 1995. "Ecological Integrity and Sustainability: Buzzwords in Conflict?" In *Perspectives on Ecological Integrity*, ed. L. Westra and J. Lemons, pp. 60–76. Dordrecht, Netherlands: Kluwer Academic Publishers.

Odum, E. P. 1997. *Ecology: A Bridge between Science and Society*. Sunderland, MA: Sinauer and Associates.

Olson, B. E. 1999. "Impacts of Noxious Weeds on Ecologic and Economic Systems." In *Biology and Management of Noxious Rangeland Weeds,* ed. R. L. Sheley and J. K. Petroff, pp. 4–18. Corvallis: Oregon State University Press.

Packard, S., and L. M. Ross. 1997. "Restoring Remnants." In *The Tallgrass Restoration Handbook,* ed. S. Packard and C. F. Mutel, pp. 63–87. Washington, DC: Island Press.

Pfister, R. D. 1993. "The Need and Potential for Ecosystem Management in Forests of the Inland West." In *Defining Sustainable Forestry,* ed. G. H. Aplet, N. Johnson, J. T. Olson, and V. A. Sample, pp. 217–239. Washington, DC: Island Press.

Phillips, O. L., and B. A. Meilleur. 1998. "Usefulness and Economic Potential of the Rare Plants of the United States: A Statistical Survey." *Economic Botany* 2:57–67.

Pisani, D. J. 1997. "Forests and Conservation, 1865–1890." In *American Forests: Nature, Culture, and Politics,* ed. C. Miller, pp. 15–34. Lawrence: University Press of Kansas.

Richards, R. T. 1997. "What the Natives Know." *Journal of Forestry* 95:5–10.

Robbins, W. G. 1997. "The Social Context of Forestry: The Pacific Northwest in the Twentieth Century." In *American Forests: Nature, Culture, and Politics,* ed. C. Miller, pp. 195–207. Lawrence: University Press of Kansas.

Salick, J., A. Biun, G. Martin, L. Apin, and R. Beaman. 1999. "Whence Useful Plants? A Direct Relationship between Biodiversity and Useful Plants among the Dusun of Mt. Kinabalu." *Biodiversity and Conservation* 8:797–818.

Shaw, E. W. 1949. *Minor Forest Products of the Pacific Northwest*. Portland, OR: U.S. Department of Agriculture, Forest Service, Pacific Northwest Forest and Range Experiment Station.

Sheley, R. L., S. Kedzie-Webb, and B. D. Maxwell. 1999. "Integrated Weed Management on Rangeland." In *Biology and Management of Noxious Rangeland Weeds,* ed. R. L. Sheley and J. K. Petroff, pp. 4–18. Corvallis: Oregon State University Press.

Srivastava, J., J. Lambert, and N. Vietmeyer. 1995. *Medicinal Plants: A Growing Role in Development*. Washington, DC: World Bank.

Steen, H. K. 1997. "The Beginning of the National Forest System." In *American Forests: Nature, Culture, and Politics,* ed. C. Miller, pp. 49–68. Lawrence: University Press of Kansas.

Struhsaker, T. T. 1998. "A Biologist's Perspective on the Role of Sustainable Harvest in Conservation." *Conservation Biology* 12:930–932.

Turner, N. C., and M. A. M. Bell. 1973. "The Ethnobotany of the Southern Kwakiutl Indians of British Columbia." *Economic Botany* 27:257–310.

Turner, N. J., and B. S. Efrat. 1982. "Ethnobotany of the Hesquiat Indians of Vancouver Island: Cultural Recovery Paper 2." Victoria, BC: British Columbia Provincial Museum.

USDA Forest Service. 1963. *Special Forest Products for Profit.* Agriculture Information Bulletin 278. Washington, DC: U.S. Government Printing Office.

———. 2000. "National Forest System Land and Resource Management Planning." *Federal Register* 65, no. 218 (November 9).

Vance, N. C., M. Borsting, and D. Pilz. 2001. *Species Information Guide to Special Forest Products in the Pacific Northwest.* Pub. no. GTR-PNW-513. Portland, OR: U.S. Department of Agriculture, Forest Service, Pacific Northwest Research Station.

Williams, J. R., ed. 1900. *Journal and Letters of Philip Vickers Fithian, 1767–1774.* Princeton, NJ: Princeton University Library.

Willson, M. F. 1996. "Biodiversity and Ecological Processes." In *Biodiversity in Managed Landscapes Theory and Practice,* ed. R. C. Szaro and D. W. Johnston, pp. 96–107. New York: Oxford University Press.

Wimberly, M. C., T. A. Spies, C. J. Long, and C. Whitlock. 2000. "Simulating Historical Variability in the Amount of Old Forests in the Oregon Coast Range." *Conservation Biology* 14:167–180.

World Commission on Environment and Development. 1987. *Our Common Future.* Oxford: Oxford University Press.

Young, C. C. 1998. "Defining the Range: The Development of Carrying Capacity in Management Practice." *J. History of Biology* 31:61–83.

The Paradox of Market-Oriented Conservation: Lessons from the Tropical Forests

Carolyn Crook and Roger Alex Clapp

Many conservationists trace the destructive exploitation, degradation, and replacement of native forest ecosystems to the perception that intact forests have little value when human alteration of these ecosystems is minimal. They gain value only when their timber resources are extracted, or when they are converted to other uses such as agricultural production or livestock rearing (Reid and Miller 1989; McNeely et al. 1990; Pearce, Markandya, and Barbier 1992). If, however, people can obtain economic benefits from biological diversity and the intact ecosystems that support it, they will have an incentive to protect them (Myers 1983; Swanson and Barbier 1992; Sedjo and Simpson 1995).

Conservation-minded economists suggest that the sustainable use of biodiversity has an economic value greater than that of destructive uses (Pearce and Moran 1994). Forest destruction appears economically rational because the arguably enormous value of the environmental services provided by intact ecosystems (Costanza et al. 1997) has not been captured in markets and, as a result, is often not recognized in decision making (Pearce 1995). In keeping with the widespread recent enthusiasm for privatization and market reforms, the 1992 Global Biodiversity Strategy (World Resources Institute 1992) recommended creating incentives for local communities to develop markets for sustainably harvested wild products. The underlying claim has become an article of faith among pragmatically minded environmentalists (Takacs 1996): the loss of biological diversity is a problem of market failure, and its solution lies in the expansion and formalization of markets. If gathering wild species generates profit and revenue, it should motivate better management of the harvested populations (Freese 1997) in order to sustain the industries and incomes based upon them. Conservation is a side effect of self-interested planning.

The choice is often posed as "use it or lose it" (Swanson 1992), with the declaration that biodiversity must earn its keep. We argue that profit is no panacea. The process of finding new markets usually means the creation of external, not local, markets, and external markets easily become commodity markets, with their attendant periods of oversupply and competition. Given the oscillating pressures imposed by market cycles, economic success may be as dangerous as failure. Low prices may generate overharvesting to meet revenue goals and make alternative uses more attractive, leading to the liquidation and replacement of the resource and its ecosystem. High prices in turn can promote the degradation of some species by attracting too many harvesters or too much capital investment, by encouraging pulse-harvesting in anticipation of falling prices later on (Vincent and Binkley 1992), or by promoting intensive management of the target resources, with consequent ecosystem simplification (Freese 1998).

The development of markets for nontimber forest products offers the appealing vision of conserving forests while improving rural incomes, thereby combining social and ecological sustainability. An alternative scenario is as likely, however: that newly commercialized NTFPs extend the economic value of intact forest ecosystems beyond timber, but exposure to market forces also repeats prior resource cycles of overexpansion followed by ecosystem disruption and socioeconomic crisis (Holling and Sanderson 1996; Clapp 1998). This chapter reviews recent research on NTFPs in the tropical rain forests and concludes by proposing a set of ecological and institutional conditions under which the sustainability of product collection would be most likely.

PLACING A VALUE ON NTFPS IN THE TROPICAL RAIN FORESTS

The potential of nontimber forest product exploitation to meet both conservation and development objectives gained widespread attention in the late 1980s and early 1990s, when a number of studies sought to determine the economic potential of NTFPs. Most of these studies focused on the sustainable exploitation of NTFPs in tropical forests, especially in Amazonia, with few comparable studies being conducted on temperate forest ecosystems. Many of the studies on tropical ecosystems concluded that the financial returns from nontimber forest products exceeded the value that could be obtained from the nonsustainable conversion of forest habitats. Peters et al. (1989a) concluded that, over the long term, the value of NTFPs available in an area near Iquitos, Peru, exceeded by two or three times the value of converting the forests to livestock rearing or plantation production. Other researchers concurred that NTFPs could provide better livelihoods than other opportunities available in the region. For example, studies in the Brazilian Amazon indicated that collecting Brazil nuts and rubber from an extractive reserve provided better economic returns to collectors than wage labor (Schwartzman 1989; Hecht 1992); that collecting rubber could provide a monthly income equivalent to double the minimum wage paid in towns (Aragon Castillo 1995); and that the sale of fruits, cacao, and rubber provided a mean annual income almost double the local average (Anderson and Ioris 1992).

Furthermore, a number of these studies measured the economic potential of only a limited number of products, suggesting that if a broader range of products were collected, the economic performance of NTFPs would even further outperform other income-generating activities. Biodiversity prospecting—the search for new medicines from organisms in the wild—has the potential to raise the economic benefits of sustainable collecting well beyond those of alternative uses of land. The collection of medicinal plants alone in areas of Belize was estimated to exceed the value of other land uses, with the net present value of collecting medicinal plants exceeding the value of land cleared for agriculture by between two to ten times (Balick and Mendelsohn 1992; Panayatou and Ashton 1992). Export earnings may be small—Madagascar has earned annual revenues of up to $750,000 from the export of medicinal plants (Rasoanaivo 1996)—but those figures do not account for domestic sales, barter, or subsistence consumption. In developing countries, a large proportion of the trade in medicinal plants (and other NTFPs) is unrecorded, and their contribution to subsistence is therefore uncertain. Finally, these estimates of the value of medicinal plants only account for their value as raw materials for current medicinal uses and do not account for the potential genetic and biochemical value that they, and other organisms, have as sources of novel drugs, food crops, or industrial inputs.

Notable examples of potential earnings (as opposed to current earnings) include the highly publicized $1.135 million advance (in cash and technology) and an undisclosed royalty that Merck Pharmaceuticals agreed to pay to the National Biodiversity Institute of Costa Rica in exchange for a two-year supply of plants, insects, and microorganisms (Reid et al. 1993). In 1991, worldwide pharmaceutical sales were approximately $150 billion (Aylward 1995). Considering that 41 percent by value of all medicines are derived from the genetic material from natural organisms (Powers 1993), close to $60 billion in annual sales are likely generated from natural organisms. If the countries that supply organisms as biological inputs were to receive a 5 percent royalty on future drugs developed from tropical plants alone, by very rough estimates, annual revenues could reach around $1–11 per hectare of tropical rain forest (Pearce and Puroshothaman 1995).

Although many studies ignore the medicinal value of organisms and thereby undervalue forest ecosystems, biodiversity prospecting is a speculative and knowledge-intensive activity with little hope of rapid reward. The likelihood of developing a drug from any given species is remote, and no royalties flow until the potential medicine passes through the decade or more required to develop and gain approval for a new drug (Crook and Clapp 1998). Given the remote possibility of economic benefits in the near term from bioprospecting, most commercial NTFP collectors will base management and harvesting decisions upon products that generate immediate returns.

Even without considering the value of organisms as sources of new medicines, many of the studies on the economic potential of NTFPs concluded that extractive activities could, over the long term, outcompete destructive land uses. This conclusion generated widespread enthusiasm for the economic potential of nontimber forest products to motivate conservation and improve rural livelihoods. Subsequently, however, some of the methodological approaches used in the studies were questioned, as was the ability of NTFPs to generate higher incomes than alternative land uses.

A number of the assumptions made in the studies had the effect of overstating the economic earnings from nontimber forest products. Peters et al. (1989a) calculated the hypothetical value of all NTFPs (except animals) found in an inventory of the study site and assumed that all NTFPs available in the forest site would be marketed (Coomes 1996). The study did not attempt to assess the quantity of each NTFP that could actually be sold and consequently overstated the value of the commercial portion of a harvest. Padoch and de Jong (1989) determined that the value of all sellable NTFPs on sites near Iquitos was only some 3 percent of the value of the total inventory (cited in Godoy et al. 1993). Consequently, the net annual revenue generated from the goods extracted and sold from the Peters et al. (1989a) site would have been close to $15/ha/year, a far cry from the reported $422/ha/year value of the full inventory.

Some studies, including those by Peters et al. (1989a) and Anderson and Ioris (1992), focused on the profitability of forest ecosystems near urban markets and cannot be extrapolated to more remote rural areas (Browder 1992). Many studies overestimated incomes because they assumed that collectors would receive the market price of products, when in fact a large portion of the ultimate price is absorbed by intermediaries, and the collectors earn only a small percentage of it (Coomes 1996). Clay (1997a) found that collectors received only 1 percent of the final retail price from Brazil nuts and 1–4 percent for palm hearts. At the peak of demand for Amazonian rubber, for example, the collectors still lived in poverty because the value of the product accrued to intermediaries (Fearnside 1989). Finally, the impact of production increases on market prices also was not considered (Southgate and Clark 1993).

INCOMES, MARKETS, AND ECOSYSTEMS

Changes in the supply of and demand for a product and associated changes in the price paid for it have an enormous impact on the gross returns that commercial NTFP harvesters earn. One factor that limits the gross returns earned is that the price of many NTFPs is low and is kept that way due to the substitutability of many products. For example, the demand for Brazil nuts can usually be satisfied by hazelnuts or other nuts, thereby limiting the price for Brazil nuts (LaFleur 1992). Another factor limiting earnings and incomes is the fact that NTFP markets are frequently subject to boom and bust cycles, largely driven by changes in external demand (Anderson 1990; Coomes 1995). While extractors may fare well during the period of the boom, the volatility of the market makes incomes unstable: good years are often followed by bad, and sometimes by market collapse. Although extractors may try to cushion the effects of these economic cycles by diversifying their collecting activities, few succeed; most collectors specialize in only a few products (Coomes 1996).

In addition to being subject to changes in consumer demand, commercial NTFP harvesters, especially those producing for international markets, are also vulnerable to changes in supply and increased competition. If collectors succeed in building a market, new producers may be drawn in, with two possible consequences. If overharvesting makes the product scarcer in the wild, higher prices may drive producers to intensify harvesting still further to take advantage of what they see as a temporary market opportunity, leading ultimately to Gordon's (1954) famous bioeconomic equilibrium—the point at which the resource is so scarce that harvesting costs exceed even scarcity prices.

Alternately, if increased harvesting does not lead to scarcity, it is likely to drive prices down. In the absence of a proportional increase in demand, an increase in supply will undermine incomes and profitability. International competition has the potential to pit poor producers in developing countries against one another to supply the international markets. This scenario suggests that NTFP harvesters may gain greater security and stability by producing for local and regional markets, where an already established demand for locally available products may provide a more stable market. In local and regional economies, producers are also likely to be more aware of local demands for and the prices and supply of a given product than is the case when supplying international markets. Nevertheless, in many areas of the tropics, local and regional markets do not generate sufficient demand for a product, making national or international markets essential.

Higher prices also increase the incentive for domestication and plantation production or for the development of synthetic substitutes. Those NTFPs for which there has been a strong and sustained demand have been domesticated and cultivated (e.g., rubber, cacao, coffee, and palm oil) or synthesized (e.g., rubber, palm oils, vanilla, and many medicinal chemical compounds) (Pendelton 1992). Cultivation will be pursued whenever possible because cultivated plants are more easily fertilized and bred to increase output and productivity (Dore and Nogueira 1994). They also provide a more uniform product than wild sources and, at least initially, a more stable and reliable supply. In the case of medicinal plants, the process of selection can yield a plant with a higher concentration of the active biochemical compound and thereby a more potent product (Sheldon, Balick, and Laird 1997).

Synthetic substitutes eliminate the risks associated with dependence on biological raw materials, including their uncertain supply, the unpredictable concentration of active chemicals, and the threat that pests will attack wild or cultivated plants. Plantations are usually more viable and profitable outside the ecosystem of origin, since exotic species are freed (at least temporarily) from the predators and parasites they face in their native ecosystems. Unless the country of origin is fairly compensated for any exported biological resources, what Shiva (1997) calls biopiracy undermines the income-earning potential of the regional ecosystem that harbored the species by evading the obligation of compensation. The mass production that occurs with domestication drives prices down, and eventually producers dependent on wild supplies cannot compete, leading to the collapse of the industry in the source country.

A final, ecological factor that limits the profitability of NTFP harvesting is that in the highly diverse tropical ecosystems, many resources are widely dispersed and usually are found at very low density. This makes collecting a labor-intensive, low-productivity activity, limiting the economic returns that collectors may earn from a given area of land.

Ultimately, estimates of the annual value of extractive production in the Amazon rain forest range from $15 to $32 per hectare (Browder 1992). Even when the speculative earnings from biodiversity prospecting ($1–11/ha) are included, extraction does not outcompete the approximate $52 per hectare earned by clearing forests for swidden agriculture (Browder 1992). Ultimately, NTFP collecting yields among the lowest returns per hectare of a number of forest-use activities (Hecht 1992). As long as there is forestland to be cleared, NTFP collection seems likely to remain a casual and irregular activity for periods when no other occupation can be found.

THE ECOLOGICAL IMPACTS OF NTFP HARVESTING

Low incomes and volatile prices force collectors to pursue a number of activities and survival strategies that compromise the sustainability of commercial NTFP collection. First, collectors may be forced to overexploit the resource base in an attempt to increase incomes. When demand is high and the resource is accessible but of limited supply, collectors are tempted to cash in on the high prices by overexploiting the resource, and so degradation of the resource base results (Aragon Castillo 1995). Where the resource is open to access by all, an increase in demand is likely to generate depletion rather than conservation, because those who would benefit from sustainable management are unable to exclude opportunistic harvesters. Unfortunately, the impact of low prices has much the same result: a fall in the price will prompt the collector to overharvest in an attempt to maintain income levels, leading to degradation of the resource base. The overexploitation of rattan in Southeast Asia, for example, has resulted in the near extinction of several species (Panayatou and Ashton 1992; Siebert 1993).

Ultimately, the income earned from NTFP collecting in the tropical forests is usually insufficient to meet the basic needs of collectors and their families, who rely on agriculture and livestock rearing for subsistence and to supplement incomes. Cropping and grazing by necessity involve clearing at least some portion of the forest. Up to a point, such activities may be compatible with conservation objectives, but evidence from Amazonia suggests that households are increasing the area under crops—in certain instances, at an annual rate of almost 21 percent (Browder 1992)—calling the sustainability, and hence the conservation effect, of NTFP collection into question. Finally, the dependence on hunting to supplement both protein intake and incomes leads to overhunting and depletion of animal resources. Subsistence hunting in Amazonia contributes significantly to the food intake of extractive families but severely reduces populations of some hunted species, especially of the large mammals (e.g., monkeys, deer, and peccaries) and birds that are preferred target species (Pendelton 1992; Redford 1992; Aragon Castillo 1995).

In an attempt to increase their earnings, collectors may try to increase the density at which economically valuable resources are usually found in tropical ecosystems. Enrichment planting—that is, increasing the number and density of economically useful plants while removing undesirable or economically unimportant species (Denevan et al. 1984; Anderson and Ioris 1992)—may lead to ecosystem simplification. Three islands in the Amazon River that had been managed to produce palm hearts and fruit lost 50 percent of their native tree species (Clay 1997b). In its extreme, forest management may mean the extermination of animal competitors, especially those that feed on fruits and nuts (Pendelton 1992), destabilizing the trophic pyramid and leading to widespread and unpredictable changes in flora and fauna.

Enrichment planting and weeding is a first step on the road toward domestication and cultivation. Once domestication is achieved, its initial effect is to intensify pressure on wild resources as collectors try to cash in on the remaining value of the product, before mass production renders these wild stocks worthless. This is not to say that domestication is ecologically sustainable, but that intensively managed agroecosystems can usually be sustained for long enough to place the wild resource in peril from the industry that it can no longer support.

ECOLOGICAL CONDITIONS FOR SUSTAINABILITY

Whether commercial NTFP gathering and conservation are compatible depends on a combination of ecological and sociopolitical conditions. Four ecological conditions limit the sustainability of nontimber forest products: the density at which the marketable resource is found; whether the resource can be harvested nondestructively; whether its regeneration is sufficiently rapid to withstand the effects of discounting; and whether sustainable harvesting in the wild provides a cheaper and more reliable product than cultivation in plantations or synthesis in the laboratory. Ecosystems that favor the sustainable commercial harvesting of NTFPs are those where the marketable resource is found at relatively high density (Peters et al. 1989b; Browder 1992; Salafsky, Dugelby, and Terborgh 1993; Freese 1997). The profitability of NTFP collecting is likely to be limited in diverse ecosystems, as the species diversity of an ecosystem is inversely related to the density of any one species, prompting an intensification of management that threatens less valued species and the complex interactions they support. Oligarchic forests, in which one or a few species dominate the ecosystem, are relatively rare in tropical ecosystems; in temperate forests economic species are more likely to occur naturally in high densities.

The harvesting process is another critical variable. If the entire organism is destroyed to obtain the marketable product, as occurs when rosewood trees are felled to obtain rosewood oil for perfume (Coomes 1995) or with the harvesting of the roots of medicinal plants, overexploitation is the inevitable result. If only certain parts of the organism are required, harvesting could be limited to a small section of the tree so as not to threaten its survival. Nevertheless, even the selective removal of bark, roots, and rhizomes may weaken the plant's resistance to pests and disease, which threatens the individual's chance of survival (Sheldon, Balick, and Laird 1997). Even when appropriate levels of selective harvesting can be identified, harvesters may knowingly exceed sustainable harvest levels to meet demand, especially in the case of valuable species. A notable example is that of the tree *Prunus africana*, a source of medicinal bark, which has been listed as a vulnerable species under Appendix II of CITES because overcollection has resulted in its genetic erosion (Sheldon, Balick, and Laird 1997).

The collection of fruit, seeds, and leaves is more likely to be sustainable, provided that harvesting is limited to a rate that does not threaten regeneration and does not threaten the food source of animals or other organisms. The continued overexploitation of the Brazil nut, as measured in the Cachoeira Reserve in Brazil, has contributed to its population decline and to the biotic impoverishment of the forest, possibly because insufficient nuts are left behind to ensure regeneration (Anderson and Ioris 1992; Nepstad et al. 1992). Harvesting levels should not allow too many essential nutrients, such as nitrogen and phosphorus, to be removed from the nutrient cycle. Seeds, fruits, and nuts are all high in nutrients, and in the nutrient-poor soils of much of the tropics their intensive collection could conceivably be unsustainable over the long term (Salafsky, Dugelby, and Terborgh 1993).

Ensuring that a level of harvesting is sustainable requires knowledge of the rate of replacement or regeneration of the harvested species. Even where such knowledge is available, economic and political pressures may cause harvesters to ignore sustainable-yield levels. When the rate of regeneration is low, discounting reduces the value of future yields to a level so low that short-term economic pressures (be they from poverty or from overcapitalization and the resulting debt burden) encourage destructive exploitation, not sustainable harvesting (Norgaard 1995). If forests are required to yield a competitive rate of return, slow-maturing species will be depleted, not managed (Clark 1991), and the complex ecosystems that support them are likely to be replaced. Only ecosystems with simple trophic structures and a small number of fast-growing species will be managed for sustained production, and predators of the harvested species may be eliminated in the name of "managing" the resource.

Valuable resources are likely to be cultivated and produced in plantations or to be replaced with a synthetic substitute, thereby undermining collection in the wild. From this perspective, the only viable NTFPs are those that are not valuable enough to warrant investment in cultivation or synthesizing; those that are too expensive or too difficult to cultivate or synthesize, or those that are of a better quality than the cultivated or synthesized counterparts. Many medicinal plants are uneconomical to domesticate and difficult or impossible to synthesize, so their collection in the wild continues. In addition, the perception that plants grown in the wild are more vigorous and therefore produce more potent medicines (Sheldon et al. 1997) supports the ongoing collection of medicinal plants in the wild, at least for traditional uses and herbal remedies, if not for the pharmaceutical industry.

INSTITUTIONAL CONDITIONS FOR SUSTAINABILITY

Reconciling commercial NTFP collecting with conservation depends upon a number of institutional conditions, including the existence of secure and equitably distributed property rights, appropriate management regimes, and independent monitoring agencies. Ultimately, fiscal incentives may be needed to augment the profitability of NTFP collecting.

Sustainability depends on who benefits from the harvest, and whether they have both the desire to use the resources in a sustainable manner and the ability to prevent others from doing otherwise. Secure and stable resource tenure, whether it covers only the target species or extends to the land around it, is vital. Both property rights and enforcement mechanisms tend to be weak in tropical forests, which then creates powerful incentives for overharvesting when market prices are high (Southgate and Clark 1993). This tendency does not imply that privatization is necessary for sustainable management; many complex common-property arrangements have been successful in sustaining biological resources (Mendelsohn and Balick 1995; Berkes 1996).

Many indigenous and traditional resource management systems also have mechanisms for restraining destructive exploitation (Posey 1996), and these may offer useful blueprints for the design of local institutions. Nevertheless, there is nothing inherently sustainable about traditional and indigenous practices: while many have stood the test of time (Nabhan 1995), the simple fact that a product has been harvested for a long period does not necessarily mean that harvesting is sustainable. Sustainability must be judged on a case-by-case basis by directly comparing the rate of extraction to the rate of natural replacement (Godoy and Bawa 1993) and allowing a substantial margin of error for unpredicted disturbance, whether natural or anthropogenic.

Ensuring sustainability of the harvest also involves devising and enforcing appropriate resource management practices and regulations. This requires detailed knowledge of both the target species and the surrounding ecosystem and presumes that rates of regeneration are known to establish sustainable harvesting levels. If conservation of biodiversity is an intended side effect of NTFP harvesting, then sustainable harvest levels must also account for the role of the target species in the ecosystem, for example, its role as a food source for other species. For most species there is a decided lack of ecological information upon which to base sustainable extraction systems. Such information is inadequate even for well-known species such as the Brazil nut and mahogany (Boot and Gullison 1995). Ensuring sustainability also presumes that the distribution of the species has been mapped so that regions where marketable resources are found in high densities may be designated for commercial NTFP extraction, while areas with small populations or at the edge of the species' range can be protected.

Strong participatory local institutions with social legitimacy are required in order to exclude poachers, to streamline transportation, processing and marketing, and to facilitate the transfer of technology and the evolving knowledge of the resource. Reducing the time between collecting, processing, and marketing of products would reduce losses of perishable items, and the adoption of new processing technologies contributes to increasing the value added locally, thus increasing productivity and incomes. Marketing cooperatives may streamline marketing channels by removing intermediaries, thereby raising (and possibly stabilizing) the prices paid to collectors

(Clay 1997a). These institutions could also promote the dissemination of management practices and regulations by facilitating training programs. The experience in the Maya Biosphere Reserve in Guatemala, where inexperienced allspice and xate harvesters were threatening these resources with their destructive harvesting methods, suggests that licensing new harvesters following an apprenticeship or training with a veteran harvester may be a useful approach to reduce resource degradation (Nations 1992). Institutions are also required to enable local populations to retain customary rights to forest resources and to buttress those with legal rights, as well as to provide compensation to those excluded.

Finally, there is a need for scientific monitoring agencies that are independent by statute. For management of NTFPs to be adaptive, it must change volume goals and harvesting methods if monitoring reveals that the assumptions about species regeneration and ecosystem stability are wrong (Noss and Cooperrider 1994). Monitoring data need to be open to public discussion and debate (Hutchings, Walters, and Haedrich 1997), and the stakeholders must be acknowledged to include national, international, and local observers (Clapp 1998). Adaptive management is an institutional problem as well as a scientific one (Grumbine 1997), and limiting intervenors to local resource-extractors is likely to favor overharvesting over needed cutbacks. Without statutory independence, resource management regimes may be unable to place ecosystem sustainability above short-term economic goals. Independent monitoring, however, adds another expense to an occupation already at or beyond the economic margin.

Experience in the tropical forests indicates that the earnings from NTFP collecting may not meet family or community needs, nor does it provide sufficient incentive to dissuade forest clearing and conversion. Incentive or subsidy programs may therefore be warranted to alter the prices of sustainably collected resources so that they outperform unsustainably collected ones. For example, subsidies could be provided to help with start-up costs for adding value locally (e.g., for the purchase of improved processing equipment). Subsidies could also compensate local communities for forgone harvesting opportunities with the purpose of achieving conservation (Altieri 1990). Many destructive land uses receive either direct or indirect government subsidies: timber extraction is subsidized through low stumpage fees charged by governments and through government support for road building to allow access to trees.

Certainly, institutions face considerable challenges in targeting incentives and subsidies in such a way that they do not promote inefficiency, inequality, or overharvesting. One subsidy program is the Brazilian price support for rubber, which at times has kept rubber prices in Brazil three times higher than international prices (Fearnside 1989). Subsidy programs and their associated economic burdens may face powerful fiscal and ideological obstacles, and tax breaks may offer a more palatable form for promoting sustainable production. In Brazil, tax breaks have in the past supported cattle ranching, which has been a major cause of deforestation (Goodman and Hall 1990; Hall 1992), so providing tax breaks for sustainable production of NTFPs would appear appropriate as a corrective measure. At the very least, the value-added taxes that some governments apply to NTFPs, such as the 12 percent tax that Brazil applies to Brazil nuts (LaFleur 1992), should be removed.

CONCLUSION

At its best, commercial NTFP harvesting does contribute to forest dwellers' livelihoods, but even then it can only support a low population density (Salafsky, Dugelby, and Terborgh 1993), so the influx of people into the forest wishing to draw on its resources needs to be controlled. In its most destructive form, commercial exploitation of NTFPs creates strong pressures of overexploitation, leading to ecosystem degradation and species loss. Management to increase profitability can lead to the erosion of genetic diversity, the loss of species diversity, and ultimately ecosystem simplification to the point where resilience is lost. Although this may be preferable to wholesale destruction, it can hardly be considered a form of conservation. Unless extractive activities are limited by strictly enforced yield levels, they run the risk of becoming yet another destructive use of forest ecosystems, although perhaps one in which the loss of biodiversity is more gradual. Although we urge caution in promoting trade as a means of conservation, we acknowledge the important role of NTFP collecting in those areas where it is most likely to be economically feasible. Highly diverse ecosystems and regions deemed particularly important for conservation (e.g., regions harboring endangered species and concentrations of endemic species) should be protected from exploitation, or at the very least should be subject to minimal exploitation.

There are perils in drawing lessons from the experiences of tropical forests in developing countries, as they may not apply to temperate regions of developed countries, where ecological and institutional conditions are different. The lower species diversity in temperate regions could mean that economically valuable nontimber forest products are found at higher densities, making NTFP collecting a more profitable undertaking. The chances for economic viability in developed countries are enhanced where prices are high and transportation costs low, as when urban specialty markets for NTFPs are nearby. The proximity of markets may also result in shorter marketing chains, with fewer intermediaries appropriating a portion of the value of the harvest. A potential limitation on the extent of earnings, however, is the lower reliance on traditional medicinal systems in developed countries and thus the reduced demand for medicinal plants.

Commercial NTFP harvesting in temperate regions may also be ecologically more sustainable. The higher density of resources reduces the temptation to practice enrichment planting or other forest management techniques that reduce biological diversity. Temperate forests are also less subject to the threat of deforestation for subsistence agriculture (Mather 1992; Grainger 1995). In addition, while nontimber forest product collectors in developed countries are still subject to economic forces that motivate overexploitation of the resource base, the existence of stronger institutions to enforce harvesting methods and levels, to ensure secure property rights, and perhaps to buffer the impact of market swings improves the chances of sustainable commercial NTFP collecting. Finally, in temperate regions where forests are protected from destructive uses (such as logging or agriculture or both) but are not designated as parks or wilderness, NTFPs offer a means to realize some economic revenues from the forests. In such cases, nontimber forest products that provide local communities with alternative incomes could make the bitter pill of forgoing timber-related income a bit more palatable.

REFERENCES

Altieri, M. 1990. "Why Study Traditional Agriculture?" In *Agroecology*, ed. R. Carroll, J. Vandermeer, and P. Rossett, pp. 551–564. New York: McGraw Hill.

Anderson, A. 1990. "Land-Use Strategies for Successful Extractive Economies." In *The Rainforest Harvest*, ed. S. Counsell and T. Rice, pp. 213–223. London: Friends of the Earth.

Anderson, A. B., and E. M. Ioris. 1992. "The Logic of Extraction: Resource Management and Income Generation by Extractive Producers in the Amazon." In *Conservation of Neotropical Forests*, ed. K. H. Redford and C. Padoch, pp. 175–199. New York: Columbia University Press.

Aragon Castillo, C. 1995. "Viability of the Extractive Reserves." In *Extractive Reserves*, ed. J. Ruiz Murrieta and R. Pinzon Rueda, pp. 19–35. Gland, Switzerland: World Conservation Union.

Aylward, B. 1995. "The Role of Plant Screening and Plant Supply in Biodiversity Conservation, Drug Development and Health Care." In *Intellectual Property Rights and Biodiversity Conservation*, ed. T. Swanson, pp. 93–126. Cambridge, UK: Cambridge University Press.

Balick, M., and R. Mendelsohn. 1992. "The Economic Value of Traditional Medicine from Tropical Rain Forests." *Conservation Biology* 6:128–139.

Berkes, F. 1996. "Social Systems, Ecological Systems, and Property Rights." In *Rights to Nature: Ecological, Economic, Cultural, and Political Principles of Institutions for the Environment*, ed. Susan Hanna, C. Folke, and K. G. Maler, pp. 87–107. Washington, DC: Island Press.

Boot, R. G., and R. E. Gullison. 1995. "Approaches to Developing Sustainable Extraction Systems for Tropical Forest Products." *Ecological Applications* 5(4): 896–903.

Browder, J. O. 1992. "The Limits of Extractivism." *BioScience* 42:174–182.

Clapp, R. A. 1998. "The Resource Cycle in Fishing and Forestry." *Canadian Geographer* 42:129–144.

Clark, C. 1991. "Economic Biases against Sustainable Development." In *Ecological Economics: the Science and Management of Sustainability,* ed. R. Costanza, pp. 319–330. New York: Columbia University Press.

Clay, Jason. 1997a. "Brazil Nuts: The Use of a Keystone Species for Conservation and Development." In *Harvesting Wild Species: Implications for Biodiversity Conservation,* ed. C. Freese, pp. 246–282. Washington, DC: Island Press.

———. 1997b. "The Impact of Palm Heart Harvesting in the Amazon Estuary." In *Harvesting Wild Species: Implications for Biodiversity Conservation,* ed. C. Freese, pp. 283–314. Washington, DC: Island Press.

Coomes, O. T. 1995. "A Century of Rain Forest Use in Western Amazonia: Lessons for Extraction-based Conservation of Tropical Forest Resources." *Forest and Conservation History* 39:108–120.

———. 1996. "Income Formation among Amazonian Peasant Households in Northeastern Perú: Empirical Observations and Implications for Market-Oriented Conservation." *Conference of Latin Americanist Geographers* 22:51–64.

Costanza, R., R. d'Arge, R. de Groot, S. Farber, M.Grasso, B. Hannon, K. Limburg, S. Naeem, R. O'Neill, J. Paruelo, R. Raskin, P. Sutton, and M. van den Belt. 1997. "The Value of the World's Ecosystem Services and Natural Capital." *Nature* 387:253–260.

Crook, C., and R. A. Clapp. 1998. "Is Market-Oriented Forest Conservation a Contradiction in Terms?" *Environmental Conservation* 25(2): 131–145.

Denevan, W., J. Treacy, J. Alcorn, C. Padoch, J. Denslow, and S. Flores Paitan. 1984. "Indigenous Agroforestry in the Peruvian Amazon: Bora Indian Management of Swidden Fallows." *Interciencia* 9.

Dore, M., and J. Nogueira. 1994. "The Amazon Rain Forest, Sustainable Development and the Biodiversity Convention: A Political Economy Perspective." *Ambio* 23(8): 491–495

Fearnside, P. M. 1989. "Extractive Reserves in Brazilian Amazonia." *BioScience* 39:387–393.

Freese, C. 1997. "The 'Use It or Lose It' Debate." In *Harvesting Wild Species: Implications for Biodiversity Conservation,* ed. C. Freese, pp. 1–48. Washington, DC: Island Press.

———. 1998. *Wild Species as Commodities.* Washington, D.C.: Island Press.

Godoy, R., and K. Bawa. 1993. "The Economic Value and Sustainable Harvest of Plants and Animals from the Tropical Forest: Assumptions, Hypotheses, and Methods." *Economic Botany* 47(3): 215–219.

Godoy, R., R. Lubowski, and A. Markandya. 1993. "A Method for the Economic Valuation of Nontimber Tropical Forest Products." *Economic Botany* 47(3): 220–233.

Goodman, D., and A. Hall. 1990. *The Future of Amazonia: Destruction or Sustainable Development.* London: Macmillan.

Gordon, H. S. 1954. "The Economic Theory of a Common Property Resource: The Fishery." *Journal of Political Economy* 62:124–142.

Grainger, A. 1995. "The Forest Transition: An Alternative Approach." *Area* 27(3): 242–251

Grumbine, E. 1997. "Reflections on 'What Is Ecosystem Management?'" *Conservation Biology* 11(1): 41–47.

Hall, A. 1992. *Making People Matter: Development and the Environment in Brazilian Amazonia*. London: Institute of Latin American Studies.

Hecht, S. B. 1992. "Valuing Land Uses in Amazonia: Colonist Agriculture, Cattle, and Petty Extraction in Comparative Perspective." In *Conservation of Neotropical Forests: Working from Traditional Resource Use,* ed. K. H. Redford and C. Padoch, pp. 379–399. New York: Columbia University Press.

Holling, C., and S. Sanderson. 1996. "Dynamics of (Dis)harmony in Ecological and Social Systems." In *Rights to Nature: Ecological, Economic, Cultural and Political Principles of Institutions for the Environment,* ed. Susan Hanna, C. Folke, and K. G. Maler, pp. 57–86. Washington, DC: Island Press.

Hutchings, J., C. Walters, and R. Haedrich. 1997. "Is Scientific Inquiry Incompatible with Government Information Control?" *Canadian Journal of Fisheries and Aquatic Sciences* 54 (May): 1198–1210.

LaFleur, J. R. 1992. *Marketing of Brazil Nuts: A Case Study from Brazil*. Rome: FAO.

Mather, A. S. 1992. "The Forest Transition." *Area* 24:367–379.

McNeely, J. A., K. R. Miller, W. V. Reid, R. A. Mittermeier, and T. B. Werner. 1990. *Conserving the World's Biological Diversity*. Gland, Switzerland: World Conservation Union.

Mendelsohn, R., and M. Balick. 1995. "Private Property and Rainforest Conservation." *Conservation Biology* 9:1322–1323.

Myers, N. 1983. *A Wealth of Wild Species: Storehouse for Human Welfare*. Boulder, CO: Westview Press.

———. 1993. "Biodiversity and the Precautionary Principle." *Ambio* 22:74–79.

Nabhan, G. 1995. "Cultural Parallax in Viewing North American Habitats. In *Reinventing Nature? Responses to Postmodern Deconstruction,* ed. M. E. Soulé and G. Lease, pp. 87–101. Washington, DC: Island Press.

Nations, J. 1992. "Xateros, Chicleros, and Pimenteros: Harvesting Renewable Tropical Forest Resources in the Guatemalan Peten." In *Conservation of Neotropical Forests: Working from Traditional Resource Use,* ed. K. H. Redford and C. Padoch, pp. 208–219. New York: Columbia University Press.

Nepstad, D. C., I. F. Brown, L. Luz, A. Alechandre, and V. Viana. 1992. "Biotic Impoverishment of Amazonian Forests by Rubber Tappers, Loggers, and Cattle Ranchers." In *Nontimber Products from Tropical Forests,* ed. D. C. Nepstad and S. Schwartzman, pp. 1–14. New York: New York Botanical Garden.

Norgaard, R. 1995. "Ecology, Politics, and Economics: Finding the Common Ground for Decision Making in Conservation." In *Principles of Conservation Biology,* ed. G. Meffe and C. Carroll, pp. 439–465. Sunderland, MA: Sinauer Associates.

Noss, R., and A. Cooperrider. 1994. *Saving Nature's Legacy.* Washington, DC: Island Press.

Panayotou, T., and P. Ashton. 1992. *Not by Timber Alone: Economics and Ecology for Sustaining Tropical Forests.* Washington, DC: Island Press.

Pearce, D. 1995. *Blueprint 4: Capturing Global Environmental Value.* London: Earthscan.

Pearce, D., A. Markandya, and E. Barbier. 1992. *Blueprint for a Green Economy.* London: Earthscan.

Pearce, D., and D. Moran. 1994. *The Economic Value of Biodiversity.* London: Earthscan.

Pearce, D., and S. Puroshothaman. 1995. "The Economic Value of Plant-Based Pharmaceuticals." In *Intellectual Property Rights and Biodiversity Conservation,* ed. T. Swanson, pp. 127–138. Cambridge, UK: Cambridge University Press.

Pendelton, L. H. 1992. "Trouble in Paradise: Practical Obstacles to Nontimber Forestry in Latin America." In *Sustainable Harvest and Marketing of Rain Forest Products,* ed. M. Plotkin and L. Famolare, pp. 252–262. Washington, DC: Island Press.

Peters, C., M. Alwyn, H. Gentry, and R. O. Mendelsohn. 1989a. "Valuation of an Amazonian Rainforest." *Nature* 339:655–656.

Peters, C., M. J. Balick, F. Khan, and A. B. Anderson. 1989b. "Oligarchic Forests of Economic Plants in Amazonia: Utilization and Conservation of an Important Tropical Resource." *Conservation Biology* 3:341–348.

Posey, D. A. 1996. "Indigenous Knowledge, Biodiversity, and International Rights: Learning about Forests from the Kayapó Indians of the Brazilian Amazon." *Commonwealth Forestry Review* 76(1): 53–60.

Posey, D. A., and G. Dutfield. 1996. *Beyond Intellectual Property.* Ottawa: International Development Research Centre.

Powers, M. 1993. "The United Nations Framework Convention on Biological Diversity: Will Biodiversity Preservation Be Enhanced through Its Provisions Concerning Biotechnology Intellectual Property Rights?" *Wisconsin International Law Journal* 12(1): 103–124.

Rasoanaivo, P. 1996. "Rain Forests of Madagascar: Sources of Industrial and Medicinal Plants." *Ambio* 19:421–423.

Redford, K. 1992. "The Empty Forest." *BioScience* 42(6): 412–422.

Reid, W. V., S. A. Laird, C. A. Meyer, R. Gamez, A. Sittenfeld, D. H. Janzen, M. A. Gollin, and C. Juma. 1993. "A New Lease on Life." In *Biodiversity Prospecting: Using Genetic Resources for Sustainable Development,* ed. W. V. Reid, S. A. Laird, C. A. Meyer, R. Gamez, A. Sittenfeld, D. H. Janzen, M. A. Gollin, and C. Juma, pp. 1–52. Washington, DC: World Resources Institute.

Reid, W. V., and K. Miller. 1989. *Keeping Options Alive: The Scientific Basis for Conserving Biodiversity.* Washington, DC: World Resources Institute.

Salafsky, N., B. L. Dugelby, and J. W. Terborgh. 1993. "Can Extractive Reserves Save the Rain Forest? An Ecological and Socioeconomic Comparison of Nontimber Forest Product Extraction Systems in Peten, Guatemala, and West Kalimantan, Indonesia." *Conservation Biology* 7:39–52.

Schwartzman, S. 1989. "Extractive Reserves: The Rubber Tapper's Strategy for Sustainable Use of the Amazon Rainforest." In *Fragile Lands of Latin America,* ed. J. Browder, pp. 150–165. Boulder, CO: Westview Press.

Sedjo, R. A., and R. D. Simpson. 1995. "Property Rights, Externalities, and Biodiversity." In *The Economics and Ecology of Biodiversity Decline: The Forces Driving Global Change,* ed. T. M. Swanson, pp. 79–88. Cambridge, UK: Cambridge University Press.

Sheldon, J., M. Balick, and S. Laird. 1997. *Medicinal Plants: Can Utilization and Conservation Coexist?* New York: New York Botanical Garden.

Shiva, V. 1997. *Biopiracy: The Plunder of Nature and Knowledge.* Boston: South End Press.

Siebert, S. F. 1993. "Rattan and Extractive Reserves." *Conservation Biology* 7: 749–750.

Southgate, D., and H. L. Clark. 1993. "Can Conservation Projects Save Biodiversity in South America?" *Ambio* 22:163–166.

Swanson, T. M. 1992. "Economics of a Biodiversity Convention." *Ambio* 21: 250–257.

Swanson, T. M., and E. Barbier. 1992. *Economics for the Wilds: Wildlife, Diversity, and Development.* Washington, DC: Island Press.

Takacs, D. 1996. *The Idea of Biodiversity.* Baltimore: Johns Hopkins University Press.

Vincent, J., and C. Binkley. 1992. "Forest-Based Industrialization: A Dynamic Perspective." In *Managing the World's Forests,* ed. N. Sharma, pp. 93–137. Dubuque, IA: Kendall-Hunt Publishing.

World Resources Institute. 1992. *Global Biodiversity Strategy: Guidelines for Action to Save, Study, and Use Earth's Biotic Wealth Sustainably and Equitably.* Baltimore: World Resources Institute.

CASE STUDY

Extractive Reserves for the United States? Lessons from the Amazonian Experience

Thomas Love

Discussions like this of extractive reserves as models for sustainable forest development draw from the prototypical experience of western Amazonian rubber tappers and Brazil nut harvesters. In this chapter I describe this experience in some detail and summarize some closer examinations of it (Browder 1992; Hecht and Cockburn 1990; Nepstad and Schwartzman 1992). The Amazonian experience offers two primary lessons: Amazonian extractive reserves emerged out of a particular historical conjuncture and are currently under debilitating internal and external pressures; and while there can be no automatic transfer of this model to U.S. (or other nations') circumstances, the Amazonian experience holds certain lessons that may enable state/legal recognition of existing practices as well as the development of new policy models that utilize NTFP harvesting to manage temperate forests more sustainably.

THE AMAZONIAN EXTRACTIVE RESERVE EXPERIENCE

Beginning in the late 1980s, a system of "extractive" reserves was created by the Brazilian government in response to pressures from rubber tappers, Brazil nut collectors, and other sustainable harvesters, aided by national and international NGO advocates. In this system, forest users are granted long-term usufruct rights to forest resources that they collectively manage (Schwartzman 1989, 151). Development pressures leading to widespread tropical forest clearance generated this grassroots Amazonian response, which came quickly to be seen in conservation circles as a more viable alternative to tropical forest conservation than the model of depopulated, U.S.–style, preservation-oriented national parks. But on the ground, advocates saw the movement primarily in terms of defending labor and land rights and only secondarily in terms of environmental protection. The extractive reserve model grew out of a specific historical experience of politically mobilized local populations dependent for their livelihood on standing forests.

The rubber tappers' movement of Acre, western Amazonian Brazil, had its origins in a series of rebellions that swept northeastern and interior Brazil in the nineteenth century (Hecht and Cockburn 1990, 161ff.). It involved "an extraordinary alliance of urban workers, slaves, *caboclos,* peasants and Indians" (Hecht and Cockburn 1990, 163) who, when it was all over, had modified labor relations in Amazonia toward more autonomy and independence from various forms of forced labor characteristic of the plantation system in the more coastal areas of the Brazil and earlier periods of the country's history.

Due to this history, as well as to the constraints imposed by large distances and vast rain forests, extraction of rubber, nuts, and other forest products came to be organized not by the typical Brazilian agrarian order of controlled laborers on estate systems, but rather by merchants who maintained personal and fictive kinship ties and extended credit to dispersed extractors in a pattern called *aviamento* (Wolf and Hansen 1972, 135). Although the rubber boom of the turn of the twentieth century temporarily reinforced estate-like conditions of harsher labor control, even in the more remote headwaters areas, when rubber export collapsed by 1915, the system reverted to its more diffuse and decentralized form. Since this collapse, the majority of rubber tappers, Brazil nut collectors, and other forest product extractors of western Brazil, eastern Peru, and northern Bolivia have lived in relative autonomy and isolation, loosely tied to wider markets (except for a period during and just after World War II when the Western Allies needed natural rubber for the war effort). To supplement irregular and unpredictable income from sale of these products, harvesters subsisted on fishing, hunting, gathering, and small-scale slash-and-burn cultivation.

However, in Brazilian Amazonia beginning in the late 1960s, the pace of change began to quicken. Road building programs sponsored by the military regimes of the 1960s stimulated the long-awaited opening up of the great Amazonian forests. Outside interests began buying up old rubber holdings and clearing the forest for export-oriented cattle ranching. The smallholding extractors had never established clear title to the forestlands they harvested. Such penetration opened up the forest not only for cattle ranching but also for the immigration of ever-growing waves of peasants from (alternately) northeastern and southeastern Brazil, made landless by expanding soybean, citrus, and other commercial farms. Generous credits from the Inter-American Development Bank, among others, facilitated road building and consequent deforestation. The sorry record of deforestation in Rondonia, and later Acre, was well publicized in (and somewhat slowed by) a series of films and articles in the 1980s.

Since the mid-1970s, Francisco "Chico" Mendes had been working quietly, patiently, sometimes even furtively, organizing dispersed smallholding rubber tappers into the rural workers' (rubber tappers') union. Their primary objective was to improve both the price of rubber and the price of products (formerly monopolized by the *aviadores*—agents of trade houses engaged in *aviamento*) exchanged in return. But as the pace of forest clearance picked up, the struggle turned more fundamentally to preservation of basic life-sustaining resources. "While the issues of slavery and peonage, found throughout the Amazon, were not struck from memory, the real issue now, as *seringais* [rubber forest holdings], *castanais* [Brazil nut forest holdings] and other forests went up in smoke, was land. Rural workers, squatters and the landless began to agitate more and more for agrarian reform" (Hecht and Cockburn 1990, 172). Standoffs began between organized forest products extractors and cattle interests over the forceful and at times violent clearing of rubber- and nut-rich forests.

It was in this context of class conflict over access to basic productive resources that the extractive reserve movement was born. The Brazilian state and its international creditors came under increasing international scrutiny over failure to control deforestation and dislocation of indigenous Amazonians by cattle ranchers and invading landless peasants. Such projects of large-scale capital interests (akin to the extensive clear-cutting of Pacific Northwest temperate forests), backed by international lending institutions and a distant state apparatus, have been termed "crash-and-burn" projects for their abject failure on social, human rights, and environmental, let alone economic and political, grounds.

Critical to the successful evolution of this new form of land tenure in western Amazonia was the intervention into this rural resource conflict by the Institute for Amazon Studies of Curitiba (in southeastern Brazil), assisted by the U.S.–based Environmental Defense Fund. Such national and international environmental interests quickly realized that extractive reserves would de facto preserve vast acreages of little-disturbed primary rain forest. State policy favoring the creation of forest reserves for extractive harvesting was developed in response to pressures from an alliance of extractive producers, the church, Brazilian social reform and human rights groups, and national and international environmental groups.

The extractive reserves model was thus born (the first being created in February 1988). Amazonian extractive reserves were essentially modeled on the old rubber estates. Forest reserves would be declared by the state, and access would be given in long-term leases to the forest product extractors who lived there. Use rights of rubber tapper households would be recognized, but holdings would not be privately owned. Most of the state of Acre was owned in overly large ranches and other holdings, vulnerable to agrarian reform. Administration of the reserves was therefore originally lodged in the agrarian reform branch of the agriculture ministry, hoping to fend off the breakup of these large deteriorated estates. However, in 1990 the program was transferred to the national environmental agency.

The reserves were more than just environmental-extractive defense structures, however. The vision was far more grand—a whole effort to promote sustainable, decentralized, locally controlled development. As such, political opposition was inevitable. "Once tenure was assured, the extractive reserves would also organize health clinics, schools and small-scale rubber-processing factories, and eventually even some manufacturing. . . . To the [ranchers], this emphasis on collective *ejido* (communally held agro-pastoral lands distributed to family cultivators) types of ownership was rank socialism, for the land rights of the great would be contested, perhaps replaced by some form of communal land ownership. The extractive reserves were an attack on private property and hence capitalism" (Hecht and Cockburn 1990, 181, 182). It was in this context that Chico Mendes was assassinated in December 1988, along with many hundreds of other forest extractors who have been murdered, tortured, and expelled from the land.

But as the extractive reserve movement quickly emerged into national and international prominence, its success was hampered by far more than the loss of its now famous leader. International markets for Brazil nuts strengthened initially but then collapsed; quality control suffered as organizational problems delayed shipments of perishable nuts. International buyers had to turn to conventional sources—nonsustainably produced through estate labor conditions—to meet demand.

Critical to the successful establishment of these reserves was linking their products with national and international markets, a greening of international trade practices. However, more intensive plantation management of selected commercially valuable products typically means that cultivated products will usually outcompete wild-harvested products in such markets, undermining the sustainability goal (Clement 1993). No household depends on extracting renewable resources for its entire income; consequently, evidence shows that when the profitability of sustained yield extraction declines, forest-dwelling populations, whatever their social orientation, are likely to deplete a renewable commercial resource or shift to other, more profitable activities, regardless of their environmental effects (Clement 1993, 175). Compounding the problem with wild-harvested rubber, in the early 1990s the Brazilian government removed import tariffs that had artifically subsidized the price of natural rubber, leading tappers to turn to farming (and forest clearance) to maintain household incomes.

These factors conspired to further reduce extractivists' already low incomes and living standards. In a review of three case studies of Amazonian extractive communities, Browder (1992, 176ff.) found that on a wide variety of measures (e.g., infant mortality, diet, residential stability, literacy) extractivists fared poorly in comparison with broader regional populations.

NTFP EXTRACTIVE RESERVES IN THE UNITED STATES

Having briefly reviewed the western Amazonian experience, what lessons can be drawn for NTFP-assisted sustainable forestry in the United States, with its profound ecological as well as social and political economic differences? Crook and Clapp (this volume) note that environmental conditions for sustainable harvesting of NTFP species may more likely occur in temperate than tropical forests. That is, fewer species exist with generally larger, or at least more concentrated, populations. Although this situation is encouraging, there is a widespread lack of basic biological information about the abundance and distribution of harvestable species. Major questions remain about renewability of these resources, especially medicinal plants, and the extent to which productivity of such species is sufficient to support extraction at more than very modest levels.

But while ecological conditions in temperate forests may foster sustainable NTFP harvesting, sociopolitical conditions—at least in the United States—suggest that communally-based nontimber forest product extraction regimes, such as those recognized in the extractive reserve model from western Amazonia, are unlikely to work in most cases. A close examination of the Amazonian model suggests a number of critical differences that hinder the application of an extractive reserves model to temperate forest NTFP harvesting in North America:

1. In Amazonia, local users had a relatively long history of organizing to defend their basic subsistence rights. In the United States, apart from Indian reservations and some pockets of traditional collective uses (e.g., New England townships), there exists little tradition of formal collective use rights to forest resources by local communities. North America (along with Australia) is one of the few major regions in the world in which a subsistence-oriented peasantry did not develop, hence there are fewer place-based traditions of communal natural resource use (Berry 1996). As this book makes clear, however, NTFP extraction is widespread and significant to many rural as well as urban North Americans (see Goodman, this volume). The point is that in North America (and Australia) these practices have not achieved nearly the degree of cultural and/or political/legal recognition that they have for much of the rest of humanity.
2. In North America, commercial interests have long maintained cultural hegemony and define property in terms that militate against formally breaking up the bundle of property rights called private through, for example, assigning partial usufruct rights to communities adjacent to forest properties. Most NTFP harvesting in the United States is done informally, barely recognized even as usufruct rights, in a system generally

characterized by neglect—benign or otherwise (see Alexander, Weigand, and Blatner's discussion of global commodity chains, this volume).

3. The Brazilian experience depended heavily on direction by a charismatic, populist leader who captured international attention and support. Such leadership appears to be absent in the United States.
4. Brazilian, U.S., and certain European environmentalist NGOs rallied to support the rubber tappers, realizing that working to secure their usufruct rights would at the same time act to conserve major tracts of high-quality primary rain forest. But such a coalition seems difficult to achieve in the United States; most potential environmentalist allies are primarily urban middle class–based, preservationist, and misanthropic—and therefore antiextractive.
5. The Brazilian state was under strong international as well as rising domestic pressures to ameliorate widespread deforestation in the Amazon basin. Increasing international pressures may eventually lead the U.S. government to alter its domestic NTFP policy, but this seems unlikely.
6. Extractors in the United States are rarely residential in the sense of in situ subsistence residents. A variety of local as well as migrant harvesters collect NTFPs from public forestlands, so with a disinterested state unwilling if not legally unable to distinguish between local and nonlocal harvesters, how will diverse usufruct claims be reconciled? (McLain and Jones 1997).

Despite these glaring differences, however, there are some similarities that suggest that creative avenues may exist for adapting the extractive reserve model to U.S. nontimber forest product harvesting, particularly on lands considered marginally productive for full-scale commercial activity. A recent case study from upstate New York (Geisler and Silberling 1992) suggests some possible leads. The Finger Lakes National Forest (FLNF) is a federally owned, community-managed agroforestry system built on an earlier, New Deal–era program of buying up small farms from impoverished farmers on marginal lands. About fifty families now gain use rights through a permit process. The income from this commons flows to private users who also have other sources of income, so locals have a direct interest in maintaining the health of this environment as well as limiting access to free riders. Drawing from the Brazilian model, the authors distill four relevant and distinctive features of de facto extractive reserves (Geisler and Silberling 1992, 60): the organized (yet decentralized) extraction of natural resources with commercial value; a property system assuring limited access to and equity (ownership) in land and related resources; a local management system that prescribes and enforces acceptable extractive behaviors by user-group members; and a strategy for social as well as environmental sustainability adapted to marginal lands.

CONCLUSIONS

Basic social data about the importance of NTFP harvesting at the household and community levels are woefully incomplete. As this book demonstrates, it is becoming increasingly clear that in the United States, harvest of wild products such as ferns, moss, salal, rhododendron, mushrooms, and cascara bark, among others, is a viable (if not thriving) cottage industry involving thousands of people and millions of dollars. It is both more extensive and intensive than most professionals or lay people realize. "Brush picking," wildcrafting, and related NTFP harvesting is poorly understood as a way of life, since it is largely an inconspicuous, if not deliberately hidden, industry. (Standard survey and census methods and instruments imperfectly capture these patterns.) Like Amazonian rubber tappers, Brazil nut collectors, and other harvesters, long-term, multigenerational "brush pickers" and other NTFP harvesters in the Pacific Northwest and elsewhere have often devised local management strategies that may well be sustainable. On-the-ground investigation is clearly needed to identify and strengthen appropriate harvesting practices. Harvest techniques and consequent environmental impacts are poorly known.

But is the extractive reserve model a viable one to help protect an industry vulnerable to disruption and in need of protection through more formal recognition of use rights? Formidable political, legal, economic, and social barriers exist. NTFP harvesters need legal guarantees for long-term access to resource areas. Such predictability is critical in order to implement the kinds of sustainable management strategies that local harvesters have developed over long periods, several generations in some cases (e.g., the FLNF case [Geisler and Silberling 1992]), or that might be developed with further experience and investigation.

Establishing formal usufruct rights in the form of stewardship contracts in extractive reserves can achieve additional policy objectives beyond simply assisting resource-dependent communities hit hard by declining timber harvests (see Ringgold, this volume). By so solidifying the local stakes in forestland management, agencies could create effective buffer zones around areas of signficant biodiversity—e.g., biosphere reserves like the Olympic Peninsula in northwest Washington, where we have carried out research on harvesters of wild edible mushrooms (Love, Jones, and Liegel 1998). Local people manage buffer areas and benefit directly from continuous sustainable harvesting, while ecosystemic integrity is maintained and taxes are generated for state monitoring and other purposes (Love 1991).

In sum, applying an extractive reserve model to temperate forest NTFP extraction is possible but generally founders on a critical socioeconomic reality: what is primarily missing in North America is a class-based movement of people whose livelihoods depend largely, if not primarily, on harvesting such products from standing forests in some system of collective rights. Central to what little success Amazonian extractive reserves have experienced is a politically mobilized set of harvesters for whom forest preservation is in their direct interest, whose rights to forest resources are constrained in some way by communal forces, and whose harvesting was understood, by themselves if not by others, as traditional. With a few notable exceptions (e.g., many resource-owning Native American groups, and these for the most part are not commercially engaged), NTFP harvesters in the United States are profoundly immobilized politically despite certain local efforts to organize them, have only the barest of institutionalized community resource practices (however interesting sociologically), and are not seen as traditional by themselves or others in ways that can be activated legally. U.S. harvesters also seem to have few class allies, which in turn rests on the economic reality that for most, NTFP harvesting generates mainly seasonal, supplemental income.

To the extent that the nontimber forest product industry continues to develop, with a formalizing of commodity chain relations out and down to ground-level forest floor extraction itself, NTFP buyers and processors could yet join forces with increasingly waged labor to develop a multiclass movement with a direct interest in preserving standing forests. Whether such a movement could wring something like extractive reserves from the state is an open and fundamentally political question, well beyond the scope of this chapter.

REFERENCES

Berry, Wendell. 1996. *The Unsettling of America: Culture and Agriculture*. San Francisco: Sierra Club Books.

Browder, John O. 1992. "The Limits of Extractivism: Tropical Forest Strategies beyond Extractive Reserves." *Bioscience* 42(3): 174–182.

Clement, Charles R. 1993. "Extractive Reserves Examined." *Bioscience* 43(9): 644–646.

Geisler, Charles, and Louise Silberling. 1992. "Extractive Reserves As Alternative Land Reform: Amazonia and Appalachia Compared." *Agriculture and Human Values* 9(3): 58–70.

Hecht, Susanna, and Alexander Cockburn. 1990. *The Fate of the Forest: Developers, Destroyers, and Defenders of the Amazon*. London: Verso.

Love, Thomas. 1991. "A System of Sustainable Development: 'Extractive' Reserves for the Pacific Northwest Temperate Rain Forest," Oregon Academy of Sciences Session on Sustainability, February 23, Monmouth, OR.

Love, Thomas, Eric Jones, and Leon Liegel. 1998. "Valuing the Temperate Rainforest: Wild Mushrooming on the Olympic Peninsula Biosphere Reserve." *Ambio Special Report* 9:16–25.

McLain, Rebecca J., and Eric T. Jones, 1997. *Challenging "Community" Definitions in Sustainable Natural Resource Management: The Case of Wild Mushroom Harvesting in the USA*. Gatekeeper Series, no. 68, pp. 1–19. London: International Institute for Environment and Development, Sustainable Agriculture Programme.

Nepstad, Daniel C., and S. Schwartzman, eds. 1992. *Nontimber Products from Tropical Forests: Evaluation of a Conservation and Development Strategy*. New York: New York Botanical Garden.

Schwartzman, Stephan. 1989. "Extractive Reserves: The Rubber Tappers' Strategy for Sustainable Use of the Amazon Rain Forest." In *Fragile Lands of Latin America: Strategies for Sustainable Development*, ed. J. Browder, pp. 150–165. Boulder, CO: Westview Press.

Wolf, Eric, and Edward Hansen. 1972. *The Human Condition in Latin America*. New York: Oxford University Press.

CASE STUDY

Certification of Nontimber Forest Products

Patrick Mallet

Harvesting nontimber forest products is not a new forest practice, but the scale and intensity of commercial harvesting has increased considerably over the last decade (Blatner and Alexander 1998). In addition, little scientific knowledge exists on the resilience of many NTFPs to harvesting pressures or on the full implications of the ecological roles played by these products. Increased harvesting levels have the potential to drive the harvest of some species to unsustainable levels (Hansis 1998).

As nontimber forest products gain in market value and harvest and production levels rise, it will become increasingly important for natural resource managers and others to acquire the capability to gauge the impact that NTFP harvesting has on the environment and on local communities. Independent certification is one way to provide incentives for harvesters and producers to employ practices less harmful to the environment and of benefit to local economies. Certification is a market-based verification system that assesses resource harvesting operations against a standard set of criteria. These criteria generally reflect widely accepted best management practices in the field to which they are applied. In this chapter, I describe a number of different certification systems that are applicable to nontimber forest products and assess the utility of certification for these products.

SYSTEMS OF CERTIFICATION FOR NTPFS

Products on the shelves of specialty stores and supermarkets are increasingly likely to carry a certification logo on their packaging, conveying a message to consumers that the product meets specific criteria for sustainable harvest. Each certification program has its own area of emphasis, but many of those focused on biotic products share the same basic components: ecological, socioeconomic, and institutional. Some of the issues associated with ecological criteria include environmental harvesting practices, conservation of biodiversity, use of chemicals, and waste management. Socioeconomic criteria address the well-being of workers and local communities, indigenous people's rights, and the economic viability of the operation. Institutional issues relevant to certification include the legality of an operation, its management plan, and monitoring of activities (Mallet 1999).

Among the international systems significant for NTFPs are the Forest Stewardship Council (FSC) that promotes well-managed forests, the International Federation of Organic Agriculture Movements (IFOAM) that addresses organic agricultural practices, and the Fairtrade Labeling Organizations (FLO) that focuses on the well-being of the producer. These organizations each play a global coordination or accreditation role for certification bodies within their respective fields. Each of these programs includes all three types of criteria to a greater or lesser extent but places an emphasis on its own priority areas. A common element in the evolution of certification, and the direction in which these systems are moving, is to develop programs that are more holistic and well rounded. In other words, these certification programs are moving toward the promotion of more sustainable production systems (Mallet 1999).

CHALLENGES FOR NTFP CERTIFICATION

Certification of nontimber forest products is a new and emerging practice. Much like the commercial NTFP industry itself, certification of these products has only recently received serious consideration. Interest in certification is due to a number of factors including trends toward certification in other resource sectors, the potential for increased market access and price premiums, and a desire by producers and harvesters to be recognized for more ecologically and socially sustainable production systems (Viana, Pierce, and Donovan 1996; Hayward and Vertinsky 1999). However, given the lack of a significant body of practical experience in this area, many of the constraints to certification have yet to be worked out.

The lack of an internationally recognized system of certification targeted specifically toward NTFPs presents a challenge to NTFP management. The absence of such a system is due in part to the fact that the term "nontimber forest product" is primarily a political categorization rather than a clearly distinct ecological or social category of products. As most certification systems are developed for products that fit within clear ecological or social production systems, NTFPs have tended to fall through the cracks. In addition to the certification systems mentioned above, a number of agroforestry certification programs may be useful for NTFP harvesting. However, these certification systems focus mainly on intensive production operations and do not deal with the specific constraints faced in the wild harvest of nontimber forest products. The lack of a distinct system for NTFPs has prompted existing certification programs to review and develop their systems to meet the specific requirements of nontimber forest product harvesting operations. This has not always proved an easy task and much of the fine-tuning through field trials and policy development is still under way.

Each system of certification has had a different approach to certifying nontimber forest products. The organic industry has had criteria for some time that address wild-harvested products. Harvesters who seek to become certified under an IFOAM-accredited label are required to meet all of the basic criteria as well as to show that only a sustained yield of products is harvested from a strictly defined collecting area; that there is no contamination of that area by prohibited substances or from conventional farming; and that the operator is clearly defined and familiar with the harvesting area (IFOAM 1998). A similar situation exists in forest management systems where the overall management of the forest is certified. NTFPs are considered an integral part of a healthy forest and are therefore incorporated into the forest assessment. FSC-accredited certifiers have recently started certifying nontimber forest products under the basic principles and criteria with additional criteria specific to the ecological management of NTFPs. Fair trade certification, on the other hand, has been developing criteria on a product by product basis that includes a number of agroforestry products. The list of products under this system continues to grow and could come to include wild-crafted products, although in the United States forestry and agriculture certification programs will be more applicable than fair trade programs.

TENURE RIGHTS

None of the systems described above is ideal for the certification of nontimber forest products. Some of the key requirements in forestry and agriculture certification systems are not well suited to the realities of many NTFP harvesting operations. One of these problematic issues is tenure requirements. Certification usually requires limited access to a defined piece of land which creates two major hurdles for nontimber forest product harvesters. The first is that limited access means clear and exclusive rights to harvest NTFPs from the land. At minimum, this requires a restricted permitting system to be in place, which is rarely the case on public land. The second hurdle, related to the first, is that the boundaries of harvesting areas need to be clearly defined, which is not a problem where harvesting always takes place in the same location. However, many individuals, such as chanterelle and morel mushroom harvesters in the Pacific Northwest, harvest wherever species grow most abundantly, shifting location with the seasons and from year to year.

Some basic questions about what these programs are certifying also need to be asked. In NTFP harvesting operations, it is not the product that is being certified but the process by which the final product was arrived at. Certification of the product itself is more appropriate for products that are identical and that meet technical specifications for size and quality. In NTFP systems that certify the process, it is an area of land that is being certified, which means that all products harvested from the certified area can be labeled as such. This qualifier is useful for forest products, rather than having to inspect and label each product coming out of the forest, but it does not address the situation described above where NTFP harvesters do not work the same piece of land on a regular basis.

An alternative solution to this problem has been attempted through a number of different projects, including some based in the United States. Programs have been developed to certify the harvesters themselves rather than a defined area of land. This type of certification focuses on the skill and management practices of the harvesters, in effect certifying the manner in which they carry out their task. These initiatives can take the form of ethical harvesting guidelines that harvesters sign on to, such as the program operated by Trinity Alps Botanicals in California. This program has developed product-specific guidelines for a range of medicinal herbs including yarrow and Saint-John's-wort (Ambrose and Johnson 1999). Initiatives also sometimes involve training programs that harvesters participate in that teach them a common set of skills such as the harvester training program operated by the Northwest Natural Resources Group in Washington State. Although these programs do not meet the strict auditing requirements of a third-party certification system, they are useful in local circumstances.

SUSTAINABLE HARVESTS

Unlike timber, comparatively little research has been done on the ecology and resiliency of most nontimber forest products. Lacking a clear idea of how much a product can be harvested without adversely affecting its reproductive capacity or ecosystem functions, it is difficult to define sustainable harvesting levels that are required for many certification systems. Ecological research on NTFP species and the development of expertise often comes as a direct response to unexpected market demands (Johnson 1992), which means that many of the lesser known species have had very little research conducted on them and could be at greater risk of overharvesting. One tool that can be used to better define harvesting guidelines for a species is to work directly with the harvesters who tend to have the best idea of its resilience.

Defining the sustainable harvest of a species also brings up the issue of whether it is necessary to define harvesting criteria for each NTFP individually, or whether it is possible to develop generic criteria that can be applied to a whole range of products. This latter option would enable broader application of certification for nontimber forest products and has been the focus of a project being coordinated by SmartWood, an FSC-accredited certifier based in Vermont. The SmartWood project has developed a set of generic criteria for NTFPs harvested from natural forests that are based on the FSC principles and criteria but that also incorporate criteria for each component of a species being harvested. These components include exudates such as resins and gums, reproductive propagules like seeds and fruit, and vegetative structures including roots, bark, apical buds, and leaves (Shanley, Guillen and Laird 1999). The draft criteria were prepared in early 1999 and have been field-tested in half a dozen countries on products ranging from Brazil nuts to gum from the chicle tree. Each field test has provided further input for the criteria that are being refined to create a final generic list. The first case of applying these generic criteria to an NTFP in the United States took place in 2000 with sugar maples in the Northeast and was successful.

ORGANIZATIONAL ISSUES

Certification programs presuppose a certain level of organizational structure within an operation that will enable long-term planning and implementation. Some of these requirements can seem quite onerous for small operations. One of the main tools in forestry certification used to assess an operation's ability to harvest sustainably is a management plan. Although this is a basic requirement for all businesses, a plan that focuses on long-term harvest levels may not be as relevant for harvesters and may be beyond their existing capacity.

Related to this is the expense of getting certified. In all certification programs with the exception of fair trade, there are a number of costs incurred by the person or organization seeking certification. Some of these costs, such as the application fee, are fixed and are therefore more burdensome to smaller operations. In addition, many of the variable costs, including assessor fees, while not fixed, are more economical for larger operations. Harvesters must determine whether they need to pursue an internationally recognized certification system or whether their customers will be satisfied with the seal of a less costly local system.

MARKETS

The final area that presents challenges to NTFP certification is the marketplace. There are three key issues here. The first is that wildcrafting is tied closely to a subsistence economy. The harvest of nontimber forest products provides an invaluable and informal economic development opportunity for many rural communities, and a major part of this harvest happens outside the formal economy (Emery 1998). Certification, on the other hand, is a market-based mechanism, and its introduction could have negative impacts on subsistence harvesting by creating market demands and consequent regulations such as a permitting system where none existed before (Pierce 1999). Negative market impacts of certification can be minimized or avoided through meaningful participation of all stakeholders in the development or implementation of the certification program.

The second issue related to market demands is the association of certified products with product quality. Certified products have historically occupied niche markets that target upper-end consumers who demand a superior and uniform level of quality in their products. These high expectations mean that getting certified does not automatically guarantee market access; it is also critical to ensure that stringent quality controls are strictly enforced. Again, this issue is less of a factor where the product is being marketed locally and where more direct relationships are created between harvesters and consumers.

The final challenge for NTFP certification is to create a price premium for certified products in the marketplace. This is already happening on a regular basis with organic produce, and certified organic wild-harvested products should theoretically be able to access this same market. A price premium for certified forest products under FSC is not yet guaranteed, however, and more research needs to be done on whether consumers will associate certified NTFPs with better forest management and be willing to pay more for those certified products. Similarly, local certification systems have to rely on consumer recognition and awareness of their label and what it stands for in order to charge a higher price for their products.

SOME STEPS FORWARD

It is clear from the challenges outlined above that certification of NTFPs will be complicated. At the same time, many of these challenges arise because of the relatively recent development of certification for nontimber forest products and can be considered growing pains through which all new certification programs have to progress. Given the myriad challenges to certification, it may be useful to provide some examples of initiatives that have taken place in the United States. The following examples show how organizations are overcoming these obstacles and also help to define when certification of NTFPs is an appropriate tool.

One of the early initiatives, beginning in 1994, was the work of the

Rogue Institute for Ecology and Economy (RIEE) in Oregon. Southern Oregon was facing a crisis time of high unemployment and mill closures. Their project looked at sustainable economic alternatives for local forest workers and started by developing an inventory protocol for NTFPs as a means to understand what was in the forest. The Rogue Institute created the protocol in collaboration with a few harvesters, several agency botanists and nontimber forest product coordinators, and other local botanists. The development of the protocol happened in conjunction with a training program, where trainees spent nearly a year collecting data on private lands and also created a pared-down version of the protocol for public lands. The inventory protocol was to provide the foundation for development of new community NTFP initiatives. RIEE intended to develop sustainable harvest guidelines and then work to develop local businesses that used NTFPs in a sustainable manner, but these projects were not pursued due to lack of funding (Borsting 1999).

Another initiative that has been undertaken in the Pacific Northwest that focuses on the training of NTFP harvesters was a partnership between the Northwest Natural Resources Group (NNRG) and Rainkist, a craft marketing program that is part of Shorebank Enterprise in Washington State. Rainkist is a local economic development program that assists harvesters and craftspeople to market their natural products. They were interested in training NTFP harvesters to a uniform level of expertise and solicited the assistance of NNRG. The training program was adapted from a much longer course that had been developed previously in the region and focused mainly on providing the harvesters with core competency skills, including map reading, first aid, and safety. In addition, best management practices (BMPs) for three species—salal, western swordfern, and evergreen boughs—were developed and included as a key component of the training program (Pranger 1999; Van Daalen 1999).

Through the Rainkist program, harvesters who completed the two-day training were able to market their products as being sustainably harvested. NNRG is currently working on expanding the list of species covered by BMPs, and the course is now going to be offered to a wider range of harvesters through NNRG and the Alliance of Forest Workers and Harvesters (Van Daalen 1999). This program is a good example of how local organizations can create a training program that is relevant to harvesters in specific circumstances and provide them with the market mechanism to benefit from the training. As the program grows beyond its association with Rainkist, an increased emphasis will have to be placed on the marketing component of the program. The potential exists to develop the certification component of the training course further and to market a label associated with specific criteria.

Maple syrup from the U.S. Northeast exemplifies how a product can become associated with quality and excellence. Maple syrup from Vermont has been regulated and labeled by the state for the past fifty years, resulting in price premiums being paid by consumers who believe they are purchasing an environmentally friendly product (Viana, Pierce, and Donovan 1996). With the growing interest in forest certification in the United States over the last couple of years, a number of woodlot owners in this region have successfully sought certification for woodlots that contain sugarbush maples. While the FSC certification they received was for timber extraction, a small number of these same woodlot owners are now seeking to certify their sugarbush maple products as well. SmartWood, the FSC-accredited certifier involved, is revising the generic certification criteria developed through their NTFP project to meet the specific requirements of the sugar maple operations (Landis 1999). This is a case where criteria are being developed on a species by species basis to adequately assess the sustainability of the harvest.

A key factor in this example is that each of the harvesting operations has already been certified for its timber harvest, which means that the additional time and financial costs for these operations to get certified for maple products are reduced. It may not have been economically viable for these sugarbush maple operations to get certified for their NTFPs alone since the added value of certification in this case is not yet proven. However, if an operation were seeking certification for timber, it would make more sense to incorporate NTFPs into the assessment.

THE REAL VALUE OF CERTIFICATION

A lot of work remains to be done in order to refine certification systems so that they meet the needs of NTFP harvesters, producers, and managers. Much of this work can be accomplished through putting existing certification programs into practice for nontimber forest products and revising or reviewing them based on the results of field experiences. It will also take an increased interest by both the harvesters themselves and by consumers seeking certified products. Based on this requirement, considerable potential exists for the development of education and awareness programs that combine useful information with practical training.

A few general lessons can be drawn from existing experiences with certification of NTFPs. First among these is the importance for certification programs to define the target market and establish whether there is any demand for internationally recognized certification. Certification tends to be more applicable when the markets are at a great distance from where the product originates. The more local the market, the less likely that consumers will require an expensive, internationally recognized certification label. In these cases, the development of a local label that sells a unique messagc may be more appropriate.

Another factor to consider is whether the costs incurred to meet certification requirements are offset by the returns expected from selling certified products. The larger expense in many certification assessments is not the cost of the assessment itself, but rather the cost of changes that need to be made in order to meet the criteria. Harvesters can get a rough idea of what changes will be required by seeking a preassessment visit from a certifier. A second component is that relevant market research needs to be undertaken and made available to harvesters in order for them to determine whether their customers are willing to pay a premium for the certified product.

Certification has the potential to promote the sustainable harvest of nontimber forest products, both ecologically and socially. It is one tool among many that can be used. As can be seen in this chapter, there are many constraints to certification of NTFPs and many issues that have yet to be worked out, but, at the same time, there are a number of initiatives that are working to solve these problems. In the end, certification of NTFPs may appeal only to a small percentage of harvesters and producers. What has to be remembered is that certification is valuable not only for those who successfully complete the assessment process. The greatest value of certification may lie in the ability of producers to apply certification criteria even without seeking certification. Certification criteria represent best management practices in their respective fields. Producers and harvesters everywhere can use these guidelines to assess and improve their own practices so that they are less harmful to the environment and more beneficial to their local communities.

REFERENCES

Ambrose, C., and C. Johnson. 1999. *Standards and Guidelines for the Harvesting of Selected Medicinal Herbs*. Burnt Ranch, CA: Trinity Alps Botanicals.

Blatner, Keith, and Susan Alexander. 1998. "Recent Price Trends for Nontimber Forest Products in the Pacific Northwest." *Journal of Forest Products* 48(10): 28–34.

Borsting, Melissa. 1999. Personal communication, Rogue Institute for Culture and Ecology, Ashland, OR. November.

Emery, Marla. 1998. *Invisible Livelihoods: Nontimber Forest Products in Michigan's Upper Peninsula*. Ph.D. diss., Rutgers University.

Hansis, Richard. 1998. "A Political Ecology of Picking: Nontimber Forest Products in the Pacific Northwest." *Human Ecology* 26(1): 67–86.

Hayward, J. and I. Vertinsky. 1999. "High Expectations, Unexpected Benefits: What Managers and Owners Think of Certification." *Journal of Forestry* 97(2): 13–17.

IFOAM. 1998. Basic standards. International Federation of Organic Agriculture Movements (IFOAM), Tholey-Theley, Germany.

Johnson, J. H. 1992. "The Secret Harvest." *American Forests* 65:28–31.

Landis, J. 1999. Personal communication, SmartWood. November.

Mallet, P. 1999. *Certification of Nontimber Forest Products: The State of the Playing Field*. Knowlesville, New Brunswick: Falls Brook Centre.

Pierce, Alan. 1999. "The Challenges of Nontimber Forest Product Certification." *Journal of Forestry* 97(2): 34–37.

Pranger, D. 1999. Personal communication. Northwest Natural Resources Group. November.

Shanley, P., A. Guillen, and S. Laird. 1999. *Generic Guidelines for Assessing the Management of NTFPs in Natural Forests*. Richmond, VT: SmartWood Program.

Van Daalen, Chris. 1999. Personal communication. Alliance of Forest Workers and Harvesters. November.

Viana, V., Alan Pierce, and R. Donovan. 1996. "Certification of Nontimber Forest Products." In *Certification of Forest Products: Issues and Perspectives*, ed. V. Viana, A. Pierce, and R. Donovan, pp. 145–163. Washington, DC: Island Press.

Between Wildcrafting and Monocultures: Agroforestry Options

Wayne S. Teel and Louise E. Buck

Agroforestry is an approach to plant and animal production that intentionally integrates natural resources conservation objectives into the system. By strategically selecting combinations of woody and herbaceous plants and managing them to perform complementary agroecological roles, often with animals, the sustainability of producing multiple products with comparatively minimal external inputs can be enhanced. Environmental benefits that agroforestry systems generate often can be captured directly by the managing landowner through the creation of niches that over time favor the production of a variety of unique and profitable products.

This chapter explores the potential for producing nontimber forest products in agroforestry systems. By identifying options for this type of practice we aim to foster appreciation for the numerous opportunities that are present, and yet to be invented, for integrating specialty forest products into farms and rural enterprises. Expanding market demand for NTFPs provides an important incentive for landowners to invest in conservation farming practices through agroforestry. Such practices can serve also to limit the overexploitation of nontimber forest products from their native habitats.

Enthusiasm for designing and managing NTFPs in agroforestry systems is growing. Such practice is complex and uncertain, however, and experience has not been widely shared. Success will depend on a constellation of factors. Strategies for investing in NTFP production through agroforesty need to consider technical, economic, social, and institutional feasibility within particular cultural and ecological settings. We draw attention to key issues that influence the potential effectiveness of agroforestry approaches to producing NTFPs and suggest some means of addressing them that may help to unblock current constraints.

WILDCRAFTING AND THE PROBLEMS OF NONTIMBER FOREST PRODUCTS

According to legend, when the English colonizers of North America arrived, a squirrel could travel from the Atlantic to the Mississippi without ever touching the ground. Forests were, and remain, the dominant ecosystem in some parts of North America. European colonists, with a strong agrarian cultural tradition, never really learned to live in or with American forests, which were used as a source of timber, fuel, and fertilizer in the form of potash. Occasionally a special forest product such as naval stores—the sap from longleaf and other pine trees (primarily used for caulking in wooden sailing vessels)—became a key resource in support of the emerging imperial economy in Great Britain. No attempt was made to conserve this resource, and converting even longleaf pine to farmland signaled the "advance of civilization" (Williams 1992).

In the colonial process of usurping land and rights to the land of native peoples, much indigenous knowledge acquired by Native Americans over the millennia was lost. But Native Americans held and continue to hold an abundance of knowledge about native vegetation and technology for its use. A notable example is the sugar maple *(Acer saccharum),* which is a major tree species of the forests in the Northeast, from Kentucky to Minnesota and Maine and on into Ontario, Quebec, and the Maritime Provinces in Canada. Indigenous people in this region knew the sweet quality of the sap and developed ways to condense the sap into syrup using stone bowls and hot rocks (Nearing and Nearing 1950), technology that over time was adapted by white people to eventually create today's maple sugar and syrup industry.

Indians taught colonists about the medicinal uses of slippery elm *(Ulmus rubra)* and coneflowers (*Echinacea* spp.) (Missouri Dept. of Conservation 1993).[1] They also identified the value of black cohosh *(Cimicifuga racemosa)* for treating the symptoms of menopause. Black cohosh, a herbaceous perennial forest understory plant, is the main ingredient in *Remifemine,* an over-the-counter botanical packaged in Germany and sold in health centers. These are just four in a wide array of so-called nontimber forest products, or special forest products (SFPs), that have modern-day international markets.[2]

Foresters have long overlooked the value of these plants and have directed their efforts to silviculture and timber extraction, and more recently to rotational production of timber in monocultures or mixed stands. Another group of forest users has tapped the resources of the understory, often without the knowledge and consent of the landowners, whether the U.S. Forest Service, timber companies, or private landlords. In the eastern mountains of North America, these folk learned to derive an income from the land in niches ignored by the mainstream (Krochmal, Walters, and Doughty 1971; Crellin and Philpott 1990). Wildcrafters, as this group is sometimes called, glean the forests for roots, fruits, bark, branches and sap, or other products that they then sell to middlemen or processors. Some wildcrafters also actively manage sections of land for production, though not necessarily in a systematic fashion (Emery 1998).

For years, the markets for many of these products were relatively small, and the supply met demand without a noticeable depletion of the resources. This trend began to change in the 1980s and accelerated in the 1990s with the boom in consumer demand for natural products, especially those with medicinal or "food supplement" uses, which constitute a wide range of products commonly referred to as "nutraceuticals." Wildcrafters experienced higher demand and better prices for the products they collected, and thus extraction from the wild expanded. There has been a corresponding decrease in natural stocks of some of the plant material.

As supply drops and prices rise, users of a commodity begin seeking alternative strategies for obtaining more product. Wilcox Natural Products, a company that was formed in the mountains of North Carolina nearly one hundred years ago, exemplified this shift until its recent closure. The firm concentrated on the production of natural medicines from wildcrafted native plants. As the company expanded, their business grew to include Christmas greenery and furs. Then, in the late 1970s, a German firm, Zuellig Group NA, purchased Wilcox and expanded the American branch substantially to become the largest buyer, supplier, and producer of native medicinal plant products in the United States. Wilcox concentrated solely on medicinal plants, actively researched cultivation techniques for herbs, and recruited private landowners as growers. The company was careful to focus on appropriate techniques for wildcrafters that did not damage wild plant populations and ensured a high quality product.[3]

Concerns about the status of native plants are not based on economic necessity alone. Many herbalists and lovers of wildflowers share a desire to keep plant populations healthy for their own sake, not just for human use. A leading example among advocates of native plant populations of medicinal or aesthetic value are the members of United Plant Savers (UpS), a group dedicated to preserving, understanding, and sustaining use of native plants in North America. Though inclusive of all plants, the group focuses on finding ways to protect endangered plants that have medicinal, aesthetic, or other value. Two of these are goldenseal *(Hydrastis canadensis)* and black cohosh (Cech 1998). UpS insists that saving these plants is not simply a matter of protecting and preserving habitat. An appropriate conservation strategy also must include domesticated production by gardeners, herbalists, and forest owners for sale and home use.[4]

Cech (1998) is a prominent promoter of a new approach to native plant production: the deliberate farming of these products within the forest environment, or in "agroforests." In October 1998, the University of Minnesota sponsored a conference called "Enterprise Development through Agroforestry: Farming the Agroforest for Specialty Products." It brought together members of the academic community, natural resources professionals, landowners, and entrepreneurs from throughout North America to discuss the possibilities, methods, economics, and marketing of a wide variety of NTFPs from goldenseal to hazelnuts *(Corylus cornuta),* matsutake (pine mushrooms, *Tricholoma magnivelare*) to pine straw. Participants agreed that many plants of economic or cultural value were potentially at risk and that alternative production systems should be considered. Determining ways to propagate and cultivate these plants in an economically viable way was deemed essential. New ways of managing and harvesting plant populations will be situated somewhere between wild grown stock and open field monocultures.[5]

GINSENG: A MODEL FOR NTFP DEVELOPMENT?

Of all NTFPs, American ginseng *(Panax quinquefolius)* stands out as one of the best understood, arguably the most endangered, and certainly one of the most economically valuable. Ginseng acquired its status by virtue of its role in Chinese medicine. The Chinese species *(Panax ginseng)* has long been valued as a tonic for increasing energy and virility. Men chew pieces of roots, which look like tiny, misshaped carrots, the best having a human-like appearance. Due to the overexploitation of Chinese forests and expanding populations, Chinese ginseng production no longer comes close to meeting demand. American ginseng has achieved status as a valuable replacement, though it is not considered an exact substitute (Foster 1995).

Wildcrafted American ginseng of acceptable quality, as determined principally by age and shape, may sell to the collector for over five hundred dollars per pound. When prices rise to such dizzying heights, more people consider expanding domesticated production. Both in China and the United States, growers have made strides in producing ginseng under artificial shade. Shade-grown ginseng is an ingredient in many products now sold in the United States: herbal teas, soft drinks with ginseng, and a variety of herbal supplements. This type of ginseng, however, does not fill the same market niche as the wildcrafted ginseng in high demand by the Chinese market. Monocropped product sells for between ten and twenty dollars a pound, hardly a profitable price, because the roots do not possess the shape, age, or color characteristics desired in the Chinese market (Hankins 1997).

Since truly wild ginseng is becoming increasingly rare, and monocropped, artificially shaded ginseng does not bring a high price in conventional markets, searches are under way for alternative production strategies. One such method is called wild-simulated production. Scott Persons, author of *American Ginseng: Green Gold* (1994), has been an active leader in this work, conducting informal research and selling seed from his Tuckasegee Valley ginseng company in North Carolina. This process involves preparing seedbeds in the plant's natural habitat, sowing seed or one-year-old rootlets, and letting nature do the rest. Producers claim that the wild-simulated product will be comparable to wildcrafted roots and sell in that high-priced market (Beyfuss 1998). Andy Hankins of Virginia State University's extension program has planted wild-simulated beds of ginseng for the last fourteen years and is just now marketing the products.[6] As he says, it is the buyers who determine the value; producers can only hope to get close to what the market demands (personal communication 1998).

Producers have tried other methods of growing ginseng in the forest understory with more intensive production techniques. Instead of simply preparing beds, landowners like Bill Slagle in West Virginia prepare an entire section of understory after thinning a hardwood stand and then plant the area with ginseng (Temperate Agroforester 1999). This mixed hardwood and ginseng production system, combined with the growing of shiitake mushrooms on the thinned oak logs, is a prime example of an agroforestry system designed for an on-farm forest. Sustaining ginseng production via Slagel's intensive method, however, depends upon the use of substantial quantities of chemical inputs, which may impair the long-term viability of this currently highly profitable strategy.

AGROFORESTRY: DEFINITION AND EXAMPLES

Agroforestry is a term coined about twenty-five years ago to connote the deliberate management of trees within the farming context. Although there is no official definition, perhaps the most authoritative comes from the International Center for Research in Agroforestry (ICRAF), based in Nairobi, Kenya: "ICRAF defines agroforestry as a dynamic, ecologically based, natural resources management system that, through the integration of trees on farms and in the agricultural landscape, diversifies and sustains production for increased social, economic and environmental benefits for land users at all levels."[7] In North America, the Association for Temperate Agroforestry (AFTA) coordinates the sharing of information about agroforestry. In conjunction with the U.S. Department of Agriculture's National Agroforestry Center (NAC) based in Lincoln, Nebraska, the association has resources to help farmers and researchers develop agroforestry systems. In the last few years, their attention has turned toward the production and marketing of NTFPs.

AFTA and NAC have identified four main characteristics of agroforestry systems:

- First, they are *intentional.* Conscious efforts are made to incorporate trees into farming systems to improve the overall productivity and health of the farm, including the on-farm forest.
- Second, such systems are *intensive.* When these systems are in place, the overall complexity and diversity of spatial or temporal use of land rises, as does the type of management interventions.
- Third, agroforestry systems are *interactive.* Relations between the trees and crops are manipulated, enhancing the production of more than one product while simultaneously providing conservation benefits such as erosion control or expanding wildlife habitat.
- Fourth, these systems are *integrated.* The trees and crops are not seen as separate units but are managed together to increase productivity and protect the farm's soil and water.[8]

Though all agroforestry systems share these characteristics, the practices themselves are highly variable, depending on the ecology of the farm, the types of products the farmers wish to grow, and the ability to market them. Until recently, some NTFPs have not been considered major components of these systems, while others have been part of some systems from the earliest stages. The NAC places agroforestry practices into five categories that vary regionally across the continent but have similar spatial characteristics. These are considered in turn, with examples of appropriate NTFP management.

Forest Farming

"Farming the agroforest" generally refers to turning the understory region of a forest environment into a production zone for NTFPs in an intentional, intensive, and integrated fashion. Forest farming involves manipulating forestlands to create conditions that are conducive to introducing agricultural or cropping techniques into the forest system (Hill and Buck 2000). Many farms, especially those in the naturally forested ecosystems east of the 100th meridian or in the wetter regions of the west, have some woodland. These areas traditionally were sources for fuelwood, fenceposts, and building material from selected woody species and sometimes provided a haven for farm animals from temperature extremes. Farm woodlands occasionally were sources for wild berries or fruits as well but for the most part were left unmanaged and underutilized.

Recent extension efforts have targeted farm woodlots as resources for managed timber production. Publications like *Woodland Management,* jointly produced by Cornell University's Cooperative Extension Program,

SUNY College of Environmental Science and Forestry, and the New York State Department of Environmental Conservation (1987), provide considerable detail about managing woods for firewood, timber, and wildlife, though they make no mention of NTFPs. However, the increased demand for alternative medicines, natural nutritional supplements, and forest-based ornamental and decorative products has turned attention to these woodlots.

Timber production is a long-term prospect, with limited opportunities for intermediate or short-term returns. Although most woodlots have some potentially harvestable material, for the most part a management strategy will concentrate on "low-grading," or taking out junk or poorly formed trees to encourage straighter, more valuable trees to mature more rapidly. This is the strategy of Paul Strauss, a forest woodland owner in Rutland, Ohio, situated on the western fringe of the Appalachian region.

Strauss owns the seven-hundred-acre Equinox Farm, about half of which is in forest that he manages for the production of NTFPs. The forest is regularly thinned and improved using a rotational pattern that limits areas of disturbance and aims to encourage growth of selected understory species. Strauss tries to lives in as self-sufficient a manner as possible, growing much of his own food and producing ginseng, black cohosh, goldenseal, blue cohosh, and more than six hundred additional herbs on the farm. Shiitake and other mushrooms are grown on the thinned timber for food, medicine, and occasionally for sale. The farm also has beehives for pollen, honey, and other products.

Although a good supply of herbs, roots, and other plant material grows on the farm, the chief sales items are value-added botanical products marketed under the name Equinox Botanicals. Though many of the products are wildcrafted from his land, Strauss works closely with a group called Land Reformers, which he helped found, to propagate most of the material using germplasm from his forest. The only outside germplasm used is for native plants that are rare or absent from the farm. He views cultivation as the best way to preserve plants such as black cohosh that are declining due to overharvesting and has been conducting this type of work for over a decade.

The value of material taken from the woodlot on an annual basis is quite likely to exceed the value of timber harvested at the end of the rotation, whether that is forty, sixty, or even more years away. Although a formal economic analysis has yet to be done, it appears that NTFP harvesting on Equinox Farm provides a suitable standard of living for four people.

Cultivating American ginseng *(Panax quinquefolius)* and goldenseal *(Hydrastis canadensis)* in their native forest settings is a practice that was advocated by agricultural professionals early in this century (Harding 1972). The driving force has been the consistent market demand from China for American ginseng and the fluctuating but generally increasing domestic and international demand for other medicinal plants, particularly "root drugs." Recommendations generally are to approximate the natural growing conditions of the plants as closely as possible to produce roots of the highest economic value.

Each region of the country will feature different understory crops. Any location with the potential to sustain a forest, however, will likely have a healthy selection of herbs, botanicals, fruits, mushrooms, and more that can be managed in the understory among the trees. An example from the southeastern United States is saw palmetto *(Serenoa repens),* a low-growing palm that occurs as a major understory plant in pine *(Pinus clausa)* scrub and savanna throughout Florida and northward into parts of South Carolina and Mississippi. This endemic plant is important to many species of wildlife for nesting and protective cover and as a food source (Tanner, Mullahey, and Maehr 1995). Human interest in the plant has grown as "enviroscaping" has expanded, saw palmetto being naturally drought- and insect-resistant and requiring no fertilizer. Landscapers have found it difficult to transplant the species from the wild and have it survive, thus nurseries specializing in native species have begun to raise plants from seed to supply this market demand (Tanner, Mullahey, and Maehr 1995). The medicinal value of the saw palmetto fruit for relief of prostate gland swelling has led to its commercialization, and in 1995 its economic value began to make the news when the price for raw fruit exceeded three dollars per pound. A strong projected demand for the fruit by European pharmaceutical companies can supply an added economic value to the pine-dominated landscape from which it originates.

Alleycropping

In years after the term agroforestry was coined, alleycropping received more research and extension attention than any other agroforestry practice. As the name implies, alleycropping involves alternating rows of trees and crops in a cultivated setting. Tree rows may be straight or follow contour lines. Spacing between rows differs based on the types of benefits desired from the trees. In tropical settings, one benefit sought was enhanced soil stability and fertility, using deep-rooted trees, commonly nitrogen-fixing, to stabilize soils and add nitrogen through leaf litter to the cropped area of the field. In this system, trees are closely planted in rows that are spaced from ten to thirty feet apart depending upon conditions. Frequent pruning of the trees is required for nutrient release and to reduce light competition. These systems have tended not to be popular with farmers due to the high levels of labor and management required to control competition and obtain their multiple benefits. Alleycropping in developing countries tends to be most successful in contour hedgerow configurations where controlling erosion is important and in commercial, cash crop situations on relatively high-potential lands.

In North America, alleycropping, or intercropping with trees, is focused less on nutrient cycling benefits and more on producing an annual crop from the tree itself. The predominant species in these systems is black walnut *(Juglans nigra),* with research on its value in field settings conducted by various institutions from Missouri to Ontario. The tree has two major sources of value: the nut, harvested annually from trees that are fifteen years old or more, and timber, especially from veneer-quality logs derived from well-pruned and managed plantations (Garrett et al. 1991). Trees are planted in rows between forty and sixty feet apart to allow for use of farm equipment and thinned and pruned in the rows to an eventual density of approximately thirty trees per acre.

Opportunities for managing NTFPs in alleycropping systems will change as the tree component matures. During the establishment stage, a sun-loving herb such as echinacea might be grown in the alleys between rows of young trees. A shade-loving plant such as ginseng or goldenseal might be planted within the rows of trees even at an early stage in the development of the system. As the trees mature and cast more shade over a wider area, increasingly shade-tolerant species could be cultivated in the alleys. There are a number of multipurpose trees that might be used in these systems such as willow for floral displays, or pine for pine rope or pine straw. Presently, however, there is little experimentation or information upon which to evaluate the potential of this type of practice. Most alleycropping efforts emphasize nut production from black walnut, pecan *(Carya illinoensis),* or various cultivars of American hazelnut *(Corylus americana),* some hybridized with the common European hazelnut *(Corylus avellana).*

Shelterbelts and Windbreaks

Shelterbelts and windbreaks have been part of North American farming systems for a long time. One or more rows of trees planted perpendicular to prevailing winds reduce wind speed, prevent or limit snowdrifts, decrease evaporation, and increase infiltration of water in properly designed systems. Although often providing secondary products, such as fenceposts and firewood, windbreaks are seldom-considered product production sites. Through the 1970s and 1980s, U.S. agricultural policies promoted efficiency in farm equipment, and commodity prices encouraged many farmers to take out windbreaks and shelterbelts. With crop prices down and incentive programs like the Conservation Reserve Program encouraging them to take erodible land out of production, farmers again are considering these practices. Many express interest in also using these sites for producing additional products.

This desire has stimulated research in fruit- and nut-producing species as components of windbreak systems. One example is the Saskatoonberry, native to the northern plains of the United States and the Pacific Northwest and well into the same areas in Canada. The Saskatoonberry, also called western serviceberry *(Amelanchier alnifolia),* is an improved selection from wild stock that produces applelike blue "berries" between one and two centimeters in diameter. These are sweet, sometimes juicy fruits that make good jams, jellies, and pies and have been sold in roadside stands for over two dollars a pound (three dollars Canadian). The plant grows to twelve feet and, if protected well over its first four years, makes an excellent addition to windbreaks and snow fences. Saskatoonberry has the potential to replace the value lost from the conversion of crop acreage into windbreaks.

Developing a marketable product from plants growing in field borders and shelterbelts has precedents. A company called Minnesota Wild developed a line of products from wild chokecherries *(Prunus virginiana)* commonly found in fencerows and other farm sites. Now many farmers manage the chokecherry for fruit production rather than as an opportunistic invader of a field border.[9] Probably the key lesson from the chokecherry is that market development pulls production more readily than surplus production can push marketing.[10]

Riparian Buffer Zones

Probably no agroforestry land use has received more recent research support than the riparian buffer zone. Work by R. C. Schultz and J. P. Colletti at Iowa State University (Schultz et al. 1993), Andrew Gordon of the University of Guelph in Ontario (Gordon and Newman 1997), and Robert Tjaden of the University of Maryland (1998) have contributed substantially to our knowledge of agroforestry-based buffer zone practice and potential. The need to protect streams from erosion, nutrient loading, chemical pollution, and other forms of degradation associated with agriculture and urban sprawl spurs this research. Resources available to address these problems are large and growing (Tjaden 1998).

Tjaden (1998) lists a number of items that could grow in riparian zones for a profit. These include aromatic herbs, Christmas trees and greens, cooking wood, decorative cones, ginseng (upper flood plain only), nuts, shiitake mushrooms, and weaving and dyeing materials. To this list we could add poplars and willows for harvest as fuel or wood shavings to use as animal bedding, various riparian florals like pussy willow or curly willow, and medicinal plants such as slippery elm. Slippery elm *(Ulmus rubra)* has an exceptionally wide range of traditional and medicinal uses by Native American groups throughout much of North America. Growing naturally in river bottoms and on low fertile hills from southern Newfoundland to central Florida, its ecological range extends west across much of North America. It is the white, inner bark of this forty- to fifty-foot tree that is used as an aromatic as well as for a variety of medicinal purposes (Harding 1972).

A study of floral production in riparian areas that was conducted by Purdue University's Department of Horticulture suggests substantial potential for raising specialty products in riparian systems, especially in areas within easy access of a large floral market such as Chicago, New York City, or Washington, D.C. Dr. Bruno Moser, who is leading the study with wildlife specialist Brian Miller and agronomist Keith Johnson, planted a filter strip composed of orchard grass and three rows of horticultural shrubs at a density of 660 per acre along streams on selected farms. Their third year of harvest yielded a potential return of five thousand dollars per acre in the Chicago market. These strips have multiple benefits, including enhanced protection for wildlife, nutrient and sediment capture, economic return, and improved stream health.

Paul Stamets of Fungi Perfecti has proposed an unusual ingredient for riparian buffers in Washington State on southern Puget Sound. He prepared a bed of organic material for Royal Stropharia mushroom spore in the bottom of a ravine leading to the sound where a neighbor harvests clams and oysters. This ravine carried cattle manure–contaminated water contributing fecal coliforms to the salt water. Once the Stropharia mushrooms were established, Stamets noticed that water passing through the organic material lacked contaminants. He had the water tested and found a 98 percent reduction in fecal coliforms that he attributed to mycofiltration. The combination of edible mushroom production and nonpoint source pollution reduction makes this an ingredient worthy of consideration in a wide variety of buffer situations.[11]

Cottonwood *(Salicaceae)* is a family of fast-growing, multipurpose trees that are suited to many riparian settings. Some also perform well in the less moist environments of shelterbelts (windbreaks). A species of cottonwood that is commonly found along streams and rivers, *Populus deltoides,* can supply medicinal products, fodder, food preservatives, specialty implements, and building materials. The tree contains aspirin and in folk medicine has been used as a gynecological aid, an orthopedic aid, and in treating scurvy (Tantaquidgeon 1942).

At present the major incentive for farmers to limit their conventional agricultural activity in riparian zones is the Conservation Reserve Program (CRP), funded through the National Resource Conservation Service and often supplemented by state-supported programs. These pay rent to farmers for land they fence off or protect along streams, and subsidize alternative watering systems for cattle, the major cause of streambank degradation. However, the programs are time limited and there is no guarantee that conservation practices will not revert to previous forms of management when they end. Establishing a permanent riparian forest crop may offer a profit incentive for maintaining protection practices beyond the limits of the CRP.[12]

Silvopastoral Systems

Upon first consideration, integrating animals with special forest products may not seem a good idea. Given unrestricted access to forestland, animals will graze the understory down to bare soil, trample roots, and often browse or strip tree boughs and bark. In a silvopastoral system grazing needs to be carefully managed, which does not mean that the productivity of the animal component of the system must suffer. In fact, there is strong evidence that intensive, rapid rotation grazing actually increases the carrying capacity of the land as well as stimulating understory and grass growth. Much of the information on such practices comes from the work of Allan Savory (1988) on holistic resource management.

The basic theory is that cattle and other grazing or browsing animals in their natural state are always on the move. They move to avoid predators, keep ahead of flies, and pursue fresh fodder. Placing animals in a single field for long periods induces selective overgrazing and promotes degradation. By making fields smaller, moving cattle regularly, and providing alternative watering systems, the animals tend to concentrate on grass and herbaceous material, do less trampling damage, and eat less woody growth. This approach can increase the survival of an established tree component and permit the harvest of tree-grown products, although understory products would suffer periodic grazing.

An example of this approach comes from the mesquite-producing region of Texas *(Prosopis glandulosa* and *P. velutina)*. In most cases, mesquite grows as a shrubby weed that is disliked by ranchers and frequently mowed. However, it is possible to turn this weed into a multiproduct silvopastoral centerpiece (Felker 1999). Mesquite is nitrogen-fixing. It produces a long, sugary pod with good protein content that sometimes is ground into flour by indigenous people of the Southwest and Mexico and is a favorite browse of animals. Its wood is very hard, shrinks less than oak or hickory, and has high value for flooring or furniture. According to Peter Felker (1999), the wood is valued at one dollar per board foot, with the possible production of seven thousand board feet per acre on a thirty-year rotation. With its potential for food, fodder, nitrogen fixation, charcoal, and hardwood, it is surprising that the tree has not been more extensively exploited. According to Felker, the main drawback has been the lack of mechanical harvesting methods. In Mexico and Brazil, where labor is less expensive, use of the mesquite pod for food and fodder is correspondingly greater.

Ranchers do not like mesquite because of its thorniness and shrubby growth. With proper management, mature trees are more widespread, grow taller with thicker trunks, and associate well with grasses, increasing nitrogen and carbon in the soil as well as the quality and quantity of available forage (Felker 1999). Managed mesquite also makes a good shade tree for cattle and is important to wildlife. The key to developing mesquite is to view it as part of a system producing a number of products, instead of just focusing on a single product, such as beef, which most southwestern U.S. land managers tend to do at present.

Acacia farnesiana is another multipurpose woody perennial that has a high potential for cultivation in silvopastoral systems in Texas and other Gulf Coast states. Cassia perfume may be distilled from the flowers. The pods and bark contain a high percentage of tannins that are used for tanning leather, and the gum that exudes from the trunk is valued in arts. The wood is hard and durable, and the seed, leaves, and bark have been used throughout the world as remedies for various ailments (Duke 1983). The plant thrives in warm, dry localities, is propagated from seed and cuttings, grows rapidly, and does not require much cultivation, watering, or care (Duke 1981).

REGIONAL AND AGROECOLOGICAL VARIATIONS IN NTFP RESOURCES FOR ON-FARM SITUATIONS

A strategy to intentionally cultivate nontimber forest products raises a number of questions. Plant geneticists have not selected for cultivars of most NTFP species under cultivation or studied the factors affecting their growth. The economic potential of NTFP species is also poorly understood, and high demand for a wild-grown product does not necessarily translate into cultivars reaping the same profits. In addition, social impacts occur after domesticating a new crop, and these can be difficult to forecast. Finally, a sophisticated network of government agencies, commercial enterprises, and private consulting firms already serves industrialized agriculture in North America by helping farmers cope with selection, cultivation, and marketing questions. Similar services are not readily available for entrepreneurial landowners interested in new-to-market NTFPs.

The following sections of this chapter identify agroecological concerns and discuss economic, social, and institutional issues on the basis of ongoing work by the authors at Cornell University and the National Agroforestry Center. We are near completion in developing an assessment tool, in the form of a diagnostic matrix, which is designed to provide rapid access to basic information about specific NTFPs in particular regions of the country.

The United States is characterized by a highly diverse mix of climates, topographies, soils, and vegetation types. The Agroclimatic Zone Map published by the USDA points to the difficulty of dividing the country into growing regions based on political boundaries. Nevertheless, some regional distinctions based on vegetation type are useful.

The USDA National Resource Conservation Service (NRCS) uses a scheme of six regions, and we follow their regional guidelines where practical. Two of the six regions lack appreciable forest cover and have relatively dry climates. The potential for NTFP production in these areas is limited, with some notable exceptions. The Southwest Region includes most of the territory between the 100th meridian in Texas and the Pacific Coast of southern California, including the dry expanses of Colorado, Utah, and Nevada. The hot, dry climate here limits most NTFPs to riparian or gallery forests or to colder, high-altitude pine, spruce, and fir forests. The Great Plains Region extends from northern Texas to Canada, east of the Continental Divide almost to the Missouri River. Like the Southwest, most of the NTFPs in this region are either riparian or in higher forest zones such as the Black Hills of South Dakota. This region, however, has spearheaded efforts to incorporate some nontimber forest products into windbreak or shelterbelt systems.

The other four regions are more diverse. The Pacific Northwest Region includes those areas dominated by Douglas fir and ponderosa pine forests, extending from the coast to the Continental Divide. State or federal agencies manage much of the forestland. Other chapters in this book discuss agroforestry uses of this region more fully. In the Midwest, bordered by the Red River and Missouri Valleys in the west and the Ohio River on the south and east, large farms rather than large forests dominate the landscape. Northern hardwood forests thrive in nonfarm areas, and numerous NTFPs grow naturally in the understory or forest border areas. The same traits hold for the Northeastern Region, extending from Maryland north to Maine, except that smallholder forests are more common and the amount of NTFP cultivation presently under way is greater. Maryland, Virginia, West Virginia, and Kentucky are transition states, having climates, soils, and vegetation that fit both the eastern regions, but they arguably fit better in the Southeastern Region, dominated by southern hardwood forests and pine forests.

Table 10 presents a list of NTFPs found in the four predominantly forested regions, arranged by product type. Some products are widely known, others less so, but all are expected to have market potential soon. Despite considerable regional overlap, especially in the East, cultivation practices in different regions may require the development of different cultivars that are adapted to regional conditions.

An example of the need for cultivars is the pawpaw (*Asimina triloba*). The native range of this fruit-bearing tree is the eastern United States from

Table 10. A sampling of important nontraditional forest products listed by product type in four regions of the United States

Pacific Northwest	Midwest	Northeast	Southeast
	DECORATIVES		
Bear grass	American bittersweet	American holly	Christmas trees
Western juniper	Black walnuts	Bankers willow	Easter red cedar
Western red cedar	Christmas trees	Birch	Grape vines
Incense cedar	Corkscrew willow	Black ash	Pine straw
Christmas trees	Hybrid poplar	Boughs (fir and pine)	Pine rope
Hybrid poplar	Red osier dogwood	Christmas trees	Spanish moss
Noble fir (boughs)	Russian olive	Corkscrew willow	*Smilax smallii*
Salal	Witchhazel	Willow	
Willows			
	MUSHROOMS		
Boletes	King Stropharia	King Stropharia	Morels
Matsutake (pine mushrooms)	Oyster	Oyster	King Stropharia
King Stropharia	Shiitake	Shiitake	Shiitake
Chanterelles			Truffles
Morels			
	FOOD: NUTS, FRUIT		
Berries (variety)	Black walnuts	Berries	Black walnuts
Hazelnuts	Chestnuts	Black walnuts	Chestnuts
Huckleberries	Chokecherries	Chokecherries	Pawpaw
Wasabe (horseradish)	Hazelnuts	Hazelnuts	Pecans
Honey	Maple syrup	Maple syrup	Persimmons
	Pawpaw	Honey	Honey
	Honey		
	HERBAL MEDICINALS		
Buckthorn	Black cohosh	Black cohosh	Black cohosh
Devil's club	Blue cohosh	Blue cohosh	Goldenseal
Oregon-grape	Ginseng	Ginseng	Saw palmetto
Pacific yew	Goldenseal	Goldenseal	Slippery elm

Alabama and Mississippi north and east to New York and west to Iowa. It commonly grows in the partially shaded understory on moister sites but does not like continuously wet conditions. Pawpaw fruit resembles a combination of mango, pineapple, and banana when fully ripened on the tree. It does not last long on the shelf, so either must be eaten fresh or preserved in some fashion. Fruit in the wild carries a wide range of traits. Sometimes fully ripened fruit is astringent to the point of unpalatability, and trees vary widely in productivity, appearance, and ripening time, among other characteristics.

Although Native Americans have eaten pawpaw fruit for millennia, few efforts to improve the stock occurred until recently. Kentucky State University is now taking the lead in this effort, coordinating the work of numerous individual growers around the country and bringing their information into a central database.[13] The KSU website lists forty-four different varieties from thirteen states and Ontario, Canada. Cultivar selection is possible for pawpaw but remains less sophisticated than for most fruits, with little capacity to select for cultivars by soil type and for specific fruit traits. As the popularity of the fruit increases, better selection options will become available.

The same could be said for a number of the products listed in the table. Some, such as shiitake mushrooms, have active commercial distribution systems, high consumer recognition, and production of cultivars for sale around the country. Others, like blue cohosh, are just in the beginning stages of identifying cultivation techniques, and few details are available about growing conditions and handling germplasm. Given the present high interest in these products and active information sharing available via websites, needed technology is likely to develop quickly.

A downside to domesticating NTFPs exists as well. Any time cultivation activities occur, selections from wild stock contain characteristics that ultimately are desired by consumers. Selection could result in plant populations under cultivation with a relatively narrow genetic base and a high vulnerability to pests and diseases. At the same time, the remaining wild stock could come under pressure from other markets for different characteristics, as has been the case with ginseng. Crook and Clapp (this volume) discuss this tendency as part of the boom-and-bust cycle in wild natural resources. Striking a balance between domesticated and wild production of these products may prove more agronomically sound than focusing all resources on cultivating within agroforestry systems.

ECONOMIC CONSIDERATIONS

Any assessment of NTFPs as a crop eventually must demonstrate that growing the item has potential for economic return. Some growers of NTFPs are wildly enthusiastic about production possibilities but often have failed to apply the same enthusiasm to market development of the product. As a result, they are left with a stockpile of product and a limited market. Economists describe this as a "push" marketing strategy, driven by the producers' hope that the availability of a product accompanied by a significant sales push will open a market. This strategy places the producer at high risk and could scare away more risk-averse potential producers entirely.

Chamberlain and Hammett (1999) advocate a different approach. They suggest that the agroforestry community in North America has stressed the development of production technologies that improve biological interactions between trees, crops, and animals, with all three components contributing to the overall productivity of the farm (Garrett et al. 1994). This emphasis shows how agroforestry benefits a farm in an ecological sense but does little to provide farmers with an economic incentive to implement the system. To increase adoption of agroforestry practices, and by association introductions of nontimber forest products, potential producers need to see that their income will climb if the new practice is adopted.

Such an approach would require a "comprehensive analysis of all factors that affect agroforestry adoption" (Chamberlain and Hammett 1999). This process identifies areas where knowledge about the production and marketing of a given product is strong or weak and guides the direction of research and extension activities. At present, researchers and extension staff concentrate on production, if they have a program at all, and leave economic factors aside until production begins. Since farmers' strengths are generally in production, however, they need more help in value-added processing and marketing of their products. If these questions were addressed first, more producers could risk introducing a new product into their farming systems.

To address the economic issues raised by each product, we propose that a series of questions be asked, which should address local, regional, national, and international markets:

- What is the current potential for landowners to generate income by producing this item as a raw commodity?
- What is the current potential for producers and/or entrepreneurs to profit by investing time or capital or both in the processing and marketing of this product?
- Who are current or potential consumers?
- What types of products are presently purchased in the market made from or with this product?
- What is the future potential for landowners and/or entrepreneurs to benefit financially from this product?
- What is the current market development for this item as raw material?
- What is the current market development for products made from this item?
- What is the potential for developing or expanding markets within a given region for this item or products made from it?
- What is the potential for developing or expanding national and/or international markets for this item or products made from it?
- What are the labor requirements for this product in its raw form and for the value-added products?
- Does the labor demand come at a complementary time to other farm labor, or does it conflict with peak labor periods?
- Will development of this product negatively impact local wild-harvested systems/household economies?
- What are acceptable levels of risk?

At present, suitable market analyses are available for only a few NTFPs. Well-known products such as ginseng (Robbins 1998) in the Northeast and matsutake mushrooms (Hosford and Pilz 1997) in the Pacific Northwest have been analyzed. For the most part, however, market and enterprise information to aid producer decisions is unavailable, even for well-known products like sugar maple (Krasny, personal communication 1999). This area stands as one of the major identified needs of NTFP development.

SOCIAL CONSIDERATIONS

Wildcrafting is a way of life for a small but significant number of people around the country. The activity is difficult to document and quantify. In the Appalachian region, wildcrafting ginseng, black cohosh, and Virginia snakeroot *(Aristolochia serpentaria)* commonly accompanies other woods-based activities such as fur trapping, small-scale logging, and moonshining. Andy Hankins, who has worked with ginseng in the wild and in wild-simulated settings for fifteen years, avoids planting ginseng in the forests of the Blue Ridge Mountains because he knows wildcrafters will pluck the product before the landowner can. Their traditional antipathy to anything and anyone related to government (referred to as revenuers) makes forest management of NTFPs risky at best (Hankins 1998).

A new factor for wildcrafters is the recent addition to the CITES list of threatened species of many NTFPs, including ginseng, black cohosh, and goldenseal. This designation requires government regulation of the harvesting of these plants. In some cases, a total ban on harvesting has been imposed in certain areas, such as the Hoosier National Forest in southern Indiana, where local wildcrafters have harvested American ginseng for years. For the most part, these are poor families at least partly dependent on the plants for income. As with wildcrafters in the Appalachians, families are reluctant to disclose locations of digging sites or information about income relating to their wildcrafting activities. At the same time, they are indignant about the regulatory restrictions and claim, with some justification, that they spend time replanting as they harvest.[14]

This example points to another question about NTFPs: what impact has traditional wildcrafting had on the present distribution and genetic diversity of the products? If the wildcrafters' claim that they do have a positive impact on plant populations within the protected areas is true, will restricting their access lead to a decline in both population and diversity? If their claim is false, are there ways they can become participants in wild-simulated or forest farming activities in designated areas to reverse their loss of income due to regulatory enforcement?

The shift in production from wildcrafting situations to agroforestry settings is likely to cause a change in beneficiaries. Most wildcrafters are resource-poor, generally having an inadequate land base to switch from wildcrafting activities to management of wild-simulated or cultivated production systems, and they generally have little interest in making such a transition (Emery 1998). Any agroforestry activity requires a land base, whether private or rented, usually with some long-term security given the nature of the system. Ultimately, this situation could lead to a transfer of wealth unless wildcrafters are included in the management decision-making process (McLain and Jones 1997). It is likely to be both socially and ecologically beneficial to formulate policy to protect NTFPs that does not victimize traditional harvesters but instead engages them in constructive conservation measures to ensure the sustainability of the wild populations and traditional livelihoods.

Concern about regulation is not limited to wildcrafters. Rapidly expanding markets for nutraceuticals (unregulated botanical products used as dietary supplements) has led to a proliferation of product labels with a wide variety of claims for health benefits. Presently, the Food and Drug Administration does not regulate or control labeling or the contents of nutraceuticals as long as the company makes no claim about medical efficacy. Most producers of these value-added products (capsules, tinctures, extracts, and other items) express concern that a few manufacturers who do not voluntarily adhere to product quality control measures and whose products could be construed as health risks could stimulate the FDA to begin regulating the industry. Additional costs of conforming to regulations are likely to put a number of small producers out of business. Because profit margins are small for growing the raw materials, certain products might become unavailable. Although better-financed companies with streamlined production systems may pick up some products, others with very limited markets may be dropped.

Growing NTFPs in agroforestry settings will alter present social relations. Some transfer of wealth is inevitable, and the focus will move from dispersed forest gathering systems to local, intensively managed production units. Ultimately, supplies of these products will increase as markets expand, enabling a broader distribution to processors and consumers. Those who profit from the present production system, particularly wildcrafters, will bear much of the cost of this transition through losses of returns to their labor. Such factors should influence agroforestry professionals to include in agroforestry system design activities people who could potentially lose as production strategies change. Only time will tell if it is possible to design systems that encompass a broad range of beneficiaries.

INSTITUTIONAL CONSIDERATIONS

Agricultural extension services based at state land grant colleges and universities are a widely accepted resource for farmers. Similar services are available from the USDA National Resource Conservation Service, state foresters, and the U.S. Forest Service and its state and private forestry for private woodland owners, primarily for timber or wood product management. Agroforestry is gaining wider acceptance in the United States, especially since the NRCS and the Forest Service established the National Agroforestry Center as a partnership between the two land management organizations (Lassoie and Buck 2000). NTFPs, however, do not fit easily into the missions of these agencies and services and do not have an established niche in any of these institutions. Institutional support for activity related to NTFP development varies widely from state to state and often is difficult to locate.

A characteristic of institutional support that currently is available is product specificity. For example, Cornell University has expertise on maple and ginseng in its Natural Resources Department but little experience with other products. The University of Missouri has a major focus on black walnut– and pecan-based agroforestry practices but so far little knowledge of other NTFPs. Kentucky State University has a strong emphasis on pawpaw, North Carolina State University's Department of Horticultural Science harbors expertise on goldenseal, the University of Florida's Range Science Program is a resource center for saw palmetto, and there are other examples of public institutional support for particular products. Few research and educational institutions, however, have a broad-based expertise in NTFPs, although several have a single staff person with a keen interest in the subject.

This situation suggests that an effective model for further development might rest on state or academic institutions that are specialized in one or more NTFPs, with such institutions becoming centers of expertise for their particular product(s) that reach beyond conventional state boundaries. Producers then would seek information from a broad range of institutions via various extension media such as the World Wide Web, Cooperative Extension services, or the NRCS. Access to useful information could be facilitated through sponsored activities such as regional assessments, workshops, or web-page development as well as specific training events. Such activities should be designed to improve the quality of information in addition to making it more readily accessible. The strategy would be a reasonably efficient means of meeting information needs about diverse species without duplicating scarce research and extension resources.

Building institutional capacity is one of the main requirements in advancing the status and utility of NTFPs. The challenge is to increase awareness about these products, their present and potential roles in the market, and the methods of production. Few people at county cooperative extension bureaus or NRCS field offices are at all familiar with NTFPs, since the topic is not included in the curriculum of their training institutions. Unless individual professionals develop an interest through contacts with producers or potential producers, field personnel have little if any information to share.

Perhaps the most hopeful sign is rapidly proliferating information from Internet websites. Some is very general, giving only plant descriptions and uses. Other information is more specific and helpful, but users generally do not know how reliable it is for their circumstances. Research-based information is badly needed.

Through our national assessment of nontimber forest products, we currently are examining the institutional capacity for aiding producers and marketers of NTFPs on a product-specific basis within NRCS regions. The effort involves attempts to establish links with various organizations—public, private, business, and nonprofit—that can provide information, services, or genetic material. The goal is not to develop a single, comprehensive source for information about NTFPs but to contribute some order to a growing network of information sources by making it easier to find answers to specific needs.

CONCLUSION

Agroforestry is an important land use option for many landowners, particularly farmers who seek to diversify their operations ecologically and economically. Agroforestry practices can provide a variety of services such as crop protection from wind, riparian zone protection, soil conservation, and habitat for pollinators and pest predators. They also can provide products for additional income, such as fenceposts, firewood, foods, herbs, nursery plants, and others. NTFPs can fit into agroforestry systems to improve overall productivity, diversity, and ecological health.

Agroforestry, however, is not a simple solution. Such practices tend to require careful planning and design and knowledge-intensive management. Nor is agroforestry development a rapid process. Most NTFPs take time to establish and may require several years to bring a significant return. In the long run, however, agroforestry systems that include NTFPs can contribute importantly to sustainable agricultural development and to forest quality improvement while generating significant economic returns to the landowner (Buck, Lassoie, and Fernandes 1999). Accepting this challenge over more conventional pathways to crop development through monocropping is a mission that can help bind natural resources professionals and practicing land managers in their quests for innovative solutions to the imperatives of natural resources conservation and sustainable economic development.

NOTES

1. Although Europeans accepted and used Native American knowledge about medicinal and food plants in the seventeenth century, in the westward expansion of the nineteenth century the dominant attitude about medicine and the critical need for Indian medicine had changed greatly. Surviving tribes retained the medicine of Indian people in the West, but in the East, where many tribes disappeared, the technology was transmitted to the mainstream medical culture.

2. There are some differences between agriculturalists and foresters over what to call products from the forests that lie outside the mainstream of forestry. Forest managers prefer nontimber forest products, while agriculturalists like special forest products, the difference being that farmers include timber as a product since it is outside their normal production sphere. Since this book is directed primarily to the forestry community, the acronym NTFP will be used, although in the context of agroforestry, timber and other wood products are included in the management strategies described.

3. Information for this paragraph comes from the Wilcox Natural Products website, *www.goldenseal.com,* and from personal communication with Ed Fletcher, manager of the Wilcox experimental farm.

4. The UpS website is *www.plantsavers.org*. The reference, Richo Cech (1998), is located at this site, originally published in the fall 1998 UpS newsletter.

5. Native medicinal plants from prairie ecosystems, like echinacea, could be grown in monocultures. However, an equally strong argument could be made for growing them in mixed cultures of native prairie vegetation, where disease and other hazards of monocultures are minimized.

6. Hankins is extension specialist in alternative agriculture, Virginia Cooperative Extension, Virginia State University, P.O. Box 9081, Petersburg, VA 23806.

7. See *http://www.cgiar.org/ICRAF/ag_facts/ag_facts.htm.*

8. See *http://www.unl.edu/nac/database/.*

9. From a talk by Jay Erckenbrack at the conference "Enterprise Development through Agroforestry: Farming the Agroforest for Specialty Products,"October 4, 1998, Minneapolis.

10. See the section entitled "Economic Considerations" in this chapter.

11. From the Fungi Perfecti website, *www.fungi.com.*

12. A major stream protection effort is currently going on in the Pacific Northwest to compensate farmers in the region for removing crop rows or cows from salmonid streams, which is a part of the effort to comply with the endangered species act. Voluntary replacement encouraged by the ability to gain an economic benefit from streambank protection systems that incorporate NTFPs might be better in the long term.

13. The web address for this site is *http://www.pawpaw.kysu.edu/.* Dr. Kirk Pomper heads up the research on the project.

14. The information for this paragraph comes from Karyn Moskowitz, a resident of the area who has written about NTFPs in other settings. She is currently involved in helping organize the ginseng diggers in southern Indiana and to try to quantify the production and economic impact of ginseng harvest.

REFERENCES

Beyfuss, R. 1998. *The Practical Guide to Growing Ginseng*. Freehold, NY: Robert Beyfuss.

Buck, Louise E., J. P. Lassoie, and E. C. F. Fernandes. 1999. *Agroforestry in Sustainable Agricultural Systems*. Boca Raton, FL: CRC Press.

Chamberlain, Jim L., and A. L. Hammett. 1999. "Marketing Agroforestry: An Alternative Approach for the 21st Century." In *Exploring the Opportunities for Agroforestry in Changing Rural Landscapes: Proceedings of the Fifth Biennial Conference on Agroforestry in North America, August 3–6, 1997,* ed. L. E. Buck and J. P. Lassoie, pp. 208–214. Ithaca, NY: Cornell University Department of Natural Resources.

Crellin, John K., and Jane Philpott. 1990. *Herbal Medicine: Past and Present.* Durham, NC: Duke University Press.

Duke, James A. 1981. *Handbook of Legumes of World Economic Importance.* New York: Plenum Press.

———. 1983. "Handbook of Energy Crops." N.p.

Emery, Marla R. 1998. "Invisible Livelihoods: Nontimber Forest Products in Michigan's Upper Peninsula." Ph.D. diss., Rutgers University.

Felker, Peter. 1999. Personal communication.

———. 1999. "A Review of Mesquite and Leucaena Agroforestry in Southwestern USA." In *Exploring the Opportunities for Agroforestry in Changing Rural Landscapes: Proceedings of the Fifth Biennial Conference on Agroforestry in North America, August 3–6, 1997,* ed. L. E. Buck and J. P. Lassoie. Ithaca, NY: Cornell University Department of Natural Resources.

Foster, S. 1995. *Forest Pharmacy: Medicinal Plants in American Forests.* Durham, NC: Forest History Society.

Garrett, H. E., J. E. Jones, J. K. Haines, and J. P. Slusher. 1991. "Black Walnut Nut Production under Alleycropping Management: An Old but New Cash Crop for the Farm Community." In *The Second Conference on Agroforestry in North America,* ed. H. E. Garrett, pp. 159–165. Columbia: University of Missouri School of Natural Resources.

Garrett, H. E., et al. 1994. *Agroforestry: An Integrated Land Use System for Production and Farm Land Conservation.* Lincoln, NE: Association for Temperate Agroforestry.

Gordon, A. M., and S. M. Newman. 1997. *Temperate Agroforestry Systems.* Pp. 48–51. London: CAB International.

Hankins, A. 1997. "Wild-Simulated Ginseng Cultivation." *Temperate Agroforester.* January.

———. 1998. Personal communication.

Harding, A. R. 1972. *Ginseng and Other Medicinal Plants.* Columbus, Ohio: A. R. Harding.

Hill, D. B., and L. E. Buck. 2000. "Forest Farming." In *North American Agroforestry: An Integrated Science and Practice,* ed. H. E. Garrett, W. J. Rietveld, and R. F. Fisher. Madison, WI: American Society of Agronomy.

Hosford, D., and David Pilz. 1997. *Ecology and Management of the Commercially*

Harvested American Matsutake Mushroom. Pub. no. PNW-GTR-412. Portland, OR: USDA Forest Service, Pacific Northwest Research Station.

Krasny, Marianne. 1999. Personal communication.

Krochmal, Arnold, Russell S. Walters, and Richard M. Doughty. 1971. *A Guide to Medicinal Plants of Appalachia*. Washington, DC: U.S. Forest Service.

Lassoie, J. P., and L. E. Buck, 2000. "The Development of Agroforestry as an Integrated Land Use Management Strategy." In *North American Agroforestry: An Integrated Science and Practice,* ed. H. E. Garrett, W. J. Rietveld, and R. F. Fisher, pp. 1–29. Madison, WI: American Society of Agronomy.

McLain, Rebecca J., and Eric T. Jones. 1997. *Challenging "Community" Definitions in Sustainable Natural Resource Management: The Case of Wild Mushroom Harvesting in the USA*. Gatekeeper Series, no. 68, pp. 1–19. London: International Institute for Environment and Development, Sustainable Agriculture Programme.

Missouri Department of Conservation. 1993. *Missouri Special Forest Products Project: Final Report*. Corvallis, OR: Mater Engineering.

Nearing, Helen, and Scott Nearing. 1950. *The Maple Sugar Book, Together with Remarks on Pioneering as a Way of Living in the Twentieth Century*. New York: Schocken Books.

Persons, W. S. 1994. *American Ginseng: Green Gold*. Asheville, NC: Bright Mountain Books.

Robbins, Christopher S. 1998. *American Ginseng: The Root of North America's Medicinal Herb Trade*. Washington, DC: Traffic North America.

Savory, A. 1988. *Holistic Resource Management*. Washington, DC: Island Press.

Schultz, R. C., J. P. Collitti, W. W. Simpkins, C. W. Mize, and M. L. Thompson. 1994. "Design and Placement of a Multi-Species Riparian Buffer Strip System." In *Opportunities for Agroforestry in the Temperate Zone Worldwide: Proceedings of the Third North American Agroforestry Conference, August 15–18, 1993,* ed. R. C. Schultz and J. P. Colletti, pp. 109–120. Ames: Iowa State University, Department of Forestry, College of Agriculture.

Tanner, G., J. J. Mullahey, and D. Maehr. 1995. "Saw Palmetto: An Ecologically and Economically Important Native Palm." Circular WEC-109. Gainesville: University of Florida, Institute of Food and Agricultural Sciences, Range Science Program. *(www.wec.ufl.edu/research/range/sawpalm/default.htm)*.

Tantaquidgeon, Gladys, 1942. *A Study of Delaware Indian Medicine Practice and Folk Beliefs*. Harrisburg, PA: Pennsylvania Historical Commission.

Tjaden, R. 1998. "Real and Potential Income Opportunities for Riparian Areas." In *Natural Resources Income Opportunities for Private Lands*: *Conference Proceedings, April 5–7, 1998,* ed. J. S. Kays, G. R. Goff, P. J. Smallidge, W. N. Grafton, and J. A. Parkhurst, pp. 199–208. College Park: University of Maryland Cooperative Extension Service.

Williams, Michael. 1992. *Americans and Their Forests: A Historical Geography*. Cambridge, UK: Cambridge University Press.

CASE STUDY

Native U.S. Plants in Honey and Pollen Production

Anita G. Alexander and Susan J. Alexander

Honeybees have been important throughout history, as pollinators and for their honey.[1] Honey is frequently mentioned as a nontimber forest product (Chakravarti and Verma 1991; Economic Commission for Europe 1993; Midwest Research Institute 1992), and honeybees pollinate a variety of common agricultural crops and native plants. Beekeeping is not a large industry, but the products and services provided by bees and beekeepers are an integral part of American agriculture (Delaplane 1996).

Although honeybees are an introduced species in North America, they are an integral part of the food chain because of their efficiency and prevalence. Pollination of agricultural crops results in enhanced product yield and quality and thus an increase in value. For all of U.S. agriculture, this increase in crop value attributable to honey bees was $9.3 billion in 1989 (Robinson, Nowogrodski, and Morse 1989) and $14.6 billion in 1999 (Morse and Calderone 2000), a 36.3 percent increase. According to Morse and Calderone (2000), 20 to 25 percent of that increase is due to inflation and the rest to growing demand for pollinated food by an expanding population. As farms grow larger and management intensifies, they predict that growers will depend less on native solitary and semisocial ground and twig-nesting bees. Honeybees continue to be the pollinators of choice because of their availability throughout the season, because they pollinate a wide variety of crops, and because they can be concentrated in large numbers as needed.

Many insects visit crops and effect pollination. There are a number of bees native to North America that pollinate agricultural crops. Bumblebees are reared commercially as pollinators of greenhouse crops, and a few solitary bee species are managed on field and orchard crops (Williams 1995). Orchard bees are raised and managed by some growers to pollinate crops such as apples. Many species of bumblebees have long tongues and can pollinate flowers that other bees cannot. Digger bees and sweat bees are good pollinators. The alkali bee pollinates alfalfa, onions, clover, mint, and celery. Squash bees pollinate squash, pumpkins, and gourds. Leafcutter bees are efficient pollinators who prefer legumes but will pollinate other crops, such as carrots (Strickler 2000). None of these native bees produce honey in harvestable quantities.

Although some growers depend on solitary and semisocial ground and twig-nesting bees, honeybees provide an estimated 80 percent of food and other agricultural crop pollination (USDA 1971). From the standpoint of agriculture, pollination is the most important function that honeybees perform. The bee selects a nectar source richest in sugar concentration and closest to the hive, and works those specific plant species until the food supply ceases. Unlike butterflies and moths, foraging honeybees usually confine their foraging to one plant species at a time. Consequently, species are cross-pollinated most efficiently by bees.

The number of honeybees in a colony is a factor in their significance in agriculture, as there are forty to sixty thousand in one hive in the summer (Moeller 1961). A colony of bumblebees is far smaller, but their longer tongue enables them to utilize different plants. A typical honeybee colony might have five to eight thousand active foraging bees, while a bumblebee colony has only a few hundred at most (Winston 1999). An average honeybee colony may have about twenty thousand bees surviving the winter months. As daylight hours increase and temperatures rise, the population of the colony will increase to about sixty thousand (Moeller 1961). Of this large number of bees, the several thousand foraging bees per colony will pollinate tremendous numbers of plants.

People who keep bees do so for a variety of reasons. Commercial beekeepers keep thousands of hives and often move them long distances for pollination contracts. Fruits, vegetables, seed crops, almonds, legumes, and many other important agricultural products require insect pollination. Farmers pay commercial beekeepers to place hives in locations where pollination is necessary for the production of a crop, such as almonds or canola. Commercial beekeepers may move hives from the Northeast to Florida and back or from Oregon to California and back in one year.

More colonies of honeybees are owned and operated in California than in any other state (Morse and Calderone 2000). Robinson, Nowogrodski, and Morse (1989) estimated that 70 percent of the colonies rented for pollination in the United States were rented in California. California is different from other states in that farms are larger and there are fewer hobby beekeepers in its agricultural areas (Morse and Calderone 2000). Most commercial beekeepers rely on both pollination fees and income from honey. Many other beekeepers have far fewer hives and refer to themselves as hobbyists. Hobby beekeepers may also derive income from pollination fees, honey and wax, and even propolis and pollen. They rely on native and agricultural sources of forage for their bees, and many market their honey as being from wildflowers.

Costs associated with keeping bees include mite and disease treatments and equipment costs. Parasitic tracheal mites were introduced to North America in 1984, and Varroa mites in 1987. They have become a leading cause of the loss of honeybees throughout the United States. As much as 80 percent of feral honeybees have been lost to mites and disease in the past decade in the United States, so beekeepers must know and use effective controls (Delaplane 1996). They must be well informed about bee diseases and care and often are members of state and national associations.

BEE DEVELOPMENT AND SEASONAL ACTIVITY

A bee colony is a highly organized interdependent unit. Unlike other insects, honeybees neither die nor hibernate in early winter. Consequently, when cold weather prevents food gathering, honeybee colonies must have ample stores of honey and pollen very near the clustered mass of bees. Flower nectar provides the carbohydrates, and flower pollen provides the minerals, vitamins, and protein needed for growth and a healthy life span. Bees can carry their own weight in nectar and use the carbohydrates for energy. Pollen contains a wide variety of nutrients that support growth and development of living organisms. Many of the nutrients, particularly certain amino acids, are essential for the development of honeybees from the egg to the mature adult. Pollen grains differ in protein and fiber content but are the only source of these essential nutrients for honeybees. A bee foraging for pollen packs it into a compact load on each hind leg and returns to the hive with it (Crane 1990). Flower nectar stored in the hive, dehydrated and then capped with a thin layer of wax, becomes honey.

Generally, pollen from insect-pollinated angiosperms provides more nutrients than does pollen from gymnosperms and other wind-pollinated plants. The grasses, sedges, rushes, and cereal grains that depend upon wind pollination have small green or dull-colored flowers, usually scentless and with no nectar. Plants attractive to honeybees are accessible to them and produce pollen and usually nectar. Flowering plants with substantial amounts of pollen but with little or no nectar have particularly large and brightly colored blooms, such as poppies and roses (Lovell 1926).

Honeybees must store pollen and nectar for their own needs in the winter and spring, particularly for the time when the weather warms in the spring but before pollen and nectar become widely available. Nectar and pollen are stored in the cells of the honeycomb. A honeybee colony uses fifty to sixty pounds of honey or a substitute fed by the beekeeper, if not more, from the time brood rearing starts in the spring until the main honey flow. Spring supplies of pollen are just as important as nectar, because brood rearing requires eight to ten pounds of pollen per month to maintain the colony and rear larvae (Scullen 1947). The honeybee digestive tract discards about 50 percent of the pollen ingested. Water is also essential to the bees' survival. As bees cannot store water, it must be available close to the hives with safe access. Water seeping or running through sand or damp earth in a place sheltered from wind is ideal (Crane 1990).

Certain plants supply reliable pollen, but the nectar supply of any given plant is subject to many variables. Latitude, temperature, soil type and fertility, and water supply determine feast or famine for the foraging worker bee. For example, fireweed yields a surplus nectar flow once every four to six years at forty-five degrees latitude. The farther north one goes, the better the nectar flow from fireweed, with increased hours of sunlight, cool nights, and sunny days to help evaporate the nectar and increase sugar concentration (Crane 1990). Many variables govern the production of nectar in various plant species, but information about native wild plants is sparse (Goltz 1999). One colony of bees needs no less than an acre of nectar and pollen sources, as a general guideline (USDA 1971). Of necessity, beekeepers select sites on the basis of identification of good food sources: flowering trees, shrubs, and herbaceous plants with high nectar or pollen content.

Good pollination of multiple plant species is of value to other wildlife. If the stigma of the blossom is fully pollinated, the resulting fruit will be fully developed, hence larger and of better quality or balance, that is, rounded apples and berries with every drupe filled. The increased size and quality benefits forest animals and insects. Many weeds are good forage plants and reproduce better if the seed supply is ample. Valuable erosion control is supplied by annual and perennial herbaceous bee plants as well as woody bee plants such as willows and black locust.

COLONY PLACEMENT

Beekeepers place colonies at specific sites for a variety of reasons. Good nectar sources are needed in the spring for increasing colony size and in the fall for winter food supply. The location must have abundant plants attractive to bees and all-weather roads suited for a loaded truck. Access should be limited to deter vandalism. Beekeepers have lost entire yards to bear damage and human vandalism. Ants, mice, skunks, raccoons, and horses will also damage bee colonies, as will disease and parasites. In addition to sharing the responsibility for fire protection, the landowner and the beekeeper must agree on a reasonable fee. The beekeeper provides part of the fire protection and obtains personal liability insurance. The costs of locating hives in many areas include long drives to remote yards (locations where many hives are kept); distance increases the time and expense of management. Hives require frequent observation, manipulation, and knowledgeable care. Even with excellent forage plants, variables such as local temperature and humidity greatly influence nectar production. Clean, safe water is needed daily because bees do not store water. If the beekeeper must haul water, time and expense increase sharply.

LAND MANAGEMENT AND POLICY ISSUES

Beekeepers with many hives are often interested in temporary locations where the bees might collect nectar for food needs or for honey production. Commercial beekeepers use such sites between pollination contracts or for overwintering. In the past, many hobby and commercial beekeepers used sites with gated access roads, often on public lands in the West. Federal land managers issued permits promptly for thirty to fifty dollars per season. The beekeeper provided fire and liability insurance; if nature was kind, bees would collect winter stores and the beekeeper would share jars of honey with district personnel. In the lower forty-eight states, fireweed would provide enough nectar flow for a surplus one year out of five. Only when the bees have more honey than they need can beekeepers remove honey from the hive, particularly for a fall or early spring crop. Fireweed honey is choice, very mild and clear, and often brings a premium price. Alaska has a more reliable fireweed flow largely due to the long summer days (Crane 1990).

Beekeepers in the Pacific Northwest now report experiencing permit delays that amount to refusals on public lands. Commercial and noncommercial beekeepers have experienced delays of three to seven months, rejection of all selected sites, and requests to locate bees along highly traveled, very public roads. The beekeepers must fill out environmental impact statements for yards of any size, and permit fees vary widely within districts or national forests. As roads have been closed and access has decreased, and areas with desirable forage plants such as fireweed have decreased in acreage, public lands have become less desirable for beekeepers. Most beekeepers are unwilling to fill out lengthy forms or pay high fees, particularly when they are accustomed to being paid to locate bees. Most people interested in wild plant honey crops would be willing to pay fees based on the number of yards or colonies if the process seemed equitable and quick. Beekeepers we interviewed, however, have not generally had positive experiences with public land agencies in the past decade or so.

PLANT SOURCES OF NECTAR AND POLLEN IN THE UNITED STATES

This section focuses on nectar and pollen sources most attractive to honeybees. Table 11 shows native sources of pollen and nectar that receive honeybee visitation for trees, shrubs, and herbaceous plants common in meadows, woodlands, and forests. Most of the plants we know as honey source plants developed in Asia or Europe, not in the Western Hemisphere. The evolution of plants in North America was largely keyed to other pollinators that exerted selection on flower color and other secondary attractants, such as odor. As a consequence, many Western plant families are not attractive to honeybees, which are not native to North America. Commercially grown fruits, vegetables, and seed crops are not included. Introduced species are included if widely naturalized, and these species have italicized common names and range descriptions in the tables. Some plants are toxic to bees or to animals (Table 12).

Table 11 lists trees that have been noted in the literature as important sources of nectar and pollen throughout the United States. All are hardwoods. Honeybees also collect sap exudates from some conifers, referred to as "honeydew" in the literature. Conifers are not included in this chapter, however, because the literature is inconclusive as to the benefit and uses of honeydew by honeybees.

Shrubs important to honeybees as sources of nectar and pollen are also listed in the table. Native shrubs reported as important nectar and pollen sources throughout the United States are included except for Hawaii, which is so different that it deserves separate treatment. U.S. territories (American Samoa, Guam, Puerto Rico, and the U.S. Virgin Islands) are not included, as they also need separate treatment. Native herbaceous plants reported as most attractive to honeybees in the literature throughout the United States (except Hawaii and U.S. territories) are included.

Table 12 lists plants that have nectar and pollen that are toxic to bees, to mammals, or to both. Although very few nectars are poisonous to bees, the nectar of any plant to which a systemic insecticide has been applied may become toxic to bees (Crane 1990). Some plants contain alkaloids that prevent the reproduction of liver cells, thereby causing irreversible liver damage in mammals (Burrill et al. 1996). Plants in Table 12 with these alkaloids include the *Apocynum* species (dogbane), *Asclepias* species (milkweeds), and *Senecio* species (stinking willie or tansy ragwort, and groundsells). All bees *(Hymenoptera)* are attracted to these plants as sources of pollen and are not harmed by them. The nectar can be used by the bees as food, but not by humans. With the exception of wingleaf soapberry, the plants in Table 12 are toxic to all mammals if ingested. Pacific poison oak is not included because it is a fine forage plant for bees and the honey is safe for human consumption. Ott (1998) reviewed the history and phytochemistry of toxic honeys, and he suggested that they may have served as indicators of psychoactive and other medicinal plants for people exploring novel ecosystems. He examined the ethnomedicinal uses of honey and proposed that psychoactive honey may have intentionally been produced by pre-Columbian Mayans.

Table 11. Plants important as nectar and pollen sources in the United States

Nectar*	Pollen*	Latin name	NRCS common name(s)	Native range *(Introduced range)*
			TREES	
x	x	*Acacia berlanderi*	guajillo	TX
x	x	*A. farnesiana*	sweet acacia, huisache	PR, SE, TX, VI
x	x	*A. greggii*	catclaw acacia	CA, SW, TX
x	x	*Acer circinatum*	vine maple	AK, CA, PNW
x	x	*A. macrophyllum*	big-leaf maple	CA, PNW
x	x	*A. negundo*	box elder	All US except AK, MW
x	x	*A. platanoides*	Norway maple	*MW, NE*
x	x	*A. pseudoplantanus*	sycamore maple	*MW, NE*
x	x	*A. rubrum*	red maple	FL, LPS, MW, NE, SE
x	x	*A. saccharium*	sugar maple	MW, NE, SE
x	x	*Arbutus menziesii*	Pacific madrone	CA, PNW
x	x	*Catalpa bignonioides*	southern catalpa	FL, LPS, MW, NE, SE
x	x	*C. speciosa*	northern catalpa	LPS, MW, NE, SE, UPS
x	x	*Cercis canadensis*	eastern redbud	FL, LPS, MW, NE, SE
x	x	*C. orbiculata*	California redbud	CA
x	x	*Cladrastis kentukea*	Kentucky yellowwood	MW, SE
x	x	*Cornus* spp.	dogwood	Widespread
x	x	*Catageus* spp.	hawthorn	Widespread
x	(x)	*Diospyros virginiana*	common persimmon	FL, LPS, MW, NE, SE
x	x	*Eucalyptus* spp.	eucalyptus	*CA, FL, HI, PNW, PR, SW, TX, VI*
x	x	*Frangula purshiana*	Pursh's buckthorn, cascara	CA, PNW, RM
	x	*Fraxinus* spp.	ash	Widespread
x	x	*Gleditsea triacanthos*	honey locust	Widespread
x	x	*Liriodendron tulipifera*	tulip-tree, tulip poplar	FL, MW, NE, SE, TX
x	x	*Malus* spp.	crabapple	Widespread
x	x	*Nyssa aquatica*	water tupelo	FL, SE, TX
x	x	*N. sylvatica*	black-gum	FL, LPS, MW, NE, SE
x	x	*Oxydendrum arboreum*	sourwood, sorrell tree	FL, MW, NE, SE
	x	*Populus* spp.	aspen, cottonwood, balsam poplar, and so on	Widespread
(x)	x	*Prunus americana*	American plum	East, South
(x)	x	*P. emarginata*	bitter cherry	CA, PNW, RM, SW
(x)	x	*P. pensylvanica*	pin cherry	MW, NE, RM, SE, UPS
(x)	x	*P. virginiana*	chokecherry	Widespread except FL
x	x	*Rhamnus* spp.	buckthorn	Widespread except AK, FL
x	x	*Robinia pseudoacacia*	black locust, yellow locust	FL, LPS, MW, NE, SE, UPS
x	x	*Tilia americana*	American basswood	FL, LPS, MW, NE, SE, UPS
x	x	*Ulmus americana*	American elm	FL, LPS, MW, NE, SE, UPS
			SHRUBS	
x	x	*Amelanchier alnifolia*	serviceberry, saskatoon	AK, CA, PNW, RM, UPS
x	(x)	*Arcotostaphylos manzanita*	whiteleaf manzanita	CA
x	x	*A. uva-ursi*	kinnikinnick	AK, CA, MW, NE, PNW, RM, SW

Table 11. Continued

Nectar*	Pollen*	Latin name	NRCS common name(s)	Native range *(Introduced range)*
			SHRUBS, continued	
	x	*Artemisia* spp.	sagebrush	Widespread
x	x	*Castonopsis chrysophylla*	giant chinquapin	CA, PNW
x	x	*Ceanothus* spp.	ceanothus, snowbrush, deerbrush, and so on	Widespread except AK, HI
x	(x)	*Cephalanthus occidentalis*	common button bush	CA, FL, LPS, MW, NE, SE
x	x	*Clethra alnifolia*	coastal sweetpepper-bush	FL, NE, SE, TX
x	x	*Cotoneaster* spp.	cotoneaster	CA, HI, MW, NE, PNW
x	x	*Gaultheria shallon*	salal	AK, CA, PNW
x	x	*G. humifusa*	alpine spicywintergreen	CA, PNW, RM
x	x	*G. ovatifoilia*	western teaberry	CA, PNW, RM
	x	*Ilex glabra*	inkberry, gallberry	FL, NE, SE, TX
	x	*I. opaca*	American holly	FL, LPS, MW, NE, SE
	x	*I. verticillata*	common winterberry	FL, MW, NE, SE, TX
x	x	*Mahonia aquifolium*	hollyleaved barberry, tall Oregon-grape	CA, PNW, RM
x	x	*M. nervosa*	Cascade barberry, dwarf Oregon-grape	CA, PNW
x	x	*M. repens*	creeping barberry	CA, PNW, RM, SW, UPS
x	(x)	*Physocarpos* spp.	ninebark	Widespread
x	x	*Purshia tridentata*	antelope bitterbrush	CA, PNW, RM, SW
x	x	*Rosa* spp.	wild rose	Widespread
x	x	*Rubus* spp.	blackberry, thimble-berry, and so on	Widespread
x	x	*Salix* spp.	willow	Widespread
x	x	*Symphoricarpos albus*	common snowberry	Widespread
x	x	*S. mollis*	creeping snowberry	CA
x	x	*S. occidentalis*	western snowberry	LPS, MW, NE, PNW, RM, UPS
x	x	*S. rotundifolia*	roundleaf snowberry	CA, RM, SW, TX
x	x	*Vaccinium* spp.	blueberry, cranberry, and so on	Widespread
x	x	*Viburnum prunifolium*	black haw, stagbush	LPS, MW, NE, SE
x	(x)	*Vitex negundo*	chastetree, vitex	*FL, LPS, VI*
(x)	x	*Yucca filamentosa*	Adam's needle	FL, MW, NE, SE, TX
(x)	x	*Y. glauca*	soapweed, yucca	LPS, RM, UPS
			HERBACEOUS PLANTS	
x	x	*Aster* spp.	aster	Widespread
x	x	*Balsamorhiza deltoidea*	deltoid balsam root	CA, PNW
x	x	*Brassica rapa*	field mustard	Widespread
x	x	*B. nigra*	black mustard	Widespread
x	x	*Centaurea cyanus*	garden cornflower	Widespread
x	x	*C. jacea*	brownray knapweed	CA, MW, NE, PNW, RM
x	x	*C. solstitialis*	yellow star thistle	Widespread except SE
x	x	*Chamerion angustifolium*	fireweed	AK, CA, MW, NE, RM, SW, UPS
x	x	*Cirsium arvense*	Canadian thistle	Widespread except FL, LPS, SE

Nectar*	Pollen*	Latin name	NRCS common name(s)	Native range *(Introduced range)*
		HERBACEOUS PLANTS, continued		
x	x	*C. vulgare*	bull thistle	Widespread
x	x	*Dipsacus fullonum*	Fuller's teasel	Widespread except FL, SE, TX
x	x	*Erodium cicutarium*	redstem stork's bill	Widespread except FL
x	x	*Fagopyrum esculentum*	buckwheat	Widespread except TX
x	x	*Phacelia* spp.	fiddleneck	Widespread except FL
x	x	*P. tanacetifolia*	lacy phacelia	CA, SW
x	x	*Scrophularia californica*	California figwort	CA
x	x	S. marilandica	carpenter's square	FL, LPS, MW, NE, SE, UPS
x	x	*S. vulgaris*	common groundsell	Widespread
x	x	*Sinapis alba*	white mustard	Widespread
x	x	*S. arvensis*	charlock mustard	Widespread
(x)	(x)	*Solidago canadensis*	Canada goldenrod	Widespread
x	x	*S. rugosa*	wrinkleleaf goldenrod	FL, LPS, MW, NE, SE
x	x	*Taraxacum officinale*	common dandelion	Widespread

Sources for tree material include Bailey Hortorium 1976; Burgett, Stringer, and Johnston 1989; Crane 1990; Dalby 1999b, 1999d; Harlow and Harrar 1937; Hitchcock and Cronquist 1976; Little 1979; Lovell 1926; Mountain et al. 1992; Peck 1961; Ramsay 1987; Russ 1999; Stanger et al. 1971; and Wilson 1974. *Sources for shrub material* include Bailey Hortorium 1976; Burgett, Stringer, and Johnston 1989; Crane 1990; Dalby 1999c; Harlow and Harrar 1937; Hitchcock and Cronquist 1976; Lovell 1926; Peck 1961; Pellett 1923; Ramsay 1987; Russ 1999; Stanger et al. 1971; and USDA 1971. *Sources for herbaceous plant material* include Bailey Hortorium 1976; Burgett, Stringer, and Johnston 1989; Burrill et al. 1996; Crane 1990; Dalby 1999a; Harlow and Harrar 1937; Hitchcock and Cronquist 1976; Larrison et al. 1977; Lovell 1926; Mountain et al. 1992; Peck 1961; Pellett 1923; Ramsay 1987; Russ 1999; Sharples 1958; and USDA 1971.

The USDA Natural Resource Conservation Service (NRCS) was the source for current Latin and common names. The website is *plants.usda.gov*.

Geographic abbreviations: AK = Alaska; CA = California; FL = Florida; HI = Hawaii; LPS (lower prairie states) = OK, TX; MW = Midwest; NC (north central states) = Illinois, Indiana, Iowa, Kentucky, Michigan, Minnesota, Missouri, Ohio, Wisconsin; NE (northeastern states) = Connecticut, Delaware, Maine, Maryland, Massachusetts, New Hampshire, New Jersey, New York, Pennsylvania, Rhode Island, Vermont, West Virginia; PNW (Pacific Northwest) = Oregon, Washington; PR = Puerto Rico; RM (Rocky Mountains) = Colorado, Idaho, Montana, Utah, Wyoming; SE (southeastern states) = Alabama, Arkansas, Georgia, Mississippi, North Carolina, South Carolina, Tennessee, Virginia; SW (southwestern states) = Arizona, Nevada, New Mexico; TX = Texas; UPS (upper prairie states) = North Dakota, South Dakota; VI = U.S. Virgin Islands.

*If sources were inconclusive about whether pollen or nectar was important from a particular species, we put the "x" in parenthesis. If the species is not a source of pollen or nectar, there is no "x."

Table 12. Plants toxic to bees and/or animals

Nectar toxic to bees	Pollen toxic to to bees	Latin name	NRCS common name(s)	Honey toxic to humans	Native range *(Introduced range)*
Yes	Yes	*Aconitum* spp.	monkshood	Yes	Widespread
Yes	Yes	*Aesculus californica*	California buckeye	No	CA

Table 12. Continued

Nectar toxic to bees	Pollen toxic to to bees	Latin name	NRCS common name(s)	Honey toxic to humans	Native range *(Introduced range)*
Yes	Yes	*Andromeda* spp.	bog rosemary	Uncertain	MW, NE, PNW
No	No	*Apocynum* spp.	dogbane	Yes	Widespread
No	No	*Asclepias* spp.	milkweed	Yes	Widespread
Yes	Yes	*Astragalus* spp.	milkvetch	Yes	Widespread
Uncertain	Uncertain	*Conium maculatum*	poison hemlock	Uncertain	*Widespread except AK, FL*
Yes	Yes	*Euphorbia* spp. (including *Chamaesyce)*	spurge	Yes	Widespread
Yes	Yes	*Hymenoxys hoopesii*	owl's claws	No	CA, PNW, RM, SW
Yes	Yes	*Rhododendron* spp.	rhododendron	Uncertain	Widespread
Yes	No	*Sapindus marginatus*	wingleaf	Uncertain	FL, PR, SE, VI
No	No	*Senecio jacobaea*	stinking willie or tansy ragwort	Yes	*Widespread*
No	No	*S. riddellii*	Riddell's ragwort	Yes	LPS, RM, SW, UPS
No	Yes	*Taxus* spp.	yew	No	West
Yes	Yes	*Veratrum californicum*	California false hellebore	Yes	CA, PNW, RM, SW
Yes	Yes	*Zigadenus venenosus*	meadow death-camus	Yes	West

Sources: Bailey Hortorium 1976; Burgett, Stringer, and Johnston 1989; Burrill et al. 1996; Crane 1990; Ramsay 1987; Stanger et al. 1971; USDA 1971; and Whittlesay 1985.

The USDA Natural Resource Conservation Service (NRCS) was the source for current Latin and common names. The website is *plants.usda.gov.*

Geographic abbreviations: AK = Alaska; CA = California; FL = Florida; HI = Hawaii; LPS (lower prairie states) = OK, TX; MW = Midwest; NC (north central states) = Illinois, Indiana, Iowa, Kentucky, Michigan, Minnesota, Missouri, Ohio, Wisconsin; NE (northeastern states) = Connecticut, Delaware, Maine, Maryland, Massachusetts, New Hampshire, New Jersey, New York, Pennsylvania, Rhode Island, Vermont, West Virginia; PNW (Pacific Northwest) = Oregon, Washington; PR = Puerto Rico; RM (Rocky Mountains) = Colorado, Idaho, Montana, Utah, Wyoming; SE (southeastern states) = Alabama, Arkansas, Georgia, Mississippi, North Carolina, South Carolina, Tennessee, Virginia; SW (southwestern states) = Arizona, Nevada, New Mexico; TX = Texas; UPS (upper prairie states) = North Dakota, South Dakota; VI = U.S. Virgin Islands.

Fortunately, plants with bad odors attract flies, not bees. Few poisonous plants attract bees, and beekeepers avoid sites thick with nectar or pollen sources poisonous to humans, such as California buckeye, meadow death-camas, and *Rhododendron* species. Table 12 indicates nectar and pollen sources that beekeepers need to avoid.

Honeybees are an integral, although often unacknowledged, part of American agriculture and American life. Almost all food plants except grasses (corn, grains) are insect pollinated, and plants used for oil, fiber, and forage seeds depend on insects. Honeybees are often considered as competitors to other flower visitors, particularly in areas where they are not native (Williams 1995; Paton 1993), but there might be beneficial interactions too. Some native plants may have lost their native pollinators because of loss of native habitat, fires, chance, or even past competition with honeybees. Honeybees may enable those plants to continue to set seed. Although there is some information and research under way about competition among bee species, there is still relatively little known about the requirements of native plants and their native pollinators and the impact of land use changes and honeybees on native pollinators. Measures that are taken to preserve good floral habitat for honeybees will help preserve native bees, as will additional measures such as providing habitat for native bee nest sites and avoiding soil cultivation to protect nests in the soil (Strickler 2000). Management of honeybees needs to balance the negative interactions against positive interactions and consider the value of the honeybee to agriculture (Paton 1993).

Alexander et al. (2000) noted that people who harvest or produce nontimber forest products do so for a variety of reasons, both commercial and noncommercial. Producers or harvesters of nontimber forest products are often categorized as commercial or noncommercial, but this division is artificial. People who participate in these activities, such as berry or mushroom picking, may pick for personal use, for trade and gifts, and for sale, and this tendency is particularly true of beekeepers. Commercial beekeepers with a thousand hives or more make large-scale food production possible. Smaller commercial and hobby beekeepers produce honey for personal use, for sale, and for trade and gifts, and they derive enjoyment and a supplemental income from honeybees.

Hobby and small commercial beekeepers are numerous throughout the United States, as evidenced by participation in local and state associations and by trade journals. They provide pollination of both native plants and agricultural crops. The total participation of hobby beekeepers in local or regional economies is not documented. The contribution of beekeepers to local or regional economies would be difficult to assess for many of the same reasons that the economic contributions of other nontimber forest product industries are difficult to document. A case study of hobby and small commercial beekeepers in an area might reveal a significant provision of pollination services, nonwage labor, and value of honey and wax production.

Wildflower honey has a special appeal to many people and is believed to have beneficial health effects. Many hobby beekeepers enjoy eating, giving away, or selling honey from wildflowers. Honey from native plants in early seral stages of forests, such as fireweed and vine maple, is particularly choice. Wildflower honey has long been a special forest product and will continue to be, but it will probably be harder to find as access and site availability decrease and permit restrictions increase. Throughout the United States, the conversion of land from native habitat to agricultural or rural use as well as insecticide and herbicide spraying practices in forests, agricultural uses, roadsides, and homes continue to impact the availability of native plant forage for honeybees and native bees. Beekeepers must deal with mites and disease, vandalism and pesticides, and trade policies that impact their ability to remain in business, or for the hobbyist, to cover costs.

NOTE

1. List of common and Latin names from the text:

alkali bee	*Nomia melanderi*
black locust	*Robinia pseudoacacia* L.
bumblebee	*Bombus* spp.
catclaw acacia	*Acacia greggii*
digger bees	*Andrena, Colletes,* and other spp.
fireweed	*Chamerion (Epilobium) angustifolium*
guajillo	*Acacia berlanderi*
honeybee	*Apis mellifera*
leafcutter bees	*Megachile* spp.
orchard mason bee	*Osmia lignaria*
Pacific poison oak	*Toxicodendron diversiloba*
squash bee	*Peponapis pruinosa*
sweat bees	*Halictidae* family
sweet acacia, huisache	*Acacia farnesiana*
tracheal mite	*Acarapis woodi*
varroa mite	*Varroa jacobsoni*
willows	*Salix* spp.

REFERENCES

Alexander, S. J., R. J. McLain, Y.-S. Kim, and R. Johnson. 2000. "Recreational Harvest of Wild Foods on the Gifford Pinchot National Forest: Resources and Issues." In *Proceedings, Society of American Foresters, 1999 National Convention*. SAF pub. no. 00-1, pp. 180–185.

Bailey Hortorium. 1976. *Hortis Third: Concise Dictionary of Plants Cultivated in the United States and Canada*. Ithaca, NY: Cornell University Press.

Burgett, D. M., B. A. Stringer, and L. D. Johnston. 1989. *Nectar and Pollen Plants of Oregon and the Pacific Northwest*. Blodgett, OR: Honeystone Press.

Burrill, L. C., S. A. Dewey, D. W. Cudney, B. E. Nelson, R. D. Lee, and R. Parker.

1996. *Weeds of the West,* ed. T. D. Whitson. Jackson Hole, WY: Western Society of Weed Science.

Chakravarti, I., and R. Verma. 1991. "Marketing of Minor Forest Products in Tribal Subplain Area through Cooperatives in Rajasthan." *Indian Journal of Economics* 71:311–320.

Crane, E. 1990. *Bees and Beekeeping; Science, Practice, and World Resources.* London: International Bee Research Association.

Dalby, R. 1999a. "Autumn Asters." *American Bee Journal* 139(9): 698–699.

———. 1999b. "Beautiful Basswoods." *Bee Culture* 127(6): 38–39.

———. 1999c. "Minor Bee Plants in a Major Key." *American Bee Journal* 139(12): 945–946.

———. 1999d. "Willows Are Wonderful." *American Bee Journal* 139(3): 220–221.

Delaplane, Keith S. 1996. *Honey Bees and Beekeeping: A Year in the Life of an Apiary.* Athens: University of Georgia/Georgia Center for Continuing Education, Cooperative Extension Service.

Economic Commission for Europe. 1993. *The Forest Resource of the Temperate Zones: The UN-ECE/FAO 1990 Forest Resource Assessment.* Vol. 2, *Benefits and Functions of the Forest.* New York: United Nations.

Goltz, L. 1999. "The Enigma of Nectar Secretion." *Bee Culture* 127(8): 23–25.

Harlow, W. M., and E. S. Harrar. 1937. *Textbook of Dendrology.* American Forestry Series. New York: McGraw Hill.

Hitchcock, C. L., and A. Cronquist. 1976. *Flora of the Pacific Northwest.* Seattle: University of Washington Press.

Larrison, E., G. Patrick, W. Baker, and J. Yaich. 1977. *Washington Wildflowers.* Seattle Audubon Society. Portland, OR: Durham-Downy.

Little, E. L. 1979. *Checklist of United States Trees (Native and Naturalized).* Agricultural Handbook 541. Washington, DC: U.S. Department of Agriculture, Forest Service.

Lovell, J. H. 1926. *Honey Plants of North America: A Guide to the Best Locations for Beekeeping in the United States.* Medina, OH: A. I. Root.

Midwest Research Institute. 1992. *Honey.* MRI Technical Paper, Kansas City, MO.

Moeller, F. E. 1961. *The Relationship between Colony Populations and Honey Production.* Wisconsin Agricultural Experiment Station Production Research Report 55. Washington, DC: U.S. Department of Agriculture.

Morse, R. A., and N. W. Calderone. 2000. "The Value of Honeybees as Pollinators of U.S. Crops in 2000." *Bee Culture* 128(3): special insert.

Mountain, M. F., R. Day, C. Quartly, and A. Goatcher. 1992. *Garden Plants Valuable to Bees.* London: International Bee Research Association.

Ott, J. 1998. "The Delphic Bee: Bees and Toxic Honeys as Pointers to Psychoactive and Other Medicinal Plants." *Economic Botany* 52(3): 260–266.

Paton, D. C. 1993. "Honeybees in the Australian Environment: Does *Apis mellifera* Disrupt or Benefit the Native Biota?" *Bioscience* 43(2): 95–103.

Peck, M. E. 1961. *Manual of the Higher Plants of Oregon.* Corvallis: Oregon State University Press.

Pellett, F. C. 1923. *American Honey Plants: Together with Those Which Are of a Special Value to the Beekeeper as Sources of Pollen.* Hamilton, IL: American Bee Journal.

Ramsay, J. 1987. *Plants for Beekeeping in Canada and the Northern USA: A Directory of Nectar and Pollen Sources Found in Canada and the Northern USA*. London: International Bee Research Association.

Robinson, W. S., R. Nowogrodski, and R. A. Morse. 1989. "The Value of Honeybees as Pollinators of U.S. Crops." *American Bee Journal* 129:411–423, 477–487.

Russ, R. 1999. "In the South, in July." *American Bee Journal* 139(7): 518–519.

Scullen, H. A. 1947. *Beekeeping in Oregon*. Oregon State Extension Bulletin 622. Corvallis: Oregon State University Press.

Sharples, A. W. 1958. *Alaska Wildflowers*. Stanford, CA: Stanford University Press.

Stanger, W. L. Foote, H. H. Laidlaw, R. W. Thorp, N. E. Gary, and L. H. Watkins. 1971. *Fundamentals of California Beekeeping*. University of California College of Agriculture Manual 42. Berkeley: California Agricultural Experiment Station Extension Service.

Strickler, K. 2000. University of Idaho website, Entomology Department; several links to extension information, in addition to personal communication. *www.pollinatorparadise.com, karens@w-idaho.net.*

U.S. Department of Agriculture. 1971. *Beekeeping in the United States*. Agricultural Handbook 335. Washington DC: U.S. Department of Agriculture.

Whittlesay, R. 1985. *Familiar Friends, Northwest Plants*. Portland, OR: Rose Press.

Williams, C. S. 1995. "Conserving Europe's Bees: Why All the Buzz?" *Trends in Ecology and Evolution* 10(8): 309–310.

Wilson, E. 1974. *Aristocrats of the Trees*. Cambridge, MA: Harvard University Press.

Winston, M. 1999. "Less Than I Thought." *Bee Culture* 127(3): 19–20.

Biological Inventory and Monitoring

Becky K. Kerns, Leon Liegel,
David Pilz, and Susan J. Alexander

Biological inventory and monitoring of nontimber forest product species are critical issues in the formulation of sustainable land management plans and policies and conservation-based economic development (USDA 2000; Von Hagen and Fight 1999). Commercial, recreational, and subsistence harvesters as well as public and private land managers and planners all ask basic questions about individual nontimber forest products or groups of products:

- Where is the species from which the product is derived?
- How much is there?
- Is it accessible, available for harvest, and of high quality?
- What level of harvest is sustainable?
- Which species need protection or conservation?
- How can resource productivity be enhanced?

Answers to these questions are the basis for assessing resource sustainability, determining product economic value and marketability, and deciding whether appropriate management is to use, conserve, or enhance the resource. Knowledge of how species quantity and quality change over time and across landscapes via natural successional changes or by human and natural disturbance is critical. Such information can be obtained from a number of sources, including local and indigenous knowledge, existing forest resource inventories, statistically designed inventories, scientific investigations, and holistic studies embracing social, political, and biophysical processes. The type, relevance, and cost of information provided by each of these approaches differ considerably, so managers, stakeholders, and policy makers will benefit from understanding the strengths and limitations of various strategies used to assess resource conditions and trends. Inventory and monitoring activities can produce knowledge that is useful and relevant to managers and stakeholders and foster sustainability of human and natural communities. However, land management decisions and policy formulation based on inadequate or inappropriate information can lead to unsustainable resource conditions and destabilize human communities.

The purpose of this chapter is to provide a detailed but relatively nontechnical overview and critique of specific methods and factors to consider when designing and implementing an inventory and monitoring program, examining or analyzing existing data, or formulating policies based on a resource assessment. When possible, we will provide specific examples or studies from the United States. We also suggest several approaches to inventory and monitoring that can guide future efforts, point out knowledge gaps, and discuss new holistic methods that incorporate epistemological diversity and integrate biological, sociocultural, and managerial strategies. Our examples center on biological, ecological, and sociocultural studies from the Pacific Northwest, where NTFP research has been conducted for over a decade. A large body of international literature also exists (Wong 2000; Lund 1998), which we mention briefly. Since we use common names of organisms when possible, Appendix A lists all scientific names and authorities used in this chapter.

DEFINITIONS

To *inventory* a resource is "to account quantitatively for goods on hand or provide a descriptive list of articles giving, at a minimum, the quantity or quality of each" (Lund and Thomas 1989). Inventories provide a snapshot of the resource at a single point in time. In contrast, resource *monitoring* is a dynamic activity that has temporal elements: "the process of observing and measuring over a period of time to detect change or to predict trends" (Lund and Thomas 1989). Because the primary goals are long-term detection of change and prediction of trends, selecting a sampling design and plot size that ensure statistical validity are crucial to a monitoring project's success.

Essential parts of any monitoring project measure the resource a first time to establish a baseline description; return at periodic intervals to remeasure the same resource (the same plots) characterized in the baseline assessment, in the same manner; compare baseline with subsequent remeasurement data to detect changes in status from the baseline assessment; and determine whether any observed change is biologically, economically, or socioculturally significant. Validity and assessment of information provided by both inventory and monitoring projects hinge on two easily confused concepts: accuracy and precision. The difference between accuracy and precision can be illustrated by the following example. Consider a target where holes are clustered very tightly but are several inches from the bull's-eye—the person is shooting precisely but not accurately.

BIOLOGICAL LIFE-FORMS AND NONTIMBER PRODUCTS

Plants and other organisms are commonly grouped into broad categories called life-forms based on their morphology, horizontal and vertical arrangement, and spatial distribution. The major life-forms we refer to are trees, shrubs, herbs, bryophtyes, lichens, and fungi. These are briefly described below; examples of nontimber forest product categories for these life-forms are listed in Table 13, with pertinent citations.

Trees are perennial woody plants that are frequently single-stemmed and form the tallest layer in the forest canopy. Shrubs are also perennial woody plants but are generally less than three meters in height and commonly have multiple stems. Herbaceous plants do not have perennial woody parts or persistent aboveground stems, and they grow near the ground. Bryophytes are nonvascular plants that have no perennial stems and grow on rocks, soil, or on trees or shrubs (epiphytes). Bryophytes include the mosses, liverworts, and hornworts. Lichens are composite organisms of algae and fungi. Fungi are nonphotosynthetic organisms that reproduce by spores.

Further subdivisions of the five major life-forms based on more detailed information regarding their growth form are common. For example, some researchers group bryophytes according to the substrates, such as the rocks, soils, and tree branches on which they grow. Some fungi, such as mushrooms, form fruiting bodies above ground (epigeal); others, including truffles, fruit below ground (hypogeal). Herbaceous plants are frequently broken out into grasses, forbs, and ferns. Other divisions can be based on the organism's life span (perennial versus annual), size (dwarf shrub), parasitism, rosette form, leaf traits, and so on. Life and growth forms provide a framework to describe terrestrial communities (Odum 1971), but other biological traits such as reproductive strategy and characteristics of the harvested portion of the plant are also used to determine which kind of inventory or monitoring protocols are most effective to achieve specific project goals.

APPROACHES TO INVENTORY AND MONITORING

Initial Considerations

The appropriate approach used to inventory and monitor NTFPs depends on the type of information needed and how it will be used. Establishing specific project goals and objectives at the outset is crucial. Project complexity and knowledge generated generally increase as one moves from simple human and natural systems to those that include many harvester groups and multiple ecosystem products (Table 14). Although certain information could be available from existing databases, new information might be

Table 13. Examples of nontimber products from different product categories organized by the major life-forms that are frequently used to inventory and monitor resources*

Sources for inventory and monitoring information on these life-forms	Medicinal and foods	Floral products, art and crafts	Industrial resins and derived products
	TREES		
Avery and Burkhart (1994); Schreuder, Gregoire, and Wood (1993); Shiver and Borders (1996)	cascara bark, chestnuts, madrone, maple syrup, Pacific yew, slippery elm bark, willow	cedar boughs, noble fir, myrtlewood, pine and juniper boughs, pinecones, and pine needles	eastern hemlock (tannin), slash pine resin (turpentine)
	SHRUBS		
Barnes and Musselman (1996); Bonham (1989); Elzinga, Salzer, and Willoughby (1998); Kent and Coker (1992)	devil's club, hairy manzanita, huckleberries, salal, saskatoon, witchhazel	dwarf Oregon-grape, evergreen huckleberry, salal, scotch broom	mesquite (gum)
	HERBS		
Bonham (1989); Elzinga, Salzer, and Willoughby (1998); Kent and Coker (1992); Lessica and Steele (1994)	*Echinacea,* black cohosh, bloodroot, camas, ginseng, goldenseal, watercress, valerian	baby's breath, bear grass, blue grama, cattail, common sunflower, deer fern, sword fern	stinging nettle, yarrow, and wild mint used in cosmetics
	FUNGI		
Amaranthus and Pilz (1996); Arnolds (1992); Castellano et al. (1999)	maitake, boletes, chantrelles, matsutakes, morels, Polypores, reishi, shiitake	artist's conk	
	BRYOPHYTES AND LICHENS		
McCune and Lesica (1992); Peck (1997); Peck and McCune (1998); Peck and Muir (1999); Vance and Kirkland (1997)	*Lobaria* spp., *Usnea* spp., *Dicranum* spp., *Sphagnum* spp., some species (black tree "moss") eaten as famine foods	many species of mosses, liverworts, and lichens occurring together are collected as mats	many species of lichens used as perfume stabilizers
	GENERAL		
	Everett (1997); Brill and Dean (1994); Foster (1995); Fisher and Bessette (1992); Hobbs (1995); Moore (1979, 1993); Stamets (1993)	Ciesla (1998); Coppen (1995); De Geus (1995); Douglass (1975); Rice (1980); Schlosser, Blatner, and Chapman (1991); Schlosser, Blatner, and Zamora (1992); Schlosser et al. (1992)	Ciesla (1995); Coppen and Hone (1995)

*Selected citations for further reading are included. Species names and authorities are included in Appendix A.

Table 14. Hierarchy of nontimber forest product inventory and monitoring approaches based on degree of knowledge required, spatial and temporal scales, and project complexity

HIERARCHY OF APPROACHES		
Knowledge required	*Kind or scale of inventory*	*Project complexity*
Where is the resource?	Presence/absence maps within watersheds, by township, county and state, ecoregions, or major forest types; remote sensing or map base; modeling	Simple qualitative approaches to complex statistical designs
How much is there? When is it available? What percentage has value?	Small- to large-scale distribution and abundance studies; past experience; harvester knowledge; existing data; timber company stand exams; lease permit maps; inventories that measure economic attributes	Simple to complex statistical designs and research
Is it threatened or endangered?	Literature reviews of known biology; 100% surveys; existing data and studies (Northwest Forest Plan)	Simple compilations and summaries to complex statistical approaches
How does species abundance change through time and space?	Repeat inventories and continuous monitoring; research and retrospective studies; past experience; harvester groups knowledge; historical studies; National Forest Service annular surveys	Compilations and summaries to complex designs and research with spatial and temporal components
Is productivity impacted by harvest? What are sustainable harvest methods?	Literature searches and surveys; experimental research studies; past experience; harvester knowledge; historical studies	Complex designs with research and collaborative participatory approaches
How can we sustain human and natural systems?	Holistic and integrated inventories	Most comprehensive and complex; epistemological diversity

needed. In developing an inventory system, the basic criterion of effectiveness is provision of adequate information for decision making at a suitable level of detail in a timely manner (Myers and Patil 1995). If existing databases are used, careful thought should be given to how appropriate the information provided is for answering the questions of interest (Appendix C). For example, unlike the extensive monitoring of nontimber forest products in temperate forests of Europe (Eriksson, Ingelög, and Kardell 1979; Glowacki 1988; Kostov and Stojanov 1985; Salo 1993; Zaitseva 1993), federal surveys of vegetation in the United States have traditionally been established primarily as statistical inventories to estimate the productivity and health of timber resources.

We have developed a question list that, coupled with the following sections discussing common inventory and monitoring approaches, can help guide the selection of appropriate methodologies and aid in the interpretation of results generated from exiting databases:

- What species, products, and life-forms are of interest?
- Is the whole organism of interest or just the harvested product?
- How is the species harvested and used as a nontimber forest product?
- What data already exist that can be used?
- Are existing data adequate to address information needs?
- Why are new data being collected?
- What will they be used for?
- What human and financial resources are available to complete the project?
- What is an acceptable balance between accuracy and overall cost and use of resources?
- How do sampling techniques vary for the products and life-forms?
- What is the size of the species of interest?
- When is the product visible and identifiable?
- What is the scale of the study area (e.g., country, state, watershed, bioregion, and so on)?
- How is the species distributed across the area of interest?
- How do temporal factors (e.g., seasonal variations) affect the data being collected?
- Will commercial product yields be estimated? How will this be done?
- Can several products or species be inventoried and monitored at once?
- Is product processing and transportation an important consideration?
- Who will collect the data and do they require training?
- How will the data be analyzed and who will do it?
- How will the data being collected answer the question or questions of interest?
- How will the information be transferred to those who need it?
- If it is a long-term monitoring project: How will data be archived? What institutional arrangements exist for continuity?

Descriptive and Nonstatistical Approaches

Some inventories are descriptive: species and habitats are characterized, but statistical methodologies and hypothesis testing are not applied (Kent and Coker 1992). Descriptive studies can be informal and qualitative or quantitative. Based on years of experience and personally developed rules, an experienced individual can informally estimate product availability, quality, and quantity. If individuals are willing to share their rules, the methodology might be applied elsewhere. Although "rule-of-thumb" methods might be accurate and precise, they are difficult to evaluate and repeat unless an individual is willing to divulge and formalize methods used for assessment. Interviews and contacts with harvesters, recreational pickers, and buyers can yield important information regarding species distribution and abundance and can also provide a context for local use, history, and customs (Lund 1998).

An example of a quantitative descriptive approach is the Braun-Blanquet or relevé method that has been used to classify most of the vegetation of Europe (Barbour et al. 1999; Mueller-Dombois and Ellenberg 1974) and map all the vegetation within the national parks of the United States (Barbour et al. 1999). The relevé method is considered descriptive because it uses subjective plot placement, which can bias results and limit inferences, although proponents of this method point out that unbiased subjective plot placement can be used (Mueller-Dombois and Ellenberg 1974).

Presence/Absence Methods

With the presence/absence approach, only the presence of the species or product is noted. The presence/absence technique is relatively rapid but limited in application, as it provides no information specific to the species, such as plant size or vigor, and it cannot be used to monitor change in abundance over time. Generally, a list of species is compiled for a particular area or for individual plots within an area of interest. For example, Bluhm (1988) lists fifty-six low- and mid-elevation Pacific Northwest native herbaceous vascular plants that might be commercially important. Vance, Borsting, and Pilz (in press) provide a species information guide for nontimber forest products that occur in the Pacific Northwest. In ethnobotanical studies, a researcher may compile a list of plants used by local peoples that occur in the area by conducting interviews (Turner and Richard 1980; Turner and Efrat 1982; Martin 1995). Some biodiversity assessments, such as Conservation International's Rapid Assessment Program (e.g., Killeen and Schulenberg 1999), include only species' presence and absence, as quickly assessing an unknown area is the primary goal.

If plots are used in an inventory, presence/absence can be quantitative and expressed as frequency or constancy of species occurrence, that is, the percentage of sampling units that contain a particular species. Frequency is dependent on sampling unit size and shape, organism size and shape, and how species are distributed in a given area, and it is sensitive to sampling unit placement (Kent and Coker 1992; Whysong and Miller 1987). Frequency is an effective monitoring technique for life-forms that respond fairly quickly to environmental change, such as some herbs, but such methods are less suitable for monitoring trees and long-lived organisms. Presence/absence is also used for multivariate statistical techniques (e.g., ordinations of plots), modeling odds of occurrence, and some nonparametric hypothesis testing.

PHOTOGRAPHIC AND REMOTE SENSING METHODS

The use of photographic techniques to inventory and monitor vegetation can be rapid, accurate, and objective (Bonham 1989). Historical photos and repeat photography are commonly used to document vegetation change (Hasting and Turner 1965; Gruell 1980; Covington and Moore 1994; Webb 1996). Hall (1999) developed a very extensive and well-documented ground-based photographic monitoring system for comparison and repeat photographic purposes. This technique can be applied to nontimber species as long as they can be identified easily on film.

Remotely sensed data from aircraft or satellites include photographs or images of electromagnetic radiation that is either reflected or emitted by vegetation (Barbour et al. 1999). Using remotely sensed data to inventory and monitor nontimber products is practical if the species or product of interest can be readily detected or is associated strongly with specific vegetation types. Thus, this technique has limited usefulness for understory species and species that have a broad range of habitat associations. Remotely sensed data can be used to delineate areas where species are likely to occur (including canopy gaps, second growth stands, old-growth stands), can aid in the creation of sampling units, and are useful for statistical stratification, landscape modeling, and assisting in navigation. Interpreting remotely sensed data requires specialized expertise and subsequent field checks. Maus (1995) established guidelines for using remotely sensed digital imagery to map vegetation in the United States.

Statistically Based Methods

Since it is rarely feasible to survey 100 percent of an area or population, estimates of species characteristics or effects of harvest activities are usually derived from statistical sampling. A decision to design an inventory program using statistically based methods depends on project objectives as well as fiscal and time constraints. Because statistical methods can provide very useful information for assessing resource sustainability, the impact of harvesting methods, and long-term monitoring, we now discuss statistical approaches in greater detail.

Data Analysis and Management

Data analysis and management are as important to the success of an inventory and monitoring program as are the underlying study design and sampling. It is crucial to give careful thought about how information will be collected in the field, organized, transferred into a database, labeled, analyzed, and archived. Numerous statistical packages (e.g., SAS, SPSS, S^+, SYS-

TAT) are available and range from simple to complex. We suggest consultation with a statistician during the project-planning phase. A helpful exercise is to create a small data set using prototype forms that will actually be used in the field, establish a database, and analyze it. A key question to ask at the end of this exercise is whether or not the prototype data created will provide the information needed based on project objectives. For many nontimber products, inventory methods do not yet exist, and pilot studies are needed.

Spatial and Temporal Variation

Both spatial and temporal variation are considered in selecting appropriate sampling methods. Spatial variation depends not only on the size of an area of interest but also on the inherent pattern or distribution of the species. Information collected at one scale might not be appropriate for addressing questions at another scale. Most species are clumped, not randomly distributed across landscapes (Kent and Coker 1992; Barbour et al. 1999). Sampling techniques (such as plot size and shape) can be modified to account for the size and distribution of a species of interest across the study area (Kenkel and Podani 1991). Sampling methods can also be designed to detect specific spatial patterns in vegetation (Kenkel, Juhasz-Nagy, and Podani 1989; Podani, Czaran, and Bartha 1993). It is also important to consider temporal variation. For example, inventory and monitoring of berry and fruit products can only be done while fruiting occurs, unless indirect methods relating some factor of plant size to fruiting have been developed. Deciduous foliage is only visible during the growing season, and certain products have the highest commercial value during particular time frames. Many herbaceous species are not even detectable except during certain restricted periods and might only be identifiable while flowering. West and Reese (1991) found that for herbaceous vegetation, very different results for plant diversity and biomass were obtained depending on when sampling was done. They suggest that multiple dates of sampling through the growing season are the best way to characterize herbaceous communities. Moreover, year-to-year variation in plant populations (presence/ absence, abundance, fruiting) can be extreme. Attention to these issues is particularly important to detect trends in monitoring. For example, detectable numbers of many herb species vary appreciably from year to year depending on annual meteorological events or previous plant performance (Lesica and Steele 1994). Edible fungi are nontimber products that exhibit large spatial and temporal variability (Appendix D).

Sampling Design

The procedure by which the sample units are selected from the population is called the sampling design (Thompson 1992). Both parameter estimation efficiency and cost-effectiveness should be evaluated when choosing a sampling design. Most sampling designs are random, stratified, systematic, or a combination of these. Random sampling is time-consuming, might not be cost-effective, and can leave large sections of an area unsampled or rare patches of vegetation undersampled (Barbour et al. 1999). Therefore, purely random sampling designs are not usually used for inventory and monitoring purposes. Many studies in forestry and plant ecology use some sort of stratified or systematic sampling (FIA, FHM, NFS, Appendix C).

Stratification is the subdivision of a study area into several homogenous regions based on factors such as soil type, elevation, seral stage, overstory cover type, or management applications. Stratification removes the major sources of variation that are easily recognized and is more cost-effective than purely random sampling. Choice of criteria for strata designation will depend on species ecology and project objectives. Traditional stratification is usually based on land cover classes delineated on maps or air photos, but De Jong and Bonner (1995) used local knowledge to aid in stratification for sampling Pacific yew. Once an area is stratified, samples can be located randomly or systematically within each stratum.

Systematic sampling involves the location of sampling units at regular or systematic intervals, such as on a grid or line, with only the origin and orientation of the grid randomly located. Systematic designs have the advantage of being well distributed across the population (Scott 1998). Many broad-scale forest inventories in the United States (FIA, FHM, NFS, Appendix C) are based on systematic arrangement of grids, as are many European forest inventories (Kohl, Innes, and Kaufmann 1994). Rarely is a penalty incurred statistically for choosing systematic over random sampling (Schreuder, Gregoire, and Wood 1993; Shiver and Borders 1996; Scott 1998), but a potential problem can occur when the sampling interval coincides with some environmental periodicity (Shiver and Borders 1996).

Regardless of whether one chooses systematic or random sampling, care should be taken that the sampling design will produce a set of independent samples. Contiguous or touching plots can never be independent, and a higher degree of spatial autocorrelation (what is present in one plot depends on what is present in adjacent plots) will result (Fortin, Drapeau, and Legendre 1989; Legendre 1993). This is especially problematic for nested plot designs and transects, both of which are discussed below.

SELECTION OF SAMPLING UNIT

Selecting a sampling unit and its dimensions is dependent on the life-form of interest, the type of information needed, time and fiscal constraints, and overall project goals and objectives. Some common sampling units used for forest and vegetation inventories are plots or quadrats, belt transects and line-intercept methods, and distance or plotless sampling.

Plots

Plots are usually square, rectangular, strip (elongated rectangle), or circular in shape and can be any size. They are recommended for studies where basic information on plant species' presence/absence, frequency, abundance, diversity, and repeatability (reusable plots) are needed. Both plot size and shape should be considered carefully. Narrow strip plots that cross major environmental gradients can capture more species compared to square or round plots that have a reduced perimeter to surface area ratio compared to rectangular plots (Borman 1953; Barbour et al. 1999). Inventories for species richness and diversity usually include plots that are rectangular (Stohlgren, Falkner, and Schell 1995). However, accuracy declines as plot length increases due to greater edge effect; that is, the more perimeter there is for a plot, the more subjective decisions are made to determine whether a plant is in or out of the plot. Clear criteria for inclusion, that are carefully applied, can minimize this drawback to use of strip plots. Circular plots have the least amount of edge, and some suggest they are easier to set up in dense forest vegetation (Schreuder, Gregoire, and Wood 1993; Shiver and Borders 1996). Circular plots are not recommended for capturing linear features such as downed woody material.

Optimum plot size will vary and is tied to the size and spatial distribution of the species, but should be large enough to estimate the parameter of interest accurately and precisely (Appendix E). Exploratory work, a pilot study, and field experience can help define both plot size and shape. Examining prior study results and variance (standard error or standard deviation of the attribute of interest) can also help define plot size. The total percentage of area sampled is another consideration. Kenkel and Podani (1991) examined the effects of plot size on parameter estimation efficiency from three plant communities (deciduous understory, coniferous understory, and mire vegetation) in central Canada and noted that estimation efficiency increased with increasing plot size. However, relative gains in parameter estimation efficiency at larger plot sizes were offset by substantial increases in sampling efforts. In evaluating cost-effectiveness, also consider the distance traveled between plots; this aspect is often ignored but can be critical for studies using small but numerous plots across a large study area (Brummer et al. 1994).

A nested plot design is an efficient approach to use for multiobjective projects where inventory and monitoring of numerous life-forms and analysis of results across multiple spatial scales are required. Nested plots have been commonly used to understand how different plot sizes affect species richness results (species areas curves) by examining how many species are captured by the different plot sizes (Mueller-Dombois and Ellenberg 1974; Barbour et al. 1999; Stohlgren, Falkner, and Schell 1995; Stohlgren et al. 1997). Stohlgren, Falkner, and Schell (1995) note that nested plot designs can be used to estimate local species richness and cover, plant diversity and spatial patterns, and trend analysis from monitoring a series of permanent plots. In order to have truly independent samples, care should be taken that samples are not contiguous or overlapping. In order to avoid the confounding influence of different plot shapes, using consistent plot shapes is also recommended (Stohlgren, Falkner, and Schell 1995).

Belt Transects and Line-Intercept Method

Belt transects have plots placed along a line (the transect) and are technically systematic plot designs. They can be used in multispecies analyses to determine variation in dominant species over fairly large distances or areas (>10,000 hectares) that cross major environmental gradients such as mountainsides, geological features, or ecotones (Barbour et al. 1999) but are also appropriate for much smaller areas. Although single transects are useful to quickly examine changes in plant communities along a gradient, because of the small spatial area involved, they only capture the most dominant species (Stohlgren, Bull, and Otsuki 1998).

Transects (lines) serve as the sampling unit for the line-intercept method. This method was designed for sampling shrub-dominated vegetation (Barbour et al. 1999). A length of tape or line is laid out, and all plant canopies projecting over the line are tallied. The fraction of the line covered by each species is the percent cover for that species, but since no area is involved, density cannot be calculated. This method works best in vegetation that is compact with a distinct growth form, such as tussock grasses, heather, shrubs, and trees (Ferris-Kaan and Patterson 1992). It also has been used effectively to measure forest canopy gaps (Battles, Dushoff, and Fahey 1996), coarse woody debris, and fuels for fire management (Brown 1974). However, because of the small size of the sample area and issues of spatial autocorrelation, the line-intercept method is not the most effective way to measure total plant diversity (Stohlgren, Bull, and Otsuki 1998).

Distance Methods or Plotless Sampling

Distance or plotless methods use the distance from a random or regular point or transect to the nearest species. Species-to-species distances can also be used. Of particular interest in most distance methods are accurate estimates of density. Numerous types of distance methods can be used, including nearest individual, point-centered quarter, nearest neighbor, the

Bitterlich variable plot method (Appendix F), and random pairs (Barbour et al. 1999; Bonham 1989; Mueller-Dombois and Ellenberg 1974). Distance measures are effective for easily seen species such as trees and shrubs found in fairly open conditions (Ferris-Kaan and Patterson 1992) but can be inaccurate for estimating density for clumped species. Plotless methods can be applied to surveys of specific trees or associated products such as mosses (Appendix G), lichens, or berries. Data from distance sampling designs can also be used to analyze the spatial distribution of species.

REPLICATION

Replication is required for statistical hypothesis testing to provide an estimate of parameter variability. The number of replicates (sample size or *n*-value) is another question that project planners agonize over and is not easily answered. Mathematically, more replicates yield more precise estimates. However, it is usually expensive to gather data from many samples. Thus, investigators seek to maximize precision within certain cost constraints.

Barbour et al. (1999) suggest that the number of sampling units can be determined empirically by plotting data for any given attribute using different numbers of samples. Sample size can be selected where fluctuations dampen, or one can sample until variability is within some previously decided, acceptable bound. If variability can be estimated from previous work, sample size requirements can be determined empirically for known population sizes (Bonham 1989; Cochran 1977; Schreuder, Gregoire, and Wood 1993). Selection of sample size should also include an examination of statistical power (the probability that the statistical conclusion is correct), which is an important consideration not only for project design but also for interpretation of results.

Many biological and ecological studies have suffered from a problem known as pseudoreplication (Hurlbert 1984). Pseudoreplication occurs in studies that have no replication at the level of the population of interest. For example, an estimation of marketable biomass of sword fern in second growth Douglas-fir stands as compared to old-growth stands, based on fifty plots in one stand of each type, would not be true replication. Inferences could be made regarding the two stands in relation to each other, but the estimates could not be applied to larger populations of the two stand types. If an investigator wanted to draw conclusions regarding the generalized population of second growth stands versus old-growth stands, replication at the stand level would be required (e.g., many stands of each type). Therefore, whether or not a study has true or pseudoreplication fundamentally depends on the population about which inferences are made. Wester (1992) points out that numerous studies have been accused of pseudoreplication because of an unclear understanding regarding this concept and what constitutes an experimental unit.

ADAPTIVE SAMPLING

Adaptive sampling refers to designs in which the procedure for selecting the sampling units depends on results as the survey progresses (Thompson and Seber 1996). For example, when sampling for a rare species, adjacent areas can be added to the sample whenever the species is encountered during the survey. Therefore, the sampling plan has the flexibility to change during the survey in response to observed patterns in the population. For nontimber forest products, adaptive sampling might be useful for species that exhibit high spatial clustering. Roesch (1993) showed that adaptive cluster sampling is potentially very effective for sampling rare and clustered hardwood trees in eastern deciduous forests. The text by Thompson and Seber (1996) provides detailed information on adaptive sampling.

ESTIMATION OF SPECIES ABUNDANCE

Some of the most common measures used to estimate the abundance of a species include rank order abundance categories, density, size, cover, and biomass. Choice of abundance measure depends on project goals and objectives and the species' life-form. For in-depth discussions of abundance measurements traditionally used in plant ecology, see Bonham (1989) and Kent and Coker (1992). Chiarucci et al. (1999) discuss differences in results and interpretation of data obtained using frequency, biomass, and cover for issues related to biodiversity.

Rank order abundance categories are generally based on defined frequency class such as 1 = dominant, 2 = abundant, 3 = frequent, 4 = occasional, and 5 = rare. Prefixes such as locally, very, and so on can be added. A rank order descriptive rating system is currently in use to estimate abundance for lichen and bryophyte epiphytes for monitoring protocols included in the Northwest Forest Plan (California, western Oregon, and western Washington) (USDA and USDI 1994). This type of system should be adequately defined to allow repeatability—one person's "frequent" should not be another's "abundant." If correctly designed and repeatability is ensured, rank order abundance categories can be used for statistical hypothesis testing.

Product or species size can be measured in a number of ways. Examples include total height, stem diameter, shrub canopy width, fruit diameter, or fern frond length. Size can be an important variable to estimate for some nontimber products (e.g., floral greens), as it is frequently linked to economic attributes (Douglas 1975; Geldenhuys and Van der Merwe 1988; Schlosser, Blatner, and Zamora 1992).

Density refers to the number of entities (individuals, stems, clumps) within a unit area. The accuracy of estimated density is theoretically independent of plot size, but precision can vary dramatically among units of different shapes and sizes (Elzinga, Salzer, and Willoughby 1998). Density estimates for individual plants require that individuals of a species be easily recognized, such as trees, or certain herbaceous species, such as annuals. For monitoring, density is an appropriate measure to use when the change expected is recruitment or loss of the entity (Elzinga, Salzer, and Willoughby 1998).

Cover is the percentage of ground occupied by the vertical projection of plant material growing above it onto a horizontal plane (usually the ground). It is relatively easy and rapid to assess and is one of the most widely applied estimates of abundance. However, ocular estimates of cover are dependant on the skill of the observer and error rates can be high (Floyd and Anderson 1987; Hatton, West, and Johnson 1986; Kennedy and Addison 1987; Sykes, Horrill, and Mountford 1983). Cover estimates can change dramatically over the course of a growing season, so sampling should be done at the same time of year for all comparative and monitoring purposes. Because of inherent sampling error, cover is commonly reported using percentage classes (such as <1%, 1–5%, 5–10%, 10–25%, and so on). Using cover classes that approximate an arcsine-square root transformation can improve the statistical properties of cover data (Muir and McCune 1988). Cover can also be recorded using grid frames (e.g., pin frames), which increase accuracy but can double or triple sampling times (Stampfli 1991).

Biomass is the amount of plant or product material present in a unit area, and production generally refers to annual yield. Commercial yield is a specifically defined aspect of biomass. Biomass can be determined directly by destructive sampling in which the portion of interest (fruit, mushroom, root, frond, or bough) is totally removed and weighed. Commercial yield may be defined using units other than mass (e.g., number of sprays or bunches of floral greenery) or sorted into quality grades. Biomass or commercial yield is usually determined via a small number of destructive samples and then estimated indirectly for the rest of the study area. This is referred to as double sampling and is accomplished by establishing relationships (regression equations or models) between a readily measured variable like plant cover, mushroom cap diameter, frond length, or basal area and the biomass or yield (Appendix E).

Studies that indirectly estimate plant biomass have been done for all lifeforms and can be found in the biological and ecological literature

(Andariese and Covington 1986; Anderson and Kothmann 1982; Brand and Smith 1985; McCune 1990; Murray and Crawford 1982; Peck and Muir 1999; Pilz, Molina, and Liegel 1998; Pitt and Schwab 1988; Smith and McLeod 1992; Thomson, Mirza, and Afzal 1998). Bonham (1989) notes that few studies have shown good relationships between tree and shrub size and biomass unless size classes and site are considered. Environmental variables such as soil type or precipitation can be included, and complex models can be developed (Andariese and Covington 1985; Kuusipalo 1988). Inventories across multiple stand conditions, soil types, landscapes, and species age classes would involve developing multiple predictive equations modeled independently for each set of conditions. This approach has been used for many years to estimate berry yields in Europe (Eriksson, Ingelög, and Kardell 1979; Glowacki 1988; Grochowski and Ostalski 1981; Raatikainen, Rossi, and Huovinen 1984). In the United States, outside of traditional timber species, only a few studies have been done that examine commercial yield (Barnes and Musselman 1996; Peck and Muir 1999; Vance, Kelsey, and Copes 1998).

MULTIPLE RESOURCE INVENTORIES

Resource managers are charged with managing a wide array of resources, and there is considerable interest in development of inventory and monitoring programs that include multiple biological and physical attributes (Appendix H). As straightforward as integration sounds, planning for multiple resource objectives is inherently complex, and designing projects that are statistically valid for multiple resources is difficult. Inclusion of nontimber species as part of multiresource projects may be constrained by available field skills, botanical skills, and field training (Kleinn, Laamanen, and Malla 1996; Wong 2000).

The Oregon Demonstration Project (USDA 1998) investigated the feasibility of incorporating multiple federal surveys of terrestrial natural resources and includes a useful list of key conclusions and recommendations. Schmoldt, Peterson, and Silsbee (1994) suggest that multiresource project development can benefit from an analytical hierarchy process that incorporates multiple objective decision-making preferences to find potential solutions. Lund (1998) stresses the importance of designing projects before data are collected by including input from inventory designers and intended users. Lund (1998) has produced one of the most comprehensive works concerning this topic and provides extensive guidelines and literature sources for designing multipurpose resource inventories.

SPECIAL CONSIDERATIONS FOR MONITORING PROJECTS AND TREND ANALYSIS

Currently, forest resource managers need appropriate criteria or protocols to monitor the sustainability of nontimber products. Peters (1995) states that the notion that commercial harvesting of nontimber forest products has very little ecological impact on ecosystems is a myth and that development of a series of indicators and procedures for monitoring is a priority issue. He suggests that species density, size-class structure, and reproduction are key factors to monitor the sustainability of nontimber products. Although Peters specifically discusses tropical forest trees, these variables are also key monitoring criteria for any nontimber species (Appendix I). Peck and McCune (1998) stress that postharvest accumulation or growth rates are also important to monitor (Appendix G). Peters (1995) presents a basic strategy for exploiting nontimber resources on a sustained yield basis: species selection, forest inventory, yield studies, regeneration studies, harvest adjustments, and serial harvest adjustments. For many plants, the impact of harvesting on the population structure and long-term productivity of the resource will be difficult to detect in the short term.

To monitor trends precisely using statistical methods, measurement techniques and sampling designs are needed that produce low error values (Brady et al. 1995; Kennedy and Addison 1987; Stampfli 1991), which is particularly true when small changes are important. Consulting a statistician is highly recommended before the onset of a new monitoring project. Monitoring also requires that accurate measurements be made on plant species or products in order to detect change that is biologically, ecologically, and/or socioeconomically significant. For example, if a 10 percent change in cover of an important medicinal plant is ecologically and economically important, using typical cover class systems (e.g., 0–5%, 6–25%, 26–50%, and so on) would be inappropriate. Moreover, Sykes, Horrill, and Mountford (1983) note that when using ocular estimates of plant cover, changes of less than about 20 percent cannot be detected from differences due to error. Rank abundance classes such as 1 = dominant, 2 = abundant, 3 = frequent, 4 = occasional, and 5 = rare present similar problems. Although careful training of personnel and well-defined rank abundance classes can decrease error, it is difficult to ensure that techniques will be consistently applied in the long term.

Sampling designs for monitoring should include some form of fixed-area permanent plots that are remeasured at periodic time intervals (Bakker et al. 1996; Scott 1998; Stohlgren, Falkner, and Schell 1995). Incorporating design features that simplify relocation and remeasurement of plots and vegetation is important. It is generally easier to find systematically placed plots than randomly placed plots in the field (Stohlgren, Falkner, and Schell

1995). For some site locations, plot locations can be referenced with Global Positioning System (GPS) coordinates, but the forest canopies can interfere with satellite acquisition by the equipment. Well-developed pace and compass mapping techniques also work very well.

In order to assess the impact of harvesting, studies might include plots with known quantities of products harvested. Results will reflect actual harvest impacts if sampling methods for product removal closely match techniques actually used by the harvesters (Barnes and Musselman 1996; Peck and McCune 1998). Using local harvesters and community members can facilitate this process, but considerable variation may be introduced. Plots that are not subject to harvesting can provide experimental controls for comparison.

More information on sampling designs and trend detection can be found in Ferris-Kaan and Patterson (1992), Goldsmith (1991), Elzinga, Salzer, and Willoughby (1998), and several articles in a special feature of *Ecological Applications* entitled "Measuring Ecological Trends" (1999). Olsen et al. (1999) discuss statistical issues in monitoring natural resources and compare and contrast many national monitoring programs. Mulder et al. (1999) present monitoring guidelines for the regional-scale approach required for the Northwest Forest Plan that can be applied to any project regardless of spatial scale. Elzinga and Evenden (1997) compiled an extensive, annotated bibliography focused on vegetation monitoring.

HISTORICAL DATA

Understanding historical conditions and ecosystem patterns can provide baseline information and serve as a target for ecosystem restoration. Land management and planning require knowledge of ecological processes, which can be gained, in part, by studying historic variation. Historical studies can provide important information for nontimber species and product abundance and distribution through time and space.

Numerous techniques are available for determining past reference conditions including historical, enthnohistorical, archival, and historical photographic information; micro- and macrofossils; tree-ring analysis and inference from population structure; use of existing natural areas; and modeling. Each of these techniques provides specific information for a particular time frame and species and thus has associated strengths and weaknesses. To provide the most information for determining historical conditions, several techniques can be combined. Detailed coverage of historical techniques are provided in Betancourt, Van Devender, and Martin (1990), Covington and Moore (1994), Moore, Webb, and Collison (1991), Morgan et al. (1994), Noss (1985), and Pearsall (1989).

INTERDISCIPLINARY OR HOLISTIC STUDIES

Historical views of natural resources have placed humans outside of and apart from ecosystems; today new concepts based on ecosystem management draw on integrated or holistic approaches that include humans and their activities (Cordell et al. 1999). Expanding on the multiple resource surveys described in a previous section, these interdisciplinary or holistic efforts collect information on the biophysical status and health of natural resources plus the social, political, and economic contexts within which management decisions are made. Policy makers require detailed scientific information, but this information can be more useful if social scientists, economists, stakeholders, and the public are involved in the monitoring or scientific process. Interdisciplinary natural resource assessments are part of a larger effort to integrate human dimensions—the social, political, and economic processes and data—with biophysical factors (Christensen et al. 1996; Endter-Wada et al. 1998; Human Dimension Study Group 1994; Kaufman et al. 1994; Slocombe 1993).

Examples of holistic studies in natural resource management are emerging. The Forest Resource Division, Food and Agriculture Organization of the United Nations (FAO), is promoting new strategies for natural resource use and conservation by combining a holistic view of the land with a dynamic relationship between ecological, economic, and social processes (FAO Draft Concept Paper 1999). Former USDA Forest Service Chief Jack Ward Thomas stressed that the Forest Service should focus efforts on the "larger environments in order to integrate the human, biological, and physical dimensions of natural resource management" (Thomas 1994). Large-scale bioregional assessments (e.g., Forest Ecosystem Management Assessment Team, Great Lakes–St. Lawrence River Basin Assessments, Interior Columbia Basin Ecosystem Management Project) have integrated a broad range of information about existing social, economic, and ecological conditions within a region to provide a comprehensive basis for decision making and management action (Herring 1999).

Examples of holistic studies concerning nontimber forest products also exist. An interdisciplinary effort was used by a team of scientists to determine the impacts of chanterelle mushroom harvests on humans and natural systems in the Pacific Northwest (Liegel, Pilz, and Love 1998; Liegel et al. 1998; Love, Jones, and Liegel 1998; McLain, Jones, and Liegel 1998; Pilz et al. 1998; Pilz, Molina, and Liegel 1998). Not only were multiple stakeholders involved in study conception, implementation, data analysis, synthesis, and report writing, but economic and social studies also were included and integrated into a holistic guide for managing chanterelle mushrooms.

Despite these examples, much confusion still exists over how interdisciplinary and holistic approaches can be accomplished. One problem is the idea that scientific inquiry related to land management issues can only be accomplished by natural scientists. Endter-Wada et al. (1998) stress that, in most cases, social considerations are included only in the decision-making and political processes during initiation and implementation of projects and programs. Social and some economic (e.g., nonmarket valuation) scientific contributions to management are often ignored or misunderstood. Moreover, Sesco and McDonald (1999) suggest that although the current ecosystem focus of land management provides an opportunity for transition to holistic approaches, it can only be accomplished by incorporating epistemological diversity or multiple theories of knowledge creation. Therefore, in addition to integrating multiple scientific disciplines, holistic approaches often challenge the idea that reductionist scientific methodology is the only way to obtain knowledge.

Richards (1997) states that determining the relationship between ecological dynamics, Native American cultural practices, and indigenous knowledge is especially important for managing plants that tribes have gathered for generations, many of which are nontimber forest products. Cortner, Wallace, and Moote (1999) stress that multiple forms of information, such as individual experiential knowledge, indigenous knowledge, and other forms of data, need to be integral parts of assessment design, from project inception through execution and report writing. Endter-Wada et al. (1998) suggest implementing intense interdisciplinary training programs designed to give all project members basic exposure to a broad array of knowledge acquisition. Because natural resource management involves complex socioeconomic and ecological issues, use of holistic methods to inventory and monitor nontimber products might be necessary to capture the appropriate information for effective management and policy-making decisions.

CONCLUSIONS AND FUTURE DIRECTIONS

Many inventory and monitoring methods exist for trees, shrubs, and herbs or are being developed for fungi and nonvascular plants that are applicable for nontimber forest products. A major problem is that available information is scattered throughout both the formal (peer-reviewed) and "gray" (unreviewed or unpublished reports) literature. Formal literature may be widely available at university libraries, but all stakeholders might not easily understand it. Unpublished reports can be difficult to obtain and often have not been critically reviewed. Also, many studies in the biological and ecological literature would never emerge in a literature search for information on nontimber forest products. Such studies often contain general and valuable information regarding sampling for particular life-forms and also include data on specific biological and ecological species traits and temporal and spatial variation. For example, experimental and retrospective studies in the Pacific Northwest have been done that examine the effects of natural and human disturbance on some major nontimber forest product species and include abundance estimates under different stand conditions (Bailey et al. 1998; Huffman and Tappeiner 1997; Thysell and Carey 2000; Stein 1995; Spies 1991). Databases including literature by species and product are needed where information across disciplines is synthesized. This synthesis and others (Wong 2000; Vance, Borsting, and Pilz, in press; Von Hagen et al. 1996) provide a starting point for bringing such information together.

Several key issues and knowledge gaps have emerged from our analysis of nontimber forest product inventory and monitoring. Achieving consistency and linking databases in federal agency resource monitoring programs is a high priority issue (Olsen et al. 1999). Linking nontimber databases and promoting consistency will allow integrated reports that summarize data acquired by federal agencies. Currently, survey objectives are different between agencies and even within agencies as exemplified by the USDA Forest Service. The 1998 Agricultural Research, Extension, and Education Reform Act contained several mandates that directed the USDA Forest Service FIA Program to make some significant inventory changes, including switching to annual surveys, developing a core program that will be implemented consistently across the United States, including the national forests, and producing comprehensive state reports at five-year intervals. Although implementation is under way, it is uncertain how long it will take to fully achieve these objectives.

It is still unclear if consistent and linked federal forest resource databases will be cost-effective, particularly for the type of nontimber information that is collected. Federal resource inventories contain little or no information on temporally and spatially ephemeral species such as edible mushrooms, bryophytes and lichens, many herbaceous species, and rare and low-cover species, and no data are collected regarding product quality. Spatial grids and temporal scales are frequently inadequate for local planning efforts. In order to formulate long-term development plans for human and natural communities, knowledge of product abundance, distribution, and quality is needed at the scale of small watersheds within individual counties and townships within counties in order to address productivity, sustainability, and market and value issues.

Existing forest inventories could be expanded to include more nontimber species and additional data collection, but spatial grids and temporal scales will need to be altered. More detailed inventory data could also be used to address other ecosystem management goals such as endangered (existing or future) species habitats and plant and habitat biodiversity and to provide information for future resource needs. For some species, inventory methods and protocols are not well developed, and designing projects that are statistically valid for the multitude of nontimber products will be difficult. European forest inventories include more nontimber attributes and using their methodologies might provide valuable insight.

An important inventory issue concerning nontimber forest products is that current guidelines lack methods, available resource databases lack attributes that assign economic value to harvestable products, and few methodologies exist for determining economic quantity and quality. Studies are needed to determine appropriate quality attributes and yield functions across multiple landscape positions. For floral greenery products, market quality is determined by numerous factors such as temporal changes in foliage age and color, overstory stand conditions, disease, and site quality. Measures of quality could be developed using input from local users and buyers and from market information. Quality condition classes for nontimber forest product species could be added to existing inventory protocols. Condition and yield data and additional biotic and abiotic information could be used to develop NTFP species site indices similar to those used for timber species.

A major gap in our current knowledge is how harvesting practices affect resource productivity, adversely or positively. For example, interviews have revealed that harvesters throw clippings and low-grade mushrooms back into the forest in the hope of "reseeding the grounds" that have been harvested (Love, Jones, and Liegel 1998). Some recreational pickers are still concerned that using rakes to move litter layers and mineral soil to find young mushrooms or truffles that fruit underground might decrease future productivity. Research studies and small-scale inventory and monitoring projects for specific products or groups of products, such as those being done for mushrooms and moss in the Pacific Northwest, would allow development and testing of sustainable harvest practices and inventory monitoring protocols. This approach may be particularly critical for species that are now intensively harvested and in immediate need of management guidelines. Information from research studies and small-scale inventory and monitoring projects for specific products could provide more useful information for stakeholders than existing regional federal surveys and databases.

For many products, additional research is also needed to develop models using stand level, geographic information systems, and satellite data. Potential product distribution and abundance might be inferred from age and structure of overstory species as well as rainfall, temperature, and other factors that influence productivity. In such modeling efforts, actual unit-area productivity for different-aged forest stands is a key input variable. One way to obtain such estimates for large landscape areas could be via cooperative work with commercial harvesters who share their daily picking totals with researchers and land managers. Moreover, satellite imagery resolution for some data is now at one meter or less. Correlations can be developed between reflectance or leaf area index of overstory trees and detailed understory cover types. By linking detailed ground surveys, satellite imagery, and broad-based resource surveys, more useful information on NTFP species distribution and abundance will eventually become available. Knowledge of stand conditions from survey data can be combined with satellite imagery to develop models that predict forest type change under different management strategies. Developing such models for ground cover types and specific nontimber products could eventually be beneficial for NTFP users.

Using holistic methods that incorporate epistemological diversity and integrate biological, sociocultural, and managerial strategies for nontimber products can be used to promote sustainable natural and human systems (Liegel et al. 1998b). Similar cross-disciplinary efforts can be implemented to identify harvester data needs and suitable field sampling methods and cycles to obtain finer resolution data. Harvester, volunteer, and indigenous knowledge can be tapped to develop techniques to summarize productivity, product extent and availability, and existing or future value in formats usable by different clients. The MAB Mushroom Study showed that the variability of chanterelle biological productivity for two harvest seasons was quite large at the landscape scale of forest types (Pilz et al. 1998; Pilz, Molina, and Liegel 1998). This variation, for edible mushrooms and other products, makes it almost impossible to assign future value to landscape areas during inventories that only cover small percentages of the total landscapes actually harvested or before crops mature. Local harvester knowledge of where particular harvest techniques are used and have been used for long time periods can be incorporated into field inventories to develop relational inferences between harvest practices and observed productivity. Contacts and relationships started in these efforts can be the foundation upon which stewardship and other programs work to maintain human and natural systems. Such efforts would help promote consistency in regulations being demanded by stakeholders across jurisdictions if applied across national forests and between agencies (Von Hagen and Fight 1999).

Finally, we note that inventory and monitoring of nontimber species is linked with many other ecosystem management goals necessary for an ecosystem management approach. For example, many NTFP species produce food and cover for wildlife or play key roles in nutrient cycling. Having a better understanding of nontimber forest product species distribution, abundance, and productivity at the appropriate spatial and temporal scales will aid in our understanding of plant and habitat biodiversity and function, effects of anthropogenic and natural disturbance on species composition and distribution, ecological integrity, and sustainable management practices.

REFERENCES

Amaranthus, M., and D. Pilz. 1996. "Productivity and Sustainable Harvest of Wild Mushrooms." In *Managing Forest Ecosystems to Conserve Fungus Diversity and Sustain Wild Mushroom Harvests,* ed. D. Pilz and R. Molina, pp. 42–61. Pub. no. PNW-GTR-371. Portland, OR: U.S. Department of Agriculture, Forest Service, Pacific Northwest Research Station.

Andariese, Steven W., and W. Wallace Covington. 1986. "Biomass Estimation for Four Common Grass Species in Northern Arizona Ponderosa Pine." *Journal of Range Management* 39:472–473.

Anderson, D. M., and M. M. Kothmann. 1982. "A Two-Step Sampling Technique for Estimating Standing Crop of Herbaceous Vegetation." *Journal of Range Management* 35:675–677.

Arnolds, E. 1992. "Mapping and Monitoring of Macromycetes in Relation to Nature Conservation. *McIlvanea* 10(2): 4–27.

Avery, Thomas Eugene, and Harold E. Burkhart. 1994. *Forest Measurements*. New York: McGraw-Hill.

Bailey, John D., Cheryl Mayrsohn, Paul S. Doescher, Eilzabeth St. Pierre, and John C. Tappeiner. 1998. "Understory Vegetation in Old and Young Douglas-Fir Forests of Western Oregon." *Forest Ecology and Management* 112:289–302.

Bakker, J. P., H. Olff, J. H. Willems, and M. Zobel. 1996. "Why Do We Need Permanent Plots in the Study of Long-Term Vegetation Dynamics?" *Journal of Vegetation Science* 7:147–156.

Barbour, Michael G., Jack H. Burk, Wanna D. Pitts, Frank S. Gillian, and Mark W. Schwartz. 1999. *Terrestrial Plant Ecology*. Menlo Park, CA: Benjamin/Cummings.

Barnes, Michael, and Victor P. Musselman. 1996. *Inventory and Appraisal Methodologies for Special Forest Products*. Prepared for North Santiam Canyon Economic Development Committee. Tigard, OR: Musselman and Associates.

Battles, J. J., J. G. Dushoff, and T. J. Fahey. 1996. "Line-Intercept Sampling of Forest Canopy Gaps." *Forest Science* 42:131–183.

Betancourt, J. L, T. R. Van Devender, and P. S. Martin. 1990. *Packrat Middens*. Tucson: University of Arizona Press.

Bluhm, Wilbur L. 1988. "Native Herbaceous Perennials of the Pacific Northwest Worthy of Commercial Production." *Combined Proceedings of the International Plant Propagators Society* 38:135–137.

Bonham, C. D. 1989. *Measurements for Terrestrial Vegetation*. New York: John Wiley and Sons.

Borman, F. H. 1953. "The Statistical Efficiency of Sample Plot Size and Shape in Forest Ecology." *Ecology* 34:474–487.

Brady, W., J. E. Mitchell, C. D. Bonham, and J. W. Cook. 1995. "Assessing the Power of the Point-Line Transect to Monitor Changes in Plant Basal Cover." *Journal of Range Management* 48:187–190.

Brand, G. J., and W. B. Smith. 1985. "Evaluating Allometric Shrub Biomass Equations Fit to Generated Data." *Canadian Journal of Botany* 63:64–67.

Brill, Steve, and Everlyn Dean. 1994. *Identifying and Harvesting Edible and Medicinal Plants in Wild (and Not So Wild) Places*. New York: Hearst Books.

Brown, J. K. 1974. *Handbook for Inventorying Downed Woody Material.* General Technical Report INT-16. Ogden, UT: U.S. Department of Agriculture, Forest Service, Intermountain Forest and Range Experiment Station.

Brummer, Joe E., James T. Nichols, Russell K. Engel, and Kent M. Eskridge. 1994. "Efficiency of Different Quadrat Sizes and Shapes for Sampling Standing Crop." *Journal of Range Management* 47:84–89.

Castellano, Michael A., Jane E. Smith, Thom O'Dell, Efrén Cázares, and Susan Nugent. 1999. *Handbook to Strategy 1 Fungal Taxa from the Northwest Forest Plan.* General Technical Report PNW-GTR-476. Portland, OR: U.S. Department of Agriculture, Forest Service, Pacific Northwest Research Station.

Castellano, Michael A., and J. M. Trappe. In press. "Survey, Inventory, and Monitoring of Sequestrate Fungi." In *Measuring and Monitoring Biological Diversity: Standard Methods for Fungi,* ed. G. M. Mueller, G. F. Bills, and M. S. Foste. Washington, DC: Smithsonian Institution Press.

Chiarucci, A., J. Wilson, J. Bastow, Barbara J. Anderson, and V. De Dominicis. 1999. "Cover Versus Biomass As an Estimate of Species Abundance: Does It Make a Difference to the Conclusions?" *Journal of Vegetation Science* 10:35–42.

Christensen, N. L., A. M. Bartuska, S. Carpenter, C. D'Antonio, R. Francis, J. F. Franklin, R. MacMahon, R. F. Noss, D. J. Parson, C. H. Peterson, M. G. Turner, and R. G. Woodmansee. 1996. "The Report of the Ecological Society of America Committee on the Scientific Basis for Ecosystem Management." *Ecological Applications* 6:665–691.

Ciesla, William M. 1998. *Nonwood Forest Products from Conifers.* Nonwood Forest Products Series 12. Rome: Food and Agriculture Organization of the United Nations.

Cochran, William Gemmell. 1977. *Sampling Techniques.* New York: John Wiley and Sons.

Coppen, J. J. W. 1998. *Flavours and Fragrances of Plant Origin.* Nonwood Forest Products Series 1. Rome: Food and Agriculture Organization of the United Nations.

Coppen, J. J. W., and G. A. Hone. 1998. *Gum Naval Stores: Turpentine and Rosin from Pine Resin.* Nonwood Forest Products Series 2. Rome: Food and Agriculture Organization of the United Nations.

Cordell, H. Ken, Anne P. Hoover, Gregory R. Super, and Cynthia H Manning. 1999. "Adding Human Dimensions to Ecosystem-Based Management of Natural Resources." In *Integrating Social Sciences with Ecosystem Management,* ed. H. K. Cordell and J. C. Bergstrom, pp. 1–12. Champaign, IL: Sagamore Publishing.

Cortner, Hanna J., Mary G. Wallace, and Margaret and A. Moote. 1999. "A Political Context Model for Bioregional Assessments." In *Bioregional Assessments: Science at the Crossroads of Management and Policy,* ed. K. N. Johnson, F. J. Swanson, M. Herring, and S. Greene. Washington, DC: Island Press.

Covington, W. Wallace, and Margaret M. Moore. 1994. "Southwestern Ponderosa Pine Forest Structure." *Journal of Forestry* 92:39–47.

De Geus, Nelly. 1995. *Botanical Forest Products in British Columbia: An Overview.* Victoria, BC: British Columbia Ministry of Forests, Integrated Resource Policy Branch.

De Jong, R. J., and G. M. Bonner. 1995. *Pilot Inventory for Pacific Yew*. FRDA Report 231. Victoria, BC: Canadian Forest Service.

Douglass, Bernard S. 1975. *Floral Greenery from Pacific Northwest Forests*. Portland, OR: U.S. Department of Agriculture, Forest Service, Pacific Northwest Region.

Elzinga, Caryl L., and Angela G. Evenden. 1997. *Vegetation Monitoring: An Annotated Bibliography*. General Technical Report INT-GTR-352. Ogden, UT: U.S. Department of Agriculture, Forest Service, Intermountain Research Station.

Elzinga, Caryl L., Daniel W. Salzer, and John Willoughby. 1998. *Measuring and Monitoring Plant Populations*. BLM Technical Reference 1730-1. Ogden, UT: U.S. Department of the Interior, Bureau of Land Management.

Endter-Wada, Joanna, Dale Blahna, Richard Krannich, and Mark Brunson. 1998. "A Framework for Understanding Social Science Contributions to Ecosystem Management." *Ecological Applications* 8:891–904.

Eriksson, L., T. Ingelög, and L. Kardell. 1979. *Blåbär, Lingon, Hallon: Förekomst och Bärproduktion I Sverige, 1974–1977* [Whortleberry, Lingonberry, and Red Raspberry: Distribution and Berry Production in Sweden, 1974–1977; in Swedish with an English summary]. Garpenberg, Sweden: Swedish University of Agricultural Sciences.

Everett, Yvonne. 1997. *A Guide to Selected Nontimber Forest Products of the Hayfork Adaptive Management Area, Shasta-Trinity and Six Rivers National Forests, California*. General Technical Report PSW-GTR-162. Albany, CA: U.S. Department of Agriculture, Forest Service, Pacific Southwest Research Station.

FAO Draft Concept Paper. 1999. Contact Jean Claude Clement, Forest Resources Division director, or Giovanni Preto, senior forestry officer, FAO, via delle Terme di Caracalla, 00100-Rome (Italy), or see *http://www.fao.org*.

Ferris-Kaan, R., and G. S. Patterson. 1992. *Monitoring Vegetation Changes in Conservation Management of Forests*. Farnham, Surrey: Forest Research Station, Alice Holt Lodge.

Fisher, D. W., and A. E. Bessette. 1992. *Edible Wild Mushrooms of North America: A Field to Kitchen Guide*. Austin: University of Texas Press.

Floyd, Donald A., and Jay E Anderson. 1987. "A Comparison of Three Methods for Estimating Plant Cover." *Journal of Ecology* 75:221–288.

Fortin, M. J., P. Drapeau, and P. Legendre. 1989. "Spatial Autocorrelation and Sampling Design in Plant Ecology." *Vegetatio* 83:209–222.

Foster, Steven. 1995. *Forest Pharmacy: Medicinal Plants in American Forests*. Durham, NC: Forest History Society.

Gagnon, Daniel. 1999. "A Review of the Ecology and Population Biology of Goldenseal, and Protocols for Monitoring Its Population." Unpublished report on file with the Office of Scientific Authority of the Fish and Wildlife Service and the author, Groupe de recherche en écologie forestière, University of Quebec at Montreal.

Geldenhuys, C. J., and C. J. van der Merwe. 1988. "Population Structure and Growth of the Fern *Rumohra adiantiformis* in Relation to Frond Harvesting in the Southern Cape Forests." *South African Journal of Botany* 54:351–362.

Gilbertson, R. L., and L. Ryvarden. 1986. *North American Polypores*. 2 vols. Oslo: Fungiflora.

Glowacki, Stanislaw. 1988. "Die Rohstoffbase von Waldfruchten auf natürlichen Standorten und Plantagen in Polen" ["The Resource Base for Forest Fruits in Natural Stands and Plantations in Poland"]. *Norwegian Journal of Agricultural Sciences* 2:151–159. In German; English abstract summary in *Conservation and Development of Nontimber Forest Products in the Pacific Northwest: An Annotated Bibliography,* ed. Bettina von Hagen et al., 1996.

Goldsmith, B., ed. 1991. *Monitoring for Conservation and Ecology.* London: Chapman and Hall.

Grochowski, W., and R. Ostalski. 1981. "Recherches sur les Productions Spontanees des Etages Inferieur de la Foret de Pologne" ["Research Concerning the Nontimber Product Production in Forest Understories of Poland"]. In *Productions spontanees; 17–20 June 1980; Colmer, France,* pp. 39–48. Paris: Institut National de la Recherche Agricole, Les colloques de l'INRA 4. In French; English abstract summary in *Conservation and Development of Nontimber Forest Products in the Pacific Northwest: An Annotated Bibliography,* ed. Bettina von Hagen et al., 1996.

Gruell, George E. 1980. *Fire's Influence on Wildlife Habitat on the Bridger-Teton National Forest, Wyoming.* Vol 1. Research Paper INT-RP-235. Odgen, UT: U.S. Department of Agriculture, Forest Service, Intermountain Forest and Range Experiment Station and Intermountain Region.

Hall, Frederick C. 1999. "Ground-Based Photographic Monitoring." Unpublished report on file with the author, senior plant ecologist, Natural Rescues Unit, Pacific Northwest Region, USDA Forest Service, Portland, Oregon.

Hasting, James Rodney, and Raymond M. Turner. 1965. *The Changing Mile: An Ecological Study of Vegetation Change with Time in the Lower Mile of an Arid and Semiarid Region.* Tucson: University of Arizona Press.

Hatton, Thomas J., Neil E. West, and Patricia S. Johnson. 1986. "Relationships of the Error Associated with Ocular Estimation and Actual Total Cover." *Journal of Range Management* 39(1): 91–92.

Herring, Margaret. 1999. "Introduction." In *Bioregional Assessments: Science at the Crossroads of Management and Policy,* ed. K. N. Johnson, F. J. Swanson, M. Herring, and S. Greene, pp. 1–8. Washington, DC: Island Press.

Hobbs, C. 1995. *Medicinal Mushrooms: An Exploration of Tradition, Healing, and Culture.* Santa Cruz, CA: Botanica Press.

Huffman, D. W., and J. C. Tappeiner. 1997. "Clonal Expansion and Seedling Recruitment of Oregon Grape *(Berberis nervosa)* in Douglas-fir *(Pseudotsuga menziesii)* Forests: Comparisons with Salal *(Gaultheria shallon).*" *Canadian Journal of Forest Research* 27:1788–1793.

Human Dimension Study Group. 1994. *The Human Dimension in Sustainable Ecosystem Management: A Management Philosophy.* Albuquerque, NM: U.S. Forest Service, Southwestern Region, and Rocky Mountain Forest and Range Experiment Station.

Hurlbert, S. H. 1984. "Pseudoreplication and the Design of Ecological Field Experiments." *Ecological Monographs* 54:187–211.

Kaufman, M. R., R. T. Graham, D. A. Boyce Jr., W. H. Moir, L. Perry, R. T. Reynolds, R. L. Bassett, P. Mehlhop, C. B. Edminster, W. M. Block, and P. S. Corn. 1994. *An Ecological Basis for Ecosystem Management.* General Technical Report PNW-318. Portland, OR: U.S. Department of Agriculture, Forest Service, Pacific Northwest Research Station.

Kenkel, N., C. P. Juhasz-Nagy, and J. Podani. 1989. "On Sampling Procedures in Population and Community Ecology." *Vegetatio* 83:195–207.

Kenkel, N., and J. Podani. 1991. "Plot Size and Estimation Efficiency in Plant Community Studies. *Journal of Vegetation Science* 2:539–544.

Kennedy, K. A., and P. A. Addison. 1987. "Some Considerations for the Use of Visual Estimates of Plant Cover in Biomonitoring." *Journal of Ecology* 75:151–157.

Kent, Martin, and Paddy Coker. 1992. *Vegetation Description and Analysis*. London: Belhaven Press.

Killeen, Timothy J., and Thomas S. Schulenberg, eds. 1999. *A Biological Assessment of the Parque Nacional Noel Kempff Mercado, Bolivia*. RAP Working Papers, no. 10. Distributed for Conservation International. Chicago: University of Chicago Press.

Kleinn, Christoph, Risto Laamanen, and Samar Bahadur Malla. 1996. *Integrating the Assessment of Nonwood Products into the Forest Inventory of a Large Area: Experiences from Nepal*. Proceedings of an international conference held in Nairobi, Kenya. Rome: FAO.

Köhl, Micheal, John L. Innes, and Edgar Kaufmann. 1994. "Reliability of Differing Densities of Sample Grids Used for the Monitoring of Forest Conditions in Europe." *Environmental Monitoring and Assessment* 29:210–220.

Kostov, P. P., and D. T. Stojanov. 1985. "Rational Utilization of Blueberry Finding Places in Bulgaria and Their Cultivation." *Acta Horticulturalis* 165:281–285.

Kozak, A., and R. C. Yang. 1981. "Equations for Estimating Bark Volume and Thickness of Commercial Trees in British Columbia." *Forestry Chronicle* 57: 115–117.

Kuusipalo, J. 1988. "Factors Affecting the Fruiting of Bilberries: An Analysis of Categorical Data Set." *Vegetatio* 76:71–77.

Legendre, Pierre. 1993. "Spatial Autocorrelation: Trouble or New Paradigim?" *Ecology* 74:1659–1673.

Lessica, Peter, and Brian M. Steele. 1994. "Prolonged Dormancy in Vascular Plants and Implications for Monitoring Studies." *Natural Areas Journal* 14:209–212.

Liegel, Leon, David Pilz, and Thomas Love. 1998. "The MAB Mushroom Study: Background and Concerns." *Ambio Special Report* 9:3–7.

Liegel, Leon, David Pilz, Thomas Love, and Eric T. Jones. 1998. "Integrating Biological, Socioeconomic, and Managerial Methods and Results in the MAB Mushroom Study." *Ambio Special Report* 9:26–33.

Lincoff, Gary H. 1981. *The Audubon Society Field Guide to North American Mushrooms*. New York: Alfred A. Knopf.

Love, Thomas, Eric T. Jones, and Leon Liegel. 1998. "Valuing the Temperate Rainforest: Wild Mushrooming on the Olympic Peninsula." *Ambio Special Report* 9:16–25.

Lund, H. Gyde, ed. 1998. *IUFRO Guidelines for Designing Multipurpose Resource Inventories*. Vol. 8. Vienna: IUFRO World Series.

Lund, H. Gyde, and C. E. Thomas. 1989. *A Primer on Stand and Forest Inventory Designs*. General Technical Report WO-54. Washington, DC: U.S. Department of Agriculture, Forest Service.

Martin, Gary J. 1995. *Ethnobotany: A Methods Manual.* New York: Chapman and Hall.

Maus, Paul. 1995. *Guidelines for the Use of Digital Imagery for Vegetation Mapping.* Prepared for the Forest Service Remote Sensing Steering Committee, Integration of Remote Sensing, Nationwide Forestry Applications Program. Washington, DC: U.S. Department of Agriculture, Forest Service.

McCune, B. 1990. "Rapid Estimation of Abundance of Epiphytes on Branches." *The Bryologist* 93:39–43.

McCune, Bruce, and Peter Lessica. 1992. "The Trade-Off between Species Capture and Quantitative Accuracy in Ecological Inventory of Lichens and Bryophytes in Forests in Montana." *The Bryologist* 95:296–304.

McLain, Rebecca J., Eric T. Jones, and Leon Liegel. 1998. "The MAB Mushroom Study as a Teaching Case Example of Interdisciplinary and Sustainable Forestry Research." *Ambio Special Report* 9:34–35.

Moore, Michael. 1979. *Medicinal Plants of the Mountain West.* Santa Fe, NM: Museum of New Mexico.

———. 1993. *Medicinal Plants of the Pacific West.* Santa Fe, NM: Red Crane Books.

Moore, P. D., J. A. Webb, and M. E. Collison. 1991. *Pollen Analysis.* Oxford: Blackwell Scientific Publications.

Morgan, P., Gregory H. Aplet, Jonathon B. Haufler, Hope C. Humphries, Margaret M. Moore, and W. Dale Wilson. 1994. "Historical Range of Variability: A Useful Tool for Evaluating Ecosystem Change." *Journal of Sustainable Forestry* 2:87–111.

Mueller-Dombois, D., and H. Ellenberg. 1974. *Aims and Methods of Vegetation Ecology.* New York: John Wiley and Sons.

Muir, Patricia S., and Bruce McCune. 1988. "Lichens, Tree Growth, and Foliar Symptoms of Air Pollution: Are the Stories Consistent?" *Journal of Environmental Quality* 17:361–370.

Mulder, Barry S., Barry R. Noon, Thomas A. Spies, Martin G. Raphael, Craig J. Palmer, Anthony R. Olsen, Gordon H. Reeves, and Hartwell H. Welsh, eds. 1999. *The Strategy and Design of the Effectiveness Monitoring Program for the Northwest Forest Plan.* General Technical Report PNW-GTR-437. Portland, OR: U.S. Department of Agriculture, Forest Service, Pacific Northwest Research Station.

Murray, M. D., and P. D. Crawford. 1982. "Timber and Boughs: Compatible Crops Form a Noble Fir Plantation." In *Proceedings of a Symposium on the Biology and Management of True Fir in the Pacific Northwest, 24–26 February 1981, Seattle,* ed. C. D. Oliver and R. M. Kendady, contribution 45. Seattle: University of Washington, Institute of Forest Resources.

Myers, Wayne L., and Ganapati P. Patil. 1995. "Simplicity, Efficiency, and Economy in Forest Surveys." In *The Monte Verita Conference on Forest Survey Designs,* ed. Michael Kohl, Peter Bachman, Peter Brassel, and Giovanni Preto, pp. 47–55. Zurich: Swiss Federal Institute of Technology (ETH), Section of Forest Inventory and Planning.

Noss, R. 1985. "On Characterizing Presettlement Vegetation: How and Why." *Natural Areas Journal* 5:5–19.

O'Dell, T. E., D. J. Lodge, and J. F. Ammirati. In press. "Measuring the Diversity of Terrestrial Macrofungi on Soil." In *Measuring and Monitoring Biological Diversity: Standard Methods for Fungi,* ed. G. M. Mueller, G. F. Bills, and M. S. Foste. Washington, DC: Smithsonian Institution Press.

Odum, E. P. 1971. *Fundamentals of Ecology.* 3d ed. Philadelphia: Saunders.

Olsen, Anthony R., Joseph Sedransk, Don Edwards, Carol A. Gotway, Walter Liggett, Stephen Rathbun, Kenneth H. Reckhow, and Linda Young. 1999. "Statistical Issues for Monitoring Ecological and Natural Resources in the United States." *Environmental Monitoring and Assessment* 54:1–45.

Pearsall, D. M. 1989. *Paleoethnobotany: A Handbook of Procedures.* San Diego, CA: Academic Press.

Peck, JeriLynn, E. 1997. "Commercial Moss Harvest in Northwestern Oregon: Describing the Epiphyte Communities." *Northwest Science* 71:186–195.

———. 1998. "Update to the Moss Harvesting Monitoring Plan." Unpublished report on file with the Siuslaw National Forest, Corvallis, OR.

Peck, JeriLynn E., S. Acker, and W. McKee. 1995. "Autecology of Mosses in Coniferous Forests in the Central Western Cascades of Oregon." *Northwest Science* 69:184–190.

Peck, JeriLynn E., and Bruce McCune. 1998. "Commercial Moss Harvest in Northwestern Oregon: Biomass and Accumulation of Epiphytes." *Biological Conservation* 86:299–305.

Peck, JeriLynn E., and Patricia S. Muir. 1999. "Commercial 'Moss' Harvesting: Estimating the Size of the Resource and Accumulation Rates." Unpublished report on file with Dr. Patricia Muir, Department of Botany and Plant Pathology, Oregon State University, Corvallis, OR.

Peters, Charles. 1995. "Observations on the Sustainable Exploitation of Nontimber Tropical Forest Products." In *Current Issues in Nontimber Forest Products Research,* ed. M. Perez, J. E. Ruiz, and M. Arnold, pp. 19–39. Proceedings of the Research on NTFP Workshop. Hot Springs, Zimbabwe: CIFOR.

Pilz, D., F. D. Brodie, S. Alexander, and R. Molina. 1998. "Relative Value of Chanterelles and Timber as Commercial Forest Products." *Ambio Special Report* 9:14–15.

Pilz, D., and R. Molina. In press. "Sustaining Productivity of Commercially Harvested Edible Forest Mushrooms." *Forest Ecology and Management.*

———. In review. *Monitoring Commercially Harvested Forest Mushrooms.* General Technical Report PNW-GTR. Portland, OR: U.S. Department of Agriculture, Forest Service, Pacific Northwest Research Station.

Pilz, D., R. Molina, and L. Liegel. 1998. "Biological Productivity of Chanterelle Mushrooms in and near the Olympic Peninsula Biosphere Reserve." *Ambio Special Report* 9:8–13.

Pilz, D., N. S. Weber, C. Carter, C. Parks, and R. Molina. In review. "Investigations of Morel Mushroom Productivity, Ecology, Taxonomy, and Population Genetics Following Wildfires and Tree Mortality in Northeastern Oregon."

Pitt, Michael D., and Francis Edward Schwab. 1988. *Quantitative Determinations of Shrub Biomass and Production: A Problem Analysis.* Victoria, BC: Research Branch, Ministry of Forests and Lands.

Podani, J., T. Czaran, and S. Bartha. 1993. "Pattern, Area, and Diversity: The

Importance of Spatial Scale in Species Assemblages." *Abstracta Botanica* 17: 37–51.

Raatikainen, Mikko, Esko Rossi, and Jarvo Huovinen. 1984. "The Yields of the Edible Wild Berries in Central Finland." *Silva Fennica* 18:199–219.

Rambo, Thomas R., Jouko Rikkinen, and Jerilynn Peck. 1998. "Bryophyte and Pin Lichen Inventories of Selected Oregon Coast Range Sites. Unpublished report on file with the Siuslaw National Forest, Corvallis, OR.

Rice, Miriam. 1980. *Mushrooms for Color*. Eureka, CA: Mad River Press.

Richards, Rebecca Templin. 1997. "What the Natives Know: Wild Mushrooms and Forest Health." *Journal of Forestry* 95:5–10.

Roesch, Francis A. 1993. "Adaptive Cluster Sampling for Forest Inventories." *Forest Science* 39:655–669.

Rogue Institute for Ecology and Economy. 1995. Field Instructions for Assessment/Inventory, Ashland, OR.

Salo, Kauko. 1993. "Yields of Commercial Edible Mushrooms in Mineral Soil Forests in Finland, 1985–1986." *Aquilo Ser Bot* 31:115–121.

Schlosser, William E., Keith A. Blatner, and R. C. Chapman. 1991. "Economic and Marketing Implications of the Special Forest Products Harvest in the Coastal Pacific Northwest." *Western Journal of Applied Forestry* 6:67–72.

Schlosser, William E., Keith A. Blatner, and Benjamin Zamora. 1992. "Pacific Northwest Forest Lands Potential for Floral Greenery Production." *Northwest Science* 66:44–55.

Schlosser, William E., Cindy Talbott Roche, Keith A. Blatner, and David M. Baumgartner. 1992. *A Guide to Floral Greens: Special Forest Products*. Pullman: Washington State University Cooperative Extension.

Schmoldt, Daniel, D. L. Peterson, and David G. Silsbee. 1994. "Developing Inventory and Monitoring Programs Based on Multiple Objectives." *Environmental Management* 18:707–727.

Schreuder, Hans, Timothy G. Gregoire, and Geoffrey B. Wood. 1993. *Sampling Methods for Multiresource Forest Inventory*. New York: John Wiley and Sons.

Scott, Charles. 1998. "Sampling Methods for Estimating Change in Forest Resources." *Ecological Applications* 8:228–233.

Sesco, Jerry A., and Barbara McDonald. 1999. "Integrating the Human Dimension and Ecosystem Management: A Consideration of Epistemological Diversity." In *Integrating Social Sciences with Ecosystem Management,* ed. H. K. Cordell and J. C. Bergstrom, pp. 225–233. Champlain, IL: Sagamore Publishing.

Shiver, Barry D., and Bruce E. Borders. 1996. *Sampling Techniques for Forest Resource Inventory*. New York: John Wiley and Sons.

Slocombe, D. Scott. 1993. "Implementing Ecosystem-Based Management." *Bioscience* 43:612–622.

Smith, Nicholas J., and Alan McLeod. 1992. "Equations for Estimating Browse Biomass of Red Huckleberry, Western Red-cedar, and Deer Fern by Vertical Profile." *Western Journal of Applied Forestry* 7:48–50.

Spies, Thomas A. 1991. "Plant Species Diversity and Occurrence in Young, Mature, and Old-Growth Douglas-Fir Stands in Western Oregon and Washington." In *Wildlife and Vegetation of Unmanaged Douglas-Fir Stands,* ed. Leonard F. Ruggiero, Keith B. Aubry, Andrew B. Carey, and Mark H. Huff, pp. 111–121.

General Technical Report PNW-GTR-371. Portland, OR: U.S. Department of Agriculture, Forest Service, Pacific Northwest Research Station.

Stamets, Paul. 1993. *Growing Gourmet and Medicinal Mushrooms*. Berkeley, CA: Ten Speed Press.

Stampli, A. 1991. "Accurate Determination of Vegetation Change in Meadows by Successive Point Quadrant Analysis." *Vegetatio* 96:185–194.

Stein, William I. 1995. *Ten-Year Development of Douglas-Fir and Associated Vegetation after Different Site Preparation on Coast Range Clearcuts*. Pub. no. PNW-RP-473. Portland, OR: U.S. Department of Agriculture, Forest Service, Pacific Northwest Research Station.

Stohlgren, Thomas J., Kelly A. Bull, and Yuka Otsuki. 1998. "Comparison of Rangeland Vegetation Sampling Techniques in the Central Grasslands." *Journal of Range Management* 51:164–172.

Stohlgren, Thomas J., Geneva W. Chong, Mohammed A Kalkhan, and Lisa D. Schell. 1997. "Multiscale Sampling of Plant Diversity: Effects of Minimum Mapping Unit Size." *Ecological Applications* 7:1064–1074.

Stohlgren, Thomas J., M. B. Falkner, and L. D. Schell. 1995. "A Modified-Whittaker Nested Vegetation Sampling Method." *Vegetatio* 117:113–121.

Sykes, J. M., A. D. Horrill, and M. D. Mountford. 1983. "Use of Visual Cover Assessment as Quantitative Estimators of Some British Woodland Taxa." *Journal of Ecology* 71:437–450.

Thomas, J. W. 1994. Statement of Dr. Jack Ward Thomas, chief, Forest Service, USDA, February 3, before the Committee on Natural Resources, U.S. House of Representatives.

Thompson, Steven K. 1992. *Sampling*. New York: John Wiley and Sons.

Thompson, Steven K., and George A. F. Seber. 1996. *Adaptive Sampling*. New York: John Wiley and Sons.

Thomson, Euan F., Sarwat N. Mirza, and Javed Afzal. 1998. "Technical Note: Predicting the Components of Aerial Biomass of Fourwing Saltbush from Shrub Height and Volume." *Journal of Range Management* 51:323–325.

Thysell, David R., and Andrew B. Carey. 2000. *Effects of Forest Management on Understory and Overstory Vegetation: A Retrospective Study*. Pub. no. PNW-GTR-488. Portland, OR: U.S. Department of Agriculture, Forest Service, Pacific Northwest Research Station.

Turner, Nancy J., and Barbara S. Efrat. 1982. *Ethnobotany of the Hesquiat Indians of Vancouver Island*. Victoria, BC: British Columbia Provincial Museum.

Turner, Nancy J., and Hebda J. Richard. 1980. "Contemporary Use of Bark for Medicine by Two Salishan Native Elders of Southwest Vancouver Islands, Canada." *Journal of Ethnopharmacology* 29:59–72.

U.S. Department of Agriculture, Forest Service. 1998. *Integrating Surveys of Terrestrial Natural Resources: The Oregon Demonstration Project*. Inventory and Monitoring Report no. 2. Fort Collins, CO: U.S. Department of Agriculture, Forest Service, Rocky Mountain Research Station.

———. 2000. *National Strategy for Special Forest Products*. Washington, DC: U.S. Department of Agriculture, Forest Service.

U.S. Department of Agriculture, Forest Service, and U.S. Department of the Interior, Bureau of Land Management. 1994. *Record of Decision for Amendments to Forest Service and Bureau of Land Management Planning Documents within the Range of the Northern Spotted Owl.* Portland, OR: U.S. Department of Agriculture, Forest Service.

U.S. Department of Agriculture and National Resource Conservation Service. 1999. National PLANTS database, National Plant Data Center, Baton Rouge, LA. *http://plants.usda.gov/plants.*

Vance, Nan C., Melissa Borsting, and David Pilz. In press. *Species Information Guide for Special Forest Products in the Pacific Northwest.* Portland, OR: U.S. Department of Agriculture, Forest Service, Pacific Northwest Research Station.

Vance, Nan C., R. G. Kelsey, and D. L. Copes. 1998. "Comparing Biomass and Taxane Concentration to Maximize Yield in Rooted Cutting of Pacific Yew (*Taxus brevifolia* Nutt)." In *Symposium Proceedings: Native Plants' Propagating and Planting,* ed. R. Rose and D. L. Haase, pp. 82–85. Corvallis: Oregon State University Press.

Vance, Nan C., and M. J. Kirkland. 1997. "Commercially Harvested Bryophytes Associated with *Acer circinatum* (Aceraceae)." In *Conservation and Management of Native Plants and Fungi,* ed. Thomas N. Kaye, Aaron Liston, Rhoda Love, Daniel L. Luoma, Robert J. Meinke, and Mark V. Wilson, pp. 267–271. Corvallis, OR: Native Plant Society of Oregon.

Vitt, Dale H., Janet E. Marsh, and Robin B. Bovey. 1988. *Mosses, Lichens, and Ferns of Northwest America.* Edmonton, Alberta: Lone Pine Publishing.

Von Hagen, Bettina, and Roger Fight. 1999. *Opportunities for Conservation-Based Development of Nontimber Forest Products in the Pacific Northwest.* General Technical Report PNW-GTR-473. Portland, OR: U.S. Department of Agriculture, Forest Service, Pacific Northwest Research Station.

Von Hagen, Bettina, James F. Weigand, Rebecca McLain, Roger Fight, and Harriet Christensen, eds. 1996. *Conservation and Development of Nontimber Forest Products in the Pacific Northwest: An Annotated Bibliography.* General Technical Report PNW-GTR-375. Portland, OR: U.S. Department of Agriculture, Forest Service, Pacific Northwest Research Station.

Webb, R. H. 1996. *Grand Canyon: A Century of Change.* Tucson: University of Arizona Press.

West, N. E., and G. A. Reese. 1991. "Comparison of Some Methods for Collecting and Analyzing Data on Aboveground Net Production and Diversity of Herbaceous Vegetation in a Northern Utah Subalpine Context." *Vegetatio* 96: 145–163.

Wester, David. B. 1992. "Viewpoint: Replication, Randomization, and Statistics in Range Research." *Journal of Range Management* 45:285–290.

Whysong, G. L., and W. H. Miller. 1987. "An Evaluation of Random and Systematic Plot Placement for Estimating Frequency." *Journal of Range Management* 40:475–479.

Wong, Jenny. 2000. "Biometrics of Nontimber Forest Product Resource Assessment: A Review of Current Methodology." *http://www.etfrn.org/etfrn/workshop/ntfp/ntfpbar.html.*

Zaitseva, Nina. 1993. "Medicinal Raw Material Resources of the Karellian Forests and Problems Concerning Their Protection." *Aquilo Ser Bot* 31:147–151.

Part Three

NATIVE AMERICAN CLAIMS

Tree of Life

A tree images life
It grows
Unwell, it heals itself
Spent, it dies

A tree reflects being
It changes
Altered, it restores itself
Ever to remain the same

A tree gives life
It abides
It lends existence yet
Endures undiminished.

Trees give me everything
Serve all my needs
To the tree I can give nothing
Except my song of praise.

When I look upon the tree
I remember that
The apple tree can
Allay my hunger
The maple can
Slake my thirst
The pine can
Heal my wounds and cuts
The bark of birch can
Form my home, can
mould my canoe and vessels
The tissue of birch can
keep the images that I draw
The balsam groves can
Shield me from the winds
Fruit of the grape vine can
Lend colour to my quills
The hickory can
Bend as my bow, while
The cherrywood provides
An arrow shaft.

The cedar ferns can
Cushion my body in sleep
The basswood can
Become my daughter's doll
The ash, as snowshoe, can
Carry me across the snows
The tobacco can
Transport my prayers to God
The sweetgrass can
Aromate my lodge
The roots of evergreen can
Bind my sleigh and craft
The stump and twig can
Warm my lodge
The rose and daisy can

Move the soul of woman
The leaves wind-blown can
Open my spirit.

—Basil Johnston (excerpted from *Ojibway Heritage*)

Indian Reserved Rights

Edmund Clay Goodman

The following chapter is a general overview of Indian reserved rights to gather forest products on public lands. It is only an initial survey of some of the issues relevant to tribal gathering rights on public lands administered by the United States. My discussion first examines the relevant federal Indian law issues concerning Indian tribal rights to gather on public lands. Second, I set out the results of some preliminary inquiries into the specific status of various tribes that currently exercise reserved gathering rights on national forestlands.

An initial note on terminology: this overview will use the term "reserved" rights, rather than "treaty" rights, to describe the rights that tribes exercise on public lands. Although many of the tribes that have such rights did in fact reserve them through treaty, there are a number of tribes whose rights derive from other government-to-government agreements (memorialized through Executive Orders and Acts of Congress). For the purposes of this analysis, the rights reserved through these latter agreements are viewed as having the same legal status as rights reserved by treaty (*Antoine v. Washington* 1975, 420 U.S. 194, 200–204). The term "reserved" rights is the term preferred by tribes themselves, since it clarifies the misconception that such rights were created or given to the tribes by treaty rather than reserved by them through such documents.

HISTORY OF TREATY AND RESERVATION PROCESS

As the United States expanded westward during the nineteenth century, the country faced the significant legal and political obstacles of tribal ownership and possession of the land base that the country sought to acquire. The United States obtained ownership of this land through two principal means: military conquest and land cessions agreed to through a government-to-government negotiation process. In both instances, the legal transfer of the lands acquired by the United States was often memorialized by treaty.[1] Most of these land cession agreements involved the reservation of a smaller area within the tribe's aboriginal territory for the tribe's exclusive use and possession in perpetuity, hence the term "reservation" to describe the lands upon which the Indians eventually settled as homelands.

A number of tribes, particularly those in the upper Midwest and in the Pacific Northwest, agreed to move onto reservations only after securing guarantees that they would continue to have the right to harvest certain resources off-reservation on the lands and waters that had been ceded. The rights reserved sought to preserve for the tribes the ability to continue a way of life that they had engaged in for centuries and that, as the Supreme Court described in the fishing rights context, was "not much less necessary to the existence of the Indians than the atmosphere they breathed" (*United States v. Winans* 1905, 198 U.S. 371, 380).

TREATIES: A RESERVATION OF PREEXISTING INHERENT RIGHTS

The 1905 decision of the U.S. Supreme Court in *United States v. Winans* has become the cornerstone for the recognition and protection of off-reservation reserved usufructuary rights. *Winans* involved a suit brought by the United States on behalf of the Yakama Indian Nation, which in its 1855 treaty with the United States had agreed to cede its aboriginal territory and remove itself to a smaller reservation but had also reserved "the right of taking fish at all usual and accustomed places, in common with the citizens of the territory, and of erecting temporary buildings for curing them" (Treaty with the Yakamas, June 9, 1855, 12 Stat. 951, 953). In the 1890s, two non-Indians who owned riparian lands excluded the Yakama tribal members from exercising their rights at one of these usual and accustomed sites (*Winans* 1905, 379; *United States v. Winans* 1896, 73 F.72, 75 [D.Wash.]).

The Court held that the right reserved through the 1855 Treaty was more than a right to equal access to the fishery with non-Indians (whom the Winans had the right to exclude); it was a servitude that burdened the land that the Winans had obtained (*Winans* 1905, 380). The Court articulated a principle of Indian treaty interpretation that has shaped the course of Indian law ever since: that Indian treaties did not involve a grant of rights *to* the Indians but were rather a grant *from* them and, therefore, a reservation of those rights not granted to the United States by the treaty (*Winans* 1905, 380–381). The Supreme Court expressly recognized that at treaty time, the tribes were sovereigns whose rights over their lands and waters existed without "a shadow of impediment," and that the treaties were instruments by which the tribes granted certain of those rights and retained those not given away (*Winans* 1905, 380–381).[2] The Supreme Court has subsequently held that these same principles of construction apply whether the instrument reserving the rights was a treaty or an Executive Order, a congressional act or some other legal instrument reflecting an agreement between a tribe and the United States (*Antoine v. Washington* 1975, 200–204). This principle concerning Indian treaties as reserving rights to the tribes (rather than granting rights to them) has been repeatedly upheld, particularly in the context of off-reservation usufructuary rights.[3]

THE SOURCE OF OFF-RESERVATION RESERVED RIGHTS

As noted above, the source of off-reservation reserved gathering rights for the majority of tribes with such rights are treaties or other government-to-government agreements with the United States. Treaties between the United States and Indian tribes are considered the "Supreme law of the land" pursuant to the U.S. Constitution and would trump or preempt any conflicting state law or regulations. Tribal reserved rights are property rights, and the abrogation of the ability of the tribes to exercise such rights by governmental action would give rise to a takings claim under the Fifth Amendment of the U.S. Constitution (*Menominee Tribe v. United States* 1968, 390 U.S. 916).

Some other tribes have off-reservation rights by virtue of actions taken after their treaties were signed. The Confederated Tribes of the Colville Reservation in northeastern Washington State continue to hold and exercise off-reservation hunting, fishing, trapping, and gathering rights on lands that originally comprised the former northern half of their reservation but were transferred to the United States pursuant to a subsequent agreement and act of Congress (*Antoine v. Washington* 1975). Although some of the northern half has been transferred to private ownership, a substantial portion remains in federal (U.S. Forest Service and U.S. Bureau of Land Management) ownership. The Klamath tribes in south-central Oregon retain hunting, fishing, trapping, and gathering rights on national forestlands that formerly constituted the Klamath Reservation but were transferred out of tribal ownership due to the policy of "termination" (*Kimball I* 1974; *Kimball II* 1979). The rights of the Klamaths, Colvilles, and similarly situated tribes are also recognized as compensable property rights (*Antoine v. Washington* 1975).

The liberal principles of construction used to interpret treaties and other intergovernmental agreements with Indian tribes have been applied to find that usufructuary rights not expressly mentioned in a treaty were nonetheless reserved by the tribes. For example, the reservation of "the exclusive right of taking fish" in the 1864 Treaty between the United States and

Klamath tribes has been interpreted as including the right to hunt (*Klamath and Modoc Tribes v. Maison* 1956, F. Supp. 634; *Kimball I* 1974, 439 F.2d 566). The treaty phrase reserving lands "to be held as Indian lands are held" has been interpreted as reserving a broad array of usufructuary rights (*Menominee Tribe v. United States* 1968, 391 U.S. 406).

Finally, some tribes retain usufructuary rights on off-reservation lands by virtue of aboriginal use and possession that have not been divested. Such aboriginal rights were not reserved by treaty or other document but are recognized as inherent in a tribe's use of an area since time immemorial (Cohen 1982, 486–493). Aboriginal rights, while they remain intact, generally have the same scope and status as reserved rights; however, such rights are more easily defeasible and do not give rise to a claim for a Fifth Amendment taking (*Tee-Hit-Ton Indians v. United States* 1955, 348 U.S. 272).

THE SCOPE OF OFF-RESERVATION RESERVED RIGHTS

The exercise of off-reservation usufructuary rights has, predictably, given rise to a great deal of litigation over the years. The three major areas that this litigation has dealt with are the ability of the state or federal government to regulate tribal exercise of the right; allocation of resources between tribal use and non-Indian users; and environmental protection of the resources.

Rights vis-à-vis State and Federal Governments Regarding Regulation

The various states on whose public lands and waters tribal members exercise reserved rights have sought for many years to regulate the exercise of those rights pursuant to state law, such as the imposition of seasonal take restrictions, bag limits, and so on. The courts have repeatedly recognized that the rights exercised by tribal members belong to the tribes as inherent sovereign entities, and that the states have no authority to bring tribal members under general state regulations except when reasonable and necessary in the interests of conservation.[4] This conservation standard has been interpreted to justify regulations necessary to protect various species from extinction (*Washington Department of Game v. Puyallup Tribe* 1973, 414 U.S. 44).

Federal regulatory authority over Indian exercise of off-reservation rights has been applied under the broad and general authority of the United States in Indian affairs, although the government has exerted little control over off-reservation hunting and fishing rights (Cohen 1982, 486–493). Since fish and game are usually the province of the states and the tribes, the United States has had little occasion to step in to regulate, although the government does maintain regulatory authority over the flora on public lands (National Forest Management Act, 16 U.S.C. 1601 *et Seq.*). I have not found any cases that address the ability of the United States to restrict tribal exercise of reserved gathering rights on public lands through regulation. Conflicts over tribal harvest of plant species on U.S. managed lands have generally been resolved through government-to-government agreements. Presumably, since the reserved right to gather is a protected property right, the ability of the United States to restrict harvest through regulation would have to be justified as reasonable and necessary for conservation purposes; otherwise, per *Menominee, supra,* such restriction would potentially subject the government to a claim for damages.

Rights to Allocation of a Shared Resource

Another contentious issue in the exercise of off-reservation rights concerns the allocation of such resources in situations of scarcity. Although at the time that the particular treaties or agreements were signed the relevant resources may have been so plentiful that no one foresaw any problem with shared use, the increase in non-Indian populations and attendant pressures have led to conflicts over who has a right to how much. Courts have generally approached this issue by finding that the tribes who had a reserved right to a common resource had a right to a 50 percent allocation of that resource (*United States v. Washington* 1974, 384 F.Supp 312).[5] The tribe's share was based on the court-created doctrine of a "moderate living standard"; the court interpreted the relevant treaties as reserving to the tribes a sufficient amount of resources to ensure that their members could obtain a moderate living, and if they could obtain such a standard by an allocation of less than 50 percent of the resource, the tribal share would be reduced (*U.S. v. Washington* 1974; *Washington v. Washington State Commercial Passenger Fishing Vessel Ass'n* 1979, 443 U.S. 658; *Sohappy v. Smith* 1969, 302 F.Supp 899).

In Wisconsin, protracted litigation between tribes and the state over allocation of usufructuary rights resources was initially resolved by finding that the tribes had a right to sufficient resources to meet a moderate standard of living with no upper limit (*Lac Courte Oreilles v. Wisconsin* 1991, 775 F.Supp 321); later, however, the same court (under a different presiding judge) determined that since the tribes could not obtain a moderate standard of living even if they were permitted to harvest all the available resources, the equitable result would be to apportion the resources by a 50 percent allocation (*Lac Courte Oreilles v. Wisconsin* 1991, 775 F.Supp 321; *Lac Courte Oreilles v. Wisconsin* 1988, 686 F.Supp 226).

One critical difference between non-Indian users and Indians is that the latter have reserved property rights, whereas the former merely have a privilege that can be licensed or otherwise qualified by the state. Absent a conservation necessity, tribal hunters, fishers, and gatherers exercising their reserved rights are guaranteed the right to access their 50 percent share without interference by state regulators (*Lac Courte Oreilles v. Wisconsin* 1988, 227).

Rights to Protection of Resources

Another issue that courts have begun to address is whether the tribes who have the right to harvest a particular off-reservation resource also have the right to environmental protection sufficient to protect that resource and thereby guarantee that the tribe's right can continue to be meaningfully exercised. The Ninth Circuit was faced squarely with this issue in phase 2 of the *United States v. Washington* (1985, 759 F.2d 1353, 1357) fisheries litigation but refused to hear the issue on ripeness grounds. In a recent decision, the federal district court for Oregon enjoined a series of U.S. Forest Service timber sales on the lands on which the Klamath tribes exercised hunting and fishing rights, requiring that the Forest Service first engage in government-to-government consultation with the tribes to ensure that their usufructuary resources be protected "to the fullest extent possible" (*Klamath Tribes* at 8, quoting *Pyramid Lake Paiute Tribe v. Morton* 1973, 354 F.Supp. 252). A number of commentators have argued that the right to harvest resources must of necessity carry a right for the protection of the resources and have pointed to a number of cases that support this proposition (Blumm and Swift 1998).

RESERVED OFF-RESERVATION GATHERING RIGHTS OF VARIOUS TRIBES

Many of the court decisions dealing with hunting and fishing rights refer to tribal "gathering" rights as well. The reference to "gathering" rights as part of the parcel of reserved usufructuary rights often follows from the broad interpretations given to tribal reserved rights under the liberal canons of construction discussed earlier. However, for the most part, the substance of gathering rights has not been subject to the same kind of contention as the taking of wild game and fish.

Chippewa Tribes of the Upper Midwest

The various Chippewa tribes (located largely in Wisconsin and Minnesota) reserved extensive off-reservation usufructuary rights, the scope and exercise of which have been subject to extensive litigation. Most of the litigation, however, has focused on the much more contentious issues involving fishing and hunting. However, since the various Chippewa treaties expressly reserved gathering rights (often, specifically, the right to gather wild rice), these rights have been addressed at various points in the litigation.

The *Lac Courte Oreilles* litigation began in 1974 with the various Wisconsin Chippewa tribes' filing of a suit to determine the extent of their off-reservation usufructuary right, and the litigation continued well into the 1990s. The courts determined that the Chippewa tribes had reserved usufructuary rights on all public lands in the northern third of the state of Wisconsin (*Lac Courte Oreilles v. Voigt* 1983, 700 F.2d 341). Although the overall subject of the *Lac Courte Oreilles* litigation was hunting and fishing rights, the courts were also faced with the issue of the scope of the tribes' reserved gathering right. The courts determined that the tribes had a right to harvest 175 different species of plants and animals (*Lac Courte Oreilles v. Wisconsin* 1987, 653 F.Supp. 1420, 1426–1427) but had not reserved the right to harvest timber commercially on those lands (*Lac Courte Oreilles v. Wisconsin* 1991, 758 F.Supp. 1262).

The Mille Lacs band of Chippewa Indians, located in Minnesota, are in the process of litigating the question of the scope and survival of their off-reservation hunting, fishing, and gathering rights. The Minnesota Chippewa treaties specifically reserved the right to "gather wild rice" on ceded lands (Treaty with the Chippewa, July 29, 1837, 7 Stat. 536, 537). In the 1930s, the Minnesota Chippewas' successful assertion of a treaty right to gather wild rice off-reservation led to the creation of a Wild Rice Lake Reserve for their exclusive use (*United States v. 4,450.72 Acres of Land* 1939, 72 F.Supp 167). The Mille Lacs' case is currently before the U.S. Supreme Court.

Pacific Northwest Tribes

In the Pacific Northwest, various tribes have gathering rights on off-reservation lands, including lands that are part of the U.S. National Forest System. While fishing and hunting rights on such lands have been subject to extensive litigation, the issues concerning gathering rights (once their existence was established as part and parcel of the other off-reservation rights) have generally been resolved through government-to-government agreements.

The Yakama Indian Nation, located in south-central Washington State, has reserved rights to gather huckleberries on national forestlands. The Nation has entered into an agreement with the U.S. Forest Service that sets aside certain huckleberry picking areas for the exclusive use of tribal members exercising treaty-reserved off-reservation gathering rights. Treaties with the Salish and Kootenai tribes and other northwestern Indian tribes also expressly reserved the right of "gathering roots and berries" on ceded lands that remained "unclaimed." Both the Klamath tribes of south-central Oregon and the Confederated tribes of the Colville Indian Reservation in northeastern Washington, as described earlier, retain off-reservation usufructuary rights on Forest Service lands. These include various gathering rights to roots, berries, and wood. For many of the tribes, the gathering right includes both an economic component (subsistence or commercial) as well as a cultural component. Gathering of various plant species is often an essential part of various religious or spiritual practices of the tribes, and such uses are often recognized and protected even where there has been no reservation of rights.

NOTES

1. In 1871, Congress prohibited any further treaties with Indian tribes, requiring that any subsequent agreements occur through Executive Order or act of Congress. Act of March 3, 1871, ch. 120, sec. 1, 16 Stat. 544 (codified as carried forward at 25 U.S.C., sec. 71).

2. The Court's rationale for this rule of construction was based on the existing principle that an Indian treaty was to be interpreted as the Indian signers would have understood it, since the treaties were negotiated and written in a language foreign to the Indians and because the United States stood in a superior bargaining position. These liberal canons of construction continue to be applied to the interpretation of documents reserving Indian rights.

3. See, e.g., *Kimball v. Callahan,* 493 F.2d 564 (9th Cir. 1974), *cert denied* 419 U.S. 1019 (1974) *(Kimball I); Kimball v. Callahan,* 590 F.2d 768 (9th Cir. 1979), *cert denied* 444 U.S. 826 (1979) *(Kimball II); United States v. Washington*, 384 F.Supp. 312 (W.D. Wash. 1974); *Sohappy v. Smith,* 302 F.Supp 899 (D.Or. 1969).

4. See, e.g., *United States v. Washington,* 384 F.Supp 312 (W.D. Wash. 1974), *aff'd* 520 F.2d 676 (9th Cir. 1975); *Sohappy v. Smith,* 302 F.Supp (D.Or. 1969), *aff'd and remanded* 529 F.2d 570 (9th Cir. 1976); *Kimball I* and *Kimball II, supra.*

5. This 50 percent allocation in the context of Northwest off-reservation fishing rights was ultimately affirmed by the U.S. Supreme Court in *Washington v. Washington State Commercial Passenger Fishing Vessel Ass'n,* 443 U.S. 658 (1979).

REFERENCES

Blumm, Michael, and Brett Swift. 1998. "The Indian Treaty Piscary Profit and Habitat Protection in the Pacific Northwest: A Property Rights Approach." *University of Colorado Law Review* 69:407–414.

Cohen, Felix. 1982. *Handbook of Federal Indian Law.* Pp. 486–493. Charlottesville, VA: Bobbs-Merrill.

Acts of Congress and Treaties

Act of March 3, 1871, ch. 120, sec. 1, 16 Stat. 544 (codified as carried forward at 25 U.S.C., sec. 71).

National Forest Management Act, 16 U.S.C. 1601 *et. Se.*
Treaty with the Chippewa, July 29, 1837, 7 Stat. 536, 537.
Treaty with the Yakamas, June 9, 1855, 12 Stat. 951, 953.

Legal Decisions

Antoine v. Washington, 420 U.S. 194, 200–204 (1975).
Kimball v. Callahan, 493 F.2d 564 (9th Cir. 1974); *cert denied* 419 U.S. 1019 (1974) *(Kimball I).*
Kimball v. Callahan, 590 F.2d 768 (9th Cir. 1979); *cert denied* 444 U.S. 826 (1979) *(Kimball II).*
Klamath and Modoc Tribes v. Maison, 139 F.Supp 634 (D.Or. 1956).
Klamath Tribes, slip op. at 8, quoting *Pyramid Lake Paiute Tribe v. Morton,* 354 F.Supp. 252 (D.D.C. 1973).
Lac Courte Oreilles Band of Chippewa Indians v. State of Wisconsin, 653 F.Supp 1420–1435 (W.D. Wis. 1987).
Lac Courte Oreilles Band of Chippewa Indians v. State of Wisconsin, 758 F.Supp 1262 (W.D. Wis. 1991).
Lac Courte Oreilles Band of Chippewa Indians v. Voigt, 700 F.2d 341 (7th Cir.); *cert. denied* 464 U.S. 805 (1983) (LCO I).
Lac Courte Oreilles Band of Lake Superior Chippewa Indians v. Wisconsin, 686 F.Supp 226, 227 (W.D. Wis. 1988).
Lac Courte Oreilles Band of Lake Superior Chippewa Indians v. Wisconsin, 775 F.Supp 321 (W.D. Wis. 1991).
Menominee Tribe v. United States, 390 U.S. 916 (1968).
Sohappy v. Smith, 302 F.Supp 899 (D.Or. 1969); *aff'd and remanded* 529 F.2d 570 (9th Cir. 1976).
Tee-Hit-Ton Indians v. United States, 348 U.S. 272 (1955).
United States v. 4,450.72 Acres of Land, 72 F.Supp 167 (D.Minn. 1939); *aff'd sub nom Minnesota v. United States,* 125 F.2d 636 (8th Cir. 1982).
United States v. Washington, 384 F.Supp 312 (W.D. Wash. 1974); *aff'd* 520 F.2d 676 (9th Cir. 1975).
United States v. Washington, 759 F.2d 1353, 1357 (9th Cir. 1985).
United States v. Winans, 73 F.72, 75 (D.Wash. 1896).
United States v. Winans, 198 U.S. 371, 380 (1905).
Washington Department of Game v. Puyallup Tribe, 414 U.S. 44 (1973).
Washington v. Washington State Commercial Passenger Fishing Vessel Ass'n, 443 U.S. 658 (1979).

CASE STUDY

Ojibwe Off-Reservation Harvest of Wild Plants

Karen C. Danielsen and Jonathan H. Gilbert

INTRODUCTION: OFF-RESERVATION TREATY RIGHTS

The Ojibwe[1] had long lived in the Lake Superior region (portions of modern-day Minnesota, Wisconsin, Michigan, and Canada) by the time European explorers first entered the area. At that time, the Ojibwe lived a seminomadic lifestyle, moving seasonally from camp to camp, harvesting from the earth (*aki*)[2] vital foods, medicines, utility supplies, and ceremonial items.

As more Europeans moved into the Lake Superior region in search of timber and minerals, the U.S. government obtained vast parcels of land from the Ojibwe through cession treaties. In many of these treaties, the Ojibwe retained the rights to hunt, fish, and gather in the ceded territories to meet economic, cultural, spiritual, and medicinal needs—in essence, to sustain their lifeway. Tribal negotiations for these rights were fastidious and purposeful, and only through the guarantee of these rights did the tribes agree to sign the treaties. Today, these reserved usufructuary rights are often referred to as treaty rights.

Treaties that reserved these rights include the Treaty of 1836, ceding land in Michigan's Upper and Lower Peninsulas and parts of the Upper Great Lakes; the Treaty of 1837, ceding land in north-central Wisconsin and east-central Minnesota; the Treaty of 1842, ceding land in northern Michigan and Wisconsin and the western part of Lake Superior; and the Treaty of 1854, ceding land in northeastern Minnesota and creating reservations for many Ojibwe tribes (Figure 3).

For many years following the ratification of these treaties, the Ojibwe continued to hunt, fish, and gather as always. However, over the years, as states passed various conservation laws, state game wardens enforced these laws against tribal members. Members exercising their off-reservation treaty rights within the ceded territories were frequently cited and convicted in state courts. Many members paid fines, endured the confiscation of their rifles and fishing gear, and suffered incarceration.

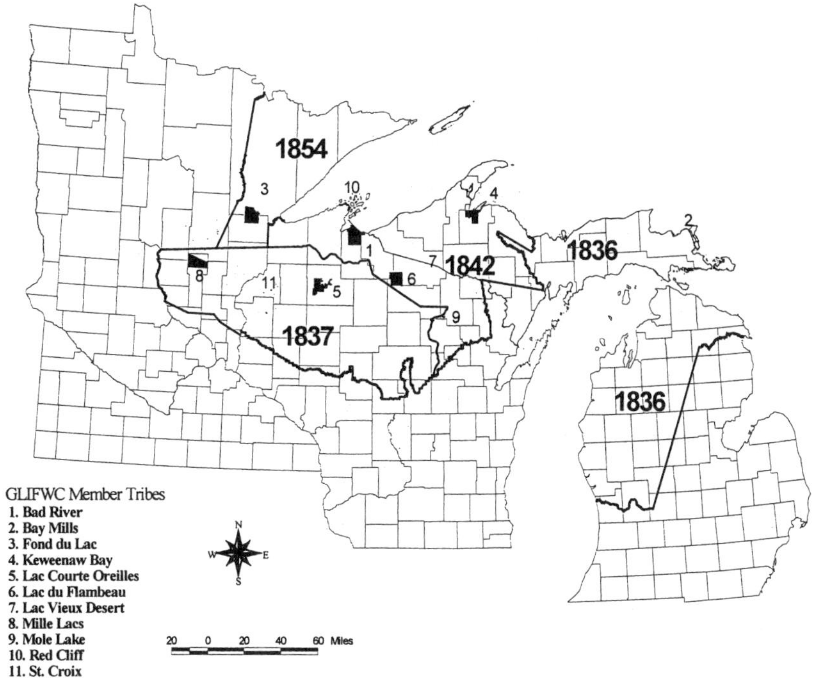

Figure 3. Map of the ceded territories and reservations of the Great Lakes Indian Fish and Wildlife Commission member tribes.

Although the Ojibwe have always believed in the continued existence of their treaty rights, it was not until the 1970s, as part of a general resurgence of tribal self-determination, that Ojibwe governments and their members more aggressively and more formally challenged state conservation laws and enforcement activities. These challenges gave rise to many federal and state court decisions that reaffirmed Ojibwe off-reservation treaty rights on public lands in the ceded territories.[3]

The courts confirmed the Ojibwe's understanding of their treaty rights: the treaties provide a "permanent" guarantee "to make a moderate living off the land and from the waters . . . by engaging in hunting, fishing and gathering as they had in the past."[4] In essence, the courts found the Ojibwe treaties to be legally binding agreements to be respected within the framework of the U.S. Constitution, which defines treaties as the "supreme law of the land."

In addition, the courts recognized that by reserving the rights to engage in hunting, fishing, and gathering, the Ojibwe also retained their sovereignty to regulate tribal members exercising these treaty rights. Sovereignty refers to the right of inherent self-government and self-determination. Thus, tribal self-regulation is a requisite of treaty rights implementation.

This chapter will focus on the implementation of off-reservation treaty rights and tribal self-regulation on public lands, specifically with respect to the gathering of wild plants (nontimber forest products). Regarding on-reservation gathering activities, many of the conclusions about tribal sovereign prerogatives and retained rights may apply even more forcefully and extensively. After all, the pursuit of a lifeway off-reservation mirrors that found on-reservation. Moreover, on-reservation gathering activities are regulated through the sovereign prerogatives of each respective tribe and thus gathering regulations often vary considerably among different tribes.

THE GREAT LAKES INDIAN FISH AND WILDLIFE COMMISSION

As the courts reaffirmed the Ojibwe's ceded territory treaty rights, a number of tribes in Michigan, Minnesota, and Wisconsin chose to enhance their self-regulatory infrastructures through the formation of the Great Lakes Indian Fish and Wildlife Commission (GLIFWC).[5] GLIFWC's mission statement reads as follows:

- To provide assistance to member tribes in the conservation and management of fish, wildlife, and other natural resources throughout the Great Lakes region, thereby ensuring access to traditional pursuits of the Chippewa people;
- To facilitate the development of institutions of tribal self-government so as to ensure the continued sovereignty of its member tribes in the regulation and management of natural resources;
- To extend the mission to ecosystem protection recognizing that fish, wildlife, and wild plants cannot long survive in abundance in an environment that has been degraded; and
- To infuse traditional Anishinaabe culture and values as all aspects of the mission are implemented.

To carry out this mission, GLIFWC maintains a permanent full-time staff of approximately sixty employees in addition to an annual seasonal hiring of approximately another sixty part-time employees. An important role for GLIFWC employees is to address the changing needs of the member tribes. Staff members assist with issues such as the application of tribal self-regulation within the off-reservation ceded territories, identification and condition assessment of treaty resources, negotiations and consultation with state and federal government agencies regarding the management of treaty resources within the ceded territories, and litigation pertaining to the treaties of member tribes. GLIFWC employees also examine and attempt to rectify social misconceptions held by the non-Indian community regarding treaty rights through a variety of informational publications and presentations.

TRIBAL OFF-RESERVATION WILD PLANT HARVEST

The Ojibwe gather over 350 wild plant species for food, utilitarian, medicinal, ceremonial, and commercial purposes (Meeker, Elias, and Heim 1993; Densmore 1928). Examples include sweet grass *(wiingashk)*,[6] white sage *(mashkiki)*, basswood *(wiigob)*, yellow birch *(wiinizik)*, paper birch *(wiigwaas)*, wintergreen *(wiinisiibag)*, red-osier dogwood *(miskoobimizh)*, bearberry *(miskwaabiimag)*, wild sarsaparilla *(waaboozojiibik)*, white water lily *(akandamoo)*, bluebead lily *(odotaagaans)*, Canada mayflower *(agongosimin)*, swamp milkweed *(bagizowin)*, wood lily *(mashkodepin)*, rue anemone *(biimaakwad)*, wild ginger *(namepin)*, blue cohosh *(bezhigojiibik)*, bloodroot *(meskwiijiibikak)*, black ash *(aagimaak)*, yarrow *(ajidamoowaanow)*, wild rose *(oginiiminagaawanzh)*, Labrador tea *(waabashkikiibag)*, sweet flag *(wiikenh)*, wild black current *(amikomin)*, wild blackberry *(odatagaagominagaawanzh)*, blueberry *(miinagaawanzh)*, nannyberry *(aditemin)*, and highbush cranberry *(annibiminagaawashk)*.

Tribal members may gather wild plants, as guaranteed by their treaty rights, on all public lands within the ceded territories. However, only intermittent tribal wild plant gathering has occurred on state and county lands, which is likely due to regulatory complexities and obstacles that have resulted from the court decisions affirming treaty rights on these lands. For example, in Wisconsin, tribal members wishing to gather wild plants on state and county lands not only must comply with tribal regulations but also must obtain gathering permits from state and county land managers.

Most tribal off-reservation wild plant gathering occurs in the national forests that constitute a large portion of the ceded territory public land base and offer excellent gathering opportunities. The rights of GLIFWC member tribes to gather on federal lands, however, have not been specifically litigated. Nevertheless, court decisions that affirm the existence of treaty gathering rights on other public lands provide overwhelming precedent.

In lieu of an unnecessary court case in the face of this strong legal precedent on treaty gathering rights, ten of the GLIFWC member tribes and the Eastern Region of the USDA Forest Service (National Forest System, Law Enforcement and Investigation Branch, and North Central Research Station) entered into a Memorandum of Understanding (MOU) entitled "Tribal–USDA Forest Service Relations on National Forest Lands within the Ceded Territory in Treaties of 1836, 1837, and 1842."

The development of the MOU took five years of negotiations and reached completion in 1998. During this long negotiation period, in order to expedite tribal wild plant gathering on national forestlands under tribal self-regulation, the tribes and the USDA Forest Service (USFS) developed an interim agreement in 1995 that was then renewed three times before the final completion of the MOU. This interim agreement served as a template for portions of the final version.

The MOU establishes a consistent set of practices related to the trust responsibility and treaty obligations of the federal government and to the gathering of wild plants (except wild rice; *manoomin*) by the GLIFWC member tribes on national forest lands. It does not apply to tribal wild rice gathering because this issue generally has been resolved between the tribes and the states. The MOU is based on the principle of government-to-government interactions. It acknowledges and recognizes inherent tribal sovereignty and the retained tribal regulatory authority regarding treaty rights. It also establishes a process for consistent and timely consultation, with a desired goal of consensus, between GLIFWC member tribes and the USFS.

Tribal members must follow a code of regulations, adopted by their tribe, for wild plant gathering on national forestlands. Tribal wardens enforce these codes, and violations are cited into the appropriate tribal court system for prosecution. The code of regulations includes a requirement for tribal members to obtain an annual off-reservation harvest permit validated for wild plant gathering on national forests (hereafter referred to as a general gathering permit). In addition, an annual tribal commercial wild plant gathering permit must be obtained by tribal members gathering and selling conifer boughs (primarily balsam fir; *aninaandag*), princess pine *(cigonagan)*, or ginseng *(jisens)*. General and commercial gathering occurs year-round. However, permits are valid beginning August 1 and expire on July 31 of the following year.

The gathering of wild plants for specific commercial purposes has associated regulations designed to protect these resources from excessive damage caused by harvesting activities. For example, conifer boughs may not be gathered from the upper half of a tree, and the gathering of northern white cedar *(giizhik)* and hemlock *(gaagaagimizh)* boughs may only be for personal use and not for commercial purposes.

MONITORING TRIBAL OFF-RESERVATION WILD PLANT HARVEST

GLIFWC staff monitor the issuance of general and commercial permits to gauge tribal members' interest in gathering wild plants. They also conduct an annual survey to document harvest amounts of select wild plants (e.g., conifer boughs, princess pine, ginseng, birch bark, and firewood). The survey is limited to those resources suspected of being sensitive to gathering because of rarity or potential harvest levels.

Monitoring data for gathering on national forestlands extends back to the 1995–1996 harvest season with the establishment of the first interim Tribal/USFS agreement and the first issuance of tribal gathering permits for national forestlands (Danielsen 2000). Tribal participation in the permitting system has escalated each year with the growing awareness of and familiarity with the system. During the 1995–1996 season, approximately 350 tribal members acquired an off-reservation general gathering permit, and that number increased to more than 2,000 members during the 1998–1999 season. Issuance of tribal off-reservation commercial wild plant gathering permits has also generally increased through the years, with 31 permits issued during the 1995–1996 season, 115 during the 1996–1997 season, and 227 during the 1997–1998 season. For reasons that are unclear, the permits issued during the 1998–1999 season declined to 182. Continued annual monitoring will illustrate whether this is an anomaly to an increasing trend or whether the number of tribal members interested in acquiring commercial permits will stabilize at around 200.

When obtaining a commercial permit, tribal members specify one or more of the products (conifer boughs, princess pine, or ginseng) that they plan to gather. Members have indicated an interest in gathering conifer boughs more often than princess pine and ginseng. Most likely, easy access to large quantities and local markets make this product more feasible and profitable for commercial gathering. In addition, for commercial purposes, tribal members seem to condone the gathering of conifer boughs more than any other wild plant (Gilbert, Sullivan, and Zorn 1996).

The number of members who reported harvest, through the GLIFWC harvest survey, has been consistently lower than the number of members obtaining a tribal commercial gathering permit. For example, during the 1998–1999 season, of the 178 members who obtained a commercial permit, only 22 reported a harvest. It appears that members procure commercial permits in order to provide the opportunity for gathering, whether or not actual harvest ensues.

The reported harvest of conifer boughs, princess pine, ginseng, birch bark, and firewood has fluctuated yearly. The annual harvest of conifer boughs has ranged from 0.8 to 1.68 tons for individual gatherers and 10 to 37 tons for all gatherers combined. The annual harvest of princess pine has ranged from 1 to 75 pounds for individual gatherers and 13 to 525 pounds for all gatherers combined. For ginseng, members reported a harvest for the 1995–1996 season, in which three gatherers harvested 0.75 pounds. Since then, however, no ginseng harvest has been reported.

Monitoring of birch bark and firewood harvest began during the 1996–1997 season because of an apparent increasing tribal interest in these products. During that season, six members reported gathering birch bark (on average, each gathering from four trees), and twenty reported gathering firewood (on average, each gathering less than an eighth of a cord). During the 1997–1998 season, no members reported gathering birch bark, and only one member reported gathering five cords of firewood. No members reported gathering either birch bark or firewood during the 1998–1999 season. These numbers contradict the notion of an increasing interest in tribal gathering of these products. Consequently, during the next few years, GLIFWC will review survey procedures to ensure accurate data results.

As monitoring continues, GLIFWC staff will be better able to recognize trends in tribal wild plant harvest. This information will help GLIFWC member tribes identify and resolve issues and concerns associated with these resources to ensure a sustainable harvest for future generations. Of course, to fully understand the sustainability of these resources, the harvest by the non-Indian population should also be monitored and analyzed.

TRIBAL OFF-RESERVATION HARVEST OF MAPLE SAP

The process of making syrup and sugar from the sap of the sugar maple *(aninaatig)* has always been important to the Ojibwe as a food resource and as a cultural and spiritual tradition. Sugarbush camps still become quite active during early spring when family and friends come together for the gathering and processing of maple sap. The Tribal/USFS MOU specifically addresses this tribal tradition and states that the signatories will cooperate to designate tribal sugarbushes on national forestlands.

Tribal members wishing to establish a sugarbush on national forestlands must work with their tribe's conservation department and consult with the USFS to develop a site management plan. Upon completion of this plan, the tribal conservation department may issue a site permit that designates the sugarbush and allows members to gather and perhaps process sap at that site. During the 1999–2000 harvest season, two tribal sugarbushes were designated on national forestlands in Wisconsin and Michigan.

TRIBAL OFF-RESERVATION HARVEST OF WILD RICE

Considered to be a special gift from the Creator, wild rice has been a central component of the Ojibwe culture for generations. It is an annual grass with abundance fluctuating yearly. Tribal members and GLIFWC staff closely monitor wild rice lakes during the summer in preparation for the harvest season in mid-August to mid-September. To harvest rice, tribal members must obtain a tribal off-reservation harvest permit validated for wild rice gathering. Other tribal regulations include length of boat, harvesting gear, and harvesting hours.

In Wisconsin, the tribes and the Wisconsin Department of Natural Resources jointly decide when to open and close regulated lakes for harvest. Rice chiefs, selected by each tribe, provide the tribal input for each of these declarations. Traditionally, rice chiefs have always retained the tribe's respect and support to direct wild rice gathering.

Off-reservation wild rice harvest in the Wisconsin ceded territories has been monitored through annual surveys since 1987, with the exception of 1988. The estimated annual tribal harvest has averaged slightly over 20,000 pounds, ranging from less than 7,000 to over 41,000 pounds. During these years, approximately 36 percent of the total off-reservation harvest was gathered by tribal ricers, with the remainder having been gathered by state-licensed ricers.

Wild rice has declined in abundance from historic levels due to habitat loss and degradation. Tribal, state, federal, and private natural resource organizations have been working together in attempts to reverse this trend through the monitoring, research, and restoration of wild rice populations (Williamson, Dlutkowski, and Soltis 2000). With the growth of this interagency effort, land managers and other interested individuals have developed a stronger appreciation for and recognition of the importance of this special resource.

TRADITIONAL ECOLOGICAL KNOWLEDGE, ECOSYSTEM MANAGEMENT, AND PUBLIC LAND PLANNING

The Ojibwe have been "managing" (e.g., respecting, observing, and utilizing) the land and its resources since time immemorial. However, tribal members seldom use the term "managing." Through the sharing of stories and spiritual beliefs, elders transfer a wide spectrum of skills and information to younger generations. Some scholars refer to this information as traditional ecological knowledge and wisdom (TEKW) (Ford and Martinez 2000).

Berkes (1999) defines TEKW as "a cumulative body of knowledge, practice, and belief, evolving by adaptive processes and handed down through generations by cultural transmission, about the relationship of living beings (including humans) with one another and with their environment." TEKW does not reflect a stagnant inventory of information but rather, without disregarding past wisdom, continues to transform through time.

Some scientists discount TEKW by characterizing it as merely anecdotal, and they point to examples where indigenous people have overexploited natural resources. However, for cultures dependent on oral traditions, the translation of resource observation, manipulation, and wisdom into teachings is a complex and involved process. Furthermore, traditional stories often reflect the understanding that human survival requires an authentic respect toward nature and that resource use must necessarily be sustainable.

TEKW and contemporary ecosystem management, though not identical, share common characteristics. A report published by the Ecological Society of America Committee on the Scientific Basis for Ecosystem Management states: "Ecosystem management is management driven by explicit goals, executed by policies, protocols, and practices, and made adaptable by monitoring and research based on our best understanding of the ecological interactions and processes necessary to sustain ecosystem composition, structure, and function." In addition, "ecosystem management assumes intergenerational sustainability as a precondition for management rather than an afterthought" (Christensen et al. 1996). Clearly, shared principles include adaptive management through observation and monitoring and an intergenerational sustainability, including the relationship and dependence of humans and all life on each other.

GLIFWC biologists support ecosystem, rather than single species, management. Tribal members gather many different types of treaty resources from a variety of habitats. Tribal customs sometimes preclude an open discussion of particular medicinal and ceremonial resources and their locations. Consequently, single species management actually becomes counterproductive to protecting and sustaining an all-inclusive set of treaty resources.

Tribal members have a vested interest in the management of public lands and the sustainability of treaty resources. When conducting government-to-government consultations regarding public land planning, GLIFWC member tribes utilize TEKW and ecosystem management principles. For example, the Tribal/USFS MOU states that all parties will "seek to collaboratively promote ecosystem management that protects and restores native communities and species, furthers the diversity of species, and ensures the sustained yield of treaty resources."

GLIFWC member tribes view the conservation of wild plants as an extremely high priority on public lands. Non-Indian gathering and utilization of these resources must be more closely monitored and, if necessary, increased regulations established. Research needs must be identified and studies implemented. Currently, most public land managers make decisions affecting the conservation and sustainability of these resources with little or no information to support these decisions.

GLIFWC member tribes routinely request public land managers within the ceded territories to educate themselves on issues regarding wild plant gathering and to utilize TEKW and ecosystem management when developing specific gathering policies and overall land management plans. The tribes remind these land managers that, as necessitated by trust responsibility and treaty law, they must ensure the availability and sustainability of wild plant harvest. Irrevocably, the Ojibwe worldview teaches values based on an understanding that humans depend on all other earth beings (Johnston 1976).

NOTES

1. There are several terms used in reference to the Ojibwe people. The Ojibwe often call themselves Anishinaabe, which in their language means Indian person or original people. The anglicized word for Ojibwe is Chippewa.

2. Ojibwe language.

3. See *People v. Jondreau,* 384 Mich 539, 185 N.W. 2d 375 (1971); *State of Wisconsin v. Gurnoe,* 53 Wis. 2d 390 (1972); *U.S. v. Michigan,* 471 F.Supp 192 (W.D. Mich. 1979); *Lac Courte Oreilles v. Voigt* (*LCO I*), 700 F.2d 341 (7th Cir. 1983), *cert. denied* 464 U.S. 805 (1983); *Lac Courte Oreilles v. State of Wisconsin* (*LCO III*), 653 F.Supp 1420 (W.D. Wis. 1987); *Lac Courte Oreilles v. State of Wisconsin* (*LCO IV*), 668 F.Supp 1233 (W.D. Wis. 1987); *Lac Courte Oreilles v. State of Wisconsin* (*LCO V*), 686 F.Supp 226 (W.D. Wis. 1988); *Lac Courte Oreilles v. State of Wisconsin* (*LCO VI*), 707 F.Supp 1034 (W.D. Wis. 1989); *Lac Courte Oreilles v State of Wisconsin* (*LCO VII*), 740 F.Supp 1400 (W.D. Wis. 1990); *Lac Courte Oreilles v. State of Wisconsin* (*LCO VIII*), 749 F.Supp 913 (W.D. Wis. 1990); *Lac Courte Oreilles v. State of Wisconsin* (*IX*), 758 F.Supp 1262 (W.D. Wis. 1991); *Lac Courte Oreilles v. State of Wisconsin* (X), 775 F.Supp 321 (W.D. Wis. 1991); *U.S. v. Bresette,* 761 F.Supp 658 (D. Minn. 1991); *Mille Lacs Band v. State of Minnesota,* 861 F.Supp 784 (D. Minn. 1994); *Mille Lacs Band v. State of Minnesota,* 952 F.Supp 1362 (D. Minn. 1997); *Mille Lacs Band v. State of Minnesota,* 124 F.3d 904 (8th Cir. 1997); and *State of Minnesota v. Mille Lacs Band,* 119 S.Ct. 1187 (1999).

4. *LCO III,* 653 F.Supp 1420, 1426 (W.D. Wis. 1987).

5. GLIFWC's current member tribes include: in Wisconsin—the Bad River Band of the Lake Superior Tribe of Chippewa Indians, Lac du Flambeau Band of Lake Superior Chippewa Indians, Lac Courte Oreilles Band of Lake Superior Chippewa Indians, Red Cliff Band of the Lake Superior Chippewa Indians, St. Croix Chippewa Indians of Wisconsin, and Sokaogon Chippewa Community of the Mole Lake Band; in Michigan—Bay Mills Indian Community, Keweenaw Bay Indian Community, and Lac Vieux Desert Band of Lake Superior Chippewa Indians; and in Minnesota—Fond du Lac Chippewa Tribe and Mille Lacs Band of Chippewa Indians.

6. Ojibwe language; see Appendix B for scientific nomenclature.

REFERENCES

Berkes, Fikret. 1999. *Sacred Ecology: Traditional Ecological Knowledge and Resource Management.* Ann Arbor, MI: Braun-Brumfield.

Christensen, N. L., A. M. Bartuska, J. H. Brown, S. Carpenter, C. D'Antonio, R. Francis, J. F. Franklin, J. A. MacMahon, R. F. Noss, D. J. Parsons, C. H. Peterson, M. G. Turner, and R. G. Woodmansee. 1996. "The Report of the Ecological Society of America Committee on the Scientific Basis for Ecosystem Management." *Ecol Appl* 6(3): 665–691.

Danielsen, Karen C. 2000. *Results of Wild Plant and Forest Products Gathering on National Forest Lands—Harvest Seasons: 1995–1996 through 1998–1999.* Odanah, WI: Great Lakes Indian Fish and Wildlife Commission.

Densmore, Frances. 1928. *Uses of Plants by the Chippewa Indians.* Bureau of American Ethnology Annual Report 44, pp. 273–379. Washington, DC: Smithsonian Institution.

Ford, J., and D. Martinez. 2000. "Traditional Ecological Knowledge, Ecosystem Science, and Environmental Management." *Ecol Appl* 10 (5): 1249–1250.

Gilbert, Jonathan, Veronica Sullivan, and James E. Zorn. 1996. *Tribal/USDA Forest Service Relations: An Off-Reservation Treaty Rights Perspective.* Administration for Native Americans grant no. 90NA1574. Odanah, WI: Great Lakes Indian Fish and Wildlife Commission.

Johnston, Basil. 1976. *Ojibway Heritage.* Lincoln: University of Nebraska Press.

Meeker, James E., Joan E. Elias, and John A. Heim. 1993. *Plants Used by the Great Lakes Ojibwa.* Odanah, WI: Great Lakes Indian Fish and Wildlife Commission.

Williamson, Lisa S., Lisa A. Dlutkowski, and Ann P. McCammon Soltis, eds. 2000. *Proceedings of the Wild Rice Research and Management Conference, July 7–8, 1999.* Odanah, WI: Great Lakes Indian Fish and Wildlife Commission.

CASE STUDY

Making Peace in the Berry Patch: The 1932 Handshake Agreement and the Promise of Cultural Use Zones

Andrew H. Fisher

Every August for at least five thousand years, Native Americans from the Columbia Plateau have traveled to the Cascade Mountains to harvest huckleberries and other forest products. The culmination of their seasonal round, *wiwnumi* ("berry month") has historically served as a time of human gathering as well, when different groups met to socialize and trade. Although berry picking for subsistence purposes has declined in the twentieth century, many Native Americans still cherish the social and religious aspects of this annual activity. "Huckleberry is very sacred to Indians," declared tribal elder Hazel Smiscon Miller in 1979. "[We] have communion with God with the huckleberry like [the] white man uses wine." Besides spiritual sustenance, berrying provides a break from routine, a source of supplemental income, and a link to cultural traditions. On the Gifford Pinchot National Forest in south-central Washington State, the Indians' ability to practice these traditions has benefited from an unusual agreement between the U.S. Forest Service and several Columbia River Indian communities.

The 1932 Handshake Agreement[1] stands out as a striking case of accommodation in a rather bleak record of bureaucratic indifference or antagonism toward Native American cultural and religious concerns. Generally speaking, the Forest Service and other federal agencies have rarely expressed much sympathy for Indian subsistence practices or the concept of sacred geography. However, when an army of unemployed non-Indians invaded tribal berry fields during the Great Depression, forest rangers set aside some three thousand acres of public land for the exclusive use of Native American gatherers. This small parcel seems insignificant compared to the 10,800,000 acres (29,000 square miles) ceded to the government by the Yakama Nation alone, yet the importance of the Forest Service's decision should not be overlooked. The Handshake Agreement guaranteed Native access to some of the most productive huckleberry fields in the world and gave the Indians a measure of privacy in which to carry on their traditions. Despite persistent problems with resource conservation and non-Indian trespassing, the agreement continues to afford Indian pickers a degree of protection unknown in other national forests. By maintaining an open dialogue with local Forest Service officials, they have turned a temporary compromise into an enduring affirmation of their treaty right to gather berries in "usual and accustomed places."

Mid-Columbia Indians traditionally harvested huckleberries from August through September. Prime picking locations shifted frequently in response to spring frosts and forest growth, but families generally returned to the same campsites every year. Following a "first-foods" feast, which expressed gratitude for the benevolence of the Creator and ensured future harvests, the women picked and preserved enough fruit to last through the winter. They originally dried the berries using heat reflected from smoldering logs, creating a raisinlike product that transported easily and kept indefinitely. By the 1930s, however, the Forest Service's fear of wildfires and the gradual adoption of canning had combined to end this practice on public land. While the women and children worked in the berry fields, the men fished in nearby lakes and streams or searched the surrounding forests for deer and elk. Despite the considerable labor involved, many Indians viewed "berry month" as the ideal season. People from many different villages and linguistic groups gathered in the Twin Buttes country near Mt. Adams, where they spent much of the summer gambling, socializing, trading, and (after 1730) racing horses. Although a poor berry crop could cut the season short, families often remained in the mountains until the first snowfall in October.

Mid-Columbia Indians valued huckleberries and other traditional foods so highly that they expressly reserved the right to harvest these resources in their treaties with the federal government. Signed in 1855, the four Plateau treaties contained virtually identical clauses guaranteeing tribes "the right of taking fish at all usual and accustomed places, in common with the citizens of the Territory . . . together with the privilege of hunting, gathering roots and berries, and pasturing their horses and cattle upon open and unclaimed land." The Indians did not recognize the legalistic difference between "rights" and "privileges," and the courts have since ruled that these terms "have no operative distinction." The Indians also applied the phrase "usual and accustomed places" to all their subsistence activities and adopted a much broader definition of "open and unclaimed land." It made no sense to reserve fishing sites while surrendering traditional hunting and gathering areas, since all three remained integral to the seasonal round. Thus, the tribes disagreed with the government's subsequent assertion that off-reservation hunting "was not intended to be a continuing right as was the fishing right." Nor did they accept the view that national parks and forests could not be classified as "open and unclaimed land" within the meaning of the treaty. For the next century, the differing Indian and white understandings of the treaty caused chronic confusion over the nature and extent of the tribes' off-reservation rights.

During the early twentieth century, many mid-Columbia Indians continued to exercise their treaty rights despite dramatic environmental changes, state legal challenges, and federal policies designed to assimilate them into mainstream American society. Instead of farming, as the government insisted they should, most Indians supplemented traditional subsistence activities with cash income from wage labor, land sales or leases, and annuity payments. As the century progressed, non-Indian uses for public land increasingly threatened Native American access to huckleberries and other forest resources. Indians visiting the Twin Buttes country found many of their huckleberry fields overgrown by forest or overrun by sheep. By 1908, when President Theodore Roosevelt created the Columbia National Forest (later renamed the Gifford Pinchot National Forest), non-Indian graziers had over 150,000 sheep on the range within its boundaries. The Indians complained that these bleating beasts damaged the huckleberry bushes, consumed pasture needed for Indian horses, and fouled the water supply. The graziers, in turn, argued that Indian horses ate forage paid for by grazing leases while allotments on the Yakama Reservation went to the highest bidder. The highest bidders were often non-Indian stockmen who sought to stop the Indians from using public lands, but the Forest Service generally sided with white grazing interests. In addition, agency officials blamed Native gatherers for setting fires in order to drive game, improve pasturage, and increase berry production.

The Forest Service made a small concession to Native concerns in 1911, when rangers excluded sheep from several berry fields near Mount Adams, including Peterson Prairie, South Prairie, and Little Huckleberry Mountain. Confrontations between Indians and graziers became increasingly common, however, and new sources of friction developed due to road construction and state regulation of Indian hunting. In 1926 the Forest Service built an improved road into the Twin Buttes country, bringing large numbers of non-Indians to the berry fields for the first time. A year later, the Washington State Supreme Court ruled that the Yakama Nation's 1855 treaty "did not foreclose the right of the state, succeeding to the sovereign power of the Federal government, to regulate and prohibit the taking of game on 'open and unclaimed' Federal lands outside the Indian Reservation." Although subsequent decisions on Indian hunting overturned this interpretation, the Forest Service shared the erroneous opinion that the Indians lacked treaty rights on public land. Frustrated with harassment from game wardens and with continuing efforts to exclude Indian horses, tribal representatives held the first of several councils with Forest Service officials in 1929. Although this meeting failed to resolve the problems plaguing the Indians, it opened a direct dialogue that would serve them well in the near future.

As the Great Depression deepened in the early 1930s, negotiations between the Indians and the Forest Service acquired an added sense of urgency. Before the stock market crash, only a few hundred non-Indians had visited the Twin Buttes country every year. Most were local residents or recreationists who picked huckleberries for home consumption. During the next three years, this trickle of tourists became a torrent of refugees that threatened to swamp both the Indians and the staff of the Mt. Adams Ranger District. In 1931 nearly seven thousand jobless non-Indians poured into the mountains, creating a sprawling sylvan Hooverville almost overnight. Besides the comfort of shared misfortune, the huckleberry camps offered plentiful supplies of water, wood, and a valuable cash crop that seemed free for the taking. With over sixty thousand gallons picked in 1931 alone, berries supported a thriving barter and cash economy among the non-Indian squatters. Local canneries purchased the fruit for fifty cents a gallon, and a productive family could make around five dollars a day. Some people tried to boost the market by driving to nearby towns once a week, where they peddled berries door to door for seventy-five cents a gallon or more. One ambitious group even loaded a truck with 240 gallons of fruit and sent it off to Texas. After two days and nights on the road, the driver planned to sell his load in Galveston for $1.75 to $2.00 a gallon.

Although some Indians devised commercial strategies of their own, most objected to the exploitation of their sacred food by Euro-American intruders. In their view, the Creator had given *wiwnu* to the Indians, who needed it for survival and treated it with the proper respect. Whites could share in this bounty, but they had no right to usurp Indian berry fields. "It is our patch and the same as a wheat field or a herd of horses or cattle," argued Wyam headman Tommy Thompson. "I wouldn't come into your place and take your crops or your stock and sell them." The invading non-Indians rarely recognized or respected Native American claims to specific patches and campgrounds, and their sheer numbers threatened to crowd out Indian families and to disrupt Native religious practices. Consequently, the Indians began pushing for exclusive access to a portion of their traditional grounds. The Forest Service ignored their pleas for two years, but in 1932 Forest Supervisor J. R. Bruckart agreed to discuss the Indians' concerns at a council held in the Sawtooth huckleberry fields.

During the council, a delegation of tribal headmen led by Chief William Yallup declared that their treaties had reserved "the right to hunt, fish, and gather berries for all time in our usual and accustomed places." They expressed special concern for the elderly women, who could not reach the more remote berry patches and faced intense competition from throngs of non-Indians. While Supervisor Bruckart could not control county game wardens or close the forest to non-Indians, he agreed to set aside some 2,800 acres and three campsites (Surprise Lakes, Cold Springs, and

Meadow Creek) for exclusive tribal use during the huckleberry season. This concession pleased the Indians, and Chief Yallup rose to thank Bruckart: "I have spoken to the end. Nothing is hidden in my heart. Your words give me happiness. You are my friend. Now all is well between my people and your people." The two men then shook hands to formalize the agreement. In the fullness of time, this rather unspectacular compromise would become a lasting confirmation of the Indians' right to gather huckleberries in their "usual and accustomed places."

Over the next six decades, while Indian hunting and fishing rights followed a tortured path through the courts, local rangers continued to honor the Handshake Agreement. Bruckart and his immediate successor met with Chief Yallup and other Indian leaders every summer between 1933 and 1936 to reaffirm the agreement, which they saw as a necessary barrier against the persistent white presence. Yallup died in 1955 at age eighty-nine, but his pact with the Forest Service survived. Today, his descendants continue to work with agency officials and are currently negotiating plans for a permanent longhouse at the Cold Springs campground. To discourage trespassing and inform the public about the agreement, rangers have developed interpretive stations and posted signs around the reserved acreage. Such measures, along with alert Natives, prevent most non-Indians from straying into the area. Rangers hear occasional objections to the Indians' "special rights," however, and some law enforcement personnel believe the agreement should be discontinued because it complicates an already difficult job.

The increasing commercialization of huckleberries has generated fresh cultural clashes and user conflicts. In 1979 Wyam elder Maggie Jim recalled almost getting into fights with non-Indians who infringed on the reserved area, while Mary Yallup complained that "Indians know when to pick the berries but whites don't know and pick them green," thereby reducing the size and quality of the remaining crop. More recently, an influx of Asian and Mexican immigrants has further heightened competition and complicated enforcement efforts. "It seems like they [non-Indians] are commercializing everything," protested one Indian elder. With huckleberries now selling for around sixty dollars a gallon, thieves have taken baskets of fruit from Indian camps, cars, and solitary female pickers. Additional law-and-order problems have resulted from the use of tribal campgrounds by non-Indians. Some bring alcohol and drugs into the forest, and their rowdy behavior intimidates Indian families. Although the Mt. Adams Ranger District has hired two Native Americans to patrol the berry fields in a Forest Service vehicle, trespassing remains a recurring problem. With no legal means to exclude people from the reserved area, voluntary non-Indian cooperation is essential to the integrity of the Handshake Agreement.

Indians and non-Indians alike face the problem of forest encroachment, which threatens the survival of the berry fields and promises to generate more user conflicts. In aboriginal times, the Indians periodically burned the fields to prevent the growth of forest and thereby preserve the conditions necessary for berry production. Since the 1920s, fire suppression has prevented anthropogenic and natural burns from doing their work. Although clear-cuts and wildfires have opened other areas to huckleberry growth, the Indians' traditional patches have shrunk by approximately one hundred acres per year. In the 1930s, the Twin Buttes fields spanned roughly twelve thousand acres; they now cover only a third of that area, while the patch reserved by the Handshake Agreement has dwindled to less than seven hundred acres. If forest encroachment continues at the present rate, the berry fields will completely disappear in under forty years.

The Yakama Nation has contributed money and manpower to the Forest Service's fitful research on huckleberry enhancement, but an effective management program has yet to be implemented. Manual and mechanical removal of foliage cannot keep up with forest growth, the Indians will not allow the use of herbicides on their sacred food, and the Forest Service remains skeptical of prescribed burning. The agency has conducted several experimental burns, however, on huckleberry fields in the Cispus Adaptive Management Area, which lies adjacent to the Yakama Reservation on the north side of Mt. Adams.

In spite of these shortcomings, the Handshake Agreement demonstrates the value of open communication and cooperation between Indian tribes and government agencies. Now written into the Land and Resource Management Plan for the Gifford Pinchot National Forest, the agreement protects Native rights that even the 1978 American Indian Religious Freedom Act (AIRFA) does not guarantee. More significantly, it provides an example for other forests to follow. As competition for nontimber forest products intensifies, it will become increasingly important for federal agencies to maintain open dialogues with the Native American "first users" of these resources. The prospects for cooperation have improved in recent decades. In response to AIRFA and tribal legal victories, many national forests and national parks have established or strengthened provisions allowing Indians to visit sacred sites and to gather traditional foods and medicinal plants on public property.

Hoping to head off future conflicts, some national forests have also requested tribal assistance in compiling inventories of significant cultural and religious areas. Because many traditional resources do not appeal to non-Indians and have little commercial value, they do not generate the intense competition that necessitated the Handshake Agreement. In areas where conflict does occur, such agreements offer hope that management systems can be devised that respect Native cultural needs and legal rights while also meeting demands for resource conservation, wilderness protection, and outdoor recreation. As anthropologists Thomas C. Blackburn and Kat

Anderson have suggested, "cultural use zones," managed for specific purposes and with Native participation, would provide both a measure of social justice and a means of preserving endangered indigenous resources.

NOTE

1. A longer version of this essay appeared as "The 1932 Handshake Agreement: Yakama Indian Treaty Rights and Forest Service Policy in the Pacific Northwest," *Western Historical Quarterly* 28 (Summer 1997): 187–217.

REFERENCES

Blackburn, Thomas C., and Kat Anderson, eds. 1993. *Before the Wilderness: Environmental Management by Native Californians*. Menlo Park, CA: Ballena Press.

Filloon, Ray M. 1952. "Huckleberry Pilgrimage." *Pacific Discovery* 5 (May/June): 4–13.

Hunn, Eugene, with James Selam and Family. 1990. *Nch'i-Wana, "The Big River": Mid-Columbia Indians and Their Land*. Seattle: University of Washington Press.

Mack, Cheryl. 1992. "Report of Archaeological Testing at Kpss-wa-nite (45-SA-265), Gifford Pinchot National Forest." Trout Lake, WA: Mt. Adams Ranger District, GPNF, USDA Forest Service, Region 6.

McCoy, Keith. 1987. *The Mount Adams Country: Forgotten Corner of the Columbia River Gorge*. White Salmon, WA: Pahto Publications.

Richards, Leverett. 1932. "Great Army of Jobless Whites Invade Old Huckleberry Sanctums of Red Men." *Sunday (Portland) Oregonian,* September 4.

———. 1983. "Enduring 1932 Handshake Treaty Threatened." *(Portland) Oregonian,* September 2, C5.

State of Washington v. Miller, 102 Wn.2d 678, 689 P.2d 81 (1984).

Swindell, Edward G., Jr. 1942. *Report on Source, Nature, and Extent of the Fishing, Hunting, and Miscellaneous Related Rights of Certain Indian Tribes in Washington and Oregon Territory Together with Affidavits Showing the Location of a Number of Usual and Accustomed Fishing Grounds and Stations*. Los Angeles: Office of Indian Affairs.

U.S. Forest Service. 1929. "Notes Taken at a Council at Meadow Creek," 25 August. Mt. Adams Ranger Station, Trout Lake, Washington.

———. 1967. *National Forest Recreation Plan, Gifford Pinchot National Forest, Indian Heaven Unusual Interest Area (Back-Country)*. Vancouver, WA: Gifford Pinchot National Forest Headquarters.

———. 1979a. "Notes from Celilo Wyam Board Meeting," 23 February. Gifford Pinchot National Forest Headquarters, Vancouver, Washington.

———. 1979b. "Older Indians Meeting, White Panther Unit, 6 P.M., Toppenish, Yakima Tribe." Gifford Pinchot National Forest Headquarters, Vancouver, Washington.

CASE STUDY

Contemporary Subsistence Use of Nontimber Forest Products in Alaska

Robert Schroeder

Alaska may provide an interesting case example of indigenous plant use. The state's forests and other ecological provinces are largely intact. The Aleut, Eskimo, and Indian societies of the state continue to maintain physical and cultural ties to traditional territories. Subsistence and other local home use of forest plants continue to account for virtually all contemporary uses of nontimber forest products. This heretofore undeveloped status of NTFPs in the state presents the opportunity to develop sound policy that will respect the existing and continuing indigenous uses and allow for ecologically sound development of forest resources.

This chapter describes some salient geographical and demographic characteristics, and the legal sidebars unique to Alaska, that are relevant to plant use in Alaska's forests. The bulk of the chapter describes some of the variety of plant species known to have subsistence uses in Alaska based on both early and recent ethnographic work and outlines the cultural importance of these uses. It presents summary level estimates of the magnitude of subsistence plant harvests for the south-central and southeast regions of the state, where the Chugach and Tongass National Forests are located. Some special plant uses are also discussed. The chapter concludes with a discussion of issues related to developing policy to direct possible commercial collection of NTFPs.

GEOGRAPHIC AND LEGAL CONTEXTS

Alaska's 586,412 square miles, or about 375 million acres, include some of the world's largest remaining areas of coastal temperate and boreal rain forest, expanses of subarctic forest or taiga, and riparian boreal forest habitat found along river systems. Tree species of the coastal and boreal rain forests consist of Sitka spruce *(Picea sitchensis),* mountain hemlock *(Tsuga mertensiana),* western hemlock *(T. heterophylla),* western red cedar *(Thuja plicata)*, and yellow cedar *(Chamaecyparis nootkensis)*. Subarctic or taiga forests consist principally of black spruce *(Picea mariana)*, white spruce *(P. glauca)*, and aspen (*Populus* spp.). Riparian forests contain willow species. An estimated 119 million acres are forested with thirty-two native tree species.[1] Of the total land base, about 44 million acres, including biologically productive forestlands, belong to Alaska Natives under Native Corporation ownership. These lands, along with a cash payment of $962 million, were part of the 1971 Alaska Native Claims Settlement Act (ANSCA), which was passed to resolve aboriginal claims in the state.[2] The 12 Native regional and more than 200 Native village corporations established by the act generally selected economically productive lands, in or near traditional-use tribal territories and important for subsistence harvests.[3]

The act left about 322 million acres in public ownership, and the State of Alaska had the option to select 124 million acres of this total. Approximately 197 million acres, or about 52 percent of the total land in Alaska, remained under federal jurisdiction. The bulk of these federal lands are managed as parks by the National Park Service, wildlife refuges by the Fish and Wildlife Service, national forests and monuments by the Forest Service, and petroleum reserves and other land statuses by the Bureau of Land Management. Apart from Native Corporation land, relatively little of Alaska is privately owned.[4] This chapter will focus on subsistence uses of nontimber forest products in a portion of this public land, mainly in the temperate rain forest. The Forest Service manages most of this rain forest. The Chugach National Forest comprises 5.3 million acres, and the Tongass National Forest, the nation's largest national forest, includes 16.9 million acres.

About 62 percent of Alaska's 621,400 people are concentrated in the cities of Anchorage, Fairbanks, Juneau, and Ketchikan, the only places in the state with populations greater than 10,000. The rest of the state's population lives in 144 incorporated cities and in unincorporated areas. About 16.6 percent of the total state population is comprised of Native Americans. Yupik and Innuit Eskimos are about 8 percent of the state's total population, Indians about 6 percent, and Aleuts about 2 percent. Parallel with the city government structure in Native communities, Alaska has 246 federally recognized tribal governments.[5] Tribal governments generally represent localized groups of Native Americans, most of which are located on and maintain ties to geographical areas that have been used for subsistence harvests of fish, wildlife, and plants. Tlingit, Haida, Tsimshian, and other Athapaskan Indians are the main cultural groups using the temperate rain forest.

Subsistence has a number of meanings in the Alaskan context. From a social science perspective, subsistence includes the rich cultural complex encompassing the production and use of food from the wild. To be sure, this complex includes an economic aspect—the efficient harvest of natural foods that are unavailable from other sources. Many Native communities and households have low cash incomes, with subsistence harvesting being a main way of putting quality foods on the table. But much more than that, the harvest of traditional foods has become the sine qua non characteristic of Native communities and a central cultural marker of what it means to be a Tlingit or Haida Indian in southeast Alaska.

For Alaska Natives, harvest and use of traditional foods are at the center of cultural identity. These activities, more than any other, provide the tie to place, belief, and history that is essential to cultural identity. Subsistence as an activity provides a vehicle for expressing or manifesting what it is to be a Native person. Prior to contact with colonial powers in the 1700s, all Alaska Native cultures relied exclusively on hunting and gathering for food supplies. Although fish, marine and land mammals, and birds were the main calorie sources, marine and terrestrial plants accounted for an important portion of the aboriginal diet and supplied nutritional items not as readily available from fish and meat sources. Plants also provide the source for much of the Native pharmacopoeia used to treat the normal range of injuries and sicknesses found in any human population.

Subsistence also has a set of special legal meanings in Alaska. ANSCA settled aboriginal land claims in Alaska but did not resolve issues of recognizing, continuing, or restricting Native subsistence hunting, fishing, and gathering. Because subsistence was still a pending issue, provisions to provide protection for subsistence were included in the 1980 Alaska National Interest Land Conservation Act (ANILCA). While the main import of this act was to put more Alaskan land in protected status through creating new national parks and national refuges and adding to existing conservation units, ANILCA provided strong provisions for continuing subsistence harvesting and use in two important areas. The act found that "the continuation of the opportunity for subsistence uses by rural residents of Alaska, including both Natives and non-Natives, on the public lands and by Alaska Natives on Native lands is essential to Native physical, economic, traditional and cultural existence and to non-Native physical, economic, traditional, and social existence."[6]

Based on this finding, ANILCA established a priority use for subsistence.[7] In times of resource scarcity or when demand exceeds biologically sound harvest levels, subsistence would have a priority over other consumptive use of resources. In practice, this means that commercial, sport, or other harvests would be curtailed by state or federal fish and wildlife management authorities before subsistence harvests would be limited. Furthermore, the act allowed the State of Alaska to manage subsistence harvests on federal land as long as it maintained this priority use in law and regulation and, by so doing, was in compliance with ANILCA. The State of Alaska complied with ANILCA until 1990, when the state supreme court found that providing a priority for rural subsistence conflicted with the state constitution. Since that time, the federal government has assumed management of subsistence on federal lands.[8] State of Alaska regulations currently cover subsistence uses on state and private land only.[9] ANILCA and the resulting federal management involve the federal government more closely in subsistence resource harvesting and use than otherwise would be the case.

A second important provision of ANILCA establishes special procedures to be followed when federal land use actions might restrict subsistence uses.[10] These procedures are something of a mirror of National Environmental Policy Act provisions. They require the federal agency to show what the effects of its actions might be on subsistence uses and to hold hearings that provide a special vehicle for public input concerning impacts to subsistence. This provision, along with associated rights to appeal land management decisions, has resulted in close examination of many proposed large-scale uses of federal land in Alaska. In southeast Alaska, for example, timber sales and forest plans in the Tongass National Forest have been hotly contested because of their likely effects on future subsistence harvests. As a result of these potential impacts to subsistence uses, plans and timber sales directing large-scale logging in this national forest have received frequent court review. Timber projects have frequently been under court injunction, modified, or abandoned because of their likely impacts on subsistence uses.

Although ANILCA has not been applied to the subsistence use of plants as thoroughly as to subsistence uses of fish and wildlife, the legislation and its implementation over the past twenty years have set the main rules of operation for government agencies in dealing with subsistence issues.[11] This modus operandi includes a heightened sensitivity to potential impacts on subsistence uses and a clear recognition that major public policy issues are at stake in this area. More specifically, federal agencies have been loath to encourage commercial exploitation of nontimber forest products where conflict with existing subsistence uses might result. Agencies are also aware of the likely Alaska Native opposition to commercialization of traditionally used plants. Federal agencies may also avoid other actions on federal lands that might have adverse impacts to subsistence uses of plants.

STATEWIDE NTFP SUBSISTENCE HARVESTS AND USE

As I have noted, most Alaska Native groups continue to occupy traditional territories. The length of time groups have been living in specific ecosystems, of course, varies. Southeast Alaska Tlingit Indians consider themselves to be the original inhabitants of this region, with songs and legends that refer to events preceding the last glacial advance. Almost all extant

Native groups continue to be found in approximately the same areas they inhabited at the time of first contact with Western explorers and colonial powers in the 1700s.[12] For many groups, indigenous history may trace occupancy back much farther in time, and the archaeological record frequently supports Native historical knowledge.[13]

The traditional territories of many groups have been well documented through ethnographic or other research. For examples, Burch (1975) has reconstructed traditional territorial areas for twenty Eskimo societies in northwest Alaska, and Goldschmidt and Haas ([1946] 1998) documented traditional clan territories for many Tlingit groups in southeast Alaska. In these studies, knowledge and use of fish, wildlife, and plants were the main ways that tribal groups identified their traditional territories. Respondents were able to document their association with traditional areas by identifying specific sites used for subsistence harvests and to describe the subsistence species they took from different traditional areas during the seasonal round of resource harvesting.

This continuity with place has some bearing on traditional use of NTFPs. Native groups have had multigenerational or multicentury association with the geographic and ecological areas they inhabit. Because of this long association, they have had sufficient time to classify the plants in their areas, experiment with the possible utilitarian uses of this biota, develop methods of collecting and preserving the plants that are used, locate sources of useful plants, and note changes in plant distribution and abundance.

General descriptions of Alaska Native cultures and both their early and contemporary subsistence hunting, fishing, and gathering patterns are found in the *Handbook of North American Indians,* volumes 5, 6, and 7, which cover arctic, subarctic, and northwest coast cultures respectively.[14] In the precontact subsistence economy of Native groups in Alaska, fish, land and marine mammals, and birds accounted for the bulk of calories consumed. Except for limited cultivation of tobacco by some groups,[15] plants were not regularly grown for consumption, although some attention was paid to maintaining favorable growing conditions for wild food sources. Wild plant products were and continue to be highly valued, and the effort expended to gather and preserve edible green plants and berries may be as great as that expended on the calorically more important fish and wildlife harvests.[16]

Table 15 lists plants whose subsistence uses have been documented in recent studies.[17] This list is by no means complete both because field research and management issues have been more focused on hunting and fishing than on plant use and because plants have more species diversity than other subsistence harvests. Many plants additional to those named have certainly been used. Field studies to identify traditionally used plants typically included interviews with village residents, recording of indigenous

Native names for plants used, and, when possible, participant observation of harvest methods and collection of specimen samples of plants used. Many of Alaska's tribes have active programs to document Native language names for plants found in their traditional territories and to describe traditional uses that may not be well known at the present time. Information from these tribal initiatives is included in the cited reports.

Table 15 provides an indication of the range of NTFP plants used for subsistence in various parts of Alaska. Research documenting Native use of plants is particularly good for those plants that continue to be used in quantities. For this reason, the table is probably most complete for edible berries and less comprehensive for edible green plants, many of which may continue to be collected in small quantities. The use of roots and tubers has become less common, and the listing of these species may be more incomplete. The small number of species listed with medicinal and craft or construction uses is only an indication of some notable uses. Many Native people in Alaska may not have made regular use of mushrooms and other fungi. In southeast Alaska, for example, aboriginal use of mushrooms appears to have been uncommon.

Because of the attention paid to federal and state management of subsistence harvests, good household and community level data have been collected (see Emery and Weigand, this volume). Data showing subsistence harvest levels by species, by community, and by household have been used by the State of Alaska and federal regulatory bodies to set seasons and bag limits for subsistence fish and wildlife harvests and, when required, to limit sport and commercial harvests to maintain adequate subsistence hunting and fishing opportunity.[18] Examples of these data are presented below. This data set is very robust in estimating overall subsistence plant use. However, the goal of the harvest assessment surveys has been to record those species taken in substantial quantities with less attention to itemizing all species that might have some use.

Use of a number of food plants has declined with the introduction of imported foods into rural communities. These would include use of various starchy roots that have largely been replaced by rice, potatoes, or pasta products. Other food plants may have always had low-volume harvests. Examples would include the spring shoots of various berries in southeast Alaska, which may never have been large dietary items but were certainly part of the plant diet breadth of the Tlingit Indians. Finally, medicinal and magical uses of plants are not well captured in the harvest assessment data and have not been comprehensively described in other sources.[19] In various parts of the state, use of plants for these purposes was actively discouraged by missionaries, and shamans and other specialists were suppressed in many areas. The breaking of shamanic traditions meant the loss of the specialized plant knowledge that these specialists maintained. As a consequence, knowledge

Table 15. Plants with documented historic or contemporary use for subsistence in Alaska

Scientific name	Common name	Use	Area	Source
Achillea spp.	Yarrow	Medicinal external compresses	Southeast	6
Allium schoenoprasum	Wild chive	Food, edible leaves or shoots	Widely used	1
Alnus rubra	Alder bark	Medicinal, effusion used as a tonic	Southeast	5
Anemone patens	Anemone	Burned to drive off mosquitoes	Interior	3
Angelica lucida	Wild celery	Food, edible leaves or shoots	Widely used	1,4,5
Arabis hirsuta and *A. lyrata kamchatka*	Rock cress	Food, edible leaves or shoots	Southeast	6
Arctostaphylos alpina	Bearberry	Food, edible berry	Widely used	1,4
Arctostaphylos rubra	Bearberry, red fruited	Food, edible berry	Widely used	1
Arctostaphylos uvaursi	Kinnickinnick, bearberry	Food, edible berry	Widely used	1
Bucephala albeola	Beach asparagus	Food, edible shoots	Southeast	5
Caltha palustris	Cowslip	Food, edible leaves or shoots	Subarctic	4
Carex aquatilis	Water sedge	Possible food	Southeast	5
Chamaecyparis nootkensis	Cedar bark	Craft, weaving and basketry	Southeast	5
Chenopodium album	Lamb's quarter	Food, edible leaves or shoots	Widely used	1,2
Chenopodium capitatum	Strawberry spinach	Food, edible leaves or shoots	Interior	2
Cornus suecica and *C. canadensis*	Bunchberry	Food, edible berry	Widely used	4
Dryopteris dilatata and other species	Fern	Food, fiddleheads and roots	Widely used	4,5
Empetrum nigrum	Blackberry, crowberry, mountain blueberry	Food, edible berry	Widely used	2,4,5
Epilobium augustifolium	Fireweed	Food, edible leaves or shoots	Widely used	1,2,4,5
Epilobium latifolium	Fireweed, dwarf	Food, edible leaves or shoots	Widely used	1,2,5
Equisetum selvaticum	"Mouse foods"	Food, root	Subarctic	4
Equisetum silvatorum and *E. arvense*	"Mouse foods"	Food, root	Subarctic	4
Eriophorum angustifolium	"Mouse foods"	Food, root	Subarctic	4
Eriophorum augustifolium	Cottongrass, tall	Food, edible root	Widely used	1
Fragaria childensis	Strawberry	Food, edible berry	Southeast	5
Fritillaria kamchatcensis	Indian rice	Food, roots	Southeast	5
Hedysarum alpinum	Eskimo potato	Food, edible root	Widely used	1,2
Heracleum lanatum	Cow parsnip	Food, edible leave or stalk	Subarctic	4
Hippuris vulgaris	Goose grass, wild onion	Food, edible leaves or stalk	Widely used	4,5
Juniperus communis	Juniper berries	Tea for colds	Interior	2,3

Scientific name	Common name	Use	Area	Source
Juniperus communis	Common mountain juniper	Food, edible berry	Widely used	1
Lathyrus palustris	Purple vetch	Food, edible leaves or seeds (peas)	Southeast	6
Ledum palustre	Labrador or Hudson's Bay tea	Tea, infusion	Widely used	1,2,3,4,5
Ligusticium scoticum	Wild parsley	Food, edible leaves or stalk	Southeast	5
Lysichiton americanum	Skunk cabbage	Food preparation	Southeast	5
Maianthemum dilatatum	Deer cabbage	Food, edible leaves or shoots	Southeast	5
Oplopanax horridus	Devil's club	Medicinal with both external and internal use	Southeast	5
Oxyria digyna	Sourgrass	Food, edible leaves or shoots	Widely used	1,4
Oxytropis mayudelliana	Yellow oxytrope	Food, edible root	Widely used	1
Pedicularis lanata (kanai)	Lousewort, wooly	Food, edible leaves or shoots	Widely used	1
Petasites frigida	Coltsfoot	Food, edible leaves or shoots	Widely used	1,4
Petasites hyperboreus	Coltsfoot	Food, edible leaves or shoots	Widely used	1
Phellinus tremulae	Birch fungus	Ashes mixed with snuff or tobacco	Widely used	2
Picea sitchensis	Spruce cambium	Food, sweet inner bark scrapings	Southeast	5
Picea sitchensis	Sitka spruce roots	Craft, weaving and basketry	Southeast	5
Plantago martima	Goosetongue	Food, edible leaves or shoots	Southeast	5
Polygonum alaskanum	Wild rhubarb	Food, stalk	Wide area	1,2,3,4,5
Potentilla pacifica	Wild sweet potato	Food, root	Southeast	5
Pteridium aquilinum	Fern, bracken	Food, fiddleheads	Widely used	4,5
Ranunculus pallasii	Pallas buttercup	Food, edible leaves	Subarctic	4
Ribes divaricatum	Gooseberry	Food, edible berry	Southeast	5
Ribes triste	Current, northern red	Food, edible berry	Widely used	1
Rosa acicularis	Rose hips	Food, edible berry; tea, infusion	Widely used	1,3
Rubus articus	Nagoonberry	Food, edible berry	Widely used	1,4,5
Rubus bracteosum	Current, blue	Food, edible berry	Southeast	5
Rubus chamaemorus	Cloudberry	Food, edible berry	Widely used	2,4,5
Rubus idaeus	Raspberry	Food, edible berry	Widely used	1,5
Rubus laxiflorum	Current, trailing	Food, edible berry	Southeast	5
Rubus parvifolium	Thimbleberry	Food, edible berry	Southeast	5
Rubus spectabilis	Salmonberry	Food, edible berry	Southeast	5
Rumex arcticus	Sourdock	Food, edible leaves or shoots	Widely used	1,4,5
Salix alexensis	Willow, big or river	Food, edible leaves or shoots	Widely used	1
Salix pulcra	Willow, sura	Food, edible leaves or shoots	Widely used	1
Sambucus callicarpa	Elderberry	Food, edible berry	Southeast	5

Table 15. Continued

Scientific name	Common name	Use	Area	Source
Saxifraga punctata	Saxifrage, grook	Food, edible leaves or shoots	Widely used	1
Sedum roseum	Roseroot	Food, edible leaves or shoots	Widely used	1
Shepherdia canadensis	Soapberry, buffaloberry	Food, edible berry	Widely used	1,5
Sphagnum spp.	Sphagnum moss	Cabin chinking	Interior	2
Streptopus amplexifolius	Wild cucumber	Food, edible leaves or shoots	Southeast	5
Thuja plicata	Cedar bark	Craft, weaving and basketry	Southeast	5
Tripleiruspermum spp.	Chamomile	Tea, infusion	Widely used	2
Tsuga heterophylla	Western hemlock branches	Substrate for herring egg deposit	Southeast	5
Urtica lyalli	Nettles	Food, edible leaves	Southeast	5
Vaccinium oxycoccus	Bog cranberry	Food, edible berry	Widely used	1,4,5
Vaccinium uliginosum, V. caespitsum, V. alaskensis	Blueberries, dwarf, early, bog	Food, berries, sometimes shoots	Widely used	1,2,3,4,5
Vaccinium vitis-idaea	Cranberry, lowbush	Food, edible berry	Widely used	1,2,3,4,5
Viburnum edule	Cranberry, highbush	Food, edible berry	Widely used	1,2,5
	Many tree, shrub, and grass species	Craft and con-strution uses, baskets, utensils, carving, and so on	Widely used	1,2,3,4,5

Sources: 1. Anderson et al. (1977); Jones (1983).
2. Caulfield (1983); Martin (1983).
3. Nelson (1973).
4. Stickney (1985).
5. Schroeder and Kookesh (1990b).
6. DeLaguna (1972).

of medicinal and magical plant uses is fragmented, and what knowledge remains is not readily shared by informants.[20] Finally, the replacement of Native Eskimo and Indian languages with English has been accompanied by a loss of the Native knowledge, taxonomic and substantive, about plants in traditional territories.

Over the past two decades, research in rural Alaskan communities has included retrospective household surveys in which respondents are asked the quantities of subsistence foods they have harvested in the previous year. Qualitative research conducted before household surveys are conducted identifies species likely to be used in study communities, including all fish, mammal, bird, invertebrate, and plant species thought to be used. Survey data are collected in units of measurement appropriate to study communities. These units may be the number of sockeye salmon taken, the number of buckets of berries picked, or other units. In order to have a common currency for comparing subsistence harvests across communities, quantity data are converted to units of food weight. Food weight is defined as the portion of a particular subsistence harvest that would be cooked or otherwise prepared for eating, and this weight is comparable to the weight of purchased foods. The food weight conversions are based on actual field measurements. For example, food weight conversion factors for harbor seals, deer, clams, and berries in southeast Alaska were based on weighing subsistence harvests.

USE LEVELS IN SOUTHCENTRAL AND SOUTHEAST ALASKA STUDY COMMUNITIES

Table 16 presents aggregate data for forty-six southcentral Alaska and thirty-three southeast Alaska communities based on the most recent surveys done in study communities.[21] (Similar data are also available for twelve arctic, twenty-one interior, forty-four southwest, and four western Alaska communities.)[22] These data show the community name and year of study. In the *resource category* column, *all resources* refers to the total subsistence fish, wildlife, bird, and plant harvest. *Vegetation* refers to the portion of the total harvest made up of edible plants and berries; seaweeds are included. A review of the more detailed species data shows that most collected vegetation consisted of various berry species. Participation rates show the percentage of households using, trying to harvest, actually harvesting, receiving, and giving a subsistence harvest. The *community total harvest* column presents food weight in pounds. *Household mean harvest* refers to the average household harvest in food weight pounds. *Per capita harvest* presents per capita food weight in pounds.

Participation rates for vegetation use, attempt to harvest, harvest, and receiving and giving are generally high in all communities. Typically 80 percent or more of survey respondents participate in the harvest and use of subsistence vegetation. Participation is particularly high in smaller communities whose economies rely on commercial fishing and other natural resource uses, for example in Point Baker and in Yakutat in southeast Alaska or in Chenega Bay and in Nanwalek in southcentral Alaska.

Overall subsistence harvests in these two regions vary from a high of 586 pounds per capita in Klukwan in 1996 to a low of 55 pounds per capita in Talkeetna in 1985. In the southcentral region, thirty-four of the forty-six study communities have total harvests over 100 pounds per capita; in the southeast, all but three of the thirty-three study communities have total harvests over this amount.[23] Overall estimated plant harvests in the southcentral region range from a low of 1.7 pounds per capita in Glennallen in 1987 to a high of 18.6 pounds per capita in Chase in 1986. In southeast Alaska, the plant harvests range from 2 pounds per capita in Skagway in 1987 to a high of 34.8 pounds per capita in Klukwan in 1996.

Table 16. Use levels of subsistence harvests in Southcentral and Southeast Alaska

Community name	Resource category	Percent households using	Percent households trying	Percent households harvesting	Percent households receiving	Percent households giving	Community total harvest	Household mean harvest	Per capita harvest
							(in food weight pounds)		
			SOUTHCENTRAL REGION						
Cantwell 1982	All Resources	100		98			15,241	324	111.6
Cantwell 1982	Vegetation	67		67			611	13	4.5
Chase 1986	All Resources	100	100	100	71	59	16,615	554	209.2
Chase 1986	Vegetation	100	100	100	6	18	1,474	49	18.6
Chenega Bay 1993	All Resources	100	96	96	100	91	27,809	993	275.2
Chenega Bay 1993	Vegetation	100	96	96	78	74	808	29	8.0
Chickaloon 1982	All Resources	100		89			15,650	522	223.6
Chickaloon 1982	Vegetation	67		67			1,143	38	16.3
Chistochina 1987	All Resources	100	100	100	75	64	20,584	710	261.5
Chistochina 1987	Vegetation	89	89	89	18	32	1,048	36	13.3
Chitina 1987	All Resources	94	89	89	72	50	11,925	628	342.4
Chitina 1987	Vegetation	89	83	83	17	33	509	27	14.6
Cooper Landing 1990	All Resources	100	94	94	81	72	23,563	238	91.5
Cooper Landing 1990	Vegetation	94	90	90	31	42	1,045	11	4.1
Copper Center 1987	All Resources	100	100	100	93	44	85,895	534	174.3
Copper Center 1987	Vegetation	88	88	88	35	6	1,911	12	3.9
Cordova 1997	All Resources	98	92	90	88	79	449,841	542	179.4
Cordova 1997	Vegetation	87	83	85	4	44	20,966	25	8.4
East Glenn Highway 1987	All Resources	100	90	90	82	68	28,800	430	132.4
East Glenn Highway 1987	Vegetation	77	77	77	27	18	621	9	2.9
Gakona 1987	All Resources	93	100	86	83	52	19,916	285	95.3
Gakona 1987	Vegetation	84	86	84	31	17	774	11	3.7
Glennallen 1987	All Resources	100	92	92	86	64	46,684	275	99.5
Glennallen 1987	Vegetation	75	65	65	28	23	778	5	1.7
Gold Creek 1986	All Resources	100	100	100	100	40	2,087	348	173.9
Gold Creek 1986	Vegetation	100	100	100	0	20	154	26	12.8
Gulkana 1987	All Resources	95	100	90	80	40	10,237	465	152.6
Gulkana 1987	Vegetation	70	70	70	30	20	176	8	2.6

Homer 1982	All Resources			86			528,558	294	93.8
Homer 1982	Vegetation	51		44	7		9,907	6	1.8
Hope 1990	All Resources	100	94	94	90	74	16,782	262	110.7
Hope 1990	Vegetation	94	94	94	36	47	865	14	5.7
Hurricane-Broad Pass 1986	All Resources	100	100	100	75	63	7,206	601	177.9
Hurricane-Broad Pass 1986	Vegetation	100	88	88	25	38	621	52	15.3
Kenai 1993	All Resources	98	89	86	81	62	534,062	235	83.8
Kenai 1993	Vegetation	61	53	53	18	22	33,282	15	5.2
Kenny Lake 1987	All Resources	100	100	100	65	29	43,692	470	136.3
Kenny Lake 1987	Vegetation	80	80	80	4	13	1,279	14	4.0
Lake Louise 1987	All Resources	100	100	100	82	47	7,009	369	179.2
Lake Louise 1987	Vegetation	94	94	94	6	18	268	14	6.9
McCarthy Road 1987	All Resources	100	100	100	82	59	8,747	460	230.2
McCarthy Road 1987	Vegetation	100	100	100	6	24	483	25	12.7
Mentasta 1987	All Resources	96	92	92	83	58	9,672	387	125.5
Mentasta 1987	Vegetation	88	79	79	17	38	1,323	53	17.2
Mentasta Pass 1987	All Resources	100	100	100	80	70	4,962	451	188.0
Mentasta Pass 1987	Vegetation	90	90	90	30	30	387	35	14.7
Nabesna Road 1987	All Resources	100	92	92	92	67	9,212	709	250.1
Nabesna Road 1987	Vegetation	100	92	92	42	33	287	22	7.8
Nanwalek 1997	All Resources	100	100	100	100	90	42,593	1,121	253.9
Nanwalek 1997	Vegetation	97	97	97	72	72	966	25	5.8
Ninilchik 1982	All Resources			92			49,897	230	76.7
Ninilchik 1982	Vegetation	54		38	17		1,664	8	2.6
Parks Highway South 1985	All Resources	87	90	87	57	33	21,282	162	58.0
Parks Highway South 1985	Vegetation	67	67	67	3	10	1,183	9	3.2
Paxson 1987	All Resources	93	100	93	71	57	11,236	661	289.1
Paxson 1987	Vegetation	79	79	79	0	21	115	7	3.0
Petersville Road 1985	All Resources	100	94	94	77	29	10,153	423	167.3
Petersville Road 1985	Vegetation	82	82	82	6	18	284	12	4.7
Port Graham 1997	All Resources	100	98	98	96	86	39,548	628	253.4
Port Graham 1997	Vegetation	91	82	82	66	55	1,403	22	9.0
San Juan Bay 1984	All Resources						4,253	709	250.2

Table 16. Continued

Community name	Resource category	Percent households using	Percent households trying	Percent households harvesting	Percent households receiving	Percent households giving	Community total harvest	Household mean harvest	Per capita harvest
							(in food weight pounds)		
SOUTHCENTRAL REGION, continued									
San Juan Bay 1984	Vegetation	100	100	100	0	33	108	18	6.4
Seldovia 1993	All Resources	95	95	95	86	79	79,063	517	183.6
Seldovia 1993	Vegetation	95	94	94	31	54	6,729	44	15.6
Slana 1987	All Resources	96	96	96	73	77	14,185	567	249.7
Slana 1987	Vegetation	96	96	96	9	36	709	28	12.5
Slana Homestead North 1987	All Resources	100	100	100	88	50	10,638	304	173.7
Slana Homestead North 1987	Vegetation	88	88	88	13	25	346	10	5.7
Slana Homestead South 1987	All Resources	94	94	94	82	65	22,606	343	121.3
Slana Homestead South 1987	Vegetation	94	94	94	18	29	344	5	1.9
Sourdough 1987	All Resources	100	100	89	78	44	3,015	301	118.0
Sourdough 1987	Vegetation	78	78	78	0	0	200	20	7.8
South Wrangell Mountains 1987	All Resources	100	100	100	100	79	6,617	288	138.9
South Wrangell Mountains 1987	Vegetation	100	100	100	43	43	518	23	10.9
Talkeetna 1985	All Resources	94	91	87	69	50	33,435	156	55.1
Talkeetna 1985	Vegetation	84	81	81	29	29	3,045	14	5.0
Tatitlek 1997	All Resources	100	94	88	100	100	32,915	1,219	406.4
Tatitlek 1997	Vegetation	100	81	75	63	69	658	24	8.1
Tazlina 1987	All Resources	100	88	69	91	53	39,182	327	107.5
Tazlina 1987	Vegetation	66	60	60	30	26	1,673	14	4.6
Tonsina 1987	All Resources	92	92	92	80	62	46,310	482	155.7
Tonsina 1987	Vegetation	73	64	64	28	22	1,296	14	4.4
Trapper Creek 1985	All Resources	100	100	100	90	63	12,391	207	65.4
Trapper Creek 1985	Vegetation	90	90	90	26	26	796	13	4.2

Tyonek 1983	All Resources			93	91	60	70,962	887	259.9
Tyonek 1983	Vegetation			79	14	19	930	12	3.4
Valdez 1993	All Resources	97	89	83	89	66	296,831	236	79.5
Valdez 1993	Vegetation	60	57	57	14	31	12,785	10	3.4
West Glenn Highway 1987	All Resources	100	93	93	97	55	25,765	243	91.8
West Glenn Highway 1987	Vegetation	93	93	93	8	32	1,176	11	4.2
Whittier 1990	All Resources	94	79	77	87	66	22,308	217	79.9
Whittier 1990	Vegetation	78	73	73	18	20	1,133	11	4.1
SOUTHEAST REGION									
Angoon 1996	All Resources	97	93	93	95	68	130,385	810	224.5
Angoon 1996	Vegetation	66	62	57	50	18	2,525	16	4.3
Beecher Pass 1987	All Resources	100		100	100	100	21,082	1,240	477.0
Beecher Pass 1987	Vegetation	100		100	40	60	571	34	12.9
Coffman Cove 1987	All Resources	97		88	90	53	34,090	514	183.4
Coffman Cove 1987	Vegetation	72		67	17	15	1,020	15	5.5
Craig 1997	All Resources	99	91	90	91	71	409,242	673	232
Craig 1997	Vegetation	74	68	68	38	35	32,938	54	18.7
Edna Bay 1987	All Resources	100		100	100	100	33,184	1,580	478.9
Edna Bay 1987	Vegetation	100		95	60	65	1,832	87	26.4
Elfin Cove 1987	All Resources	100		100	100	92	15,715	827	262.5
Elfin Cove 1987	Vegetation	100		100	54	46	1,644	87	27.5
Game Creek 1996	All Resources	100	100	100	100	83	11,935	796	187.2
Game Creek 1996	Vegetation	100	92	92	100	58	1,267	84	19.9
Gustavus 1987	All Resources	100		100	90	90	36,681	569	240.8
Gustavus 1987	Vegetation	100		100	44	39	1,504	23	9.9
Haines 1996	All Resources	98	93	91	97	72	421,430	535	195.8
Haines 1996	Vegetation	87	84	83	41	37	31,309	40	14.5
Hollis 1987	All Resources	100		88	93	59	14,507	452	182.7
Hollis 1987	Vegetation	88		80	30	29	887	28	11.2
Hoonah 1996	All Resources	97	95	95	90	78	331,453	1,184	372.0
Hoonah 1996	Vegetation	84	79	79	55	60	26,627	95	29.9
Hydaburg 1997	All Resources	100	90	90	100	80	154,874	1,182	384.1
Hydaburg 1997	Vegetation	92	78	78	51	47	7,570	58	18.8
Hyder 1987	All Resources	97		91	76	33	26,890	689	345.3

Table 16. Continued

Community name	Resource category	Percent households using	Percent households trying	Percent households harvesting	Percent households receiving	Percent households giving	Community total harvest	Household mean harvest	Per capita harvest
		SOUTHEAST REGION, continued					(in food weight pounds)		
Hyder 1987	Vegetation	82		76	18	12	521	13	6.7
Kake 1996	All Resources	99	89	85	96	75	133,794	537	179.1
Kake 1996	Vegetation	90	77	74	69	44	6,633	27	8.9
Kasaan 1987	All Resources	100		100	100	86	7,264	519	181.6
Kasaan 1987	Vegetation	100		93	43	36	249	18	6.2
Klawock 1997	All Resources	100	93	91	94	77	271,071	895	320.4
Klawock 1997	Vegetation	82	71	71	41	41	20,519	68	24.2
Klukwan 1996	All Resources	100	94	94	100	90	67,746	1,882	608.3
Klukwan 1996	Vegetation	100	90	90	97	87	4,918	137	44.7
Metlakatla 1987	All Resources	100		77	99	53	109,016	261	70.1
Metlakatla 1987	Vegetation	85		71	42	32	7,619	18	4.9
Meyers Chuck 1987	All Resources	100		100	80	60	12,416	1,242	413.9
Meyers Chuck 1987	Vegetation	90		90	20	30	430	43	14.3
Pelican 1987	All Resources	100		92	99	78	85,017	1,032	355.1
Pelican 1987	Vegetation	84		78	47	39	2,241	27	9.4
Petersburg 1987	All Resources	97		94	93	87	739,048	658	197.7
Petersburg 1987	Vegetation	78		70	30	33	32,259	29	8.6
Point Baker 1996	All Resources	100	100	100	100	75	13,707	721	288.6
Point Baker 1996	Vegetation	100	100	100	38	38	573	30	12.1
Port Alexander 1987	All Resources	100		100	94	86	33,222	901	311.7
Port Alexander 1987	Vegetation	97		97	47	47	3,026	82	28.4
Port Protection 1996	All Resources	100	92	92	96	76	44,004	1,100	450.9
Port Protection 1996	Vegetation	92	88	88	44	52	2,912	73	29.8
Saxman 1987	All Resources	97		83	95	45	24,192	318	93.5
Saxman 1987	Vegetation	85		74	45	29	1,047	14	4.1
Sitka 1996	All Resources	97	85	83	93	74	1,749,772	573	205.0
Sitka 1996	Vegetation	70	61	60	29	28	5,9671	19	7.0
Skagway 1987	All Resources	96		68	93	38	28,025	137	48.1
Skagway 1987	Vegetation	46		44	20	15	1,151	6	2.0

Tenakee Springs 1987	All Resources	100		90	97	68	31,234	702	329.9
Tenakee Springs 1987	Vegetation	87		81	32	32	1,001	23	10.6
Thorne Bay 1987	All Resources	100		97	87	66	90,418	578	189.0
Thorne Bay 1987	Vegetation	90		82	34	17	1,707	11	3.6
Whale Pass 1987	All Resources	100		100	67	72	9,134	507	179.1
Whale Pass 1987	Vegetation	100		100	22	44	237	13	4.7
Whitestone Logging Camp 1996	All Resources	100	96	96	67	50	25,295	617	178.4
Whitestone Logging Camp 1996	Vegetation	63	63	63	4	8	765	19	5.4
Wrangell 1987	All Resources	95		80	90	63	440,612	435	155.2
Wrangell 1987	Vegetation	76		65	41	32	12,263	12	4.3
Yakutat 1987	All Resources	96		96	93	99	234,205	1,385	397.8
Yakutat 1987	Vegetation	89		85	47	54	10,258	61	17.4

Size of a community closely correlates with total vegetation gathering, shown as *community harvest total.* In southcentral Alaska study communities, total vegetation harvest varied from 108 pounds in San Juan Bay in 1987 to over 33,000 pounds in Kenai in 1993. Twenty of the forty-six southcentral study communities have estimated vegetation harvests over 1,000 pounds in the study year. Similarly, in southeast Alaska, total community vegetation harvests varied from 237 pounds in tiny Whale Pass in 1987, to over 56,000 pounds in Sitka in 1996. Twenty-five of the thirty-three southeast Alaska study communities had vegetation harvests over 1,000 pounds in the study year.

These data show substantial vegetation harvests in southcentral and southeast study communities, although the quantity of vegetation harvested is frequently dwarfed by the very large quantities of other subsistence resources that are used.

SPECIFIC HARVEST LEVELS OF PLANTS USED IN SELECTED SOUTHEAST ALASKA COMMUNITIES

In household surveys conducted in southeast Alaska since 1996, respondents were asked about their previous year's harvest of fourteen varieties of berries and twenty edible plant categories. I examined the plant harvests for six southeast communities—Hoonah, Hydaburg, Kake, Klawock, Klukwan, and Sitka[24]—to identify characteristics of harvest.

Sitka's population is about 20 percent Native Alaskan; the other five study communities are predominantly Native. The harvest patterns in these communities are illustrative of land plant harvests in other southeast communities.[25] Not surprisingly, household participation in berry picking and berry harvest levels are higher than for other land plants. Participation in harvesting or using berries ranged from 68 to 94 percent in these study communities. Various species of blueberries, huckleberries, and salmonberries in the genera *Rubus* and *Vaccinium* generally account for most of the berries harvested. Nagoonberries *(Rubus articus),* soapberries *(Shepherdia canadensis),* strawberries *(Fragaria childensis),* and thimbleberries *(Rubus parvifolium)* are not found near or taken in all communities. High harvest of highbush cranberries *(Viburnum edule)* took place in Klukwan, where these berries are found in abundance.

Harvests of other land plants show similar ranges of variability and lower overall harvest levels than those found for berries. Beach asparagus *(Bucephala albeola),* Hudson's Bay tea *(Ledum palustre),* and goosetongue *(Plantago martima),* for example, are harvested by relatively few people, who only pick a small portion of available forest stocks. Overall household participation in harvesting or using other land plants ranged from 23 to 68 percent. Looking across communities, I found that from 6.2 percent to 16.1 percent of interviewed households used devil's club *(Oplopanax horridus)*. Tlingit and Haida Indians use this plant for medicinal purposes, with parts of it used as a dressing or poultice and other parts used to make infusions for internal use.[26] Overall, these data show continued general food use of berries and plants in southeast Alaska and reflect the significant effort expended to collect and preserve these subsistence foods.

OTHER NOTABLE PLANT USES

Subsistence plants and berries and other foods also figure in Native ceremonies. Tlingit society is organized into traditional houses, clans, and moieties or sides. Every Tlingit belongs to one and only one house, clan, and moiety. A person from Hoonah, for example, might be from Ice House, Dakdeintaan clan, on the Raven side. A person inherits his or her house, clan, and moiety memberships from his or her mother. After a person dies, other members of his house, clan, and moiety are expected to host a major feast or payoff party[27] to honor the deceased and to pay off the opposing side for the assistance they gave in burying the dead and in other death duties. At the payoff party, the dead symbolically eat the food that is prepared and given to the living guests. The selection of food should include large quantities of the traditional subsistence foods that the deceased favored, which ideally should come from the harvesting areas used by the deceased. In practice, a payoff party requires large quantities of subsistence foods to be harvested by clan members. Plant foods typically served to guests include berries for immediate consumption and for taking home. Smaller quantities of other land plants may also be distributed.[28]

Other plant uses merit brief mention and description. Both bark and roots have craft and artisan uses. People cut long strips of cedar bark from living trees. The bark is cleaned, softened, and separated into smaller strips used for weaving and basketry.[29] Spruce roots are gathered for basketry from sandy soils, where ecological conditions encourage the trees to send out long, straight surface roots with little branching. Weavers claim that forest edge situations with sandy soils produce the best roots for weaving. Spruce roots are cleaned and split for weaving.[30]

On the west coast of Prince of Wales Island, near Sitka, and elsewhere in southeast Alaska, there are major herring spawning areas, and hemlock branches are used to collect the eggs. Tlingits and Haidas recognize two varieties of hemlock, one with smooth bark and one with more variegated bark. The smooth bark variety is used in the herring egg harvest. Before the spawning begins, subsistence harvesters cut hemlock boughs and small hemlock trees to use as depositional substrate and bring them to saltwater bays where herring are likely to spawn. The hemlock branches or trees are weighted so that they are suspended in the water column just below the surface at midtide. A fishing float or tag line leading to the beach may be used to help locate the hemlock sets. After herring spawn, layers of eggs become attached to the suspended hemlock boughs or trees. When the spawn encasing the boughs is thick enough, the harvester removes the boughs or trees, which are then cut up into usable pieces for immediate consumption, distribution to other people, or storing in a freezer for later use.[31]

The ethnographic literature on southeast Alaska societies includes interesting material on Native medicinal uses of plants. DeLaguna (1972), Emmons (1991), Suttles (1990), and Turner (1992) provide helpful descriptions of numerous plant remedies believed to have been used in the region. Although recent field research in Native communities in the area has not focused on medicinal use of plants, interview and participant observation data indicate that people still use plants for medicinal purposes. The use of devil's club *(Oplopanax horridus)* is openly discussed, and its use both as a topical treatment and as a tonic is reasonably well understood. Other plant uses are less well understood. I have gathered red alder *(Alnus rubra)* bark with a Tlingit elder from Hoonah to make an infusion thought to be good for treating cancer. Whether this is a common treatment is unknown at this time. In interviews in Hydaburg, informants described making medicines for internal ailments. However, for cultural reasons, Hydaburg healers are not able to discuss exactly which plant species and which plant preparations were used, where they were gathered, or which maladies were treated.[32]

Both in Hoonah and Hydaburg, persons interviewed stressed that all individual plants of a single species are not the same. Medicine made from the same plant species but collected from different locations would likely have different effects. This view has both an ecological and a spiritual dimension. Ecologically, Native informants believe that the community of plants—the soil, water, aspect, and other physical conditions—influence the medicinal characteristics of the plant being gathered. Spiritually, elders refer to speaking to plants before taking them. They emphasize that the plant world is living and animate and that a proper code of behavior is necessary if medicines are to work. These examples point to a continuing tradition of medicinal use of plants, but describing its prevalence and complexity awaits further research.

NTFP POLICY ISSUES

The data presented above indicate that consumptive and other utilitarian uses of NTFPs by Native and non-Native residents of rural communities take place throughout Alaska. The southcentral and southeast Alaska data include the communities that make the most use of the Chugach and Tongass National Forests, respectively. To date, much harvesting of NTFPs that has taken place in these forests, and on the ecologically similar adjacent or encapsulated Native Corporations lands, has been exclusively an indigenous harvest.

Although most harvesting of NTFPs takes place for home use, use in local ceremonies, and use in crafts by the harvester, there is some level of traditional trade and exchange of forest products. In the regional data presented in Table 16 and in the recent southeast Alaska studies, the percentage of households using vegetation or specific plant species is generally higher than the percentage of households actually harvesting the item. The data showing the percentage of households receiving and giving plants reflect the trade and exchange that takes place. NTFPs also flow in intercommunity trade through which plant foods or other forest products move from communities where they are more abundant to communities where they are not found or are in short supply. Although some subsistence trade and exchange do take place, harvests tend to be self-limiting because a harvester would have no reason to take more than he or she is able to use.[33]

Although there is no established commercial market for NTFPs from the Chugach and Tongass National Forests, some interest has been expressed in possible commercial harvesting of devil's club, other medicinal plants, or ornamental moss from these areas.[34] Because of this nascent interest in commercializing NTFPs on national forestlands in Alaska, Region 10 of the Forest Service is developing a policy for special forest products.[35] Not surprisingly, tribal governments whose members use national forestlands for subsistence have strongly opposed possible commercialization. Their opposition appears to be rooted in ideas of traditional territory, ethics, and the practicality of Native participation in possible commercial harvests. Although ANCSA settled Native legal claims, Natives continue to identify traditional territories as the cultural property of the clans that own them according to traditional law.[36] Clans (and tribes) may believe that they should have authority over what activities take place on clan property, particularly if a new activity affects traditional uses of that land.

Second, Natives share a general widespread concern about commercializing what has been exclusively a traditional harvest activity. Natives have seen fish and wildlife resources transformed from what were solely traditionally used resources to general common property resources that are allocated by state and federal agencies to competing users and uses. Not only do many Alaska Natives believe that the state and federal governments have disenfranchised them from the benefits of commercial fishing and that Natives have lost hunting opportunities, but they also may dislike the transformation itself. In recent years, southeast Alaska Natives have opposed commercialization of sea cucumbers and sea urchins largely on these cultural grounds. Natives have experienced the loss of their ability to harvest other subsistence resources when commercial harvests have overwhelmed traditional ones.[37]

Several ethical questions are related to Native uneasiness with commercialization of resources that have had only traditional uses. The subsistence ethic calls for a harvester to take what is needed and no more, and this ethic emphasizes that subsistence foods should not be wasted. Need is finite and defined by the uses a person can make of the subsistence product. Second, while subsistence harvests tend to be efficient, they do not appear to always be driven strictly by economic logic. A berry or plant harvest area is likely both to have a good supply of the target species and to be a traditional gathering area for the harvester. A third ethical consideration may deal with spirituality and Native conceptions of the correct way to gather NTFPs. Traditionally, Tlingits, for example, saw themselves as spiritually connected with the forest and its resources. There was a proper way of showing respect for plants to be harvested. These ethical areas may make Natives uneasy with commercial harvesting.[38]

Finally, Natives perceive that they have been disenfranchised from many of the other Alaskan booms of resource extraction that have occurred. They are concerned that large-scale commercialization of NTFPs could result in non-Natives receiving most of the benefits from the harvests. At worst, commercial harvests of some species could negatively impact existing tradition subsistence harvests and result in little or no economic return to residents of small communities.

The Forest Service has been working with a Special Forest Products Task Group, composed primarily of Native subsistence users and their tribal representatives, to develop a policy to cover commercial use of NTFPs in the Chugach and Tongass National Forests. This group included representatives of the twenty-two federally recognized tribal governments whose members use plants in the Chugach and Tongass National Forests. The draft policy attempts to address the concerns of tribes about possible adverse effects of commercialization of forest plants on existing traditional subsistence uses.[39] The policy directs the agency to proceed carefully in permitting possible commercial uses of NTFPs in the Tongass and Chugach National Forests, and it recognizes that ANILCA provides a priority for subsistence uses. Under this policy, commercialization of devil's club will not be permitted on Forest Service lands. Areas used for subsistence plant harvesting are to be avoided if possible. Tribes are included in the permitting process, and the expectation is set that National Environmental Policy Act provisions may require preparation of assessment or impact statements for commercial plant collection. Further, this Forest Service Region 10 policy sets harvest and regeneration guidelines that will ensure that plant distribution and abundance are maintained.

Development of this policy had representatives of potentially affected tribes working with Forest Service planners and actively discussing traditional plant use and grappling with ways that plant use might be managed. As a result, the tribes have become more focused on this aspect of their traditional subsistence use patterns. A number of tribes have increased the attention they pay to plant use and are exploring ways that they might better document traditional ecological knowledge of the plants in their areas.

Alaska is fortunate in that traditional plant uses by Native people continue to take place in much of its national forests and that significant market commoditization of Chugach and Tongass National Forests' NTFPs has yet to take place. Perhaps this advantageous situation will allow the development of Forest Service policy and management practices that both respect continued traditional plant use and allow for other responsible use of NTFPs.

NOTES

1. Most of this, 106 million acres, is composed of interior subarctic forest or taiga, little of which is commercial forest. Almost all commercial forestland is found in coastal Alaska, primarily in the Tongass and Chugach National Forests. White spruce, black spruce, quaking aspen, paper birch, and balsam poplar are characteristic of some stands in the state. See Viereck and Little (1972) and Viereck (1974).

2. The discovery and push to develop North Slope oil resources provided the impetus to pass this legislation. Oil development could only proceed after Native claims were resolved.

3. See Berger (1985) for a discussion of the effects of the Alaska Native Claims Settlement Act and the formation of corporations.

4. The 44 million acres in Native Corporation ownership, 124 million acres under State of Alaska selection, and 197 million acres in federal status account for about 365 million of Alaska's 375 million acres, leaving about 10 million acres unaccounted for in this tally. This 10 million acres is in municipal, private, or other ownership status.

5. Demographic data are based on U.S. decennial censuses with updated estimates. The latest updates are for July 1998; see Alaska Department of Labor (1999).

6. See ANILCA, Title VIII, Sec. 801, or 16 USC 3111. Note that "subsistence" applies to rural residents, not only to Natives. Nevertheless, this provision of ANILCA is frequently seen deserving the special legal consideration given to Native legislation.

7. See ANILCA Title VIII, Sec. 804, or 16 USC 3114.

8. The State of Alaska has been unable to amend its constitution to make it possible to comply with ANILCA requirements or to interest the U.S. Congress in changing ANILCA. This issue has become a continuing rift zone between Alaska's Natives who rely on ANILCA protections and other Alaska groups who oppose federal management or Native subsistence protections or both.

9. Under State of Alaska subsistence law and regulations, all Alaskans, including urban residents, are considered subsistence users. Under federal law and regulations, only rural residents are covered by subsistence protections.

10. See ANILCA Title VIII, Sec. 810, or 16 USC 3120.

11. ANILCA defines "*subsistence uses* as the customary and traditional uses . . . of wild renewable resources for direct or family consumption as food, *shelter, fuel,* clothing, *tools,* or *transportation*" (emphasis added); see ANILCA Title VIII, Sec. 803. However, the act is less clear or legally tested on the mechanisms for protecting plant use than it is for use of fish and wildlife.

12. Clearly, very significant population and place changes have taken place. These would include the tragic population declines early in the colonial period due to disease, social disruption, or, in the case of the Aleuts, forced labor. In the late 1900s, settlement patterns changed. Most Native groups began living year-round in larger permanent villages, often at the sites of earlier winter settlements, and making less residential use of seasonally occupied camps.

13. The legends and songs of Northern Tlingit Indians, for example, describe events of the little ice age, perhaps 500–600 years before present. This group also identifies with cultural material found at the Ground Hog Bay site, dated back to nine thousand years ago; cf. Ackerman (1968).

14. When completed, this series will provide coverage for all American Indian populations as well as a number of special topics; see Damas (1984), Helm (1981), and Suttles (1990). Turner (1992) provides an excellent description of Native use of plants in British Columbia; coastal uses are similar to those in southeast Alaska. See Norton (1981) for interesting information on Haida Indian plant use.

15. In southeast Alaska, *Nicotiana quadrivalvis* was probably cultivated.

16. Based on personal field observations in western, northwestern, interior, southwestern, and southeastern regions of the state.

17. Although original citations are listed, much of these data have been summarized in Schroeder et al. (1987).

18. The Division of Subsistence, Alaska Department of Fish and Game, has been the agency most concerned with collecting these data. Field data collections take place with tribal and community approval and participation.

19. DeLaguna (1972) provides a fascinating description of magical medicines in her ethnography of Yakutat. Included are "no strength" medicine that a person chews, robbing dangerous animal or human opponents of their strength or will to fight, "marksmanship" medicine that works both for hunting and basketball, "grabbing" medicine that would make prey approach, and "glare" medicine that would keep rival hunters away from spotted game.

20. In addition, Fortuine (1992) maintains that many Native cultures abandoned traditional shamanic practices and the use of some traditional plant remedies as a consequence of epidemics in the late 1700s and throughout the 1800s. Undoubtedly, the epidemics did cause breaks in the transmission of traditional knowledge because of the disruption caused by the high mortality during epidemics and perhaps because of the crisis of faith in traditional worldview that epidemics and the colonial rule engendered.

21. Because of the cost and burden on informants, surveys are not conducted on a yearly basis. However, a number of years of data are available for many com-

munities, particularly in southeast Alaska where studies were repeated because of potential logging impacts and in southcentral Alaska where repeat studies were done following the *Exxon Valdez* oil spill.

22. Original reports are referenced at *http://www.state.ak.us/local/akpages/FISH.GAME/subsist/subhome.htm*; the Community Profile Database may be downloaded from this site.

23. The average American diet includes about 225 pounds of meat, fish, and poultry. A subsistence harvest of 100 pounds or more, most of which is meat, fish, and poultry, would indicate substantial reliance on wild foods. The lower harvest levels in these data sets occur in less traditional communities with less orientation to wild resource harvest.

24. Similar detailed data are available for other communities in southeast Alaska and for other regions of the state.

25. Native communities tend to harvest more seaweed than non-Native communities, but land plant use is comparable.

26. In the screening of possible medicinal plants used in British Columbia, McCutcheon et al. (1992) found that devil's club *(Oplopanax horridus)* had a high level of antibiotic activity against two bacteria, *Mycobacter phlei* and *Staphylococcus aureus* methicillin-sensitive. Note that Tlingits use devil's club to dress wounds, and devil's club preparations are also taken internally. See Turner (1982) for a discussion of Native American uses of this plant and Smith (1982) for a discussion of its pharmacology. The 6.2 percent rate of use for Sitka probably reflects lower use of devil's club among non-Natives in that community.

27. This is often referred to as a potlatch, although contemporary Tlingit refer to the event as a payoff party; cf. Kan (1989).

28. Quantities of berries can be quite large. The author attended a payoff party in 1998 in which large vats of berries were carried ceremonially into the hall where the party was taking place and distributed to guests. He estimates that over two hundred gallons of berries were given away. Blueberries and salmonberries were the main species groups. Although this example is from southeast Alaska, subsistence foods and related traditional uses of plants figure importantly in death rites and various cultural ceremonies of other Native cultural groups.

29. Culturally modified trees—cedar trees showing scars from bark stripping—are good markers of historic and prehistoric camp locations in southeast Alaska; see Mobley and Eldridge (1992). No doubt some areas were used as camps because of this resource.

30. Teri Rofkar (1999), personal communication. She also notes a resurgence of interest in weaving and basketry and some interest in the use of traditional dyes.

31. Schroeder and Kookesh (1990a) estimate that about 100,000 pounds of herring eggs were harvested in this manner from Sitka alone in a typical year. Large quantities of herring eggs are shipped to other Native communities where herring do not spawn in abundance. The total southeast Alaska harvest would be much higher.

32. In Hydaburg, knowledge of how to make plant medicines is taught through a traditional relationship and is not publicly discussed. Medicine appeared to be made only for someone else, perhaps a person of a different clan. Purchase or payment was not appropriate, suggesting that the healer-patient relationship was embedded in larger cultural beliefs and practices.

33. In contrast to commercial harvesting where there may be an economy of scale such that profits go up at higher harvest levels, the marginal utility of subsistence harvests drops to zero or below when personal or household needs are met. Taking an additional deer, boatload of fish, or bucket of berries becomes all cost and no benefit.

34. There may be some potential for matsutake, morel, and other mushroom harvests from some parts of the forest.

35. Although disposed to encourage commercial utilization of forest resources, the Forest Service is well aware of user conflicts, environmental harm, and management problems associated with NTFP harvests in the Pacific Northwest and elsewhere.

36. See Goldschmidt and Haas ([1946] 1998) for mapping of traditional territories for Tlingit Indians. In Native communities in southeast Alaska, clans give very great importance to which clan owns which part of a community's traditional territory. Ownership is encoded in and validated by traditional songs, clan crests, and personal names and titles. Clans and their heads continue to have some authority over activities in clan territory. Both clan and personal identity are tied to clan territory.

37. Harvesting of abalone provides a good example. Abalone were gathered at minus tides by residents of some southeast Alaska communities, but commercial exploitation has lowered the population such that dive gear is now needed for harvesting.

38. These ethical considerations also apply to logging, particularly logging on Native Corporation land. A great deal of conflict has occurred in this area, with tribal governments frequently opposing timber harvesting activities of Native Corporations as well as logging permitted on Forest Service lands.

39. See the draft plan at *http://www.fs.fed.us/r10/issues.htm.*

REFERENCES

Ackerman, Robert E. 1968. *The Archeology of the Glacier Bay Region, Southeastern Alaska: Final Report of the Archaeological Survey of the Glacier Bay National Monument.* Report of Investigations, no. 44. Pullman: Washington State University.

Alaska Department of Labor. 1999. *Alaska Population Overview.* Juneau: Alaska Department of Labor.

Anderson, D. D., R. Bane, R. K. Nelson, W. W. Anderson, and N. Sheldon. 1977. *Kuuvangmiit Subsistence: Traditional Eskimo Life in the Latter Twentieth Century.* Washington, DC.: National Park Service, U.S. Department of the Interior.

Berger, Thomas R. 1985. *Village Journey.* New York: Hill and Wang.

Burch, Ernest, 1975. *Eskimo Kinsmen: Changing Family Relations in Northwest Alaska.* American Ethnological Society Monograph 50. St. Paul, MN: West Publishing.

Caulfield, R. A. 1983. *Subsistence Land Use in Upper Yukon–Porcupine Communities.* Division of Subsistence Technical Paper 61. Juneau: Alaska Department of Fish and Game.

Damas, David, ed. 1984. *Handbook of North American Indians.* Vol. 5, *Arctic.* Washington, DC: Smithsonian Institution.

De Laguna, Frederica. 1972. *Under Mount Saint Elias: The History and Culture of the Yakutat Tlingit.* Washington, DC: Smithsonian Institution, Bureau of American Ethnology.

Emmons, George Thornton. [late 1800s (?)] 1991. *The Tlingit Indians.* Seattle: University of Washington Press.

Fortuine, Robert. 1992. *Chills and Fevers: Health and Disease in the Early History of Alaska.* Fairbanks: University of Alaska Press.

Goldschmidt, Walter R., and Theordore H. Haas. [1946] 1998. *Haa Aani Our Land: Tlingit and Haida Land Rights and Use.* Introduction by Thomas F. Thornton. Seattle: University of Washington Press.

Helm, June, ed. 1981. *Handbook of North American Indians.* Vol. 6, *Subarctic.* Washington, DC: Smithsonian Institution.

Jones, A. 1983. *Nauriat Niginaqtuat: Plants That We Eat.* Kotzebue, AK: Maniilaq Association.

Kan, Sergei. 1989. *Symbolic Immortality: The Tlingit Potlatch of the Nineteenth Century.* Washington, DC: Smithsonian Institution Press.

Martin, G. 1983. *Use of Natural Resources by the Residents of Dot Lake, Alaska.* Division of Subsistence Technical Paper 19. Juneau: Alaska Department of Fish and Game.

McCutcheon, A. R., S. M. Ellis, R. E. W. Hancock, and G. H. N. Towers. 1992. "Antibiotic Screening of Medicinal Plants of the British Columbia Native Peoples." *Journal of Ethnopharmocology* 37:213–223.

Mobley, Charles M., and Morley Eldridge. 1992. "Culturally Modified Trees in the Pacific Northwest." *Arctic Anthropology* 298(2): 91–110.

Nelson, Richard, 1973. *Hunters of the Northern Forest.* Chicago: University of Chicago Press.

Norton, Helen H. 1981. "Plant Use in Kaigani Haida Culture: Correction of an Ethnohistorical Oversight." *Economic Botany* 35(4): 434–449.

Rofkar, Teri, 1999. Raven Art, Sitka, Alaska. Personal communication.

Schroeder, Robert F., David B. Andersen, Rob Bosworth, Judith M. Morris, and John M. Wright. 1987. *Subsistence in Alaska: Arctic, Interior, Southcentral, Southwest, and Western Regional Summaries.* Division of Subsistence Technical Paper 150. Juneau: Alaska Department of Fish and Game.

Schroeder, Robert F., and Mathew Kookesh. 1990a. *The Subsistence Harvest of Herring Eggs in Sitka Sound, 1989.* Division of Subsistence Technical Paper 173. Juneau: Alaska Department of Fish and Game.

———. 1990b. *Subsistence Harvest and Use of Fish and Wildlife Resources and the Effects of Forest Management in Hoonah, Alaska.* Division of Subsistence Technical Paper 142. Juneau: Alaska Department of Fish and Game.

Smith, G. Warren. 1982. "Arctic Pharmacognosia II: Devil's Club, Oplopanax Horridus." *Journal of Ethnopharmacology* 7 (1983): 313–320.

Stickney, Alice, 1985. *Coastal Ecology and Wild Resource Use in the Central Bering Sea Area: Hooper Bay and Kwigillingok.* Division of Subsistence Technical Paper 85. Juneau: Alaska Department of Fish and Game.

Suttles, Wayne, ed. 1990. *Handbook of North American Indians.* Vol. 7, *Northwest Coast.* Washington, DC: Smithsonian Institution.

Turner, Nancy J. 1982. "Traditional Use of Devil's Club *(Oplopanax horridus;*

Araliaceae) by Native Peoples in Western North America." *Journal of Ethnobiology* 2(1): 17–38.

——. 1992. *Plants in British Columbia Technology*. Victoria: Royal British Columbia Museum.

Viereck, Leslie A. 1974. *Guide to Alaska Trees*. Agricultural Handbook 472. Washington, DC: USDA Forest Service.

Viereck, Leslie A., and Elbert L. Little Jr. 1972. *Alaska Trees and Shrubs*. Agriculture Handbook 410. Washington, DC: USDA Forest Service.

CASE STUDY

American Indian Management of Federal Lands: The Maidu Cultural and Development Group

Jonathan K. London

After centuries of physical displacement, forced assimilation, and genocide, often initiated or condoned by the federal government, many American Indians have been rendered landless and disenfranchised in their native land (Horsman 1992; Prucha 1995). This status has forced many American Indians into a dependence on land now controlled by the federal government for access to critical natural and cultural resources (Huntsinger et al. 1994). In the last decade, however, American Indians have made significant progress in increasing their participation in the management of natural resources and, in particular, nontimber forest products on federal lands, including those in the national forest system (USDA 1997).

This case study of the Maidu people in California's northern Sierra Nevada emphasizes two points about the participation of American Indians in nontimber forest product management.[1] First, federal tribal recognition, or the lack thereof, is a significant factor mediating Indians' voice in managing NTFPs on federal lands. Second, ecosystem management is opening up new opportunities for American Indian participation in NTFP management for federally unrecognized tribes. However, defining those opportunities is often the a process of conflict rather than collaboration.

The first section will examine the role of federal recognition in mediating Indian resource claims for NTFPs. I begin with a brief treatment of the historical construction of federal recognition and its relevance for Indian participation in resource management on federal lands. This discussion will serve as the framework to explore the historical relationships between the Maidu and the federal government in regard to land claims and political representation.

The second section will introduce the Maidu Cultural and Development Group (MCDG) and its attempts to gain a greater role in the stewardship of the Maidu homeland now contained primarily within the national forest system. I will describe the MCDG's Maidu Stewardship Project (part of the Forest Service's Stewardship Pilot initiative), which includes a significant emphasis on the restoration and care for nontimber forest products as part of an integrated approach to ecosystem and cultural revival. I will also address the dynamics of conflict and cooperation with the Forest Service during the Maidu Stewardship Project's approval and initial implementation stages. The case study concludes by setting out several broader lessons that the example of the Maidu and the MCDG might offer for policy formation and agency practice in regard to indigenous peoples and NTFP management.

CASE CONTEXT

The Maidu people have inhabited the subalpine valleys and midelevation slopes of the northern Sierra Nevada in northeastern California for at least a thousand years, and perhaps since the last ice age ten thousand years ago (Dixon 1905). Maidu is part of the California Penutian language family and is divided into three major dialects spoken by the three Maidu cultural groups: Nisenan or "Southern Maidu," Concow or "Valley Maidu," and northeastern Maidu or "Mountain Maidu."[2] It is this latter group of Mountain Maidu that is the subject of this case study.

As a result of a complicated history to be briefly summarized below, the roughly one thousand Mountain Maidu (hereafter simply Maidu) are not represented by a unified and federally recognized tribal entity and consequently have no reservation lands or treaty rights to their ancestral homeland. The Maidu's homeland is currently contained primarily in the northeastern California counties of Plumas and Lassen, which in turn consist mainly of lands within the Plumas and Lassen National Forests. Private timberlands and ranch and utility lands, interspersed with small towns and hamlets, make up the majority of nonfederal land in the region. Most Maidu live in the Indian and American Valleys in Plumas County and the Honey Lake Valley (including Susanville) in Lassen County. However, many Maidu have been forced by limited employment opportunities to migrate temporarily or permanently to the larger cities surrounding their homeland (e.g., Redding, Reno, Oroville).

Although usage of NTFPs has greatly declined as the Maidu have adopted a "modern" lifestyle, many Maidu still collect forest products for food, medicinal, and ceremonial uses. Many also work in the forest sector as loggers or with the Forest Service. The Maidu's historic and contemporary baskets—made from willow, bear grass, redbud, and other species—are a source of pride for them and are highly prized by collectors around the world. With no lands of their own, the Maidu gather forest products on an informal—or as some of them describe, an "invisible"—basis from the national forests and private lands in the area. This arrangement offers the Maidu little ability to ensure the protection or engage in the management of these vital components of their culture and is the source of significant frustration and concern.

RECOGNITION AND RESOURCE CLAIMS

The Wolf Timber Sale

The Maidu's difficulties in effectively asserting their voice in the management of NTFPs on federal land can be illustrated by the case of the Wolf timber sale on the Plumas National Forest. In 1994, Plumas National Forest personnel enlisted the help of several Maidu basket weavers to develop site maps of a prized bear grass gathering site on national forestland with the promise that such documents would help the agency protect the bear grass. Although some of the Maidu elders whose families had frequented the site for generations were reluctant to share their knowledge with the Forest Service, they agreed to do so as a measure of last resort.

That same summer, a timber sale was conducted in the area without reference to the bear grass maps. When Maidu gatherers returned to the site, they found it devastated: the slopes that had once supplied bear grass for their baskets were broken earth, skid trails, and grease pits. The Maidu's request that the Forest Service use the logging contractor's bond to restore the site was refused with the response that such funds could not be allocated back to the project site and would have to go through a forestwide prioritization process. To date, no bear grass restoration has occurred.

Some Maidu understood the episode as a result of the agency's compartmentalized structure in which the department recording the maps did not communicate with the department administering the sale. However, many other Maidu viewed the destruction as a clear signal that protecting gathering sites would be better achieved by "going underground" and maintaining silence about their practices than through collaborating with the Forest Service. This episode was especially demoralizing for the Maidu weavers who struggle with the irony of practicing an art form with worldwide appeal but whose viability is threatened locally as the weaving materials and the human repositories of weaving knowledge die out without replacement. Many Maidu attribute the Forest Service's failure to protect or restore the site to their lack of legal standing as a recognized tribe.

Losing Ground in Maidu Country

How does the recognized or unrecognized status of a tribe affect its ability to represent its interests in the management of nontimber forest products with federal agencies such as the Forest Service? The answer to this question, as exemplified here by the Maidu, necessitates a clearer definition of the notion of federal recognition.

Federal recognition, as it is defined today, is the legal status granted by the federal government to certain Indian tribes that qualifies them to engage on a government-to-government basis with Congress and federal agencies (ACCIP 1997). Only recognized tribes are able to serve as beneficiaries of trust resources (including land), recipients of federal Indian programs, and holders of treaty rights. Even though individuals may self-identify as Indian based on their ancestry and cultural affiliation, recognition as a political, legal, and economic entitlement is only possible as an enrolled member of a recognized tribe. To be recognized, a tribe must demonstrate that it has been a stable cultural, social, and political unit over time.[3] To many Indians, the federal government's application of "stability" as a test for recognition is deeply ironic given the government's primary role in disrupting this stability over hundreds of years. The fact that the tribes themselves bear the burden of proof to legitimate claims to land and other resources they view as their birthright only adds to the sense of injustice (ACCIP 1997).

Considering that in California two-thirds of self-identified Indians are not members of recognized tribes and that only one of the forty applications for recognition filed through 1997 was accepted by the Bureau of Indian Affairs suggests that the Maidu's problems are part of a systematic pattern (ACCIP 1997). A brief history of this peculiar political, economic, and cultural institution may help to explain some of the Maidu's current difficulties in managing and protecting NTFPs on federal lands.

During the 1700s, relationships between the newly formed United States and Indian groups were nation-to-nation treaties, similar to those signed with European powers, signifying the recognition of Indian nations as sovereign entities. However, by the time that Anglo-American settlement came to California in the 1800s, the nation-to-nation phase had passed. Instead the country was in the throes of the Indian removal period (1828–1871) during which treaty making was largely predicated upon military defeat of Indians as "suits of peace" between unequal adversaries (Barsh and Henderson 1980).

As one of the first acts of the federal government in the newly formed state of California, federal Indian agents encouraged the Maidu to become a signatory to one of the eighteen treaties of 1851 in which upwards of half of the California Indian tribes agreed to vacate their lands in return for new reservation lands elsewhere and federal assistance (Anderson, Allison, and Heizer 1978; Heizer 1972). The Maidu agreed to sign the treaty under the duress of conflicts with gold miners who killed hundreds of them directly through massacres and disease and indirectly through degrading the streams that carried critical food sources such as salmon, eel, river otter, and waterfowl. Although the Maidu, like many Indians, left their lands in anticipation of protection and support on reservations (they were promised a roughly ten-square-mile reservation along the Feather River), the U.S. Senate refused to ratify the treaties and furthermore kept their decision under seal for fifty years, thus precluding any subsequent efforts to gain a secure land base or political status as a recognized tribe (Heizer 1972). At the same time, Congress passed the Land Claims Act of 1851 designating all lands in California as public domain unless valid claims were presented to specific parcels within two years. Because no Indians were informed of this policy, few claims were so registered, and most Indian lands, including that of the Maidu, passed into the public domain (Anderson, Allison, and Heizer 1978).

This era of political land alienation was followed in the 1860s by a policy of forced removal as federal troops marched many of the remaining Maidu to reservations in the Central Valley and prison camps near San Francisco. Those who survived and were able to escape often found their lands held by settlers who rarely were willing to relinquish their new claims. In particular, many ranchers' massive holdings encompassed multiple Maidu villages and the critical acorn belt on the slopes above the valleys. Faced with the decline of their original food base and the alternative of certain death if they contested ranchers' new claims, most Maidu accepted a kind of landed slavery in which they continued to live in their own villages and worked for board as ranch hands. Although oppressive, the working relationship between ranchers and Maidu reduced the outright extermination that occurred in many other areas of California and allowed the Maidu to remain on their ancestral lands, at least for a time.

The Dawes or General Allotment Act, passed in 1897 to break up the tribal structure through individual parcelization of tribal lands, resulted in the alienation of most of the remaining Maidu lands.[4] Unlike Indian groups that earlier had been granted reservations and therefore faced their disassembly, for the Maidu, who had no such reservation, the loss of land occurred as the federal Office of Indian Affairs sought to transfer newly designated forested land allotments to whites. This policy was based on a period ideology in which Indians' forest-based hunting and gathering lifestyle was viewed as retarding incorporation into the mainstream society and in need of replacement by sedentary agriculture (Lewis 1994). Typically, the purchasers of these Indian allotments—at far below market value and often under suspicious circumstances—were large logging and hydroelectric companies seeking to consolidate their holdings in the area.[5] Harassment by whites (typically miners) also led to many Maidu selling or simply abandoning their allotments. As a result of this massive transfer of Maidu lands, by the time the Plumas and Lassen National Forests were created in 1907, the government's negotiations were largely conducted with the logging and hydroelectric firms. Maidu land and resource claims were not even on the table for discussion.

Compounding their loss of legal title to the land itself, ecological changes prompted by the Forest Service's fire suppression policies resulted in the loss of much of the oak woodlands and the associated species used for food, medicinal, and weaving materials that provided their cultural and economic foundation. The Forest Service's fire suppression efforts initiated a large-scale ecological shift from an oak and pine open-canopy forest with a diverse understory that depended on a regular low-intensity fire regime toward a fir-dominated and closed-canopy forest.[6] Running conflicts between the Forest Service and Maidu seeking to maintain their traditional burning practices continued into the 1980s when the last of the Maidu actively engaged in these practices died. It gives the Maidu bittersweet solace that the Forest Service and other resource scientists are finally convinced that fire is a necessary part of the ecosystem and must be reintroduced to promote forest health.

Faced with the abject poverty of the few remaining California Indians who survived the massacres, epidemics, and starvation of the preceding century, the federal government established a series of rancherias as "homes for homeless California Indians" during the first three decades of the twentieth century (Dyer 1975). Several were established in the Maidu's region, including the Greenville, Susanville, and Taylorsville rancherias, but provided them with little political power or access to land. Like other rancherias, these lacked treaty rights and consisted mainly of the land surrounding the housing units themselves (Prucha 1995).

The detribalization emphasis at the turn of the century was replaced by a retribalization policy under the Roosevelt administration's Indian Reorganization Act (IRA) of 1934, which developed processes and standards to establish tribal governments (Barsh and Henderson 1980). These standards became the foundation of the current system of federal recognition. No Maidu tribal council was established during this period, a fact largely attributable to the fragmentation of their land base and political structures in the preceding century.

The IRA's bold, if ambiguous, social experiment was short-lived, however, as a series of "termination" acts focused federal policy on "freeing" Indians from federal control and the newly formed tribal governments. The (California) Rancheria Act of 1958 served to terminate forty-one rancherias, including the Greenville and Taylorsville rancherias to which many Maidu belonged (ACCIP 1997). Upon termination, the land formally held in trust was turned over to the residents in fee simple. Most new titleholders, faced with the inability to pay property taxes, soon sold out to whites.

The 1970s saw yet another swing of the pendulum as tribes petitioned to become "unterminated" and the federal government reinitiated government-to-government relationships with newly recognized Indian tribes. As part of the settlement in a case brought by dozens of terminated California rancherias (the Tillie Hardwick case), the Greenville rancheria was unterminated in 1983. A progressive tribal council soon developed plans for obtaining a Maidu land base combining forest management areas, housing, and tribal enterprises. Unfortunately, this upswing in tribal power was short-lived. In an action many Maidu suspect was supported if not initiated by the Bureau of Indian Affairs (BIA), the Greenville Rancheria Council purged from the tribal roles all but a handful of lineal descendants of the former inhabitants of the rancheria site. This action both stalled most efforts in self-development and produced fractures in the Maidu community between those families purged and those remaining in the rancheria that persist to this day.

Currently, the Greenville rancheria includes only a small fraction of the total Maidu population as members, has a local land base large enough for only a few houses, and is administered from Red Bluff, a Central Valley town 150 miles away from the central Mountain Maidu population center. The Susanville rancheria, which includes a number of Maidu as members, is dominated by other Indian groups (e.g., Paiute) and has no land base other than its own housing development area. Neither rancheria has been effective as a champion of a Maidu voice in forest management. Although many Mountain Maidu have been adopted into Concow Maidu rancherias in the Central Valley, their lack of full voting status and the rancherias' focus on their own geographic areas has precluded these entities from playing a significant role in forest management in the Mountain Maidu homeland.

Various groups of Maidu have launched several efforts to achieve federal recognition since the 1970s, but to date none have made their way through the system. As described above, this inability to gain federal recognition is largely due to the historical disruptions faced by the Maidu that make meeting the BIA's standards of cultural, social, and political continuity a severe challenge.

The lack of the political and economic entitlements associated with federal recognition has had significant cultural implications for the Maidu. Some Maidu attribute the decreasing interest among the younger generations in basket weaving and other lifeways to the problems of gaining access to land from which to gather these materials and to participate in the ceremonies that invest these objects with meaning. Coupled with a generation of elders shaped by a policy of forced enrollment in Indian boarding schools established to leach out Indian culture from their charges and continued experiences of subtle (and not so subtle) racism, many Maidu view their lack of federal recognition as reinforcing the message that "you don't exist."[7] High rates of alcoholism, family violence, school failure, and intergenerational alienation are deemed as symptomatic of the historical assault on the bases of the Maidu's sense of cultural pride.

Despite these tremendous challenges, however, there remains a strong determination among many Maidu to maintain a sense of cultural identity. The efforts of the Maidu Cultural and Development Group to restore a "sense of place" in their homeland are an important development in this community initiative.

THE MAIDU CULTURAL AND DEVELOPMENT GROUP: NAMING AND CLAIMING PLACE

Formation and Initiatives of the MCDG

The Maidu Cultural and Development Group (MCDG) was formed in 1995 by several Maidu community leaders and non-Maidu supporters who sought to increase the role of the Maidu in the forest management and economic development activities in the area. Group members shared the belief that the ecological vitality of the forest and the social vitality of the Maidu community could only be achieved through a revival of the land-based Maidu culture in which natural and social systems were tightly linked. The MCDG's *Maidu Sense of Place Action Plan* (Gorbet, 1998) articulates this connection between ecological and cultural vitality: "Spiritual strength and material livelihoods come from healthy land. When the land is sick, the spirits go away; communities fall apart."

Because most of the original Maidu members of the MCDG were not part of any recognized tribal entity, they viewed the group as a vehicle through which to rally support for their vision within the Maidu community and advocate it with the Forest Service and other agencies. Many members describe being motivated to form the organization by the urgency of revitalizing the community before the last generation with direct experience of traditional Maidu lifeways passes away. Non-Maidu members of the MCDG, mostly county and federal agency personnel, saw the group as a venue in which to support the nonrecognized Maidu community in ways that otherwise would be impossible.

The MCDG's first project, supported by a Rural Community Assistance grant from the Forest Service, was the Maidu Sense of Place Map, which indicated the Maidu names for prominent landmarks in Indian Valley. While current place-names reflect the history of white settlement and conquest, the Maidu names evoke the mythic origins as well as the earlier uses and natural characteristics of these sites. The MCDG has taken further steps to request that these names be included by the Forest Service and the

U.S. Geological Survey on their official maps. In the absence of formally recognized land claims, this map can be seen as a way for the Maidu to address their legal alienation from the land by reestablishing a kind of symbolic ownership.

In 1998, the MCDG created a *Maidu Sense of Place Action Plan* that outlined a strategy to use Maidu culture as the basis for integrated economic development in Indian Valley. At the same time, the MCDG submitted a special use permit to the Plumas National Forest as the administrative means to implement key elements of the action plan, including the creation of a Maidu "living village" educational facility, ethnobotanical nature trails, and vegetation restoration sites. The Plumas National Forest rejected the group's special use permit application, citing the mismatch between the MCDG's attempt to secure a large land base (fifteen hundred acres) for a significant time period (ninety-nine years) and the more limited parameters of special use permits. The Forest Service response also noted that the group's application represented an inappropriate substitution of public land for a use that should occur on private or tribal lands. This response was the subject of much criticism by the MCDG for its perceived ignorance of the history of the Maidu's loss of land, much of it at the hands of the federal government, and the Maidu's status as original inhabitants of the land now controlled by the Forest Service.

Undaunted, the MCDG repackaged their plans in the form of a proposal to become a site in the National Stewardship Pilot program, which is part of the Forest Service's efforts to "reinvent" its timber management program as ecosystem management and to explore new contractual work arrangements.[8] The MCDG's proposal, which was eventually selected as one of twenty-one pilot sites nationwide, combines land management, cultural education, and economic development objectives as part of an overall program of Maidu Stewardship. The MCDG's vision of stewardship is a multilayered approach to simultaneously restoring the ecological health of the land, institutional relationships with the Forest Service, and the sense of pride and cultural vitality within the Maidu community. The *Maidu Sense of Place Action Plan* presents the logic of the group's approach: "The land has been abused. It is getting trashy—a kind of wilderness. The plants and animals are going away because they have not been respected and taken care of. The spirit is leaving the land. . . . All this degradation is a result of the near ecological extinction of Indian people. . . . 'good science' is not possible without TEK [traditional ecological knowledge]; and TEK will die if the People die culturally" (MCDG 1998).

The land for the proposal included and expanded beyond that requested in the special use permit to cover twenty-one hundred acres: fifteen hundred acres of riparian land at the north end of Indian Valley and six hundred acres surrounding a sacred lake on the slope above the valley. MCDG members purposely selected "wounded land" to demonstrate and relearn their resource management practices, such as prescribed fire to restore the land back to health. One member described the group's response to the Forest Service's offer of a smaller area with richer stands of timber instead of the degraded lands that the group proposed: "We told them, we don't want the trees, we want the land!" The area's riparian character was also crucial for its provision of key basket weaving species such as willow. The easy access to roads and population centers was considered important to promote the educational and economic development aspects of the plan, such as the living village and ethnobotanical trails. The six hundred acres surrounding the sacred lake contributed to the MCDG's goals of cultural education by promoting recreation that respected the cultural importance of the site and its protection from improper usage such as motorized vehicles.

Both sites are being used to develop two sets of "protocols," one guiding the application of traditional Maidu ecological knowledge to the analysis, planning, and implementation of ecosystem management projects and the other guiding collaboration and communication between the Maidu and the Forest Service. Traditional ecological knowledge (TEK) teams, including Maidu experts assisted by technical consultants from other Indian groups, will assist in the development of both sets of protocols.

Agency Response to the Maidu Stewardship Proposal

The MCDG's proposal received top ranking through the selection process, which included screening at the regional (Region 5) and national levels of the Forest Service. At the regional level, the proposal was selected for consideration because its unique character (native American stewardship) put it in its own category and thus precluded any competitors. At the national level, it received top ranking again for its nearly unique character and its minor funding requirements (principally for program coordination).[9]

Beyond these formal selection criteria, the Maidu Stewardship Proposal also received significant support in the Washington office because it coincided with and served several institutional trends within the agency. As ecosystem management replaces multiple use as the dominant credo of the Forest Service, multigenerational knowledge, like that held by the Maidu, becomes increasingly important as a source of information on "historical range of variability," "reference conditions," and disturbance regimes such as wildfires and flooding. Indigenous knowledge is seen as potentially contributing to management techniques such as prescribed fire, the sustainable management of NTFPs, and understory systems as a whole as well as ecosystem restoration. Improved understanding and application of indigenous management techniques are seen as critical, given new analyses of ecosystems as "cultural landscapes" shaped by centuries of intentional manipulation by indigenous populations and potentially benefiting from the reintroduction of these cultural resource management systems (Blackburn and Anderson 1993; Anderson 1996; Keystone Center 1996).

Linked to this growing appreciation of indigenous knowledge is the increased emphasis on Indian groups as important organizational partners in environmental and natural resource management in light of tribes' increasing assertion of their government-to-government relationships with federal agencies (USDA 1997). Coupled with the Forest Service's need to legitimate their own role as stewards of their vast landed jurisdiction during a period of government downsizing and in a "New West" where amenity economies are overtaking extractive economies (at least in the public eye), strategic partnerships with Indian groups such as the MCDG are seen as a much needed feather in the agency's slightly threadbare cap.

At the same time that the MCDG was embraced by the Forest Service's regional and national levels, they were embroiled in conflict with the local level of the agency. It took nearly two years and multiple revisions of its action plan after the pilot project was approved in Washington for the Plumas National Forest to provide final approval of the MCDG's project and release the funds. This seeming contradiction can be explained by the MCDG's role in promoting institutional transformations that are not fully welcomed by forest-level leadership.

Unlike all of the other national stewardship pilots, the Maidu Stewardship Proposal was produced *for* its local forest, not *by* it. Although the other pilot projects were initiated by the local forest and produced with varying degrees of input from the local community, the MCDG turned this typical "community participation" on its head when they initiated their own proposal and then asked for support from the local forest. In fact, contrary to the account by the MCDG, the forest-level leadership maintains that they were not informed about the pilot proposal until just before it was submitted. Beyond an instance of simple miscommunication, the MCDG's proposal was seen by the forest leadership as potentially detracting from its institutional autonomy and authority, which was perceived to occur as forest management was initiated in the community from "below" the local forest and was then enforced from "above" at the regional and national levels of the agency, the administration, and Congress. Perceived impacts on forest-level autonomy were also prompted by the land base specified by the Maidu Stewardship Project that spans the Plumas and Lassen National Forests. This stipulation required the two forests to collaborate with each other, a task that individual forests typically resist for its perceived infringement on the autonomy of forest-level leadership.

Tensions between the MCDG and the Plumas National Forest leadership have also arisen over the meaning of the term "stewardship." Although the Maidu include both the ecosystem and cultural restoration components of their proposal as fundamental and indivisible constituents of stewardship, the local forest has consistently attempted to partition off the cultural elements from the pilot project. They claim these are outside the purview of the National Stewardship Program and therefore detrimental to the long-term viability and funding of the MCDG's project. The MCDG, in turn, views the requests to alter their project as reflecting an unwillingness to acknowledge the Maidu's worldview and an inappropriate imposition of a Western scientific overlay.

The local Forest Service leadership has also consistently asked the Maidu to specify the exact land management techniques to be used and the ecological knowledge underlying these techniques. The Maidu have consistently demurred, noting that decisions about restoration and other management efforts must be made on a site-by-site basis over time, by "listening to the land," and not as part of a formalized set of standards. The MCDG Action Plan describes the MCDG's orientation to time as follows: "It is to be remembered that Native Americans have a different sense of time than the non-native community (so-called 'Indian time' when things happen when they are supposed to happen). It does not mean that we sit back and wait, but that we work with the timeframes of Nature. The caretaking of the land is never done; it is a lifetime project" (MCDG 1998).

The MCDG also refuses to divulge all their knowledge to the agency, mindful of the long history of having their knowledge appropriated without compensation or even used against them. The group's unwillingness to provide explicit details about their management strategy to the Forest Service has made it difficult for local forest officials to accommodate the MCDG into their standard administrative procedures of planning, budgeting, and reporting. One local forest official deemed this problem of fit as trying to put a "square peg into a round hole."

MCDG members have often complained that the local Forest Service leadership has not worked with the Maidu as equal partners because of their lack of recognized status. They attribute the Plumas National Forest's delay in releasing the pilot project funds and their pressure to change elements of the Stewardship Project (e.g., dropping the living village) to their lack of clout as a nonrecognized entity. Forest Service staff deny this charge and explain that their repeated requests for revisions of the MCDG's plan are based on their desire to see the project succeed. Indeed, the forest leadership has explained its hesitancy in approving the transfer of funds as based on a concern that the pilot project would fail and reflect badly on them.

Conversely, some observers speculate that the forest leadership may be concerned that the MCDG's possible success may set a precedent for much larger land claims in the future, even culminating in a formal reversion of some of the national forest to one or more of the Maidu groups seeking federal recognition status. Some MCDG members have questioned whether the problems in collaboration with the Forest Service might extend beyond tribal status to the forest leadership's perceived loss of control associated with engaging with other community-based collaborators, whether Indian or not (especially those with national connections).[10] In this case, the MCDG's status as a nonfederally recognized Indian organization might simply exacerbate this more generic problem.

Despite these difficulties, implementation of the Maidu Stewardship Project is going forward, as are attempts to facilitate the collaboration between the MCDG and the local forests. As of this writing in summer 2000, the MCDG has completed its first year of the Maidu Stewardship Project and has produced drafts of the traditional ecological knowledge and communications and collaboration protocols. Relations with the local forests have also improved as the MCDG has demonstrated its capacity to the agency and as new staff assignments (particularly a newly designated district ranger) have enhanced communication and mutual trust.

BROADER IMPLICATIONS OF THE CASE OF THE MAIDU CULTURAL AND DEVELOPMENT GROUP

The case of the Maidu people and the MCDG represents both the positive potentials for collaboration between public agencies and Indian groups in NTFP management and the challenges that historical patterns of exclusion and mutual distrust pose to this collaboration. Several lessons can be gleaned from this case with implications that may extend to other Indian groups and other areas of the country.

First, secure entitlements to land, including arrangements designated by treaty or more administrative means such as special use permits or stewardship pilot status, are a critical variable in affecting whether Indians can play a substantive role in the management of NTFPs or any other resource. The lack of federal recognition, in turn, is a central variable affecting the range of entitlements available to Indian groups. In contrast to the Maidu, the neighboring Washoe—a federally recognized tribe holding a number of treaties and reservation areas—were recently granted a large-scale permit on the Tahoe National Forest to run a resort and education center. The Washoe also played a prominent role in the 1998 Tahoe Summit attended by top members of the Clinton administration and have been integrally involved in Forest Service planning efforts regarding protection of sacred sites on Lake Tahoe (Reynolds 1996).

This is not to say that federal recognition, or lack thereof, is a determining factor in Indians' empowerment in federal land management. In many cases, nonrecognized—but well-organized—Indian entities such as the California Indian Basketweavers Association can have significant clout in issues such as promoting the ability of their members to gather weaving materials on public lands. In other cases, lack of recognition may simply be a convenient administrative justification for not incorporating the concerns of Indians as opposed to a formal barrier to doing so. Nevertheless, identifying and addressing the legal and administrative barriers to full participation in nontimber forest product management decisions by all Indians, regardless of formal status, will be important to ensure that NTFP management does not further marginalize nonfederally recognized Indian groups.

Federally unrecognized Indians such as those in the MCDG often have special concerns in regard to the sharing of ecological knowledge with federal agencies. While most Indians are hesitant about the exploitation of their knowledge, for unrecognized tribes that lack most other collective material resources (e.g., land, resource rights), their ecological knowledge is all the more precious and precarious. Therefore, in order for federal agencies to benefit from this vital source of information, great strides in building trust and mutual respect are imperative. The MCDG's development of a "communications protocol" with the Forest Service and the continued attempts to improve collaborative relationships with the agency are critical steps in this direction.

The ability to manage and obtain access to NTFPs is critical as a means of cultural regeneration, which can be especially important for nonrecognized and landless tribes. Playing an active role in the protection and management of nontimber forest products on public lands, after generations of displacement, can provide nonrecognized tribes with the opportunities to reproduce and, in many cases, relearn the art forms and lifeways included in their heritage.

Being positioned as agent as opposed to the object of land management decisions can also provide an individually and collectively empowering experience. The extent of this empowerment is greatly influenced not only by the control of material resources but also by the ability to define the management terms and meanings. For example, the MCDG has struggled with the Plumas National Forest over whether projects that the forest deems "cultural," such as a living village re-creation, are legitimate elements to their forest stewardship plans. Although the forest leadership views such cultural facilities as outside the mandate of the stewardship framework, for the MCDG, culture and stewardship are inseparable. How inclusive the definitions of NTFP and ecosystem management are allowed to be and who gets to define these terms will have a significant impact on the outcomes for Indian people.

Finally, despite the potential match between Indian expertise and growing agency interest in NTFPs, there is a potential tension in the very term "NTFP" itself that may make for an uncomfortable fit between Indians and this new agency management emphasis. Some Indians object to the use of the word "product," with its implications of commodification, as out of keeping with the noneconomic and often sacred values associated with these species. Similarly, defining these species by what they are not (i.e., non*timber*) as opposed to what they are (a particular set of forest species) casts them as a derivative or secondary object and thereby continues to elevate timber as the primary forest product. Conversely, Indians involved in timber harvesting (including many Maidu) have expressed concern that the association of Indians with NTFP management as an exclusively cultural as opposed to an economic practice may serve to confine them to margins of the forest economy. Attention to such cultural issues and their real political and economic implications will be important as Indians become increasingly involved in NTFP policy and management.[11]

NOTES

1. This case study draws upon interviews with members of the Maidu Cultural and Development Group, other members of the Maidu community, the USDA Forest Service, and various informants conducted for the author's dissertation research (London 2001). To safeguard confidentiality, no personal attributions are made.

2. The term "Maidu" itself simply means people. For more ethnographic detail on the Mountain Maidu, see Dixon (1905); Kroeber (1925); Riddell (1968, 1978); Powers (1877); Potts (1977); Shipley (1997); Margolin (1981); Ogle Benner (1998); Coyote Man (1973a, 1973b).

3. To gain federal recognition as tribes, Indian groups must prove that they can be identified by historical evidence as being an Indian tribe; that their members are descendants of an Indian tribe that inhabited a specific area, and that descendants now live in a community identified as Indian, distinct from other populations; that the group has maintained government authority over its members as an autonomous unit over time until the present; that the membership of the group consists principally of persons who are not members of other tribes; and that the tribe has not been subject to congressional termination (Pevar 1992).

4. Nationwide, between 1897 and 1934, this policy resulted in the passing of 60 million of the 138 million acres of Indian lands into the public domain, with an additional 27 million acres sold directly to non-Indians (Limerick 1987).

5. Quit claims deeding the allotment to a logging or hydroelectric company were often signed soon after the original allotment claim was granted (typically only with an "X"). Fraud was rampant: one Maidu elder recounted that her father supposedly signed a quit claim to his allotment that was dated after he died.

6. See Huntsinger et al. (1994) for an account of the economic and cultural impacts of federal fire suppression policies on the Yurok people of California's north coast, particularly the loss of acorns as oaks were succeeded by Douglas fir and other conifers that thrived in the absence of fire.

7. One Miwok woman married to a local Maidu man related the following parable-like story about the social meaning of federal nonrecognition: "Suppose

you wake up one morning and there's a man at the door with a three-piece suit serving you a notice that says, 'By the power of the President of the United States and the U.S. Congress, you are hereby notified that you no longer exist. You no longer are recognized as a people and no longer have the rights and privileges as a tribe.' You look in the mirror and ask, how can I not exist? You hear people say, oh they are all dead, they used to be here but they're gone now, but you're sitting right there, and you are thinking 'I'm right here, I'm right here, I'm right here.' And you'd rather be dead than be 'walking dead.' "

8. The National Stewardship Pilot initiative was developed through a collaboration between the Ecosystem Management sector of the USDA Forest Service (Washington office) and the Pinchot Institute for Conservation, a Washington, D.C.-based conservation organization.

9. The remainder of project support is expected to be secured through a combination of donated labor and materials, private foundation grants, and allocations from the Herger-Feinstein Quincy Library Group Forest Recovery Act, which directs forest management on a 2.5-million-acre segment of national forestland including the MCDG's pilot site. The Quincy Library Group has formally endorsed the Maidu Stewardship Proposal.

10. The case of the Quincy Library Group, a coalition of timber firm executives and local environmentalists that is using federal legislation to require the adoption of new forest management plans on parts of the Plumas, Lassen, and Tahoe National Forests, represents similar issues of institutional change, albeit on a much larger scale. Indeed, the fact that these forests are struggling in their attempts to adjust to this new configuration of power may amplify the perceived implications of the MCDG's much smaller claim. See London, forthcoming.

11. See Berkhofer (1978), for treatment of the power of "primitive" and other imagery of Indians as a means of control and oppression. See also works by Stuart Hall (1992), for example, for incisive treatment of the cultural politics of race and ethnicity.

REFERENCES

Advisory Council on California Indian Policy. 1997. *The ACCIP Recognition Report: Equal Justice for California*. Sacramento, CA: ACCIP.

Anderson, George E., W. H. Allison, and Robert F. Heizer. 1978. *Treaty Making and Rejection by the Federal Government in California, 1850–1852*. Ballena Press Publications in Archeology, Ethnology, and History, no. 9. Menlo Park, CA: Ballena Press.

Anderson, M. Kat. 1996. "Tending the Wilderness." *Restoration and Management Notes* 14(2): 154–166.

Barsh, Russel Lawrence, and James Youngblood Henderson. 1980. *The Road: Indian Tribes and Political Liberty*. Berkeley: University of California Press.

Berkhofer, Robert F., Jr. 1978. *The White Man's Indian: Images of the American Indian from Columbus to the Present*. New York: Vintage Press.

Blackburn, T. C., and M. Kat Anderson, eds. 1993. *Before the Wilderness: Native Californians as Environmental Managers*. Menlo Park, CA: Ballena Press.

Coyote Man. 1973a. *Sun Moon and Stars: Part One the Trilogy: Old People of the New World—A Source Book*. Berkeley, CA: Brother William Press.

———. 1973b. *The Destruction of the People: Part Two the Trilogy: Old People of the New World—A Source Book*. Berkeley, CA: Brother William Press.

Dixon, R. B. 1905. "The Northern Maidu: The Huntington California Expedition." *Bulletin of the American Museum of Natural History* 17:119–346.

Dyer, Ruth Caroline. 1975. *The Indian Land Title in California: A Case in Federal Equity 1851–1942*. San Francisco: R and E Research Associates.

Gorbet, Lorena 1998. *Maidu Cultural and Development Group: Action Plan for the Living Village and Stewardship Area*. Greenville, CA: privately printed.

Hall, Stuart. 1992. "Cultural Studies and Its Theoretical Legacies." In *Cultural Studies*, ed. L. Grossberg, C. Nelson, and P. Treichler, pp. 277–294. New York: Routledge.

Heizer, Robert Fleming. 1972. *The Eighteen Unratified Treaties of 1851–1852 between the California Indians and the United States Government*. Berkeley: Archaeological Research Facility, Department of Anthropology, University of California.

Horsman, Reginald. 1992. *Expansion and American Indian Policy, 1783–1812*. Norman: University of Oklahoma Press.

Huntsinger, Lynn et al. 1994. *A Yurok Forest History*. Presented to the Bureau of Indian Affairs. Berkeley: Department of Environmental Science Policy and Management, University of California.

Keystone Center. 1996. *The Keystone National Policy Dialogue on Ecosystem Management: Final Report*. Keystone, CO: Keystone Center.

Kroeber, A. L. 1925. *Handbook of California Indians*. Bureau of American Ethnology Bulletin 78. Washington, DC: U.S. Government Printing Office.

Lewis, David Rich. 1994. *Neither Wolf nor Dog: American Indians, Environment, and Agrarian Change*. New York: Oxford University Press.

Limerick, Patricia. 1987. *Legacy of Conquest: The Unbroken Past of the American West*. New York: W. W. Norton.

London, Jonathan. 2001. "Placing Conflict and Collaboration in Community Forestry." Ph.D. diss., University of California, Berkeley.

Margolin, Malcolm, ed. 1981. *The Way We Lived: California Indian Reminiscences, Stories, and Songs*. Berkeley, CA: Heyday Books.

Ogle Benner, Beverly. 1998. *Whisper of the Maidu: My Indian Ancestors of the Humbug Valley*. Privately printed.

Pevar, Stephen L. 1992. *The Rights of Indian Tribes: The Basic ACLU Guide to Indian and Tribal Rights*. 2d ed. Carbondale: University of Southern Illinois Press.

Potts, Marie. 1977. *The Northern Maidu*. Happy Camp, CA: Naturegraph Publishers.

Powers, Stephen. 1877. *Tribes of California*. Vol. 3, *Contributions to North American Ethnology*. Department of the Interior, U.S. Geographical and Geological Survey of the Rocky Mountain Region. Washington, DC: U.S. Government Printing Office.

Prucha, Francis Paul. 1995. *The Great Father: The United States Government and the American Indians*. Lincoln: University of Nebraska Press.

Reynolds, Linda A. 1996. "The Role of Indian Tribal Governments and Communities in Regional Land Management." In *Sierra Nevada Ecosystem Project, Final Report to Congress,* vol. 2, *Assessment and Scientific Basis for Management Options*. Davis: University of California, Centers for Water and Wildland Resources.

Riddell, Francis A. 1968. "Ethnogeography of Two Maidu Groups I: The Silom Ma-a Maidu." *Masterkey* 42(2): 45–52.

———. 1978. "Maidu and Concow." In *Handbook of North American Indians,* vol. 8, ed. R. F. Heizer, pp. 370–386. Washington, DC: Smithsonian Institution.

Shipley William, ed. and trans. 1991. *The Maidu Indian Myths and Stories of Hanc'ibyjim*. Berkeley, CA: Heyday Books.

U.S. Department of Agriculture. 1997. *Working Together: California Indians and the Forest Service, Accomplishment Report 1997*. Albany, CA: USDA Forest Service, Pacific Southwest Research Station.

Part Four

POLICY AND MANAGEMENT

Federal Nontimber Forest Products Policy and Management

Alexios Antypas, Rebecca J. McLain, Jennifer Gilden, and Greg Dyson

Nontimber forest products harvesters, buyers, and sellers deriving their products from federal lands must negotiate a complex network of laws and land and resource use policies pertaining to these lands. People obtain NTFPs from federal lands administered by five agencies, including the National Forest Service, the National Park Service, the Bureau of Land Management, the U.S. Fish and Wildlife Service, and the Departments of the Army, Navy, and Air Force. Each agency has its own management mandate and is governed by laws and regulations particular to it. At the same time, each agency also falls under the purview of some broad federal laws that pertain to all federal agencies, notably the Endangered Species Act and the National Environmental Policy Act.

Cutting across the various federal land ownerships and specific legal instruments governing federal agency policies are natural resource management practices institutionalized through long application and maintained by universities and professional societies. Professionals in these scientific and managerial communities work within a common set of assumptions and practices, which are then applied to resource management across jurisdictions. Additionally, since the early 1990s federal agencies have had an administratively imposed mandate to apply ecosystem management principles to their management practices. The ecosystem management mandate fosters greater collaboration across federal resource management regimes. While still evolving, ecosystem management constitutes the governing scientific and ideological paradigm for federal land management, at least at the level of broad principle. Since the issuance of Executive Order 12898 in 1994, federal agencies, including land management agencies, have an administrative mandate to ensure that federal land and resource management actions take into account the effects on minority and low-income groups. This environmental justice mandate has enormous potential to affect NTFP management on federal lands.

In this chapter we review and analyze major federal environmental laws, policies, and regulations important for NTFPs. We begin with a discussion of the concepts of ecosystem management and environmental justice as they are used within the federal land management context and describe possible implications of these concepts for nontimber forest products. We then examine three key overarching federal laws that directly or indirectly affect NTFP management: the Endangered Species Act, the Lacey Act, and the National Environmental Policy Act. The discussion of these three laws is followed by a review of specific NTFP policies of the U.S. Forest Service, the Bureau of Land Management, the National Park Service, the U.S. Fish and Wildlife Service, and the Department of Defense. Finally, we end with a discussion of how environmental justice and ecosystem management policies might interact in ways that could be beneficial for people for whom nontimber forest products are important parts of their lives.

ECOSYSTEM MANAGEMENT AND NTFPS

In 1992, the U.S. Forest Service adopted ecosystem management as the guiding policy for managing the lands within their administrative jurisdictions (Robertson 1992). By spring 1994, sixteen additional federal agencies, including the Bureau of Land Management, the U.S. Fish and Wildlife Service, the National Park Service, the Department of Defense, and others, had formally committed themselves in agency policy documents to the principles of ecosystem management (Morrissey, Zinn, and Corn 1994). Considerable ambiguity surrounds the definition of ecosystem management, with each agency using its own definition to guide its ecosystem planning and management efforts. Themes common to all definitions are the notions of managing for biological sustainability in ways that simultaneously incorporate human needs and values (Keiter 1990).

The scientific foundations of ecosystem management run largely counter to those of the traditional resource management sciences developed during the nineteenth-century Progressive Era's conservation reforms (Hays 1959). In many cases, the scientific foundations of ecosystem management conflict with traditional guiding principles of forest resource management aimed at producing high volumes of wood fiber (Franklin 1989). Moreover, ecosystem management contains a political program that some social scientific analysts believe runs counter to the political program of traditional resource management (Cortner and Moote 1999). Ecosystem management is not yet a fully coherent and transparent set of principles upon which the great majority of forest stakeholders agree. Rather, it is a contested ideological field on which industrial, scientific, managerial, and environmentalist factions struggle to define ecosystem management in pursuit of marginal advantages in an antagonistic political setting.

Natural resources policies fall into the category of distributional policies generally. They determine who gets what, when, where, and how. In traditional management regimes, access and rights to resources pass to competing social actors on the basis of availability, efficiency, and, in some cases, social objectives such as rural development. In such cases, resource policy borders on redistributional policy.[1] Ecosystem management has thrown a new component into the debate on the distributional aspects of resource policies because its strongest proponents contend that certain rights and benefits should be granted to ecosystems themselves.

Although still lacking an explicit legislative mandate to pursue ecosystem management, federal land management agencies have increasingly incorporated its principles into their planning and implementation. For example, as noted later in this chapter, the National Park Service and the U.S. Fish and Wildlife Service have shifted the scale of their planning efforts from administrative units, such as parks or refuges, to ecological units, such as watersheds or bioregions. Rather than managing areas for one species or one type of product or service, federal land management agencies now manage for suites of species in ways that maintain critical ecosystem processes and structures. The focus on maintaining ecosystem integrity fundamentally shifts how we manage forests. Rather than emphasizing "what the forests should produce," attention has shifted to "what the forest should be" (Flick and King 1995, 6).

The shift toward ecosystem management carries enormous implications for nontimber forest products and the people who use and manage them. Forests managed for ecosystem integrity and maximum biodiversity will produce much different sets of NTFPs than forests managed principally for single products or uses, such as timber, forage, or recreation. Certain NTFPs will be produced in greater abundance, while others may become less abundant. For example, past fire policies in the western United States favor periodic large-scale fruitings of morel mushrooms in burned areas. New fire management policies designed to decrease the frequency of large-scale fires may also decrease the volume of morels that fruit each year. On the other hand, new fire management policies may encourage the production of other NTFPs, such as huckleberries or grasses and shrubs used as fibers by basket weavers.

The focus on ecosystem management compels agencies to account for the effect of any management actions on a much broader array of species and harvesting activities than in the past. Nontimber forest products are now appearing in environmental impact statements, environmental assessments, and other land planning documents. This development is a double-edged sword for NTFP harvesters and buyers. On the one hand, the visibility of NTFPs in public land planning processes can protect existing product uses and the livelihoods or cultural traditions that are linked to them. For example, after much public debate in the early 1990s, the Oregon Dunes National Recreation Area decided to maintain a commercial matsutake harvesting program because such harvesting was an important local economic activity (Oregon Dunes National Recreation Area 1993). On the other hand, visibility can lead to decisions to shut down commercial NTFP harvesting over large areas, as has happened for matustake mushrooms in the late-successional reserves established in parts of central Oregon under the Northwest Forest Plan (Deschutes, Fremont, and Winema National Forests 1994).

ENVIRONMENTAL JUSTICE AND NTFPS

Further complicating ecosystem management is the as yet unknown role that federal environmental justice policy will or could play in setting rules for resource access and use (see McLain, this volume). Environmental justice calls attention to the need for government policies and actions to reduce the disproportionate health risks that minorities and the poor bear as a result of industrial and waste facilities siting decisions. As a social movement, environmental justice also seeks to redress possible racial and class biases of mainstream environmentalism (Tesh and Williams 1996). This movement has spawned its own scholarly literature and a federal policy response that establishes formal rules and procedures to assure nondiscrimination in federal land management.[2]

The environmental justice debate is now taking a further step. Some scholars argue that environmental justice should be conceived more broadly to encompass the political rights of all persons to be involved in natural resource management decisions, regardless of race or ethnic status (McLain and McDonald 2000). In this case, the right to participate meaningfully in decisions regarding one's environment is seen as the principal benefit to be achieved through environmental justice. In this chapter, we point to trends in ecosystem management policy that are disturbing from the point of view of democratic politics. Executive Order 12898 issued by President Clinton in 1994 seeks in part to expand the issue of power discrepancies into natural resources policy and is as much a part of federal NTFP policy as ecosystem management. Indeed, environmental justice can fit into ecosystem management quite easily because ecosystem management already acknowledges the legitimacy of incorporating social aims into resources management.

Recent studies of the social organization of NTFPs in the United States (Hansis 1998; Richards and Creasey 1996; Love, Jones, and Liegel 1998; Rosengarten 1994) suggest that a number of minority groups, including African Americans, Southeast Asians, Hispanics, and Native Americans, depend upon these products for subsistence goods and income. Nontimber forest products also are extremely important as either a source of primary income or as an economic buffer for low-income rural Euroamericans (Emery 1998; Love, Jones, and Liegel 1998; McLain 2000). The environmental justice executive order thus could come into direct application in the NTFP arena. Land management agencies, in contrast to the Environmental Protection Agency, have not yet taken a lead in applying the environmental justice standards. Perhaps this lack of attention in the forest management agencies is linked to the existence of politically well-organized timber and lumber mill workers. In the case of NTFP users, however, such a high degree of political organization has not yet occurred, making it clear that the agencies have a political imperative to identify and empower these diffuse and underrepresented constituencies under the environmental justice executive order.

OVERARCHING FEDERAL LAWS AFFECTING NTFPS

The five federal agencies with major direct land management responsibilities include the U.S. Forest Service, the Bureau of Land Management, the National Park Service, the U.S. Fish and Wildlife Service, and the Department of Defense. Each agency has its own particular land management mandate as well as laws, policies, and regulations that apply specifically to it. In addition, each agency is subject to the provisions of a number of overarching laws that apply to all federal agencies. Three of the more important federal laws governing land management by federal agencies include the Endangered Species Act, the Lacey Act, and the National Environmental Policy Act. This section examines the major provisions of each of these laws and discusses how they have affected or could potentially affect NTFP harvesting and management.

The Endangered Species Act

Of the three federal laws that most directly pertain to NTFPs, the Endangered Species Act (ESA) is certainly the most well known and controversial. Briefly, the ESA provides a formal procedure through which federal agencies classify species of plants and animals as either threatened or endangered under the law, providing them with stringent protection. The ESA protects plant and animal habitats and in fact intends "to provide a means whereby the ecosystems upon which endangered species and threatened species depend may be conserved" (16 USC Sec. 1531[b]). Despite acknowledging the importance of ecosystems, the ESA focuses fundamentally on preserving species. It does not discriminate among species by their comparative ecological "importance" but rather treats them all equally by providing for their protection and the protection of their habitats as needed in the context of a threatened or endangered species listing. The ESA makes it illegal to harm any individual of a listed species, whether found on private or public land. Only Native Americans may take listed species for subsistence and cultural purposes.

The ESA is a formidable weapon in the fight against the loss of biological diversity. It is a "biologically forcing" law in that the administering agencies[3] may only consider biological criteria when determining whether or not to list a species. Economic, social, and political factors may not be taken into account. This provision of the law is the source of the controversy about it.[4] Giving stakeholders no recourse, and not allowing for a ranking of species in order of ecological importance (with variable obligations to protect them), has created a fear that the ESA threatens private property rights and that it puts the rights of plants and animals above those of humans.

In most cases, the ESA applies without controversy to preserve species and habitat through negotiations with stakeholders. Negotiations might, for instance, involve some limited economic restrictions on private property use. In many cases, only federal or state agencies are involved, and understandings can quickly be reached. However, some cases have engendered deep controversy over the act following the discovery, or suspected discovery, of a threatened or endangered species. Although other laws, such as the National Forest Management Act, are arguably more important in a strictly legal sense, the ESA has become a symbol of oppression and injustice for people who argue that thousands of families and hundreds of communities were jeopardized for the sake of the northern spotted owl in the Pacific Northwest.

To make the ESA more flexible, the U.S. Fish and Wildlife Service has instituted a program under which it makes voluntary agreements with private landowners that allow them to harm species "incidentally" in the course of otherwise lawful activities. The agreements, known as Habitat Conservation Plans (HCPs), were made possible under the 1982 amendments to the ESA but have only come into widespread use under the Clinton administration.[5] An HCP is not an exemption from the ESA but commits landowners to apply land use practices that will minimize harm to species listed as threatened or endangered and provide other biological benefits. HCPs are intended to be win-win solutions to otherwise difficult conflicts over resources and are clearly more popular with private landowners and resource users than across-the-board restrictions imposed by the federal government.

That some species of NTFPs will eventually be listed as endangered or threatened seems quite likely. American ginseng and goldenseal are the most likely candidates at the moment, as both appear in the Convention on International Trade in Endangered Species (CITES) Appendix. Both species are under review by the U.S. Fish and Wildlife Service. Should these species receive federal protection, harvesting them will become illegal. Because their taking would be deliberate and for commercial purposes rather than incidental to another activity, HCPs that include ginseng and goldenseal thus would not be an available instrument for private landowners wishing to exempt their actions from the protections afforded those species by the ESA. However, the ESA is sensitive to the regional distribution and abundance of species, and only in areas where a species is depleted to being threatened or endangered with extinction will it be listed. Also, the domestic production and harvest of species listed in the wild is permitted in the case of plants. Domestication is not always a perfect solution, as some species are thought to be more potent when grown in the wild (e.g., American ginseng). However, domestication does provide the industry with an alternative to complete product substitution. The ESA is likely to affect the ability of NTFP harvesters to gain access to a number of plants they have gathered and should be kept in mind as the regimes for nontimber forest products continue to develop.

The Lacey Act

The Lacey Act became law in 1900 during a time when illegal interstate trade in wildlife, especially birds, was at its height in the United States. Killed for sport, plumage, and the dinner table, game and nongame bird species faced rapid population declines in the latter years of the nineteenth century. The Lacey Act addressed the problem by stemming national trade in which people sometimes shipped across state lines tens of thousands of animals and birds that had been illegally killed in one state (Dunlap 1989). The original act prohibited the interstate transport of game animals and birds killed in violation of state or territorial game laws. Prosecutions immediately followed passage of the legislation to demonstrate the seriousness of the federal government in this matter.

The law also requires that wildlife moved across state lines for commercial purposes be clearly marked, bans the importation of certain invasive species (e.g., house sparrows, European starling, fruit bats) that could harm U.S. agriculture, and directs the federal government to conserve and restore game bird species. The Lacey Act has been amended three times—1935, 1945, and 1981—each time expanding its scope. The 1935 amendments make conducting interstate commerce illegal for species killed in violation of federal or foreign laws, the 1945 amendments ban the importation of wildlife under "inhumane or unhealthful" conditions, and the 1981 amendments overhauled the law, adding fish and rare plants to the list of protected species, expanding the definition of fish and wildlife, adding felony violations, increasing fines and maximum prison terms, and including violations of tribal law and federal treaties under the protection of the act.

The Lacey Act as amended in 1981 is now a comprehensive fish, wildlife, and plant protection statute. It is also a law enforcement statute implemented by Department of the Interior, Department of Agriculture, and Department of Commerce agents with police powers. The act authorizes the U.S. Fish and Wildlife Service to prosecute individuals and organizations who trade in any wild animal illegally taken under federal, state, tribal, treaty, or foreign law, "whether alive or dead, including without limitation any wild mammal, bird, reptile, amphibian, fish, mollusk, crustacean, arthropod, coelenterate, or other invertebrate, whether or not bred, hatched, or born in captivity, and includes any part, product, egg, or offspring thereof" (16 USC Sec. 3371 [a]). Plants covered by the Lacey Act are "any member of the plant kingdom, including roots, seeds, and other parts thereof (but excluding common food crops and cultivators) which is indigenous to any State and which is either (A) listed on an appendix to the Convention on International Trade in Endangered Species or Wild Fauna and Flora, or (B) listed pursuant to any State law that provides for the conservation of species threatened with extinction" (16 USC Sec. 3371 [f]). The law covers all aspects of commerce, including import, export, transport, selling, receiving, acquiring, and buying.

In 1999 the U.S. Fish and Wildlife Service alone conducted over fifteen hundred Lacey Act investigations, although most involved wildlife rather than plants. The act is still primarily used to prosecute violations of wildlife law. One of the most relevant cases for NTFPs was *United States v. McCullough* (1995), based on an Ohio law that regulates ginseng.[6] The court held that ginseng fell into the category of a "common food crop" not protected by the act and therefore did not consider the merits of the government's case. The ruling employs circular reasoning: The more a plant is harvested, the more likely it is to be considered a common food crop, regardless of whether the species is in danger of extinction and protected by state or federal law or the CITES treaty. The McCullough ruling suggests that the Lacey Act may not play a significant role in the NTFP world. However, its specific function of enforcing other laws in the area of interstate and transboundary commerce gives it the potential to become a factor for NTFPs if the responsible agencies focus more energy on pursuing violations involving plants and if courts narrow the definition of "common food crop."

The National Environmental Policy Act

The third important federal law in which NTFPs are implicated is the National Environmental Policy Act (NEPA). Signed into law in 1969 by

President Nixon, the NEPA was a part of the fundamental shift that the federal government made at the end of the 1960s and beginning of the 1970s to recognize and address modern environmental problems.[7] Although the ESA is substantive and the Lacey Act punitive, the NEPA consists of two parts, one substantive and one procedural. The substantive aspect, which states a federal commitment to harmonize relations between humans and nature for the benefit of present and future generations, has not translated into any legally enforceable provisions. Far more important is the act's procedural component, which creates the environmental impact statement (EIS) as an instrument of environmental policy.

The EIS is an interdisciplinary analysis, incorporating both social and natural sciences, of the effects of a proposed action on the human and natural environment. An EIS is required when an initial environmental assessment finds that impacts of major federal actions are likely to be significant. If a finding of no significant impact is found, an EIS is not required and the action can proceed on the basis of the assessment. An EIS must consider a range of alternatives, not merely the one an agency prefers, but it does not require that the least environmentally harmful alternative be chosen or if least harm can be known in advance. The NEPA applies to all federal agencies.

Judicial interpretation of "major federal action" has been quite broad. In 1974 the Forest Service argued before the 8th U.S. Circuit Court that timber sales do not require an EIS because they do not meet the standard of being a "major federal action."[8] The Forest Service maintained that the applicable phrase in the NEPA—"major federal action significantly affecting the quality of the human environment"—was in fact a two-part test. The first part involved determining whether an action was "major." If it was, then the second test determining significance came into play. The court disagreed, holding that the phrase in fact constituted a single test in which an action would be considered major if it significantly affected the environment. A timber sale could not be considered "minor" simply because it was routine, relatively small, or for another reason that did not first take into account its effects on the environment.

In another case (*Hankey v. Kleindienst* 1972), the 2nd U.S. Circuit Court held that significance depends on the presence of a substantive dispute surrounding the size or nature or effects of an action. Agencies should consider whether the negative environmental consequences of an action would exceed consequences of present actions, including cumulative effects. Moreover, the court held that agencies should employ a precautionary approach, preparing an EIS in borderline cases, rather than risk lawsuits and delay. Preparing an EIS is contingent on whether an action by a federal agency will harm the environment in excess of present harm, whether its effects are disputed or in doubt, and whether effects can be considered a small link in a longer chain of causation involving other anticipated or past actions.

In the case of cumulative impacts, the analysis must consider direct and indirect impacts of present, past, and "reasonably foreseeable" actions on a given geographic area (*Fritiofson v. Alexander* 1985). However, "reasonably foreseeable" refers only to proposed actions. If an action has not yet been officially proposed, even if it seems inevitable due to the commitment of resources made in actually proposed actions, the courts have held that it cannot be considered "reasonably foreseeable" (*National Wildlife Federation v. Federal Energy Regulatory Commission* 1990). EIS's must also consider in a single analysis all discrete proposed actions in any functionally or economically related set of actions. Environmental justice is an integral part of these statements as well.

Over the past decade, the federal land management agencies have started to integrate nontimber forest products into their NEPA process. For example, many national forests now include NTFPs in their forest plans. Many also include NTFPs in at least one or more of the following kinds of planning documents: environmental assessments, environmental impact statements, landscape analyses, social impact assessments, watershed analyses, geographic area analyses, and biological assessments. An increasing number of forests are developing NTFP-specific planning and management documents. For example, the Klamath National Forest in northern California has issued an environmental assessment on mushroom management (Klamath National Forest 1993), and the Deschutes, Fremont, and Winema National Forests in central Oregon have issued a joint matsutake mushroom management environmental assessment (Deschutes, Fremont, and Winema National Forests 1994). As noted below, the Bureau of Land Management, the National Park Service, and the U.S. Fish and Wildlife Service also have begun to incorporate NTFPs into their planning processes.

NTFP POLICIES OF FEDERAL LAND MANAGEMENT AGENCIES

U.S. Forest Service

Permanent federal ownership of forestlands for the purpose of long-term management began late in the nineteenth century. The 1891 Creative Act established a system of forest reserves out of public domain lands in the West (Williams 1992, 410), and in 1911 Congress authorized the government to purchase forestlands in the East to add to the system (442). Today the Forest Service manages over 190 million acres of land, most of it in the West, including Alaska. The original intent of the reserves was to protect water and forest resources and to provide timber in times when the private sector could not meet the nation's demands (415). In the 1897 Organic Act, Congress further mandated that residents in and around the forests should have access to resources on the reserves for domestic uses (Steen 1997, 63–64). The agency has developed the dual-purpose mission of resource protection and national and local economic development (Emery 1998).

Until the 1980s, the Forest Service paid little attention to nontimber forest products. In some areas, such as the temperate rain forest on the Pacific Northwest coast, ranger districts, the lowest administrative unit of the Forest Service, developed permit and lease systems for NTFPs such as sword fern, huckleberry branch tips, and salal branch tips, harvested on an industrial scale. However, these systems usually were poorly enforced (McLain 2000). Past inattention to nontimber forest products likely is due to the agency's bias in favor of timber management over other activities and to the fact that timber generated far more revenue than NTFP resources. In the 1980s, as commercial demand for nontimber forest products increased and as the ecological value of these species became more widely acknowledged, the Forest Service began to expand its NTFP regulatory system (Molina et al. 1993; McLain, Christensen, and Shannon 1998).

Four laws play a key role in how the Forest Service currently manages NTFPs: the 1897 Organic Act, the National Forest Management Act (NFMA), the Multiple-Use Sustained-Yield (MUSY) Act, and the National Environmental Policy Act, previously described. The Organic Act sets forth the purposes of the forest reserve system; it also gives the Forest Service authority to establish regulations governing the occupancy and use of national forests and to protect them from destruction. The MUSY Act sets forth management objectives. As the title of the act suggests, these objectives specify that a range of resources be harvested sustainably over time. Among other things, the NFMA provides for a planning procedure for national forests that includes active public participation in the development of forest plans.

The MUSY Act and the NFMA both direct the U.S. Forest Service to provide for and integrate renewable resource management, including timber, range, watershed, fish and wildlife, wilderness, and recreation. As renewable resources, NTFPs fall under the general purposes of both laws, though neither law explicitly mentions them. Regulations in the U.S. Forest Service Manual (USFSM) explicitly state that nontimber forest products can be sold "where it will serve local needs and meet land management objectives" (USFSM 2567.02) set forth in forest plans, subject to fees at fair market value when this is "practical" (USFSM 2467.03).

A number of ranger districts and national forests are also studying NTFPs and the people who harvest them in their jurisdictions. For example, the Rio Grande National Forest in Colorado has recently completed a scientific study of NTFP uses and users to serve as background for future management and planning initiatives (Spero and Fleming, this volume). The Winema National Forest, the Siskiyou National Forest, and the Oregon Dunes National Recreation Area have been partners since the early 1990s in collaborative research efforts with the Forest Service's Pacific Northwest Research Station on matustake mushroom productivity, prices, and harvesting impacts (Hosford et al. 1997). The Gifford Pinchot and Mount Hood National Forests are collaborating on experimental management of huckleberry grounds with the Yakama Nation and Warm Springs Confederated Tribes.

Permits and small sales contracts are the most common ways in which commercial nontimber forest product users gain legal access to NTFPs on national forestlands.[9] The small sales contracts tend to be for woody products, such as firewood, Christmas trees, and boughs. Other products sometimes sold through small sales contracts include ginseng, moss, pine straw, and transplants. Many forests issue free-use permits to noncommercial harvesters; in some cases forests charge for these permits (e.g., firewood permits), while in other cases they are free of charge (e.g., wild mushrooms). Other forests allow harvesters to gather small amounts without obtaining a permit, and some national forests issue buying permits for people wishing to establish temporary buying stations. A few Oregon national forests have established commercial campsites for wild mushroom harvesters. The campsites allow the Forest Service to better monitor and enforce wild mushroom permit requirements; they also provide a means for controlling litter and campfires by concentrating people into a single monitored area. Many harvesters resent the centralized camping system, however, which is at odds with the dispersed camping tradition they had established prior to NTFP regulation (McLain 2000).

At the national level, the Forest Service has given NTFPs more prominence in management concerns since the mid-1990s. In 1994, the Washington office issued a draft strategic plan for nontimber forest products (USDA-FS 1994), the first national document focused on NTFP issues. Although the Washington office has yet to release a final version of that strategy, the draft strategy provides some insights into the directions in which the Forest Service is moving with its NTFP policies. The draft strategy emphasizes integrating nontimber forest products into Forest Service ecosystem management and inventorying and monitoring efforts; it also focuses attention on the importance of public involvement and collaborative management with other agencies, local communities, and nongovernmental organizations in the development and implementation of NTFP-related programs. The draft strategy stresses the community assistance aspect of its NTFP programs as well as greater attention to these products as a means to assist communities in diversifying their economies.

In the fall of 1999, the U.S. Congress included a provision to P.L. 106-

113, the Consolidated FY2000 Appropriations Act, that made the Forest Service the first federal land management agency to receive a legislative mandate regarding how it should manage nontimber forest products (see Appendix to P.L. 106-113 [H.R.3423] Sec. 331). The NTFP section, entitled "Pilot Program of Charges and Fees for Harvest of Forest Botanical Products," includes four provisions that, if applied widely, could greatly affect many NTFP industries that rely heavily on national forestlands. These provisions include fees for harvesting NTFPs that are at least equivalent to their fair market value and also include the costs of running the permitting system, including those associated with environmental or other analyses; analyses to determine whether NTFP harvesting in national forests is sustainable; a prohibition against unsustainable harvest levels; and a special account for the fees so they can be redistributed back to the originating administrative unit to administer NTFP programs and conduct NTFP inventories, studies, and restoration activities.

The law has generated great uncertainty in the nontimber forest product community, which reacted in surprise to its appearance. In an informal survey of ten ranger districts in Oregon conducted in winter 2000 by one of the authors of this chapter, most NTFP coordinators did not know how the rider would affect their programs in upcoming years. Two districts considered shutting down their NTFP programs entirely when they initially received news of the law because of concerns about lawsuits from environmental organizations. Both districts subsequently reversed course after the regional office issued a memo clarifying that the law merely established pilot programs in a few areas and was not meant to apply everywhere.

One difficulty presented by the law is establishing and updating fair market values for the hundreds of nontimber forest products now harvested in national forests. A second point of controversy concerns the requirement that permit fees cover the costs of administration, environmental and social impact analyses, and monitoring and enforcement costs. This requirement may lead to fees too high for most harvesters to pay and may exclude economically marginalized participants for whom NTFPs provide an important buffer against financial uncertainty and hardship. A third point of controversy concerns the sustainable harvest requirement. As other chapters in this book have pointed out, the existing body of scientific knowledge on sustainable harvest for most NTFPs is limited.

The above overview of U.S. Forest Service policies and regulations suggests that the agency has taken steps to extend its capacity and authority to incorporate NTFPs into its planning and management programs and activities. The agency has sought to bring order to NTFP harvesting on national forestlands by creating systems that allow it to identify and keep track of harvesters and, to a lesser degree, of quantities of NTFPs harvested. At the same time, however, many of the agency's laws and regulations directly or indirectly affecting NTFP management are developed with little understanding of nontimber forest product ecology, markets, or cultural traditions, and enforcement is often resource-intensive. A similar situation exists with respect to the Bureau of Land Management, whose policies and regulations pertaining to NTFPs are described below.

Bureau of Land Management

The Bureau of Land Management (BLM) was created in 1946 from the General Land Office (established in 1812) and the Grazing Service (established in 1934) and is a subdivision of the Department of the Interior (Cawley 1993). The BLM is a relatively decentralized agency with field office managers exercising considerable discretion. It is divided into state offices, which oversee and coordinate activities of districts, which in turn oversee and coordinate the activities of resource areas, the field administrative units of the agency. The BLM manages 269 million acres of land in the United States, most of which is located west of the Mississippi or in Alaska. With the exception of heavily forested lands in western Oregon, northern California, and Alaska (much of which is managed as wilderness), the BLM's holdings are predominantly grasslands, dry montane forests, desertlands, and arctic tundra.

The Federal Land Policy and Management Act (FLPMA) of 1976 serves as organic legislation for the Bureau of Land Management, providing the agency with its mandate and guiding principles for managing the lands under its jurisdiction. Under FLPMA, the nation's public lands are managed "on the basis of multiple use and sustained yield unless otherwise specified by law" (P.L. 94-579, Sec. 102[a][7]). The act requires the BLM to manage the lands under its jurisdiction in ways that protect a broad array of cultural, ecological, and aesthetic values as well as fish and wildlife habitats, outdoor recreation settings, and settings for other types of human use and occupancy. At the same time, FLPMA also requires that the lands be managed "in a manner which recognizes the Nation's need for domestic sources of minerals, foods, timber, and fiber" (P.L. 94-579 Sec. 102[a][12]). Thus, like the U.S. Forest Service, the BLM has mandates for both environmental protection and economic development. Moreover, the agency has a mandate to obtain fair market value for uses of those lands (P.L. 94-579 Sec. 102[a][9]). Like the National Forest Management Act, FLPMA also contains requirements for developing land use plans through a public involvement and review process.

Although the act does not mention nontimber forest products directly, FLPMA's provisions call for multiple use, protecting values and habitats on public lands, meeting the nation's needs for raw materials, and obtaining fair market values, which also apply to NTFPs. Nontimber forest products located on BLM land in Alaska are subject to the provisions of the Alaska

National Interest Lands Conservation Act and thus are treated differently from NTFPs located on other agency holdings (see Schroeder, this volume).

The Bureau of Land Management is not currently working on a national strategy for managing NTFPs on its holdings. However, the BLM was the first federal land management agency to appoint a major task force to review NTFP management for forestlands under its authority and was also the first to publish an official handbook that focuses specifically on NTFP management procedures. The agency's Special Forest Product (SFP) Task Force and the subsequent SFP *Manual Supplement* originated in debates during the late 1980s and early 1990s over how to manage NTFPs in the BLM-administered forests in Oregon (BLM 1992, 1994).

The agency's interest in addressing NTFP management issues grew out of a series of events that took place in the Pacific Northwest during the 1980s (BLM 1992). Chief among these events was the downturn in timber sales in the early 1980s that resulted in massive layoffs in forest-related industries and a decline in agency revenues from the sale of timber. To maintain some revenues, the BLM explored possibilities for expanding sales of other forest products. Through these sales activities, agency staff developed familiarity with NTFPs. At the same time, the controversy over the northern spotted owl and old-growth forest management led the BLM to pay closer attention to biodiversity and protecting threatened and endangered species and habitats. A sudden increase during the 1980s in commercial demand for large amounts of NTFPs (Pacific yew bark, bear grass, and wild mushrooms) further expanded the agency's institutional awareness of nontimber forest products as potential commodities. The increase in demand for NTFPs prompted fears within the agency that the prevailing low levels of product regulation and enforcement were inadequate to prevent ecological damage from NTFP harvesting.

In late 1991, a team of BLM administrative and field staff members identified key issues that they felt inhibited effective management of NTFPs in Oregon (BLM 1992). These issues included difficulties with contract and permit administration, consistent contract forms and provisions, pricing, meeting NEPA requirements, tracking quantities sold, inventory and monitoring, developing staff qualified to handle NTFP management and law enforcement, public education, and road maintenance concerns. During 1992, the task force identified a range of options available to address these issues, and a number of the recommended solutions were subsequently incorporated into the policies and guidelines of the *SFP Procedure Series: BLM Manual Supplement Handbook 5400-2*. The handbook constituted a first step in the agency's effort to develop more uniform standards and guidelines for NTFP management.

Responsibility for NTFP programs in the BLM rests with the district managers, who in turn can delegate responsibility to the managers of the different resource areas. The resource area managers then assign staff members to administer and monitor nontimber forest product program activities, including inventories, sales, and enforcement. Administration of NTFP sales and permits and enforcement of sale and permit provisions tend to be handled by separate sections of the agency, and coordination between the two sections is often poor. Only BLM employees or other designated federal employees are authorized to collect sale revenues for nontimber forest products. From the harvesters' standpoint, this policy complicates NTFP harvesting, since hours for selling products are restricted and low staffing levels can negatively affect the ability of the agency to deal with the demand for permits. This is less of a problem for products such as floral greens, where timing of harvests is less critical for product quality than for ephemeral or perishable wild foods products.

The handbook (BLM 1994) lists eighteen of the most important federal regulations that affect NTFP management on BLM lands. Many of these regulations provide guidelines for how to conduct sales and other forms of product disposal, specifics of contract provisions and bonds, and circumstances under which products may be available free of charge. Other regulations guide people's behavior in the woods, including trespass, littering, fire prevention, and use of firearms. Oregon laws regarding unlawful harvest and transport of nontimber forest products as well as littering, species protection, and fire prevention also affect NTFP activities on BLM lands in that state.

The Bureau of Land Management has three use categories for plant resources on its lands: incidental use, personal use, and commercial use (BLM 1994). Incidental use includes such things as gathering branches for campfires and gathering small quantities of wild mushrooms or berries, generally for immediate consumption. Incidental use, however, is not permitted for very valuable, threatened, or endangered species. Persons wishing to remove plant resources from BLM lands for personal or commercial use must obtain a written contract or permit from the agency office responsible for administering that area. Persons who remove materials for anything other than incidental use and who fail to obtain a contract or permit are liable for prosecution as trespassers.

The BLM has three major mechanisms for selling nontimber forest products: negotiated sales, advertised sales, and leases (BLM 1994). Most agency NTFP program managers rely on negotiated sales to provide people with commercial access to NTFPs. Negotiated sales use a one-page form and apply to resources valued at less than $2,500 and with little likelihood of damage to natural resources or BLM investments, such as roads, ditches, or culverts, from NTFP harvests. Negotiated sales serve the public interest when it is best to remove the resource quickly, when the product is spatially scattered, when product values and demand are low, and when the BLM cannot guarantee access to the site. Advertised sales are required when products are valued at $2,500 or more. As a rule of thumb, the BLM manual suggests that program administrators advertise NTFP sales when doing so is in the agency's best financial interest, when there is a large concentrated resource supply, when the product has a high value, and when demand exceeds supply.

Whether negotiated or advertised, no sales can cover a period of longer than thirty-six months, and most contracts are for less than a year. Long-term leases for NTFPs are permitted, but few districts in Oregon make use of leases as mechanisms for disposing of these products. Generally, long-term leases are used when the districts involved want to encourage longer term investment and maintenance activities. For example, the Medford district in southern Oregon is considering using such contracts for harvesting conifer boughs under power lines.

The BLM can allow people to collect reasonable amounts of common flowers, berries, nuts, seeds, cones, and leaves for noncommercial use. However, for products in high demand, such as firewood, quinine conk, and prince's pine, the agency charges a fee for the noncommercial use permit. For other products, such as mushrooms and berries, no fee is charged. Where state laws regarding maximum noncommercial quantities are more restrictive than BLM regulations, state law prevails (BLM 1994).

Harvesting NTFPs for sale or barter is prohibited on large areas of agency lands (BLM 1994), including wilderness areas, areas of critical environmental concern, recreational sites, research natural areas, designated riparian reserves or management areas, outstanding natural areas, recreation sites, Wild and Scenic River segments, and areas where there are endangered, threatened, or special status species. In addition, some areas covered by treaties or other agreements with Native Americans are also off-limits to commercial harvesting. The sale and harvest of NTFPs is not permitted on timber harvesting units once the rights to harvest those units have been sold or the unit has been cruised by the timber purchaser.

Like the U.S. Forest Service, the Bureau of Land Management has sought to respond both to the rise in economic, recreational, and cultural demands for NTFPs as well as the ecological concerns voiced over the increased levels of harvesting of such products on federal lands. Common to both agencies is the existence of three-part user categorization systems, in which NTFP harvesters are classified into commercial harvesters, personal use harvesters, and incidental harvesters. As noted earlier in this volume (Alexander, Weigand, and Blatner; Jones and Lynch; Spero and Fleming), many NTFP harvesters move back and forth between commercial and personal use harvesting, and as a result, conflict over what constitutes commercial harvesting pervades nontimber forest product policy discussions (BLM 1992; McLain 2000). Both agencies have also taken steps to incorporate NTFPs into their planning processes, including the development of environmental assessments and environmental impact statements for these products in areas where their harvesting is controversial. At the same time, NTFP harvesting has become increasingly limited spatially, as more and more areas are declared off-limits to commercial and/or noncommercial harvesting of plants and fungi. The result has been a progressive concentration of harvesters in those areas still legally open to NTFP uses. While such concentration facilitates monitoring and enforcement of NTFP harvesting regulations, it may in some cases be ecologically counterproductive.

National Park Service

Unlike the Forest Service and Bureau of Land Management, which have dual mandates of protection and development, the role of the National Park Service (NPS) is to protect natural resources and settings (NPSSP 1997b). Congress created the agency within the Department of the Interior in 1916 with the passage of the National Park Service Act (Sellars 1997). It now comprises 378 units covering more than 83.3 million acres in every state except Delaware.[10] These include national parks, national monuments, historic sites and parks, battlefields, military parks, lakeshores, seashores, recreation areas, scenic rivers and trails, and the White House.

The National Park Service Act directs the agency to "provide for public enjoyment while leaving resources unimpaired for future generations." This broad directive allows a degree of autonomy for the superintendents of each NPS unit; however, park regulations also emphasize nonconsumptive park uses. The National Park Service does not manage its lands for multiple uses, but rather for ecological integrity and nonconsumptive recreation. Harvesting NTFPs is allowed only when specifically authorized by treaty rights, federal laws, or other existing rights (36CFR2.1[c] and [d]). Each park's superintendent may permit specified traditional activities such as berry picking and fishing within specified regulatory parameters. These include that harvesting be limited to personal consumption, that it not harm wildlife, plants, or other resources, and that it not be for religious or ceremonial purposes already prohibited by law or treaty (36 CFR 2.1[c] and [d]). The sale or other commercial use of products obtained from national parks is prohibited.

National parks permit subsistence uses of NTFPs, but only if laws or treaties protect those activities. Moreover, the NPS allows subsistence uses only when they are "consistent with sound management principles and managed so that the composition, condition, and distribution of native plant and animal communities and ecosystem dynamics are not significantly altered" (NPSSP 1997c). An example of non-Indian gathering of NTFPs can be found at Big Cypress National Park in Florida, where the superintendent has permitted the gathering by hand of tree snails *(Liguus fasciatus)* for personal use, provided that no significant adverse impacts result to park resources, wildlife populations, or visitor enjoyment of resources (36 CFR 7.86[e]).

The American Indian Religious Freedom Act (42 USC 1996) states that "it shall be the policy of the United States to protect and preserve for American Indians their inherent right to freedom to believe, express, and exercise the traditional religions of the American Indians, Eskimo, Aleut, and Native Hawaiians, including but not limited to access to sites, use and possession of sacred objects, and the freedom to worship through ceremonials and traditional rites." This act allows Native Americans to use traditional resources located in NPS units where protected by treaties and other legislation. However, where access to sites and resources is not specifically guaranteed by preexisting law, "requests to conduct Native American activities will be subject to the same criteria as other special park uses" (NPSSP 1997a). Examples of Native American use of NPS resources include Miccosukee tribal members' cutting of bald cypress for domestic use in Big Cypress National Preserve, tribal mining of catlinite at Pipestone National Monument, and Navajo collection of medicines and dyes at Glen Canyon. Members of unrecognized or nontreaty tribes abide by the same regulations as non-Indians (NPSSP 1997a).

An interesting development that may have indirect implications for NTFP users on NPS lands has occurred at Yellowstone National Park.[11] After the discovery of heat-loving, or thermophilic, microbial organisms in Yellowstone's geysers in the 1970s, a private firm used a specimen of one type of organism to develop the Polymerase Chain Reaction process, which resulted in sales of over $500 million. The Park Service was not compensated. In response, it has begun to develop policies and relationships that will allow further research on thermophilic organisms leading to commercial applications but with direct financial benefits to the agency. One contract has already been signed, but a lawsuit by the Edmonds Institute, International Center for Technology Assessment, and Alliance for the Wild Rockies has stopped the program. These organizations claimed that while firms stood to reap large profits, the public would be inadequately compensated under the existing scheme. The federal district court for the District of Columbia agreed and ordered an environmental assessment. This case demonstrates that the Park Service may allow commercial uses of its resources, although harvesting microbes may not harm the resource base in the ways that harvesting other products might.

U.S. Fish and Wildlife Service

The U.S. Fish and Wildlife Service's (USFWS) approach to NTFPs lies in between the Forest Service's and the BLM's more commodity production–

oriented approach and the National Park Service's prohibition of most commercial and many recreational uses of nontimber forest products. The USFWS, which is the third largest federal land management agency in the United States, is charged with managing the National Wildlife Refuge System (NWRS). The NWRS is composed of 509 refuges covering an area of almost 93 million acres.[12] USFWS policies are made at the national level and are fairly centralized compared to other land management agencies, such as the Forest Service and the Bureau of Land Management. The USFWS's lands are divided into seven administrative regions, each of which has some autonomy in refuge policies. Under the provisions of the National Wildlife Refuge System Administration Act of 1966 (NWRSA Act), the individual refuges were joined into a system but retained a high degree of autonomy in terms of purposes and planning. The passage of the National Wildlife Refuge Improvement Act (NWRIA) (P.L. 105-57) in 1997, however, created a more centralized system, with policies and regulations spelled out in the USFWS manual rather than in refuge manuals.

The USFWS is currently rewriting its policies to conform to the requirements of the NWRIA. One goal of rewriting existing policies is to attain greater consistency in policies within the agency and, to the extent possible, to develop policies that are consistent with those of other state and federal agencies. This policy revision is expected to take from three to five years and is likely to have some effect on the ways in which NTFPs are managed on USFWS lands. One debate concerns the policy that the agency should adopt about allowing bioprospecting activities on national wildlife refuges. In addition, any efforts to make NTFP harvesting rules on national wildlife refuges consistent with each other or with state and other federal agency regulations governing these products could also affect NTFP resources and users (possibly by making them more restrictive).

National wildlife refuges are different from Forest Service and BLM lands in that their main purpose is the protection of fish, wildlife, and plant resources and their habitats rather than multiple use. The NWRIA states that "the mission of the System is to administer a national network of lands and waters for the conservation, management, and where appropriate, restoration of the fish, wildlife, and plant resources and their habitats within the United States for the benefit of present and future generations of Americans" (Sec. 4). Although NTFP management is not specifically addressed in the act or in any national USFWS strategy documents, the mission of the new national wildlife refuge system includes plant resources and habitats in the list of resources to be conserved, managed, or restored; it also requires that the agency maintain the "biological integrity, diversity, and environmental health of the system" (NWRIA Sec. 5[4][B]). These two provisions give the agency clear jurisdiction over the use and management of a wide variety of nontimber forest products located on national wildlife refuges as well as their habitats. Importantly, however, both commercial and noncommercial NTFP harvesting are potentially allowable on national wildlife refuges, provided such use is compatible with the purposes of the refuge and does not jeopardize public safety. The NWRIA requires refuges to prepare conservation plans within fifteen years of enactment. The plans must take NTFPs into account, whether they are identified as consumable species or not.

USFWS regulations on specialized uses also affect the conditions under which NTFPs can be harvested on national wildlife refuges (USFWS Refuge Manual 5 RM 17.1–17.14). Specialized uses, which can involve "funds, refuge products, or exchange of goods, services, or privileges," can be authorized only by establishing a "permit, contract, agreement, or other form of authorization for documentation purposes" (USFWS Refuge Manual 5 RM 17.3). A fee is generally required for specialized use permits, although there are exceptions that potentially could apply to some NTFP activities. These include a fee exemption if administrative costs consume most of the money gained by the fees or if the system proves impractical. Exemptions are also possible if the market demand for the use is low and the refuge derives some benefit from the use that compensates for the costs incurred in supporting it. Noncommercial firewood cutting is one of the uses specifically mentioned in the regulations. Fair market value is usually the basis for the fee rate unless that value is insufficient to cover government costs, in which case the highest prevailing rate is assessed. Fair market value is established either through a competitive bid process or is based on the use of prevailing rates in the private sector.

Although the regulations recommend that managers use an unbiased system such as a lottery, auction, or first-come, first-served permit process to allocate uses where demand exceeds supply, they allow a preference-ranking approach for cases where a priority system might be more appropriate. Previous permittees and cooperators take precedence over other users, followed by former landowners, former tenants, resident neighbors, nonresidents, and, finally, applicants from outside the local vicinity. Fees can be set either at the refuge or the regional level, depending on the refuge manager's warrant authority. Although the regulations recommend that managers issue annual or short-term permits, the fact that preference can be given to previous permittees sets up the potential for relative tenure security and thus, in the case of NTFP harvesting, provides tenure incentives for permittees to use sustainable harvesting practices.

Department of Defense

The Department of Defense manages 25 million acres of public lands ranging from the arid Mojave Desert to coastal rain forests. These lands include habitat for approximately two hundred federally listed plants and animals (Leslie et al. 1996). Apart from their primary mission of national defense, the army, navy, and air force manage their lands for multiple uses, some of which include recreation, agricultural leases, sales of timber products, and protection of endangered or rare plant and wildlife habitat. Regulations governing the Department of Defense that potentially affect NTFPs include the Sikes Act, the Forest Resources Conservation and Shortage Relief Act, the Military Construction Authorization Act, the Outdoor Recreation–Federal/State Programs Act, and the Defense Appropriations Act of 1991 Legacy Program. The Sikes Act provides a framework for managing natural resources on military lands (see *Federal Wildlife and Related Laws Handbook*, chap. 4). Under the Sikes Act, the secretary of defense plans for the development, maintenance, and coordination of fish, wildlife, and game conservation and rehabilitation in each military reservation in cooperation with the secretary of the interior and appropriate state agencies. Cooperative planning provides for habitat improvements, range rehabilitation, and protection of plants, fish, and wildlife that are considered threatened or endangered. Sales and leases of land must be compatible with cooperative plans, which are reviewed every five years. State fish and wildlife agencies are given priority in managing fish and wildlife activities on military reservations.

The Sikes Act also specifies that the secretary for each command (army, navy, and air force) manages the natural resources of his or her respective military reservation under the jurisdiction of the secretary of defense in a manner that is both consistent with the reservation's military mission and provides for sustained multiple use of resources and public access to resources. The act also authorizes the secretary of defense to carry out outdoor recreation programs on military reservations in cooperation with the secretary of the interior and state agencies.

The Forest Resources Conservation and Shortage Relief Act regulates the export of unmilled timber originating on federal land, and the Military Construction Authorization Act provides for the leasing of public lands and the production and sale of forest products. Both acts potentially affect NTFPs through the indirect effect of these regulations on military reservations' forest management. Timber cutting programs, for example, can greatly affect the supply and quality of understory plants and fungi sought by NTFP harvesters. However, neither law mentions NTFPs explicitly. The Outdoor Recreation–Federal/State Programs Act, which defines the management of lands for recreation, potentially could restrict recreational harvesting of nontimber forest products. Similarly, the Defense Appropriations Act of 1991 Legacy Program, which established a program for the stewardship of biological, geophysical, cultural, and historic resources on Department of Defense lands, could potentially include NTFPs in its stewardship efforts.

At the present time, the army, navy, and air force do not have very active NTFP programs. All three branches have adopted ecosystem management, allow timber harvesting, and emphasize rare species protection.[13] However, some nontimber forest products are made available to the public, including fuelwood, Christmas trees, conifer boughs, and floral greens on army lands and firewood on air force lands. The extent to which other NTFPs are actually harvested on Department of Defense lands is unknown. Commanding officers of individual branch units make decisions regarding resource uses. Consequently, a significant degree of variation of NTFP access and use exists across the hundreds of military installations in the United States.

CONCLUSION

At first glance, nontimber forest products seem to occupy a marginal place in federal resource management. Within the two largest federal land management agencies, the Bureau of Land Management and the Forest Service, NTFPs have neither the economic clout nor the organized constituency that other resources and uses like timber and recreation have. On National Park Service and USFWS lands, NTFP harvesting is permitted only within the constraints of those agencies' ecological protection mandates. On Department of Defense lands, NTFP harvesting is secondary to the agency's military defense mandate. However, developing NTFP markets and communities of users is a responsibility that land managing agencies need to examine more carefully. With the shift away from heavy timber production on federal forests and the adoption of ecosystem management policies, NTFP development exemplifies low-impact, multiresource use that is more compatible with diverse and increasing uses. In this period of rapid change in federal land management policies, incorporating NTFPs more fully into forest management can allow land managing agencies to design programs that meet some people's expectation that federal lands be managed for ecological sustainability as well as for social and economic benefits.

For policy makers, ecosystem management represents an attractive alternative to traditional timber industry–oriented policy because it promises some resource output, addresses conflicts over rare species, and prevents policy paralysis. The hope among policy makers that ecosystem management will provide some certainty for federal land use by keeping species off the threatened and endangered lists should not be underestimated as a motivating force behind the adoption of ecosystem management policy. Policy makers and scientists thus have what might be called a convergence of interests, with policy makers seeking the assistance of scientists in solving a potentially long-term political problem in the resources field (i.e., ever greater numbers of threatened and endangered species, making long-range planning and management impossible). Reciprocally, scientists need the decision-making authority of policy makers to implement what they believe are better ways to manage land and resources. Indeed, even interest groups have stood to gain, with environmentalists being encouraged, for instance, by the 80 percent reduction of timber harvested on federal lands in the Northwest following the implementation of ecosystem management, and the industry relieved to have some certainty upon which to make long-term planning and higher prices for wood due to the reduced cut. Missing in the equation is a way to include stakeholders in federal resources and lands who are not organized into interest groups and who may have different ideas about managing federal resources.

Proponents of ecosystem management frequently comment that people should understand themselves as parts of ecosystems. In this view, ecosystems are complex wholes, with people and all other organic and inorganic elements being parts. But people are not a part of ecosystems, nor is society somehow integrated into ecosystems as a constituent part. The very ability of human beings to transcend, destroy, and redesign systems characterizes their special place on the planet. Far from being limited by either instinct or environmental conditions, as are all other organisms in nature, human society continues to evolve at a rate that makes the rate of natural evolution look glacial. Human social evolution is not an orderly sequence, nor are human social systems subject to well-engineered interventions that produce predictable outcomes. Instead, human society is a loosely organized constellation of disparate and often antagonistic elements, each of which has a high degree of autonomy to determine its own future. Furthermore, in an American society characterized by democratic politics, the notion that society must serve nature (or ecosystems) before it serves itself is doomed to failure when the interests of society and ecosystems come into sharp conflict.

Although some agencies, notably the Forest Service and the BLM, have developed rudimentary policies and management regimes for NTFPs, the lack of participation by major stakeholders is troubling. In addition, federal agencies continue to rank NTFPs as secondary to other resources. Operating under ecosystem management mandates, agencies have an unprecedented opportunity to meet societal needs for resources while also addressing ecological concerns. However, ecosystem management is also potentially a tool with which land managers and policy makers can exclude NTFP users from resources. Principles of environmental justice should extend to nontimber forest product interest groups to ensure that NTFP users participate meaningfully in the management of these products. Indeed, the case for participation is especially strong for NTFPs because for many species, the harvesters themselves know more about forest species than agency staffs do or can, given limited resources. This "local" knowledge should not be squandered but rather translated into verifiable ecological knowledge. The growing scope of NTFPs offers the federal land management agencies an opportunity to integrate social and ecological policy, to achieve sustainability of resources, social institutions, legitimacy, and justice. These should be the goals of the federal land managers and policy makers as they draw upon the potent conceptual and practical resources contained within the ecosystem management and environmental justice frameworks.

NOTES

1. Some environmentalists have long argued that national forest management policy has in fact been redistributional in the sense that it subsidized the timber industry with public resources by providing below-cost sales. For the classic presentation of this argument, see Randall O'Toole, *Reforming the Forest Service* (Washington, DC: Island Press, 1988).

2. For a comprehensive discussion of the range of issues involved in the environmental justice movement up to this point, see David Schlosberg. *Environmental Justice and the New Pluralism* (Oxford: Oxford University Press, 1999).

3. The U.S. Fish and Wildlife Service is responsible for listings of terrestrial species and freshwater species, and the National Marine Fisheries Service for marine mammals and anadromous fish.

4. The most famous case involves the Tellico Dam in Tennessee and a small fish called the snail darter, but other cases such as the California gnatcatcher, the northern spotted owl, and the Snake River salmon have galvanized conflicts between conservationists and proponents of private property rights.

5. By 1992, only 14 HCPs had been prepared; by the end of 1999, over 290 were in effect.

6. Ohio Revised Code §1518.24.

7. Other contemporaneous or nearly contemporaneous developments included the creation of the Environmental Protection Agency and the Council on Environmental Quality and passage of the Clean Air Act, Clean Water Act, and Endangered Species Act.

8. *Minnesota Public Interest Research Group v. Butz,* 498 F.2d 1314 (8th Cir. 1974).

9. Data on the U.S. Forest Service's NTFP policies and management practices are derived from preliminary analysis of an e-mail survey that the editors of this book sent out to national forests across the United States during 1999.

10. See the National Park Service's official website: *http://www.nps.gove/legacy/acreage.html* for a description of the extent and types of national parks.

11. See the following websites for additional details on conflicts over bioprospecting in Yellowstone National Park: National Park Service (1999), "Bioprospecting in Yellowstone," located at *http://www.nps.gov/yell/nature/thermophiles/biopro.html;* Alliance for Wild Rockies news release, March 28, 1999, at *http://www.wildrockiesalliance.org/programs/publications/networkers/*

networker.html; Sue Consolo-Murphy and Tami Blackford, April 28, 1998, "First Bioprospecting Agreement Targeted in Yellowstone," Center for Resources, Yellowstone National Park, located at *http://www.aqd.nps.gov/pubs/yr_rvw97/chapter06/chapter06_a01.html.*

12. Information on the USFWS refuge system was obtained from the Fish and Wildlife Service's official website, *http://www.fws.gov.*

13. See for example, Air Force Instruction 32-7064 (July 1994), which provides guidelines on how installations should manage their natural resources. It defines forest products as "plant materials in wooded areas that have commercial value." Forest management objectives include maintaining biological diversity and balance, protecting watersheds and wildlife habitat, and managing forestlands for multiple use. The only specific reference to "minor" forest products is in section 8.3.2: "Users may harvest minor forest products such as firewood for picnic and camping sites without charge if the forest management component of the integrated natural resources plan details such use." The priority of ecosystem protection is reflected in section 8.3.6, which states that commercial harvesting of forest products must include safeguards for ecosystem structure and function. Similar provisions are included in Army Regulation 200-3 (Natural Resources—Land, Forest, and Wildlife Management) and Chief of Naval Operations Instruction (OPNAVINST) 5090.1B, chapter 22.

REFERENCES

Bureau of Land Management. 1992. *Managing Special Forest Products in Oregon and Washington: BLM Task Force Draft Report.* Portland, OR: Bureau of Land Management, Oregon State Office.

———. 1994. *Special Forest Products Procedure Series: BLM Manual Supplement Handbook 5400-2.* Portland, OR: Bureau of Land Management, Oregon State Office.

Cawley, R. McGregor. 1993. *Federal Land, Western Anger: The Sagebrush Rebellion and Environmental Politics.* Lawrence: University Press of Kansas.

Cortner, Hannah, and Margaret Moote. 1999. *The Politics of Ecosystem Management.* Washington, DC: Island Press.

Deschutes, Fremont, and Winema National Forests. 1994. *Matsutake Mushroom Management Plan.* USDA Forest Service, Pacific Northwest Region.

Dunlap, Thomas R. 1989. "The Federal Government, Wildlife, and Endangered Species." In *Government and Environmental Politics: Essays on Historical Developments since World War Two,* ed. Michael J. Lacey, pp. 209–232. Washington, DC: Woodrow Wilson International Center for Scholars.

Emery, M. R. 1998. "Invisible Livelihoods: Nontimber Forest Products in Michigan's Upper Peninsula." Ph.D. diss., Rutgers University.

Flick, Warren A., and William E. King. 1995. "Ecosystem Management As American Law." *Renewable Resources Journal* (Autumn): 6–11.

Franklin, Jerry. 1989. "Towards a New Forestry, " *American Forests* (November/December): 37–44.

Hansis, R. 1998. "A Political Ecology of Picking: Nontimber Forest Products in the Pacific Northwest." *Human Ecology* 26(1): 67–86.

Hays, Samuel P. 1959. *Conservation and the Gospel of Efficiency: The Progressive Conservation Movement, 1890–1920.* Cambridge, MA: Harvard University Press.

Hosford, David, David Pilz, Randy Molina, and Michael Amaranthus. 1997. *Ecology and Management of the Commercially Harvested American Matsutake Mushroom.* USDA Forest Service General Technical Report 412. Portland, OR: Pacific Northwest Research Station.

Keiter, Robert B. 1990. "NEPA and the Emerging Concept of Ecosystem Management on the Public Lands." *Land and Water Law Review* 25(1): 43–60.

Klamath National Forest. October 1993. *Environmental Assessment: Mushroom Management,* USDA Forest Service.

Leslie, M. G. K. Meffe, J. L. Hardesty, and D. L. Adams. 1996. *Conserving Biodiversity on Military Lands: A Handbook for Natural Resources Managers.* Arlington, VA: Nature Conservancy.

Love, Thomas, Eric Jones, and Leon Liegel. 1998. "Valuing the Temperate Rainforest: Wild Mushrooming on the Olympic Peninsula Biosphere Reserve." *Ambio Special Report* 9:16–25.

McLain, Rebecca J. 2000. "Controlling the Forest Understory: Wild Mushroom Politics in Central Oregon." Ph.D. diss., University of Washington, Seattle.

McLain, Rebecca J., Harriet H. Christensen, and Margaret A. Shannon. 1998. "When Amateurs Are the Experts: Amateur Mycologists and Wild Mushroom Politics in the Pacific Northwest, USA." *Society and Natural Resources* 11:615–626.

McLain, Rebecca J., and Eric T. Jones. 2001. "Expanding NTFP Harvester/Buyer Participation in Pacific Northwest Forest Policy." *Journal of Sustainable Forestry* 13(3/4): 147–161.

McLain, Rebecca J., and Kim McDonald. 2000. "Exploring the Boundaries of Environmental Justice: Excluded Stakeholders in Natural Resource Policymaking." Paper presented at the Natural Resources Law Center's Workshop on Environmental Justice, Denver, April 14–15.

Molina, Randy, Thomas O'Dell, Daniel Luoma, Michael Amaranthus, Michael Castellano, and Kenelm Russell. 1993. *Biology, Ecology, and Social Aspects of Wild Edible Mushrooms in the Forests of the Pacific Northwest: A Preface to Managing Commercial Harvest.* USDA–Forest Service General Technical Report PNW-GTR-309. Portland, OR: Pacific Northwest Research Station.

National Park Service Strategic Plan (NPSSP). 1997a. Native American Use, at *www.nps.gov/planning/mngmtplc/upna.html.*

———. 1997b. Park Planning Home Page, Natural Resource Management, at *www.nps.gov/planning/mngmtplc/npsmptoc.html.*

———. 1997. Special Park Uses, at *www.nps.gov/planning/mngmtplc/upsp.html,* pp. 6–7.

Oregon Dunes National Recreation Area. September 1993. *Environmental Assessment: Mushroom Harvesting,* Siuslaw National Forest, USDA Forest Service.

Richards, Rebecca T., and Max Creasey. 1996. "Ethnic Diversity, Resource Values, and Ecosystem Management: Matsutake Mushroom Harvesting in the Klamath Bioregion." *Society and Natural Resources* 9:359–374.

Robertson, F. Dale. June 4, 1992. "Memo to Regional Foresters and Station Directors Regarding Ecosystem Management of the National Forests and Grasslands, U.S. Department of Agriculture–Forest Service." Washington, DC. Pp. 1–3 plus Attachment 1 entitled "Working Guidelines for Ecosystem Management," Attachment 2 entitled "Clear-Cutting on the National Forests," and Attachment 3 entitled "USDA to Eliminate Clear-Cutting as Standard Practice on National Forests." Documents on file with author.

Rosengarten, Dale. 1994. "'Sweet Grass Is Gold': Natural Resources, Conservation Policy, and African-American Basketry." In *Conserving Culture: A New Discourse on Heritage,* ed. Mary Hufford, pp. 152–163. Urbana: University of Illinois Press.

Sellars, Richard West. 1997. *Preserving Nature in the National Parks: A History.* New Haven, CT: Yale University Press.

Steen, Harold K. 1997. "The Beginning of the National Forest System." In *American Forests: Nature, Culture, and Politics,* ed. Char Miller, pp. 49–68. Lawrence: University Press of Kansas.

Tesh, Sylvia N., and Bruce A. Williams. 1996. "Identity Politics, Disinterested Politics, and Environmental Justice." *Polity* 18(3): 285–305.

USDA Forest Service. October 27, 1994. Memo from Jack Ward Thomas to reviewers entitled "Draft Strategic Plan for Managing Special Forest Products," Washington office.

Williams, Michael. 1992. *Americans and Their Forests: A Historical Geography.* Cambridge, UK: Cambridge University Press.

Legal Decisions

Fritiofson v. Alexander, 772 F.2d 1225 (5th Cir. 1985).

Hanley v. Kleindienst, 471 F.2d 823 (2d Cir. 1972).

Minnesota Public Interest Research Group v. Butz, 498 F.2d 1314 (8th Cir. 1974).

National Wildlife Federation v. Federal Energy Regulatory Commission, 912 F.2d 1471 (D.C. Cir. 1990).

United States v. McCullough, 891 F.Supp. 422 (N.D. Ohio 1995)

CASE STUDY

Business As Usual: The Exclusion of Mushroom Pickers in Wild Mushroom Management in Oregon's National Forests

Rebecca J. McLain

Environmental justice in the United States historically has focused on the inequitable burdens that racial and ethnic minorities have borne with respect to industrial pollutants and waste facility siting (Tesh and Williams 1996; Capek 1993). More recently, Executive Order 12898, signed by President Clinton on February 11, 1994, now requires that federal agencies incorporate environmental justice concerns into their actions and expands the concept of environmental justice to include economically impoverished groups. Additionally, the order extends environmental justice concerns at the federal level into new arenas, including natural resource management and examination of environmental impacts.

Issues of justice and equity in natural resource management have also been a major concern internationally (Johnston 1997; Brosius, Tsing, and Zerner 1998). In addition to exploring race, ethnicity, and low-income considerations in environmental degradation, international scholars interested in environmental justice also emphasize the importance of gender and involvement in resource-dependent livelihoods as factors that need to be taken into account when striving to encourage the formulation and implementation of just and equitable resource management policies (Peet and Watts 1996). International environmental justice scholars increasingly stress the role that involvement in land-based work plays in the formation and maintenance of cultural and personal identities of rural cultures (Peet and Watts 1996; Zerner 2000). At the same time, they note that local ecological knowledge embedded within rural cultures can play an important role in the formulation of environmentally sound natural resource management strategies.

The following case study examines the difficulties that migrant wild mushroom pickers are encountering in maintaining access to wild mushroom grounds located on national forestlands in central Oregon.[1] It illustrates a situation in which natural resource workers are inadvertently excluded from public involvement processes that purport to be open to all stakeholders. Not all wild mushroom harvesters are people of color nor are they all poor. What wild mushroom harvesters share in common is the position of chronic powerlessness in natural resource management policy processes that have resulted in decisions that force upon them an undue burden in terms of the costs of natural resource protection.

Every spring, several hundred commercial wild mushroom pickers and a handful of itinerant buyers travel to the forests near Sisters, Oregon, to look for wild morels and boletes. The Sisters "pick" is just one of many wild mushroom "picks" along the mushroom circuits that thousands of commercial pickers follow each year from Alaska to Mexico and from the Pacific Coast to the Rockies. Although no one area produces commercial quantities of wild mushrooms all year, pickers and buyers can make a living year-round by moving around the various circuits. Pickers and buyers unwilling or unable to follow the circuits typically engage in other occupations such as farming, berry picking, moss harvesting, construction work, logging, or mill work to produce a year-round income (Hansis 1998; Love, Jones, and Liegel 1998). Although some pickers and buyers make a good living and can afford their own homes and newer vehicles, many exist on the margins of survival, wondering whether the day's harvest will cover the cost of their gas for the next trip out.

Sociocultural diversity characterizes the Pacific Northwest wild mushroom industry (Hansis 1998; Love, Jones, and Liegel 1998, Richards and Creasey 1996). A variety of ethnic groups participate in the commercial harvest of wild mushrooms, with the majority being Euroamericans, Southeast Asians (mostly Khmer, Lao, and Mien), Native Americans, and Latinos (mostly Mexican, Guatemalan, and Salvadoran). At Sisters, Euroamericans constitute 70 percent of the pickers with legal authorization to pick. In southwestern Oregon, northern California, and parts of southwestern Washington, Southeast Asians compose the bulk of pickers.

Many Euroamericans who participate in the Sisters pick entered the wild mushroom industry after layoffs in the 1980s and early 1990s from timber-related positions with private companies and public agencies. For those who began picking during timber industry slumps, wild mushroom gathering was a way for them to continue working in the woods. For many Euroamerican pickers at Sisters, wild mushroom picking is an extension of long-standing family traditions of reliance on nontimber forest products as seasonal and supplemental sources of income. For Southeast Asian and Hispanic pickers at Sisters, most of whom are immigrants, wild mushroom gathering offers an opportunity for them to make a living or supplement income earned at other jobs despite their often poor English-language skills or limited technical skills. Gathering mushrooms also provides them an opportunity to work in the woods, a choice that many find preferable to the choices that face them in the cities or agricultural fields. Irrespective of ethnicity, mushroom pickers at Sisters participate in the harvest in part because it is a profession where they can work independently or as a part of small-scale kinship and friendship units, thus exercising considerable control over the structure of their lives.

Approximately three-quarters of the commercial pickers who work the Sisters spring pick come from somewhere else. Most Euroamerican pickers come from rural towns and cities in the Willamette Valley or the Oregon Coastal Range; the majority of Southeast Asian pickers come from large urban centers, including Seattle, Tacoma, Sacramento, and Redding; and the Latino pickers come from rural towns in the Willamette Valley. Regardless of where the pickers come from, they share one thing in common—their livelihoods depend on their ability to move with the mushroom crops. In the unpredictable business of wild mushrooms, where microclimatic changes in soil moisture and temperature drastically affect the location, quantity, and quality of mushroom fruitings, a picker has to be ready to go where the mushrooms are if he or she wants to make a living.

The National Forest System administers much of the forested land in Washington and Oregon, which together form the core of Pacific Northwest mushroom circuits. Consequently, many pickers and buyers rely to some degree on mushroom grounds located on national forests for their livelihoods. National forest management decisions that restrict wild mushroom harvesting activities and resulting management actions that affect wild mushroom habitat and productivity thus potentially affect picker and buyer livelihoods.

Commercial mushroom gathering appeared on national forest management agendas in the Pacific Northwest in the mid-1980s, when demand for wild mushrooms on domestic and international markets was expanding (Hosford et al. 1997; McLain, Christensen, and Shannon 1998). At the same time, more pickers entered the woods as recently arrived immigrants from Southeast Asia established a foothold in the commercial wild mushroom industry, previously dominated by Euroamerican pickers. By the late 1980s and early 1990s, the Sisters Ranger District, along with other ranger districts throughout Oregon and Washington, began to institute and enforce regulations on wild mushroom harvesting and related activities, such as buying and camping (Hosford et al. 1997; Love, Jones, and Liegel 1998; Richards and Creasey 1996; McLain, Christensen, and Shannon 1998; Parks and Schmitt 1997). The push for regulation came both from within the Forest Service, which was faced with having to manage large, temporary influxes of pickers on national forestlands, and from outside the agency. Amateur mycologists were particularly active in pushing for state and federal regulation of wild mushrooms during the mid and late 1980s, arguing that large-scale commercial harvesting was potentially destructive to mushroom beds (McLain, Christensen, and Shannon 1998). Despite the lack of scientific evidence that commercial harvesting is damaging to forest ecosystems, ecological health protection arguments have played an important role in cautious Forest Service decisions to limit picker access to large tracts of forested land in the Pacific Northwest (McLain 2000).

Harvesting permits were the first mechanism that the national forests used to regulate wild mushroom harvesting in the late 1980s. Through issuing permits, the U.S. Forest Service sought to better understand how many people were picking wild mushrooms on national forestland (McLain 2000). Many mushroom programs were poorly enforced due to the general feeling among district staff that resources could be better spent on more pressing resource management problems. In the early 1990s, however, news of conflicts over mushroom harvesting appeared on the front page of a number of regional and national newspapers and journals (Egan 1993; McRae 1993; Lipske 1994), drawing attention to the issue and creating pressure on the Forest Service to expand its enforcement. By the mid-1990s, Sisters and neighboring ranger districts began to regulate mushroom harvests by hiring full-time technicians responsible for special forest product enforcement and oversight; by limiting buying to designated areas so that law enforcement officers can easily check for permits; by establishing periodic roadblocks with legal options for search and seizure; and by instituting regular patrols by law enforcement officers through centralized mushroom camps (McLain 2000).

Efforts by the Forest Service at Sisters to involve mushroom pickers in regulatory decisions affecting their lives have been minimal (McLain 2000; McLain and Jones 2001). Neither buyers nor pickers were consulted in 1994 when the Sisters Ranger District designated a specific site as the buying camp location, nor were they consulted in determining the layout of the camp. Five years later, the camp is still controversial because its linear shape greatly favors the buyer who is lucky enough to obtain the site at the camp entrance. The district's regulations are fixed in conjunction with several adjacent national forests. The spring season rules are established at an in-house meeting that usually takes place in January or February. The Sisters Ranger District also participates in a fall-season meeting with district staff from three other national forests to discuss changes to fall-season regulations. The fall meetings are nominally open to the public, including wild mushroom pickers and buyers.

Until fall 1998, participation in these meetings by wild mushroom pickers and buyers was limited. Prior to 1998, the fall meetings were held weeks or months after the actual harvest, at a time when most people impacted by the changes were not able to attend because they had long left the area for other harvesting sites. Although the Forest Service now holds camp meetings during the fall mushroom season, the meetings are held at a site on the east side of the Cascades, some seventy miles south of Sisters.

This site is convenient for the Forest Service since it is centrally located for the various districts that participate in the joint permit system in which the Sisters Ranger District also takes part. It is also convenient for those matsutake pickers who are based at the site during the fall season. However, pickers who focus on the spring harvest or who harvest on the west side of the Cascades in the fall season, as many pickers at Sisters do, face a three- to four-hour drive one way to reach the fall mushroom meetings.

In years with major changes in the regulations, such as in 1998 when the Sisters Ranger District decided to shut down the matsutake harvest and when significant changes were made to the matsutake season closing date, the four forests have also held public meetings in the summer months to discuss the upcoming changes. These meetings function more as forums for the Forest Service to disseminate information than as participative information gathering from the public or as decision-making venues. The summer meetings occur at a time when all but a few local pickers and buyers are working elsewhere.

In advertising its public mushroom meetings, the Forest Service follows standard procedures for other types of public involvement: posting notices on local bulletin boards, mailing notices to people who have asked to have their name placed on the "mushroom" mailing list, and posting notices in the classified section of the local newspapers. None of these methods, however, is suited to reaching a migrant population of pickers and buyers. Rarely are pickers present at the times when the notices are posted locally, many do not have reliable mailing addresses, and others are unable to check their mail on a regular basis. Although the fall mushroom meetings are advertised on the east side of the Cascades, they are not advertised in the west side newspapers or public bulletin boards. Thus, west side pickers who do not pick on the east side during the fall rarely hear about the fall meetings. Yet the rules developed in the fall meetings also pertain to districts on the west side.

Moreover, ensuring wide public participation in these meetings is not a high priority for many special forest products managers in the participating national forests.[2] Many Forest Service staff officers simultaneously manage other programs, such as small sales (post and poles), firewood, and so forth and place a low priority on the importance of their commercial mushroom program. Neglect on the part of some special forest products program managers coupled with the inability of traditional public involvement techniques to reach a politically disorganized and highly mobile user group population has resulted in the inadvertent but nonetheless real disenfranchisement of many wild mushroom pickers and buyers in national forest management decision making.

Attempts by the wild mushroom industry to organize economically and politically have had limited success. Wild mushroom pickers and buyers in the Pacific Northwest have not yet formed any industry or worker associations that are broad-based enough to legitimately represent "the" interests of the industry, or even large segments of it, or to serve as reliable conduits of information in ways that other forest user associations do. Wild mushroom and floral greens buyers' efforts to create an industrywide association during the late 1980s and 1990s as a means for them to acquire political legitimacy in the eyes of the Forest Service and other agencies also failed (McLain and Jones 2001). This failure was due in large part to divisions within the association about whether pickers should also be allowed to be voting members, as well as divisions between the floral greens and mushroom industries about what types and level of regulation are appropriate. The association's lack of internal cohesion rendered it politically ineffective.

More recently the Jefferson Center, a small nongovernmental organization based in southwestern Oregon that supports broad-based learning and analysis, especially among low-income and multicultural groups, has been working with wild mushroom pickers and buyers to expand their opportunities for participating in forest management decisions that affect their lives. The Jefferson Center (1998a, 1998b) has worked to bring together pickers and buyers of all of the ethnic groups active in the wild mushroom industry through a series of meetings held during the middle and late 1990s to discuss mutual interests regarding wild mushroom regulation. Over the years it has also been successful at getting Forest Service managers on the Deschutes, Winema, and Siskiyou National Forests to take part in community-led meetings that facilitate, rather than discourage, picker and buyer participation.

For example, under pressure from and with the help of the Jefferson Center and interested pickers and buyers, the Forest Service instituted a series of mushroom camp meetings during the fall matsutake season at Crescent in 1998 and 1999 (Jefferson Center 1998a, 1998b). These meetings served as a forum for pickers, buyers, and Forest Service staff to air their concerns in a setting and style less alienating to pickers and buyers than formal public meetings. One of the outcomes of the mushroom camp meetings was a decision to hold the 1999 end-of-season meeting before, rather than after, the official closing date, thus ensuring that at least some nonlocal pickers would have an opportunity to participate in the discussions. In 1998 and 1999, the Jefferson Center also invited Forest Service staff from the four forests to take part in public discussions of wild mushroom and brush harvesting issues in Crescent, Redding, Stockton, Sacramento, Oroville, Fresno, and Hoopa. In 2000, Cambodian and Lao pickers cosponsored the agency-picker meetings with the Jefferson Center. Unlike most Forest Service public meetings, where agency employees tend to outnumber pickers and buyers, these community-based meetings are numerically dominated by pickers and buyers. The center is a liaison in developing picker-based wild mushroom monitoring systems in southwestern and central Oregon, and the agencies are involved as participants rather than as the leaders of these multiparty efforts.

The Jefferson Center has also served as a liaison among the picker communities, notably enhancing contacts between Euroamerican, Native American, and Southeast Asian pickers in southwestern Oregon and northern California. Its efforts to facilitate participation by Euroamerican and Latino wild mushroom pickers and buyers in central and northwestern Oregon, however, have met with limited success (Brown 2000). The center works with community leaders, who then organize what happens within their communities. Thus far, the center has been unable to identify anyone within the Euroamerican and Latino harvesting communities in central and northwestern Oregon with the ability to motivate the widespread participation of those ethnic groups in meetings with the Forest Service or other land management agencies. My work at Sisters suggests that Southeast Asian pickers are relatively tightly connected into widespread kinship and sociocultural networks, while Euroamerican pickers, and possibly Latino pickers as well, tend to operate as independent entrepreneurs or in weakly connected kinship groups (McLain 2000).

As a result, disseminating information and generating widespread political participation among Euroamerican and Latino picking communities requires a much greater investment in time and human resources. Euroamerican and Latino pickers thus continue to be largely absent in the current public participation framework for developing wild mushroom regulations in central Oregon's national forests. Here is an instance where more active intervention by the Forest Service is needed to assure that a new single ethnic group does not come to dominate the mushroom harvest in national forests. Culturally based ways of dealing with kinship should not be the determinant of who learns about public meetings, and the Forest Service may have to spend more time with some groups to assure equity of inclusion.

From this case study we can draw several lessons related to applying environmental justice in natural resource management policies with respect to public participation in nontimber forest product industries. The wild mushroom case illustrates that standard Forest Service public involvement processes are ill-suited to bringing politically disorganized, economically weak, and geographically mobile stakeholders, irrespective of their race or ethnicity, to the table to formulate policy. The Jefferson Center has begun to make inroads into opening up processes for policy formulation in central Oregon, but doing so has required an intensive effort on the part of their small and poorly funded staff to create alternative venues that are more appropriate to the mobile lifestyles of pickers and buyers. Participation by wild mushroom pickers and buyers in decisions affecting the spring mushroom harvests and harvests in national forests continues to be extremely limited where the Jefferson Center has not focused its efforts. Despite inconclusive scientific evidence that current commercial wild mushroom harvesting presents ecological risks (Hosford et al. 1997, 45–54; Liegel et al. 1998, 28–29; Parks and Schmitt 1997, 11–13), all commercial wild mushroom pickers have been excluded from access to larger and larger areas of the Pacific Northwest's national forests and thus to the resources that they would like to have access to in order to make a living. Although excluding commercial pickers appears to be unintentional on the part of the Forest Service, the negative effects on wild mushroom pickers' lives are quite real.

The mushroom case points to a core consideration when addressing issues of environmental injustice in natural resource allocation: whether the existing legal avenues for formal and informal public participation inadvertently but systematically exclude whole categories of resource users. Identifying the points of exclusion and developing alternative forms of public participation that include more people constitute important avenues by which environmental justice can be supported. The case study suggests that mediating organizations, such as the Jefferson Center, may aid in developing and implementing needed alternative public participation mechanisms. It further illustrates the obligation for natural resource management agencies to develop their capacity to undertake the economic, sociological, and policy analyses that would enable them to develop and implement broader based public participation strategies.

The wild mushroom case also underscores the limits of relying on specific minority groups to be involved in decision making as a measure of whether environmental justice has been achieved sufficiently in natural resource management. Indeed, Southeast Asian wild mushroom pickers have been able to gain a much greater voice in wild mushroom regulation on certain national forests through the pressure that the Jefferson Center has placed on the Forest Service to modify its informal public involvement processes. However, can we therefore call this result a success for environmental justice? The answer is "No" as long as migrant Euroamerican and Latino pickers continue to lack access to decision-making processes that affect their livelihoods. Until the Forest Service public participation processes are structured in ways that invite the participation of *all* mushroom picker groups, environmental justice will not have been achieved in this area.

Beyond fairness to individuals, the wild mushroom case also raises the question of whether sustainable forest management is promoted when land managers either deliberately or inadvertently exclude people who have extensive local ecological knowledge from decision-making processes about forests and their products. People whose daily lives are impacted by natural resource laws and policies may possess important knowledge about local ecosystems and their species. Indeed, given the lack of scientific knowledge about wild mushrooms, exclusion of wild mushroom pickers from management decisions may well be counterproductive. Ethnographic studies of wild mushroom pickers indicate that many have accumulated considerable knowledge of both mushroom and forest ecology (Love, Jones, and Liegel 1998; Richards 1997; McLain 2000). Incorporating that knowledge into forest management might lead to regulations that are ecologically sounder and more likely to be respected by wild mushroom pickers rather than autocratic decisions based primarily upon a limited, if at all relevant, body of scientific knowledge.

NOTES

1. This case study draws upon data gathered as part of an ethnographic study of wild mushroom politics conducted by the author in western and central Oregon from 1995–1998. Unless otherwise noted, data about the characteristics of pickers and buyers at Sisters as well as information about the wild mushroom policy process in national forests in central Oregon are drawn from this study. Additional details about the project can be found in McLain (2000).

2. Forest managers generally place wild mushrooms into a product/species management category referred to as either special forest products or nontimber forest products. The term "special forest products" still dominates within the United States, while the term "nontimber forest products" dominates in the international forest policy arena. Special forest products include a wide variety of understory products, including moss, floral greens, barks, roots, and fungi. During the past decade, many ranger districts in national forests have developed special forest products programs and assigned staff to coordinate those programs.

REFERENCES

Brosius, Peter J., Anna Lowenhaupt Tsing, and Charles Zerner. 1998. "Representing Communities: Histories and Politics of Community-Based Natural Resource Management." *Society and Natural Resources* 11:157–168.

Brown, Beverly. 1998. "Voices from the Woods." *American Forests* 103(4): 35–37.

———. July 9, 2000. Personal communication.

Capek, Stella M. 1993. "The 'Environmental Justice' Frame: A Conceptual Discussion and an Application." *Social Problems* 40(1): 5–24.

Egan, Timothy. June 28, 1993. "Rushing to Gather Up Cash on the Northwest's Forest Floor." *New York Times,* A1, A10.

Hansis, Richard. 1998. "A Political Ecology of Picking: Nontimber Forest Products in the Pacific Northwest." *Human Ecology* 26(1): 67–86.

Hosford, David, David Pilz, Randy Molina, and Michael Amaranthus. 1997. *Ecol-*

ogy and Management of the Commercially Harvested American Matsutake Mushroom. USDA Forest Service General Technical Report 412. Portland, OR: Pacific Northwest Research Station.

Jefferson Center. 1998a. "Matsutake Season a Bust, but Communications among Pickers, USFS, Improve." *Jefferson Center Newsletter* 1(4): 3.

———. 1998b. "Mushroom Pickers and U.S. Forest Service Discuss Matsutake Program." *Jefferson Center Newsletter* 1(3): 1, 3.

Johnston, Barbara Rose. 1997. "Introduction: Life and Death Matters at the End of the Millennium." In *Life and Death Matters: Human Rights and the Environment at the End of the Millennium,* ed. Barbara Rose Johnston. Walnut Creek, CA: Alta Mira Press.

Liegel, Leon, David Pilz, Tom Love, and Eric Jones. 1998. "Integrating Biological, Socioeconomic, and Managerial Methods and Results in the MAB Mushroom Study." *Ambio Special Report* 9:28–29.

Lipske, M. 1994. "A New Gold Rush Packs the Woods in Central Oregon." *Smithsonian* 25:35–46.

Love, Thomas, Eric Jones, and Leon Liegel. 1998. "Valuing the Temperate Rainforest: Wild Mushrooming on the Olympic Peninsula Biosphere Reserve." *Ambio Special Report* 9:16–25.

McLain, Rebecca J. 2000. "Controlling the Forest Understory: Wild Mushroom Politics in Central Oregon." Ph.D. diss., University of Washington, Seattle.

McLain, Rebecca J., Harriet H. Christensen, and Margaret A. Shannon. 1998. "When Amateurs Are the Experts: Amateur Mycologists and Wild Mushroom Politics in the Pacific Northwest, USA." *Society and Natural Resources* 11:615–626.

McLain, Rebecca J., and Eric T. Jones. 2001. "Expanding NTFP Picker/Buyer Participation in Pacific Northwest Forest Policy." *Journal of Sustainable Forestry* 13(3/4): 147–161.

McRae, M. 1993. "Mushrooms, Guns, and Money." *Outside* 18(10): 64–69, 151–154.

Parks, Catherine G., and Craig L. Schmitt. 1997. *Wild Edible Mushrooms in the Blue Mountains: Resource and Issues.* USDA Forest Service General Technical Report PNW-GTR-393. Portland, OR: Pacific Northwest Research Station.

Peet, Richard, and Michael Watts, eds. 1996. *Liberation Ecologies: Environment, Development, Social Movements.* London: Routledge.

Pilz, David, Randy Molina, and Leon Liegel. 1998. "Biological Productivity of Chanterelle Mushrooms in and near the Olympic Peninsula Biosphere Reserve." *Ambio Special Report* 9:8–13.

Richards, Rebecca Templin. 1997. "What the Natives Know." *Journal of Forestry* 95(9): 5–10.

Richards, Rebecca T., and Max Creasey. 1996. "Ethnic Diversity, Resource Values, and Ecosystem Management: Matsutake Mushroom Harvesting in the Klamath Bioregion." *Society and Natural Resources* 9:359–374.

Tesh, Sylvia N., and Bruce A. Williams. 1996. "Identity Politics, Disinterested Politics, and Environmental Justice." *Policy* 18(3): 285–305.

Zerner, Charles, ed. 2000. *People, Plants, and Justice: The Politics of Nature Conservation.* New York: Columbia University Press.

CASE STUDY

Applying Stewardship Contracting Principles to Nontimber Forest Products

Paul Ringgold

Stewardship contracting is a complex and often misunderstood concept that has evolved in many directions over the past several years. Within the context of the national forest system, the term refers to innovative uses of new and existing resource management contracting tools to attain better stewardship of public resources. This chapter provides a brief overview of the concept and its recent history as applied within the national forest system. It also outlines some of the ways in which these new contracting mechanisms may affect nontimber forest product management on national forestlands.

BACKGROUND TO STEWARDSHIP CONTRACTING

In 1992, the U.S. Forest Service adopted ecosystem management as its official guiding management principle. Due to pressure from environmental organizations, recreational associations, tourist industry associations, and a host of other social actors, the Forest Service now operates in a sociopolitical context requiring it to manage national forestlands for a much broader range of uses, goods, and services than it did during much of the past century. For example, timber harvesting on lands administered by the Forest Service is no longer seen solely as a means for the agency to meet sustained-yield production targets. Instead, timber harvesting is viewed as only one component of a diverse set of activities used to meet ecosystem management objectives (USDA Forest Service 2000). The ability of the Forest Service to implement ecosystem management, however, is severely hampered by its organizational and funding structures, which continue to reflect the agency's historical reliance on timber revenue. In particular, the agency's NTFP programs typically have been funded primarily through timber harvest receipts, notably through special accounts, such as the Knudsen-Vandenberg and Brush Disposal Funds.

With recent cutbacks in the federal timber program, the Forest Service is no longer able to fund many land stewardship activities, such as reforestation, brush disposal, and thinning, which it had financed through the use of special timber-derived funds. Yet many small businesses have the skills and experience needed to carry out these activities. Moreover, the forest products that could be harvested in the course of carrying out these types of activities represent a significant potential source of sustainable income and employment for rural and nonrural inhabitants. Unfortunately, under existing regulations governing its management activities, the Forest Service has had difficulty matching this growing need for land stewardship services with those businesses and communities willing and able to provide such services.

The notion of stewardship contracting emerged from efforts by environmental groups, local and regional community groups, and Forest Service employees to address this gap between the lack of contractual and funding mechanisms within the Forest Service for carrying out forest stewardship activities and the existence of firms with the ability and interest in performing such tasks. Environmental groups have supported stewardship contracting primarily because of their concerns about the negative impacts of past and present management practices on ecosystem health. Community groups, while often sharing many of the environmental groups' concerns, also see stewardship contracting as a way to promote local involvement in the management of federal lands and to strengthen local economies. Forest Service employees view stewardship contracting as an opportunity to increase collaboration between the Forest Service and other groups, address ecosystem health concerns, and improve contracting flexibility and efficiency in times of shrinking personnel rosters and budgets. All of these groups share a desire to develop management strategies that promote long-term sustainability but are flexible enough to meet dynamic ecological, social, and economic conditions.

Early contracting mechanisms to address these goals included "land management services contracts," which were designed to bundle a variety of management activities under a single contract. These contracts, which were first tested on the national forests during the 1980s, sought to save public funds by making contract administration more efficient (Ringgold and Mitsos 1996). In addition to consolidating multiple timber management activities under a single contract instrument, they allowed more flexibility in how the contractees executed the contract. This flexibility was achieved through the use of descriptions in the contract that provided the contractor with information on the desired goals of the activity. Rather than working according to a strict set of specifications, contractors were allowed to use their own judgment as to how to best achieve the intended results of the project.

Although initially developed to facilitate traditional timber management activities, such as timber sale layout, site preparation, reforestation, and thinning, over time these contracts evolved toward ecosystem management through the inclusion of such objectives as wildlife habitat improvement, development and maintenance of dispersed recreational facilities, and soil and water conservation practices. These more recent contracting approaches, which encompassed both timber and nontimber objectives, are commonly referred to as stewardship contracts. These types of contracts make use of the following mechanisms: end-results objectives rather than rigid specifications to define contract activities; the use of cooperative agreements and research authorities; and the bundling of management services and product sales within a single contract (Ringgold 1998).

APPLICATION OF STEWARDSHIP CONTRACTING MECHANISMS TO NTFP PROJECTS

In 1998, Congress authorized the Forest Service to develop up to as many as twenty-eight pilot projects to contract "services to achieve land management goals for National Forests and rural community needs" and, in connection with these contracts, "to apply the value of timber or other forest products removed as an offset against the cost of services received" (§347, P.L. 105-277; Omnibus Appropriations Act, FY 1999). The number of authorized pilot projects was increased to fifty-two in 2000 (§338, P.L. 106-291; Department of Interior and Related Agencies Appropriations Act, FY 2001). Although the Forest Service has yet to select some of the authorized pilots, most of the pilot projects in progress are related to fuel management involving the removal of small-diameter, low-value wood products (Mitsos and Ringgold 2000). The focus on fuel management projects is due to the immediate need (perceived or otherwise) to address forest health and fire safety concerns in many forested areas of the western United States.

One unintended consequence of the recent legislation is that stewardship contracting risks being misinterpreted as synonymous with "goods for services" contracts. "Goods for services" is the general term applied to situations in which an agency provides the contractor with public goods in exchange for services rendered. With limited exceptions, the Forest Service does not have legal authorization to make use of a "goods for services" approach to management, as it would give the agency potentially undue control over the disposition of public resources, as well as allow for agency budgeting of projects at levels potentially exceeding congressional appropriations. Nonetheless, the goods for services approach may be useful in situations where the agency has limited funds to perform work that needs to be done and where contractors are available who value the product that they will be removing.

Other less controversial contractual mechanisms exist that are more likely to be applicable to projects involving NTFPs. One such mechanism is the cooperative agreement, which can be used to facilitate and formalize a relationship between the federal agency and an outside cooperator, where both parties stand to benefit equally from a given project or activity. The use of these agreements is limited to projects in which the agency and the cooperator share mutual interests and benefit in the same qualitative way from the objective of the agreement. One example is the use of a formal cooperative agreement between federal agencies and local resource users that clearly defines the respective roles and responsibilities for the management of nontimber forest products in conjunction with other forest management activities.

The integration of nontimber forest products into broader forest management objectives requires the development of a better understanding of appropriate, sustainable NTFP harvest levels. For example, an ongoing project in northern California has involved the development of a native medicinal plant research and management agreement between the Forest Service and two local interests—a Native American tribe and Trinity Alps Botanicals, a small business engaged in the wildcrafting of botanical products. This partnership focuses on developing techniques for the sustainable management of native plants to support ecosystem functions as well providing resources for cultural and commodity uses (Johnston 2000). The project also may alleviate potential conflicts between diverse NTFP users in the project area.

The Forest Service may be able to gain control over the amounts of product being harvested through entering into agreements with local harvesting cooperatives. In exchange for the right to exclusive use of a certain area, the harvesters would pay an established permit fee and would police the area to avert overharvesting, thereby promoting the long-term sustainability of NTFPs in their area. This kind of agreement rests on the ability of the Forest Service to enter into long-term agreements. The legal authorities for the agency to engage in long-term service contracts do exist; however, questions remain as to whether these authorities could be applied within the framework of a permit system. If the NTFP program was carried out as part of a broader ecosystem services contract, there would be an increased opportunity to apply long-term, or even indefinite, contract authority.

A recent development that is likely to affect how such cooperative agreements are structured in the future is a federal pilot program to establish charges and fees that will recover fair market value for forest botanical products on national forestland (see Antypas et al., this volume). Although this program may prompt much needed attention on the analysis of sustainable harvest levels for these products, it is yet unclear how the fee and fund structures created by the program will influence the flexibility that remains a cornerstone of the stewardship contracting concept. As in the case of low-value timber products, the rationale for the use of "low value" as a means of either trading goods for services or using other marginal value related authorities often disappears as a higher value is found for the product.

REFERENCES

Johnston, Christina. 2000. Personal communication on January 26.

Mitsos, Mary K., and Paul C. Ringgold. 2001. "Testing Stewardship Concepts on Federal Lands." In *Understanding Community Based Ecosystem Management in the United States,* ed. G. Gray, M. Enzer, and J. Kusel, pp. 305–320. New York: Haworth Press.

Ringgold, Paul C. 1998. *Land Stewardship Contracting in the National Forests: A Community Guide to Existing Authorities*. Washington, DC: Pinchot Institute for Conservation.

Ringgold, Paul C., and Mary K. Mitsos. 1996. "Land Management Stewardship Contracts: Background and Legislative History." White paper. Washington, DC: Pinchot Institute for Conservation.

USDA Forest Service. 2000. "USDA Forest Service Strategic Plan (2000 Revision)." Washington, DC: USDA Forest Service.

Part Five

CUSTOMARY CLAIMS TO USE RIGHTS ON PUBLIC LANDS

Nontimber Forest Products Customary Claims

Edmund Clay Goodman

This chapter summarizes rights on public lands based on customary law or claims. I begin by defining and discussing the concept of customary law as well as the larger concept of legal pluralism. Together these two concepts provide a useful theoretical framework to understand conflicts between customary claims and formal law. Next, I explore several international examples in which customary claims conflicted with formal law, and how such conflicts played out. I then analyze customary claims to public land and resources in the United States, focusing especially on national forestlands, and conclude with some possible scenarios for how conflicts between customary and formal claims on public lands might evolve and their potential effects on NTFP management.

CUSTOMARY CLAIMS, FORMAL LAW, AND LEGAL PLURALISM: CONTEXT AND DEFINITIONS

Customary claims to usufructuary rights on public lands are generally claims made outside, and often in conflict with, the formal, official law of the state/nation where such lands are found (Fortmann 1990, 195). Such claims may arise from a long-standing practice (custom) of the land use at issue, a use that formal state law may prohibit, restrict, or regulate in a manner that prevents the customary use. Claims may also arise from assertion of a customary law that governs the area—again, a law in place for a sufficient time to grant the law, and assertions under the law, legitimacy and enforceability even when enforceability is outside the jurisdiction of official law enforcement. Although a person may assert such claims, the authority to do so generally resides in the person's membership in a community in whose name such customary claims or customary law can be made (Hviding and Baines 1996, 71–72).

Customary law or claims consist of six key elements: (1) a set of "legal" norms, rights, and privileges, (2) within an identifiable area, (3) continued over sufficient duration, (4) legitimized by a certain community, (5) existing in opposition to, or in conflict with, the formal state system of laws, (6) yet maintaining a degree of enforceability within its community. Customary claims to public lands in the United States are use rights recognized by the local community because the community recognizes the long-standing existence of such uses (Fortmann 1990, 195).

Each element of "customary" law is problematic, particularly in the context of nonindigenous claims to customary use on federally managed public lands. By contrast, customary claims in many other countries mostly arise in the context of indigenous communities that have been in place for many hundreds or even thousands of years. The customs at issue are nearly as enduring, and the communities are relatively stable, identifiable, and intact (Ostrom 1990). In the United States, on the other hand, nonindigenous customs are relatively recent, particularly for western public lands, where nonindigenous settlement dates in many cases to less than two hundred years. Further, the United States is a highly heterogeneous and mobile society, making defining and maintaining the community necessary for customary claims more difficult (Fortmann and Roe 1993, 142–143).

"Legal pluralism" provides a useful theoretical framework for considering the assertion of customary claims and the conflicts arising from their assertion within the state legal system. Griffiths has defined legal pluralism as "that state of affairs, for any social field, in which behavior pursuant to more than one legal order occurs" (1986, 2). Legal pluralism recognizes that various overlapping and contradictory legal orders govern the actions and behaviors of people, a "dynamic condition" in which "social action always takes place in a context of multiple, overlapping, 'semi-autonomous social fields'" (38). Griffiths contrasts the "fact" of legal pluralism with the "ideology and myth" of legal centralism, which asserts that "law is and should be the law of the state, uniform for all persons, exclusive of other law, and administered by a single set of state institutions" (3). Galanter asserts that the official state legal system is often a secondary focus of regulation and that "what we find instead is a multitude of associations and networks, overlapping and interpenetrating, more fragmentary and less inclusive" (1981, 20-21).

Legal pluralism allows for analyzing legal systems in ways that recognize the existence and potential enforceability of certain usufructuary claims based on local custom, even if the custom is relatively recent, the community within which it is based is fluid, and the practices are dynamic. Legal pluralism analyzes various local systems, whose form and content likely differ considerably from region to region. Finally, legal pluralism, particularly in Galanter's formulation, assumes that the various legal orders overlap in their application to specific persons in particular regions.

It also assumes that overlapping legal systems may conflict, creating points of tension.

CUSTOMARY USE CLAIMS AND CONFLICTS WITH FORMAL LAW: INTERNATIONAL EXAMPLES

Numerous examples exist of conflicts between various modes of customary legal orders concerning usufructuary rights and those of official state law. Many of these conflicts are legacies of colonialism, in which colonial governments attempted to establish a central, unified state system often at odds with local, customary systems. The governments established upon independence from colonial powers inherited these unified state systems. However, these conflicts are not uniquely colonial in origin, nor do significant anomalies between the state system and the local, customary systems always result in conflict.

Allemansrätt: Public Right to Forest Recreation in Sweden

In Sweden, a tradition of outdoor life is linked to the right of public access to the countryside, a right known in Swedish as *allemansrätt*. Every person in Sweden has a right, "within certain restrictions, to move freely across private landholdings, pick mushrooms, flowers and berries, etc." (Sandell 1996, 6). *Allemansrätt* is a right derived from traditional use, and although various laws support it, facilitating countryside access, the right is not codified (as it is, for example, in Norway). As Sandell notes, "The public right of access in Sweden is in common law and can be seen as the 'free space' between various restrictions, mainly: (i) economic interests; (ii) people's privacy; and (iii) conservation" (6). Thus, the formal state system protects various sets of interests, but *allemansrätt* operates as a mode of customary law—arising outside of the formal system, sometimes in conflict with it, but established in and evolving from a different legal order (Sandell 1996).

Sandell notes that the right is traceable back to the Middle Ages and is regarded as a "tradition" deriving from preindustrial society. But he also notes that a confluence of two relatively recent factors led to contemporary recognition and development of the right: the shaping of the Swedish nation and the development of a national identity; and the rising material standard of living and the shortening workweek, which made it possible "for the broad mass of people to have, and make use of, leisure time" (1996, 5). Further, he notes that Sweden's sparse population decreases the likelihood of conflict with other interests.

However, *allemansrätt* has also played a prominent role in a local population's opposition to creating a national park in northern Sweden. As

Sandell describes it, "The local people are very much in favor of snowmobiling, accessibility through the use of roads, and activities like hunting and fishing. The tourists from far off, however, often accord high priority to silence, hiking, scenic views and cross-country skiing" (1995, 140). Local people assert that developing the park, with the resulting influx of competing users, would in effect intrude upon their right of public access. In effect, local rural users are asserting *allemansrätt* to prevent a perceived urban elite, with different views of "the outdoor life," from usurping and displacing *allemansrätt* as they practice it.

Because custom and practice, rather than formal law, protect *allemansrätt,* the increasing industrialization of Swedish life is slowly eroding the right. The custom of *allemansrätt* had previously been strong enough to protect and enforce it through indirect legislative action—for example, protection of shores against new buildings, prohibiting obstacles to enjoyment of the outdoor life, requiring landowners to facilitate people passing across their lands. The "free space" in which *allemansrätt* can effectively operate is narrowing, not by any legislative enactment or repeal but because of the increased power and precedence of other political and economic sectors and legal orders. To use a phrase currently much applied in the recent Balkans' conflicts, the emerging order is creating "facts on the ground" that work to undermine the customary field of the *allemansrätt.*

Customary Open Use of Forests and Fields in England

Rose has noted that "customary claims originated in ancient British legal doctrine, whereby residents of given localities could claim rights as 'customs of the manor' overriding the common law" (1986, 740). Under British law, "custom" had traditionally supported a community's claims to use a variety of lands in common: for example, manorial tenants' rights to graze animals, gather wood, or cut turf on the manor commons. However, by the nineteenth century, customary use had all but disappeared from the British countryside, and customary claims are, for the most part, no longer recognized as legitimate under British law (Rose 1986).

The erosion of customary open use of forests and fields in England began in the seventeenth century, but the main thrust against customary use came through the Black Act of 1723 (Thompson 1975). The act constitutes another example of creating facts on the ground that usurped the customary law of open fields and forests by replacing custom with partitioning, enclosures, and private property. The Black Act aimed to brutally suppress protests by the rural populace in support of customary use of rural England's forests and fields. It was part of a larger process to displace a body of indigenous law and practice in conflict with a newly emerging legal order backed by more economically and politically powerful interests (Thompson 1975).

Forested lands in Berkshire and Hampshire had, over the course of many centuries, developed an intrinsic and complex local economy based on an open fields access system for forest resources, including subsistence hunting, livestock grazing, timber and firewood harvest, and peat cutting. The use of these practices over time, and the informal system for allocation and distribution of resources, constituted a body of local customary law among local forest users. Local uses coexisted for many years with the use of the same lands by the nobility and the local gentry as sport hunting grounds. After the Norman conquest in the eleventh century, a series of laws often attributed to William the Conqueror protected deer and other wild game for hunting by the king and the nobility (Schama 1995, 145–147). Although the forest laws and courts generally protected the sport hunting and income of the nobility, they also made efforts to incorporate and recognize customary use and practices as a means for achieving some semblance of balance between conflicting uses (Thompson 1975, 34–41).

With the ascendancy of the Whig political faction following the Restoration of the English monarchy in the seventeenth century, Whig politicians needed to legitimize their claims to land and power. They increased appropriation of "common" forestland by enclosure, and local conflict erupted, culminating in the actions of the "Blacks," organized protestors who blackened their faces and committed acts of vandalism and depredation against deer, deer parks, and artificial fish ponds. The government's response was the Black Act, which created a long list of capital offenses aimed at the protesters. The Black Act instituted the death penalty not only for deer poaching and destruction of fish ponds but also for blackening one's face and for writing threatening letters (Thompson 1975, 21–22). Enforcement of the act, particularly in its first two decades, expanded to cover many previously recognized customary rights to the forest, that is the very customs and practices that the protesters sought to preserve. The Black Act was part of a larger effort by an emerging set of powerful economic and political interests to displace an existing customary legal order using state force against that order (258–269).

Dahlmann (1980) offers another view on the transformation of the British "open fields" system to a system of state sanctioned and enforced enclosure: actors within the system transformed land tenure arrangements using a property rights and transaction costs analysis. This analysis determined that a private property–based enclosure system was institutionally superior to the open fields system. Dahlmann argues that the open fields system made economic sense to the participants as long as natural resources were abundant and competition relatively insignificant. As resources became scarce and competition for them more intense per economic unit, a system of private property rights and protection became economically rational (73–75).

Public Forests, Ancestral Lands, and Community-Based Natural Resource Management in the Philippines

The Philippines has a long history of conflict between the central government's claims to ownership of public forestlands and the customary claims of local residents and users to those same lands. Over 60 percent of the land mass of the Philippines is considered "public domain," lands that are also home to approximately one-third of the population (Lynch 1997, 16). The central government's ownership claims over such land are based on one of the last acts issued by Spanish colonists, the Maura Law of 1894. The Maura Law provided that all lands whose ownership was not registered with the Crown would revert to the new central government (11–12). For much of the twentieth century, the conflict was abstract because the unregistered lands were largely remote. Customary use and ownership prevailed because the central government was unable to assert authority and control. Since the early 1970s, however, the federal government has licensed intensive timber harvests on these lands, and severe deforestation and displacement of large numbers of indigenous people have resulted. These environmental and sociological disruptions have intensified conflicts, not only between the government and the local users but also between local users competing for increasingly scarce forest resources.

During the last two decades, community activists and nongovernmental organizations have organized and lobbied for change. They have mapped out territories and asserted the validity of ancestral, customary land use and ownership rights. These groups succeeded in persuading the Philippines Supreme Court to hold that lands occupied by un-Hispanicized groups for more than thirty years were to be considered not only ancestral but "private," and thus not public lands (Lynch 1997, 16–19). The Supreme Court's judgment, growing community activism, and ongoing civil unrest in the remote areas resulted in a 1995 Executive Order mandating "community-based forest management" as the "national strategy to achieve sustainable forestry and social justice" (18). Although the Executive Order is a significant movement toward resolving the dispute between the federal government and the customary practices and claims of local, indigenous forest communities, it still supports centralized authority and control. The Executive Order resulted in the creation of new government institutions to implement the national strategy, and the political and financial elite still control these institutions. The largely poor local users thus remain marginalized (18–21).

Local indigenous groups, however, see the concept of community-based natural resource management (CBNRM) as part of a long-term strategy for national recognition and protection of customary use rights and practices in the Philippines's public forests. Activists assert that customary rights draw support and legitimacy from the community in which they operate. These rights derive from long-term relations between local users and the resources that have sustained people, and constitute a more effective and enforceable means than state institutions for managing forests for long-term use (Lynch 1997, 23–24). CBNRM, the activists assert, must involve rights and authority emanating from the community, empowering and enhancing local institutions and recognizing property rights of local users as well as competing and overlapping uses. Customary use activists in the Philippines have found strong support in the 1994 Baguio Declaration, in which fourteen Asian and Pacific Island nations committed themselves to certain principles, including the principles underlying CBNRM (26–27). The declaration is not enforceable, but local users and activists have been able to appeal to it to build and legitimize local institutions to counter the power of the central government. This change in perceptions provides for the greater recognition and protection of customary claims (Lynch 1997).

Forestry Management and Customary Community Practices in Zimbabwe

Much of sub-Saharan Africa has had to deal with the legacies of colonialism in the postcolonial era. One of the most vexing legacies has been the often conflict-rife relations between the formal, centralized legal systems created during colonial administrations and generally continued by postindependence governments and the indigenous, customary practices of land use and land tenure found at the local level. The World Bank and the Land Tenure Center at the University of Wisconsin funded a series of studies on land tenure and agriculture in sub-Saharan Africa to examine questions of land tenure, land security, investment in land, and land productivity in instances of conflict between customary systems of land tenure and centralized, formal law systems of ownership and title (Bruce and Migot-Adholla 1994). The various studies, which employed differing methodologies and covered a wide range of agroecological conditions, arrived at the same general conclusion: customary practices of land tenure were not disincentives to or cause declines in agricultural investment or production (as compared with the more formal systems of title and registration). The researchers made similar policy recommendations concerning the importance, viability, and legitimacy of customary land tenure practices for attaining agricultural production, subsistence, and social cohesion (Bruce and Migot-Adholla 1994).

The World Bank also commissioned a study of forestry practices in Zimbabwe, again focusing on land productivity when centralized, formal approaches to land use management conflict with customary law (Bradley and McNamara 1993). The study identifies and analyzes ongoing significant problems with Zimbabwe's forests, including resource degradation, loss of soil productivity, and adverse impacts to hydrologic functions. Customary practices were managed and enforced in communities and had provided for sustainable resource use and stewardship. The customary systems for managing communal forestlands in Zimbabwe consisted of four local mechanisms operating in a variety of contexts: sacred controls, including traditional religious beliefs, internalized norms, and community sanctions; pragmatic controls, both long-standing and recently developed norms to ensure a steady flow of a particular product; informal civil contracts or norms of civility that govern daily conduct; and the initiation of new institutions and rules to address changing circumstances (Nehira and Fortmann 1993). Colonialism and postcolonialism, however, disrupted these customary systems, imposing a centralized legal and land tenure system that generally focused on resource extraction for profit and relied on nonlocal central governmental regulation and sanction to protect resources. The colonial and postcolonial systems also modified customary social mechanisms as well. Significant exploitation of resources resulted from outside the community and undermined community control over local users. Over the longer term, supplanting traditional resource management institutions has harmed the resources considered in the study.

The World Bank study demonstrates the failure of the centralized, formal legal system in protecting against such resource depredation, describing how the colonial and postcolonial systems significantly disrupted the customary, communal mechanisms for resource management. The study also shows the critical importance of customary systems in managing natural resources as well as the importance of local approaches and institutions. Further, it demonstrates that customary systems included the flexibility necessary to address changing circumstances. The study makes recommendations based on these findings. First, central directives regulating resource use would continue to be ineffective, and locally derived solutions should replace them. It also advocates reforming existing legislation to give local communities greater control over resource use and management. Further, the study directs that the central government empower customary systems and institutions by providing them with the necessary authority to carry out local natural resource management. Finally, it asserts that the myriad of situations at the local level, along with social and economic diversity, preclude the success of a single, centralized forestry policy. A diversity of policies and approaches better reflects local conditions and customary management systems.

CUSTOMARY USE CLAIMS AND CONFLICTS WITH FORMAL LAW: UNITED STATES

Nonindigenous customary use claims in the United States highlight the importance of analyzing legal pluralism in view of the conclusions reached in the African and Philippines studies about the importance of local institutions and local control. The American legal system over the past two hundred years has significantly delegitimized and marginalized the claims of indigenous peoples in the United States. However, these rights have a certain place within the centralized national system. Although the formal U.S. federal system recognizes and protects indigenous customary claims, it does not provide similar protection or recognition for nonindigenous customary claims. Yet, nonindigenous claims still have a certain legitimacy and enforceability—in certain contexts and under certain circumstances—that demonstrate the existence of a pluralistic legal order.

The concept of customary claims to use of open fields and forests in English law developed in ancient Britain, but the claims had been effectively invalidated before the early nineteenth century (Rose 1986, 740). The U.S. courts have followed British common law and have generally refused to recognize the legitimacy of claims to property and resource use based on "customary" law outside of indigenous peoples' rights (741). However, in some instances, the formal U.S. legal system has accepted or tacitly recognized customary claims.

A number of factors in the United States complicate the recognition and legitimation of nonindigenous customary law, particularly in regard to natural resources use. Piccone (1987) asserts that the rise to power and dominance of a new class of scientific managers employed by federal and state natural resource management agencies has disempowered local communities so that no political space exists to exercise customary claims. The power and pervasiveness of this new class, along with its proclivity for micromanagement, have usurped the authority of local communities to determine issues critical to their lifestyle, culture, and identity (Piccone 1987). Fortmann and Roe (1993), however, have disputed Piccone's assertion. They argue that, particularly in the modern United States, the idea of "community" is a "shifting and contested conceptual, social and political terrain." Further, they claim that population mobility, community openness, and fragmentation are long-term elements of the American political landscape, and these factors have rendered many communities "functionally incapable" of organizing themselves as organic, autonomous communities (142–143). These community traits also undermine the ability of such communities to develop, legitimize, and enforce customary claims or systems for resource use and management since stable autonomy is a prerequisite for effectively exercising community-based resource management (Ostrom 1990). The difficulties associated with recognition of customary rights on behalf of an ill-defined and fluctuating "community" have been a frequently voiced concern in court decisions rejecting such claims (Rose 1986, 740–741).

As Rose (1986) demonstrates in her analysis of customary claims in the nineteenth and early twentieth centuries, U.S. law in fact validated "customary" uses and claims in several cases, even if not necessarily using that term. She notes that U.S. common law recognizes two distinct types of "public" property: property owned or managed by a governmental body; and "property collectively owned or managed by society at large, with claims independent of and indeed superior to the claims of any purported governmental manager" (720). Rose refers to this latter type as "inherently public property" and analyzes the rights to use roads and to use navigable waterways as the most prominent examples (720–724). One significant precondition necessary for recognizing these societywide rights in the courts was that the "public" use of such resources was not greedy, rapacious, and disorganized, as characterized by Garrett Hardin's *Tragedy of the Commons,* but rather that public use based on "custom" comprised a set of rules and understandings regulating such use (746). Rose proposes two essential elements for court recognition of customary public rights: "first, the property had to be physically capable of monopolization by private persons—or would have been without doctrines securing public access against such threats. Second, the public's claim had to be superior to that of the private owner, because the properties themselves were most valuable when used by indefinite and unlimited numbers of persons—by the public at large" (774).

Aside from U.S. common law of a public right to use of roadways and navigable waterways, perhaps the most significant recognition by the formal legal system of customary uses are beach access cases, exemplified by Oregon's *Thornton v. Hay* decision (1969). Florida and Hawaii have recognized similar rights of beach access based on custom (*City of Daytona Beach v. Tona-Rama* 1974; *Application of Ashford* 1968). In *Thornton v. Hay,* beachfront property owners challenged an Oregon law that protected the right of the public to access the "dry sand" area of the entire Oregon coast, that is, the area between the high tide mark and the limit of vegetation. The Oregon Supreme Court upheld the law as valid, specifically finding that it was justified based upon the common law notion of "custom" (*Thornton* 1969, 595). The court found that the public's use of the dry sand beach met all the criteria for customary use set out in Blackstone's book on property: long-term (ancient); uninterrupted; peaceable; reasonable; definable with certainty; obligatory on all burdened by the custom; and not repugnant to other customs or law (597).

The Oregon court also rejected the landowners' argument that British common law custom requires use since "antiquity," and that the United States was too young to recognize any such use. Although the U.S. legal system might be relatively young and most of its law codified, "this truism does not, however, militate against the validity of a custom when the custom does in fact exist" (*Thornton* 1969, 597). In support of the validity of such customary claims under U.S. law, the court stated: "Because so much of our law is the product of legislation, we sometimes lose sight of the importance of custom as a source of law in our society. It seems particularly appropriate in the case at bar to look to an ancient and accepted custom in this state as the source of a rule of law. The rule in this case, based upon custom, is salutary in confirming a public right, and at the same time it takes from no man anything which he has had a legitimate reason to regard as exclusively his" (597–598).

Public roads, navigable waterways, and beach access cases provide examples of legitimizing customary uses by the centralized formal legal system. Customary use had developed within and protected a specific legal space for exercising use rights outside the practices of the state. In these instances, when the state legislated the areas in which customary uses prevailed, codification recognized and protected the space created and enforced by the customary claims. Other examples of formal legitimation of custom include incorporating usufructuary claims of "bona fide settlers, miners, residents, and prospectors" in the National Forest System by statute (16 USC §477); the preference given to "bona fide settlers" under the Taylor Grazing Act (43 USC §315b); and recognizing certain customary uses on public lands in the New Mexico territory by former Mexican nationals pursuant to the Treaty of Guadalupe-Hidalgo (Falen and Budd-Fallen 1994). Further, the complex of law governing hard rock mining on public lands initially grew out of customary practices by independent mining districts outside of federal policies. In fact, an 1866 mining law specifically recognized "local customs or rules of the miners in the several mining districts" (Klyza 1996, 35). In these four examples, the formal legal system recognized and protected, through statute, certain customary uses and users on lands that the federal government otherwise reserved and restricted.

The centralized, formal legal system has not incorporated all customary claims, however. Rather, as suggested by legal pluralism analyses, a number of customary claims exist outside that system. Louise Fortmann notes the existence of U.S. customary law in the diversity of local legal cultures, in the differing interpretations of the general statutes, and in the observance of customary mercantile laws in business practices (1990, 197). Robert Nelson describes the powerful and broad-based opposition to the Reagan administration's 1982 proposal to sell large areas of public lands as evidence of a de facto set of private property claims—based on custom and use—to the U.S. public lands: "The administration soon discovered . . . that a wide array of public land users considered themselves as holders of vested rights to continue existing land uses. The administration was unable to sell the lands because in an important sense it did not really own them" (1995, 345).

CUSTOMARY USE CLAIMS TO PUBLIC FORESTLANDS

The National Forest System originally served to protect forests (and their water resources) located on lands remaining in the public domain in the western United States from private lumbering operations (Klyza 1996, 68). Two central proponents of the National Forest System were President Theodore Roosevelt and his first forestry chief, Gifford Pinchot. Both men favored and were instrumental in developing a "stewardship" approach to the national forests, which professional foresters were to manage to ensure a steady, sustained supply of timber (68–76).

At the inception of the National Forest System, timber harvest was a privileged use on national forestlands. However, certain users with resource claims based on custom also had their customary claims incorporated into the National Forest Organic Act. Under the act's provisions, "bona fide settlers, miners, residents, and prospectors" retained the right to continue their customary practices on national forestlands, including taking wood for buildings, mine timbers, and fuelwood (16 USC §477). As the National Forest System evolved, other uses have also come to command a privileged position (never completely displacing timber production, but certainly making significant inroads on its primacy). Nontimber uses and the legal protection that Congress passed for such uses stem from the exercise and assertion of customary use claims to national forestlands.

The first nontimber use evolving from customary practice into legislatively protected right was livestock grazing. Grazing in the national forest preserves was initially prohibited, but by 1898, pressure from western ranchers resulted in lifting the ban and instituted a permitting system (Klyza 1996, 110). The Taylor Grazing Act of 1934 enshrined and protected the interests of ranchers having a customary practice of grazing livestock on public lands (110–116). As with hard rock miners, many ranchers had developed their own "extralegal" set of rules and regulations to govern grazing on public lands in the absence of a federal role in regulation and enforcement. The Taylor Grazing Act formally implemented ranchers' customary law on public lands, including Forest Service lands, and it required the Division of Grazing to cooperate with "local associations of stockmen" in administering grazing districts (113). This requirement led to creating local "grazing advisory boards" to institutionalize the ranchers' prior customary management and allocation systems, and these boards had a statutory basis as of 1939. Although the grazing advisory boards were abolished in the 1960s, the Federal Land Policy and Management Act (FLPMA) resurrected them again in the 1970s (123).

The next significant customary use with eventual legislative protection in national forests concerned wildlife conservation: hunters, hikers, campers, and wildlife enthusiasts came together to advocate setting aside public lands for wildernesses. Advocacy for wilderness set-asides began in the 1930s and intensified through the 1950s and early 1960s, culminating in the Wilderness Act of 1964 (Klyza 1996, 76–77). The Forest Service had actually begun its own wilderness reserve system prior to 1964 in response to the wilderness activists and in reaction to increasing expropriation of national forestlands by the growing National Park System. The complex strategy of the wilderness coalition groups involved congressional and administrative lobbying, public relations, and litigation through the 1980s and 1990s to bring about further significant changes to national forestland management. This strategy has resulted in additional allocation of national forestlands for recreational use, wildlife conservation, and hunting. Certain land management statutes have recognized these customary uses, but ultimately the multiple-pronged strategy conferred protection by involving the centralized, formal legal system—the same legal system that for many years ran counter to wilderness interests.[1]

Louise Fortmann analyzes assertions of customary claims to national forestlands near a rural town in California, which she calls "Adamsville" (1990). Unlike the examples discussed above, the customary claims that she identifies in the actions of Adamsville's citizens have no basis in the formal, centralized legal system. Instead, the claims arise primarily from assumptions about local custom and usage, and their enforceability relies on mechanisms outside the formal legal system. In some instances, however, the claims rely upon the formal system in indirect ways. She analyzes three situations: opposition to the U.S. Forest Service imposing a woodcutting fee that would increase the cost of getting firewood from the local national forest; opposition to a proposed wood-burning power plant perceived as a threat to the supply of subsistence firewood; and opposition to a decrease in the allowable timber harvest for fear of resulting local job losses. Fortmann sees two customary claims at work in the local community: a claim to access to sufficient forest resources for subsistence purposes and a claim to a preferential livelihood based on access to forest resources. They arose from local people using natural resources of the local national forest for subsistence and for livelihood for more than a century. The claims existed outside the formal law because there is no formal "right" within national forest legislation to subsistence use or preferential livelihood (201).

Fortmann also identifies the concept of "truncated customary property law": the claims to the right to use are separate and distinct from the responsibility for management (1990, 196). She notes that rights to use are intricately linked with management responsibilities and rules to protect the resource in many customary systems, but, in certain instances, the management aspects will either atrophy or disappear or may have not yet developed because the custom is relatively young. Atrophy, for example, occurs when the customary system comes under a national legal system, leaving only the sense of right. Based on her analysis of "Adamsville" customary uses, Fortmann argues:

> (1) Local people make claims to customary usufructuary rights to natural resources that are not enforceable under U.S. formal property law;

(2) these claims to rights are legitimized in the minds of local users by their historical and continuing proximity to the resource; (3) these claims can be distinguished from conventional local practice by their articulation and defense as rights; (4) they should be understood as claims to a truncated form of customary property law co-existing with U.S. formal property law; and (5) the conflict between claims of local residents to customary usufructuary rights and claims made under formal law can trigger rural protest. (196)

In Fortmann's analysis (1990), the critical factors for customary claims are factors two and three: The claims are legitimate in the minds of local users because of continuing proximity and use, and such claims are asserted as "rights," not simply local conventions. Further, as Fortmann notes, enforceability of the custom, in the case of customary rights asserted against the state, may involve protest or other direct or indirect means of defending the right as a means of "holding [the customary right] up as the rule that ought to be used to settle the dispute" (200): "If claims to rights can be enforced through the claimants' ability to use other sources of power to defend their claims despite the lack of a specialized coercive force, then it is possible to argue that the claimants have a *de facto* though not a *de jure* right" (199).

The "rural protest" that Fortmann identifies emerged in response to actions that the local community sees as infringing on their customary rights. In the Adamsville case, it took the form of letter writing, editorials, community mobilization, symbolic protests, and the use of other formal legal processes that would hamper enforcement through the formal legal system. She notes that, in one instance, the use of indirect legal methods (a challenge to the permits needed by the power plant) led to the defeat of the move to build the plant. Some members of the community also defied the formal system and continued to practice their threatened rights by harvesting fuelwood without buying a permit from the U.S. Forest Service.

HOW WILL THESE CONFLICTS PLAY OUT IN THE FUTURE AND WITH RESPECT TO NTFPS?

The theory of legal pluralism suggests that conflicts involving assertions of customary claims to the use of national forests will continue in the coming years. Local communities, such as Adamsville, as well as defined user groups, such as environmentalists, ranchers, miners, and plant gatherers, will continue to assert customary claims to their particular use while opposing other uses that threaten their claims. The likelihood of continued conflict is high, but foreseeing the outcomes of conflict involving customary claims to national forestlands and other publicly managed lands is more difficult. Scholars of land use and property rights propose at least three paradigms that may provide insight into the future: evolution into private property rights; absorption and realignment of claims by a formal legal system; and survival as customary rights within an ongoing legally pluralistic environment.

Evolution into Private Property Rights

Several scholars posit that customary claims and the common property resource regimes in which they are often based will ultimately follow a trajectory toward recognition as private property rights. This trajectory relies on the assumption that people act as rational maximizers, weighing competing uses, values, and transaction costs to determine the most efficient way to maximize resource use. Dahlmann (1980) argues that transforming the British open fields and forests system into a private property regime stemmed from the view of an economic and political elite class that the open fields system increased population pressures, competition, and resource scarcity. As a matter of economic sense, the elite proposed transforming the open fields system into a private property rights regime. Dahlman asserts that the "self-interested acquisitive behavior of humans" will lead to private property institutions evolving from the commons approach when resources become scarce (73–75).

Similarly, Nelson (1995) outlines an evolutionary process by which common pool resources regulated under customary regimes in the United States become private property rights. Initially, access to a resource through custom is open to all because the resource is not scarce. As demands for use of the resource grow and create significant conflicts among users, the quality of the resource deteriorates and incentives to invest in its improvement disappear. There is demand for some kind of governmental regulation, usually in the form of a permit system. The evolution continues as the initial recipients of use rights gain political strength and gradually acquire greater and greater effective security in those rights. According to Nelson, users are able to resist changes to the terms of their permit rights as well as the encroachment of other users: "In the fragmented American political system with its highly decentralized power and great weight of organized user groups, the preferences of existing users generally prevail" (346). These permit rights, now the de facto property of existing user groups, become an economic commodity that users may buy or sell, achieving "full saleability . . . when the government officially recognizes the rights of a user to sell use rights without restriction" (346). The final stage "occurs when the government regulatory agency formally transfers use rights to the private user and then ceases its regulatory activities" (347). At this point, the use right is held like any other private property and is subject to the laws and procedures governing such property.

Under this paradigm, as certain customary usufructuary rights assert their way into the political system, they may solidify the political power of the users through long-term use. Ultimately, customary rights become full private property rights. For example, if this paradigm is applied to the NTFP sector, users who now gather certain nontimber forest resources would grow into a larger and more powerful group, ultimately commanding sufficient recognition of their "rights" to harvest that such rights eventually would ultimately become fully alienable private property gathering rights.

Absorption and Realignment of Interests by a Formal Law System

Another group of scholars see a different trajectory for asserting customary claims to shared resources (Lynch 1997; Rose 1986; Klyza 1996). These scholars envision the same initial evolution from common resources to governmental involvement and control. Scarcity and resource degradation would lead to calls for governmental regulation and permitting. Under governmental intervention, one user group may benefit at the expense of another, thereby relegating other competing users to assert and exercise their claims via preexisting customary systems and methods. The terrain of governmental control remains contested, and customary user groups with the power to assert their claims may ultimately succeed in having their uses recognized, absorbed, and acknowledged by the central, formal legal system. In this paradigm, there is no end, such as full privatization, but rather an ongoing, dynamic process of alliances and empowerment, absorption and marginalization.

Lynch's analysis of the growth and political empowerment of community-based natural resource management in the public forests of the Philippines demonstrates how assertion of customary claims by local users through a wide spectrum of tactics is altering a formal legal system inherited from colonial Spain. The transformation to CBNRM is far from complete, but Lynch describes the ways in which the current system is absorbing and adjusting to such claims. Rose's description of the evolving recognition of "public" rights to roads, waterways, and (in some states) beach access shows a similar transformation by the formal system to accommodate custom, reversing the trajectory proposed by the private property rights theorists.

Klyza (1996) discusses the impacts of the assertion of customary claims by user groups on public land policies. His focus is on the state and state structures, and his definition of these concepts portrays them as complex and "fragmented" networks of actors and interests variously allied and positioned in political maneuvers (7 n. 15). This network allows legal pluralism to operate to change and oppose state structures. He describes how

U.S. federal law governing hard rock mining incorporated the customary regulatory system developed by miners (28–30, 35). Klyza also describes in detail how through political pressure and mobilization wilderness preservation interest groups prevented the Reagan administration's plan to explore for gas and oil in wilderness areas. Even though the plan was consistent with the 1872 Mining Law, the alignment of interests and sense of entitlement to unspoiled wilderness for recreation and wildlife habitat led to the administration's bowing to the interest group pressure (57). Klyza also describes the movement for wilderness preservation in national forests and the changes in U.S. Forest Service policy in response to varied political pressures, including the fear of the National Park System usurping Forest Service land ownership.

Under this paradigm, shifting alliances, competing political and economic interests, and conflicting institutional missions and agendas create a fragmented state space that permits the assertion, absorption, recognition, and protection of certain customary rights on public lands. Even though such usufructuary rights may not currently be recognized by the formal legal system and may conflict with current, prevalent uses, significant political pressure from the interest groups supporting particular uses, critical alliances with other powerful groups, and unique configurations of political and economic circumstances could lead to the formal legal system recognizing such uses.

Legal Pluralism and Ongoing Customary Law Regimes

A third possible trajectory for conflicts between customary rights and formal law in the national forests is the continued coexistence of a formal, state system and customary regimes. Customary rights and practices would not diminish or become part of the formal legal system of private or state property rights. If threatened, people used to engaging in forest uses under customary regimes would likely respond with a variety of oppositional strategies ranging from violent protest to nonviolent overt defiance to legal action (Fortmann 1990).

Scholars of conflicts between state and customary natural resource management regimes have identified instances of this type of trajectory in countries from continents as diverse as Africa, Asia, and North America, demonstrating the resilience and persistence of local, customary systems. The studies in Bruce and Migot-Adholla (1994) show that attempts of central governments in sub-Saharan Africa to impose a centralized, formal legal order over the customary rights system have not completely displaced local systems. Rather, customary systems continue to operate at the local level in conjunction with, and sometimes in opposition to, formal, centralized legal systems.

The existence of this trajectory questions the basic assumptions of the first two trajectories: That common, customary use of resources will eventually cause increased resource competition and degradation and require either government intervention or private property rights to prevent the "tragedy of the commons." Ostrom (1990) has demonstrated that customary systems for management of shared resources held in common have operated in a number of instances for hundreds and even thousands of years without degrading the shared resources. Her research also shows that customary systems for managing what she calls "common pool resources" —systems often outside the formal, centralized legal regime—are sometimes quite effective in protecting resources and dealing with difficult issues of allocation and conservation.

Under this scenario, customary uses of national forestlands would continue and evolve in a system parallel to, and in occasional conflict with, the central, formal legal regime. The theory of legal pluralism views the official state legal system as a secondary, rather than a primary, site of regulation. What actually exists "is a multitude of associations and networks, overlapping and interpenetrating, more fragmentary and less inclusive" (Galanter 1981, 20–21). Sufficiently stable and localized communities that assert use rights would ultimately develop their own customary system for managing common pool resources.

NOTE

1. For a historical analysis of the source of such claims to forest wilderness for its own sake, see Schama (1995, 185–240).

REFERENCES

Bradley, P. N., and K. McNamara, eds. 1993. *Living with Trees: Policies for Forestry Management in Zimbabwe*. Washington, DC: World Bank.

Bruce, John W., and S. E. Migot-Adholla, eds. 1994. *Searching for Land Tenure Security in Africa*. Dubuque, IA: Kendall/Hunt.

Dahlmann, C. J. 1980. *The Open Field System and Beyond: A Property Rights Analysis of an Economic Institution* New York: Cambridge University Press.

Falen, F., and K. Budd-Falen. 1994. "The Right to Graze Livestock on the Federal Lands: The Historical Development of Western Grazing Rights." *Idaho Law Review* 30:505–524.

Fortmann, L. 1990. "Locality and Custom: Non-Aborginal Claims to Customary Usufructuary Rights as a Source of Rural Protest." *Journal of Rural Studies* 6: 195–208.

Fortmann, L., and J. W. Bruce, eds. 1988. *Whose Trees? Proprietary Dimensions of Forestry.* Boulder, CO: Westview Press.

Fortmann, L., and E. Roe. 1993. "On Really Existing Communities—Organic or Otherwise." *Telos* 95:139–146.

Galanter, M. 1981. "Justice in Many Rooms: Courts, Private Ordering, and Indigenous Law." *Journal of Legal Pluralism* 19:1–47.

Griffiths, J. 1986. "What Is Legal Pluralism?" *Journal of Legal Pluralism* 24: 1–55.

Hviding, E., and G. Baines. 1996. "Custom and Complexity: Marine Tenure, Fisheries Management, and Conservation in Marovo Lagoon, Solomon Islands." In *Resources, Nations, and Indigenous Peoples,* ed. R. Howitt, J. Connell, and P. Hirsch, pp. 56–65. Melbourne: Oxford University Press.

Klyza, C. M. 1996. *Who Controls Public Lands?* Chapel Hill: University of North Carolina Press.

Lynch, O. 1997. "Legal Concepts and Strategies for Promoting Community-Based Natural Resource Management: Insights from the Phillippines and Other Nations." Paper presented at the conference "Representing Communities: The Politics and History of Natural Resource Management," June 1–3, 1997, Helen, GA. *www.ciel.org/publications/olpaper2.html.*

McEvoy, A. 1986. *The Fisherman's Problem: Ecology and Law in the California Fisheries, 1850–1980.* New York: Cambridge University Press.

Nehira, C., and L. Fortmann. 1993. "Local Woodland Management: Realities at the Grassroots." In *Living with Trees: Policies for Forestry Management in Zimbabwe,* ed. P. N. Bradley and K. McNamara. Washington, DC: World Bank.

Nelson, R. H. 1995. *Public Lands and Private Rights: The Failure of Scientific Management.* Lanham, MD: Rowman and Littlefield.

Ostrom, E. 1990. *Governing the Commons: The Evolution of Institutions for Collective Action.* New York: Cambridge University Press.

Piccone, P. 1987. "The Crisis of American Conservatism." *Telos* 74:3–29.

Rose, C. 1986. "The Comedy of the Commons." *University of Chicago Law Review* 53:711–781.

Rowton Simpson, S. 1991. "Land Tenure and Economic Development: Problems and Policies in Papua New Guinea and Kenya." *Melanesian Law Journal* 19: 103–119.

Sandell, K. 1995. "Access to the 'North'—But to What and for Whom? Public Access in the Swedish Countryside and the Case of a Proposed National Park in the Kiruna Mountains." In *Polar Tourism: Tourism in the Arctic and Antarctic Regions,* ed. C. M. Hall and M. E. Johnston, pp. 131–146. New York: John Wiley and Sons.

_____. 1996. *Sense of Place—Sense of Sustainability.* Paper presented at the Sixth International Symposium on Society and Resource Management, Pennsylvania State University, University Park, May.

Schama, S. 1995. *Landscape and Memory.* New York: Alfred A. Knopf.

Thompson, E. P. 1975. *Whigs and Hunters: The Origin of the Black Act.* New York: Pantheon Books.

Wilkinson, C. 1992. *Crossing the Next Meridian.* Washington, DC: Island Press.

Legal Decisions

Application of Ashford, 440 P.2d 76 (S. Ct. Hawaii 1968): Recognizing that long-standing public use of Hawaii's beaches has ripened into a customary right.

City of Daytona Beach v. Tona-Rama, Inc., 294 So.2d 73 (S. Ct. Florida 1974): Recognizing that long-standing public use of Florida's beaches has ripened into a customary right.

Thornton v. Hay, 254 Or. 584 (1969): Upholding public right of access to Oregon beaches.

APPENDIX A

Scientific Names of Species Listed by Common Name in Text

Common Name or Products Used in Text	Scientific Name
Trees	
cascara; cascara sagrada; Pursh's buckthorn	*Frangula purshiana* (DC.) Cooper; old name *Rhamnus purshiana* DC.
cedar	species in the Cupressaceae (Cypress) Family
chestnut	*Castanea* spp.
eastern hemlock	*Tsuga canadensis* (L.) Carr.
juniper	*Juniperus* spp.
madrone	*Arbutus menziesii* Pursh
maple	*Acer* spp.
myrtlewood; California laurel	*Umbellularia californica* (Hook. and Arn.) Nutt.
noble fir	*Abies procera* Rehd.
Pacific yew	*Taxus brevifolia* Nutt.
pine	*Pinus* spp.
slash pine	*Pinus elliottii* Engelm.
slippery elm	*Ulmus rubra* Muhl.
willow	*Salix* spp.
Shrubs	
devil's club	*Oplopanax horridus* Miq.
dwarf Oregon-grape; dull Oregon-grape; cascade barberry	*Mahonia nervosa* (Pursh) Nutt.; old name *Berberis nervosa* Pursh
California huckleberry; evergreen huckleberry	*Vaccinium ovatum* Pursh
huckleberry	*Vaccinium* spp.; *Gaylussacia* spp.[1]
manzanita; hairy manzanita	*Arctostaphylos columbiana* Piper
mesquite	*Prosopis* spp.
salal	*Gaultheria shallon* Pursh
saskatoon; serviceberry	*Amelanchier* spp.

Common Name or Products Used in Text	Scientific Name
Shrubs, continued	
Scotch broom	*Cytisus scoparius* (L.) Link
vine maple	*Acer circinatum* Pursh
witch hazel; American witch hazel	*Hamamelis virginiana* L.
Herbs	
baby's breath	*Gypsophila paniculata* L.
bear grass; common bear grass	*Xerophyllum tenax* (Pursh) Nutt.
black cohosh; black bugbane	*Cimicifuga racemosa* (L.) Nutt.
bloodroot	*Sanguinaria canadensis* L.
blue grama	*Bouteloua gracilis* (Willd. ex Kunth) Lag. ex Griffiths
camas; common camas; small camas	*Camassia quamash* (Pursh) Greene
cattail	*Typha* spp.
common sunflower	*Helianthus annuus* L.
deer fern	*Blechnum spicant* (L.) Sm.
ginseng; American ginseng	*Panax quinquefolius* L.
goldenseal	*Hydrastis canadensis* L.
stinging nettles	*Urtica dioica* L.
sword fern; western sword fern	*Polystichum munitum* (Kaulfuss) K. Presl
valerian; garden valerian	*Valeriana officinalis* L.
watercress	*Rorippa nasturtium-aquaticum* (L.) Hayek
wild mint	*Mentha arvensis* L.
yarrow; common yarrow	*Achillea millefolium* L.
Fungi	
artist's conk	*Ganodermaa applanatum* (Pers. Ex Wall.) Pat.
boletes	*Boletus* spp.
chanterelle	*Cantharellus* spp.
matsutake; American matsutake	*Tricholomaa magnivelare* (Peck) Redhead
morels	*Morchella* spp.
Polypores:	
western varnished conk	*Ganoderma oregonese* Murr.
hemlock varnished conk	*Ganoderma tsugae* Murr.
reishi	*Ganoderma lucidum* (w. Curt.: Fr.) Karst.
shiitake	*Lentinula edodes* (Berk.) Pegler
Lichen	
black tree "moss"	*Bryoria fremontii* (Tuck) Brodo and D. Hawksw.

1. The common name for the genus *Vaccinium* is blueberry, and species in the genus *Gay-*

lussacia are considered the true huckleberries; in the United States, the distribution of *Gaylussacia* is restricted to east of the Mississippi River.
Sources: Information and authorities for plant species based on the PLANTS database (USDA and NRCS 1999) for vascular plants, Lincoff (1981) and Gilbertson and Ryvarden (1986) for fungi, and Vitt, Marsh, and Bovey (1988) for lichens.

APPENDIX B

Names of Referenced Plants

Common	Ojibwe	Scientific Nomenclature
balsam fir	aninaandag	*Abies balsamea* (L.) Miller
basswood	wiigob	*Tilia americana* L.
bearberry	miskwaabiimag	*Arctostaphylos uvaursi* (L.) Sprengel
black ash	aagimaak	*Fraxinus nigra Marshall*
bloodroot	meskwiijiibikak	*Sanguinaria canadensis* L.
blue cohosh	bezhigojiibik	*Caulophyllum thalictroides* (L.) Michx.
bluebead lily	odotaagaans	*Clintonia borealis* (Aiton) Raf.
blueberry	miinagaawanzh	*Vaccinium angustifolium* Aiton
Canada mayflower	agongosimin	*Maianthemum canadense* Desf.
ginseng	jisens	*Panax quinquefolia* L.
hemlock	gaagaagimizh	*Tsuga canadensis* L. Carriere.
highbush cranberry	annibiminagaawashk	*Viburnum opulus* L.
Labrador tea	wabashkikiibag	*Ledum groenlandicum* Oeder.
nannyberry	aditemin	*Viburnum lentago* L.
northern white cedar	giizhik	*Thuja occidentalis* L.
paper birch	wiigwaas	*Betula papyrifera* Marshall
princess pine	cigonagan	*Lycopodium obscurum* L.
red-osier dogwood	miskkoobimizh	*Cornus sericea* L.
rue anemone	biimaakwad	*Anemonella thalictroides* (L.) Spach.
sugar maple	aninaatig	*Acer saccharum* Marshall
swamp milkweed	bagizowin	*Asclepias incarnata* L.
sweet flag	wiikenh	*Acorus calamus* L.
sweet grass	wiingask	*Hierochloe odorata* (L.) P. Beauv.
white sage	mashkiki	*Artemisia ludoviciana* Nutt.
white water lily	akandamoo	*Nymphaea odorata* Aiton
wild black current	amikomin	*Ribes americanum* Miller

Common	Ojibwe	Scientific Nomenclature
wild blackberry	odatagaagomina-gaawanzh	*Rubus allegheniensis* T. C. Porter
wild ginger	namepin	*Asarum canadense* L.
wild rice	manoomin	*Zizania palustris* L.
wild rose	oginiiminagaawanzh	*Rosa virginiana* Miller
wild sarsaparilla	waaboozojiibik	*Aralia nudicaulis* L.
wintergreen	wiinisiibag	*Gaultheria procumbens* L.
wood lily	mashkodepin	*Lilium philadelphicum* L.
yarrow	ajidamoowaanow	*Achillia millefolium* L.
yellow birch	wiinizik	*Betula alleghaniensis* Britton

APPENDIX C

USDA Forest Service Resource Inventories and NTFPs

Inventory and monitoring of forested lands in the United States have been accomplished at various scales by three different programs: Forest Inventory and Analysis (FIA), Forest Health Monitoring (FHM), and the National Forest Resource Inventories (NFS). Efforts are presently under way to merge and standardize the field data collection aspect of these programs; however, the degree of standardization and inclusion of nontimber species are highly variable. Researchers and managers have just begun to analyze distribution and abundance data on nontimber species using these databases.

Forest Inventory and Analysis is a broad-scale inventory and monitoring program that conducts surveys on all forested lands outside of the national forests. This program is the major source of state-level forest inventory information across the United States. In the Pacific Northwest Region, sampling units are located 3.4 miles apart along a systematic grid. This spatial scale might be appropriate for some species and assessment of their distribution and abundance, but it is inadequate for rare and ephemeral species, nonvascular plants and fungi, and local planning efforts requiring more detailed information. However, FIA data could be used to predict the distribution and abundance of species that are strongly associated with specific plant communities or overstory conditions. The National Forest Health Monitoring program samples landscapes even more sparsely but includes data on lichens. No data are collected on shrubs, herbs, or fungi at the species level, but full vegetation structure studies are being piloted.

Within each national forest, land managers conduct National Forest Service Resource Inventories, which are generally done at local scales used for project-level management activities. Sampling designs and data collected vary among the nine Forest Service Regions as well as within regions. In the Pacific Northwest, these databases have been used to generate general NTFP information by plant association (Schlosser, Blatner, and Zamora

1992). The rapid growth in collection of certain nontimber forest products has prompted some NFS land managers to establish inventory and monitoring programs for particular species (Peck 1998; Rambo, Rikkinen, and Peck 1998).

APPENDIX D

Edible Mushrooms—Unique Inventory and Monitoring Considerations

Edible forest mushrooms are the reproductive structures (fruits) of fungi that live in the soil or in decaying organic matter. Because the organism is so thoroughly imbedded in the substrate where it lives, sampling it directly is impractical. Fortunately, the fruiting bodies (mushrooms) are the nontimber product of interest, but their temporal occurrence is extremely variable. Mushroom fruiting varies immensely from year to year and is often associated with complex and unpredictable weather patterns. Each species of mushroom typically fruits during a particular limited season of the year; fruiting seasons of some species often do not, or only partially, overlap those of other species. Within each mushroom's fruiting season, multiple flushes of fruiting occur, and most commercially harvested edible forest mushrooms fruit in clusters that are unevenly distributed across the forest floor.

Because the size or extent of a mushroom colony in its substrate is difficult to measure directly, the only currently practical way to assess potential productivity of a site is to average the highly variable seasonal estimates of mushroom production over many years. Likewise, detecting statistically valid trends in productivity requires many years of sampling to separate real effects from annual variation. If abundance or productivity is the monitoring goal, multiple sampling visits are needed each fruiting season to record the repeated flushes and to obtain seasonal productivity totals.

Unlike many products derived from plants or vegetation, mushrooms are quite ephemeral. The average longevity of a particular species of mushroom dictates the interval between sampling visits. For example, morels are relatively short-lived and weekly sampling is appropriate (Pilz et al. in review), whereas chanterelles are relatively long-lived and intervals of up to three weeks will still capture all fruiting in a specific location (Pilz, Molina, and Liegel 1998). More than one sampling visit per season would generally not be informative for most other nontimber products unless the rate or timing of seasonal changes such as growth or maturation are of interest. Additional information in edible mushroom sampling methods can be found in Castellano and Trappe (in press), O'Dell, Lodge, and Ammirati (in press), Pilz and Molina (in press), and Pilz et al. (in review).

APPENDIX E

Estimating Commercial Quantities of Floral Greens

Barnes and Musselman (1996) developed inventory and appraisal methods for four products found in the Pacific Northwest that are used in the floral greens market: salal, sword fern, bear grass, and noble fir boughs. Their goal was determining product-specific marketable quantities across a fairly small landscape: estimated marketable product volume and value per unit area. Prior to data collection, workers participated in inventory training sessions. Aside from general knowledge of field sampling techniques, product recognition, quality standards, and harvesting methods were also essential knowledge. Training took place in the classroom and in field situations.

The area sampled was different for each product; thus no attempt was made to inventory multiple products using the same sampling design. Only areas near roads were surveyed. Plot size was based on the overall size of the species and if it had a clumpy or more uniform distribution. For example, salal exhibited a patchy distribution and required a larger plot size (one-tenth acre) and a greater number of plots compared to bear grass (one-fiftieth acre), which is a smaller plant and was more uniformly distributed across the site of interest. All plots were circular. Data collected in each plot for salal, sword fern, and bear grass included the number of marketable units per plot (e.g., a salal bunch equaled one and three-quarter pounds, a sword fern bunch equaled fifty to fifty-two fronds,) percent cover, number of plants, age, condition, spacing, associated plant types, tree species, and other environmental variables such as slope and aspect. Regression equations from plot data relating percent cover to marketable units were then used to estimate total yield across the study area.

For noble fir, harvestable quantities of product were predicted using a series of equations and by the grade of the individual tree (1 = good, 2 = fair). Marketable harvestable quantities of boughs could then be determined for each tree by just measuring the tree height and crown in the field, and plot-level estimates were determined by counting the number of trees in each plot.

APPENDIX F

Traditional Forestry Methods to Inventory Tree Characteristics

Tree inventories date back to the beginning of forest management at the end of the Middle Ages in Europe (Schreuder, Gregoire, and Wood 1993). Often the primary resource of interest is tree wood quality and quantity, although in some cases information is collected about key understory species as an aid to site class determination. Several methods of determining wood volume and grade have been developed and are used in the United States (Avery and Burkhart 1994). The Bitterlich Variable Plot method, sometimes called variable radius plot sampling, angle count sampling, point sampling, or plotless cruising, is a distance or plotless sampling method primarily used to calculate stem basal area. The method is extremely fast, comparatively inexpensive, and has been widely adopted by foresters (Barbour et al. 1999; Schreuder, Gregoire, and Wood 1993).

Although basal area is used to calculate board feet of lumber, it can be used more generally as a measure of tree species abundance. Numerous equations have been developed and are used to indirectly predict tree volume or biomass from characteristics such as stem diameter at breast height (4.5 feet), height, and tree form. Most of these equations are for timber species and wood volume, but equations exist to estimate various components of tree biomass including foliage and bark volume (Bonham 1989; Kozak and Yang 1981). When combined with estimates of wood grade, highly accurate estimations of tree volume and value can be obtained for a wide range of landscapes. Because such equations are specific to both species and site characteristics, they are not widely applicable to other species and sites.

APPENDIX G

Inventory Methods for Commercial Moss Harvest

In the Pacific Northwest, many moss species are increasingly being harvested for the multimillion-dollar floral industry. In order to manage commercial moss harvest, estimates of existing amounts of harvestable moss and accumulation rates are needed. Peck and McCune (1998) described a retrospective method to estimate available biomass of harvestable moss growing on understory trees and accumulation rates on sites in northwestern Oregon.

Ten sites were selected specifically for harvestable moss in the coast range of northwestern Oregon and ten additional sites in the Cascade Range. Sites spanned a broad range of stand ages, species composition, structure, and management applications. At each site, one transect 200–300 meters in length (fifty meters from the nearest road) was established. Points were sampled every fifty meters along the transect using the point-centered quarter method; at each sample point, four quadrants were established using the transect line and a perpendicular line. Moss was removed from the closet stem on a one-meter-long subplot located one-half meter below the two-meter vertical cutoff point on the host stem. To approximate methods used by moss harvesters, commercial criteria of moss quantity and quality were used for sampling. Thus, only moss of commercial value and quantity was collected. Stem diameter was also recorded, and increment cores or cross sections were removed to determine stem age in order to calculate accumulation rates.

Harvestable moss biomass was variable among all the sites; variability was attributed to site quality and the amount of suitable substrate. Moss accumulation rates were also highly variable. Variability was attributed to elevation, aspect, and proximity to standing water, exposure to fog, canopy cover, propagule supply, and density of host shrubs. The amount of litterfall from higher in the canopy (as a source) can also be an important factor for moss accumulation rates (Peck, Acker, and McKee 1995).

APPENDIX H

Rogue Institute for Ecology and Economy Special Forest Products Inventory

The Rogue Institute for Ecology and Economy (1995) developed field procedures for an ecological assessment and NTFP inventory in cooperation with the Rogue River National Forest and the Bureau of Land Management (BLM). This study incorporates NTFPs into a multiresource inventory system to be used by federal agencies. Field procedures were developed using a statistical approach, and accuracy standards are provided. For small ownerships, systematic sampling is used, and stratified random sampling is suggested for large areas. The sampling protocol involves use of a one-fifth-acre ecosystem assessment plot spatially consistent with Forest Service (Rogue River National Forest) and BLM (Medford District) sampling protocols. The design includes variable radius plots for estimating tree basal area and nested fixed-radius plots for estimating poles, seedlings, and saplings. Auxilliary circular plots are used to sample threatened and endangered species and nontimber forest product species.

Data collection includes a wealth of information consistent with the wider objectives of completing an ecological assessment. Nontimber vegetation is recorded by species; abundance and distribution are estimated using a detailed prevalence class (rare, few, one patch, several individuals, a few patches, several well-spaced clumps, and so on) on 20 x 20 meter plots for low shrubs, herbs, and mosses, and 100 x 100 meter plots for tall shrubs and trees. The prevalence class system is unique and provides important information regarding species distribution; it lacks compatibility with other understory inventory methods (FIA, NFS, and so on), which generally use canopy cover. Special forest product (SFP) plots are separately sampled and include eight one-square-meter herb subplots and four 2.14-meter-radius shrub subplots. Four of the herb subplots are nested within the shrub subplots and four are separate. Information collected includes species (only locally known NTFP species are recorded), number of stems, cover, health, phenology (stage in life cycle), and plant community information.

APPENDIX I

Monitoring Wild Goldenseal Populations

Goldenseal is a slowly growing herb that occurs in deciduous forests of eastern North America. Harvesting of this species for the medicinal trade, which began in the mid 1800s, coupled with habitat loss, has drastically reduced wild populations. In the United States, a national program to regulate export and monitor wild populations is being implemented by the U.S. CITES Authority and the U.S. Fish and Wildlife Service (Gagnon 1999).

Gagnon (1999) proposed two levels of population monitoring for goldenseal: low intensity and high intensity. Low-intensity protocols involve monitoring of ten to twenty populations per state. Criteria for population selection for both levels of monitoring include a minimum number of one hundred individual plants with at least two leaves, no evidence of harvesting, a remote location, similarity of habitat types, and no evidence of recent natural disturbance. For each population, yearly visits are made where the total number of plants is recorded for each size class. Gagnon also suggests recording the number of fruits per size class. Because goldenseal has a single flower for each plant that produces a raspberry-like fruit, this is a relatively simple task.

High-intensity monitoring focuses on collecting data for population demographic analysis with yearly visits to an additional five to ten populations per state. Year-to-year precise identification and mapping of individual plants are required. Since goldenseal is a clonally propagated species, it is difficult to follow the fate of individual plants. "Mother" plants are identified as are vegetative offshoots produced each year, which generally involves removal of leaf litter to reveal roots or rhizomes. Additional data collected are plant height, width of each leaf, percent area browsed, and number of seeds per fruit. Suggested data collection includes slope, aspect, landform position, bedrock, and the species and cover class for associated species. Gagnon includes an overview of appropriate plant demographic analysis methods.

CONTRIBUTORS

ANITA G. ALEXANDER is a beekeeper, horticulturist, and award-winning plant hybridizer. She is past editor of the *American Primrose Society Quarterly* and a member of numerous professional horticultural societies. She is a certified Canadian beekeeper, an active member and past officer in several U.S. and international beekeeping organizations, and maintains an Oregon state-certified honey extraction and bottling facility, registered under Mountain Dew Honey.

SUSAN J. ALEXANDER is a natural resource economist with the USDA Forest Service Pacific Northwest Research Station in Corvallis, Oregon. Her research focuses on nonmarket valuation and imperfect markets. She has expertise in values and economic contributions of North American NTFP industries. She is a co-owner of Mountain Dew Honey.

ALEXIOS ANTYPAS is a professor of environmental policy at the Central European University in Budapest. His research areas include the history of ecosystem management in the United States, the roles of science and scientists in the formation of natural resource policy, and international environmental policy.

KEITH A. BLATNER is professor and chair, Department of Natural Resource Sciences, Washington State University. A resource economist, his current research interests are focused in two areas: production and marketing of timber and nontimber products, and the changing role of nonindustrial private forest owners in the forest products sector of the Pacific Northwest.

LOUISE E. BUCK is a senior extension associate at the Department of Natural Resources at Cornell University and an associate scientist of the Cornell International Institute for Food, Agriculture, and Development (CIIFAD) and the Center for International Forestry Research (CIFOR). A recent NTFP publication is entitled "From Wildcrafting to Intentional Cultivation: The Potential for Producing Specialty Forest Products in Agroforestry Systems in Temperate North America."

ROGER ALEX CLAPP is an associate professor of geography at Simon Fraser University in British Columbia. His research examines the ecological effects of resource industries, including NTFPs. Recent publications include "The Resource Cycle in Forestry and Fishing" and "Tree Farming and Forest Conservation in Chile: Do Replacement Forests Leave Any Originals Behind?"

CAROLYN CROOK received her Ph.D. in geography at the University of Toronto. Her research areas include bioprospecting, tropical deforestation, and biodiversity conservation.

KAREN C. DANIELSEN is an ecologist of the Great Lakes Indian Fish and Wildlife Commission, an intertribal organization charged with implementation of off-reservation treaty rights in Michigan, Minnesota, and Wisconsin. Her work focuses on tribal NTFP gathering.

GREG DYSON is an attorney for the Mt. Hood Stewardship Council, where he codesigned a project using NTFPs to move forest management away from timber management and toward biodiversity conservation.

MARLA R. EMERY is a cultural geographer with the USDA Forest Service Northeastern Research Station in Burlington, Vermont. Her research focuses on the role of nontimber forest products in household economies and other direct human-forest interactions. She has conducted comprehensive studies of contemporary NTFP use in the Upper Midwest and the Northeast.

ROGER FIGHT is a principal economist for the Forestry Sciences Laboratory in Portland, Oregon. He is the U.S. scientist-representative on the nonwood forest products study group of the North American Forest Commission of FAO. He is coauthor of "Opportunities for Conservation-Based Development of Nontimber Forest Products in the Pacific Northwest."

ANDREW H. FISHER is an instructor at Portland Community College. His research examines Native American environmental history and treaty conflicts. He recently published "The 1932 Handshake Agreement: Yakama Indian Treaty Rights and Forest Service Policy in the Pacific Northwest" in *Western Historical Quarterly.*

CAROL FLEMING is a graduate of Emory University in anthropology who has done ethnography with Rio Grande National Forest NTFP harvesters.

JONATHAN H. GILBERT is a wildlife biologist and leader of the Wildlife Section of the Great Lakes Indian Fish and Wildlife Commission, an intertribal organization charged with implementation of off-reservation treaty rights in Michigan, Minnesota, and Wisconsin.

JENNIFER GILDEN is a researcher at the Institute for Culture and Ecology in Portland, Oregon, and a faculty researcher at Oregon State University. Recent publications include "An Oregon Case Study: Gender Roles, Families, and Timber Communities in Transition" and "Human and Habitat Needs in Disaster Relief for Pacific Northwest Salmon Fisheries."

EDMUND CLAY GOODMAN is the project manager for the Oregon Water Trust. Recent publications include "Indian Tribal Co-Management of Natural Resources on Public Lands" and "Rivers, Jurisdiction, and the Role of Tribal Regulation."

RICHARD HANSIS is the coordinator of the Environmental Science Program at Humboldt State University. Recent publications include "A Political Ecology of Picking: Nontimber Forest Products in the Pacific Northwest" and "The Siouxon Valley, Gifford Pinchot National Forest."

PAUL JAHNIGE is the director of the Community Resources in Baltimore, Maryland, started a program on urban NTFPs, and has published an article entitled "Exploring Urban Nontimber Forest Products."

ERIC T. JONES is a codirector and researcher at the Institute for Culture and Ecology in Portland, Oregon. He has written numerous international and domestic publications on NTFP sociocultural problems, community forestry, land tenure, and political ecology theory.

BECKY K. KERNS is a plant community ecologist for the USDA Forest Sciences Laboratory in Corvallis, Oregon. Relevant research has focused on understory forest vegetation dynamics, monitoring protocols, and modeling NTFP species distribution and abundance. Recent publications include "Diagnostic Phytoliths in a Ponderosa Pine–Bunchgrass Community near Flagstaff, Arizona" and "Estimating Forest-Grassland Dynamics Using Soil Phytolith Assemblages."

LEON LIEGEL is a senior forest scientist for the USDA Forest Sciences Laboratory in Corvallis, Oregon. His research has looked at regional and national forest health monitoring data, integrating NTFPs in resource inventories, and the sustainability of temperate and tropical human and natural resource systems. Recent publications include "Overstory Mortality as an Indicator of Forest Health in California" and "Integrating Biological, Socioeconomic, and Managerial Methods and Results in the MAB Mushroom Study."

JONATHAN K. LONDON is cofounder and codirector of Youth in Focus, a nonprofit consulting group that promotes youth leadership through youth-led research, evaluation, and planning. Recent publications include "Coordinated Resource Management for the Feather River: A Case Study of Community-Based Watershed Management" and "Common Roots and Entangled Limbs: Earth First! and the Growth of Post-Wilderness Environmentalism."

THOMAS LOVE is a professor of anthropology at Linfield College in McMinnville, Oregon, and has studied NTFP extractive reserves in Peru and wild mushroom and brush gathering in the U.S. Pacific Northwest. Recent publications include "Grounds for Argument: Local Understandings, Science, and Global Processes in Special Forest Products Harvesting" and "Valuing the Temperate Rainforest: Wild Mushrooming on the Olympic Peninsula Biosphere Reserve."

KATHRYN LYNCH is a codirector and researcher at the Institute for Culture and Ecology in Portland, Oregon. As a Fellow of the Tropical Conservation and Development Program, she investigated medicinal NTFPs. Recent publications include "Gender, Healing, and Conservation in the Northern Peruvian Amazon." Her current research with the MERGE (Managing Ecosystems and Resources with a Gender Emphasis) Program critically evaluates the role of education in conservation strategies in Ecuador.

PATRICK MALLET coordinates the certification and marketing program at the Falls Brook Centre in Canada and is an international expert on NTFP certification. He recently published "Certification of Nontimber Forest Products: The State of the Playing Field."

REBECCA J. MCLAIN is a codirector and researcher at the Institute for Culture and Ecology in Portland, Oregon. Her research interests include community forestry, participatory management, and nontimber forest products policy. Recent publications include "Inclusive Community Forest Management: Lessons for the United States from Mali, West Africa" and "Participatory Non-Wood Forest Products Management: Experiences from the Pacific Northwest, USA."

DAVID PILZ is a botanist at the USDA Forest Sciences Laboratory in Corvallis, Oregon. He has published numerous articles on the sustainability and productivity of wild mushroom harvesting, including "Mushrooms and Timber: Managing Commercial Harvesting in the Oregon Cascades" and "A Proposal for Regional Monitoring of Edible Forest Mushrooms."

PAUL RINGGOLD is director of stewardship for the Peninsula Open Space Trust in Menlo Park, California, where his responsibilities include land acquisition, stewardship planning, and resource management. Recent publications include a guidebook titled "Land Stewardship Contracting in the National Forests" and "Testing Stewardship Concepts on Federal Lands."

ROBERT SCHROEDER is a research social scientist at the USDA Forest Sciences Lab in Juneau, Alaska. He has conducted cooperative research with tribal and nontribal groups in southeast and other areas of Alaska to document contemporary subsistence hunting, fishing, and gathering and to delineate traditional harvest territories.

VINCE SPERO is an archaeologist for the Rio Grande National Forest and Bureau of Land Management San Luis Resource Area in Colorado. His position involves heritage resource management, and he recently has undertaken a comprehensive research program on NTFP harvesting.

WAYNE S. TEEL is an agroforestry researcher at James Madison University in the integrated science and technology program. Recent publications include "Catching the Rain: Soil Conservation and Tree Establishment in Nampula, Mozambique" and "Woodland Management and Agroforestry Potential among Dairy Farmers in Lewis County, New York."

NAN C. VANCE is a supervisory plant physiologist at the USDA Forest Sciences Laboratory in Corvallis, Oregon, a member of the graduate faculty, College of Forestry, Oregon State University, and an adviser to Forest Service NTFP regional and national policy development. Publications examining NTFPs have appeared in the *American Journal of Botany, Journal of Sustainable Forestry* (in press), *Journal of Phytochemistry,* and Island Press.

JAMES WEIGAND is a natural resource economist for the U.S. Forest Service. Recent publications have examined nontimber forest product agroforestry systems to jointly produce matsutake mushrooms and timber and NTFP conservation and development systems.

INDEX

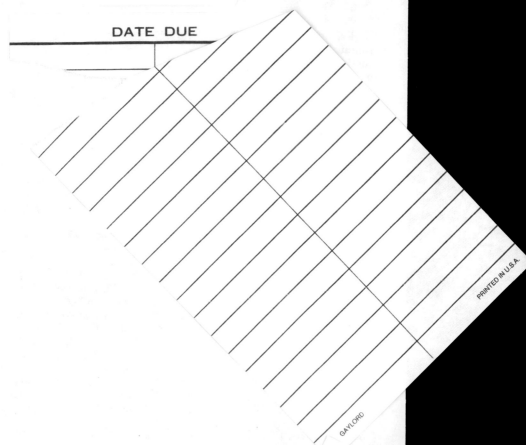